IE5 Dynamic HTML Programmer's Reference

Brian Francis
Alex Homer
Chris Ullman

Wrox Press Ltd. ®

IE5 Dynamic HTML Programmer's Reference

Published by Wrox Press Ltd
Arden House, 1102 Warwick Road, Acocks Green, Birmingham, B27 6BH, UK
Printed in USA
ISBN 1-861001-74-6

Trademark Acknowledgements

Credits

Authors
Brian Francis
Alex Homer
Chris Ullman

Additional Material
Larry Roof
Dan Kohn

Editors
Ian Nutt
Lisa Stephenson

Index
Martin Brooks

Technical Reviewers
Jeff Benjamin
Robert Chang
Damien Foggon
Jeff Rule
Jesse Reisman
Anthony Warden
David Whitney

Design/Layout
Mark Burdett

Cover
Andrew Guillaume
Image by Rita Ruban

About the Authors

Brian Francis

Brian Francis is the Technical Evangelist for NCR's Retail Self Service Solutions. From his office in Duluth, Georgia, Brian is responsible for enlightening NCR and their customers in the technologies and tools used for Self Service Applications. Brian also uses the tools that he evangelizes in developing solutions for NCR's customers. He has worked extensively with Wrox Press as a technical reviewer and has also co-authored on a number of projects.

Alex Homer

Alex Homer lives and works in the idyllic rural surroundings of Derbyshire, UK. His software company specializes in office integration and Internet-related development, and produces a range of vertical application software. He has worked with Wrox Press on several projects.

Chris Ullman

Chris Ullman is a computer science graduate, who has not let this handicap prevent him becoming a programmer fluent in Visual Basic, Java, SQL, DHTML and ASP. When not cutting up pictures by old masters to re-assemble them as dynamic jigsaws on his preferred browser, he's either found down at his local soccer ground urging on his favorite team, Birmingham City, or at home trying to prevent his two young cats from tearing up the house and each other.

HTML

Table of Contents

HTML

Introduction

After many years of boring, static HTML, Internet Explorer 4.0 ushered us into the world of **Dynamic HTML.** It released the web site creator from the strait-jacket that had limited so many of the things that could be done, and the effects that could be achieved. In fact, it provided a whole new way to make pages more interesting, more attractive, more like traditional documents, and – of course – more dynamic. Now, with the advent of **Internet Explorer 5.0**, we are seeing the refinement of the Dynamic HTML technologies coupled with a more refined and optimized browsing platform.

The refinement of Dynamic HTML in Internet Explorer 5.0 includes the integration of support for what is currently the newest and most exciting language on the web – eXtensible Markup Language (XML). IE5 also introduces optimizations of HTML and Cascading Style Sheets (CSS) that make the creation of dynamic pages easier and more robust. We will take a look at these new technologies, as well as looking at Dynamic HTML as a whole, to see how to take advantage of this new web-page paradigm.

What is this Book About?

In 1996, the World Wide Web Consortium (W3C) began working on proposals for an updated version of HTML, version 4.0 – code named *Project Cougar*. One of the main innovations in HTML 4.0 was the ability to let the user update and manipulate text and graphics on a screen dynamically, without the need for a page refresh. This innovation is the reason why the technology is known as **Dynamic HTML**.

Dynamic HTML differs from HTML in that it doesn't rely on tags alone to achieve these effects – it also makes use of JavaScript and VBScript. This book aims to bring you up-to-date with the standard outlines for Dynamic HTML, and to explain what DHTML offers you and how closely the new proposals are followed in Microsoft's new browser, Internet Explorer 5.

Dynamic HTML allows the web author to work with the contents of the page in a fundamentally different way. This book isn't a dry list of specifications and discussion documents. You'll find that it's been split into two distinct sections. The first is a lightning tour and demonstration of all the features that Dynamic HTML offers. We make references to the HTML standard, detailing what is (and what isn't) supported, throughout the book. The second section is a comprehensive reference guide to everything an HTML programmer could possibly need. This includes a cross reference of all the new and old properties, events and methods, a listing of all the Dynamic HTML tags that Internet Explorer 5 supports, a browser object model reference and much more.

Why Internet Explorer 5 Edition?

In 1997, the world saw its first two DHTML-compatible browsers. Microsoft released Internet Explorer version 4, which supported much of DHTML. Netscape also released a new browser, named Communicator 4, and it too supports a version of Dynamic HTML. However, the version supported by Netscape differed widely from the version supported by Internet Explorer.

With the release of IE5, Microsoft has continued to follow the standards being set for Dynamic HTML by the W3C. That is not to say that IE5 *completely* supports all aspects of the W3C specification, nor that IE5 has not introduced its own enhancements to Dynamic HTML. But arguably, IE5 supports the W3C specification for Dynamic HTML more closely than any other existing browser.

We are used to minor differences in the tags and attributes that different browsers support, and the different ways that they sometimes interpret them, but the current situation means that there is very little common ground between the Dynamic HTML features in the two main browsers. HTML authors continue to be in a difficult position. Producing pages and scripts that will work correctly on both browsers will continue to be a difficult task until both browsers fully support the standard.

Who Should Read This Book?

You should read this book if you want to use the latest techniques to create exciting and attractive web pages. Dynamic HTML is a combination, or perhaps even a culmination, of two (originally very different) web page coding techniques. The appearance of the page is created using **HTML**, but much of the control of the way it looks and works is down to embedded **scripting code**. On top of that, the use of **style sheets** adds extra ways of controlling and specifying the product's layout.

Therefore, a basic knowledge of a scripting language will be useful. (We've provided a fast-track VBScript tutorial for the uninitiated, and VBScript and JScript appendices, in the second section of the book.) You should also be reasonably familiar with HTML and style sheets, as we won't be providing a full tutorial on these subjects. However, we have included some tips on how they work in our examples, and a full reference section at the back of the book.

As long as you've created a few pages before, and have done a little scripting before, you'll have no problems keeping up with what's going on.

What Do I Need to Use This Book?

All you'll need to create Dynamic HTML documents yourself is a text editor capable of saving files in ASCII format, and a browser that supports Dynamic HTML. This book uses Internet Explorer version 5. You can download this browser for free, from:

http://www.microsoft.com/windows/ie

Everything else you need is here in this book. The examples and screenshots in this book were all taken from a PC running a Microsoft Windows operating system, and using Windows Notepad as the text editor. However, HTML is a platform-independent language, so you'll get the same results using a Macintosh or other operating system – as long as you have a suitable browser.

Where you'll find the Sample Code

You can try out all the examples in this book, by running them straight from our web site:

http://webdev.wrox.co.uk/books/1746

Alternatively, you can run them on your own server – all the code is available for download and reuse, for free, at the same location.

What is the World Wide Web?

The concept of the World Wide Web, or simply the web, was born in 1983 at the CERN laboratory in Geneva, when Tim Berners-Lee was looking for a way of disseminating information in a friendly, but platform-independent, manner. The scheme he devised was placed in the public domain in 1992, and the World Wide Web was born.

There are many standards and technologies involved in making the World Wide Web function, and most of the development of these standards has now been transferred from CERN to the World Wide Web Consortium (W3C). Their web site, at http://www.w3.org is a good starting place if you want to discover more about the Web. Here is the home page of the World Wide Web Consortium:

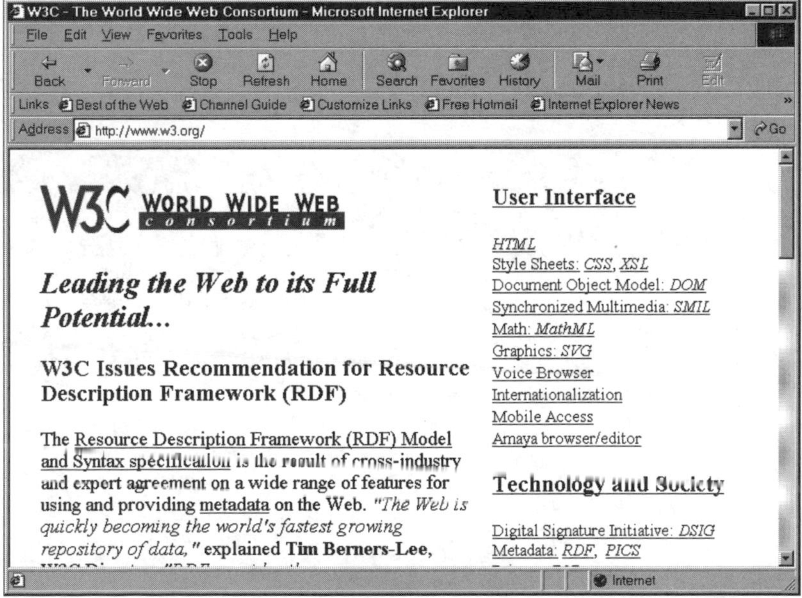

In this book, we won't be examining how the World Wide Web works; however, it is important to understand the basics that make it possible. There are three parts to this technology:

- The server that holds the information
- The client that is viewing the information
- The protocol that connects the two

Documents (things like text, images, sounds and other types of information) are held on a **server** computer; they are viewed on a **client** computer; and they are transferred between the two using the HyperText Transfer Protocol (**HTTP**).

When a client (the computer or workstation being used by the person who wishes to view the document) makes a request to the server, it uses the HTTP protocol across a network to request the information from the server. The request is made in the form of a URL. The server processes the request and, again, uses HTTP to transfer the information back to the client. As well as transferring the document itself, the server must tell also the client what type of document is being returned. This is usually defined as a MIME type. The client must then process the information before it presents it to the human viewer.

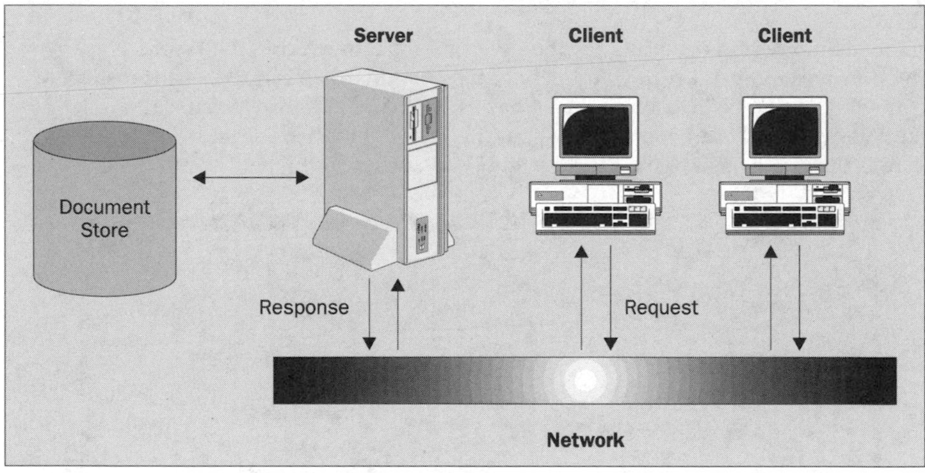

In this simplified diagram, we have shown the documents as fixed; however, in some cases, they can be dynamic documents, created 'on the fly' by the server as the client requests them. Perhaps the simplest example of a dynamic document is the ubiquitous 'hit counter' that appears on many pages.

Some Terminology

Before we get too far into the book, it might be a good idea to define some terminology.

DTD (Document Type Definition) – a set of rules on how to apply SGML (see definition below) to a particular markup language.

HTML (Hyper Text Markup Language) – the basic subject of this book.

HTTP (Hyper Text Transfer Protocol) – this is the protocol used to transfer information between the client and server computer. Although vital for the operation of the web, it is not generally necessary to know any details of HTTP in order to provide information across the web.

MIME (Multimedia Internet Mail Extension) – this was originally intended as a way of embedding complex binary documents in mail messages, but is now used much more widely. When a server serves web information to a client browser, it first tells the client the type of information it is going to send, using a MIME type and a subtype. The browser can then decide how it wishes to handle that document type. It may choose to process it internally, or invoke an external program to handle the information. MIME types consist of a main type and subtype. For example, plain text is `text/plain`, while `image/mpeg` specifies an image stored in `mpeg` format.

RFC (Request For Comments) – this is something of a misnomer, as almost all of the protocols and conventions that make the Internet function are defined in documents called RFCs. For example, RFC1725 defines POP3, the protocol often used for retrieving Internet mail, and HTML 2.0 can be found in RFC1866. All RFC documents can be found on the Internet.

SGML (Standard Generalized Markup Language) – a standard for defining markup languages.

XML (Extensible Markup Language) – a subset of SGML that is becoming a standard for data and information exchange between applications. The syntax is similar to HTML, but the definition of the tags and elements are not part of the standard. They are defined using a Document Type Definition (DTD).

URL (Uniform Resource Locator) – this is a way of specifying a resource. It consists of a protocol name, a colon (`:`), two forward slash characters (`//`), a machine name, and a path to a resource (using `/` as a separator). For example, the Wrox Press home page can be found at `http://www.wrox.com/`. URLs are the way that all resources are specified on the web. Note that URLs can specify more than just web pages. For example, to retrieve RFC1866 using FTP, we could specify `ftp://ds.internic.net/rfc/rfc1866.txt`. URLs are often embedded inside web pages, to provide links to other pages, as we shall see later.

Conventions

We have used a number of different styles of text and layout in the book to help differentiate between the different kinds of information. Here are examples of the styles we use and an explanation of what they mean:

> *Advice, hints, or background information comes in indented paragraphs of italic text, like this.*

> **Important pieces of information come in boxes like this.**

Bullets appear indented, with each new bullet marked as follows:

- **Important Words** are in a bold type font
- Words that appear on the screen, in menus like the File or Window, are in a similar font to that which you see on screen
- Keys that you press on the keyboard, like *Ctrl* and *Enter*, are in italics

Code has several fonts. If it's a word that we're talking about in the text – for example, when discussing the `For...Next` loop – it's in `this font`. If it's a block of code that you can type in as a program and run, then it's also in a gray box:

```
Response.Write("Hello World")
```

Sometimes you'll see code in a mixture of styles, like this:

```
<%
  Dim strLastName
  strLastName = Request.Form("LastName")
  Response.Write("Your surname is " & strLastName)
%>
```

The code with a white background is code we've already looked at and that we don't wish to examine further.

Tell Us What You Think

We've worked hard on this book to make it useful. We've tried to understand what you're willing to exchange to hard-earned money for, and we've tried to make the book live up to your expectations.

Please let us know what you think about this book. Tell us what we did wrong, and what we did right. We take your feedback seriously – if you don't believe us, then send us a note. We'll answer, and we'll take on board whatever you say for future editions. The easiest way is to use email:

`feedback@wrox.com`

You can also find more details about Wrox Press on our web site. There, you'll find the code from our latest books, sneak previews of forthcoming titles, and information about the authors and editors. You can order Wrox titles directly from the site, or find out where your nearest bookstore with Wrox titles is located.

Customer Support

If you find a mistake, please have a look at the errata page for this book on our web site first. Appendix K gives more details of how to submit errata, if you are unsure. You'll find the errata page on our main web site, at:

http://www.wrox.com

If you can't find an answer there, tell us about the problem and we'll do everything we can to answer promptly!

Just send us an email to `support@wrox.com` or fill in the form on our website:

http://www.wrox.com/contacts.asp

HTML

Chapter

– The Next tion

…) was released, everything was just …version 3.2 – that everyone seemed to … new tags and attributes, and how to use … Navigator sing…

…ML was really comprised of three … (version 4.0), a scriptable object model …d Cascading Style Sheets (CSS). With it …gain. This time, Microsoft were singing …mplementation of Dynamic HTML in …) standard, while Netscape's version was …d to learn how to develop Dynamic …d the vast amount of flexibility that it

…time' again, so we can take a look at …mic HTML. The move to the new …uantum leap from HTML 3.2 to Dynamic …n of DHTML sees a solidification of the …es and functionality are also …g to move beyond the bounds of just …s well.

…ds easier development of web pages. To … skills of a content specialist, a designer …With the new technology called **behaviors**, …g aspects of a page, just like Cascading …visual appearance.

Total 40.61
VISA 40.61
4502284928737019
005572 0902
Change Due 0.00
JOIN THE INDIGO CIRCLE
SAVE 10% ON BOOKS & EARN
IC POINTS ON EVERY PURCHASE
GST# 89266-5175-RT

we look at the reasons that these new features are being added to the web browser, we see that the 'web-based application' paradigm has nearly reached parity in terms of user interface functionality, with 'traditional' applications such as those developed in C++ or Visual Basic.

In this chapter, we'll aim to cover:

- The foundations of Dynamic HTML
- The similarities and differences between DHTML and static HTML
- What we can do with DHTML, and what we need to learn

The Foundations of Dynamic HTML

Dynamic HTML is a development of the 'traditional' HTML that we already use to create web pages of all kinds. HTML is intended as a *standard* way of representing information, so that it can be displayed by any different types of client browser. Before we go too deeply into Dynamic HTML itself, we'll take a brief look at the background to HTML, and the other **document definition languages** from which it originated.

Document Definition Languages

The documents that were first used in the World Wide Web were written in the format we call **HyperText Markup Language** or **HTML**. Perhaps the two most important features of this were that a basic HTML document was simple to create, and that HTML was almost totally platform- and viewer-independent.

HTML is a **markup language** that tells the client, in general terms, how the information should be presented. For example, to define a heading in an HTML document, you might write:

```
<H2>This is a heading</H2>
```

This tells the client that the text 'This is a heading' should be displayed as a level-2 heading, but allows the client to decide the most appropriate way of displaying it. As HTML has developed, this original concept has become more diluted: more and more specific information (such as fonts, point size and colors) can now be defined *for* the client.

> *An interesting side-effect of this way of defining documents is that it allows people with visual disabilities to use special browsers, that render the documents in a form that is easier to read.*

The first version of HTML was a fairly loosely-defined standard. Version 2 of HTML was more rigorously defined in terms of another standard, known as SGML.

SGML

The purpose of the **Standard Generalized Markup Language** (or **SGML**) is very simple. At the time it was developed, there were several other markup languages in existence – but none of them were particularly portable between platforms, or even between software packages. The purpose of SGML is to allow a formal definition of markup languages that can then be used to give complete flexibility and portability of information display between applications and platforms.

It is tempting for the newcomer to view SGML as a markup language in its own right – defining a set of tags and so on, and providing meanings for them. This is not the case. What SGML *does* do is describe the relationship of components within a document. As such, SGML is not a competitor with the likes of TeX or Postscript (which define such things as layout). SGML is a way of describing what the document 'is', rather than how it should be 'rendered'.

DTD

The purpose of the **Document Type Definition** (or **DTD**) is to define the legal productions of a particular markup language. A simple DTD would do nothing more than, say, define a set of tags that can be used by a particular markup language.

The HTML 4.0 standard is a formally-defined SGML DTD. In other words, the definition of HTML 4.0 is itself specified using the SGML meta-language. This allows HTML specifications to be rigorously defined.

To fully define HTML 4.0, two different specifications are required. The first is the relatively small SGML definition that defines general features, such as the character set and size limits. The second, larger part of the definition is contained in the DTD: this defines the detail, such as the tags and attributes, about which we will learn more later.

The HTML 4.0 DTD can be found at the World Wide Web Consortium (W3C) web site at http://www.w3.org/tr/wd-html40.

Hypertext Markup Language (HTML)

HTML 4.0 is the latest standard to be endorsed by the W3C, and is an outgrowth of the widely used HTML 3.2 standard. HTML 3.2 itself incorporated all of HTML 2.0, with some very minor changes, and many of the proposals that were in the HTML 3.0 draft specification, plus additional features such as tables and applets.

After the HTML 3.2 standard was proposed, additions continued to be made to new browsers – over and above the requirements of the standard – so that the 3.2 standard itself was overtaken before it reached the stage of final ratification.

So there were several subtle changes that required a new standard to be defined. The primary reason for HTML 4.0 was to make the HTML standard compatible with the other two components that make up Dynamic HTML: Cascading Style Sheets and the Document Object Model. Otherwise, HTML 4.0 is not *that* different from HTML 3.2.

Hopefully, as there is less need for new tags and new attributes, HTML 4.0 should see the standard settling down at long last. Only when there is a stable standard that the major companies adhere to, do we have any chance of achieving a fully standardized and platform-independent way of viewing information from across the planet.

Extensible Markup Language (XML)

So far, we have heard about two markup languages, SGML and HTML. Another markup language that is at the forefront of application discussions today is **eXtensible Markup Language**, or **XML**. Like HTML, XML is a subset of SGML; but there are a few differences between HTML and XML. For example, XML is a much more rigid language than HTML. Every tag in XML must have a corresponding closing tag. Also, XML supports a wide range of existing DTDs, as well as an unlimited number of yet-to-be-defined DTDs.

The flexibility of XML has led to it becoming more than just a web-specific language. For example, XML has been employed as a foundation for standards in desktop management, messaging and software distribution. XML's greatest potential strength lies in its utility in data representation. Instead of storing information separate from its description (as metadata), XML allows us to integrate the data itself, and the description of what the data is.

Let's look at an example. You're probably familiar with a comma-delimited list of information, in which the first row identifies each of the fields:

```
Name,address,city,state,postalcode,country,phone
Brian Francis,123 Main Street,Atlanta,GA,30029,USA,(404)555-02931
Jeremy Beacock,1102 Warwick Road,Birmingham,West Mids,B27 6BH,UK,0121-6874100
```

By using XML, this information can be represented in a much more readable format, both to the human reader and to the computer program:

```
<MAILLIST>
   <AUTHOR>
      <NAME>Brian Francis</NAME>
      <ADDRESS>123 Main Street</ADDRESS>
      <CITY>Atlanta</CITY>
      <STATE>GA</STATE>
      <POSTALCODE>30029</POSTALCODE>
      <COUNTRY>USA</COUNTRY>
      <PHONE>(404)555-02931</PHONE>
   </AUTHOR>
   <AUTHOR>
      <NAME>Jeremy Beacock</NAME>
      <ADDRESS>1102 Warwick Road</ADDRESS>
      <CITY>Birmingham</CITY>
      <STATE>West Mids</STATE>
      <POSTALCODE>B27 6BH</POSTALCODE>
      <COUNTRY>UK</COUNTRY>
      <PHONE>0121-6874100</PHONE>
   </AUTHOR>
</MAILLIST>
```

As you can see, while the XML takes up more space, it describes the data better. Beyond that, it describes the relationships between the individual pieces of the data. We'll look at XML later in the book – in particular, we'll examine how XML can be used as a data source within a page in IE5.

What's New in Internet Explorer 5

Internet Explorer 4.0 was considered to be a big leap forward in functionality. The addition of Dynamic HTML changed the way that people were able to develop web pages. No longer were they dependent on some applet or object to provide a dynamic presentation. Other features, such as integration with Remote Data Services, lessened the need to make multiple trips to the server. Internet Explorer 4.0 changed the web page paradigm away from static pages, towards dynamic pages with rich interactions.

Internet Explorer 5.0 builds on this foundation. As forthcoming standards (such as XML and Cascading Style Sheets) have been, or will be, realized, IE5 has been enhanced to support these new standards. Microsoft also used this new release to improve on the performance of the browser itself. This feature will just add to the better browsing experience that DHTML has provided for us.

What Hasn't Changed

As what could (hopefully!) be the start of a future trend, the implementation of Dynamic HTML in Internet Explorer 4.0 was actually compliant with the HTML 4.0 and Document Object Model (DOM) specifications before they were even ratified. This means that the DHTML support that was in IE4 remains relatively unchanged in IE5. This will allow nearly all of the pages developed for IE4 to be readily viewed from IE5.

IE5 continues to support all ActiveX Scripting-compatible engines. For most of us, this means that VBScript and JScript will continue to be the primary scripting languages employed in IE5. Microsoft has made considerable enhancements to the both of these languages, but the scripts developed for the previous versions will continue to run.

The Cascading Style Sheet (CSS) support in IE4 introduced a very powerful feature known as **filters and transitions**. This allowed developers to add a rich visual transformation (such as drop shadows or opacity) to standard HTML elements. Transitions allowed for a rich visual effect when using scripting to dynamically change the visual representation of the page.

IE4 also gave us the ability to access data from different data sources without requiring an interaction with a server. This technology, known as **data binding**, allowed these data sources to be easily bound to a set of elements on a DHTML page for display. The data was cached at the client-side, making it very efficient to filter and browse through the data. This technology continues in IE5 – but with some cool new features, brought about by the recent release of ActiveX Data Objects (ADO) 2.0.

What's Actually New

Internet Explorer 5.0 would not have been much of a release if Microsoft hadn't added any new features to it. Hence, they've added functionality that greatly enhances the role of Internet Explorer as the user interface for more than just web pages. Microsoft has been talking about the **Windows Distributed interNetworked Applications** (or **Windows DNA**) architecture. In this architecture, the role of interfacing with the end user is primarily the responsibility of Internet Explorer. This means that, rather than writing custom interface applications in Visual Basic or Java, the user experience is provided via a web page hosted by Internet Explorer.

To better support this new application architecture and use for the browser, Microsoft has added a number of new features and functions to IE5. These will provide for better performance, more code reuse and access to new formats of data.

Styles and Layout

In IE4, the visual style of the elements being displayed could be set using CSS. These style sheets supported CSS Level 1 standard (CSS1), as ratified by the W3C. With IE5, Microsoft has added support for most of the functionality of the CSS Level 2 (CSS2) specification. To make working with style properties easier, some additional events and methods have been added to the object model. For example, we have a new event called `onpropertychange`, which is fired whenever the value of any property on an element in the object model is changed.

In an effort to increase the performance of IE5, Microsoft has added some additional functionality to designing tables. With traditional tables, the browser must read the entire table in order to determine the sizes of each of the columns. Over a slow link, this means that the browser can't begin to draw the table until *all* of the table has been read. By adding support for fixed layout tables, where the column sizes are determined up front, IE5 can display tables more quickly.

Behaviors

With the introduction of behaviors in IE5, developers now have a way of encapsulating the scripting logic that makes DHTML pages dynamic. A behavior is defined by its interface in much the same way that a COM object is defined by its interface – that is, the interface allows a set of properties, methods and events to be exposed. A behavior can also listen for events that happen in the document that is hosting it, and perform some action based on that event.

Behaviors allow a web page developer to attach an element (or elements) on their page to a behavior, and that element will 'behave' in the way defined by the behavior. For example, you will have seen pages in which DHTML is used to make a part of their page react when a mouse moves over it. By putting that interactivity code into a behavior, it allows that code to be used on any page; moreover, it can be used by web page designers who don't necessarily have experience in scripting.

Object Model and Scripting Changes

The object model includes several new objects that allow the developer to provide greater control and interactivity between the page and the browsers. For example, the `dataTransfer` object gives much finer control over information being moved through the clipboard or via drag-and-drop.

IE5 also has a usability feature called **form auto-completion**. The `autocomplete` property is one of the new properties that have been added to the object model – it allows the developer to control the form auto-completion feature from script.
In promoting IE5 from being a simple web browser to an application deployment platform, Microsoft has added more control for the developer over the interaction between the document and the mouse. The new `setCapture` method gives the developer control over where mouse events are handled: with this method, drop-down menus and context menus can be easily created without the use of a custom control.

Persistence of User Data

Persistence will enable you to specify an object to persist on the client during the current and future sessions using DHTML behaviors. This will allow you to store more detailed information than can be stored in just a cookie. Persistence allows IE5 to retain web page information, styles, variables and state. For example, if you have an expandable list of information on a page, you can store what levels are currently visible, so that when the user returns to the page, they see the same information.

Native XML and XSL Support

IE5 supports direct browsing of XML source files using CSS or XSL (eXtensible Stylesheet Language), just as users can browse HTML documents. For example, a user can add XML files to his Favorites folder, and can inspect XML files in the History list. By using eXtensible Style Sheets to define what an XML file should be displayed as, these files can be shown directly in the browser, or as part of another HTML file. Some XML pundits are predicting that the combination of XML and XSL may replace all of HTML, since it is intrinsically more powerful and facilitates richer search engine technologies since content is truly separated from layout control.

An XML Data Island allows data represented in XML format to be a part of an HTML document. Rather than using a style sheet to display the information directly in the browser, the Data Island can be accessed via script.

HTML Applications

One of the ways that Microsoft is making IE5 a true application development platform is through the addition of HTML Application support. These are full-fledged Windows applications, just like those created in C++ or in Visual Basic. The application developer has complete control over the menus, icons, toolbars and title information that is normally all determined by Internet Explorer itself.

> *However, programming the browser and the Active Desktop are beyond the scope of this book. We'll focus on Dynamic HTML as a language, and learn how to create pages that conform to the Dynamic HTML as supported in IE5.*

Working with DHTML

The remainder of this chapter, is a preview of some of the things that Dynamic HTML can do for our web pages – and see how they provide opportunities to do things we can't accomplish using static HTML pages.

In later chapters we'll get down to arming you with knowledge to build these pages. One difficulty with things like browsers that have to retain a lot of backward compatibility is the accumulation of older implementations that are no longer the way to create new applications, so there's more than one way to achieve any given task. Hopefully this book will also give you enough information to choose the most appropriate ways to make things happen in DHTML.

Accessing the Elements in the Page

In traditional HTML, it's impossible to 'get at' most of the contents of a web page once it's been rendered (i.e. displayed) by the browser. You can write scripts that read or change the values in text boxes, checkboxes and other HTML controls. You can also include objects in the pages, such as ActiveX controls or Java applets, and access them through script code. And, of course, you can change the background color of the page, or the color of the links on the page, through script. What you can't do is read or change anything else. You can't change the text on the page – either in headings, lists, tables or body text. You can't change the font or style of the text, add or remove images, or change their position. In fact, you can't do much at all.

Of course, the Web itself (and in particular, the browser that displays the pages) was originally designed as an information delivery system. The whole idea was that you (the end-user) got a page full of text and graphics to read. In those days, no-one expected you to want to *play* with it...

With Dynamic HTML, all this changes. As a developer, DHTML allows you to build pages whose appearance is dependent on the user's actions. In principal, you can give the user the power to change almost anything in the page, even while it's being displayed. All the elements of your web pages are accessed through scripting languages, so all you have to do is write the scripts that give the end-user this control, and build them into your code.

As an example, this page (named `ListChange.htm`) displays its list items in a different color, size and font style when the mouse pointer moves over them. Notice that they're not even hyperlinks – it's just a normal unordered list created with the `<UL>` tag. It's done using script code that detects the position of the mouse, and then changes the style of the text.

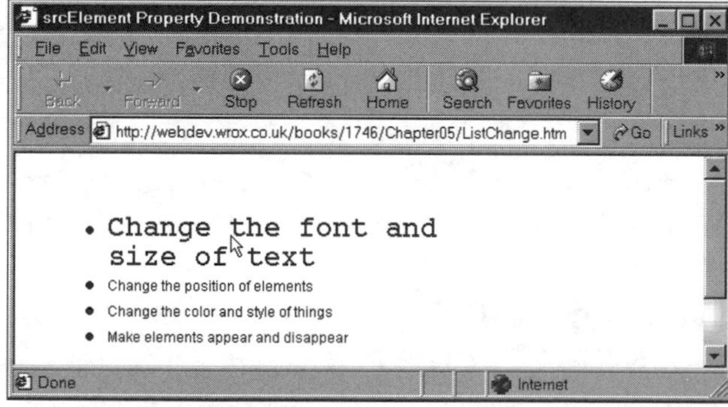

You can download (or just browse) all the samples for this book from our web site – at http://webdev.wrox.co.uk/books/1746. *We'll be returning to* `ListChange.htm` *in Chapter 5.*

Properties, Styles and Style Sheets

In the previous example, we saw that a scripting language like JavaScript or VBScript can change some relatively minor aspects of a loaded page by responding to movements of the mouse over the parts of the page. In recent versions of the mainstream browsers, it's been possible to control the size and font face of the text in a page, although it could only be set in a page as it was being designed, and not on-the-fly while it was being displayed.

This was done using either the `<FONT>` or `<STYLE>` HTML tags. The simplest way was to enclose text in `<FONT> </FONT>` tags, and specify the font face, size, color and other effects:

```
<FONT FACE="Arial Black" SIZE=4 COLOR=green>
   This is some text in big green letters
</FONT>
```

Instead of specifying these styles with every occurrence of the `<FONT>` tag, you could use the `<STYLE>` tag to define a set of named styles, then allocate them to different parts of the text. By using the standard formatting tag names, it was possible to avoid having to specify which style applied to which part of the text. If you wanted some `<H2>` text to be large and green, you just defined this in a `<STYLE>` section at the start of the page:

```
<STYLE>
   .biggreen {font-family:"Arial Black"; font-size=18; color=green}
</STYLE>
<BODY>
   <H2 CLASS=biggreen>This is some text in big green letters</H2>
   ...
```

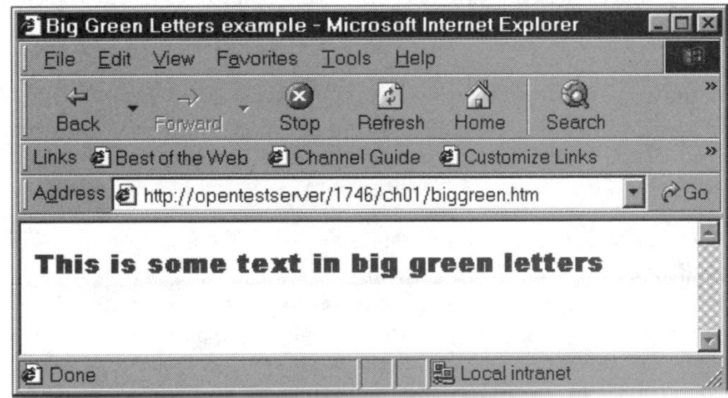

An even better way, if you wanted a lot of pages to have the same style, was to put the `<STYLE>` definition into a separate file, called a **cascading style sheet** (CSS), and link your CSS to each page. Then you could change the styles in all the pages just by changing the entry in the style sheet file.

> *Don't worry if you're not up to speed on using styles like this. We'll be looking at how it's done in more depth in the next chapter, and we've included full details in the Appendices at the back of the book.*

But, why are we talking about existing methods? The point here is that Dynamic HTML uses the characteristics you specify for the items in the page to provide **properties** for each one. In other words, we now have to think of every part of the page as an individual **element** or **object**, and not just as a tag. Using DHTML, the text between the `<H2>` and `</H2>` tags is now part of that heading element, and it has a whole range of properties that are accessible from script code. The `font-size` is no longer *just* a number in a `<STYLE>` or `<FONT>` tag – rather, it is also the `fontSize` property of an `H2` element object.

We'll be looking at style sheets in a lot more detail later. For the moment, you just need to appreciate that they provide a link between the definition of all the parts of the page in HTML, and that they can react to the script code within the page in a new way – as properties of that element's object in the Document Object Model.

The Extended Browser Object Model

So, all the pages we load into our shiny new browser are going to consist of hundreds of different objects, rather than a static page full of text and graphics with a few HTML controls, or ActiveX and Java objects. It sounds like trying to program all this lot in scripting code will be a terrifying experience. However, as in most other programming environments, the browser provides an object model which organizes all the different objects and elements in a way that makes them manageable. If you've programmed using VBScript or JavaScript before, you'll have used this concept.

To cope with the flood of all kinds of new objects, Dynamic HTML includes several additions to the browser object model. Bear in mind that this object model is a proposed standard with the W3C, so it will be available in all browsers that will host the standard Dynamic HTML. This means that, as long as we write our pages and scripts to this standards-based model, they *should* work in all the other browsers that support it.

> *Unfortunately, at this time the utopia of standard DHTML is still not reality. The DHTML supported by Netscape is different than the one supported by Microsoft. Until both browsers are compliant with the same standard, the idea of true cross-browser DHTML will probably remain just a dream.*

We'll look in detail at the object model in later chapters, and it's fully documented in the appendices at the back of this book. You'll see how it becomes part of everything we do when we work with scripts in Dynamic HTML.

Absolute Positioning and the Z-order

One of the biggest criticisms of static HTML it that it is difficult to gain accurate control of the page's appearance. Before the implementation of styles, as we saw earlier, everything was displayed in a default font (usually something like Times Roman), in default colors, and almost at random within the browser window. The most you could do was specify where a paragraph should start or end, and whether graphics or other elements should align to the left, center or right of the page. Everything moved about as the user resized the browser window, and that could be a big problem if you were trying to present a specific user interface design.

To some extent the use of tables helped to solve this, and when frames became more universally supported they allowed even more control. There is another technique – a special ActiveX control called the **Layout Control** – which appeared with Internet Explorer 3 (along with support for ActiveX controls). The Layout Control provided an area of the page that behaved like a form – you could place controls and other objects on it in fixed positions. It was rather like the screen window that fronts a normal Windows application.

One of the biggest advances in Dynamic HTML is the support for positioning and sizing, which allows us to achieve this result in the page *without* having to use frames or ActiveX controls. Elements can be sized and positioned in the browser window exactly as the author requires. As you'll see in the next chapter, this very useful feature has evolved from these earlier techniques. Also, the **z-index** allows us to overlay elements in a specific order more easily than ever before.

The new concept of laying out pages is therefore very similar to desktop publishing techniques. (Unfortunately, however, the tools available to help still have some way to go – at the time of writing, Macromedia's *Dreamweaver* is closest to this goal, but it is still not fully there yet.) To see the difference it makes, here's another of the sample pages from this book (the 'dancing buttons' page, from Chapter 5). The first screenshot shows the page as it appears in IE5; the second shows the same page loaded into IE3, which does not support direct positioning of elements. As you can see, the layout of the buttons on the two pages, derived from the same HTML file, is completely different.

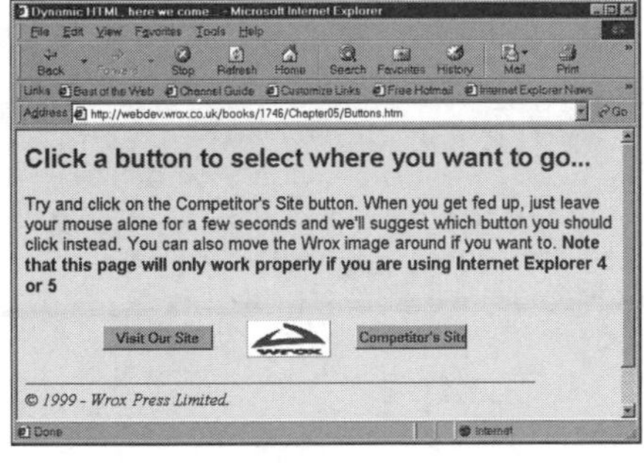

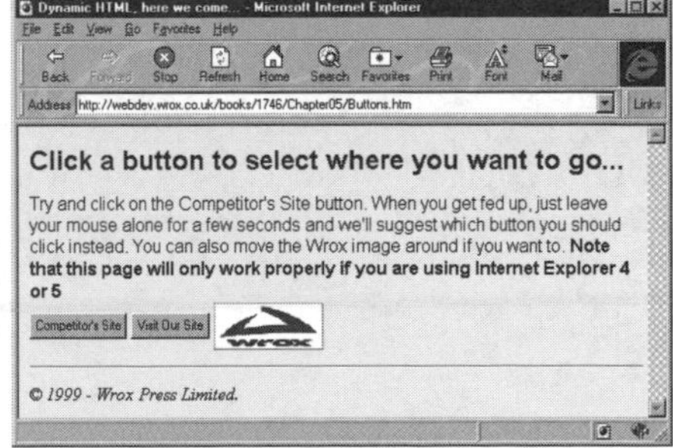

Movement and Dynamic Page Re-Drawing

The fact that we can accurately position elements on the page immediately prompts the next question. If we can put them exactly where we want them, can we move them around as well? The answer is 'yes' – in fact, this is one of the most visible advantages that Dynamic HTML provides. It's linked to the fact once the page has loaded from the HTML stream, a live object model exists in IE5 that can be manipulated by script. The original HTML stream can then be discarded.

This rather unusual effect can be seen if you load a Dynamic HTML page, then carry out a task which changes the page – such as moving an element to a new position. The usual View Source option in the browser opens the original HTML code in NotePad, but it doesn't reflect the currently displayed page: this only shows the *original* source that created the page in the first place. As you'd expect, clicking the Reload button in the browser reloads this original version of the page again.

Of course, Internet Explorer always had the ability to redraw parts of the page. If you changed the value in an HTML text box using script code, the new value was visible on the page. The big difference with Dynamic HTML is that the entire stored page representation, which can itself be manipulated by the code, will show these changes on screen as soon as they happen.

You may already have seen this in the `buttons.htm` example we showed you on the previous page. In this example, the Competitor's Site button jumps out of the way of your mouse, while the Visit our Site button creeps towards it when you stop moving the pointer around.

Handling and Bubbling Events

The reason that the samples you've seen so far behave as they do is that the code in the pages is designed to react to **events**. For example, we can generate an event by clicking on the page displayed in the browser window, or even just by moving the mouse pointer. These are examples of user-generated events – there are other events going on in the background that are generated by the operating system, not by the user. The browser, being the active window, reacts to these events by passing them on to the code in the page through the object model.

In fact, this happens in most applications. It used to happen in pre-DHTML capable browsers. What's new is that there is now a whole heap of options when it comes to reacting to the events in our scripting code. These not only give us more choice about how we create pages, but can also make the job of writing the code easier. We can provide one routine to handle an event in several objects, or several different events for one object.

Probably the two most useful features of Dynamic HTML are **event bubbling** and **source element identification**. With event bubbling we can choose whether or not to allow an event to 'bubble up' through the browser's object hierarchy. By allowing the event to bubble up, we can handle the same event at different levels. We can identify which of the page's elements fired the event (or to be more precise, which was the 'topmost' element that received the event being fired).

Source element identification is used to detect mouse movement events – by allowing us to identify which element the mouse is moving onto, and which element the mouse is being moved from. This allows behaviors to be composed together and enables authors and developers to amass stock script code to use throughout sites and web applications.

To see how useful event bubbling can be, try the `buttons.htm` sample page again. You'll find that you can push the Competitor's Site button underneath the central Wrox logo, and it still responds to mouse movements – even though the pointer is actually over the logo graphic. This is because the button is still picking up the events caused by the mouse.

Graphic Filters

Finally, one of the biggest advances in Dynamic HTML is the inclusion of multimedia effects that are fully programmable via style sheets and scripting properties. These effects are enabled through the **Visual Filter** and the **Reveal Transition Filter**. These allow the developer access to a multitude of effects.

The Visual Filter makes it easy to manipulate images and text, and to add simple effects that were once the preserve of art packages such as *Corel Draw* and *PaintShop Pro*. It has 14 effects available, allowing anything from a simple (horizontal or vertical) image flip to a motion blurring effect, and even an X-ray filter! We have a simple program (shown here) that demonstrates what all the filters can do to text and images – we'll discuss it in Chapter 4.

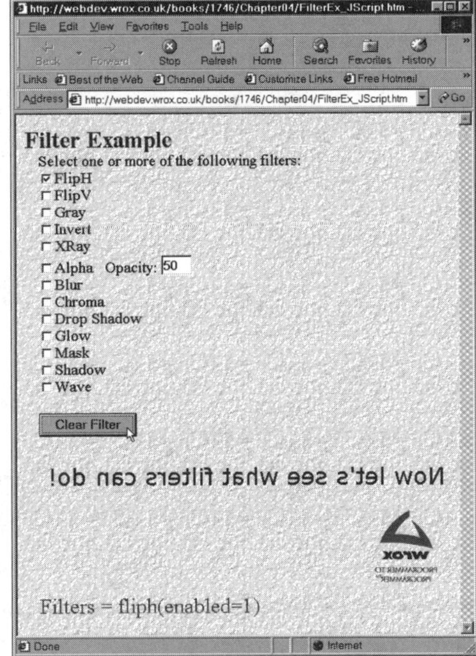

The Reveal Transition Filter allows you to reveal or hide any element (or group of elements) gradually, using any of the 23 predefined patterns. For example you make an image fade away, in the form of a vertical blind, while at the same time making another one appear. This example also allows you to select any of the effects on offer. Again, we'll be looking at this in Chapter 4.

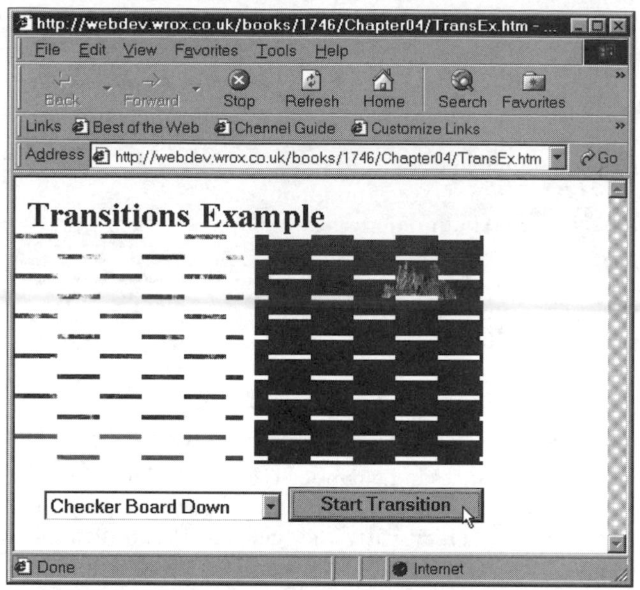

You can take a look at these graphical effects in action, by navigating to http://webdev.wrox.co.uk/books/1746.

In your average programming language, these effects would have taken quite some programming. With DHTML, they're all easily available through just a one-line method call together with parameters. Being a graphics whiz has never been easier.

We've skipped through the list of new and exciting features in Dynamic HTML very briskly here. This is intentional, both to let you see what's new (and hence, what you're going to learn about in this book), and to give you an understanding of the terminology and how it all fits together. In the remainder of this chapter, we'll look at what you'll need.

Getting Started with Dynamic HTML

By now you should appreciate that Dynamic HTML is not exactly a revolution – it's more an evolution of existing techniques and technologies. You don't need to sit down and learn a whole new language, just develop and extend your existing knowledge of HTML and browser scripting.

The Background Knowledge You'll Need

In this book, we're assuming that you already have some background in both of these areas – in other words that you know how to create a traditional web page using HTML tags, and that you have at least a rudimentary grasp of how scripts are used in web pages.

It doesn't matter whether you're more familiar with VBScript or JavaScript, because we're only using them to manipulate the elements and do basic number crunching. Both languages accomplish this in similar ways, although the details of syntax are different. While VBScript is definitely easier for the newcomer to grasp, JavaScript has now been adopted by ECMA (the European Standards Organization) as the standard scripting language. JavaScript is very likely to remain the dominant scripting language, and therefore it might be worth the extra work to learn it (Netscape software does not support VBScript, and future releases are unlikely to). In this book we feature examples in both languages.

We've included sections on VBScript and JavaScript in the appendices of this book. If you want to learn more about JavaScript or VBScript, look out for *Instant JavaScript* (Wrox, ISBN 1-861001-27-4), *JavaScript Objects* (Wrox, ISBN 1-861001-89-4) and *Instant VBScript* (Wrox, ISBN 1-861000-44-8). If you want to know more about HTML 4.0, look up *Instant HTML Programmer's Reference* (Wrox, ISBN 1-861001-56-8).

Choosing a Text Editor

When creating pages in HTML, many people use an authoring tool such as HotDog, HotMeTaL Pro or even Microsoft Word 97. This is fine for a static page, which just uses the normal HTML tags to create the appearance the user sees. FrontPage can also add WebBots, which provide some interactivity when HTML controls (such as text boxes and lists) are included.

However, these tools hide the actual structure of the page – the tags that do all the work – from the author. They are also unable to create much in the way of script. The bad news is that none of these are going to be much help when we come to use Dynamic HTML.

FrontPage 98

FrontPage 98 is a very powerful tool that Microsoft has upgraded to include Dynamic HTML usage. FrontPage is a very versatile application that allows you to create web pages graphically, and then generates the HTML automatically.

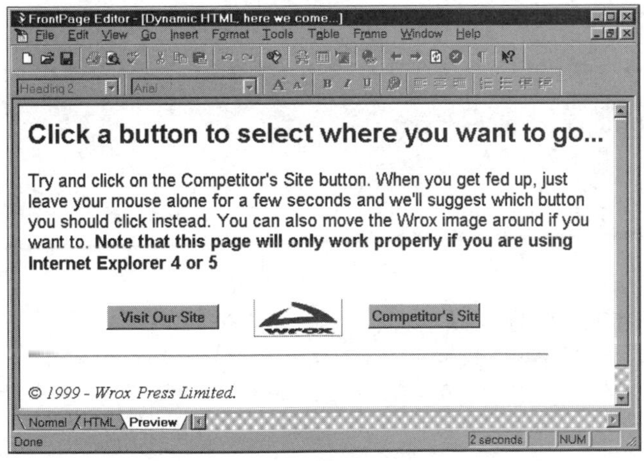

DHTML Code Editors

However, getting a tool to generate your code for you won't help you to get to grips with the language underneath. You'll get a lot more freedom if you actually understand what's going on under the hood – and that's very much what Dynamic HTML is about.

In this book, we're going to be using the single most popular Web page development tool of all time: the NotePad text editor that comes with Windows. It doesn't add frills or decorations, and it won't design your pages for you, but it does allow you to write the programs yourself.

There are two other popular candidates for DHTML code editor. Visual Interdev, part of the Microsoft Visual Studio package, is excellent for HTML and script writing, and features an integrated script debugger. The other candidate is the HomeSite editor from Allaire. You can find more information about this editor at http://www.allaire.com.

There's no reason why you can't use any other text editor that you prefer. One that provides line numbers is particularly useful when you come to look at finding and fixing script errors. You can even use Microsoft Word for this, as long as you remember to save your files with a `.txt` extension in Word 97 (and then rename them as HTML files later). Otherwise, it will automatically convert them into HTML files, and, next time you open one, you'll see the results rather than the actual source HTML tags and script which create the page.

WYSIWYG DHTML: Dreamweaver

One of the drawbacks of writing DHTML pages is that most web development tools don't support DHTML. Even the visual editors, like Front Page, do not offer a way to utilize some of the cool features that DHTML provides. Macromedia's *Dreamweaver* is a tool that provides a way to develop DHTML pages visually. In fact, it can develop pages that will run in Internet Explorer and in the Netscape browser. This is not an easy feat, given that Netscape chose not support the DHTML standard in their browser.

For learning how to program a DHTML page, *Dreamweaver* may not be the best choice. While it does make developing pages easier, it hides all of the scripting code and details from the developer. Like FrontPage, you create pages using its interface, and the DHTML is created behind the scenes.

However, for learning everything that is going on, and being able to do things that the tool won't support, there is nothing better than a simple text-based editor like NotePad or HomeSite.

The Browser – Internet Explorer 5

Finally, of course, you'll need a browser that supports Microsoft's Dynamic HTML. Internet Explorer 5 is available from a number of different sources. You can download IE5 from the Microsoft Web site at http://www.microsoft.com/windows/ie/ie5. Alternatively, you can obtain the browser on CD from a number of different sources; it may have even come preinstalled on your new computer.

So, now that we've assembled our tool kit, both mental and physical, let's get on and look at how Dynamic HTML works in more detail. The first step is to get a more complete understanding of how style sheets and style tags are used in web pages; then we'll see how this affects what we do in Dynamic HTML. This is the subject of the next chapter.

Summary

In this chapter we've taken a view of what it is that makes Dynamic HTML different from plain HTML, and explored some of the ways we can use the its features to create more dynamic web pages. In the broadest terms, the major features are:

- All the elements in the page (tags, images, text, etc.) are now accessible to script written in the page
- An extension to the implementation of styles and style sheets provides more hooks to the page elements from scripting code
- Extensions to the browser object model are included, thus providing more programmability for the scripting languages used in the pages
- Absolute positioning of elements, including control of the z-order, allows a desk-top publishing style of authoring
- Dynamic re-drawing of any or all parts of the page allows changes to a loaded page to be made visible. Pages no longer need to be reloaded to show the updated version
- New event-handling techniques are supported, including bubbling events up through the object hierarchy

We have also introduced some of the new DHTML functionality that is included with IE5, including behaviors and native XML support.

In the rest of the book, we'll explore each of these concepts in depth, and see how we can use them in the pages we create.

2

Style Sheets, Absolute Positioning and Z-Order

In Chapter 1 we looked briefly at what's new in Dynamic HTML, we saw some examples of dynamic pages, and we discovered the things that we have to learn in order to start working with it. Just to review, Dynamic HTML is really the combination of three technologies: Cascading Style Sheets, the Document Object Model, and HTML 4.0. We're now ready to delve a little deeper into the workings of DHTML.

We'll begin with style sheets, which we can use to connect the elements in the page (such as text or graphics) to the scripts. In standard HTML, styles were either specified in the attributes of tags or in style sheets, and they couldn't be changed without refreshing the whole page. One of the main innovations in Dynamic HTML is that it allows the user to alter properties dynamically, which in turn allows the elements of the page to be changed or moved – without the need to refresh the page each time. DHTML also allows much greater control over positioning of elements on a page – to the nearest pixel, in fact. It also allows us to place elements on top of other elements, and to move an element in front of another.

The basis for all of this stems from style sheets. In case you're unfamiliar with style sheets, we'll begin with a quick look at how they work and how they can be used to enhance the layout of your pages. Then we'll look at the properties that DHTML introduces and how they work. This chapter is concerned with how to build pages that leverage the power of DHTML to produce pages that look exactly the way the author intended.

So we'll be covering:

- How styles and style sheets work in general
- How we can use style tags to achieve absolute positioning
- What z-order is, and how we can control the z-order of elements in the page

- How we achieve a 'two-and-a-half-D' effect
- How to use style sheets to connect scripts to page elements
- How to create dynamic styles, whose values change automatically without scripting

With this, we'll reinforce our understanding of the way styles are used, and introduce a couple of new style attributes. We've supplied a full style reference at the back of this book to help you out.

Using Styles and Style Sheets

As we discussed in Chapter 1, style sheets are the principal way in which we provide a link between the elements in our dynamic web pages and the code that manipulates them. In this chapter, we'll take a more detailed look at how this link works; but for the moment we'll concentrate on how style sheets are used in the traditional way. You'll need to be familiar with this concept before you can start to take advantage of the extensions to the technique that DHTML offers.

At the present time, there are two main ways to implement style sheets (both of which have ugly acronyms). Internet Explorer 5 implements style sheets through the use of **Cascading Style Sheets Level Two**, or **CSS2** (CSS2 is not a standard yet, but IE5 supports *most* of it). CSS2 is designed to be easy to use and implement, and consequently it has something of a lead over the alternative, **DSSSL-Online**. DSSSL-Online is more comprehensive, but it's rather more difficult to use and is therefore not supported by IE5.

> ***DSSSL-Online** is the web version of **Document Style Semantics and Specification Language**, a remarkably large and complex standard supported by the ISO.*

CSS2 was supported by W3C and the major browsers in HTML version 3.2 – and is now well on the way to becoming the *de facto* standard for web style sheets. Dynamic HTML, in the HTML 4.0 standard, extends style sheets by adding some new attributes.

Why use Style Sheets?

There are three primary advantages to using style sheets. First, style sheets have universality of application. This means that we can develop a style sheet and then apply it to any document (or group of documents), simply by setting each document so that it refers to the style sheet we created. This universality has an additional benefit: we can make consistent changes to the appearance of *all* our pages, simply by changing the style sheet.

Second, style sheets can convey greater typographic control than is normally possible. CSS, for example, provides a number of properties that can be used to create effects such as drop-caps, overlapping text, shadowed text and so on.

Third, style sheets (unlike other methods of display control) retain the content/presentation split, which means that style sheet information is separate from the actual text information. This can result in smaller file sizes. For example, we can have five 10 KB documents that all reference the same 5 KB style sheet – these take less space than five 15 KB documents that each contain their own style information. Not only does this lead to smaller file sizes, but since the style sheet can be cached by the browser, it will only have to be downloaded once. Furthermore, the split allows better skill management, because content can be altered without having to re-format each document with the appropriate HTML tags.

The CSS Example

The following picture is achieved using all text, with no bitmaps (the giant WE appears in red type in the original):

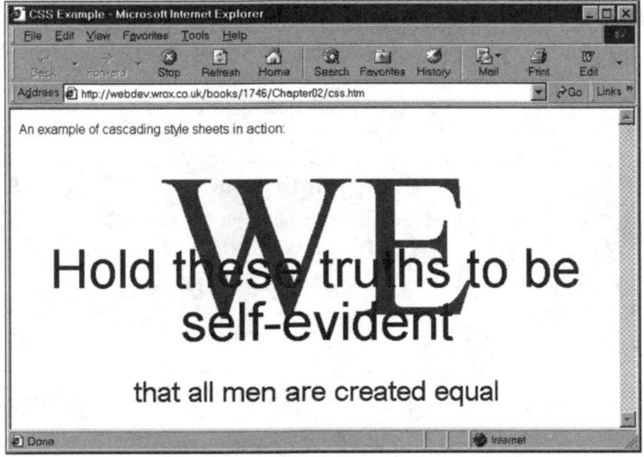

You can run this page from our web site, at *http://webdev.wrox.co.uk/books/1746.*

Here's the HTML file that generates this page:

```
<HTML>
<HEAD>
<TITLE>CSS Example</TITLE>
<STYLE TYPE="text/css">
<!--
BODY {color:        black;
      font-size:    16px;
      font-family: Arial }
.base { color: red;
        weight:       medium;
        margin-top:   10px;
        font-size:    250px;
        line-height: 250px;
        font-family: Times }
.layer1 { color:        black;
          margin-top:   -130px;
          weight:       medium;
          font-size:    65px;
          line-height: 65px;
          font-family: Arial }
```

```
.layer2 { color:         black;
          margin-top:    30px;
          weight:        medium;
          font-size:     35px;
          line-height:   45px;
          font-family:   Arial }
-->
</STYLE>
</HEAD>
<BODY>
  An example of cascading style sheets in action:
  <CENTER>
    <TABLE WIDTH=730 CELLPADDING=0 CELLSPACING=0 BORDER=0>
      <TR>
        <TD ALIGN=CENTER VALIGN=TOP>
          <DIV CLASS=base>WE</DIV>
          <DIV CLASS=layer1>Hold these truths to be self-evident</DIV>
          <DIV CLASS=layer2>that all men are created equal</DIV>
        </TD>
      </TR>
    </TABLE>
  </CENTER>
</BODY>
</HTML>
```

Notice that this HTML file doesn't contain any images. This is an example of the sort of thing that we can do with style sheets, without resorting to special workarounds or tricks. Anyone viewing this page would only have to download a little over 1 KB, which is significantly smaller than the equivalent page constructed from images.

We'll start our study of style sheets with a look at how to set about specifying the rules that go to a make up a style sheet.

Creating Style Sheets

A style sheet is essentially a declaration of display rules, specifying the display attributes of particular HTML constructs. These rules are easy to write – they consist of combinations of tags, property names and values.

Note that we place `<STYLE>` declarations in HTML comment tags, `<!--     -->`, which are used for masking blocks of code. This is in order to hide the code from older browsers that are not able to interpret it.

Syntax

The official term for a CSS declaration is a **selector**. Each selector follows the same format:

```
TAG { property : value }
```

For example, to set all level-1 headings to white, we could use either of the following statements:

```
H1 { color: white }
```

```
H1 { color: #FFFFFF }
```

As you can see, both of these lines declare that everything enclosed by an <H1> tag will have the color white (or hex #FFFFFF) applied to it.

There's a list of the color names and values in Appendix F of this book.

We can apply a single property to multiple tags by grouping the tags in the selector statement. In this example, we set level-1, level-2 and level-3 headings to display in black:

```
H1, H2, H3 { color: #000000 }
```

As well as grouping tags, we can also group properties. We simply enclose our multiple property declarations inside the curly braces and separate them with semicolons. In the following example, we've spread the selector across multiple lines to make the code easier to read. This has the same effect as placing it all on one line. In both cases, though, don't forget the closing brace.

```
H2 {
      color: #000000;
      font-size: 14pt;
      font-family: monaco
   }
```

This example will display all level-2 headings in 14 point Monaco, in black (unless the client doesn't have access to the Monaco font, in which case it will revert to the default font). Here we specified the size of the text in typeface points (`pt`), but we could have used any one of the available measurement units.

There are four relative measurement units: `em`, `en`, `ex` are typographic terms, and refer to the sizes of certain characters, while `px` refers to a measurement in screen pixels (`px` is generally only meaningful for display on computer monitors and depends on the user's display resolution setting).
There are also five absolute units: `in` gives the measurement in inches, `pc` is in picas, and `pt` is in typeface points (72 points = 6 pica = 1 inch). There are also two metric units: `cm` for centimetres, `mm` for millimetres. These units are generally only useful when you know what the output medium is going to be, since browsers are allowed to approximate if necessary.

In our CSS example above, we've defined a style for the <BODY> tag:

```
BODY {color:       black;
      font-size:   16px;
      font-family: Arial }
```

This means that all text without a specific style assignment that appears between the opening and closing <BODY> tags will automatically default to the style specified, just as the An example of cascading style sheets in action: text on the page does.

In that example, we also applied groups of properties to sections of text, without restricting those properties to any particular tags:

```
.layer2 { color:       black;
          margin-top:  30px;
          weight:      medium;
          font-size:   35px;
          line-height: 45px;
          font-family: Arial }
```

```
<DIV CLASS=layer2>that all men are created equal</DIV>
```

We do this by defining a **class**, `layer2`. We'll look at how classes work later in this chapter.

Inheritance

One of the best features of CSS is that it allows one tag to **inherit** the properties of an enclosing tag. This means that we don't need to specify every property of every single tag. For example, if we neglect to set a property for `<EM>` it will simply acquire the characteristics of whatever tag encloses it. Consider the following:

```
<H3>Section Four: <EM>Colossal</EM> Widgets</H3>
```

If our style sheet specified that all `<H3>` items were to be in green, but didn't say anything about `<EM>`, then the word Colossal would be green, just like the rest of the line. If, on the other hand, we carefully specified that `<EM>` was blue, the word Colossal would appear as such. This system of inheritance follows through all of the possible properties. This allows us to set default values – we then only need to worry about the exceptions to our rules (the best way to do this is to set all default properties in the `<BODY>` tag, and then deal with the exceptions using the appropriate tags where necessary).

Even better, we can specify that a property will have a value that is *relative* to its parent property:

```
<STYLE TYPE="text/css">
<!--
BODY {font-size:   16pt;}
.fivetimes { font-size:   500%; }
.seventimes { font-size:   700%; }
-->
</STYLE>

<BODY>
Here's some body text in 16 point<BR>
<DIV CLASS=fivetimes>Here's some at five times the size</DIV>
<DIV CLASS=seventimes>Here's some at seven times the size</DIV>
</BODY>
```

In this instance, the font size of the two classes is defined as a percentage of font size of the body text. This is useful when we come to revise the styles later, since it automatically ensures that our font sizes will instantly change whenever we change the font size of the body text. If we had declared each font size explicitly, we would need to change it manually – a task that's easily forgotten in the heat of designing a site.

Contextual Selectors

Another useful feature of inheritance is that it can be used to apply styles contextually. For example, not only can we set <H3> to green and <EM> to blue, but we can also set all instances of <EM> that occur in <H3> as yellow, without affecting either of our other declarations. This is remarkably easy to achieve:

```
H3 EM { color: yellow }
```

Here the style sheet is specifying that any instance of <EM> that occurs inside <H3> will be shown as yellow. This does not affect any other instance of <EM>. You must be careful to omit the comma between the tags when using this method – or the declaration will be interpreted as meaning that both <H3> *and* <EM> should be yellow.

This technique can be applied in great detail. For example, it is possible to specify that all emphasized words are in red, in small print, but only when they appear in a listing that is itself enclosed by <I>:

```
I EM { color: red; font-size: 75%; }
```

These types of declarations are termed **contextual selectors,** since they select values based on their context.

It is also possible to specify values for several contextual selectors within a single statement, by dividing them with commas. This can shorten pages with lots of style information, and as we all know, shorter pages mean faster download times! For example:

```
H3 EM, H2 I { color: yellow }
```

has the same effect as:

```
H3 EM { color: yellow }
H2 I { color: yellow }
```

One of the first things that budding CSS designers do is go crazy with the control they've just acquired. Sure, you can make your links all appear in pink 24pt Times, but do you really want to? Changing properties, simply because you can, is a recipe for reader dissatisfaction. If visitors can't figure out 'what is a link' versus 'what is just an emphasis', or 'why all of the lines are in 6pt type', they probably won't bother visiting your site again.

A full list of style sheet properties can be found in Appendix E.

Cascading Style Sheets

One of the niftiest (and most confusing) capabilities of CSS is the ability to have style sheets that **cascade** – hence the name **Cascading Style Sheets**. Compliant browsers are supposed to allow multiple style sheets to have control over the same document at the same time. Thus it is possible to have two (or more) separate style sheets trying to format a document at once. This is actually more useful than it sounds.

When authors set up documents and refer to style sheets, they are expressing their preferred mode of display. Browsers have their own 'default style' that they prefer to use when displaying pages, and when the browser interprets documents on the web, it will display them in the default style. However, if it runs across a document that uses CSS, it will give way to the preferences stated in that style sheet (unless the user specifically tells the browser to do otherwise). The basic idea is that 'normal' HTML documents have nothing to lose by being formatted according to browser preferences, but documents using CSS ought to be displayed the way the author intended (or else they wouldn't have been formatted that way in the first place).

With IE5, a user can create their own style sheet that can be applied to every document that they view. This makes it easy for a user with a visual impairment to view all documents with the text 50% larger, or for those who have a special font preference to make their favorite font the new default font. You can set the user style sheet for IE5 using the Accessibility dialog box, which can be displayed by selecting Tools, then Internet Options..., and finally the Accessibility... button:

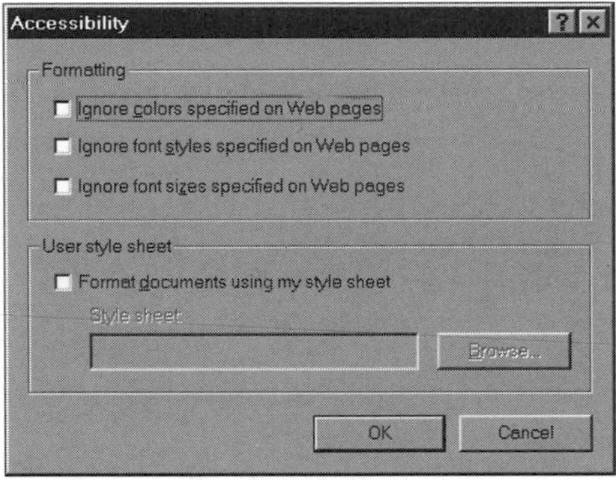

How Styles Cascade

"Cascading" in CSS specifies how an element instance is affected by styles of different types: inline style, embedded style sheet, linked style sheet and imported style sheet. The logic is quite simple: CSS cascades from general to specific, and from top to bottom.

This simple example will show us how styles work together as they cascade:

```
<STYLE>
<!--

  BODY { background-color: yellow; }
  P { margin-left: 25px; }
  .MyFontClass { font-family: "Tahoma"; font-size: 14pt; color: DarkBlue;}
  #myParagraph { text-align: left; font-weight: bold; }

--></STYLE>

<BODY>
<P ID="myParagraph" CLASS="MyFontClass">Three different styles - all take
effect</P>
</BODY>
```

If you view this page in your browser, you will see the following (this is dark blue text on a yellow background).

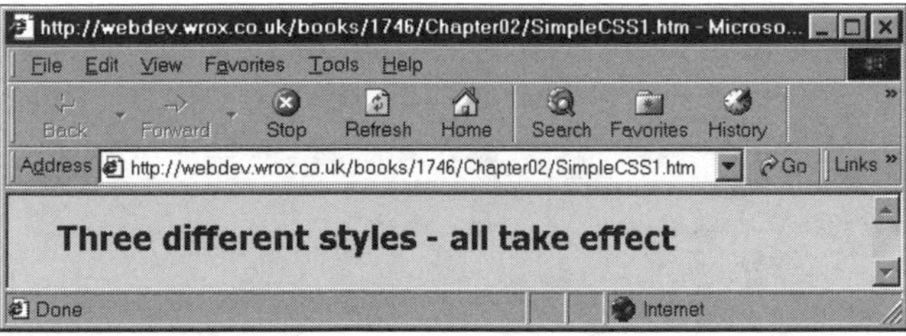

We've assigned the paragraph a name (or **ID**), `myParagraph`:

```
<P> ID="myParagraph" CLASS="MyFontClass">Three different styles - all take
effect</P>
```

This allows us to specify style rules that only apply to a paragraph with that ID:

```
#myParagraph { text-align: left; font-weight: bold; }
```

However, the paragraph formatting is also affected by the style rules for `<BODY>`, `<P>` and `MyFontClass`. These potentially conflicting styles are resolved through the laws of cascading and inheritance:

- First, the background-color style for the `<BODY>` tag is applied to the `<BODY>` element (the whole document)
- Next, the `left-margin` value is applied to the `<P>` element
- Then, the font formatting is applied to all elements with the `MyFontClass` class
- Finally, the styles specifically assigned to the `myParagraph` element are applied.

As the styles cascade and conflicts occur, the rules are applied in this order, with the top of the list having the most weight:

- Inline styles (not shown in this example)
- ID
- CLASS
- HTML element.

Since there were no conflicting style assignments – for example, the background color for the paragraph was set only in the `<BODY>` rule, and the font size was set only in the `MyFontClass` style rule – the styles "cascaded" through each assignment unchanged.

The next example will show what happens when style settings conflict:

```
<STYLE>
<!--

  BODY { background-color: yellow; }
  P { margin-left: 25px; }
  .MyFontClass { font-family: "Tahoma"; font-size: 14pt; color: DarkBlue;}
  #myParagraph { text-align: left; font-weight: bold; color: Red;}

--></STYLE>

<BODY>
<P ID="myParagraph" CLASS="MyFontClass">Three different styles - one
conflict</P>
</BODY>
```

You can see that the style defined in the `ID` takes precedence over the style defined in the `CLASS` (the higher the style is in the preceding list, the more precedence it has). If you view this page in your browser, the result is like this (this time it's *red* text on a yellow background):

In addition to having multiple styles affecting one element, it is also possible to have multiple style sheets all appearing at once on the page. This is actually a benefit, since it allows you to create multiple focused style sheets, and then apply them in different combinations to different documents. Unfortunately, however, this is neither particularly easy nor very intuitive, and requires careful use of the correct **implementation tags** within the document.

Implementing Style Sheets

So the next question is this: how do we actually incorporate the style sheet functionality into our HTML document? There are several ways to do this and they each have slightly different effects. It is important to decide which method suits your purpose, since they're not functionally identical.

Using <LINK>

The first method is a special use of the `<LINK>` tag. This can be used to reference independent style sheets, which can then be applied to the document at will. To use the `<LINK>` method, we place the following in the `<HEAD>` of our document:

```
<LINK REL=STYLESHEET TYPE="text/css" HREF="http://foo.bar.com/style"
      TITLE="Style">
```

Obviously, you would need to change the `HREF` to point to your own style sheet.

You should note that this means you can apply style sheets that reside on completely different servers. This can be particularly useful in an Intranet situation, where one department can set up several 'approved' styles to be used within all documents. As a point of Internet etiquette, it is a good idea to ask the original style sheet author for permission before 'borrowing' their style sheet in this manner.

Using <STYLE>

Alternatively, we can employ a style sheet by using the <STYLE> element. The idea here is to enclose the style sheet data in the <STYLE> tag, so that it can be parsed and applied as the document is loaded. To this end, we use the following code, placed in the <HEAD> of our document:

```
<STYLE TYPE="text/css">...style info goes here... </STYLE>
```

This seems quick and easy (and it is), but there are a few things you should be aware of. One problem is that older browsers will ignore the <STYLE> tag, and will try to handle the style data as if it were normal text. This can be avoided by enclosing the whole line in HTML comment tags as we did in the "We Hold These Truths..." example (earlier in this chapter), since style-aware browsers will still find the style information and handle it appropriately.

Another problem with using the <STYLE> tag in this manner is that we need to include a complete style sheet in every document. This not only increases the time needed to create a document and the size of the files, it also makes it more difficult to change a complete site's appearance. In effect, this method erases two of the three advantages conferred by style sheets, and should be used selectively in your pages.

Using @import

Fortunately, there is a way to automatically apply style sheets and still keep the file sizes down. You can use a special notation in the Cascading Style Sheets specification that was designed for this very purpose:

```
<HTML>
<HEAD>
<TITLE>CSS Example</TITLE>
<STYLE>
@import URL("http://webdev.wrox.co.uk/books/1746/style.css");
</STYLE>
</HEAD>
<BODY>
  An example of cascading style sheets in action:
  <CENTER>
    <TABLE WIDTH=730 CELLPADDING=0 CELLSPACING=0 BORDER=0>
      <TR>
        <TD ALIGN=CENTER VALIGN=TOP>
          <DIV CLASS=base>WE</DIV>
          <DIV CLASS=layer1>Hold these truths to be self-evident</DIV>
          <DIV CLASS=layer2>that all men are created equal</DIV>
        </TD>
      </TR>
    </TABLE>
  </CENTER>
</BODY>
</HTML>
```

This notation tells the browser to get the style sheet `style.css` from the server at `webdev.wrox.co.uk`, in the virtual directory named `books/1746/`. If we place the `@import` line between <STYLE> tags in the <HEAD> of our document, the style will be automatically retrieved and applied before our document is displayed.

Style Sheet Precedence

In the previous section, we saw how the precedence of style assignments was handled. Now that we have three methods for including style assignments on a page, we need to look at the precedence of those three methods as well. The precedence determines what the final set of styles assigned to an element will be:

- The <LINK> tag has the lowest precedence. It can be overridden by any of the other style assignments.
- Styles included with the `@import` tag are next in precedence. This tag is placed at the beginning of the <STYLE> block, so its styles will be overridden by any conflicting styles that come after it.
- The styles set in the <STYLE> block have the highest precedence of styles set in a style sheet. Of course, in-line styles still have the highest precedence.

All of these methods, when used on their own without additional tags, apply their style sheets to the entire document. In the next section, we'll look at some techniques used to style text more selectively.

Applying Style Sheets to Specific Text

If you've linked the style sheets into a document, but you don't want it to apply to the whole document, you need a way of identifying the text to which you wish to apply the style.

Using the STYLE Attribute with Individual Tags

One way of doing this is to specify the CSS information as part of the tag that we want it to affect:

```
<P STYLE="color: green">This paragraph will be green</P>
```

This is extremely flexible and easy to use, but it does have the major drawback that we need to specify each tag individually. (This, of course, removes two of the major advantages of style sheets). In Dynamic HTML, all text and graphics tags now support the `STYLE` attribute and the new properties that we will discuss shortly. To provide more control over how things are formatted, CSS utilizes the concept of a **class**.

Classes

There are two ways that you can define a class. A class can be defined as a property, not specifically assigned to a tag or other declaration; or it can be defined as a subset of a previous declaration. We can specify properties on a class-wide basis, so that the same properties apply to all instances of that class – even when used with different element tags altogether. Declaring the properties of a class is easy. In our CSS example we define a class called base, as follows:

```
.base { color: red;
        weight: medium;
        margin-top: 10px;
        font-size: 250px;
        line-height: 250px;
        font-family: Times }
```

Notice the period (full-stop) that appears before base – this establishes that we are naming a class and defining its properties. We then use the CLASS attribute of the <DIV> tag to apply it solely to the text WE:

```
<DIV CLASS=base>WE</DIV>
```

The <DIV> tag is used to define different areas of the web page – we'll talk about <DIV> again in a moment.

We can also create a subset of a previous declaration. For example if we specify that <H3> is blue, we can create a subset of <H3> that is white (#FFFFFF). This subset will retain any other properties we've given the parent, and must be referenced by name (in order to separate it from the parent.) The following code demonstrates this by creating a new class named second to apply to <H3> tags:

```
H3 { font-size: 14pt; font-family: monaco; color: #0000FF }
H3.second { color: #FFFFFF }
```

To implement our newly created class, we must call it explicitly like this:

```
<H3 CLASS=second> This is in white fourteen-point monaco </H3>
<H3> This is in the default color and fourteen-point monaco </H3>
```

There's a distinct advantage to defining a class as a property, rather than as a subset. Suppose we define it as a property, as follows:

```
.second { color: #FFFFFF }
```

Now we can then apply the properties of second wherever we call it, *without* having to set up every conceivable combination of tag and class:

```
<H1 CLASS=second> Level One </H1>
<EM CLASS=second> Emphasis </EM>
```

In this example, both items of text will be in white: each will have whatever characteristics were defined as the properties of .second, without having to explicitly define the properties of H1.second and EM.second.

You may remember that earlier in the chapter (in the CSS example) we used a tag that didn't introduce any new styling but instead identified sections of text. This was the <DIV> tag; we'll finish this section with a quick look at that.

The <DIV> Tag

This tag is used to define an area of the page, or **document division**. Anything between the opening and closing tag is referred as a single item. The <DIV> tag doesn't allocate any particular style to the text, it just allocates an area. When used together with the CLASS attribute, you can apply sets of styles (such as colors and font sizes) to this 'area' or to any individual element. Later on in the book, you will see how this element can be used to 'contain' other elements, allowing you to work with groups of elements at a time. This will quickly become your favorite element to use with Dynamic HTML.

This tag was used in our style sheets example to enclose each of the separate bits of text and to allow the different bits of text to be layered on top of one another. In early versions of HTML, the tag doesn't allow for any more direct manipulation of the individual 'layers':

```
<DIV CLASS=base>WE</DIV>
<DIV CLASS=layer1>Hold these truths to be self-evident</DIV>
<DIV CLASS=layer2>that all men are created equal</DIV>
```

In the css.htm example, the text which has the style layer1 appears over the top of the text with the style base. The order of the <DIV> tags is all that the browser has to go by to decide which sheet should appear on top of which in the page. If we changed around the <DIV> tags attached to the base and layer1 style classes, the text layering would also be reversed. Prior to Dynamic HTML, we are not able to specify the order of the text layers. This problem is addressed in DHTML by **2.5-D layering**, which we'll look at later in this chapter.

Another limitation of static HTML is that it isn't possible to define absolutely where a division should appear on a page (for example using x and y type co-ordinates). It is possible to define the height, width and margin size of document divisions, and even where they can be positioned in relation to each other, but not much more. So, while style sheets offer greater flexibility in these terms over standard HTML, they're still not the answer to everything. Dynamic HTML introduces some new ways to position elements.

Dynamic HTML Style Properties

Having taken a refresher in how style sheets are used, let's now see exactly what advantages Dynamic HTML provides in page formatting. First, DHTML provides support for seven additional properties, and extends the properties available in HTML for formatting the background and setting margins (or borders) around elements.

The seven all-new properties that we'll be looking at in particular are:

```
left            top            z-index
position        visibility     overflow
text-justify
```

You can find a list of all the properties available in Appendix B.

The extensions to static HTML border properties are:

`border-color`	`border-style`
`border-right-width`	`border-left-width`
`border-top-width`	`border-bottom-width`
`border-collapse`	

The extensions to the background formatting properties are:

`background-attachment`	`background-color`
`background-image`	`background-position`
`background-repeat`	

We will be looking at some other extensions to Cascading Style Sheets in IE5 later in this chapter. We'll see how to use script to change the value of a style property, using a script method or function. The new dynamic properties capability in IE5 allows you to set an expression for a style, and have the browser automatically recalculate that expression whenever something in the browser changes. Some of the other new extensions that have been added in IE5 are:

`behavior` style property	`table-layout` style property
`currentStyle` property	`onscroll` event
`runtimeStyle` property	`textRectangle` object
`getBoundingClientRect` method	

You'll find a complete listing of all the style properties available in Appendix E.

Displaying and Positioning Elements

The seven new style properties allow us to create pages in a way akin to desktop publishing techniques. The reason is simple, and can be seen in the names of just three of the new properties: `left`, `top` and `z-index`. Prior to Dynamic HTML, either we depended on the browser to place our elements in consecutive order as they were rendered on the page, or we used a style sheet with positive or negative margin settings. However, in Dynamic HTML, we can simply specify the *x*, *y* and *z* coordinates (in pixels) of each element on the page.

This is just like the way we design the forms or dialogs for a normal Windows application, using a 'real' programming language. The new `top` and `left` properties of the `STYLE` attribute can be used to define – with pixel point accuracy – where on a page a tag should go:

- The `left` property (the *x* coordinate) is used to specify the number of pixels between the left of the window (or container) and the element. Values are stored as strings, in the form `100px` (which would denote 100 pixels)
- The `top` property (the *y* coordinate) specifies the number of pixels between the top of the window (or container) and the element
- The `z-index` property adds a new dimension (or more accurately, a series of layers) to the page. The higher the value of an element's `z-index` property, the 'closer' it appears on the page. By this we mean elements with higher `z-index` value will appear on top of elements with lower `z-index` value

So you can see that we can work with DHTML to produce a 3-D style page layout. While it does provide a 'kind' of 3-D appearance, and we specify the three standard *x*, *y*, and *z* coordinates, we can't achieve real 3-D. For this reason, it's often referred to as **two-and-a-half-D** layout.

Going 2.5-D in a Web Page

The first step in creating a 2.5-D layout using DHTML is to understand how document divisions work. For each division we want to create on a page, we can specify its `top`, `left`, `width` and `height` properties. We combine these with the `left`, `top` and `z-index` properties of the elements inside of the `DIV` to get a display that looks as if it was created by using tables or static images. This is the sample page `2point5d.htm`:

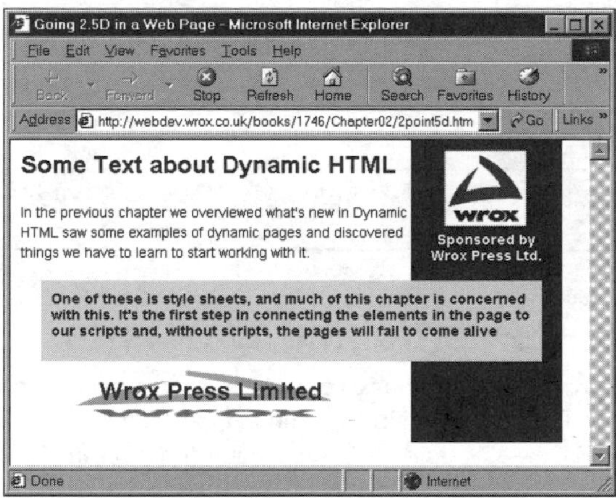

You can run this page from our web site at http://webdev.wrox.co.uk/books/1746.

Notice how the central band of text overlaps the right-hand dark-colored column. This kind of layout would be difficult to achieve with tables, but it's easy using DHTML. In fact, this page demonstrates several ways of using the new properties to build more free-form, desktop-publishing-like web pages. Here, so that you can see the overall contents, is the complete HTML source code for this page:

```
<HTML>
<HEAD><TITLE> Going 2.5D in a Web Page </TITLE></HEAD>
<STYLE>
P          { font-family: "Arial, sans-serif"; font-size: 14 }
P.bluetext { font-weight: Bold; color: darkblue }
P.reverse  { font-weight: Bold; color: white }
H2         { font-family: "Arial, sans-serif"; font-size: 24;
             font-weight: Bold; color: darkblue }
</STYLE>

<BODY>

<DIV STYLE="position: absolute ; top: 0; left: 0; width: 400; height: 100;
            margin: 10">
<H2> Some Text about Dynamic HTML </H2>
<P STYLE="line-height:140%">
In the previous chapter we overviewed what's new in Dynamic HTML saw some
examples of dynamic pages and discovered things we have to learn to start
working with it.</P>
</DIV>

<DIV STYLE="position: absolute; top: 0; left: 400; width: 150; height: 300;
            background: darkblue">
<IMG SRC="wrox0.gif" STYLE="position: relative ; top: 10; left: 33;
                            width: 82; height: 76;">
<DIV STYLE="text-align: center;">
<P CLASS="reverse" STYLE="margin-top: 10">Sponsored by<BR>Wrox Press Ltd.</P>
</DIV>
</DIV>

<DIV STYLE="position: absolute; top: 130; left: 0; width: 500; height: 80;
            background: yellow; margin-top: 10; margin-left: 30;
            margin-right: 30">
<P CLASS="bluetext" STYLE="margin-top: 10; margin-left: 10">
One of these is style sheets, and much of this chapter is concerned with
this. It's the first step in connecting the elements in the page to our
scripts and, without scripts, the pages will fail to come alive </P>
</DIV>

<DIV STYLE="position: absolute; top: 225; width: 400; left: 0;
            text-align: center;">
<H2 STYLE="color=darkred; line-height:200%">  Wrox Press Limited</H2>
<IMG SRC="wrox1.gif" STYLE="position: absolute; top: 0; left: 50;
                            z-index: -1 " width: 295; height: 54;">
</DIV>

</BODY>
</HTML>
```

As you can see, there are five main sections to the code. The first is the `STYLE` tag that sets the font styles, sizes, colors and so on for each kind of text style we are going to use in the page. You'll notice that it creates a style for the standard `<P>` paragraph tag, then two sub-class styles based on this. These have a bold font weight, and different colors. The final style is used to create the headline `<H2>` style. Of course, these style definitions could just as well be a separate style sheet, to permit easier updating of several pages in one go.

However, what we're really interested in are the other four sections of the page – the 'working parts'. These are the four `<DIV>` tags, which work in the following way.

Working with Document Divisions

We can think of the <DIV> document division tags as creating sections within the page –we can place other elements within each division, and the divisions can overlap each other. Each section becomes a **container**, and its contents can be placed accurately within this container using the DHTML `left` and `top` style attributes. These positioning attributes are now relative to the container, not to the page as a whole. You'll see later in the book that if we change the position of a `DIV`, all of the elements it contains will move right along with it. We've been able to divide our page up into separate sections that overlap by using divisions.

To present the page as a set of separate divisions, we need to use another of the DHTML style properties, `position`. This is used to specify where the browser will place the division, and can also be applied to any other elements that can be positioned using the `left` and `top` properties.

The DHTML Position Property

The element's `position` property, in conjunction with its `top` and `left` properties, allows us to determine how elements are placed within the browser window. It can be set to one of three values:

- `static` positioning means that the element will be placed automatically by the browser as the page is being laid out. Any value set in the `top` or `left` property will be ignored. Static positioning is the standard way that web pages have been laid out since Day 1, and is the default value of the `position` property
- `relative` positioning is similar to static positioning, in that the browser will determine where the element goes on the page. However, the browser only determines the point at which the element *should* go; then, the `left` and `top` properties are used to move the element from the point chosen by the browser. In the following example, the first line of text has its `position` property set to `relative` and its `left` and `top` properties set to 0: it appears in the same position in the page as if there were no positioning attributes included. The 'normal' position of the second line of text would be immediately below the first line; but it has a `position` property of `relative` and `top` and `left` properties set to 100, so it's actually placed 100 pixels down and 100 pixels to the right of its 'normal' position:

```
<DIV STYLE="position: relative;">
  Line 1 is positioned where the browser chooses
</DIV>
<DIV STYLE="position: relative; top: 100; left: 100;">
  Line 2 is positioned relative to where the browser chooses
</DIV>
And line 3 is positioned as if line 2 wasn't moved
```

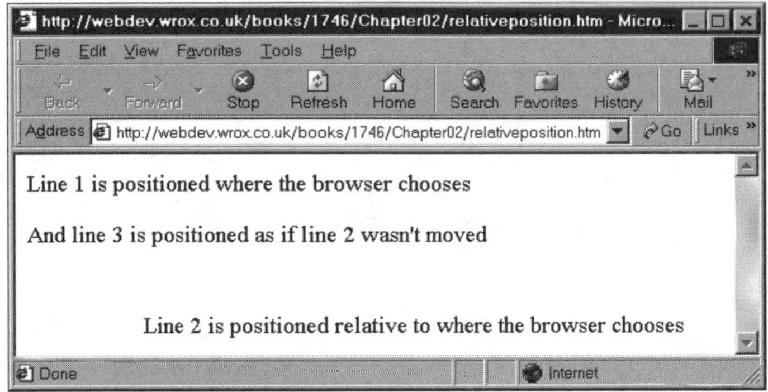

Any elements that follow this one will use the 'normal' position of line 2 to determine where they should be placed (provided that their `position` property is set to `static` or `relative`). Hence, the position of line 3 is independent of the `top` and `left` values of line 2.

- `absolute` positioning means that the element will be placed at an absolute position with respect to the top left hand corner of its container, which could be a DIV or the page itself. This effectively removes it from the HTML source as far as its influence on following elements is concerned. For example, specifying `left` and `top` values will position the element at those *x* and *y* coordinates with respect to the division that contains it. If it is not within a division, it is placed in that position with respect to the top left corner of the page. Its actual position will not affect any elements that follow it in the HTML source:

```
Line 1 is positioned where the browser chooses
<DIV STYLE="position: absolute; top: 100; left: 100;">
  Line 2 is positioned absolutely where we want it
</DIV>
<DIV STYLE="position: relative;">
  And line 3 is positioned as if line 2 wasn't there
</DIV>
```

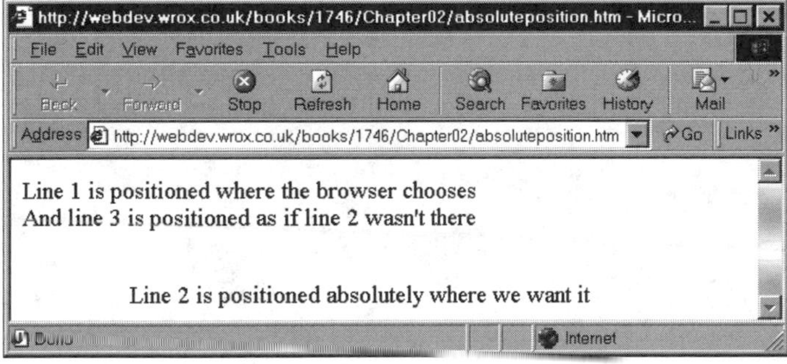

We can use the `position` property to place our document divisions accurately in the page. In the 2.5–D example above, we used these four divisions to build up the basic structure of the page:

```
<DIV STYLE="position: absolute; top: 0; left: 0; width: 400; height: 100…">
  ...
</DIV>
<DIV STYLE="position: absolute; top: 0; left: 400; width: 150; height: 300…">
  ...
</DIV>
<DIV STYLE="position: absolute; top: 130; left: 0; width: 500; height: 80…">
  ...
</DIV>
<DIV STYLE="position: absolute; top: 225; width: 400; left: 0">
  ...
</DIV>
```

Notice that there is no `height` property set for the last one. If we omit any properties like this, the division will assume default values. For example, if we omit the `width` property, it will span the width of the browser window by default.

Document divisions also act in a different way to the normal page. Text will flow across division boundaries if it won't all fit within the division in which it has been declared; however, other elements (such as images) are cropped. When the browser window is resized, text in a division does not reflow like text displayed directly on the page. With careful design, both of these properties can be used to advantage in our pages. In particular, it means that our designs are now independent of the size of the browser window, and the user must adjust the size, or scroll the page, to see it all.

Using Divisions in Specifying DHTML Layout

Having placed our document division containers on the page, we can now get on and fill them with our page elements. Anything enclosed in a `<DIV>...</DIV>` tag pair will appear within the area of the screen designated to that division. The first division is simple enough – it just displays the heading and some introductory text:

```
<DIV STYLE="position: absolute ; top: 0; left: 0; width: 400; height: 100;
            margin: 10">
<H2> Some Text about Dynamic HTML </H2>
<P STYLE="line-height:140%">
In the previous chapter we ... etc.
</P>
</DIV>
```

The next division is the dark colored section to the right of the page, which contains a logo and some text. Notice that we've specified the image element with a `position` property of `relative`. This effectively just offsets it while 'reserving' its place in the HTML source, so that the text that follows will appear below it:

```
<DIV STYLE="position: absolute; top: 0; left: 400; width: 150; height: 300;
            background: darkblue">
<IMG SRC="wrox0.gif" STYLE="position: relative ; top: 10; left: 33;
                            width: 82; height: 76;">
<DIV STYLE="text-align: center;">
<P CLASS="reverse" STYLE="margin-top: 10">Sponsored by<BR>Wrox Press Ltd.</P>
</DIV>
</DIV>
```

If we had declared the `position` property for the image as `absolute`, instead of `relative`, it would appear in the same place, but the text would be displayed at the top of the division, overlaid by the image as shown below. The image would have 'disappeared' from the HTML source as far as its effect on the following text is concerned.

You'll also see that the usual formatting tags work normally within a division. We've used the `text-align:center` style property to center the text in the division and applied the `P.reverse` style we defined earlier, just as we would in a traditional web page.

The next division is very similar to the first. It uses some extra style properties to set variable margins around the text, so that it fits nicely into the One of these is style sheets... division (the middle one in the 2.5-D screenshot):

```
<DIV STYLE="position: absolute; top: 130; left: 0; width: 500; height: 80;
         background: yellow; margin-top: 10; margin-left: 30;
         margin-right: 30">
<P CLASS=bluetext> One of these is style sheets, and ... etc. </P>
</DIV>
```

Layer Control with the Z-index Property

The final division demonstrates one more technique. Here, we have an `<IMG>` tag overlaid by text. In traditional web pages, this is nearly impossible to do, and the trick to doing it makes the resulting HTML very confusing to read. The text is wrapped around any images on the page, unless you arrange for the image to be used in the `<BODY>` tag as the page background.

Dynamic HTML provides a property called the `z-index`, which allows the web page author to specify at what level (or layer) an element is displayed. This can be relative to the body text or headings in the page, or any other elements. The body text and headings are displayed in level zero, or layer `0`, and so have a `z-index` of zero.

Specifying the Z-index

We can arrange for our elements to appear above the body text by specifying positive `z-index` numbers, and below it by specifying negative numbers We can also layer individual text and non-text elements with respect to each other by using higher or lower `z-index` values.

In the fourth division of our example page, we have some text, and a logo inside an `<IMG>` tag. The text is defined first in the HTML, and uses the `line-height` style property to give it the correct vertical spacing inside the division. Then the logo is specified, using absolute positioning to get it centered with respect to the text. (If the logo were relatively positioned, it would follow the previous text. Then it would no longer fit into the division and it would simply be clipped.) Finally, to make it appear with the text rendered on top, we set its `z-index` property to -1:

```
<DIV STYLE="position: absolute; top: 225; width: 400; left: 0;
            text-align: center;">
<H2 STYLE="color=darkred; line-height:200%">  Wrox Press Limited</H2>
<IMG SRC="wrox1.gif" STYLE="position: absolute; top: 0; left: 50;
                              z-index: -1 " width: 295; height: 54;">
</DIV>
```

The result isn't terribly pretty, but it serves to demonstrate the point.

Overlaying Document Divisions

No doubt you've realized that the browser sets the `z-index` of elements automatically as it renders the page. When two elements with an equivalent 'default level' are defined in the HTML source for the page, the one that comes last will have the highest `z-index`. Therefore, if these two elements are made to overlap, the second one will appear on top of the first one. If you look back at the previous example, you'll see that the third (yellow) document division overlays the second (dark blue) one, because it was declared later in the HTML.

By setting an element's `z-index` in a style tag (or, as you'll see later on, dynamically with script code) we can control this layering process to provide exactly the effect we want.

Fixed Table Layouts

In trying to increase the performance of IE5, Microsoft has provided a number of optimizations that will increase the speed at which pages will be loaded and displayed. One of these optimizations is support for **fixed table layouts**. In earlier browser, table performance was slow if every element in the table didn't have a height and width tag since the whole table had to be downloaded before rendering.

By setting the `tableLayout` property to `fixed`, Internet Explorer 5 will incrementally render the table, providing users with information at a faster pace. Other browsers, that don't support fixed size tables, will just ignore this property and continue to render the tables in the old way. When using the `tableLayout` property as `fixed`, the layout of a table is determined in the following order:

- Columns with assigned widths (via the `WIDTH` property of the `COL` or `COLGROUP` object) are rendered first.
- Row height is determined by the height of the table's first row.
- Columns of unspecified width will be rendered equally.

If the content of a cell exceeds the determined width of the column, the content will be wrapped. If wrapping is not possible, then the content will be clipped. When the row height is specified, wrapped text will be clipped if it exceeds the set height.

Setting the property to `fixed` significantly improves the table rendering speed, particularly for longer tables. Setting row height further improves rendering speed.

This enables the browser's parser to begin displaying the row immediately, without first having to examine the content of each cell in the row to determine row height.

Fixed table layouts can be used to great advantage when displaying information from databases. Since you probably would not be writing static HTML pages that have very long tables, there would be little speed gained in these types of pages. However, when displaying information from a database, especially tables with fixed length fields, using Active Server Pages, or some of the technologies in Chapter 7, a fixed table layout will let IE5 begin to display the information much sooner. This will make the browsing experience seem faster for the user.

Controlling Overflow and Visibility

In this chapter, we've seen how four of the DHTML style properties can be used to create pages in a fundamentally new way, by accurately positioning elements and controlling the layering. The new properties we've used are the `left`, `top` and `z-index` properties, which effectively define the *x*, *y*, and *z* coordinates, plus the `position` property, which defines how the coordinates are used and what effect the positioning has on other elements that follow in the HTML source. In this section we'll look at two more properties, which are used to control the `overflow` and `visibility` of elements.

Using the Overflow Property

The `overflow` property is used to determine what should happen when an element's contents exceed the height or width of a window, or a container such as a `DIV`. It can be set to one of three values:

- A value of `none` indicates that no clipping is to be performed. For example, preformatted text that extends past the right edge of an element's boundaries would be rendered anyway
- A value of `clip` indicates that clipping should be performed with no scrolling mechanism
- A `scroll` value causes a scrolling mechanism to be invoked

Using the Visibility Property

The last new style property in DHTML is `visibility`. As the name suggests, this controls whether the element will be visible on the page. When we create wholly static pages, using only absolute positioning, it isn't terribly useful. After all, if an element won't be seen, there's not a great deal of point in including it in the HTML source.

The `visibility` property *is* useful when we come to add scripting code to our page. It can change the properties of the elements in the page, thereby making them visible or invisible as required, while the page is displayed. One example would be in a data entry web page, where the page reacts to user input by adding or removing visible data entry fields.

However, there is one case where the `visibility` property can be useful when formatting a static page. Looking back at our '2.5-D' example (`2point5d.htm`), we found that the text below the Wrox image in the right-hand division depended on the image tag having a `position` property value of `relative`. This prevents the text from appearing at the top of the division. If we remove the image tag, the text will not be in the same position, because there is no relative image to move it down the page.

If for some reason we wanted to 'remove' the image and not move the text, we can set the image's visibility property to `hidden` (the default is `visible`). The result is that everything else stays the same, but the image itself is not rendered on the page:

Easy 3-D Text Effects

Next on our agenda is using DHTML properties to provide an easier way of displaying 3-D style titles. By using document divisions and the absolute positioning abilities of DHTML, we can achieve better results, much faster. Here's an example page, named `3Dtitles.htm`:

> *You can run this page from our web site at* ***http://webdev.wrox.co.uk/books/1746.***

Here's the HTML that creates this page. It consists of a `<STYLE>` section that defines the three text styles, and three document divisions denoted by the `<DIV>` and `</DIV>` tags. The `<STYLE>` section defines a standard paragraph format using a large red font, then two subclasses with the same font, but in different colors:

```
<HTML>
<HEAD><TITLE> Cheating with 3D Title </TITLE></HEAD>
<STYLE>
P { font-family: "Impact, sans-serif"; font-size: 96; color:red }
P.highlight { color: silver }
P.shadow { color: darkred }
</STYLE>
<BODY BGCOLOR=#408080>
<DIV STYLE="position: absolute; top: 5; left: 5; width: 600; height: 100;
          margin: 10">
```

```
<P CLASS=shadow> Wrox Press </P>
</DIV>

<DIV STYLE="position: absolute; top: 0; left: 0; width: 600; height: 100;
           margin: 10">
<P CLASS=highlight> Wrox Press </P>
</DIV>

<DIV STYLE="position: absolute; top: 2; left: 2; width: 600; height: 100;
           margin: 10">
<P> Wrox Press </P>
</DIV>

</BODY>
</HTML>
```

The three divisions are identical except for their `top` and `left` properties, and – since they are all defined with a `position` property of `absolute` – they will appear at these slightly different positions, but display different colored text. The order that they are defined in the page controls the `z-index`, so we end up with the dark red shadow overlaid by the silver highlight, and then by the top-level bright red text.

If we wanted to change the ordering of the colors, we could simply add a `z-index` style to the `DIV` that we wanted to move. Changing the appearance, shadow depth and colors is simply a matter of changing the `top`, `left`, `z-index` and `color` properties, and this can create some very different appearances.

Adding Script to HTML Pages

So far, you might be forgiven for thinking that many of the effects we've demonstrated could have been achieved – albeit with a little more effort – with cascading style sheets and without any DHTML properties. Well, this is true to some extent, but that's because we haven't used the real power that DHTML offers – the ability to dynamically manipulate properties with a **script** and therefore update the positions and styles of elements in the page.

At its most basic, a scripting language is just a way of making your pages reactive, enabling them to interact with the user so that they're more than just code. Scripting has been present in both Internet Explorer and Netscape Navigator since version 3. Internet Explorer 5 supports both JScript (Microsoft's implementation of JavaScript) and VBScript, while Navigator 4 (without the aid of a proprietary add-in) supports only JavaScript. The focus of the book is IE5, and we'll be using examples in both VBScript and JScript. There is a full reference to the two languages in Appendices I and J.

Instead of starting by talking about how to make your page react to events in too much detail, we've chosen to describe how to manipulate the new DHTML properties first and include only simple event code. In Chapter 5, *Scripts and Event Handling*, we'll look in more detail at how both VBScript and JScript are used with the object model.

However, there are a couple of things you will need to know before you start. We'll briefly show you how script code appears in a page, and how we create code routines. This will be enough to carry you through to Chapter 5.

Where to Place Your Script

Scripting code is placed in the page within the HTML <SCRIPT> and </SCRIPT> tags. These tell the browser that the code between the tags is to be interpreted and executed as the page is loaded. Inside the opening <SCRIPT> tag, we use a LANGUAGE attribute to tell the browser which interpreter to use. If omitted, the browser will assume it's JScript, and getting it wrong will provoke error messages as the page loads:

```
...
<SCRIPT LANGUAGE=VBSCRIPT>
... VBScript code goes here
</SCRIPT>
...
```

```
...
<SCRIPT LANGUAGE=JAVASCRIPT>
... JavaScript code goes here
</SCRIPT>
...
```

The script section can be placed almost anywhere in the page. The favorite position is often at the end, so that the rest of the page is loaded and rendered by the browser before the interpreter loads and runs the code. However, if we are using the code to insert something into the page, like the time and date, we need to place the <SCRIPT> section in the appropriate position within the HTML source:

```
...
The date and time is
<SCRIPT LANGUAGE=VBSCRIPT> document.write(Now) </SCRIPT>
<P>
...
```

This causes the browser to execute the VBScript Now function and pass the result to the write method of the document object. This method writes the information into that page at the point where it's called.

Another time we might not want to place the <SCRIPT> section at the end of the page is if we are using an onload script, which is run when the page is loaded: then the code for the script is better put *before* the BODY tag.

If this page is loaded into a browser that doesn't support VBScript, the code itself will simply be displayed as text on the page. The traditional way to prevent this is to enclose the contents of the <SCRIPT> section in an HTML comment tag, like this:

```
...
<SCRIPT LANGUAGE=VBSCRIPT>
<!-- hide from older browsers
... script code goes here
-->
</SCRIPT>
...
```

Non-script enabled browsers will ignore the code contained between the `<!--` and `-->` tags, while browsers that do support scripting will still be able to interpret and execute it (unless of course they only support JavaScript, in which case the script will be ignored). Of course, we're aiming our page at DHTML-enabled browsers, and support for a scripting language is a prerequisite for this anyway. However, it doesn't hurt to hide the scripting code with the HTML comment tags just in case the page is loaded by an older browser – even though it will probably still look odd because the browser won't support the other layout features of DHTML either.

Script can also be placed in a separate file. Thus, the scripts used by your page can be kept separate from the page itself. This means that it's much easier to reuse the script code, in other pages. To utilize this feature you use the `SRC` parameter of the `<SCRIPT>` tag. The `SRC` parameter is used to set the file name that contains the scripts that you want to be loaded into this page. In this example, the file `myScript.js` contains JScript code:

```
...
<SCRIPT SRC=myScript.js></SCRIPT>
...
```

Creating Script Routines in a Page

The other technique you need to be familiar with is how we create separate code routines in a page that are *not* executed as the page is loading. Much of the dynamic nature of modern web pages is down to script code that reacts to **events** occurring within the browser. We can change the contents of a page by executing script as it loads, and this does provide a dynamic page; but doesn't provide the true dynamic page refresh that we're seeking.

To prevent VBScript code being executed as the page loads, we place it inside a **subroutine** or a **function**. There are only two differences between subroutines and functions. First, they are defined in different ways in the script; and second, a function produces a value that gets passed back to the code that called it. It is up to the script developer to decide what to do, if anything, with this return value. As far as this book is concerned, we'll mainly be using subroutines.

> *If you want to know more about VBScript and its applications than we cover in this book, try* Instant VBScript *(Wrox, ISBN 1-861000-44-8).*

```
<SCRIPT LANGUAGE=VBSCRIPT>
  Sub MyNewRoutine()
  .. VBScript code goes here
  End Sub

  Sub window_onLoad()
  ..VBScript code to be executed when the window object gets an onLoad event
  End Sub

  Function GetAnyNumber()
  ..VBScript code goes here - don't forget to set the return value
  GetAnyNumber = 42
  End Function
</SCRIPT>
```

These routines will only run when we call them from code elsewhere, or when an event occurs in the browser that calls them automatically. In the case of the `window_onLoad` routine, the code will run when the window begins loading a new page.

In JavaScript, things are slightly different, because it doesn't explicitly support subroutines, only functions. (However, you can have functions in JScript that don't return a value, just like a subroutine.) We also have to write the code a little differently:

```
<SCRIPT LANGUAGE=JAVASCRIPT>
  function MyNewRoutine()
  {
    .. JavaScript code goes here;
  }

  function GetAnyNumber()
  {
    .. JavaScript code goes here, including setting the return value;
    return 42;
  }
</SCRIPT>
```

JavaScript requires the code in a routine to be enclosed in curly braces, and each line within a function to be separated by a semicolon.

Using a Script to Manipulate the DHTML Properties

We're going to look at an example that shows how we can dynamically update the properties of an element on the page with a script, to make it move across the screen. However, before we can do that, we need to understand how we can update properties using code. This is all done via the `style` object.

The STYLE Attribute

The various style properties of elements are the most useful properties of all, and the ones we'll use in most of our dynamic pages. They are decided by the element's `STYLE` attribute, within the tag that creates the element. We can get at any of the properties defined here and, best of all, we can change most of them within our code.

As an example, we can declare our heading tag like this:

```
<H2 ID=MyHeading STYLE="font-family: Arial; color: red; font-size: 48"> ...
```

With this, we can retrieve *and change* the font, size and color in our code. Remember that styles can be inherited as well, so we can have properties that are set either by a `<STYLE>` section in that page, or by a linked style sheet.

Using the Style Object

Every element that supports the HTML STYLE attribute has an equivalent style object. This is how we can get at the style properties for that element. It's important to realize that there are two different ways of setting the properties for an element in the HTML source, and correspondingly there are two different ways to access these properties in our code.

We can define an <IMG> tag like this:

```
<IMG ID=MyImage SRC="mypic.gif" WIDTH=100 HEIGHT=100>
```

In this line we are controlling the width and height using traditional HTML attributes. The width and height properties are then direct properties of the object, and we can refer to them in our code using:

```
MyImage.width
MyImage.height
```

However, we can't define the top and left properties using normal HTML attributes – we have to include them in a STYLE attribute like this:

```
<IMG ID=MyImage SRC="mypic.gif" STYLE="position: absoloute;
                                      top: 50; left: 200">
```

The values in the STYLE attribute are now properties of the image's style object, not direct properties of the image element. We refer to these using:

```
MyImage.style.top
MyImage.style.left
```

Of course, we can also set the image's width and height properties in the STYLE tag. (This over-rides the values in the traditional HTML attributes, if they are set there as well):

```
<IMG ID=MyImage SRC="mypic.gif" STYLE="position: absolute; top: 50;
                                left: 200; width: 150; height: 75">
```

Now we can refer to the width and height through the style object, and the HTML width and height properties will not be defined:

```
MyImage.style.top       'value is 50px
MyImage.style.left      'value is 200px
MyImage.style.width     'value is 150px
MyImage.style.height    'value is 75px

MyImage.width           'not defined
MyImage.height          'not defined
```

Just note that, while these properties have the same name as the various STYLE attributes and HTML attributes defined in the HTML source, this isn't always the case. For example, the font-size and font-weight attributes are referenced by the fontSize and fontWeight properties.

There's a full listing of the properties of the `style` object in Appendix A, and a list of properties and the equivalent style attributes in Appendix B.

Using the currentStyle object

We have just seen how to use the `style` object of an element to access the style properties of that element. But this will only work if those styles have been *explicitly* set on that element. If the element has had its style properties set through a linked or cascading style sheet, then the `style` object will not be able to retrieve them: you will need to use the `currentStyle` object instead. The `currentStyle` object has the same object model as the `style` object, so you can access the properties in the same way.

For example, suppose we have these simple style declarations, and some elements that use them:

```
<STYLE>
<!--
     .red {color: red;}
     H3   {font-family: Tahoma; font-weight: bold;}
-->
</STYLE>

<DIV ID=myDiv class=red>Here is some red text</DIV>
<H3 ID=myHeading>Some heading text</H3>
```

Now we can use each element's `currentStyle` object to look at some of the style property values of these elements:

```
myDiv.style.color                  'not defined
myDiv.currentStyle.color           'value is "red"

myHeading.style.fontWeight         'not defined
myHeading.currentStyle.fontWeight 'value is "bold"
```

The `runtimeStyle` object functions as a combination of the `style` object and the `currentStyle` object. Whereas the `currentStyle` object give read-only access to the current style settings, the `runtimeStyle` object allows you to both retrieve and set style information. It has the functionality of the `style` object, while returning the current style information as the `currentStyle` object does.

Moving Elements around a Page

Here's the bit you've been waiting for. Suppose we define an image tag like this:

```
<IMG SRC="MyPic.gif" STYLE="position: absolute; left: 200; top: 100>
```

With this, not only can we retrieve the image's `left` and `top` properties, but we can also change them – effectively moving it automatically around the screen while the page is displayed.

However, things aren't quite that simple. While we can freely set new values for the `left` and `top` property (and the `width` and `height` if we want to), we often want to know where the element is first. For example, we might want to just move it five pixels to the right.

The problem is that, as we mentioned earlier, the `left` and `top` properties are stored in pixels (the default) unless we specify another unit such as `em` or `pc`. If we retrieve these properties from the example above, we get the string values `200px` and `100px`, rather than numbers. This means that we can't do any calculations with the `left`, `top`, `width` and `height` properties unless we strip off the `px` from the string first. It is more convenient to use another set of properties instead.

The posLeft, posTop, posWidth and posHeight Properties

The `posLeft`, `posTop`, `posWidth` and `posHeight` properties are set by the browser when it sizes and positions the element using the `STYLE` attributes, and they return the left, top, width and height as numeric values automatically. They can also be changed using script, and the browser will reposition or resize the element as appropriate. Also, each `pos`... property is linked to its corresponding string property, so that if one is changed in script, the other is automatically changed to represent the new value. For example, if you change the value of `posTop`, then the string contained in `top` will change as well:

```
MyImage.style.posTop      'value is 50
MyImage.style.posLeft     'value is 200
MyImage.style.posWidth    'value is 150
MyImage.style.posHeight   'value is 75
```

Moving Elements around a page Example

Right, it's time to take a look at an example. We're going to 'move' an element across the screen, making it move behind one element and then in front of another by simply updating one property. The element will start its journey on the far left of the screen and move gradually to the right:

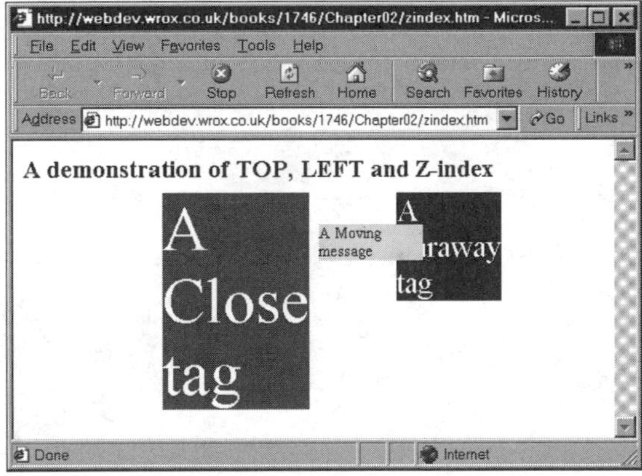

You can run this page from our web site at http://webdev.wrox.co.uk/books/1746.

The initial *x* and *y* co-ordinates of the tags are set out in the `STYLE` attributes of the `<DIV>` tags. Each `<DIV>` tag is assigned a unique name with an ID attribute, so it can be identified in the script. Here's the full code:

```
<!DOCTYPE HTML PUBLIC "-//IETF//DTD HTML//EN">
<HTML>
<HEAD>
<TITLE></TITLE>
</HEAD>

<BODY>
<H3>A demonstration of TOP, LEFT and Z-index</H3>
<DIV Id=CloseDiv STYLE="position: absolute; top: 50; left: 140; height: 130;
                        width: 100; color: white; background: red;
                        font-size:60; z-index: 4">
A Close tag
</DIV>

<DIV Id=FarDiv STYLE="position: absolute; top: 50; left: 360; height: 30;
                      width: 100; color: white; background: blue;
                      font-size: 30; z-index: 2">
A Faraway tag
</DIV>

<DIV ID=MovingMessage STYLE="position: absolute; top: 80; left: 0;
                             height: 30; width: 100; background: yellow;
                             font-size: 15; z-index: 3">
A Moving message
</DIV>

<SCRIPT LANGUAGE=VBSCRIPT>
setTimeout "MoveLeft",10,"VBScript"
Sub MoveLeft
  MovingMessage.style.posLeft = MovingMessage.style.posLeft + 1
  If MovingMessage.style.posLeft < 500 Then
    setTimeout"MoveLeft",10,"VBScript"
  End If
End Sub
</SCRIPT>
</BODY>
</HTML>
```

The script is very simple: it just obtains the `posLeft` property of the `MovingMessage` element and then increments it by one. This moves the element rightwards by one pixel:

```
MovingMessage.style.posLeft = MovingMessage.style.posLeft + 1
```

So after this procedure had been executed 10 times, the message would be in this position:

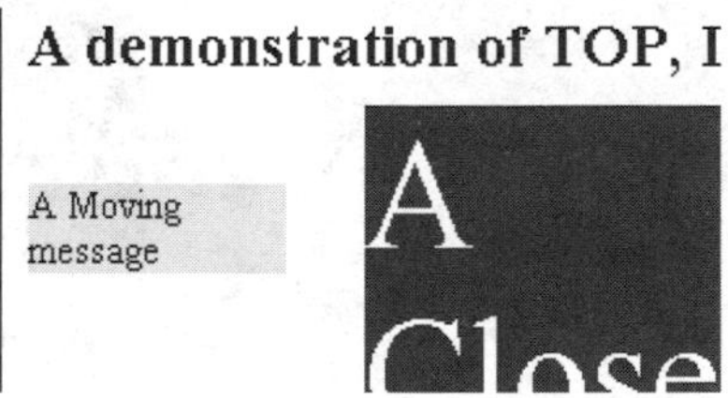

The script checks to see if the DIV has reached 500 pixels across the screen. If it has not, then it will set the timer to run the script again. If it has reached or passed that position, then it will not set the timer.

There is one minor thing that complicates the script. If you just keep moving the block across the screen and calling the procedure again, the screen won't have time to display the block as it moves. So we need to slow it down, by using a timeout, which gives DHTML time to update the position of the element on the screen...

```
If MovingMessage.style.posLeft < 500 Then
  setTimeout"MoveLeft",10,"VBScript"
End If
```

This is a very simple example, but it demonstrates something that just wasn't possible in HTML or style sheets before DHTML.

Dynamic Properties

IE5 offers a new way to work with style properties that enables web authors and developers to vastly improve the appearance and rendering of their web pages. By now, you're familiar with the idea of declaring property values using constants; but with IE5, using the power of dynamic properties, it's also possible to declare the value of a property using an **expression**.

The expressions used in a **dynamic property** can also reference property values from other elements. For example, this means that, rather than setting the width of an element to be 50 pixels, you can set it to be 0.25 times the width of another element. By doing this, your element's width is directly based on the width of another element; so if the other element's width changes, the width of your element will change as well.

More generally, with this feature you can set the values of properties or attributes to change automatically, based on the values of other aspects of the page. For example, some of the uses of dynamic properties include:

- Automatically moving elements based on a timer
- Anchoring elements to the bottom or right edge of the browser window
- Easily build tool tips whose position is always relative to the current mouse position

You can declare expressions in a style sheet or in the element's declaration, using the `expression` keyword:

```
<DIV ID=div1 STYLE="background-color: blue; width: 100;
                    height: 50; left: 20;">
Div 1</DIV>

<DIV ID=div2 STYLE="position: absolute; background-color: green;
                    top: expression(body.clientHeight - div2.clientHeight);
                    width: expression(div1.offsetHeight/2);">
Div 2</DIV>
```

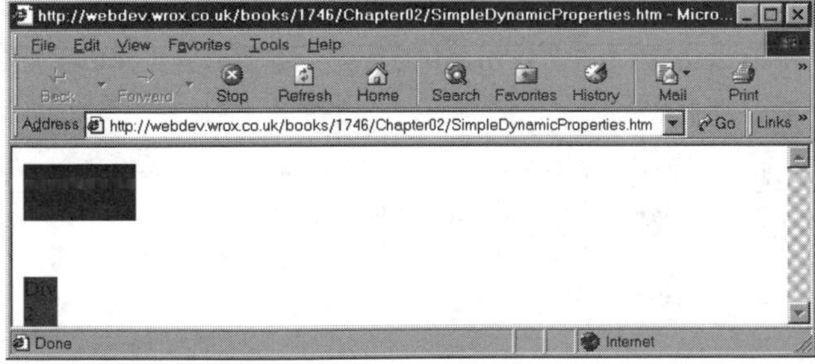

If you run this example, you'll see that no matter how you resize the window, Div 2 remains anchored to the bottom of the screen. The `expression` contains all of the script code that is needed to do this is.

You can also use scripting to set up dynamic property expressions. There are four methods that can be used to control dynamic properties.

Method	Usage
`setExpression`	Assigns the expression to the particular style of the element
`getExpression`	Returns the current expression for a style of the element
`removeExpression`	Removes the current expression from the style
`recalc`	Forces the browser to recalculate all dynamic styles in the page – called on the `document` object

The syntax for `setExpression` is as follows:

```
object.setExpression(sPropertyName, sExpression, sLanguage)
```

The *`object`* parameter is the object that will have the dynamic style set on it. The *`sPropertyName`* parameter indicates the property that will by dynamically changed and *`sExpression`* is the script code that causes the dynamic behavior. Finally, *`sLanguage`* is the scripting language that you used to write the script.

You could have used the following script to create the same effect as the example above:

```
<DIV ID=div1 STYLE="background-color: blue; width: 100;
                    height: 50; left: 20;">
Div 1</DIV>

<DIV ID=div2 STYLE="position:absolute; background-color: green;">
Div 2</DIV>

<SCRIPT LANGUAGE=JSCRIPT>
div2.style.setExpression("width", "div1.offsetHeight/2", "jscript");
div2.style.setExpression("top",
                "body.clientHeight - div2.clientHeight", "jscript");
</SCRIPT>
```

A Dynamic Property Example

One of the 'flashy' uses of DHTML is to move elements around on the screen: implementing a little animation can bring your page to life. We've already seen that you can do this by writing a script routine and tying it to a timer function. Alternatively, you can set up a dynamic property that will automatically move the element around on the page – this uses much less script:

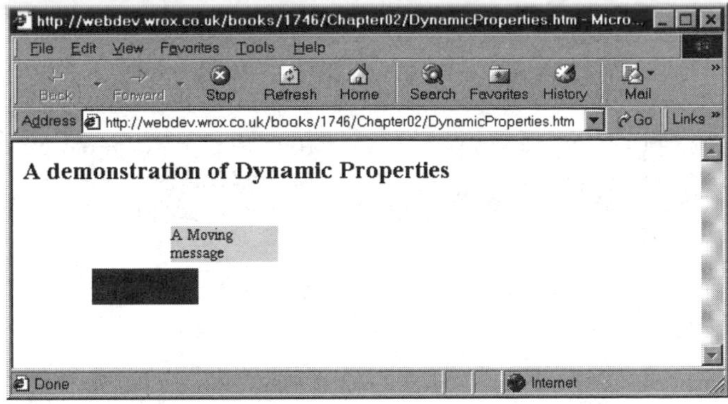

You can run this page from our web site at http://webdev.wrox.co.uk/books/1746.

This script is similar to the one we looked at earlier in the chapter. We are just showing the `MovingMessage DIV` along with a new `DIV` called `FollowingMessage`.

```
<HTML>
<BODY>
<H3>A demonstration of Dynamic Properties</H3>

<DIV ID=MovingMessage STYLE="position: absolute; top: 80; left: 0;
                              height: 30; width: 100; background: yellow;
                              font-size: 15; z-index: 3">
A Moving message
</DIV>

<DIV ID=FollowingMessage STYLE="position: absolute; top: 120;
        left: expression(MovingMessage.style.posLeft * 0.5);
        height: 30; width: 100; background: red; font-size: 15; z-index: 3">
A Following message
</DIV>

<SCRIPT LANGUAGE=JScript>
var iDelta = 1;
function MoveLeft()
{
  MovingMessage.style.posLeft = MovingMessage.style.posLeft + iDelta;
  if (MovingMessage.style.posLeft >= 500 || MovingMessage.style.posLeft < 0)
    iDelta = iDelta * -1;
}
setInterval ("MoveLeft()",50)
</SCRIPT>
</BODY>
</HTML>
```

The `FollowingMessage DIV` will follow the `MovingMessage DIV` as it moves across the page. Rather than having to compute the position of both elements in each timer loop, we use a dynamic property expression to relate the left position of the `FollowingMessage DIV` with the left position of the `MovingMessage DIV`.

```
<DIV ID=FollowingMessage STYLE="position: absolute; top: 120;
        left: expression(MovingMessage.style.posLeft * 0.5);
        height: 30; width: 100; background: red; font-size: 15; z-index: 3">
A Following message
</DIV>
```

The dynamic property expression is recalculated whenever the left position of the `MovingMessage DIV` is changed. The left position of the `FollowingMessage DIV` is set to 50% of the left position of the `MovingMessage DIV`, making it appear to move at half the speed of the `MovingMessage DIV`.

Dynamic HTML opens up a lot of possibilities: for instance, what happens if you get the movement to be triggered by the click of a mouse? But before we get carried away, we need to look at the HTML object model, and see how scripting makes use of it. That will be the subject of the next chapter.

Summary

In this chapter, we've seen how the formatting of pages in DHTML is far more dependent on `styles` than earlier versions of HTML. In particular, the seven new style properties provide ways to control the positioning, layout and z-order (or z-index) of the various elements in the page. Many HTML authors have shunned style sheets in the past, but now is the time to understand them better, because you are going to have to get used to them in the long term.

DHTML provides style properties that control the layout and appearance of pages:

- `left` and `top` define the *x* and *y* coordinates of the element within its container. This can be a document division, or the page itself
- `z-index` defines the *z* coordinate, or layer, in which the element will appear. It's set initially by the ordering of the elements in the HTML, if not specified directly
- `position` defines how the left and top values are interpreted with respect to the element's position within the HTML source, and how it affects the elements that follow
- `overflow` defines whether an element is allowed to flow beyond division boundaries, or if it is to be clipped with or without a scrolling mechanism
- `visibility` defines whether the element will be visible in the page when it is rendered. An element can be hidden, but still keep its place in the HTML source

In addition to being able to manipulate the style properties of an element using script, we can also use dynamic property expressions. These expressions allow you to relate the value of a style property in one element to a value derived from somewhere else on the page. This makes it easier to control the styles of elements, and reduces the amount of script that needs to appear on the page.

And of course, we can still use the style properties from HTML 4.0 to control the other aspects of our design – as we did throughout this chapter. We also looked at how to manipulate some of these new properties with the aid of a script. We used the `style` and `currentStyle` objects to access all of the new properties, and dynamically update the screen as they are changed. However, to understand how we can get the best out of scripting, we need to understand the **object model** on which the browser is built – and this is the subject of the next two chapters.

3

The Dynamic HTML Browser Object Model

Now that we've explored the properties that are available in the Dynamic HTML implementation of style sheets, we can move on to look at the other major difference between traditional and Dynamic HTML. Since the advent of Netscape 2 (the first browser to provide a documented **object model**), it has been possible to use the scripting code in a page to access both the browser environment and the contents of the page itself. These early object models made access OK for controls, but access was still limited when it came to most other things in the page. So while you could access such things as HTML text boxes and list boxes, and Java applets or ActiveX controls, you couldn't get at the real contents of the document. The text, images, headings and other page contents remained temptingly out of reach.

This all changed with the introduction of DHTML. Almost anything that's visible in the page, plus many things that aren't, can be accessed through the extensions to the object model. This is the subject of this chapter. We'll take an overview of the whole structure, then investigate the most useful objects. We'll continue this process in the next chapter, by looking at the objects that are most useful for integrating our script into a web page.

In this chapter, we'll cover:

- The browser object model in outline – how it compares to older browsers
- A brief tour of the basic window objects
- A look at some of the more useful objects and collections

We can't hope to give an in-depth explanation of the entire structure in this book, and there's no real need to do this anyway. Much of the structure is simple, and some is only used in very special cases. You will, however, find definitions and listings of the items that make up the structure in Appendix A of this book.

Introducing the Browser Object Model

If you haven't used scripting code in a web page before, you may not have realized that the browser is built around a structured set of **objects**. It's these objects that provide an interface between the HTML that creates the page, and the internal workings of the browser itself. To make the whole thing easier to visualize and work with, the various objects are organized into a structure called the **object model**.

Why Do We Need An Object Model?

When we define a normal static web page with HTML, we don't need to know about the browser's object model or the structure of the browser itself. Even when we display several documents in different frames, we just give each frame a name, and then TARGET new pages to the appropriate one. For example, suppose we have defined a frameset which contains a frame named mainwindow, like this:

```
<FRAMESET>
  <FRAME NAME="mainwindow" SRC="http://www.wrox.com">
  ...
</FRAMESET>
```

Then we can load a different page into it using the TARGET attribute of the <A> tag:

```
<A HREF="http://webdev.wrox.co.uk" TARGET="mainwindow">Web Developer's
website</A>
```

So why do we need an object model?

The Object Model and Scripting

If you've used a scripting language like VBScript or JavaScript before, you'll know that the example above gives an extremely simplified view. In reality, all the frames in the browser window are stored by the browser as **child** objects of the main window. They are organized into a **collection** (a structure rather like an array – we'll come back to collections later). To refer to the main window in a scripting language, we can reference it using the keywords parent or top, depending on its position in the hierarchy. The parent keyword refers to the window immediately above the current window in the hierarchy, which may be the top window, while top always refers to the topmost window. If we were in one window in a frame, and wanted to refer to another window (named mainwindow) held in the same frameset, we would use the following code:

```
parent.frames ("mainwindow").location.href = "http://webdev.wrox.co.uk"
```

Don't worry about the code we've used here for the time being – we'll look at what all of these references mean later in the chapter.

> **Throughout this chapter we'll be using VBScript in our examples, unless we specifically mention otherwise. However, many of the properties and methods definitions in code are identical in JavaScript (remembering that JavaScript is case-sensitive, while VBScript is not).**

> *You may well have met the 'page targeting' keywords `_top` and `_self` before. In the `TARGET` attribute of an <A> tag, `_top` is used to load a page into the main browser window, instead of into a frame within the window – effectively replacing the frameset. `_self` can be used to load a page into the current window and maintain the current frame layout, though this is rarely used. The `top` and `self` keywords in scripting languages have the same meaning as these.*

The concept of things belonging to collections and having parents and children implies that there is an underlying object model structure. In this chapter, we'll start to explore the object model, and see how to use it in Dynamic HTML.

The Object Model in Overview

The browser object model is, in fact, simply an **interface** between the DHTML source code in the page, and the browser software routines that create the window and fill it with the elements defined in the page. Exactly how these routines fill the browser window (or **render** the page) is unimportant to us. Dynamic HTML simply defines what the results should be, not how the processes should be implemented.

We can think of the browser object model as being a part of the browser, while Dynamic HTML is (in theory at least) a universal *browser-independent* document definition language. This means that all browsers that host Dynamic HTML must provide the same core objects in their object model. Otherwise, it would be impossible to create pages that performed properly on different browsers.

So, we can think of the browser's object model as being a way of connecting our pages to the browser. The object model provides a range of **objects**, **methods**, **properties** and **events** that are present and active within the browser's software, and are exposed to the HTML and scripting code in the page. We can use these to communicate our wishes back to the browser, and hence to the viewer. The browser will carry out our commands, and update the page(s) it displays.

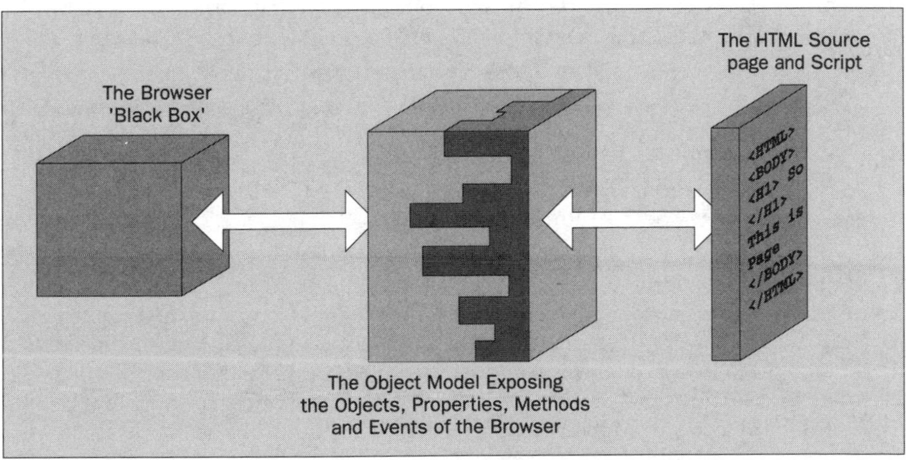

Objects, Methods, Properties and Events

So far we've talked about objects, methods, properties and events – and assumed that you're familiar with these terms. No doubt you've heard them used many times, but we'll recap briefly here before going on to look at the browser object model itself.

Objects

Modern software design is very much concerned with **objects**. Objects are self-contained parts of a program such as the browser, and each object carries out specific functions. The key is that each object will usually store its own data in its own format, and will also contain the code routines (called methods – see the definition below) that are required to manipulate that data.

You can think of an object as being rather like a video recorder, in that we put the tapes in and set the timer, but all the work of recording and playing back goes on inside the black box. We just tell it to record or play back, and we don't need to know what's actually going on inside. The video recorder stores its data (our TV program) itself, in its own format (a video cassette), without us having to worry about how it's doing it.

Methods

Methods are an object's way of letting us do something with it. Our video recorder has methods built in that allow us to record or play back TV programs. The big advantage of having an object provide methods is that it takes away the worry of knowing what's going on inside the object. Rather than telling the video recorder the exact patterns of magnetism to lay down on the tape, and how to interpret the sound signal, we execute its `Record` method by pressing a couple of buttons.

Events

If methods are our way of telling an object what to do, **events** can be thought of as the object's way of telling us that something happened. It's likely that our trusty video recorder will have something we could term an `EndOfTape` event. This occurs when the end of the tape is reached, and stops the motor to prevent it tearing the tape off the spool. Here, the event is being used internally to execute the `Stop` method of the `TapeWindingMotor` object inside the video recorder.

However, it's likely that the video recorder will also tell us that the end of the tape has been reached, by changing the display on the front or by rewinding and automatically ejecting the tape. This allows us to respond to the event, perhaps by putting the tape back in its library case – this is called **event handling**.

Properties

Properties should be no problem to grasp by now. We regularly used the term in Chapter 2, when we were referring to the style properties of the elements in the page. All we really mean by a property is some setting, or stored value, that applies to an object. The object will usually expose a set of properties that affect the appearance or behavior of the object, and some that just provide information about it.

In our video recorder example there are **read/write properties** – these are properties that we can change in order to adjust the behavior or appearance of the video recorder. These might include the record speed setting and the time setting on the clock. The video recorder will also have some **read-only properties** – these might include the age, the price, and the working condition. As you can see, there are often read-only properties that we would like to be able to change, but can't – and DHTML is no exception.

The Object Model Diagram

Being able to describe the object model of the browser is a necessity if we are to understand how all the parts of the hierarchy fit together. The usual way to do this is to show a tree-style diagram, with the main objects at the top and the subsidiary ones below: this is what we've done here. The object model diagram is really an abstract representation of the available objects and how they are related to one another. In a real page scenario, we work with instances of these objects, whose relationship reflects the structure that is shown here.

The top-level object in the browser hierarchy is the **window**. This is the parent object for every other object in the structure.

> *You'll notice that some of the 'things' in the object hierarchy are **objects**, and some are **collections**. In general, collections have a plural name, i.e.* `anchors` *rather than* `anchor`*. The one that breaks the rule is the* `all` *collection – we can only assume that calling it the* `alls` *collection would have sounded a little odd.*

The diagram shows how each of the objects is related – and there are quite a few of them altogether. If you've used VBScript or JavaScript in any depth before, you'll recognize many of them. To maintain backwards compatibility with pages designed for older browsers, the object model for DHTML is a superset of that found in prior versions of Internet Explorer.

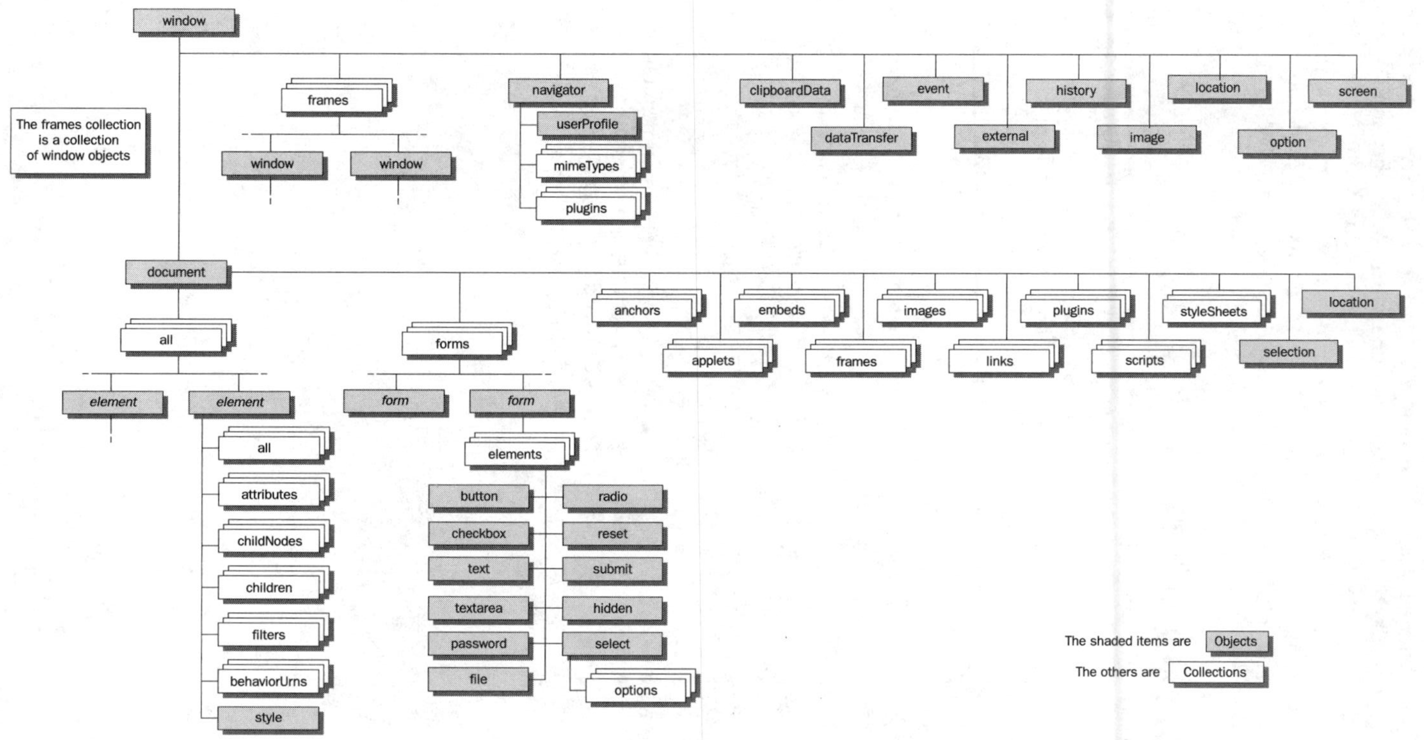
window
The frames collection is a collection of window objects
frames
window
window
navigator
userProfile
mimeTypes
plugins
clipboardData
dataTransfer
event
external
history
image
location
option
screen
document
all
element
element
all
attributes
childNodes
children
filters
behaviorUrns
style
forms
form
form
elements
button
radio
checkbox
reset
text
submit
textarea
hidden
password
select
file
options
anchors
applets
embeds
frames
images
links
plugins
scripts
styleSheets
selection
location
The shaded items are Objects
The others are Collections

Looking at the Structure

Looking at the diagram you can see that, although the `window` object is at the top of the tree, it's the `document` object that's really at the heart of things. This isn't surprising, because the bulk of our page and its contents exist within the `document` itself. The `window` is just the container that holds it.

If you are worried about remembering this structure, don't panic – a lot of it is of only minor importance when creating pages, and much of it is repeated. For example, a window can hold a selection of `frames`, but each frame is actually a `window` in its own right. Once you understand how to use the `window` object, you can use it in all the separate windows created by a frameset document.

Much the same thing happens with the `document` object. Each `window` object can contain a single `document` object. Every occurrence of a `document` object contains the set of other objects and collections that you see in the diagram.

In this chapter, we'll look at the `window` object and its subsidiary objects and collections. We'll postpone coverage of the other major object in the hierarchy – the `document` object – until the next chapter, where we'll have room to do it justice.

Understanding Collections

You can see from the diagram that many parts of the object model are implemented as **collections**. A collection is something like the arrays that you meet in programming languages, where each item is held in structure and related to its neighbors. A collection of `frames` is just a way of holding one or more frame objects together in such a way that they can be accessed in code. We can retrieve details of a frame in a browser window using either its name or its numerical position in the collection:

```
window.frames("mainframe")       'both of these refer to frames in a window
window.frames(0)                 'this is the first frame, with index zero
```

The browser assumes that the *active* `window` object (which may, of course, be a frame inside another window) is the default object for script in the page. Therefore, in most cases we don't need to specify it. The following lines of code have the same meaning as the two lines above:

```
frames("mainframe")
frames(0)
```

In the browser object model's collections, the first item is indexed zero. The actual ordering of the frames in a collection depends on their order in the HTML source. Frame zero will be the first frame defined in the `<FRAMESET>` tag. The same applies to other collections, such as the `forms` or `images` in a document.

Understanding Parents and Children

The expression `window.frames(0)` in the example above refers to the first frame in the *current* window. But what do we mean by the *current* window? One of the most confusing topics when looking at the object model is the relationship between windows and frames.

If you look back at the object tree, you will see that the top of the tree is the window object, and one of its subsidiary objects is a frames collection. This collection holds all of the frames in that current window. Imagine a case where there are three frames in a window. As far as we are concerned, they would be indexed 0, 1 and 2 in the frames collection:

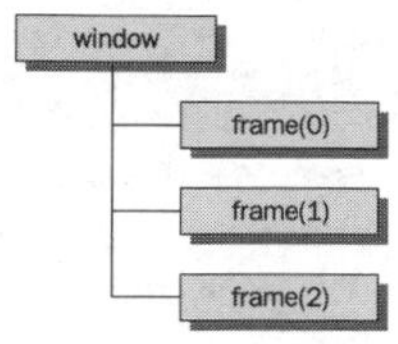

You can see from the object diagram that this window object has three frame objects as children. Now, if we take a look at each of these frame objects in a bit more detail, you'll see that each one of them has another window object as a child:

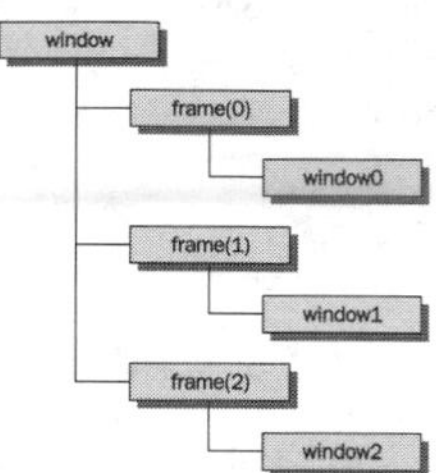

We have called these window objects window0, window1 and window2, and these objects have the same characteristics as our main window object. This means that each of them displays the contents of an HTML page. These pages can include script code as well.

One of the things that a script developer may want to do is be able to refer to objects in another window in the hierarchy. It is here that the concept of children becomes important. Let's say that we are running some script code in window1, and we want to refer to an object in window2. How would we do this?

Looking at the diagram, you can see that there is a line that connects window1 and window2, but it is not a direct path. In fact, the only way to get from window1 to window2 is to actually go back up one level, to our original window, and then back down to window2. This 'going back a level' really means obtaining a reference to the parent of window1. In the following code, we name the parent objParentWindow:

```
Dim objParentWindow
Set objParentWindow = window1.parent
```

Now that we have a reference to the parent window, we can get access to window2 by referring to the window that is the child of the second reference in the frames collection:

```
Dim objWindow2
Set objWindow2 = objParentWindow.frames(2).window
```

Notice that when moving upward through the hierarchy we can use the parent property, but when moving from parent to child, we have to specify which child we want by the frame that it is in.

We can always refer to the topmost window in the object model (the browser window itself, in effect) by using the keyword top, instead of having to specify the correct number of parent keywords. This is useful in a complex page with several layers of frames.

Of course, now that we've discovered Dynamic HTML, we won't need to use so many layers of frames. Things that could only be done in the past using frames can now be done in other ways.

The Window Object

As far as the browser object model is concerned, the `window` object is the 'top-of-the-tree' and everything else in the DHTML object model revolves around it. Once we understand the `window` object, we'll have a pretty good grasp of how we relate to the object model in our pages. When we refer to the `window` object in the code for a DHTML page, we mean the window that is displaying the page, or the *current* window. This may be the top-level window, but it might equally be a window that is within a frame created by a `<FRAMESET>` in another document. If the window is divided into frames (i.e. its document does contain a frameset) it will have a frames collection – as we saw earlier:

Collection	Description
`frames`	Collection of all the frames defined within a `<FRAMESET>` tag.

The `window` object also has a range of properties, methods and events. We'll look at these next – we'll concentrate on the most useful ones, but there's also a complete listing in Appendix A.

The Properties of the Window Object

The following table shows the most commonly-used properties of a `window` object. It includes the `parent`, `self` and `top` properties we mentioned earlier (which allow us to refer to objects throughout the hierarchy), and the `name` property (which reflects the name we give to a window in a `<FRAMESET>` tag).

Properties	Description
`parent`	Returns the parent window of the current window.
`self`	Returns a reference to the current window.
`top`	Returns a reference to the topmost window.
`name`	Name of the window.
`opener`	If the current window was opened by script, this refers to the window that that script was running in.
`closed`	Indicates if a window is closed.
`screen_Left`	Indicates left position, in pixels, of the window, on the screen.
`screenTop`	Indicates top position, in pixels, of the window on the screen.
`complete`	Indicates that the page is completely loaded.

Properties	Description
`status`	The text displayed in the browser's status bar.
`defaultStatus`	The default text from the browser's status bar.
`returnValue`	Allows a variable to be returned from a modal dialog window.
`offscreenBuffering`	Boolean value indicating if elements are drawn offscreen before they are displayed.
`document`	Read-only reference to the window's `document` object.
`event`	Read-only reference to the global `event` object. Each browser instance, no matter how many windows, has one `event` object.
`history`	Read-only reference to the window's `history` object.
`external`	Relates to an IE5 session 'hosted' within another application. A read-only reference to the object model of the host application (thus extending the IE5 object model)
`location`	Read-only reference to the window's `location` object, which contains information on the URL of the current page.
`navigator`	Read-only reference to the window's `navigator` object.
`clientInformation`	Returns a read-only reference to the window's `navigator` object. This is exactly the same reference as the `navigator` property.
`screen`	Read-only reference to the global screen object. Just like the `event` object, each browser instance has one `screen` object.

The `opener` and `closed` properties are usually used when we create new browser windows, as you'll see later in the book. The `status` and `defaultStatus` properties refer to the text displayed in the status bar at the bottom of the browser window. The `status` property is useful when we want to display progress messages to the user, or for debugging script. We can display anything we like in the status bar while the script is running:

```
window.status = "The value of the variable 'MeaningOfLife' is usually 42"
```

The Methods of the Window Object

The `window` object's methods provide many ways of manipulating a window, and carrying out tasks within it. We'll start this section with a full list of the methods of the `window` object and then look at some of these in more detail in the following sections.

Methods	Description
`open`	Opens a new browser window.
`close`	Closes the current browser window.
`showHelp`	Displays a 'help' window as a modeless dialog.
`showModalDialog`	Displays a new browser window as a modal dialog.
`showModelessDialog`	Displays a new browser window as a modeless dialog.
`alert`	Displays an Alert dialog box with a message and an OK button.
`prompt`	Displays a Prompt dialog box with a message and an input field.
`confirm`	Displays a Confirm dialog box with a message, and OK and Cancel buttons.
`navigate`	Causes the URL passed as a parameter to be loaded into the current window.
`blur`	Causes the window to lose focus, and then fire its `onblur` event.
`focus`	Causes the window to receive the focus, and then fire its `onfocus` event.
`print`	Prints the document associated with the window.
`scroll`	Scrolls the window to a specified x and y offset in the document.
`scrollBy`	Scrolls the document in the window by the number of x and y pixels specified.
`scrollTo`	Scrolls the document in the window to the position specified.
`moveBy`	Moves the browser window on the screen by the number of x and y pixels specified.
`moveTo`	Moves the browser window on the screen to the position specified.
`resizeBy`	Resizes the browser window on the screen by the number of x and y pixels specified.

Table Continued on Following Page

Methods	Description
`resizeTo`	Resizes the browser window on the screen to the width and height specified.
`setInterval`	Denotes a code routine to execute repeatedly every specified number of milliseconds. Cancel using `clearInterval`.
`setTimeout`	Denotes a code routine to execute once after a specified number of milliseconds. Cancel using `clearTimeout`.
`clearInterval`	Cancels an interval timer that was set with the `setInterval` method.
`clearTimeout`	Cancels a timeout that was set with the `setTimeout` method, before the event fires.
`execScript`	Executes the script code passed as a parameter. The default language is JScript.
`attachEvent`	Sets the function to be called when an event in the window is fired. Used for Behaviors.
`detachEvent`	Clears the function to be called when an event in the window is fired. Used for Behaviors.

New Browser Windows

If we want to create a new browser window from a web page, or close an existing one, we can use the `open` and `close` methods.For example, the following code creates a new browser window containing the page `newpage.htm`:

```
window.open "newpage.htm"
```

We can also add other arguments to the method to get more control over how the new window is presented. The full syntax is:

`window.open` *`URL, name, features, replace`*

The `name` parameter is used to set the name of the new window. If you pass the string `"_search"` then the browser will open the new window in the Search pane. The *`features`* parameter can be a string of instructions concerning the position, size and type of window, and whether it should contain scrollbars, a toolbar, etc. The Boolean *`replace`* parameter indicates if this new page should be added to the browser's history list or not.

Dynamic HTML also adds support for modal and modeless dialogs that can contain HTML code:

```
window.showModalDialog "dialogpage.htm"
window.showModelessDialog "modeless.html"
```

This is effectively a new browser window that is displayed on top of the existing window and, in the case of modal dialogs, the viewer has to close it before they can continue browsing. We'll look at modal dialogs, modeless dialogs and help dialogs in more detail in Chapter 7 of the book, together with new browser windows generally.

Built-in Dialogs

There are three built-in dialogs that we can display using `alert`, `prompt` and `confirm` (these were originally designed for use with JavaScript, which doesn't have its own dialogs or message boxes):

```
window.alert "You'll have to choose where to go next."
strLocation = window.prompt("Enter your preferred location", "Birmingham")
blnResult = window.confirm("Are you ready to load this page ?")
```

Here's an example that uses these dialogs to load a new page. The page `dialogs_vb.htm` consists of a single script section, containing this code:

```
<SCRIPT LANGUAGE=VBSCRIPT>
window.alert "You'll have to choose where to go next."
strLocation = window.prompt("Enter your preferred location", "Birmingham")
If strLocation <> "" Then
  If strLocation = "Birmingham" Then          'default text for the confirm
                                              'dialog
    strAddress = "http://webdev.wrox.co.uk"
  Else
    strAddress = "http://www.wrox.com"
  End If
  window.status = "New location will be " & strAddress
  If window.confirm("Are you ready to load this page ?") Then
    window.navigate strAddress
  End If
End If
</SCRIPT>
```

You can run this sample on our web site – http://webdev.wrox.co.uk/books/1746.

The first line displays an `alert` dialog with a simple message, like this.

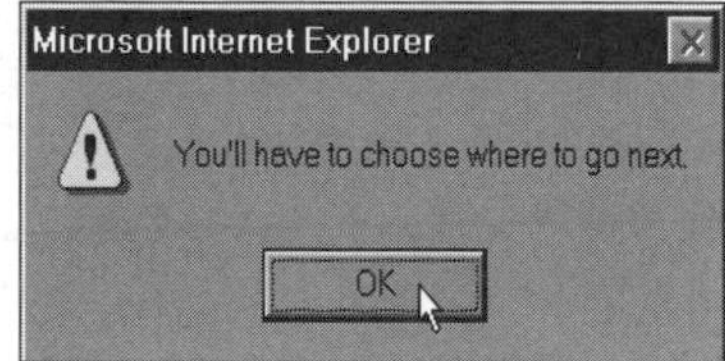

The second line uses the `window` object's `prompt` method to display a dialog where the user can enter some information. The first argument is the prompt itself, and the second is the default value for the text box in the dialog:

The value in the text box is returned to our code when the user clicks the OK button, and we assign it to a variable named `strLocation`. Now we can see what they actually entered – if anything. If they clicked the Cancel button in the dialog, or deleted all the text and didn't enter anything, we'll get an empty string back from the `prompt` method. We test for this first by comparing `strLocation` to an empty string (`""`), and only execute the following code if there actually is a value.

If the value is still Birmingham (the default), we set the value of the `strAddress` variable to the address of Wrox's UK web site. If not, we set it to the main US site address:

```
If strLocation <> "" Then
  If strLocation = "Birmingham" Then    'default text for the confirm dialog
    strAddress = "http://webdev.wrox.co.uk"
  Else
    strAddress = "http://www.wrox.com"
  End If
  ...
```

By now, we know we've got an address to go to, so we can display a message in the browser's status bar by setting the `window` object's `status` property. We use some text and add the address string from the variable `strAddress` to the end of it like this:

```
  window.status = "New location will be " & strAddress
```

Now we can perform a final check to see if they really want to do it. We use the `window` object's confirm method to display the OK or Cancel dialog. The string argument is the message displayed, and it returns `True` or `False` depending on which button the user clicks. Once they've clicked a button, we can check the result and load the new page if it is `True`:

```
  If window.confirm("Are you ready to load this page ?") Then
```

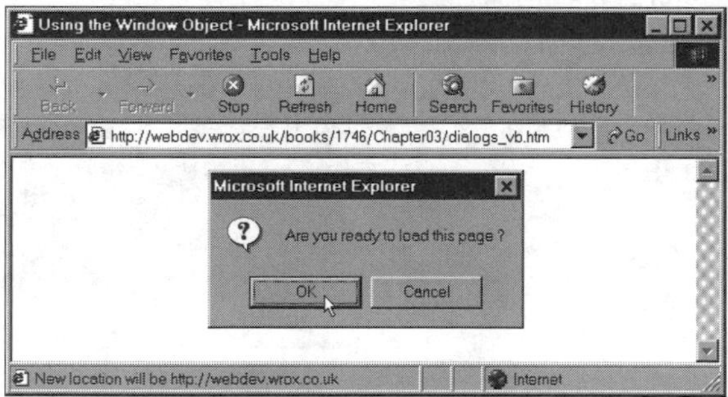

Notice that the status bar is displaying our message as well. Finally, the line that actually loads the new page uses the `navigate` method of the window object. We're supplying the address argument as the string variable `strAddress` we set earlier:

```
    window.navigate strAddress
```

Using JavaScript Instead

In the previous example, we used VBScript (despite the Explorer User Prompt displaying to the contrary). If you're just getting into scripting then VBScript is generally considered to be easier to work with than JavaScript (those with a background in Java, C or C++ will disagree!). Here's the same routine in JavaScript, and it too can be found on our web site at http://webdev.wrox.co.uk/books/1746/:

```
<SCRIPT LANGUAGE=JAVASCRIPT>
window.alert("You'll have to choose where to go next.");
strLocation = window.prompt("Enter your preferred location", "Birmingham");
if (strLocation != "")
{
  if (strLocation == "Birmingham")
  {
    strAddress = "http://webdev.wrox.co.uk"
  }
  else
  {
    strAddress = "http://www.wrox.com"
  }
  window.status = "New location will be " + strAddress;
  if (window.confirm("Are you ready to load this page ?"))
  {
    window.navigate(strAddress)
  }
}
</SCRIPT>
```

You can see that the syntax of the methods and properties is exactly the same, but that JavaScript uses curly braces to define blocks of code like the `if...` section, rather than the VBScript's `If...End If` structure.

Focus, Scrolling and Timers

If there is more than one browser window open, we can switch the **focus** between them using the `blur` and `focus` methods. These effectively change which is the 'active' window. The `blur` method moves the focus *from* the window where the code is being run to the next window (like pressing *Alt Tab*), while `focus` moves it *to* the window where the code is. We can also load a new document into a window using the `navigate` method. Again, you'll see more of these methods, combined with new browser windows, in Chapter 7.

When our page is larger than the browser window, the user has to scroll it around to see the contents. Alternatively, we can move the page around for the user with another of the window object's methods, `scroll`. For example, to scroll the page so that the point 250 pixels across and 150 pixels down is visible in the browser window, we could use:

```
window.scroll 250,150
```

Finally, there are two methods we can use to set a timer that causes part of our code to be executed after a certain number of milliseconds. The first is the `setTimeout` method. In this VBScript example, we create a timer that will wait for 5 seconds before executing a routine named `MyTimer` (the language argument can be omitted if the routine is in a script section where the language has already been specified):

```
TimeoutID = window.setTimeout("MyTimer", 5000, "VBSCRIPT")
```

We can react to the timer event by writing a subroutine that catches the `MyTimer` event:

```
Sub MyTimer()
  window.alert "Time's up!"
End Sub
```

However, once the timer has fired, we would need to reset it again if we wanted to repeat the process. The other method, `setInterval`, functions in the same way as `setTimeout`, except that the `setInterval` method is called repeatedly every so many milliseconds:

```
TimeoutID = window.setInterval("MyTimer", 5000, "VBSCRIPT")
```

So if you ran the program now, the Time's up dialog would appear at 5000-millisecond intervals until the `clearInterval` method is called:

```
window.clearInterval(TimeoutID)
```

The Events of the Window Object

The `window` object has eleven events:

Events	Description
`onblur`	Occurs when the window loses the focus.
`onfocus`	Occurs when the window receives the focus.
`onhelp`	Occurs when the user presses the *F1* or Help key.
`onresize`	Occurs when the element or object is resized by the user.
`onscroll`	Occurs when the user scrolls a page or element.
`onerror`	Occurs when an error loading a document or image arises.
`onbeforeunload`	Occurs just before the page is unloaded, allowing the unload event to be cancelled.
`onbeforeprint`	Occurs just before the page is printed.
`onafterprint`	Occurs just after the page is printed.
`onload`	Occurs when the page has completed loading.
`onunload`	Fired after `onbeforeunload`, immediately prior to the page being unloaded. When this fires, the unload cannot be cancelled.

If there is more than one browser window open then the user can switch between them, initiating the `onblur` event in the window losing focus and the `onfocus` event in the window receiving focus. Notice that these can also be fired when the `window` object's `blur` and `focus` methods are called by our code:

```
Sub window_onfocus()
  window.alert "I've now got the focus."
End Sub

Sub window_onblur()
  window.alert "Oh no, I've lost it again."
End Sub
```

If the user presses the *F1* (or Help) key, the window receives an `onhelp` event:

```
Sub window_onhelp()
  window.alert "Tell me your problems..."
End Sub
```

If the browser window is resized, either through script or by using the mouse, the window receives an `onresize` event:

```
Sub window_onresize()
  window.alert "Metamorphosizing..."
End Sub
```

If some of the display is not visible, and the user scrolls the display to view it, the window receives an `onscroll` event:

```
Sub window_onscroll()
  window.alert "Scrolling..."
End Sub
```

There's also a very useful event called `onerror`, that fires if an error occurs during the download of an image, object, or any element on the page. It fires whether an error occurred or whether the transfer was aborted manually, which can allow the program to try and download the object again or take appropriate action:

```
Sub window_onerror()
  window.alert "Error occurred during download, please try again!"
End Sub
```

Finally, let's look at these three related events:

- `onload` occurs when the window loads a page
- `onbeforeunload` occurs just before the page is unloaded. During the handling of this event, the unloading of the page can be aborted. This is done by setting the `returnValue` property of the `event` object to a string, which is then presented to the user in a dialog that gives the user the option to stay on the page
- `onunload` fires as the page is unloaded: either immediately before opening a new page or when the browser is closing down

```
Sub window_onload()
  window.alert "Finished loading the page."
End Sub

Sub window_onbeforeunload()
  window.alert "About to unload the page"
End Sub

Sub window_onunload()
  window.alert "Unloading the page."
End Sub
```

The Window's Subsidiary Objects

You'll have noticed from the object model diagram (earlier in the chapter) that the `window` object a number of subsidiary objects (as well as the one collection, `frames`), all of which are referenced through the `window` object. In this section we'll look at five of them: `history`, `navigator`, `location`, `event` and `screen`.

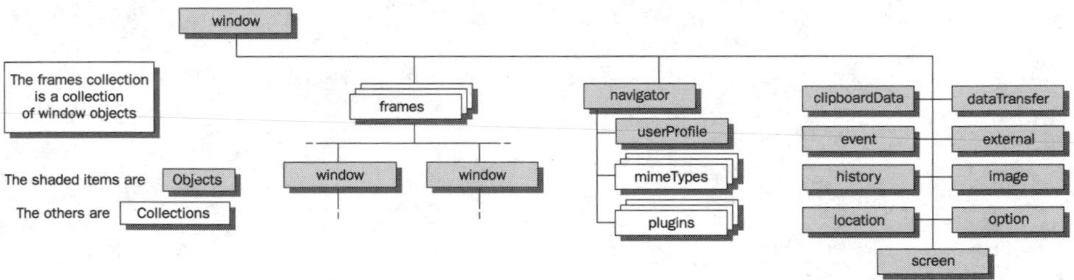

The History Object

The `history` object contains information about the URLs that the browser has visited in this session, as stored in the `History` list. It also allows us to move through the list using script code, loading the pages it contains. There is one property, the `length` of the list, and three methods:

Properties	Description
`length`	Returns the number of items in the browser's `History` list.
`back`	Loads the previous URL in the browser's `History` list.
`forward`	Loads the next URL in the browser's `History` list.
`go` *n*	Loads the page at position *n* (0-based) in the browser's `History` list.

We can use these properties and methods to move through the list. In the following example, we'll go to the first entry in the list, then jump to the sixth one after checking that there are enough available. Notice that we have omitted the default `window` object from the code:

```
history.go 1
If history.length > 5 Then history.forward 5
```

The Navigator Object

The `navigator` object represents the browser application itself, providing information about its manufacturer, version and capabilities. It has twelve properties, one collection and two methods:

Properties	Description
`appName`	The product name of the browser.
`appVersion`	The platform and version of the browser.
`appMinorVersion`	The minor version of the browser.
`browserLanguage`	The current language setting of the browser. The default value is `us-en`.
`cookieEnabled`	Denotes if cookies are enabled in the browser.
`userAgent`	The user-agent (browser name) header sent as part of the HTTP protocol.
`appCodeName`	The code name of the browser.
`cpuClass`	The CPU that the browser is running on.
`onLine`	Denotes if the global `onLine` state is enabled or disabled. This is changed by the user selecting Work Offline from the File menu in Internet Explorer.
`platform`	The platform that the browser is running on.
`systemLanguage`	Default language of the system.
`userLanguage`	Current language of the system.

Collections	Description
`plugins`	Collection of all the `embedded` objects in the page.

Methods	Description
`taintEnabled`	Returns `False` – data tainting is not supported by any version of Internet Explorer, so this is just included for compatibility with other browsers.
`javaEnabled`	Indicates if execution of Java code is enabled by the browser.

The Location Object

The `location` object contains information about the URL of the current page. It also provides methods that will reload the current page or load a new one. The properties consist of one that holds the complete URL string, `href`, and several which hold various parts of the URL string:

Properties	Description
href	The entire URL as a string (e.g. protocol://hostname:port/pathname#hash?search)
hash	The bookmark string following the # symbol in the URL.
host	The hostname:port part of the location or URL.
hostname	The hostname part of the location or URL.
pathname	The file or object path name following the third slash in a URL. (e.g.pathname in http://www.servername.com/pathname)
port	The port number in a URL.
protocol	The initial sub-string of the URL, indicating the URL's access method (e.g. file, http, ftp, etc).
search	The querystring or data following the ? in the complete URL.

If we take a look at a location that includes all these properties, we would have a URL that looked like:

```
protocol://hostname:port/pathname#hash?search
```

We can use these properties to change the page that is being displayed. The usual way is to reset the href property to a new value, which has the same effect as calling the window object's navigate method:

```
window.location.href = "http://webdev.wrox.co.uk"
```

The three methods provided by the location object can be used to either load another page, reload the current page or replace it in the browser's history list:

Methods	Description
assign	Loads another page. Equivalent to changing the window.location.href property.
reload	Reloads the current page.
replace	Loads a page replacing the current page's history entry with its URL. The page being replaced is no longer in the browser history.

The Event Object

The `event` object allows the scripting language to get more information about any event that occurs in the browser. In effect, it is global to all the objects. The `event` object provides a range of properties, a full list of which can be found in Appendix A. For the moment, we will be concentrating on the following:

Properties	Description
`x`	Returns the x coordinate of the mouse relative to the parent element when the event was fired.
`y`	Returns the y coordinate of the mouse relative to the parent element when the event was fired.
`clientX`	Returns the x coordinate of the mouse relative to the window when the event was fired.
`clientY`	Returns the y coordinate of the mouse relative to the window when the event was fired.
`offsetX`	Returns the x coordinate of the mouse pointer when an event occurs, relative to the object firing the event.
`offsetY`	Returns the y coordinate of the mouse pointer when an event occurs, relative to the object firing the event.
`screenX`	Returns the x coordinate of the mouse pointer when an event occurs, in relation to the screen.
`screenY`	Returns the y coordinate of the mouse pointer when an event occurs, in relation to the screen.
`button`	The mouse button, if any, that was pressed to fire the event.
`altKey`	Returns the state of the *Alt* key at the time the event occurred.
`ctrlKey`	Returns the state of the *Ctrl* key at the time the event occurred.
`shiftKey`	Returns the state of the *Shift* key at the time the event occurred.
`keyCode`	ASCII code of key pressed. Can be changed to send a different character.
`reason`	Indicates whether data transfer to an element was successful, or why it failed. (We'll look at the `dataTransfer` object below.)
`type`	Returns the name of the event as a string without the on prefix – e.g. if `event.name` is `onclick` then `event.type` returns `click`.
`dataFld`	Returns the data column affected by the event. Used with data binding.

Table Continued on Following Page

Properties	Description
`recordset`	Returns the recordset associated with the event. Used with data binding.
`propertyName`	The name of the property that has changed.
`srcFilter`	Indicates the filter that fired the event.
`srcURN`	Indicates the behavior that fired the event. Behaviors are covered in chapter 8.
`repeat`	True if the event is being repeated – only set during the `onkeydown` event.
`fromElement`	Element being moved from in an `onmouseover` or `onmouseout` event.
`toElement`	Element being moved to in an `onmouseover` or `onmouseout` event.
`returnValue`	Specifies a return value for the event.
`srcElement`	Object that fired the event.
`cancelBubble`	Can be set to prevent the current event from bubbling up the hierarchy.

The first thirteen properties return values that indicate what was going on when the event occurred. If it was a mouse event, these include the `x` and `y` position of the mouse pointer on the screen, and the mouse `button` that was pressed. If it was a key-press event, the `keyCode` property returns the ASCII code of the key combination that was pressed. The `altKey`, `ctrlKey` and `shiftKey` properties indicate whether the *Alt*, *Ctrl* and/or *Shift* keys were being held down at the time.

The `reason` property indicates whether a data transfer was successful, and returns an integer indicating either success, aborted transfer or error. The `type` property just creates a string of the event name which can be used within your program. The `dataFld` and `recordset` properties are used with data-bound elements, which will be covered in Chapter 7. The `dataFld` property indicates which data column in a table was affected by the `oncellchange` event.

When a property of an element is changed, the element fires the `onpropertychange` event. The `propertyName` property of the `event` object indicates which property in that element was actually changed. Likewise, when a visual filter changes state, it will fire an `onfilterchange` event. The filter that changed state can be identified with the `srcFilter` property.

The `onmouseover` or `onmouseout` events occur when the mouse is moving over or on the point of leaving an element (or the page itself). The properties indicate which element the mouse pointer was moving *onto* (`toElement`) and which element it was moving *off* (`fromElement`). These can be used to change the way an object is displayed when the mouse is over it, like the 'coolbar' you see in the latest windows programs (including Internet Explorer).

Read-Write Event Object Properties

The properties of the `event` object are set when an event occurs, and most of them are read-only. For example, we can't really expect to be able to change the `button` property, as it reflects the mouse button that was clicked. However, a couple of the properties are read/write. The `keyCode` property reflects the key that was pressed, but we can change this in code to cause a different value to be used when the event is actually handled. As an example:

```
...
If (event.keyCode < 48) Or (event.keyCode > 57) Then event.keyCode = 0
...
```

This code simply checks if the key is a number key (*0* to *9*) by looking at its UNICODE value. If it isn't, it changes the UNICODE value to the value zero (not the *0* key, which has an UNICODE value of 48). When this code is received by an element on the page, like a text box, it will be ignored.

The event object also supports the `returnValue` property that indicates if the event, or a modal HTML dialog, should return a value which can be used by the code in the page. Setting it to `False` prevents the code receiving a return value – you'll see more when we come to look at events and modal dialogs later on.

Event Bubbling Properties

The final two properties are concerned with an aspect of scripting called **event bubbling**, which is supported by Dynamic HTML. Briefly, the `srcElement` property indicates which element in the page or other container (such as a division) was 'topmost' when the event occurred. It could be the element under the mouse pointer for a `mousemove` event, or the textbox with the focus for a key-press event.

Depending on how we decide to handle the event, we can set the `cancelBubble` property of the event object to `True` to prevent the event being 'bubbled up' the object hierarchy to objects higher up.

We'll be looking into the whole subject of event handling in depth in Chapter 5. In the mean time, you just need to appreciate that the `event` object contains two properties, `srcElement` and `cancelBubble`, which are used to in conjunction with event bubbling.

The Screen Object

The `screen` object provides information about the viewer's screen resolution and rendering abilities. There are eight properties:

Properties	Description
`width`	Returns the width of the user's display screen in pixels.
`height`	Returns the height of the user's display screen in pixels.
`availWidth`	Returns the available width of the user's display screen in pixels, removing the Windows Task Bar.
`availHeight`	Returns the available height of the user's display screen in pixels, removing the Windows Task Bar.
`bufferDepth`	Specifies the number of bits per pixel used for colors in the off-screen bitmap buffer.
`colorDepth`	Specifies the number of bits per pixel used for the browser display.
`fontSmoothingEnabled`	Returns or sets the font smoothing option in the browser.
`updateInterval`	Sets or returns the interval between screen updates on the client.

The first two, `width` and `height`, are useful when we want to create new browser windows, or change the size of the existing one, in code. The `availWidth` and `availHeight` tell you how much of the screen can actually be used, taking into account the Windows Task Bar. For example, we can use them to decide where to put a new window:

```
If screen.width > 800 Then
  open "newpage.htm", "SmallWindow", "top: 100; left: 600; width: 200"
End If
```

The next two properties, `bufferDepth` and `colorDepth`, are useful for deciding which images to display, and instructing the browser how to display them. Without going into a discussion of how colors are represented, just accept that the browser can display images in a variety of color depths – from two colors (for a monochrome display) up to 16 million colors ('True Color'). These properties describe the color depth in terms of the number of 'bits per pixel', so `8` means 256 colors and `32` is 'True Color'.

If we display an image containing 256 colors, but the color depth of the user's system is only set to 16 colors, then the user will see a degraded version of the image. If we query the `colorDepth` property first, we can use the result to decide which of a series of images we display:

```
If screen.colorDepth < 8 Then
  'display monochrome image
Else
 'display 256 color image
End If
```

This can help to minimize download times as well. There's no point downloading a 'true-color' image if the user is working in 256 colors – we might as well send them a 256-color version instead. We can also instruct the browser to buffer the image and display it with a different color depth by setting the `bufferDepth` property.

On higher-color displays, Windows can play some tricks with the way that fonts are displayed in order to improve how they look. When a font is drawn against a background, jagged edges sometimes appear around the fonts. To alleviate this problem, the transition between the character and the background is smoothed through the use of shaded colors. This is known as **anti-aliasing** or **font smoothing**, and the `fontSmoothingEnabled` property can be used to turn this feature on or off.

The `updateInterval` property can be used to set or retrieve the update rate for the screen. This means that any graphical changes to the window are buffered and then can be drawn at intervals. This is aimed at preventing glitches impairing the overall painting performance, such as when rapid animations are taking place. This is a powerful property and extreme values will adversely affect the page rendering response, so take care when using it.

The dataTransfer Object

The `dataTransfer` object is new in Internet Explorer 5, and is used to support robust data transfer between elements on the page and between applications. The object is used for both the source of the transfer and the destination. There are two properties:

Properties	Description
`dropEffect`	Determines the mouse cursor that will appear over the target element when a drop is attempted
`effectAllowed`	Specifies which data transfer operations are allowed. Possible values are `copy`, `link`, `move`, `copyLink`, `copyMove`, `linkMove`, `all`, `none` and `uninitialize`.

There are three methods that are used to manipulate the `dataTransfer` object:

Methods	Description
`setData`	Set the data and data type to be transferred
`getData`	Retrieves the data and data type being transferred
`clearData`	Clears the data for the specified type being transferred

You can use the `dataTransfer` object in script to transfer information from one element to another. If you utilize the mouse control that we'll look at in the next chapter, you can implement true drag-and-drop support, both within your web page and with other Windows applications.

There is one `dataTransfer` object for each browser window, and you'll interact with this object from both the source element and the destination element. The steps to follow are:

- Put some data into the `dataTransfer` object, using the `setData` method. You can set the `datatype` for this data to be either `text` or a URL.
- Grab the data from the `dataTransfer` object using the `getData` method. You can determine the type of information by reading the `datatype` parameter in this method.

In the following example you can drag the image and drop it on the yellow DIV. When the image is dropped, the `dropIt()` function will add some text to the DIV.

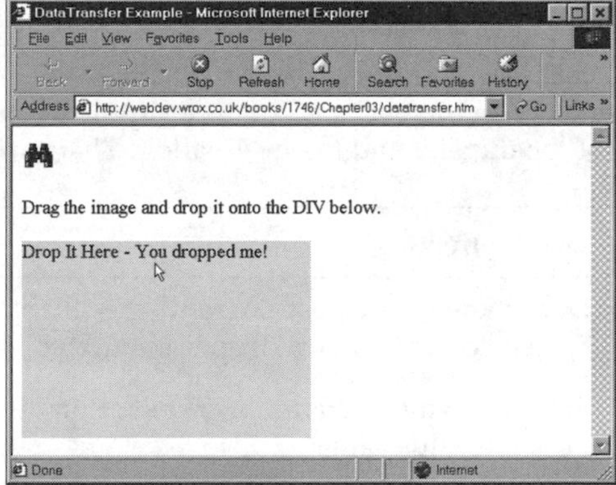


```
<HEAD>
<SCRIPT>

function beginDrag() {
  event.dataTransfer.setData("Text", "You dropped me!");
  event.dataTransfer.effectAllowed = "copy";
}
```

```
function dropIt() {
  event.returnValue = false;
  event.dataTransfer.dropEffect = "copy";
  myDropTarget.innerHTML = myDropTarget.innerHTML + " - " +
                           event.dataTransfer.getData("Text");
}

function dragOverIt() {
  event.returnValue = false;
  event.dataTransfer.dropEffect = "copy";
}

</SCRIPT>
</HEAD>

<BODY>
<IMG ID=mySourceImg SRC="binocs.gif" ondragstart="beginDrag()">
<P>Drag the image and drop it onto the DIV below.</P>
<DIV ID=myDropTarget style="background:yellow; width:300; height:200;"
       ondragenter="dragOverIt()"
       ondrop="dropIt()"
       ondragover="dragOverIt()">Drop It Here</DIV>
</BODY>
```

A Window Object Example Page

To finish up this chapter, here's another page, `DocObject.htm`, that we've provided on our web site at http://webdev.wrox.co.uk/books/1746/ for you to try out. It simply retrieves the values of properties from several of the objects we've looked at in this chapter, and displays them in a table:

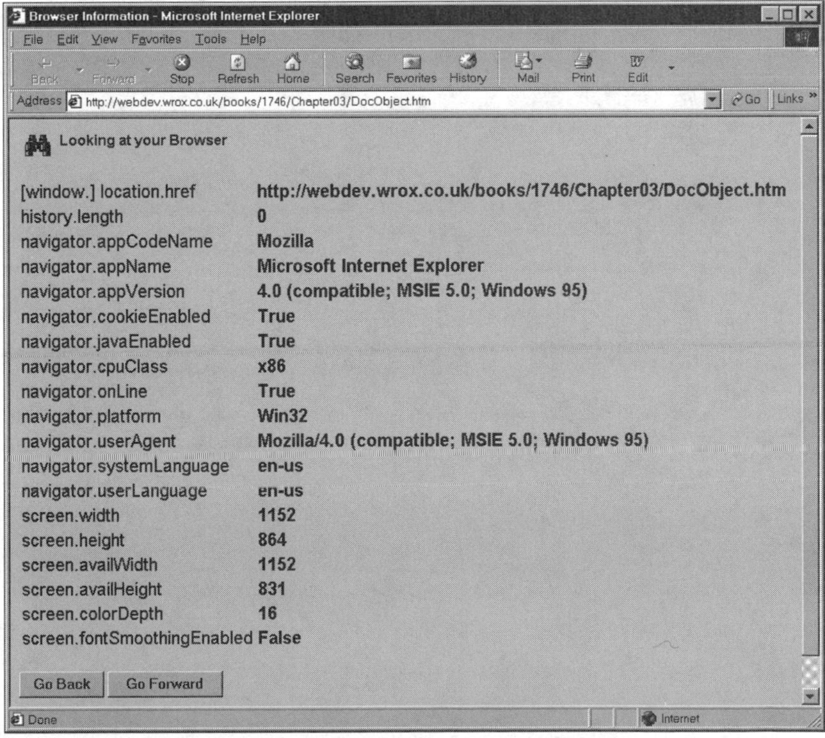

The code that creates the page looks like this:

```
<HTML>
<HEAD><TITLE> Browser Information </TITLE></HEAD>

<STYLE>
<!--
   H1 {font-family: "Arial"; font-size: 16; color: blue}
   H2 {font-family: "Arial"; font-size: 10}
   {font-family: "Arial"; font-size: 14}
-->
</STYLE>

<BODY BGCOLOR=#FFC0A0>
<H1><IMG SRC="binocs.gif" HSPACE=5 ALIGN=MIDDLE>
Looking at your Browser </H1>

<SCRIPT LANGUAGE="VBSCRIPT">
<!--
Dim strInfo
strInfo = "<CENTER><TABLE WIDTH=100%>" _
          & "<TR><TD>[window.] location.href</TD>" _
          & "<TD><B>" & window.location.href & "</TD></TR>" _
          & "<TR><TD>history.length</TD>" _
          & "<TD><B>" & history.length & "</TD></TR>" _
          & "<TR><TD>navigator.appCodeName</TD>" _
          & "<TD><B>" & navigator.appCodeName & "</TD></TR>" _
          & "<TR><TD>navigator.appName</TD>" _
          & "<TD><B>" & navigator.appName & "</TD></TR>" _
          & "<TR><TD>navigator.appVersion</TD>" _
          & "<TD><B>" & navigator.appVersion & "</TD></TR>" _
          & "<TR><TD>navigator.cookieEnabled</TD>" _
          & "<TD><B>" & navigator.cookieEnabled & "</TD></TR>" _
          & "<TR><TD>navigator.javaEnabled</TD>" _
          & "<TD><B>" & navigator.javaEnabled & "</TD></TR>" _
          & "<TR><TD>navigator.cpuClass</TD>" _
          & "<TD><B>" & navigator.cpuClass & "</TD></TR>" _
          & "<TR><TD>navigator.onLine</TD>" _
          & "<TD><B>" & navigator.onLine & "</TD></TR>" _
          & "<TR><TD>navigator.platform</TD>" _
          & "<TD><B>" & navigator.platform & "</TD></TR>" _
          & "<TR><TD>navigator.userAgent</TD>" _
          & "<TD><B>" & navigator.userAgent & "</TD></TR>" _
          & "<TR><TD>navigator.systemLanguage</TD>" _
          & "<TD><B>" & navigator.systemLanguage & "</TD></TR>" _
          & "<TR><TD>navigator.userLanguage</TD>" _
          & "<TD><B>" & navigator.userLanguage & "</TD></TR>" _
          & "<TR><TD>screen.width</TD>" _
          & "<TD><B>" & screen.width & "</TD></TR>" _
          & "<TR><TD>screen.height</TD>" _
          & "<TD><B>" & screen.height & "</TD></TR>" _
          & "<TR><TD>screen.availWidth</TD>" _
          & "<TD><B>" & screen.availWidth & "</TD></TR>" _
          & "<TR><TD>screen.availHeight</TD>" _
          & "<TD><B>" & screen.availHeight & "</TD></TR>" _
          & "<TR><TD>screen.colorDepth</TD>" _
          & "<TD><B>" & screen.colorDepth & "</TD></TR>" _
          & "<TR><TD>screen.fontSmoothingEnabled</TD>" _
          & "<TD><B>" & screen.fontSmoothingEnabled & "</TD></TR>" _
          & "</TABLE></CENTER><P>"
document.write strInfo

Sub cmdBack_onclick()
  Dim intPlaces
  Randomize
  intPlaces = CInt((Rnd() * 3) + 1)
  alert "Trying to go back " & intPlaces & " places."
  history.back intPlaces
End Sub
```

```
Sub cmdForward_onclick()
  Dim intPlaces
  Randomize
  intPlaces = CInt((Rnd() * 3) + 1)
  window.alert "Trying to go forward " & intPlaces & " places."
  history.forward intPlaces
End Sub
-->
</SCRIPT>
<INPUT TYPE=button VALUE="Go Back" NAME="cmdBack">
<INPUT TYPE=button VALUE="Go Forward" NAME="cmdForward">
<H2>&copy;1999 Wrox Press Limited</H2>

</BODY>
</HTML>
```

How It Works

The first section, up to the opening <SCRIPT> tag, just provides the title and heading for the page, and defines the styles for the text.

Inside the script section, we've defined a string variable named `strInfo`, and then filled it with a set of <TABLE>, <TR> and <TD> tags to create a two-column table:

```
Dim strInfo
strInfo = "<CENTER><TABLE WIDTH=100%>" _
          & "<TR><TD>[window.] location.href</TD>" _
          & "<TD><B>" & window.location.href & "</TD></TR>" _
          & "<TR><TD>history.length</TD>" _
          & "<TD><B>" & history.length & "</TD></TR>" _
...
```

The first column contains the names of the object and property we are querying, and the second column contains the actual value. The underscores at the end of each line are VBScript's way of indicating that the statement continues on the next line – remember to leave a space between the underscore and the previous text, or an error will be generated. There are two lines of script (corresponding to one row of the table) for each property we want to query.

Once we've got the table into our string variable, we can print it into the page. The browser doesn't know that the information is coming from our code, it just accepts it as though it were part of the HTML source stream coming from the server in the usual way. To put it into the page, we use the `write` method of the `document` object (you'll see more about this in the next chapter):

```
document.write strInfo
```

Jumping to Another Page in the History List

At the end of the page are two push buttons, created with the usual <INPUT> tag, named `cmdBack` and `cmdForward`:

```
<INPUT TYPE=button VALUE="Go Back" NAME="cmdBack">
<INPUT TYPE=button VALUE="Go Forward" NAME="cmdForward">
```

When a button is clicked, the browser looks for a subroutine in the <SCRIPT> section that is a combination of the event and the name of the element that caused it – in our case either `cmdBack_onclick()` or `cmdForward_onclick()`. We've provided both of these in our page. They simply create a random number and use the `back` and `forward` methods of the `navigator` object to load the relevant page. Here's the `cmdBack` routine again:

```
Sub cmdBack_onclick()
  Dim intPlaces
  Randomize
  intPlaces = CInt((Rnd() * 3) + 1)
  alert "Trying to go back " & intPlaces & " places."
  history.back intPlaces
End Sub
```

This VBScript code declares a variable named `intPlaces`, uses the `Randomize` statement to seed the random number generator, and then the `Rnd` function to produce a pseudo-random number between 0 and 1. This is converted into an integer (whole) number between 1 and 3 by the VBScript `CInt` (convert to integer) function. Finally, it displays a message, and executes the `back` method of the `history` object specifying that number of places to jump.

Summary

In this chapter, we've begun our tour of the Dynamic HTML **object model**. We started with the main browser object, the `window`, and looked at its properties, methods and events. Then we covered its subsidiary objects and collections, consisting of:

- The `frames` collection, which holds details of all the windows in a frameset within the current window
- The `history` object, which represents the browser's `History` list
- The `navigator` object, which represents the browser application itself
- The `location` object, which represents the URL of the page being displayed in the browser
- The `event` object, which represents the events that occur in the browser
- The `screen` object, which represents the browser's color rendering abilities
- The `dataTransfer` object, which can move information between elements on the page, or between applications. This object is new in IE5

However, the main object we use in much of our code is actually the `document` object, and its subsidiary objects and collections. These are the subjects of the next chapter.

The Dynamic HTML Document Object

In the previous chapter we discovered why we need an **object model** to use Dynamic HTML, and we saw what the DHTML browser object model looks like. We also examined the top-level `window` object and its subsidiary objects. By now, you should be familiar with some of the techniques for using scripting code, like VBScript and JavaScript, in your web pages.

Of course, there is still a lot to learn. We're continuing our exploration of the browser object model by moving on to the central object in the hierarchy, the `document` object. We've isolated this object because it merits particular attention. The `document` object represents the HTML document in the browser window. You can use this object to get all sorts of information about the document, via its properties and methods; you can also use it to modify the HTML elements and text on the page. And by using the related `TextRange` object, you can even do things like looking for a particular word on the page and replacing it with another word (this is no great shakes for Word 97, but for an HTML page, without using a page refresh, it's an entirely new trick!). The `document` object, as you might expect, can also be used to process events.

So in this chapter, we'll be looking at:

- The properties, methods and events generally supported by most of the objects on the page
- The properties, methods and events supported by the `document` object
- The `document` object's collections, which are provided to organize all the other items within the page
- The subsidiary `selection` object, which allows us to work with elements of the document selected by the user
- The `TextRectangle` object, which allows you to determine the pixel locations of text on the screen
- Visual Filters and Transitions, which allow you to add visual multimedia effects to various elements on your page

The Document Object

The whole reason for using Dynamic HTML, or any other form of HTML, is to produce pages that we can display in a browser. The page itself is technically referred to as the **document**, and the object model provides a `document` object (plus subsidiary objects and collections), to organize the document itself and all the contents. Let's look at the relevant section of the object model diagram again:

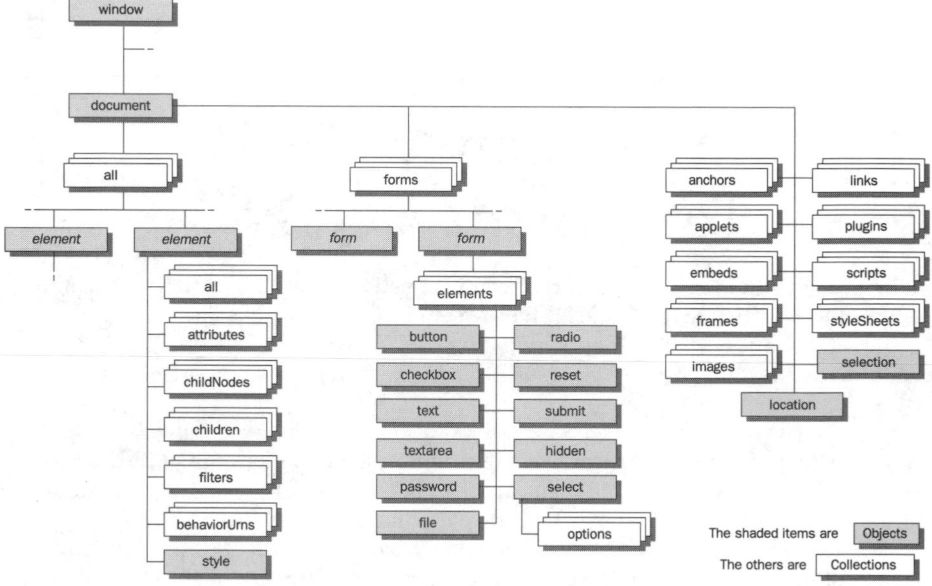

As you can see, the `window` object contains exactly one `document` object, which represents the fact that the browser displays a page (i.e. a document) within a window.

We'll start with a look at the properties, methods and events of the `document` object, then move on to look at the collections and subsidiary objects that it supports. The `document` object has more properties, methods and events than the other objects in the hierarchy, so we've divided them up into categories – this should make it easier to understand them. Appendix A lists all the objects in alphabetical order, and provides a full list of their properties, methods and events.

The Properties of the Document Object

In this section we'll look at the properties that are specific to the `document` object. They can be classified into three types:

- **Informational** properties, which hold information about the document and the disk file in which it's stored
- **Color** properties, which define the colors of various parts of the document
- **Other** document properties – a group of three other properties that provide other information about the document

The Informational Document Properties

The informational properties are mainly concerned with the document and its disk file; they provide information that can help the HTML author decide how to handle them. Most of these properties are self-explanatory, although we will look at the `domain` property in more detail. You'll find an example that demonstrates some of these properties, later in this chapter.

General Properties	Description
`title`	The title of the document as defined in the `<TITLE>` tag.
`body`	Read-only reference to the document's `body` object, as defined by the `<BODY>` tag.
`selection`	Read-only reference to the document's selection object.
`url`	The uniform resource locator (address) of the page.
`location`	A reference to the document's location.
`domain`	The security domain of the document.
`cookie`	The value of a cookie stored by the browser.
`lastModified`	Date that the document was last modified.
`fileCreatedDate`	Date the file was created.
`fileModifiedDate`	Date the file was last modified.
`fileSize`	File size in bytes
`protocol`	Protocol used to access this document, usually `http:`
`charset`	Character set of the document
`defaultCharset`	Set or retrieve the default character set of the document
`parentWindow`	Returns the parent window that contains the document.

Secure Domains

Dynamic HTML allows pages to have a `domain` property, initially the domain part of the document's URL. Imagine a situation in which a frameset is displaying pages from two different sites (or domains). In this situation, code in one page would usually be able to access the contents of the other page, even if it was loaded from a secure domain. However Dynamic HTML does *not* allow this. This helps to prevent suspect pages accessing secure information in others.

We'll return to this issue in the examples that come later in this chapter. The `domain` property returns the domain of the document; it can be used to check that access is available and to prevent code errors.

The Document Color Properties

These properties provide read/write access to the colors of various parts of the page. In particular, they allow us to write code to read and change the color of the page background, the default color of the text, and the colors of unvisited hyperlinks, visited hyperlinks and active hyperlinks. Of course, any style sheets that are applied to the document will overwrite the colors specified using these properties.

Color Properties	Description
`bgColor`	Background color of the page.
`fgColor`	Color of the document foreground text.
`linkColor`	The color for unvisited links in the page.
`aLinkColor`	The color for active links in the page (i.e. the color of the link while the mouse button is held down over the link).
`vLinkColor`	The color for visited links in the page.

These properties are really leftovers from earlier versions of the object model. We would normally use style properties to change the colors (as we did in Chapter 2), so as to keep the entire document formatting in one place. That way, if you need to make a change, you only need to go to one place to make that change.

Other Document Properties

The remaining properties of the `document` object are summarized in the following table:

Other Properties	Description
`activeElement`	The element that has the focus
`documentElement`	Returns a reference to the root node of the document
`expando`	Specifies if the document can have arbitrary variables
`designMode`	Toggles between browsing and editing the document – when on, scripting does not run
`uniqueID`	An auto-generated unique ID for the document
`readyState`	The current state of an object being downloaded
`referrer`	URL of the page that referenced the current page

The activeElement property provides a read-only reference to the element on the page that currently has the input focus. We can use this to display messages in the status bar, or just track where the focus is going in the document.

The documentElement property will return the contents of the document as an element object. This will allow you to use the text-handling features (that we'll look at in Chapter 6) to edit the entire contents of the document.

The expando property is a Boolean that indicates whether the object can support extra properties. These extra properties can be defined by the user, and will be treated just like any of the other properties of the object. You need to take care when working with a case-sensitive language like JScript that you use the proper spelling of properties. If you misspell a property with the expando set to true, IE will not return any kind of error.

The uniqueID property is a unique number generator. When creating elements dynamically, you can use the uniqueID property of the document object to generate a unique ID for the new element. Each time you access the uniqueID property, a new value will be returned. This can be useful when dynamically adding elements to the document, to ensure that they have unique names.

The readyState property provides a value that indicates the current 'download state' of the document. Other objects (such as ActiveX controls, Java Applets, images or scripts) that are embedded in the page each have their own readyState properties as well, and this can be useful to discover if they are ready to accept instructions from our code. This solves a problem encountered previously, when the code in the page attempted to execute a method of an object that was not fully downloaded. The possible values are shown as follows:

Value	Description
uninitialized	Document is not initialized
loading	Document is currently loading data
loaded	Document has finished loading all of its data
interactive	Document is ready to be interacted with, but may not be fully loaded
complete	The entire document is completely loaded

The referrer property survives from the object model of previous browser versions (although it never worked properly in IE3). The good news is that it does work in IE4 and beyond, and is fully supported in Dynamic HTML.

The Methods of the Document Object

The `document` object's methods fall neatly into three groups: **general** methods, **hierarchy** methods and **command** methods. We'll look at the general methods first, because they will be the methods that are most familiar to you.

General Document Object Methods

Here's a summary of the general methods offered by the document object:

General Methods	Description
`open`	Opens new document to collect the output of the `write` and `writeln` methods
`write`	Writes text and HTML to a document in the specified window.
`writeln`	Writes text and HTML followed by a carriage return.
`close`	Closes an output stream.
`clear`	Clears the contents of the selection.
`recalc`	Recalculates the dynamic properties of the document.
`elementFromPoint`	Returns the element at the specified *x* and *y* coordinates.
`clearAttributes`	Removes all attributes from the document.
`mergeAttributes`	Copies all read/write attributes to the specified element.
`attachEvent`	Binds the specified function to the specified event.
`detachEvent`	Unbinds the specified function from the specified event.
`releaseCapture`	Removes data that was captured using the `setCapture` method.

Let's briefly focus in on some of these methods.

Writing Text and HTML to the Document

As we saw in Chapter 3, we can write text and HTML into a page using the `write` method of the `document` object. This is often used to create pages where the content is only decided by the browser's environment – things like the current date and time, and properties of the browser itself.

There is a second related method, `writeln`, which acts in the same way, but appends a carriage return to the string it writes into the page. Of course, this has no effect most of the time, unless the string is being placed inside HTML tags such as `<PRE>`, which preserve line formatting.

Related to the write and writeln methods are three other methods: open, close and clear. The open method allows us to open an existing page (after the browser has finished rendering it) – we can then replace the text and HTML. Once complete, the close method is used to close the document – this also updates the browser display automatically. To remove the complete HTML source of the page, we can use the clear method – this will only work if open has been called first.

The open method accepts a MIME type parameter, indicating the type of contents that will be displayed:

```
document.open "text/html"                'open the document
document.write "Some text and HTML"      'write some text
document.close                           'close it again
document.clear                           'and then clear the contents
```

In Chapter 6, you'll see many more ways of using these methods; we've also included a simple example later in this chapter, which uses these methods to create a listing of the contents of the document in a new browser window.

Document Hierarchy Methods

Here's a summary of the methods offered by the document object that can affect the hierarchy of elements and objects in the document:

General Methods	Description
createElement	Creates a new element of the specified type.
createStyleSheet	Creates a new style sheet for the document.
createTextNode	Creates a text string.
getElementByID	Returns a reference to the first element in the document with the specified ID
getElementsByName	Returns a collection of elements with the specified name
getElementsByTagName	Returns a collection of elements with the specified element name

Creating and Referencing Elements

We can create instances of certain types of new elements using the createElement method. This is limited to IMG image tags, list box OPTION tags and image-map AREA tags, and allows us to create a new element in code, and set its properties.

The element itself isn't displayed until it's added to the appropriate collection:

```
set objImage = document.createElement("IMG")
objImage.src = "element.gif"      'set the image element's src property
MsgBox objImage.src               'and then display element.gif's src
                                  '                          in a message box
```

You'll see an example of this in Chapter 7.

We can also get a reference to an element by specifying the *x* and *y* coordinates in relation to the top-left of the browser window, using the `elementFromPoint` method. The following line of code will show this message box if and only if the `element.gif` graphic is displayed at the location `100,70`:

```
MsgBox document.elementFromPoint(100, 70).tagName
```

You can see this at work in the Document Object and Collections *example, later in this chapter.*

The Document Object's Command Methods

The document also provides a set of `Command` methods that are used to manipulate ranges, such as that of a `TextRange` object. We're not ready to look at any of the range methods in depth here, although you will see a little more in the final example of this chapter. In Chapter 6, we'll be devoting a lot more attention to this whole subject.

Command Methods	Description
`execCommand`	Executes a command over the selection or range.
`queryCommandEnabled`	Denotes if the specified command is available at the current time, given the state of the document.
`queryCommandIndeterm`	Denotes if the specified command is in the indeterminate state.
`queryCommandState`	Returns the current state of the command.
`queryCommandSupported`	Denotes if the specified command is supported
`queryCommandValue`	Returns the current value of the specified command.

The Events of the Document Object

The `document` object provides us with a wide range of events, which we can use to react to almost any action taken by the user. We've divided them into three groups: **mouse** events, **key-press** events and the others. Remember that, unlike many other languages, Dynamic HTML bubbles events up through the object hierarchy – so these events can occur for the `document` even when the user targets their actions to an element on the page. Don't worry if this seems a strange concept; we'll be covering event bubbling and event handling in more detail in the next chapter.

Mouse Events in the Document

As you would expect, mouse events occur when the user performs some action using the mouse. In particular, the `onmouseover` and `onmouseout` events are very useful for providing effects such as the latest 'coolbar' toolbars. The `onmouseover` event occurs when the mouse pointer first enters an element, and the `onmouseout` event occurs just after the mouse leaves an element – these allow the code to change the way that element appears when the mouse pointer is over it. Here's a list of all of the mouse events:

Mouse Events	Description
`onclick`, `ondblclick`	Occurs when the mouse button is clicked (resp. double-clicked) on the document.
`oncontextmenu`	Occurs when the user right-clicks a mouse button.
`onmousedown`	Occurs when the user presses either mouse button down (i.e. not a complete mouse-click, but the downward part only – compare with `onmouseup`)
`onmousemove`	Occurs when the user moves the mouse pointer.
`onmouseover`, `onmouseout`	Occurs when the mouse pointer first enters (resp. leaves) the element.
`onmouseup`	Occurs when the user releases a mouse button.
`ondragstart`	Occurs when the user first starts to drag an element or selection.
`ondrag`	Occurs when the user moves the mouse while dragging.
`ondragend`	Occurs when the user releases the mouse button after a drag.
`ondragenter`, `ondragleave`	Fires on the target element when the object being dragged enters (resp. leaves) a valid drop target during a drag.
`ondragover`	Fires continuously on the target element while the object being dragged is over a valid drop target during a drag.
`ondrop`	Fires on the target element when the mouse button is released to end a drag.

The `onmousedown`, `onmousemove` and `onmouseup` events provide information regarding the position of the mouse pointer, the button pressed, and the state of the *Shift*, *Ctrl* and *Alt* keys. The `ondragstart` event is used when the user presses down a mouse button and starts to move the mouse pointer (while holding the button down). The `ondragend` event tells you when the user stops dragging. We'll be looking at how we handle all the document mouse and key-press events in detail in subsequent chapters, and we'll show you a simple example towards the end of this chapter.

Note that, in some cases, the `onclick` event can also be fired from the keyboard. For example, the `onclick` event is fired when a button element has the focus and the user hits the return key or the space bar. This shouldn't be surprising: in most Windows applications you can 'click' on the active button by pressing the Return *key or space bar.*

Key-Press Events in the Document

As well as providing information on the events created by the mouse, the `document` object also provides a set of key-press events:

Key-press Events	Description
`onkeydown`	Occurs on the down-stroke of a key.
`onkeypress`	Occurs when the user presses a key. If the key is held down then multiple `onkeypress` events occur.
`onkeyup`	Occurs when the user releases a key.
`onhelp`	Occurs when the user presses the *F1* or 'help' key.

The `onkeydown` and `onkeyup` events provide information on the state of the *Shift*, *Ctrl* and *Alt* keys. The `onkeypress` event occurs when a key is pressed (and continues to occur if the key is held down) and then returns an ASCII code modified to take account of the state of the *Shift*, *Ctrl* and *Alt* keys. The `onhelp` event occurs in Windows when the user presses the *F1* key, the appropriate 'help' key in other environments or when they click on the What's This? (question mark) button and then click on a control or object.

Other Events in the Document

Before we move on, let's just list the other events supported by the `document` object, and quickly focus on a few of them:

General Events	Description
`onbeforecopy`	Fires on the source object before the selection is copied to the system clipboard.
`onbeforecut`	Fires on the source object before the selection is deleted from the document.
`onbeforeeditfocus`	Fires prior to a control entering a "UI-activated" state.
`onbeforepaste`	Fires on the target object before the selection is pasted from the system clipboard to the document.
`onbeforeupdate`	Occurs before a element containing data-bound controls is unloaded.

General Events	Description
onafterupdate	Occurs when data transfer to the data provider is complete.
onerrorupdate	Fires when a data update is canceled.
onpaste	Fires on the target object when the data is transferred from the clipboard to the document.
onpropertychange	Fires when a property changes on the element.
onreadystatechange	Fires when the readyState property of the element changes
onstop	Fires when the Stop button is clicked.

You'll notice that the onreadystatechange event is linked to the readyState property, which we met earlier. The onreadystatechange event fires each time the value of the readyState property changes. This means that we don't have to constantly monitor the readyState property to see if an element has finished loading – the onreadystatechange event does it for us.

Microsoft's implementation of Dynamic HTML supports **data-binding**, where control elements on the page are linked (or **bound**) to individual fields in a data source – normally a database on the server. We'll come to this topic in Chapter 7, although it is not the core subject of this book. When the data in a bound control is changed, and the user indicates that they are ready to update the source, two events – onbeforeupdate and onafterupdate – occur for that control. If the user attempts to unload the page before the changed data is saved, the events occur for the document itself.

The user may just move the focus to another control on the page, load another page, or close the browser. In each case, the onbeforeupdate event occurs before the new data is sent to the source – this allows the script code to validate the data and cancel the update action if appropriate. Once the source has been updated, the onafterupdate event occurs.

The Document Object's Collections

Having covered the properties, methods and events of the document, it's now time to look at the range of **collections** that the document object provides. A web page contains a vast amount of information, which must be organized in a sensible and usable way so that we can access it using Dynamic HTML. This organization is achieved through 12 collections:

Collection	Description
`all`	Collection of all the tags and elements in the body of the document.
`anchors`	Collection of all the anchors in the document.
`applets`	Collection of all the objects in the document, including intrinsic HTML controls, images, applets, embeds and other objects.
`childNodes`	Collection of all the `document` object's children.
`children`	Collection of all the `document` object's direct descendents.
`embeds`	Collection of all the `<EMBED>` tags in the document.
`forms`	Collection of all the forms in the page.
`frames`	Collection of all the frames defined within a `<FRAMESET>` tag.
`images`	Collection of all the images in the page.
`links`	Collection of all the links and image-map `<AREA>` blocks in the page.
`scripts`	Collection of all the `<SCRIPT>` sections in the page.
`styleSheets`	Collection of all the individual style property objects defined for a document.

We'll look at how we can work with these collections next, although some are intrinsically more useful than others. We'll concentrate on the collections that you're likely to come across most often.

Working with Document Collections

We looked briefly at collections in the previous chapter, where we saw how we can access other frames in a window using the `window` object's `frames` collection. We considered two ways of accessing the members of the `frames` collection:

```
window.frames(1)            'the index of a frame in the "frames" collection
window.frames("mainframe")  'the name of a frame in the "frames" collection
```

Here's a quick debugging trick that you can use to verify that your frameset pages are working properly. Check the `length` property of the `frames` collection: any value other than the number of frames you expect suggests a problem with your design. Pages that perform various indirections and targeted anchors can make frame management tricky if you're not careful.

The document object supports a range of collections, and we can use the same techniques to access the members of all of them. For example, to access the second image on a page, we can use:

```
document.images(1)      'the index of an image in the "images" collection
```

You should remember that `images(1)` *references the* second *image in the collection – because the* `images` *collection, like all collections, is zero-indexed.*

If we have named the image (using the NAME attribute in the HTML <IMG> tag), we can also access it like this:

```
document.images("MyImage")  'the name of an image in the "images" collection
```

As an example, here's part of a page that includes an image named MyImage:

```
<IMG SRC=element.gif NAME="MyImage">

<SCRIPT LANGUAGE=VBSCRIPT>
<!--
  Sub document_onclick()
    MsgBox document.images("MyImage").src
  End Sub
-->
</SCRIPT>
```

Clicking on the page fires the document's onclick event, which activates the document_onclick() event handler as shown in the screenshot. The document_onclick() routine uses the images collection to get a reference to the image named MyImage. It then displays the value of the image's src property, which is the Dynamic HTML equivalent of the value of the SRC attribute in the <IMG> tag.

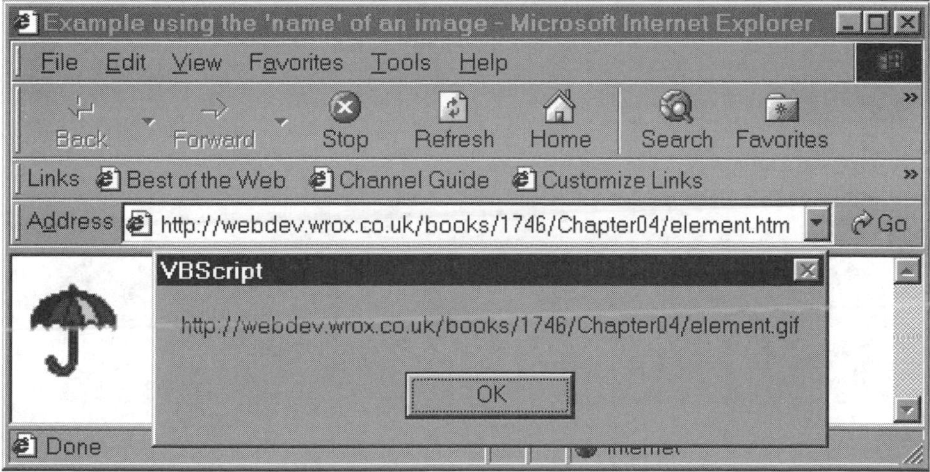

Collection Length and Filtering

When working with a collection, we may well need to find out how many items there are in the collection, or retrieve a list of the objects that are available in that collection. We can easily achieve this by using the collection's `length` property, which returns the number of items in the collection. Here's a little VBScript that uses the `length` property to control a `For...Next` loop, to list all the tagnames in the `all` collection:

```
For objItem = 0 to document.all.length-1  'all the elements in the document
  MsgBox document.all(objItem).tagName    'display the text of the tag
Next
```

Iterating a Collection with For Each

Another solution is a special construct that works with collections in VBScript – `For Each...Next`. This automatically executes the code for each object in the collection, and provides for more compact and neater code:

```
For Each objItem In document.all
  MsgBox objItem.tagName
Next
```

Filtering a Collection

There may also be occasions when we want to select only *certain* members of a collection. We can do this by **filtering** the collection, using its `tags` method. This returns a new collection, which contains only the members of the original collection which have that particular `tagName`. For example, to create a collection that contains only the text paragraphs (that is, the elements with a `P` tag), we can use the following:

```
Set NewCollection = OldCollection.tags("P")
```

Here's a simple example. It contains six paragraphs and four images. The code in the script section uses the `length` property and the `tags` method to display information about the page, and create a collection of the images only. Of course, we could have used the `images` collection directly, but this demonstrates the technique we've been discussing:

```
...
<P ID=para1>paragraph 1</P>      <IMG ID=img1 SRC="image1.gif">
<P ID=para2>paragraph 2</P>      <P ID=para3>paragraph 3</P>
<IMG ID=img2 SRC="image2.gif">   <P ID=para4>paragraph 4</P>
<P ID=para5>paragraph 5</P>      <IMG ID=img3 SRC="image3.gif">
<P ID=para6>paragraph 6</P>      <IMG ID=img4 SRC="image4.gif">

<SCRIPT LANGUAGE=VBSCRIPT>
  MsgBox document.all.length                'displays 15 (elements in "all")
  Set colImages = document.all.tags("IMG")         'creates a new collection
  MsgBox colImages.length                'displays 4 (images in "colImages")
  MsgBox colImages("img4").src                           'displays path to file
</SCRIPT>
...
```

All the collections work in this same way, providing easy access to any element on the page. However, one collection is slightly different from the others – it's the `forms` collection.

Using the Forms Collection

Web page authors can create pages that contain one or more sections defined as **forms**, by enclosing them in the <FORM> and </FORM> tags. Forms have special abilities. They can contain the `SUBMIT` and `RESET` types of <INPUT> tag: the `SUBMIT` type sends the contents of the other HTML form elements in that form to the server for processing, while the `RESET` type resets the controls to their default values.

This means that the forms in a document can themselves act as containers to hold other elements and objects. To manage this, each member of the `forms` collection (i.e. each `form` object) has its own sub-collection of `elements` – this is a collection of all the controls and other elements in the form.

This collection can be accessed in much the same way as the `document` collections - this time with the collection name added to the end of the statement:

```
'access the third element in the first form on the page
document.forms(0).elements(2)

'access the element named MyTextBox in the second form on the page
document.forms(1).elements("MyTextBox")

'access the element named MyTextBox in a form named MyForm
document.forms("MyForm").elements("MyTextBox")
```

Accessing Properties and Methods

Of course, the items in any collection are themselves objects. It's very likely that we will need to access the properties and methods of an object that belongs to a collection – just as we did earlier when retrieving the source file from an image element. Here are some property retrievals:

```
strFileName   = document.images("MyImage").src          'image source
strTheValue   = document.forms(0).elements(2).value     'control value
strElementId  = document.forms(3).elements(0).id        'element identifier
strAddress    = document.links("MyLink").href           'URL of a hyperlink
strPlugin     = document.plugins(0).name                'name of a plugin
```

In each of the above we assign the value of the specified property to a variable. In the following, we specify an object that lives in a collection, and call one of its methods:

```
document.forms(0).elements(2).focus     'set the focus to this control
document.images(3).scrollIntoView       'bring this image into view
```

Here we're calling the `focus` method of the third element in the first form, and the `scrollIntoView` method of the fourth image in the page.

The `scrollIntoView` method is provided for all visible elements, and simply brings that element into view in the browser window. You'll see it used in Chapter 6.

A Document and Collections Example

The one collection we haven't mentioned is the `all` collection, although we have already used it in some of the examples. The `all` collection contains all the elements in the document, including the `BODY`, `TITLE`, `HEAD`, etc. To show you how we can use this collection, and to demonstrate several of the properties of the `document` object at the same time, we've provided a simple example page called The Document Object and Collections (`DocObject.htm`), which you can see working on our web site at http://webdev.wrox.co.uk/books/1746/:

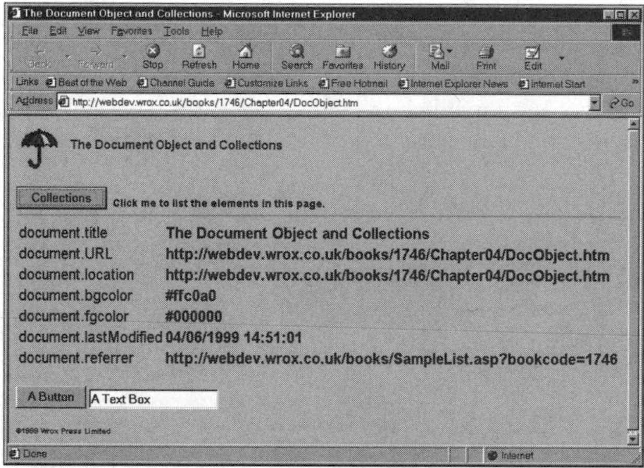

The page uses the same techniques as the `DocObject.htm` example (in Chapter 3) to display the values of several properties from the `document` object. The text box and button are included simply so that you can see how their tags and attributes appear within the `all` collection.

Using the All Collection

Go on then, click the Collections button at the top of the page. This opens a new browser window, which lists all the elements in the original document:

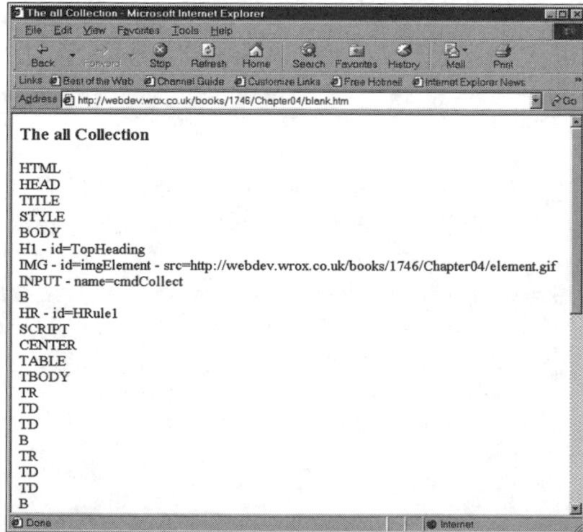

Some of them include extra information, such as an `id`, `name` or `src`. The code uses a `For Each..Next` loop to iterate through the entire `all` collection, and places properties of each member into the page. In our case we've used the `tagName` property (the text of the tag itself, a property that every element has), and the `id`, `name` and `src` properties where they are available.

Ignoring Scripting Errors

It's worth noting a side issue concerning this demonstration. As you might expect, different types of elements have different properties – for example, some of the elements in our page don't actually *have* a `src` property. This means that, as we try to list the `src` property of every element, we may generate some errors.

So, for the purposes of this script we will use the VBScript statement `On Error Resume Next`. This statement simply tells the code to ignore any errors that occur, and to continue processing the script at the next line. With this in place, we're choosing to ignore the errors that occur when we query a property that doesn't exist – so the whole thing doesn't collapse in a heap.

> *Of course, using the* `On Error Resume Next` *statement means that we have chosen to ignore* all *errors that are generated by the script – including any other types of errors that you might wish to be notified of.*
>
> *There is currently no direct JScript equivalent to VBScript's* `On Error Resume Next` *statement, though the new version of JScript introduced in IE5 includes* `try..catch` *exception handling for dealing with errors. See Appendix J.*

The Collections Button Code

Here's the complete code of the `cmdCollect_Onclick()` routine, which runs when the Collections button is clicked:

```
Sub cmdCollect_OnClick()
On Error Resume Next
  Set NewWindow = window.open("blank.htm")
  NewWindow.document.write "<HTML><HEAD><TITLE>" _
                        & "The all Collection </TITLE></HEAD><BODY>" _
                        & "<H3>The all Collection</H3>"
  For Each objItem In document.all
    NewWindow.document.write objItem.tagName
    if objItem.id <> "" Then
      NewWindow.document.write " - id="  & objItem.id
    end if
    if objItem.src <> "" Then
      NewWindow.document.write " - src="  & objItem.src
    end if
    if objItem.name <> "" Then
      NewWindow.document.write " - name="  & objItem.name
    end if
    NewWindow.document.write "<BR>"
  Next
  NewWindow.document.write "<HR></BODY></HTML>"
  NewWindow.document.close
End Sub
```

Having 'turned off' error handling with `On Error Resume Next`, we open a new browser window using the `window` object's `open` method. The source is a file called `blank.htm` – this file should have been placed on your system when you installed the browser (and the program will error if it isn't present). The `Set` expression assigns the new window object to a variable `NewWindow` – notice that we have to use the `Set` keyword, because we are assigning an object (and not a simple value) to the `NewWindow` variable. Once we've done that, we can access the object in our code.

Once we've got our new window, we can start to write to it with the `write` method of the `document` object. At first, the new window is empty, because we loaded a blank page, `blank.htm`, into it. (We'll say more about `blank.htm` shortly). We create the content within the code in `DocObject.htm`, and then we write that content to the new page. Of course, the new page is in the new browser window (not the original window), so we need to call the `write` method of the `NewWindow.document` object.

Listing the Contents of the Collection

The next step is to list the members of the collection, and to add some property values where appropriate. The `For Each..Next` construct will step through the complete collection automatically, and for each iteration it sets the variable `objItem` to that member of the collection:

```
For Each objItem In document.all
  NewWindow.document.write objItem.tagName
  if objItem.id <> "" Then
    NewWindow.document.write " - id="  & objItem.id
  end if
  ' ... write the other property values to the new window ...
Next
```

Within the loop, all we have to do is `write` the `tagName` and other properties to the new page. Note that *every* element has an `id` property; however, the value of an `id` property is always blank until it is assigned a value. Some elements (like `H1` and `IMG`, shown in the `blank.htm` screenshot) have non-empty `id` properties – these have been assigned within the HTML source. In the `For..Next` loop, we examine the value of each element's `id` property – and we only display the `id` property in the new page if it's not empty.

We haven't taken the trouble to check the values of the other properties, though you could soon implement this if it was important. And apart from this, the other properties look after themselves. If we reference a property that doesn't exist then the script will raise an error. Our code then ignores this line, and goes on to the next one.

Another Word on Secure Domains

One interesting point arises from this example, and is connected with our earlier discussion of the `document` object's `domain` property. Suppose we create a new window, but we don't specify a file name of a page to display in it. Then, the browser will load a default page named `blank.htm` from your `Windows/System` folder (if it exists); otherwise it will create an empty blank document itself.

If the browser loads blank.htm from a directory or site that differs from the page where the main document was loaded (that is, from a different domain) then the code will fail with a security breach error. It won't be able to access the page in the new browser window. To avoid this, we've supplied a blank.htm file in the same directory as the calling page (DocObject.htm), and specified that page when calling the window object's open method:

```
Set NewWindow = window.open("blank.htm")
```

Demonstrating the document.elementFromPoint Method

The DocObject.htm page also demonstrates the document object's elementFromPoint method, that we first looked at earlier in this chapter. Right-click on any part of the page to see the tagName of the element under the mouse pointer. Here is the routine that handles the right-click event:

```
Sub document_onmousedown()
  If window.event.button = 2 Then
     MsgBox document.elementFromPoint(x, y).tagName
  End If
End Sub
```

The Selection Object

One of the subsidiary objects of the document object is its selection property. This provides information about the current selection made when the user drags over the page using the mouse. The selection object allows us to access all the selected elements, including the plain text, within the page.

The selection object has a single property, type, which returns a value depending on the type of elements selected:

Property	Description
type	The type of the selection, i.e. a control, text, a table or none.

The type property can take any of the following values:

Value	HTML Constant	Description
0 - None	htmlSelectionNone	No selection.
1 - Text	htmlSelectionText	Body text and text in any type of formatting tag.
2 - Control	htmlSelectionControl	A control element.
3 - Table	htmlSelectionTable	All or part of a table.

The selection object has three methods, which provide us with a way to retrieve the selection into a TextRange object, to delete the selected items from the page, and to remove the highlighting when we have finished using it:

Method	Description
`createRange`	Creates a `TextRange` object from the current selection.
`clear`	Clears the contents of the selection.
`empty`	Deselects the current selection and sets selection type to None.

The TextRectangle object

The `TextRectangle` object is used to represent a line of text in an element or a `selection` object. The `TextRectangle` object allows you to determine the screen location of the line of text, and then perform some action based on that – such as highlighting the line. When you query an element for its `TextRectangle` objects, it will return a collection to you, with each element in the collection being a `TextRectangle` object for each line in the element.

You'll see a lot more about how we can work with text and selections and the `TextRectangle` object in Chapter 6, where we explore the whole concept of working with the contents of a document. In the meantime, here's a simple example that uses the `selection` object, and introduces the concept of a `TextRange`.

Selections and Text Ranges

A `TextRange` is an object in its own right, and we'll examine it carefully in Chapter 6. For the time being, you can think of a `TextRange` as a way of storing a 'chunk' of a document in such a way that we can access different things within that 'chunk'.

Although the document is created by an HTML source stream – basically a string of text – we often want to retrieve it in other formats. The `TextRange` object allows us to work with our document chunk in the form of an HTML stream, or in the form of the text as it is displayed on the screen. The `TextRange` object also provides information on the start and end positions of the 'chunk' within the original page, plus a whole heap of methods that we can use to work with it.

A Selection Object Example

In our example, we're using a `TextRange` object to store the selection in the document, so that we can examine it later. Here's the page, `select.htm`, which you can run from our web site at http://webdev.wrox.co.uk/books/1746.

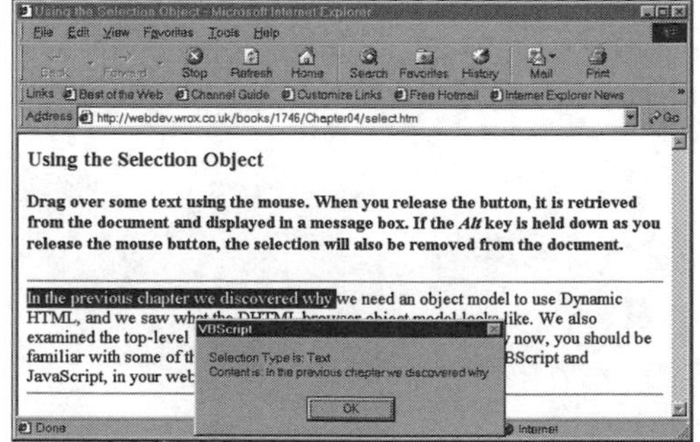

The code in the page's <SCRIPT> section is remarkably compact, when you consider what it is doing. There's one thing to remember: to work with a selection, we have to respond to an event that occurs *when the selection is made*. If we put a button on the page for the user to click with the mouse in order to get information about the selection, the result will always be `None` – because the act of clicking the button cancels the selection from the page.

Therefore, we're responding to the `onmouseup` event for the document, which occurs when the mouse button is released. This event also provides four arguments that indicate which button was pressed, which other keys were held down and the coordinates of the mouse pointer:

```
Sub document_onmouseup()
  Set MyRange = document.selection.createRange
  strMsg = "Selection Type is: " & document.selection.type & Chr(10) _
        & "Content is: " & MyRange.text
  MsgBox strMsg
  If (window.event.altKey = true) And (document.selection.type <>"None") Then
    document.selection.clear
  End If
  document.selection.empty
End Sub
```

The first step is to capture the selection into a new `TextRange` object, which we've called `MyRange`. Again, we have to use the `Set` keyword, because we are assigning an object to the variable `MyRange`, and not just a simple value. The expression `document.selection.createRange` calls the `createRange` method of the `document` object's `selection` object, which returns the `TextRange` object we need.

Now we can examine the user's selection. We need to know what kind of selection we're dealing with, and we establish that through the `selection` object's `type` property. We also need to know the contents of the selection – we get that from the `TextRange` object's `text` property. The `selection` object doesn't expose the text contents of the selection – that's why we had to assign it to a `TextRange` object in the first place.

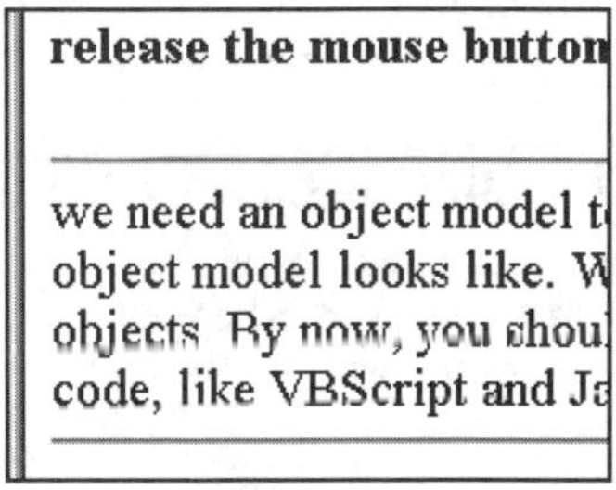

Now we can display the results in a VBScript message box, then decide if we need to delete it from the document. If the user is holding down the *Alt* key as they release the mouse button, then the `altKey` property supplied by the `onmouseup` event will be `true`. We check this, and make sure that the selection type is not `None` before we remove the selection using the `selection` object's `clear` method. To clean up afterwards, we use the `selection` object's `empty` method which un-highlights the selection on the screen ready for the user to select some more of the page.

You'll see more about the way we react to events like `onmouseup`, and use the arguments it provides, in the next chapter. We'll be looking at the whole subject of manipulating the text of the document in more detail in Chapter 6.

The Filters Collection

The `filters` collection isn't really a collection of the `document` object at all, so you might wonder why we're going to talk about it here. The reason is that `filters` is a collection that pertains to many of the elements that go to make up the `document` object. A `filters` collection is available on every element; it allows our scripts to access individual filters that are specific to an element. They are also available as properties within cascading style sheets.

What is a Filter?

A filter is an effect for enhancing the look of the graphics and text within your web pages. Internet Explorer 5.0 supports visual filter and transition filter effects through its Cascading Style Sheets. For example, we can use filters to flip our text or images upside down, or to make them disappear in a random checkerboard pattern. These filters can be applied to HTML elements that are controls – elements such as `BODY`, `DIV`, `IMG`, `TABLE` and `TEXTAREA`. Note that we can't apply these filters to windowed controls such as an `IFRAME`, a `P` element or Java applets.

There are two distinct kinds of filter available to the programmer in Internet Explorer. The first are the **visual filters**. These alter the appearance of an object (such as a block of text or a graphic), and are static: once we apply a visual filter the result persists. There are 14 visual filter effects, which allow you to manipulate and alter your elements by applying various effects, from merely reversing your image to creating an 'x-ray' of your image.

The second set of filters are known as **transition filters**. These cause a change to an image over some (usually short) amount of time. For example, the transition filter called Random dissolve fades one image into another. This means that instead of an immediate transformation being applied to your element (as with the visual filter), the element is gradually dissolved or made to emerge. There are 23 transition effects available (plus one that selects randomly from the other 23).

The Visual Filter Effects

We'll start by looking at the visual filter effects and demonstrating all 14 of them. Each of these effects can be applied by the means of a Cascading Style Sheet (CSS), or by setting properties in the browser object model. We'll look at how they're done in CSS first:

```
filter: filtername(fparameter1, fparameter2, etc)
```

There's really no difference between programming filters and programming any other CSS attribute. The following code applies the `flipH` filter effect to an image which flips the image horizontally:

```
<STYLE>
.effect {filter: fliph}
</STYLE>

<IMG SRC=wrox.gif>
<IMG CLASS=effect SRC=wrox.gif>
```

You can see the effect that the filter has on the `wrox.gif` image. The original is on the left, and the flipped image is on the right.

You can achieve the same effect through script by setting up an `ID` attribute for the image, then calling the `filter` method of the image through the `style` object. You must encase the filter name in quotes for it to work correctly, otherwise nothing will happen:

```
<IMG SRC=wrox.gif>
<IMG ID=Image1 SRC=wrox.gif>

<SCRIPT LANGUAGE=VBSCRIPT>
Image1.style.filter = "fliph"
</SCRIPT>
```

Here's a complete list of all of the visual filters, what parameters they take and what they do.

Filter effect	Parameters Needed	Description
`alpha`	`style`, `opacity`, `finish opacity`, `startx`, `starty`, `finishx`, `finishy`	Sets a uniform transparency level
`blur`	`add`, `direction`, `strength`	Creates a movement effect
`chroma`	`color`	Makes one color transparent
`dropshadow`	`color`, `offx`, `offy`, `positive`	Makes a silhouette of an object
`fliph`	none	Creates a horizontal mirror image
`flipv`	none	Creates a vertical mirror image
`glow`	`color`, `strength`	Creates the effect that an object is glowing
`grayscale`	none	Changes an object to monochromatic colors
`invert`	none	Reverses all hue, saturation and brightness values

Table Continued on Following Page

Filter effect	Parameters Needed	Description
`light`	none	Shines a light source onto an object
`mask`	`color`	Creates a transparent mask from an object
`shadow`	`color, direction`	Creates a silhouette of an object offset from the object
`wave`	`add, freq, lightstrength, phase, strength`	Creates a sine wave distortion of an object along the *x* axis
`xray`	none	Shows just the outline of an object

Visual Filters Example

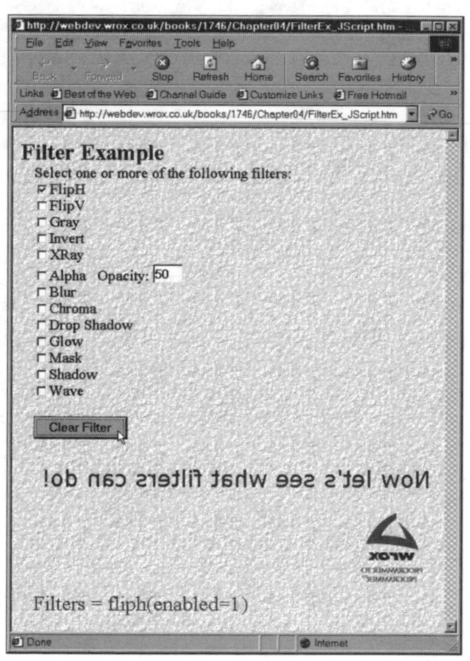

To really appreciate what some of these filters do, you need to see them in action. We've provided an example that allows you to apply each of the filters (or several of them at the same time!) to some text and graphics. Here's the page, `FilterEx_JScript.htm`, which you can run from our web site at http://webdev.wrox.co.uk/books/1746/.

As you can see, the filter is able to effect both the image and the text at the same time. You can apply several filters at the same time if you wish, simply by selecting a number of checkboxes. Once you've applied a set of filters, you have to clear them before you can apply any more. Let's take a look at some of the code behind the example.

How It Works

In this example, we will be using JScript instead of VBScript. All of this example's functionality can be just as easily implemented in VBScript. (In fact, you'll find a VBScript version of this example at http://webdev.wrox.co.uk/books/1746.)

The first part of our script declares one global variable – `bFilterApplied`. This is a Boolean value, which we use to determine whether or not a set of filters has been applied to our text and image:

```
<script LANGUAGE="JScript">
var bFilterApplied;
```

Next we need some code to execute when the browser first loads, triggered by the `window.onload` event. It isn't possible for a filter to have been applied yet, and so we set the value of `bFilterApplied` to false to indicate this:

```
function window.onload()
{
  bFilterApplied = false;
}
```

The subprocedure `ApplyFilter()` is the one where all the interesting things happen:

```
function ApplyFilter()
{
  if (bFilterApplied)
  {
    divAB.style.filter="";
    bFilterApplied = false;
    startFilter.value = "Apply Filter";
    filterString.innerText = "";
  }
```

The first part of this procedure checks to see if the `bFilterApplied` value is `true`. If a filter has been applied, then we need to reset the display, set the value of `bFilterApplied` to `false`, change the button name to Apply Filter and clear the name of the filter string. The filter string is the part we use to store a set of instructions for the browser to use on the text and images. It's stored in a variable `strFilters`. So if `bFilterApplied` is `false`, then the text and image is ready for us to apply a visual filter(s):

```
  else
  {
    var strFilters;
    strFilters = "";
    if (FlipH.checked)
      strFilters = strFilters + "fliph(enabled=1) ";
    if (FlipV.checked)
      strFilters = strFilters + "flipv(enabled=1) ";
    '...
    'code for other filters
    '...
    if (Wave.checked)
      strFilters = strFilters +
                   "wave(freq=2, strength=6, phase=0, " +
                   "     lightstrength=0, add=0, enabled=1) ";
```

The variable `strFilters` is the collection of all of the instructions that the browser will need to process in order to execute the filter selection. We build up this string gradually, one selection at a time. When the user clicks the Apply Filter button, the script examines all of the checkboxes, to see which are selected – for each selected checkbox we add an instruction to the end of the `strFilters` string. By the end of this process, `strFilters` might be very large indeed!

The page also displays the contents of `strFilters` on the screen, below the filtered image:

Once we have a set of instructions for the browser to execute we then can get around to the business of applying the filters:

```
        filterString.innerText = "Filters = " + strFilters;
        divAB.style.filter = strFilters;
        startFilter.value = "Clear Filter";
        bFilterApplied = true;
    }
}
</SCRIPT>
```

We apply the `filter` method of the `style` object of the `DIV` element `divAB`, which contains both our target text and image, by setting it to `strFilters`. The string that you see displayed on the page, below the image and text, is the actual text we assign to the `style` property. The string sets the parameters needed for each filter as well as setting the different filter types. Next, we change the name of the button to Clear Filter as we don't want to reapply filters to our `DIV` element. Finally we change the value of `bFilterApplied` to indicate this. So now somebody has to clear all of the filters before they can select any more.

This short script deals with all the possible outcomes in the program within one short function and demonstrates all of the different filter effects in action. If you're unsure of what any of them does or how they work, then go ahead and try them out. Now let's move on to transition filters.

The Transition Filters Effects

The one main difference between transitions and visual filters is that a transition takes place between two states, i.e. a visible image and an invisible one (or vice versa). Therefore, when you use a transition filter you must first set the `visibility` of the image (to either `hidden` or `visible`) somewhere in the code – then call the transition in order to change its state.

The transition filters are divided into two types – **blend** and **reveal**. In a sense, they have exactly the same purpose – to make an element appear or disappear from the browser's display. The blend filter makes the element gradually blend in or out of the surroundings in a continuous, even way. For more control over the visual transition effect, the reveal filter makes the element gradually appear or disappear in one of 23 predefined patterns. These patterns include checkerboards, blinds, and wipes, just to name a few – we'll see the full list later in this section.

You can set these effects either with Cascading Style Sheet properties or via script. The length of the transition and its type are specified in parameters. Their syntax is as follows:

```
filter: blendtrans{duration = duration}
filter: revealtrans{duration = duration, transitionshape = transition}
```

You'd expect a working example where we blend the Wrox logo slowly in over a 10 second duration from a previously blank background to look something like this:

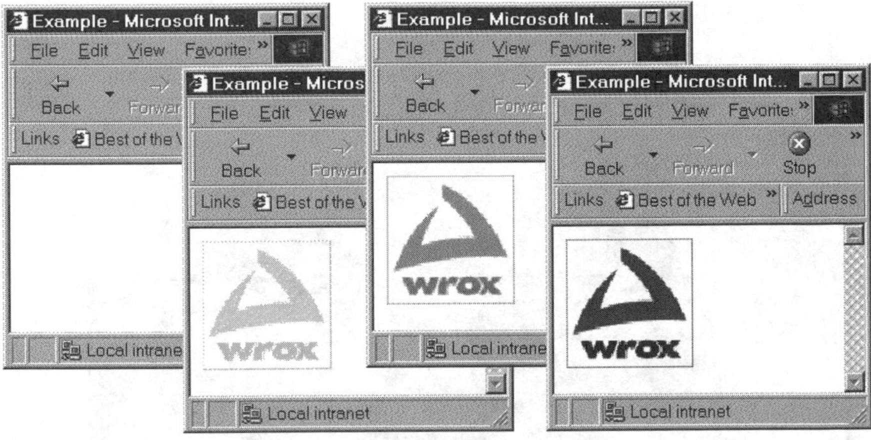

To get the desired effect, first set the `filter` type to `blendtrans` (within a `style` property), and then set the duration parameter within a scripting language (the parameter of the `play` method). At the beginning of the transition you have to freeze the image with the `Apply` method, then you have to make it visible, then finally supply the number of seconds you wish the transition to take in the `play` method. This final line of script effectively starts the transition:

```
<SCRIPT LANGUAGE=VBSCRIPT>
<!--
Sub document_onclick()
  Image1.filters.item(0).Apply()              // Freeze the image
  I1.style.visibility = "visible"             // Make the image visible
  Image1.filters.item(0).play(10)             // Start the transition
End Sub
-->
</SCRIPT>

<BODY>
<DIV ID = Image1 CLASS = effect STYLE="position: absolute; height: 100; _
                        width: 100; left:10; top:10; filter: blendtrans" >
<IMG ID=I1  STYLE="position: absolute; height: 100; width: 100; _
                                        visibility: hidden" SRC=wrox0.gif>
</DIV>
</BODY>
```

There is only one type of blend transition. To change a blend transition to a reveal transition requires only one extra line of script and an amendment to the style property setting. The extra line of script selects one of the 23 transition filter effects available (we've set it to 2, which is a 'circle in' transition):

```
<SCRIPT LANGUAGE=VBSCRIPT>
<!--
Sub document_onclick()
  call  Image1.filters.item(0).Apply()     // Freeze the image
  I1.style.visibility = "visible"          // Make the image visible
  Image1.filters.item(0).Transition = 2    // Selects the type of transition
  Image1.filters.item(0).play(10)          // Start the transition
End Sub
-->
</SCRIPT>
```

```
<BODY>
<DIV ID = Image1 CLASS = effect STYLE="position: absolute; height: 100; _
                        width: 100; left:10; top:10; filter: revealtrans" >
<IMG ID=I1  STYLE="position: absolute; height: 100; width: 100; _
                                        visibility: hidden" SRC=wrox0.gif>
</DIV>
</BODY>
```

This would have the following effect:

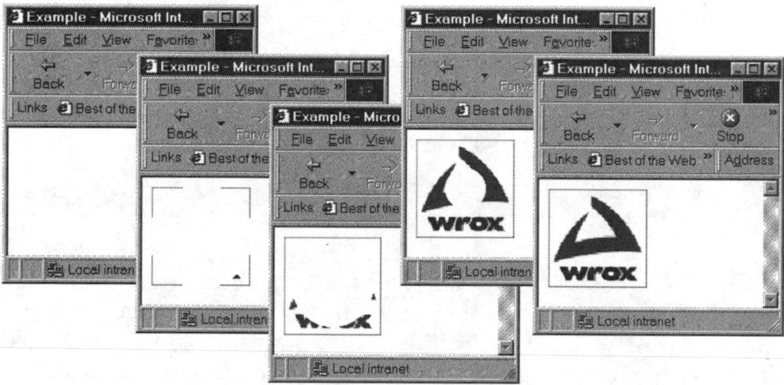

You can choose any of the 23 transition effects, simply by changing the value of the `Transition` parameter. A full list can be found later in this chapter, and also in Appendix E. In the next example you can try out any of the transition effects for yourself.

Reveal Transition Filters Example

In this example we've put two pictures together side by side, although one of the two is always hidden using the style sheet `visibility` property. The user can select the type of transition desired; when they click on the Start Transition button, one picture will appear as the other disappears using the same reveal transition filter effect. The page, `TransEx.htm` can be run from our web site at http://webdev.wrox.co.uk/books/1746/. Here we're using one of the checker board effects:

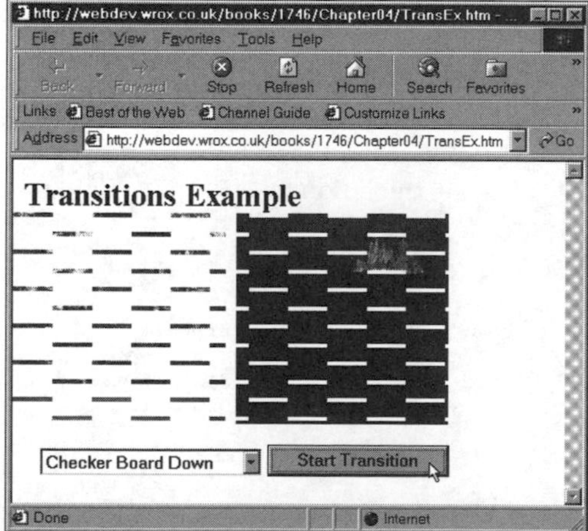

Each time a transition is begun, the chosen effect reverses the visibility of the two pictures, to reveal the previously hidden image and hide the visible. Here's a list of all of the different types of transition that are available. Most of them will be fairly self-explanatory from the name, but you can try them all out, if you're uncertain about what any of them do.

Transition Type	Number	Transition Type	Number
Box in	0	Random dissolve	12
Box out	1	Split vertical in	13
Circle in	2	Split vertical out	14
Circle out	3	Split horizontal in	15
Wipe up	4	Split horizontal out	16
Wipe down	5	Strips left down	17
Wipe right	6	Strips left up	18
Wipe left	7	Strips right down	19
Vertical blinds	8	Strips right up	20
Horizontal blinds	9	Random bars horizontal	21
Checkerboard across	10	Random bars vertical	22
Checkerboard down	11	Random selection of (0-22)	23

How It Works

We've already hinted at how this one works in our earlier example, using the Wrox logo. In addition, we need to pass the user's transition of choice from the list box to the script code, and we must also prevent the user from choosing another transition while one transition is already executing. The first part of our script declares some global variables:

```
<SCRIPT LANGUAGE="VBScript">
dim transDuration
dim transDirection
dim bTransInProgress

transDuration = 2.5
transDirection = 2
```

The first variable, `transDuration`, is used to store the duration of the transition – you can see that we've preset this to 2.5 seconds.

This example has two images, and we're going to have one image disappear as the other appears. Therefore, we use the second variable, `transDirection`, to the direction of the transition: a value of 1 indicates that the transition is to be made from right to left – i.e. the picture on the right disappears as the one on the left appears. After a 'right-to-left' transition we set the value to 2 – subsequently, the variable effectively seesaws between the two values. Finally, a Boolean value called `bTransInProgress` is set to `True` if the transition is currently in progress.

In the next section of code, we use two events to help set the global variable `bTransInProgress`:

```
Sub Window_onLoad()
  bTransInProgress = False
End Sub

Sub divAB_OnFilterChange()
  bTransInProgress = False
End Sub
```

The `Window_onLoad` event sets its value to `False` when the window is first loaded, as it isn't possible for there to be a transition currently in progress. The `OnFilterChange` event is triggered when a transition has completed. It can be used with both visual and transition filters; it fires when a visual filter changes state or when a transition filter completes a transition. In this case, when the transition completes and the event is triggered, the `bTransInProgress` value is set to `False`.

However, it's the `TransImage()` subprocedure that does the real work:

```
Sub TransImage()                          'Update the text display
  if bTransInProgress then Exit Sub
  divAB.filters.item(0).Apply()    'Freeze the image

  if TransDirection = 1 then
    TransDirection = 2
    Image3.Style.Visibility = ""
    Image2.Style.Visibility = "hidden"
  else
    TransDirection = 1
    Image2.Style.Visibility = ""
    Image3.Style.Visibility = "hidden"
  end if
  divAB.filters.item(0).Transition = TransChoice.selectedIndex
  divAB.filters.item(0).play(transDuration)
  bTransInProgress = True
End Sub
</SCRIPT>
```

The script first checks to see if the transition is in progress, and immediately exits if it is. After that we basically follow the routine we learned earlier. We freeze the image, and then we check the direction of the transition. Depending on the direction we make one of the images visible and hide the other one. Then we set the transition type to the choice selected in the user list box. Finally we set the duration of the transition to our preset global variable. One last thing is that we set the Boolean variable `bTransInProgress` to indicate that we can't start another transition for the duration of this one. That's all there is to it.

Summary

In this chapter, we've completed our tour of the Dynamic HTML **object model** by looking at the central character it provides – the `document` object. We've also looked at the other subsidiary objects and collections that it supports, and seen some ways we can use them in our pages. We looked at:

- How the entire content of the page being displayed by the browser is accessible through the `document` object and various other objects and collections
- How we can use the `document` object's properties, methods and events to manipulate the document, or just get information about it
- How we can access the various elements on the page, using the `document` object's collections
- How we can interact with the user through the `selection` object, and by reacting to events
- How we can access visual and transition filters using Cascading Style Sheet properties and scripting properties

You've probably also seen some new ways of using scripting in this chapter. We're going to be concentrating on scripting in the next chapter, and in the remainder of the book. Now you know what's inside the browser, it's just waiting for you to play with it through scripting code. OK, there are a few more things to learn – so turn the page, and let's get started.

5

Scripts and Event Handling

So far, we've covered a lot of the basics of Dynamic HTML. We've studied style sheets and style tags, looked at the new design opportunities they offer for static pages, and discovered the object model that lurks inside the browser and how to get at it. We've also seen some ways of taking advantage of all these features. What we still haven't done is create any really wild dynamic pages.

Well, the time has now come. We know enough about the way Dynamic HTML interfaces with the browser and the pages it displays to start getting into script code in a big way. As we saw back in Chapter 1, most of what happens in script is in response to an event. This can be initiated by the end-user, by the browser they're using, by a component within the page, or even by Windows itself.

When an event occurs, the browser passes it to our script code through the object model we've been exploring, and we can then choose to react to it if we want to. To do this, we need to know more about how we hook our scripts up to the event, and how we use the exposed methods and properties that this same object model provides to actually manipulate the page contents.

In this chapter, you'll see:

- What events are, and where they come from
- How we connect our script to an event
- How we can decide which events to react to
- The kinds of things we can do when reacting to an event

Understanding the nature of events, and how we create the link between an event and our code, are the crucial steps. It's these that we'll look at first.

What are Events?

Most people have heard the term **event-driven programming**, and connect this with the way Windows works. But what does this actually mean? Why should a program be driven by events, rather than by any other method? And what alternatives are there anyway?

These are questions that don't normally concern the web page author, but you need to know a little about how Windows works to use Dynamic HTML to anything like its full potential. We'll take a brief overview of the subject, and then see how we can use events in our pages.

What is Event Driven Programming?

Before Windows in particular, and graphical user interfaces in general, users usually worked with one application at a time rather than having several open simultaneously. Within that application, the user carried out tasks by navigating from one 'menu' screen to another, and had only a finite set of choices available at any one time.

In a graphical user interface like Windows, users can run several applications at the same time, change the size of the screen windows as they go along, and switch from one to another. More importantly, the applications have no fixed 'route' through them. The user can click different buttons or select from any of the menus, to decide for themselves which course they want to take in the program.

As an example, consider a program that carries out technical calculations. In the years BW (Before Windows), on starting the application we would have been presented with a main menu, from which there were a fixed number of choices. Selecting an option would display more screens collecting information, then display the result. We would have followed this same course every time we wanted to carry out the query.

In the equivalent Windows program, or the equivalent in other graphical user environments, we can generally choose which windows to open, and open several at once. We can fill in text boxes, make selections from lists, set other controls, and click a range of buttons – in almost any order we like. To keep control of all this, the operating system has to work in a fundamentally different way.

Where Do Events Come From?

When you carry out some action in Windows, say clicking on a window with the mouse, the operating system raises an **event**. This is simply a signal that something has happened. Windows examines the event to decide what caused it and what to do about it. This isn't always as simple as it may seem. For example, the user may have clicked on a window that was not currently active (i.e. not part of the application they were working with).

In this case, Windows has to work out where the mouse pointer is on the screen and which application is under the pointer, bring this application's window to the front, and tell the other application that it is no longer the active one. And this is only a simplified view. In reality there will be a lot more happening 'under the hood' – a stream of messages is being sent to all the applications by the operating system. Each application can choose to either do something about the message, or simply ignore it.

However, some events may not be aimed at any application in particular. For example, pressing a key when Microsoft Word is active will normally cause that character to appear in the page. But if there is another application running at the same time, and the key-press is *Alt-Tab*, Windows brings up its own task-switching window instead of passing the event onto Word.

Events in Dynamic HTML

In the case of the browser and Dynamic HTML, this constant barrage of messages provides a way for us to react to things that are going on in the browser. We can link code in our pages to the events that are occurring, and use them to interact with the viewer of our pages.

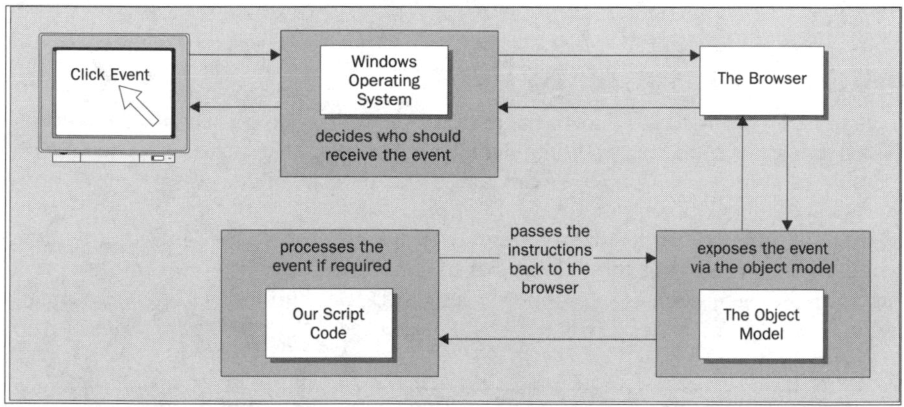

For example, just clicking the mouse button creates several events, descriptively named `onmousedown`, `onmouseup`, and `onclick`. Each message is collected by the Windows operating system, which then decides what to do with it. If the user pressed the mouse button while the pointer was on the screen over the browser window, Windows sends a message to the browser. It includes information on which button was pressed, what other keys were held down, and where the pointer was on the screen.

The browser then decides if it is going to handle the event. If they clicked on one of the browser toolbar buttons, it just gets on and does whatever is required – perhaps printing the page, refreshing it, or loading the user's Home page. If, however, the click was over the page itself, the browser then **exposes** it, by passing it on to our script code via the browser's object model. At this point, we can react to the event ourselves if we want to.

The reverse path is taken if we actually do decide to respond. The instructions in our code are passed back to the browser via the object model. It decides what effect this will have on the page and tells Windows. Windows then updates the screen to show the new page. The great thing is that, as Dynamic HTML programmers, all we have to do is decide which events to respond to, and what instructions to give the browser. Everything else is looked after automatically.

Reacting to Browser Events

To be able to react to an event, we have to be able to detect it happening. If we don't react to it, the browser will just carry on regardless – perhaps carrying out some action of its own. And even if we do decide to react, we can still let the browser carry out the original task as well. If this sounds confusing, think about the following example.

When we have a Submit button on a page, and the user clicks it, the browser sends the information from all the HTML control elements on the form to the server. However, it also fires an event called `onsubmit`, prior to submitting the information – and we can react to that event. If we want to, we can have a look at what the user entered, and decide if we want to submit the form or not. If we don't, we can instruct the browser to ignore the event as though it never happened. We'll explore this in more detail later in the chapter.

Connecting Script to Events

So, we're now getting to the crux of the matter. All we have to do is capture the event, by connecting our code to it, and then decide how to react to it ourselves. The first step, then, is to understand how we can connect code to an event.

There are 59 different events that the browser exposes to our script – but for any one element in the page, only a limited number of these are available. For example a heading in the page, such as `<H2>Some Text</H2>`, only provides 32 events, while an image tag, `<IMG>`, provides 33 different events and the `<TITLE>` tag provides only one event!

> **You'll find a description of all the events in Appendix B of this book's reference pages. Appendix C lists the events available for each HTML element tag.**

We took a brief look at event-handling routines in Chapters 3 and 4, to demonstrate the object model in action. Here, we'll summarize the way event handlers are written, and show you the other ways you can link your code to events.

Event Handling in VBScript

In VBScript, we have four ways of connecting our code to an event. The main one we've used so far is to create a subroutine or function whose name is a combination of the *element* name and the *event* name. To react to a click on some heading text, we can use:

```
<H2 ID=MyHeading> Some Text </H2>

<SCRIPT LANGUAGE=VBSCRIPT>
  Sub MyHeading_onclick()
    MsgBox "You clicked me!"
  End Sub
</SCRIPT>
```

With VBScript 5, which comes with Internet Explorer 5, you can now take advantage of function pointers to associate events with event handlers. A function pointer is a variable that, instead of containing a string or a number, contains a reference to a function. With a function pointer, you have the freedom to associate any method with an event to be handled, regardless of the name of the method. You can also dynamically change what method should be called to handle a particular event. This can come in handy – for example, if you only want an event to be handled after a certain condition has been met. This is now possible, since you can set a function pointer at any time. Let's take another look at the previous example, this time using function pointers:

```
<H2 ID=MyHeading> Some Text </H2>

<SCRIPT LANGUAGE=VBSCRIPT>
  Sub ClickMyHeading()
    MsgBox "You clicked me!"
  End Sub

  Set MyHeading.onclick = getRef("ClickMyHeading")
</SCRIPT>
```

Alternatively, we can create a routine with almost any name, and link it to the event and the element by declaring the name of the routine in the element tag. We don't need an `ID` in this case:

```
<H2 LANGUAGE=VBSCRIPT ONCLICK="MyClickCode"> Some Text </H2>

<SCRIPT LANGUAGE=VBSCRIPT>
  Sub MyClickCode()
    MsgBox "You clicked me!"
  End Sub
</SCRIPT>
```

We can also use inline script code, which does away with the need for a separate code routine. We simply write the code inside the tag, as the value of the event name attribute. Notice how we have to use single quotes inside the `ONCLICK` attribute, because this itself is a string. Also, since the `ONCLICK` attribute is part of the HTML tag, it is not case sensitive. However, the standard convention is for it to be in upper case:

```
<H2 LANGUAGE=VBSCRIPT ONCLICK="MsgBox 'You clicked me!'"> Some Text </H2>
```

The final method is to use a different script section for each event. This is done by identifying the element and the event in the `<SCRIPT>` tag:

```
<H2 ID=MyHeading> Some Text </H2>

<SCRIPT LANGUAGE=VBSCRIPT FOR=MyHeading EVENT=ONCLICK>
  MsgBox "You clicked me!"
</SCRIPT>
```

Event Handling in JScript

In JScript (Microsoft's implementation of JavaScript), we have similar options for connecting events to our code. The two things we have to watch out for are that JScript only supports functions, and the language interpreter is case-sensitive in all browsers.

The most usual way of making the connection between the function and the element is by defining the name of the function in the element tag itself. Notice that we need `MyClickCode()`, not just `MyClickCode`, to satisfy the JScript syntax requirements. We also have to use the browser's built-in `alert` dialog, rather than `MsgBox`, which is part of VBScript:

```
<H2 ONCLICK="MyClickCode()"> Some Text </H2>

<SCRIPT LANGUAGE=JSCRIPT>
function MyClickCode()
  {
    alert("You clicked me!");
  }
</SCRIPT>
```

We can also use inline code within the element tag:

```
<H2 LANGUAGE=JSCRIPT ONCLICK="alert('You clicked me!');">Some Text</H2>
```

And because JScript is the default language in the browser, we can omit the `LANGUAGE` attribute if we want to, making our code more compact:

```
<H2 ONCLICK="alert('You clicked me!');"> Some Text </H2>
```

Alternatively, we can create separate `<SCRIPT>` sections for each event, just like we did for VBScript. However, when using JScript we have to make sure that the name of the event is all lower-case, as JScript is a case-sensitive language:

```
<H2 ID=MyHeading> Some Text </H2>

<SCRIPT LANGUAGE=JSCRIPT FOR=MyHeading EVENT=onclick>
  alert("You clicked me!");
</SCRIPT>
```

This is fine for connecting script to specific elements in the page, but what about when we want to connect event handlers to the document itself? In this case, we simply put them all in the `<BODY>` tag (you can use this same technique with VBScript as well):

```
<BODY ONMOUSEMOVE="MyMouseMoveCode()" ONCLICK="MyClickCode()">
```

You can also use function pointers in JScript. The only difference between JScript and VBScript is that you no longer have to use the `getRef` function:

```
<SCRIPT LANGUAGE=JSCRIPT>
function beenClicked()
  {
    alert("I've just been clicked!");
  }
MyHeading.onclick = beenClicked;
</SCRIPT>
```

Handling Window Events in JScript

We've seen how we can place event handler declarations, such as `onmousemove`, in the `<BODY>` tag of the document to cause them to occur at `document` level. The other situation is how we handle events at `window` level. This can also be done using the VBScript syntax we looked at earlier. In Internet Explorer, we can place the event handler declarations on the opening `<HTML>` tag:

```
<HTML ONMOUSEMOVE="MyMouseMoveCode()" ONCLICK="MyClickCode()">
...
</HTML>
```

Alternatively, we can use a technique similar to the VBScript method of naming an event handler inline with the `ID` of the element and the event name. This time, we separate the two with a period (full stop) rather than an underscore as used in VBScript. This works because the functions are themselves actually stored as properties of the element object:

```
<H2 ID=MyHeading > Some Text </H2>

<SCRIPT LANGUAGE=JSCRIPT>
function MyHeading.onclick()
  {
    alert("You clicked me!");
  }
</SCRIPT>
```

The same works for the main browser objects as well, such as the `document` and `window`:

```
<SCRIPT LANGUAGE=JSCRIPT>
function window.onload()
  {
    alert("I've just loaded!");
  }
</SCRIPT>
```

The `LANGUAGE` attribute in a script or element tag can take one of four values. `VBSCRIPT` and `VBS` both instruct the browser to pass the script to its VBScript interpreter, while `JAVASCRIPT` or `JSCRIPT` pass it to the Internet Explorer JScript interpreter. Omitting the attribute altogether sends the script to the JScript interpreter.

Canceling an Event Action

Some events, such as `onsubmit`, allow us to provide a return value that controls how the browser behaves. As you'll recall from Chapter 3, to return a value in VBScript we have to use a `function` rather than a `subroutine`. In JScript, everything is a `function` anyway. The following example uses JScript to define a form section with a single text box named `Email`, and a Submit button:

```
<FORM ID=MyForm ONSUBMIT="return CheckAddress()"
      ACTION="http://www.somesite.com/scripts/doit.asp">
  <INPUT TYPE=TEXT ID=Email>
  <INPUT TYPE=SUBMIT>
</FORM>

<SCRIPT LANGUAGE=JSCRIPT>
function CheckAddress()
{
  strAddress = document.forms["MyForm"].elements["Email"].value;
  if (strAddress.indexOf("@") != -1)    // contains @ somewhere
    return true
  else
  {
    alert("You must supply a valid email address.");
    return false
  }
}
</SCRIPT>
```

This code uses the `indexOf()` function to find the position of the first @ character in the string the user enters into a textbox named `Email` on the form. If there isn't a @ character in the string, the function returns -1. In this case, we can assume it's not a valid email address, display a message, and cancel the submission of the form by returning `false`. Notice that we have to use the `return` keyword in the element's `ONSUBMIT` attribute as well, so that the result is fed back to the browser's own form submission code:

```
<FORM ID=MyForm ONSUBMIT="return CheckAddress()"
      ...
```

You can also see how we have to use the browser's object model to get at the text in the text box. The string we want is the `value` property of the element object named `Email` in the `elements` collection of the form named `MyForm`, which is stored in the `forms` collection of the `document` object. (We could have started with `window.document`, but – as you'll recall – the `window` object is the default anyway.)

Instead of returning a value from the function directly, we can also cancel the default action for any event by setting the `returnValue` property of the `event` object. You'll see this technique used in an example later in the chapter.

Responding to Events

Now that we've found ways of connecting our code to an event, we can start to write the code that tells the browser what we want it to do. In general, this involves three tasks – getting information about the event, finding out about the element the event occurred for, and carrying out the task. This is where the links between our code and the elements in the page (as exposed by the object model) come into play.

Getting Information about an Event

All the ways you've seen here of connecting code to an event were equally valid in the pre-DHTML releases of browsers which supported scripting (though the object model did not expose events for most elements - only a very limited subset of controls did this previously). Dynamic HTML also adds another way of getting information about an event.

In Chapter 3, we briefly mentioned the `event` object. This was added to the document object model in IE4 and is a subsidiary object to the top-level `window` object. The `event` object is constantly being updated to include information about each event that occurs in our page - it is global to all events in this sense. When an event occurs, we can query the `event` object's properties to learn more about the event.

Mouse Information and the Event Object

As you've seen in Chapter 3, the `event` object provides a whole range of properties that tell us about an event that has just occurred. We simply query these properties inside our event handler to find the information we need to make a decision on what to do. Here's how we can query the properties of the `event` object to get information about the mouse button that was pressed, and the position of the mouse pointer when the event occurred:

```
<H2 ID=MyHeading> Some Text </H2>

<SCRIPT LANGUAGE=VBSCRIPT>
Sub MyHeading_onmousedown()
  strMesg = "You clicked the "
  If window.event.button = 1 Then strMesg = strMesg & "left "
  If window.event.button = 2 Then strMesg = strMesg & "right "
  If window.event.button = 4 Then strMesg = strMesg & "middle "
  strMesg = strMesg & "button, at position x = " & window.event.x _
          & ", y = " & window.event.y
  strMesg = strMesg & Chr(10) & "and you held down the "
  If window.event.shiftKey Then strMesg = strMesg & "Shift key "
  If window.event.ctrlKey Then strMesg = strMesg & "Ctrl key "
  If window.event.altKey Then strMesg = strMesg & "Alt key "
  MsgBox strMesg
End Sub
</SCRIPT>
```

Here's the result, when the *Shift* and *Ctrl* keys are held down while clicking on the heading:

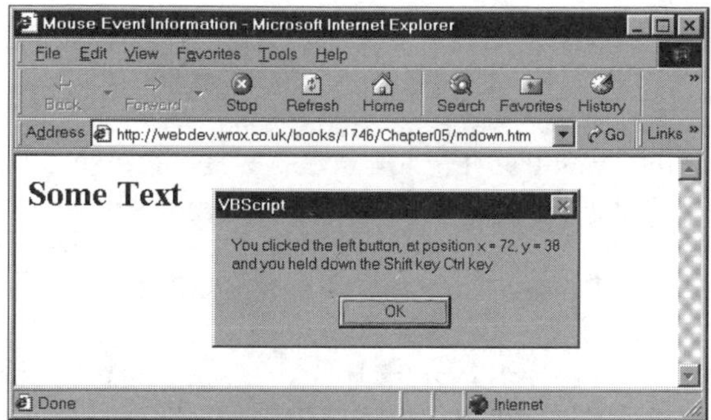

Notice that in this example, we've preceded the `event` object with the default `window` object. This is not necessary in JScript (or JavaScript), but must be done in VBScript to prevent a clash between the `event` object and the VBScript `event` keyword.

Key-Press Information and the Event Object

If we query the `event` object for a key-press event, we can use the same techniques as we did for a mouse event to find out where the mouse pointer is, and use the `shiftKey`, `ctrlKey` and `altKey` properties. However, more than that, we can use the read-only `keyCode` property to find out which key was pressed. In this example, we're reacting to the `onkeypress` event of the `document`:

```
<SCRIPT LANGUAGE=VBScript>
Sub document_onkeypress()
  strMesg = "You pressed the " & Chr(window.event.keyCode) & " key, " & _
            "which has an ASCII value of " & window.event.keyCode
  If window.event.shiftKey Then strMesg = strMesg & Chr(10) & _
                                "while holding down the Shift key"
  strMesg = strMesg & Chr(10) & "The mouse pointer is at position " & _
             "x = " & window.event.x & ", y = " & window.event.y
  MsgBox strMesg, vbInformation, "The Event object parameters"
End Sub
</SCRIPT>
```

Here's the result. Look where the mouse pointer is in the screenshot, and at the values of the mouse position retrieved from the `event` object. It still works if the pointer isn't over the page:

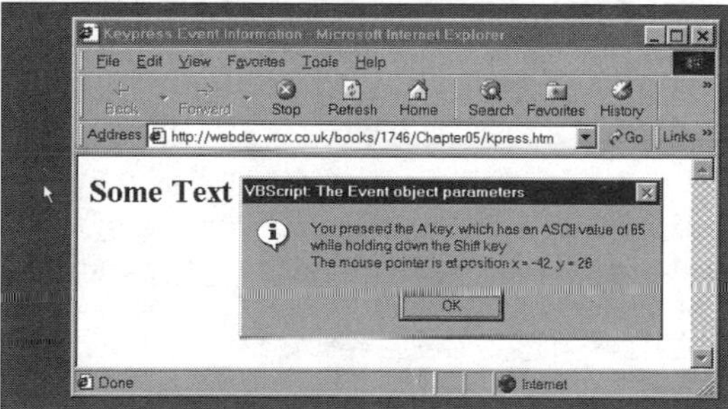

Both of the above pages, `mdown.htm` and `kpress.htm`, can be run directly from our web site at http://webdev.wrox.co.uk/books/1746.

Examining the Source of an Event

Often the first step in reacting to an event is to find out more about the event itself and the element for which the event occurred. We've seen how we can find out more about the actual event from the `event` object. The next question is how do we find out more about the element that originally raised the event?

Examining an Element's Properties

Every element in a page has a set of **properties**, and you'll find a complete list of these in the reference section at the back of the book. For example, this `<H2>` heading has an `align` property, which indicates how we aligned the text when we created the page in HTML:

```
<H2 ID="MyHeading" ALIGN=CENTER> Some Text </H2>
```

We can query the element's `align` property in code using the `Me` keyword (which provides a reference to the element that the event is bound to) like this:

```
Sub MyHeading_onclick()
  MsgBox Me.align
End Sub
```

In JScript or JavaScript, the equivalent to `Me` is the keyword `this`.

In this case, our heading will have the value `center` for it's `align` property. (Notice that the value is returned in lower case.) This is one useful way in which Dynamic HTML exposes the properties of the elements within the page, and allows them to be changed in our code. There are a whole range of different properties available for different element tags, depending on which HTML attributes are valid for that tag. For example, an `<IMG>` tag has (among many others) the `width`, `height` and `src` properties, while the `<BODY>` tag can have `aLink`, `bgColor` and `scroll` properties. As you would expect, updating the properties causes the change to appear dynamically on the page where appropriate.

One point you need to watch out for is that many elements return an empty string as the value of a property that has not been set explicitly. For example, the default alignment of a <H2> tag is `left` if no `ALIGN` attribute is included. However, the `align` property in this case returns an empty string.

Among the standard properties of all elements is the `id`. As you've seen, we use the `id` property, which we define in the `ID` attribute of the tag, to give an element a unique name that we can use to refer to in our script code:

```
<H2 ID=MyHeading> Some Text </H2>
```

We can always retrieve this value using `Me.id`, though you'll see other ways of identifying elements later on.

Element Properties versus Style Attributes

While setting the attributes of an element is an accepted way to control its alignment, appearance, etc., there is another method, which is quickly becoming the preferred way. All the visible elements on a page also have a `style` object, and this can be used to control the way the element appears – as well as or instead of the traditional attributes of its HTML tag.

We met the `style` object in Chapter 2 and you should remember that we can use it to set, retrieve and change style attributes for elements in our code, from the font size and font color, to the positioning of the text and graphics on the page:

```
<H2 ID=MyHeading STYLE="font-family: Arial; color: red; font-size: 48">
  Some Text
</H2>
```

We can align our text heading in the same way, and in fact this is the technique recommended by W3C for version 4.0 of the HTML standards:

```
<H2 ID=MyHeading STYLE="text-align: center"> Some Text </H2>
```

Once we've applied a style attribute like this, we have to remember to query the element's `style` object to get the value – in this case the `textAlign` property:

```
<SCRIPT LANGUAGE =VBSCRIPT>
  Sub MyHeading_onmousedown()
    MsgBox Me.style.textAlign
  End Sub
</SCRIPT>
```

Here's the equivalent in JScript:

```
<SCRIPT LANGUAGE=JSCRIPT>
function MyHeading.onmousedown()
  {
    alert(this.style.textAlign);
  }
</SCRIPT>
```

Remember that when we align text using a `STYLE` attribute like this, the `align` property of the element returns an empty string unless those styles have been explicitly set on that element. If the element has had its style properties set through a linked or cascading style sheet, then the style object would not be able to retrieve them. In order to do so, you would need to use the `currentStyle` object. This object has the same object model as the `style` object, so you can access the properties in the same way.

Manually Firing Events

As well as setting the values of properties and calling the methods of various objects within the browser's object model, our code can also explicitly fire events. Because all the event routines we write are available to our code, we can call them directly. The routine will run just as if that event had occurred, although the browser and Windows itself won't behave as if they had received the event. Also, if the event handler is expecting to examine the `event` object when handling the event, the expected values may not be present if the event was explicitly fired.

As an example, imagine we have a page with a button named `cmdUpdate`, which updates some part of the page. We can call this code directly from elsewhere in the page like this:

```
Sub cmdUpdate_onclick()
  '.. some code to update the page
End Sub

Sub cmdOther_onclick()
  '.. do something else to change the page
  cmdUpdate_onclick  'run the cmdUpdate routine
End Sub
```

This updates the page as if the `cmdUpdate` button had been clicked, even though that event didn't actually happen.

Bubbling and Canceling Events

One major topic that makes Dynamic HTML different from scripting in earlier versions – either with VBScript, JScript, or any other language – is the way that the browser manages the events that are occurring in the page. We've already seen this to some extent when we looked at the `event` object earlier.

However, the `event` object plays another major role in the way we create script routines in Dynamic HTML. It not only stores the values of the environment as each event comes along, it also plays a part in controlling how these events are propagated to our code. It does this through two properties, `cancelBubble` and `srcElement`.

The Event Object's Control System

When an event occurs in a page, the `event` object gets the first look at it and decides which element should receive it. Take the situation shown below where we have an `<H3>` heading inside a `<DIV>` document division on the page:

```
<DIV ID=MyDiv STYLE="background-color=aqua">
  <H3 ID=MyTitle> Click Here To Fire An Event </H3>
</DIV>
```

When the `event` object receives an `onclick` event, it looks to see which element the mouse pointer was over at the time. If it was the heading line (which has the `ID` of `MyTitle`), it looks for a routine connected to this event, and – if it finds one – executes it:

```
Sub MyTitle_onclick()
  ...
End Sub
```

Bubbling Events to the Container Element

However, it doesn't stop there. It now looks to see which element is the **container** of the heading tag. In our case, it's the `<DIV>` tag named `MyDiv`, so it runs the `onclick` event code for this as well:

```
Sub MyDiv_onclick()
  ...
End Sub
```

This process continues while there are containers available. In our case, the only remaining one is the document itself, so it looks for the equivalent event code for this and executes it:

```
Sub document_onclick()
  ...
End Sub
```

This probably isn't what you were expecting, and perhaps it's difficult to see why it should work this way. After all, if the viewer clicks on a heading, surely we just want to know about that heading? In fact **event bubbling**, as this process is called, is very useful. For one thing, it helps to minimize the code we have to write, by letting one routine handle an event for several elements. Now that all the elements support events, this is particularly helpful.

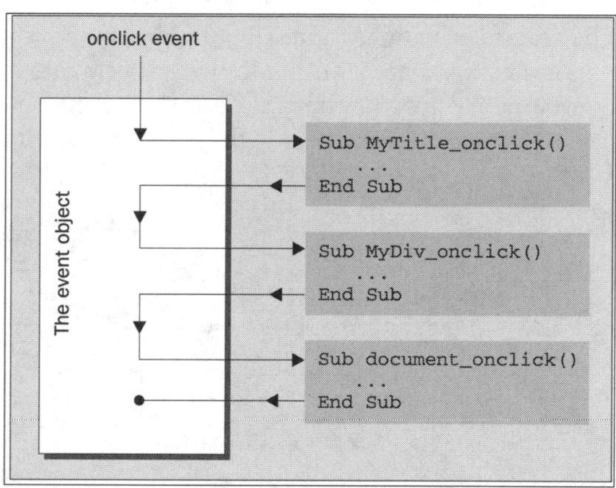

Using a Single Event Handler

To see why event bubbling can help to reduce the amount of code we write, think about what happens when we have a lot of similar elements on the page. This is the case with the Jigsaw example shown here. There are 24 image elements holding the different pieces of the puzzle.

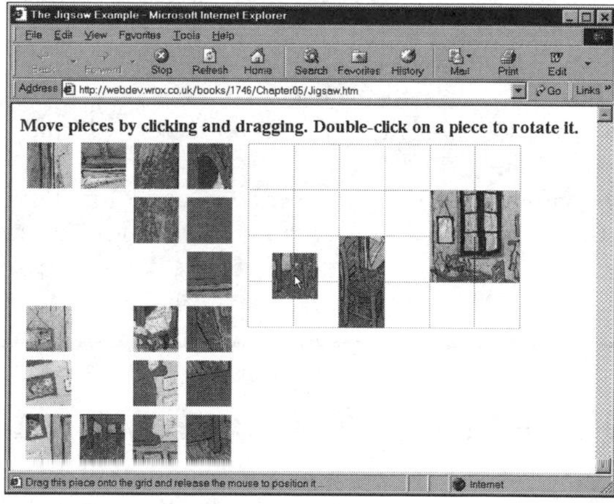

This page, and the code that creates it, can be loaded from our web site at http://webdev.wrox.co.uk/books/1746.

However, there is only one event-handling routine, and this takes care of rotating any one of the pieces when the user double-clicks on it. The routine responds to the `ondblclick` event at document level, and uses the `srcElement` property of the `event` object to figure out which of the images was clicked. Then it can apply the rotation code to just that image. If we didn't have event bubbling, we would have to attach every one of the images to an event handler that rotated the piece separately.

We'll be looking at how we identify the correct image in a while. For the moment, let's consider another way that event bubbling is useful.

Using Containers in Dynamic HTML

The second advantage that event bubbling offers is that it allows us to work with the concept of **containers**. In HTML, when we create a list of items in the page, we group them together in `<UL>` or `<OL>` tags. You can use the following code to create the `ListChange` example page, which we first saw in Chapter 1:

```
<STYLE>
.notover     {font-family=Arial; font-weight:normal; font-size:12;
              color:blue; visibility: show}
.color       {font-family="Arial Narrow"; color:red; font-size:12}
.sizechange  {font-family=courier; font-size:26; color:blue}
.disappear   {font-family=Arial; font-weight:normal; font-size:12;
              visibility: hidden}
</STYLE>

<DIV ID=DivTag STYLE="position:absolute; top:50; left:30;
                      height:200; width:400; cursor:default">
  <UL ID=MyList>
    <LI ID=Item1 CLASS=notover> Change the font and size of text</LI>
    <LI ID=Item2 CLASS=notover >Change the position of elements</LI>
    <LI ID=Item3 CLASS=notover> Change the color and style of things</LI>
    <LI ID=Item4 CLASS=notover> Make elements appear and disappear</LI>
  </UL>
</DIV>
```

Notice that we've given the list and each item in it an `ID` here, and used style classes to create the styles for the list. We've also wrapped the whole list in a `<DIV>` tag, so that we can position it absolutely and move it around in our code.

We can react to the `onmouseover` event for all the items in the list by creating one single event handler for the list itself – the **container** of the list items:

```
Sub MyList_onmouseover
  ...
End Sub
```

Finding the Source Element

OK, so we can react to an event by using a handler that collects the event when it gets up to the `document`, or up as far as the element's container. The only thing is that we generally need to know where it actually came from – either to move the correct piece of the jigsaw or do something with the items in our list. This is where the `srcElement` property of the `event` object comes in.

The srcElement Property in Action

Inside any event routine, we can identify the object that was 'topmost' and active when the event occurred (in this example, when the user clicked the page) from the event object's `srcElement` property. For example, if they click on a heading tag inside a document division on the page, the topmost element is the heading tag. If they click on the division, but not the heading, the topmost element is the division. If they click on the blank page, there is no topmost element, and the event goes straight to the document.

In the `ListChange` example below, we use the `srcElement` property to discover which element the mouse is over. We're reacting to two events: `onmouseover`, which occurs when the mouse first moves onto an element, and `onmouseout`, which occurs when it moves off it again:

```
Sub MyList_onmouseover    'occurs when the mouse enters any item in the list
                                 'get a reference to the source of the event
  Set objItem = window.event.srcElement
                'change it's style class as required, depending on the item
  If objItem.id = "Item1" Then objItem.classname = "sizechange"
  If objItem.id = "Item2" Then DivTag.style.pixelLeft = 100
  If objItem.id = "Item3" Then
    objItem.classname="color"
                                  'we also make the last item re-appear here
    document.all("Item4").classname = "notover"
  End If
  If objItem.id = "Item4" Then objItem.classname = "disappear"
End Sub
```

```
Sub MyList_onmouseout     'occurs when the mouse leaves any item in the list
                          'again, get a reference to the source of the event
  Set objItem = window.event.srcElement
          'if it's not the last item, change it's style class back to normal
  If objItem.id <> "Item4" Then objItem.classname = "notover"
              'move the division back to the normal position, in case it got
                          'moved by the onmoueover event changing it's style
  DivTag.style.pixelLeft = 30
End Sub
```

In each case, we get a reference to the list item that was topmost, i.e. the one that received the event first, using `Set objItem = window.event.srcElement`. We have to use the `Set` keyword in Visual Basic, because we are assigning an *object* (the list item element) to the variable here.

Although the code looks more complex than this, it's just a matter of changing the `classname` property of that element to the appropriate class (except for the positioning of elements, which requires the `style` property to be updated). When the mouse pointer enters the element, we set it to the appropriate value:

```
  If objItem.id = "Item1" Then objItem.classname = "sizechange"
```

When the mouse pointer moves out of the element, we return the `classname` to `notover` (except for the fourth item where hiding the element actually causes an `onmouseout` event, so we only reset this one when the mouse returns to the third item in the list):

```
If objItem.id <> "Item4" Then objItem.classname = "notover"
```

You can run the `ListChange.htm` *example from our web site at* http://webdev.wrox.co.uk/books/1746.

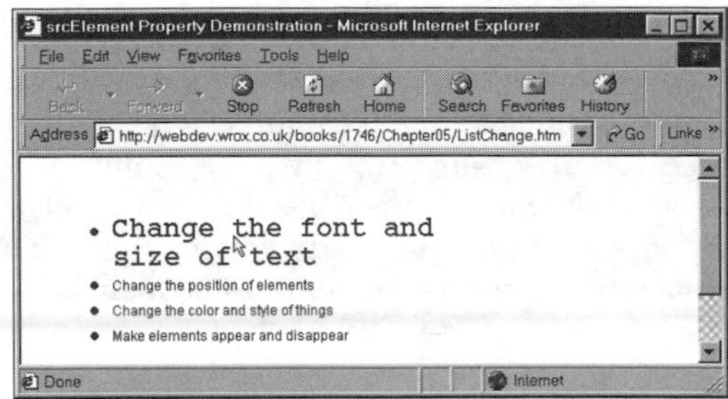

The cancelBubble Property in Action

The other situation is that sometimes we want to be a little more selective about the way we react to an event. For example, we may want most of the elements on a page to react to an event, while one or two particular ones do not. In cases like this, we can use the `event` object's `cancelBubble` property to give us that extra control.

All we do is create an event handler that reacts to the event for just this element. Normally, once the code in this event handler has finished executing, the event will be bubbled up the object hierarchy to the next container, or to the top-level document object. To prevent this, all we have to do is set the `event` object's `cancelBubble` property to `True`.

For example, if we wanted to do this for an element with the `ID` of `picture`, we just need to add the `cancelBubble` property assignment to the `onclick` event handler of that element:

```
Sub picture_onclick()
  'some code to react to the onclick event
  'now stop the event being bubbled to any other event handlers
  window.event.cancelBubble = True
End Sub
```

This breaks the chain of events, and the `document` object will not receive this `onclick` event. Of course, we can set the `cancelBubble` property in any of the events in the chain, and stop the processing at any point we choose. There's not much point in doing it in the `document` event handler, which is at the end of the chain, and we can't stop the first event handler from running because this is our first chance to set the `cancelBubble` property.

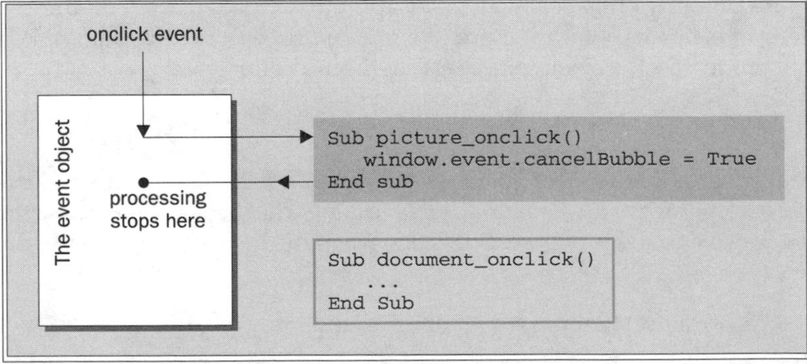

To see the cancelBubble property in action, run the sample Bubbling.htm, which you'll find on our web site at http://webdev.wrox.co.uk/books/1746. It provides a <H3> heading within a <DIV> document division on the page, plus a checkbox where you can choose to cancel event bubbling in the onclick() event for the heading, instead of letting it bubble up through the hierarchy:

```
<BODY ONCLICK="DocClickCode()">

<CENTER>
<DIV ID=MyDiv ONCLICK="DivClickCode()"
     STYLE="position:relative; width:400; background-color:aqua">
  <H3 ID=MyTitle ONCLICK="HeadingClickCode()"> Click Here To Fire An Event
  </H3>
</DIV>
<INPUT TYPE=CHECKBOX ID=chkBubble ONCLICK="CheckClickCode()"> Cancel Bubble
</CENTER>
```

The script section is all JScript this time, just for a change. It contains event handlers for each element on the page, and in each one it uses the srcElement property of the event object to reference the element that the event originally fired for. In an alert dialog, it provides this element's tagName and id properties, so that you can trace the event bubbling up through the hierarchy:

```
function HeadingClickCode()
{
  strMesg = "MyTitle onclick event fired.\n"
          + "Source tag name is " + event.srcElement.tagName + "\n"
          + "srcElement is " + event.srcElement.id;
  alert(strMesg);
  if (document.all["chkBubble"].checked)
  {
    event.cancelBubble = true;
  }
}

function DivClickCode()
{
  strMesg = "MyDiv onclick event fired.\n"
          + "Source tag name is " + event.srcElement.tagName + "\n"
          + "srcElement is " + event.srcElement.id;
  alert(strMesg);
}

function DocClickCode()
{
  strMesg = "document onclick event fired.\n"
          + "Source tag name is " + event.srcElement.tagName + "\n"
          + "srcElement is " + event.srcElement.id;
  alert(strMesg);
}

function CheckClickCode()
{
  event.cancelBubble = true
}
```

Notice that we've included code to cancel event bubbling for the checkbox element chkBubble. If we didn't do this, the message box from the document_onclick() event would appear when you changed the checkbox setting, because the event would bubble up to the document. Here's a compounded screen shot showing the result when we do allow event bubbling to take place:

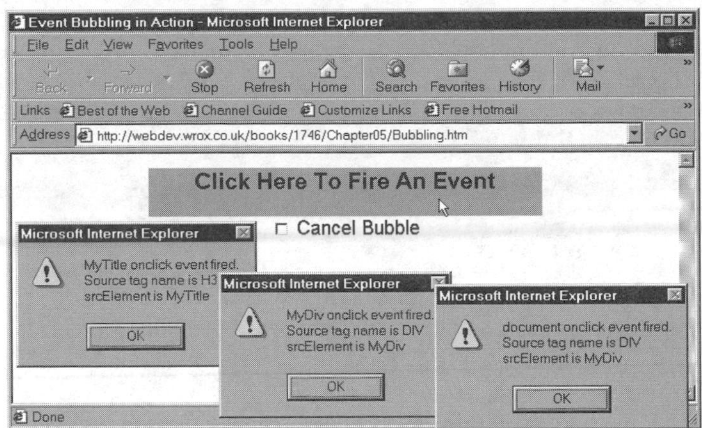

Now, if we set the Cancel Bubble checkbox and click the heading again, we only get the first message box.

The fromElement and toElement Properties

Two other properties of the `event` object that are useful for finding out what's going on in a Dynamic HTML page are `fromElement` and `toElement`. As the mouse moves into and out of elements, it fires the `onmouseover` and `onmouseout` events, as we saw in the `ListChange` example. These are useful for updating the object that the event is fired for, but not much use in telling us about what's going on in other elements.

By adding a line to the `onmouseover` code, we can display the value of the `event` object's `fromElement` or `toElement` property as an event is received. The useful one here is `fromElement`, which returns a reference to the element that the mouse was leaving when the event was fired:

```
Sub MyList_onmouseover
  ...
  window.status = window.event.fromElement.id
End Sub
```

In this partial screenshot, you can see that it was previously over the `Item3` element – the last but one item in the list – and is now over `Item2`.

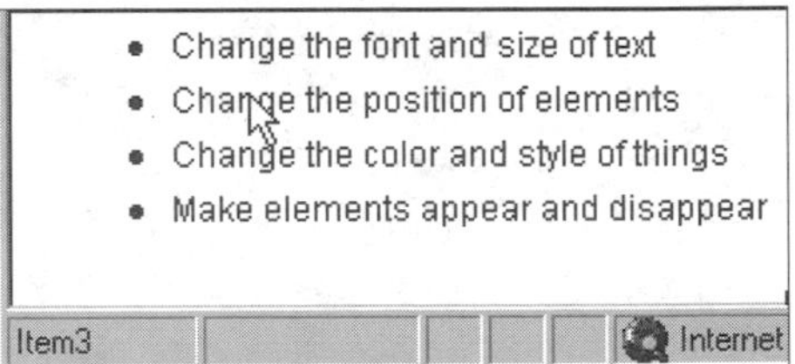

The returnValue Property

Earlier in this chapter, we saw how some events allow us to handle them with a `Function` rather than a `Subroutine`, and prevent the browser's default action taking place by setting the return value of the function to `False`. The example we looked at was a form submission, and we found that we could use this method to prevent the browser's default action of sending the data in the form to the server.

The `event` object in Dynamic HTML allows us to use another technique. All we have to do is set the `returnValue` property of the `event` object to `False`. This cancels the default action. For example, here's a page containing an `<A>` tag, which jumps to our home page when clicked:

```
...
<A ID=MyLink HREF="http://www.wrox.com">Wrox Press Limited</A>

<SCRIPT LANGUAGE=VBSCRIPT>
Sub MyLink_onclick()
  If MsgBox("Go to our site?", vbYesNo + vbQuestion, "Jump?") = vbNo Then
    window.event.returnValue=False
  End If
End Sub
</SCRIPT>
...
```

Clicking on the link in the page runs the `MyLink_onclick()` event handler code, which displays a message box asking the viewer to confirm their action. If they select No, we just have to set the `returnValue` property to `False` and the browser ignores the jump, as though they hadn't clicked it in the first place.

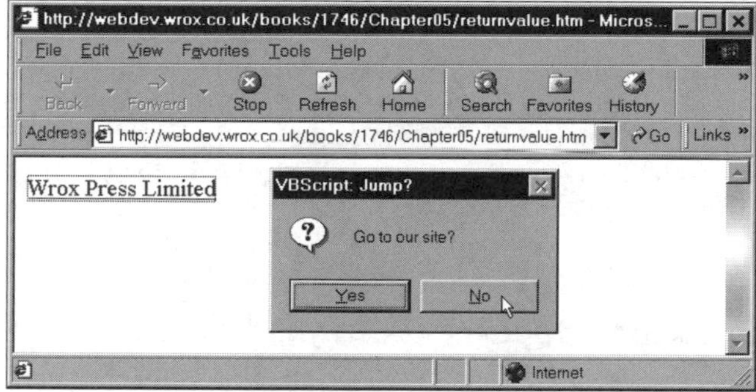

Notice how we've used the built-in VBScript constants to define the `MsgBox` *function parameters. You'll find a list of these in Appendix I, at the back of this book.*

Dynamic Element Positioning

In a couple of the examples, we've used the various 'position' properties of the `event` object to find out where the mouse pointer was when the event occurred. In fact, as you may recall from Chapter 3, there are several 'sets' of these properties. The event object provides four pairs of position properties: `offsetX` and `offsetY`, `clientX` and `clientY`, `screenX` and `screenY`, and plain `x` and `y`.

The Event Object's Position Properties

The `screenX` and `screenY` properties return the mouse pointer position in absolute terms, with respect to the screen. So the bottom right corner in vanilla VGA mode will be `screenX = 800` and `screenY = 600`. The other sets of properties return values that are based on the mouse pointer position with respect to the browser window and document.

In many cases, such as our earlier examples using mouse and key-press events, all except screenX and screenY should return the same values. This is because when we don't have any containers in the page, the offsetX and offsetY, clientX and clientY, and x and y properties all revert to being based on the document itself. However, once we add containers like document divisions, all this changes. Furthermore, the client- and offset- properties can behave unpredictably, depending on whether borders, margins or padding are included in the element dimensions. The position properties are defined as follows:

- clientX and clientY return the position of the mouse pointer in relation to the 'client area' of the browser window. This is the part of the browser that displays the page itself, excluding the window frame, scrollbars, menus, etc.
- offsetX and offsetY return the position of the mouse pointer in relation to top left corner of the element that actually received the event. If the element is a container itself, and the contents of the container are not all visible and have been scrolled within it, the values reflect the position of the top left corner of the content with respect to the top left corner of the container. Where there is no container, the values returned are with respect to the document itself.
- x and y return the position of the mouse pointer in relation to the top left corner of the container which holds the element that received the event. If an element is absolutely positioned, or is not the child of an absolutely positioned element, the x and y properties return coordinates relative to the BODY element.

Some Event Position Property Examples

To help you understand these different sets of properties we've provided a simple page that contains two nested containers. These are both <DIV> tags, with the inner one relatively positioned within the absolutely positioned outer one. Here's the HTML that creates the page:

```
<BODY ID=MyBody>
  <DIV ID=OuterDiv STYLE="position:absolute; left:50; top:50; width:300;
                          height:100; background-color:blue">
    <DIV ID=InnerDiv STYLE="position:relative; left:50; top:25; width:200;
                          height:50; background-color:yellow">
    </DIV>
  </DIV>
</BODY>
```

The code itself is simple – it just retrieves the values of the various properties, and displays them in a message box. Notice here how we've created a reference to the event object, to save having to keep using the full window.event.*property* syntax:

```
<SCRIPT LANGUAGE=VBSCRIPT>
Sub document_onclick()
  Set e = window.event
  strMesg = "srcElement is " & e.srcElement.id & chr(10) _
          & "clientX = " & e.clientX _
          & ", clientY=" & e.clientY & chr(10) _
          & "offsetX = " & e.offsetX _
          & ", offsetY = " & e.offsetY & chr(10) _
          & "screenX = " & e.screenX _
          & ", screenY = " & e.screenY & chr(10) _
          & "x = " & e.x & ", y = " & e.y & chr(10)
  MsgBox strMesg
End Sub
</SCRIPT>
```

Clicking outside either of the divisions produces the following result. The `clientX` and `X` values are equal, as are the `clientY` and `Y` values (the value of `offsetX` and `offsetY` differ by 2, due to the inclusion of a border in the calculation):

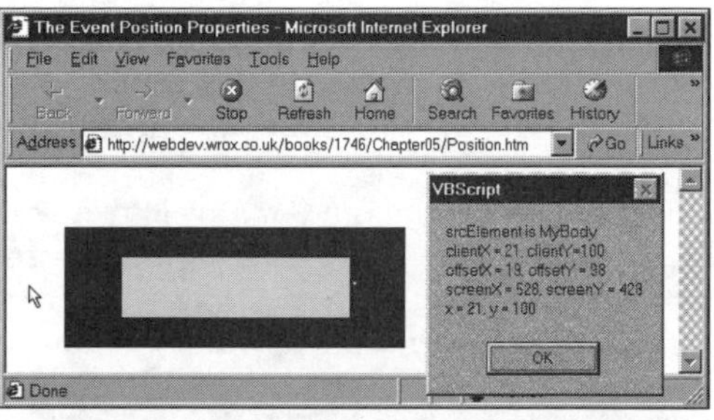

When we click inside the outer division, the `clientX` and `clientY`, and the `x` and `y` properties, are still the same as each other. However, the `offsetX` and `offsetY` properties now reflect the position of the mouse pointer within the outer division:

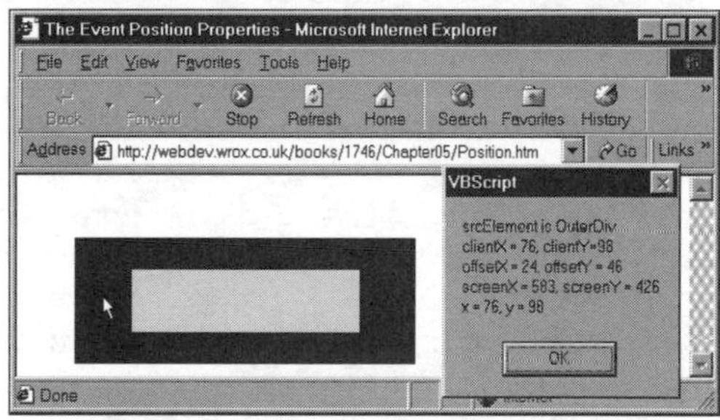

Finally, clicking inside the inner division produces different values for the properties. Now, the `x` and `y` and the `offsetX` and `offsetY` properties reflect the position with respect to the inner division. The `clientX` and `clientY` properties still show the position with respect to the document – i.e. the client area of the browser:

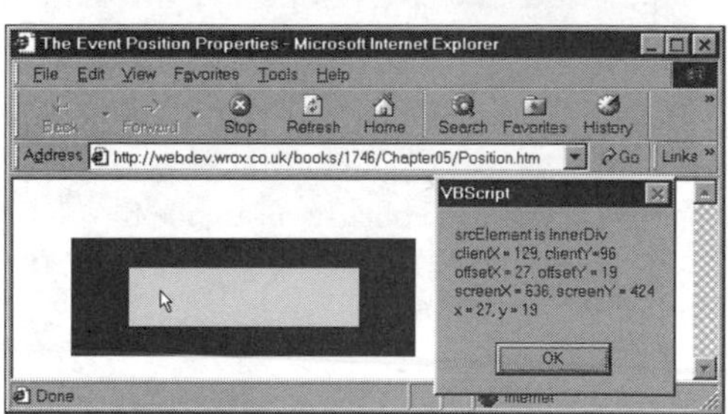

You can run this page, `Position.htm`, from our web site at *http://webdev.wrox.co.uk/books/1746.*

Capturing The Mouse

Mouse capture support has been added to IE5, allowing an object to handle all mouse activity on a page. Mouse capture offers several advantages that enable authors to enhance the interactivity of a web page. Prior versions of Dynamic HTML supported handling of mouse events through event bubbling. This could allow for a certain event to be blocked when the event bubbling was cancelled. With mouse capture, a single object can control the mouse events of the entire page, regardless of where the mouse event came from.

This method has a number of advantages over event bubbling. For example, it makes support of drag-and-drop functionality much simpler. In the past, if you were dragging an element and dropping it on another element on the page, then both elements had to have the proper scripting code in order to correctly handle the drag-and-drop. With mouse capture, this scripting code exists only in one place.

There are two methods and one event that are needed to implement mouse capture functionality. The `setCapture` method is used to begin capturing mouse events by a particular element, and the `releaseCapture` method is called to end capturing of events. To begin capturing the mouse for an element, we use this syntax:

```
<SCRIPT LANGUAGE=VBSCRIPT>
  myElement.setCapture
</SCRIPT>
```

The `setCapture` method takes one Boolean parameter. The default value of `true` will cause all mouse events on the page to be handled by this object's event handlers. If the parameter value is `false`, then only mouse events on that particular object will be captured. All other mouse events on the page will be ignored.

When an element has captured the mouse, it will receive all of the normal mouse events. The `srcElement` property of the `event` object will refer to the element that was under the mouse when the event was fired, not the element capturing the mouse.

To stop capturing the mouse, we use the `releaseCapture` method. This can be called on either the element that has captured the mouse, or on the `document` object. We can therefore call this method on the document object, and end capturing at any time without having to explicitly reference the element that has captured the mouse. An element can also lose mouse capture automatically if a certain event takes place. These events are:

- Opening a context menu by right-clicking on the document
- Invoking the `alert` method in script
- Scrolling through the document
- Losing focus on the web browser window

When an element loses the mouse capture, the `onclosecapture` event is fired on the element that had captured the mouse. You can use this event to perform any cleanup that needs to be done, such as hiding an element that was serving as the drop-down menu or moving a dragged element into a specific position.

Using Mouse Capture

In this example, we will look at how to use mouse capture to create a popup window inside an HTML page. While previous versions of DHTML have allowed you to create menus using elements on top of other elements, it was always difficult to deal with handling mouse clicks while that menu was open. By using the `setCapture` method, we can create and handle a popup menu with very little code. Here is the HTML code that will display a popup menu:

```
<HTML>
<BODY>
<H1>Mouse Capture Example</H1>
<SPAN ID=MenuBth ONCLICK="openMenu();" STYLE="color:blue;">
<U>Click for menu</U>
</SPAN>
<P>
Here is some text for the menu to open over.
<P><I>This method has a number of advantages over event bubbling.
It makes support of drag-and-drop functionality much simpler.
In the past, if you were dragging an element and dropping it on
another element on the page, then both elements had to have the
proper scripting code in order to correctly handle the drag-and-drop...</I>

<DIV ID=popupMenu STYLE="visibility:hidden; text-align:center;
                          background-color:#DDDDDD; width:200;
                          position:absolute; border-style: groove;">
This is the popup menu.  If you click on the document, nothing will happen.
If you click on the menu, it will go away.</DIV>

<SCRIPT>
  function openMenu()
  {
    var x,y;
    x = event.clientX;
    y = event.clientY;
    popupMenu.style.posTop = y;
    popupMenu.style.posLeft = x;
    popupMenu.style.visibility = "visible";
    popupMenu.setCapture();
  }

  function popupMenu.onclick()
  {
    var src = event.srcElement
    if (src.id == "popupMenu")
    {
       popupMenu.style.visibility = "hidden";
       document.releaseCapture();
    }
  }
</SCRIPT>
</BODY>
</HTML>
```

There are three key components to creating the popup menu. First, there is the link on the screen that will handle the initial mouse click. When the user clicks on this element, it will display the popup menu:

```
<SPAN ID=MenuBth ONCLICK="openMenu();" STYLE="color:blue;">
<U>Click for menu</U>
</SPAN>
```

The second component is the popup menu itself. The menu is created as a `DIV` with a different background color and a visual border. Since the menu is normally not displayed, the `visibility` property of the `DIV` is set to hidden:

```
<DIV ID=popupMenu STYLE="visibility:hidden; text-align:center;
                         background-color:#DDDDDD; width:200;
                         position:absolute; border-style: groove;">
This is the popup menu.  If you click on the document, nothing will happen.
If you click on the menu, it will go away.</DIV>
```

The final component for creating the popup menu is the script code that will provide the interactivity. First, we need to handle the click that will display the menu:

```
function openMenu()
{
   var x,y;
   x = event.clientX;
   y = event.clientY;
   popupMenu.style.posTop = y;
   popupMenu.style.posLeft = x;
   popupMenu.style.visibility = "visible";
   popupMenu.setCapture();
}
```

One frill that has been added to this popup menu is the ability to position its top left corner at the place where the mouse was clicked. To do this, we will grab the position of the mouse from the `event` object, then set the top and left position of the popup menu `DIV` to that position. With the menu in place, we can display it by setting the `visibility` property to `visible`. Finally, we want to capture the mouse to this element by calling the `setCapture` method of the menu element itself.

Now that the mouse has been captured, we need an event handler to deal with the mouse clicks for the popup menu. Since we have captured the mouse to that element, *all* mouse clicks in the document will be fed to this event handler:

```
function popupMenu.onclick()
{
   var src = event.srcElement
   if (src.id == "popupMenu")
   {
      popupMenu.style.visibility = "hidden";
      document.releaseCapture();
   }
}
```

For this popup menu, the functionality is defined so that the menu will go away if the user clicks on it. If they click anywhere else in the document, the mouse click will be ignored. To accomplish this, we need to check the `srcElement.id` property of the `event` object. Remember that when the mouse is captured, this property will return the `ID` of the element that the mouse was over, not the element handling the event. If the mouse is clicked over the popup menu, then the `DIV` is hidden, and the mouse capture is released.

Working with Text Rectangles

Another user interface enhancement in IE5 is the ability to relate lines of text within a particular element to a physical location on the screen. This is done through the use of the `TextRectangle` element. This element defines a rectangle that encompasses a single line of text within the element. There are four properties of the `TextRectangle` object, and they define the `top`, `bottom`, `left`, and `right` positions of the element. These properties are a bit different from the style properties of an element – the style properties define the `top` and `left` position along with the `width` and `height` of the element, while the `TextRectangle` object defines the four corners of the object.

When a `TextRectangle` is created for an element, what is actually generated is a collection of `TextRectangle` objects. Each element in this collection is used to define the rectangle surrounding one line of text. To obtain a `TextRectangles` collection, you call the `getClientRects()` method on an element. For example, look at this block of text in an HTML page:

> **So far, we've covered a lot of the basics of Dynamic HTML. We've** *studied style sheets and style tags, looked at the new design opportunities they offer for static pages, discovered the object model that lurks inside the browser and how to get at it. We've also seen some* **ways of taking advantage of all these features. What we still haven't done is create any really wild dynamic pages.**

There is an `<I>` element in this block of text and there are three `TextRectangle` objects inside of this `<I>` element. The rectangle objects are:

- Rectangle 1: "studied style sheets and style tags,"
- Rectangle 2: "looked at the new design…that lurks"
- Rectangle 3: "inside the browser and how to get at it. We've also seen some"

If the browser window is resized, then all of the `TextRectangle` objects will change. You would need to handle the `onresize` event, and call the `getClientRects()` method to refresh the `TextRectangle` objects.

The `getBoundingClientRect()` method will return a rectangle that encompasses all of the `TextRectangle` objects in a collection. This will be the smallest rectangle that holds all of the text rectangles in the collection.

Text Rectangle Example

In this example, we will see how you can use the `TextRectangle` object to highlight selective areas of your page. We will be showing the example text we looked at earlier in an HTML page, and then cycle through highlighting each section of it.

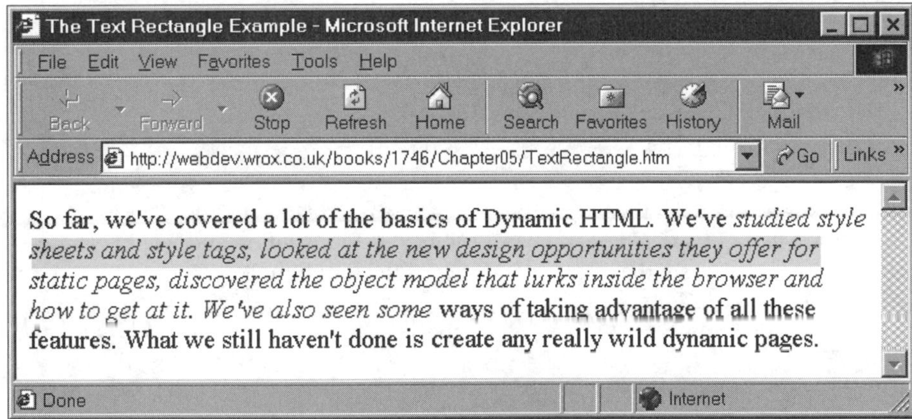

To make this page work, we have a block of text, a `DIV` element used as a highlight, and then some script code to determine the location of the highlight.

We need two text elements:

```
<DIV ID=divHilight STYLE="position:absolute; left:5; top:400;
                          z-index:0; background-color:'yellow';
                          display:'none'; zindex:-5;"></DIV>
<P STYLE="position:absolute;">
  So far, we've covered a lot of the basics of Dynamic HTML. We've
    <SPAN ID=myTR STYLE="font-style:italic;">
      studied style sheets and style tags, looked at the new design
      opportunities they offer for static pages, discovered the object model
      that lurks inside the browser and how to get at it. We've also seen
      some
    </SPAN>
  ways of taking advantage of all these features. What we still haven't done
  is create any really wild dynamic pages.
</P>
```

The first is a `DIV` named `divHighlight`. It is initially hidden, but will be moved and resized dynamically, then shown to provide the highlight. The other element is a block of text with an embedded `SPAN` tag that is adding an italicized text effect to the text.

The first step in the script code is to retrieve the collection of client rectangles that encompass the italicized portion of text in our page. We know how many rectangles are in the collection by examining the `length` property:

```
<SCRIPT>
var oRcts, iLength;
var iRight, iLeft, iTop, iHeight;
var iPos = 0;

function displayRects()
{
  oRcts = myTR.getClientRects();
  iLength= oRcts.length;
```

We maintain a counter value that denotes which rectangle is currently being highlighted. If this counter is past the end of the collection, then we will reset it to 0, hide the highlighting element, and then exit the function. You will see why we exit the function at this point:

```
  if (iPos >= iLength)
  {
    iPos = 0;
    divHilight.style.display = 'none';
    return;
  }
```

Next, we retrieve the bounding properties for the current text rectangle. These properties are its right and left positions, as well as its top position and height. These values are then used to set the position and size of the highlight `DIV`.

```
  iRight = oRcts[iPos].right;
  iLeft = oRcts[iPos].left;
  iTop = oRcts[iPos].top;
  iHeight = oRcts[iPos].height;

  divHilight.style.posLeft = iLeft;
  divHilight.style.top = iTop;
  divHilight.style.width = (iRight-iLeft) - 5;
  divHilight.style.posHeight = iHeight;
  divHilight.style.display = 'inline';
```

Once it has been sized and positioned, the highlighting element is made visible. We then need to set our position so that the next time the function is called, the next rectangle will be highlighted. To call the function again, we use the `setTimeout` method of the `window` object to call the `displayRects` function after five seconds have elapsed. Finally, we connect the `onclick` event of the document object to the `displayRects` function as the event handler:

```
  iPos = iPos+1;
  window.setTimeout("displayRects()", 5000);
}
document.onclick = displayRects;
</SCRIPT>
```

The Dancing Buttons Page

To finish off this chapter, we'll take a brief look at another example that uses events and style properties to provide a dynamic page – which includes moving button elements around, as well as moving images. We saw what this page does in Chapter 1, and here we'll see how some of the effects are achieved with techniques we've learned in this chapter. The full source for this example is available at the Wrox Press web site, at http://webdev.wrox.co.uk/books/1746.

The HTML that creates the Dancing Buttons page is simple enough. First, we define a single event handler for the `onmousemove` event in the `<BODY>` tag. Then comes the introductory text for the page, followed by an absolutely positioned division named `divDoc`, which contains two buttons and an image. These, again, are absolutely positioned within the division. Finally, a second division contains the horizontal rule and the copyright text for the bottom of the page:

```
<BODY BACKGROUND="bg.gif">

<FONT FACE="Arial">
<H2>Click a button to select where you want to go...</H2>
Try and click on the Competitor's Site button. When you get fed up..
..
</FONT>

<DIV ID="divDoc" STYLE="position:absolute; top:0; left:0;
                        width:600; height:350">
  <INPUT ID="btnTheirs" TYPE=BUTTON VALUE="Competitor's Site"
         ONCLICK="cmdTheirsClick()"
         STYLE="position:absolute; top:225; left:400; width:130; height:28">
  <INPUT ID="btnOurs" TYPE=BUTTON VALUE="Visit Our Site"
         ONCLICK="cmdOursClick()"
         STYLE="position:absolute; top:225; left:100; width:130; height:28">
  <IMG ID="imgWrox" SRC="wrox0.gif" NAME="imgWrox" WIDTH=100 HEIGHT=42
         STYLE="position:absolute; top:220; left:270">
</DIV>

<DIV STYLE="position:absolute; top:355; left:10; width:600; height:100">
  <HR><CITE>&copy; 1999 - Wrox Press Limited.</CITE>
</DIV>
```

Here's how the page appears when you first load it:

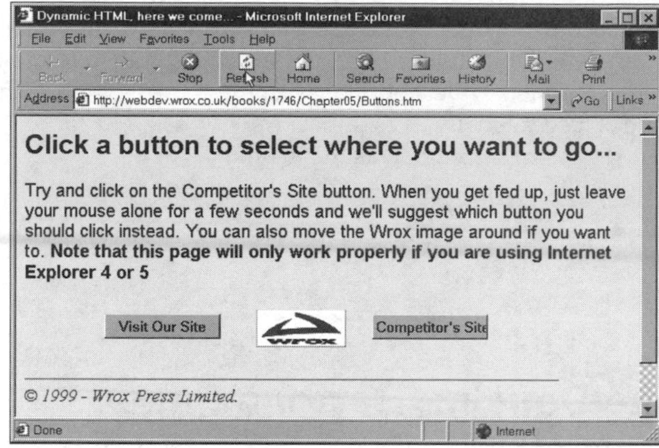

How It Works

Inside the <SCRIPT> section of the page, a subroutine is used to respond to the `onmousemove` event. We've switched to JavaScript for this example, so that you can see how it is used to reference the various items in the page:

```
function MouseMoveEvent()
{
  ...
  objDiv = document.all["divDoc"].style;
  ...
  if (event.srcElement.id == "imgWrox" && event.button == 1)
  {
    // move the Wrox image element around...
  }
  else
  {
    // move the Competitor's Site button away from the mouse pointer...
  }
};
```

Storing References to Objects

Notice how, in the first few lines of the code, we use the browser object model to get at the style properties that we are going to need for our page. We're using the `all` collection of the `document` object, which contains all the elements in the page. We refer to the document division we want, which we've given an `ID` of `divDoc` in the HTML, using `document.all["divDoc"]`. Remember that the window is the default object, so we don't need `window.document.all["divDoc"]` in this case.

However, the properties we want aren't *direct* element properties, but those stored in the element's `style` object. To get at this, we just add it to the end of the statement:

```
objDiv = document.all["divDoc"].style;
```

Now we have a reference to the division's `style` object, and we can use it to make our code more compact and easier to read. Instead of using `document.all["divDoc"].style.pixelWidth` to get the width of the division, we can simply use `objDiv.pixelWidth`.

Checking the Source Element

We want to allow the user to drag the Wrox logo around the page by holding down the left mouse button, but allow the mouse to 'chase' the Competitors Site button underneath the logo if they are not holding down the mouse button. To do this, we need to know two things: which element was the source of the `onmousemove` event, and was the left mouse button pressed at the time?

We've seen how to discover both of these things in this chapter. In our example, we use the `event` object's `srcElement` property to get a reference to the element that first received the event (the one the mouse pointer was over), and compare its `id` to that of our Wrox logo tag. At the same time, we check if the button parameter of the `onmousemove` event is `1`, indicating that the left button is pressed. If both are `true`, we move the logo. If not, we move the Competitors Site button away from the mouse pointer:

```
if (event.srcElement.id == "imgWrox" && event.button == 1)
{
  // move the Wrox image element around...
}
else
{
  // move the Competitor's Site button away from the mouse pointer...
}
```

Moving the Elements

Moving the Wrox logo is easy enough. Here's the code we use – it simply places some text in the window's status bar, then calculates the new horizontal and vertical positions for the image using the `pixelWidth` and `pixelHeight` properties and the `x` and `y` mouse coordinates. Below, we've reprinted the whole of the first part of the `MouseMoveEvent` function, so that you can see how we find out about the position of the image before we move it. We've set the values of three variables `dh`, `dw`, and `db` previously, to refer to the height and width of the document division, and the minimum distance we want to get to the edge of it. Once we've calculated the new position, we just assign it back to the image element's `pixelLeft` and `pixelTop` properties:

```
function MouseMoveEvent()
{
  db = 15;                          // how close to the edge
  objDiv = document.all["divDoc"].style;
  dw = objDiv.pixelWidth;           // main layer width
  dh = objDiv.pixelHeight;          // main layer height
  blnCreeping = false;              // and reset the global flag
  x = event.x;                      // get x and y position of
  y = event.y;                      // mouse pointer as of now
  lastX = x;                        // store x and y position of
  lastY = y;                        // mouse for timer routine
  if (event.srcElement.id == "imgWrox" && event.button == 1)
  {
    // move the Wrox image element around
    window.status = "Drag me to a new position";
    window.clearInterval(timMoveID);  // reset the creep interval
    timMoveID = window.setInterval("timMove()", 4000);
    objImage = document.all["imgWrox"].style;
    iw = objImage.pixelWidth;          // width of the image
    ih = objImage.pixelHeight;         // height of the image
    nx = x - (iw / 2);                 // new horizontal position
    if (nx < db) nx = db;              // stop at left and right edges
```

```
    if (nx > (dw - db - iw)) nx = (dw - db - iw);
    ny = y - (ih / 2);                // new vertical position
    if (ny < db) ny = db;             // stop at left and right edges
    if (ny > (dh - db - ih)) ny = (dh - db - ih);
    objImage.pixelLeft = nx;
    objImage.pixelTop = ny
  }
  else
    ...
```

Moving the Competitors Site Button

Moving the Competitors Site button follows the same process, but is complicated by the fact that we need to find out the position of the sides of the button in relation to the mouse pointer, and decide which direction to move it. In fact, there are around fifty lines of code to do all this, though the principle is no different to that of moving the image.

We just retrieve the current position, calculate the new position and assign it back to the buttons' `pixelTop` and `pixelLeft` properties. You can open and view the source code for the page to see it in detail, and we've commented it throughout to help you.

Reacting to Button Clicks

The only other code in this page that we want to consider is that for the two buttons. The Visit Our Site one is obvious – it just changes the window object's `location` object's `href` property, which loads the new page:

```
function cmdOursClick()
{
  location.href = "http://www.wrox.com"
};
```

The Competitors Site button shouldn't need any code, because the whole idea is that the user won't be able to get the mouse pointer over it. However, we're going to cover the occasion where they load the page into a browser that doesn't support Dynamic HTML:

```
function cmdTheirsClick()
{
  strMsg = "You aren't using InternetExplorer 4 or higher then ?\n" +
           "If you were, you wouldn't have been able to " +
           "click the button.\nTo see why you'll have to" +
           "install it and come back again...";
  alert(strMsg);
  location.href = "http://www.wrox.com"
};
```

For example, here it is running in Internet Explorer 3:

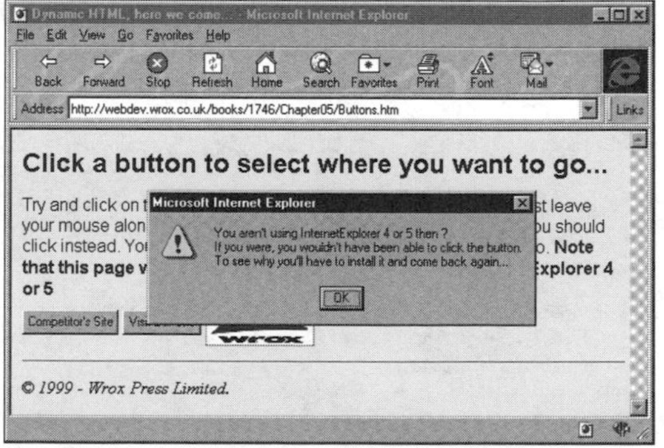

Moving the Visit Our Site Button

Of course, we haven't yet considered how the other dynamic effect of the page is achieved. If you stop moving your mouse for a few seconds, the Visit Our Site button creeps towards the mouse pointer. It's obviously not responding to an event that we are causing, because it happens when we aren't doing anything.

In fact, this event is powered by the browser's built-in interval timer—the `setInterval` and `clearInterval` methods that are part of the `window` object. If you look at the code for the page, you'll see that we have done a few extra things that aren't part of moving the Competitors Site button or the Wrox image.

At the start of the `<SCRIPT>` section, we declare three variables that will be global. We can store values in these variables that will be available all the time the page is loaded. The first is a flag to show if we are currently moving the Visit Our Site button, and the other two are the last known x and y positions of the mouse pointer as it passed over the page division:

```
<SCRIPT LANGUAGE=JAVASCRIPT>

var blnCreeping;     // our button is creeping
var lastX;           // last kown X position
var lastY;           // last know Y position
var timMoveID;       // timer reference variable
```

Working with Interval Timers

The last line of the code above declares and initializes an interval timer using the `setInterval` method of the widow object. This is very similar to the `setTimeout` method that was available in Internet Explorer 3 and other browsers, but fires repeatedly until cleared, rather than just firing once. The first parameter is the name of the function we want to execute when it fires, and the second is the time in milliseconds between firings.

In the `MouseMoveEvent` code, which runs when the user moves the mouse over our page, we have a few things to do. First, we set the global 'creeping' flag to false to indicate that our Visit Our Site button should not be moving while the user is moving the mouse. Secondly, we store the current position of the mouse pointer, ready for when they stop moving it. Thirdly, we clear our current interval timer, and reset it with a value of 4 seconds:

```
function MouseMoveEvent()
{
  ...
  dh = objDiv.pixelHeight;          // main layer height
  blnCreeping = false;              // and reset the global flag
  x = event.x;                      // get x and y position of
  y = event.y;                      // mouse pointer as of now
  lastX = x;                        // store x and y position of
  lastY = y;                        // mouse for timer routine
  if (event.srcElement.id == "imgWrox" && event.button == 1)
  {
    // move the Wrox image element around
    window.status = "Drag me to a new position";
    window.clearInterval(timMoveID);   // reset the creep interval
    timMoveID = window.setInterval("timMove()", 4000);
    ...
```

Now, four seconds after the user stops moving the mouse, the interval timer will fire and run our `timMove()` event code. This checks to see if the button is already moving (i.e. if `blnCreeping` is already `true`). Of course, it won't be the first time, because we set it to `false` in every `mousemove` event. Instead, our `timMove()` function sets it to `true`, and changes the interval from four seconds to one of less than a second:

```
function timMove()
{
  if (blnCreeping == true)
  {
    // Move the Visit Our Site button towards the mouse pointer
    ...
  }
  else
  {
    // Set the interval timer to a short interval
    blnCreeping = true;
    window.clearInterval(timMoveID);
    timMoveID = window.setInterval("timMove()", 200);
    window.status= "Please click me ...";
  };
};
```

After the interval has expired, the `timMove()` code runs again. This time `blnCreeping` is `true`, and so the first part of the function is executed instead. This simply mirrors the code used to move the **Competitors Site** button. You can open the page and view the source yourself to see it in detail.

```
  if (blnCreeping == true)
  {
    ...
    objDiv = document.all["divDoc"].style;
    dw = objDiv.pixelWidth;           // main layer width
    dh = objDiv.pixelHeight;          // main layer height
    objOurs = document.all["btnOurs"].style;
    hw = objOurs.pixelWidth / 2;      // half button width
    hh = objOurs.pixelHeight / 2;     // half button height
    nx = objOurs.pixelLeft;           // left of button
    ny = objOurs.pixelTop;            // top of button
    ...
    // calculate the new coordinates, nx and ny
    ...
    objOurs.pixelLeft = nx;           // move the button to
    objOurs.pixelTop = ny;            // the new position
  }
```

The process of moving the **Visit Our Site** button continues every 200 milliseconds until the user moves the mouse pointer again. This sets the interval back to four seconds, and clears the `blnCreeping` flag so that the whole cycle can be repeated.

> *Remember that you can try the **ListChange**, **Jigsaw** and **Buttons** pages – and download the complete code for these pages – by visiting our web site at **http://webdev.wrox.co.uk/books/1746**.*

Summary

In this chapter, we've spent a lot of time studying the basics we need to know to work with script code in Dynamic HTML. As you'll appreciate, scripting is at the heart of any Dynamic HTML page where we want to make it interactive, and responsive to the user. Only pages that use the positioning abilities of Dynamic HTML, and are not truly *dynamic*, can manage without some code.

Thankfully, the changes to the object model and workings of Dynamic HTML from earlier versions of browsers that supported scripting, mean that we can often create these exciting pages using very little actual script code. In particular, the new `event` object makes it easier to get information about the elements in the page, and manipulate them, than ever before.

We've seen how:

- **Events** are Windows' way of telling applications that something has happened
- The browser exposes many events to our script code through its **object model**
- We can respond to these events if we want to, or just ignore them
- Each element maintains a set of **properties** – either directly or through a `style` object – whose values we can access, and often change to make the page dynamic
- By default, all events bubble up through the browser object hierarchy, from the source element to the document
- We can use the `event` object to get information about an event, and prevent event bubbling taking place

With this chapter, we've completed our tour of the main parts of Dynamic HTML. It's now time to see some other techniques in action, and learn more about some of the other objects we haven't covered in depth so far. The next chapter begins this process by discovering how we can use the various properties of the elements in the page, and the `TextRange` object, to retrieve and manipulate the text and the page's contents.

6

Manipulating the Contents of the Page

With our coverage of how scripts and events worked in the previous chapter, we completed our overview of the basics needed to create attractive and dynamic web pages with Dynamic HTML. In Chapters 6 and 7 we'll be exploring some more advanced techniques, such as manipulating the text and other content in a page, using separate browser windows, and working with tables, forms and databases.

In this chapter we'll explore the final major difference between 'traditional' HTML and Dynamic HTML. As you'll already have discovered, Dynamic HTML makes almost all the elements of the page available to our scripting code – and this means that we can achieve all kinds of effects that just weren't possible before. One thing that we often want to get at is the normal text displayed in the page (either in the `BODY` of the document, or in things like lists and tables) – and that's the subject of this chapter.

In fact, one of our examples focuses directly on tables, and shows you just some of the things that are possible. Dynamic HTML is a language that offers so much freedom to work with the page that it's probably only the limits of your imagination that will hold you back.

In this chapter, we'll look at how we can:

- Reference and retrieve the text from a loaded page
- Change the text displayed in a document dynamically
- Search for text in a document that is displayed in the browser
- Manipulate the contents of HTML tables using scripting code

As we'll see in a moment, there are two basic methods for manipulating the actual contents of a document – and we'll cover both in this chapter.

Changing the Elements in a Page

In existing static HTML technologies, very little of the page's display is available to our script code. Having the ability to change the appearance of a web page by altering the displayed content *while it's displayed* is a huge advance. Now, we can actually get at almost anything that is displayed there – including the plain body text.

Up to now, almost everything we've done in Dynamic HTML has involved changing the properties of elements on-the-fly – either by changing the properties on the objects directly (such as the `src` of an image), or by changing the style properties (such as `pixelTop`).

However, neither of these techniques really changes the element itself. They simply change its appearance, by altering the way that the element is displayed or the source data that is used when it is rendered. But now, with Dynamic HTML, we can change the actual *content* of the element – even to the extent that it 'becomes' a different element. For example, we can change the text displayed in a normal paragraph on the page; we can even replace a text heading with a graphic.

The two methods we can use to achieve these kinds of effects are:

- Working with the content manipulation properties and methods, such as `innerText`, `outerHTML` and `insertAdjacentHTML`
- Working with `TextRange` objects that we create to refer to particular parts of the page

We'll look at these in the next two sections of this chapter.

Content Manipulation Properties and Methods

The easiest way to manipulate the contents of a page is to use the special properties that are supported by the majority of visible elements. These properties expose the contents of each part of the document to the page author – almost as they appear in the source code. By assigning new values to these properties, we can change the contents of the page that is being displayed.

By **document**, we mean a stream of characters that consists of both text and HTML, and represents the current page. Be careful not to confuse the document with the *actual* HTML source code. The browser translates the source code into its own representation of the page – the document – and then displays that. Thus, changing the contents of an element on the page does not update the original HTML source – just the browser's internal representation of it.

In fact, the examples later in this chapter show how the browser's internal representation of the page really does differ from the original HTML source.

The Element 'Content' Properties

There are four properties that are supported by most of the visual elements in the page:

Property	Description
innerText	The complete text content of the element, including the content of any enclosed element, but excluding any HTML tags. We can assign a new string to the `innerText` property. Note this replaces only the *content* of the element: any new HTML tags are rendered as text, and are not interpreted.
outerText	The complete text content of the element, including the content of any enclosed elements and the surrounding HTML tags. It returns the same string as `innerText`, but assigning a new string to it replaces the entire element, including the HTML tags. As with `innerText`, any new HTML tags are rendered as text, and are not implemented.
innerHTML	The complete text and HTML content of the element, including the content of any enclosed element. Assigning a new string to it replaces only the content of the element, and HTML tags within it are rendered correctly.
outerHTML	The complete text and HTML content of the element, including the start and end tags of the element and the entire text and HTML content of any enclosed element. It returns the same string as `innerHTML`, but assigning a new string to it replaces the entire element, including the HTML tags. The HTML content of the new string is rendered correctly.

You can see that there are two 'classes' of property: those that preserve the HTML tags within the element and those that ignore them. Which we use depends on the task we want to accomplish. We'll use JScript in our following examples to illustrate what the different properties do.

The innerText Property

For example, suppose we have an HTML source that contains a simple element such as the following heading:

```
<H3 ID=Heading1>This is my Heading</H3>
```

In this case, we can use the `innerText` property to change the text in the heading to And this is my NEW Heading:

```
objHead1 = document.all["Heading1"];
objHead1.innerText = "And this is my NEW Heading";
```

This preserves the original `<H3>` tags, and only replaces their content. However, if the heading also contained additional formatting, we would also need to contend with that – and so we would consider using the `innerHTML` property instead. Why is this?

Well, let's see what happens if we try to persist with `innerText`. For example, suppose that this was the original HTML source:

```
<H3 ID=Heading1>This is <I>my</I> Heading</H3>
```

and we apply the same action to it:

```
objHead1.innerText = "And this is my NEW Heading";
```

In this case, we'll lose the formatting of the `<I>` and `</I>` tags, because the `innerText` (and `outerText`) properties don't preserve it. Conceptually, the resulting HTML will be:

```
<H3 ID=Heading1>And this is my NEW Heading</H3>
```

In fact, if we use `innerText` to try to change the assignment to include the HTML tags we want, like this:

```
objHead1.innerText = "And this is <I>my</I> NEW Heading";
```

we *still* get the wrong result. In this case the page will display the heading And this is <I>my</I> NEW Heading – in other words the `<I>` and `</I>` tags will be visible as text, and the word my will not be italic. Remember that `innerText` and `outerText` do not interpret any HTML within the strings – it's just rendered as text.

The innerHTML Property

OK, let's try using the `innerHTML` property instead of `innerText`. This gives is the result we want:

```
objHead1.innerHTML = "And this is <I>my</I> NEW Heading";
```

This is because the 'HTML' content properties cause the browser to interpret any HTML within the strings correctly. In fact, it's worth noting that they are clever enough to force the new content to be structurally correct – although we might not get quite the result we want. For example, if we only provide an opening `<I>` tag in our new content, the browser will add the closing `</I>` tag automatically to prevent the rest of the page being affected. Using:

```
objHead1.innerHTML = "And this is <I>my NEW Heading";
```

will actually produce the following conceptual HTML:

```
<H3 ID=Heading1>And this is <I>my NEW Heading</I></H3>
```

Of course, this time the words NEW Heading will also be rendered as italic – so while the browser has corrected the structural error in our code, it's failed to guess that we actually wanted the closing `</I>` tag to go after the word `my`. Later in this section we'll be using a simple example page to show you more about how these properties work. You can also use this example page to experiment with the properties yourself.

> **Not every visible element supports all four 'content' properties – some only support the 'text' properties. Others may offer read-only support for some properties – for example the `<TD>` tag (as you'll see later) supports `outerText` as a read-only property.**

The Element insertAdjacent Methods

As well as the four properties mentioned above, the following two methods can also be used to change an element's contents (these are supported by many of the visible elements):

Method	Description
`insertAdjacentText`	Inserts text into or adjacent to the element. Any HTML tags are interpreted as text. Text can be inserted at the start or end of an element within the element's tags, or immediately before or after the element – outside its opening and closing tags.
`insertAdjacentHTML`	Inserts text and HTML into or adjacent to the element. HTML within the string is correctly rendered after insertion. Text and HTML can be inserted at the start or end of an element within the element's tags, or immediately before or after the element – outside its opening and closing tags.

You can immediately see that in some respects these two methods mirror the workings of the content properties we saw in the previous section. The first disregards an HTML content (rendering it as plain text), while the second causes the browser to render it correctly. The syntax of the methods is:

```
object.insertAdjacentText(where, text_to_insert)
object.insertAdjacentHTML(where, HTML_and_text_to_insert)
```

The *`where`* parameter controls where the new content is inserted. It is a string that can be one of the following:

Parameter value	Meaning
`"BeforeBegin"`	Immediately before the element's opening tag.
`"AfterBegin"`	Immediately after the element's opening tag.
`"BeforeEnd"`	Immediately before the element's closing tag.
`"AfterEnd"`	Immediately after the element's closing tag.

Again, the `insertAdjacentHTML` method will preserve the structure of the document, by adding a closing tag if it is omitted in the new string. However, this again may not behave exactly as you would expect. For example, if we use the `insertAdjacentHTML` method to insert a `<B>` tag before the beginning of an element, with the intention of inserting the `</B>` tag after the end, we don't actually get any formatting of the element's content:

```
objHead1.insertAdjacentHTML('BeforeBegin', '<B>');
```

This results in the following conceptual HTML:

```
<B></B><H3 ID=Heading1>And this is <I>my NEW Heading</I></H3>
```

A Content Manipulation Sample Page

So that you can experiment with the various document manipulation techniques, and see their results, we've provided a sample page for you to try out. It's called `DocChange.htm`, and you can run it or download it from our web site at http://webdev.wrox.co.uk/books/1746.

When you first load it, you see a single line of formatted text, and a selection of text boxes, lists and buttons:

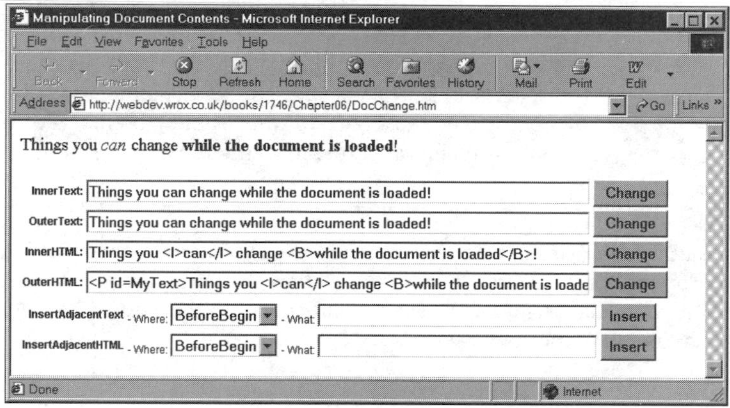

The first four controls show the content properties of the line of text at the top of the page. You can see that the `innerText` and `outerText` properties are the same. This is what we would expect because they only return the *text* content, and ignore any HTML. Therefore, even though the `outerText` property 'includes' the opening and closing tags, these don't appear in the value of the property. However, there is a reason for providing both, as you'll see in a while.

The HTML Part of the Page

The page is created using tables and traditional HTML controls. We've defined an event handler for the `ONLOAD` event of the page by placing its name, `DisplayProperties()`, in the `<BODY>` tag. It is used to fill the text boxes with the current property values when the page is first loaded. After it, you can see the text and HTML with a `<P>` and `</P>` tag pair that creates the line of formatted text at the top of the page:

```
<BODY ONLOAD="DisplayProperties()">

<P ID=MyText>Things you <I>can</I> change
<B>while the document is loaded</B>!</P>

<TABLE>
<TR>
  <TD ALIGN=RIGHT><B>InnerText:</B></TD>
  <TD><INPUT ID=txtIText TYPE=TEXT SIZE=70></TD>
  <TD><INPUT ID=cmdIText TYPE=BUTTON VALUE="Change"
             ONCLICK="UpdateProperties(this)"></TD>
</TR>
...
  HTML for other content properties controls are placed here...
...
</TABLE>
```

Each of the four content properties has a text box and a button – when the button is clicked, the `UpdateProperties()` code runs. We'll look at this code later on. The rest of the HTML part of the page consists of the code to create the `insertAdjacentText` and `insertAdjacentHTML` controls. In these two cases, the buttons are connected to two code routines named `InsAdjText()` and `InsAdjHTML()` (not shown):

```
<TABLE>
<TR>
  <TD ALIGN=RIGHT><B>InsertAdjacentText</B></TD>
  <TD> - Where:
    <SELECT ID=lstTPosn SIZE=1>
      <OPTION SELECTED>BeforeBegin</OPTION>
      <OPTION>AfterBegin</OPTION>
      <OPTION>BeforeEnd</OPTION>
      <OPTION>AfterEnd</OPTION>
    </SELECT>
  </TD>
  <TD> - What: <INPUT ID=txtInsText TYPE=TEXT SIZE=38></TD>
  <TD><INPUT TYPE=BUTTON VALUE="Insert" ONCLICK="InsAdjText()"></TD>
</TR>
...
  HTML for insertAdjacentHTML control is placed here...
...
</TABLE>
```

The remainder of the page is the `<SCRIPT>` section that does all the work. We'll look at that in the following subsections.

Displaying the Property Values

The first thing our code has to do is retrieve the values of the four content properties when the page first loads. This is done in the `DisplayProperties()` function, which is attached to the `ONLOAD` event of the document as we saw earlier. Here's the complete function:

```
function DisplayProperties()
{
  objSampleText = document.all("MyText");
  if (objSampleText == null)
  {
    document.all["txtIText"].value = null;
    document.all["txtOText"].value = null;
    document.all["txtIHTML"].value = null;
    document.all["txtOHTML"].value = null
  }
  else
  {
    document.all["txtIText"].value = objSampleText.innerText;
    document.all["txtOText"].value = objSampleText.outerText;
    document.all["txtIHTML"].value = objSampleText.innerHTML;
    document.all["txtOHTML"].value = objSampleText.outerHTML
  }
}
```

All we do is create a reference to the `<P>` element named `MyText` at the top of the page, then check that it actually exists. Yes, this seems odd, because we know it's there – we wrote it in the original HTML. But remember, this is a dynamic page and, like your waistline, it might not be there forever. If it has disappeared, we place the value `null` in each text box. Otherwise, we can look up the relevant property for each one and drop it in instead.

Updating the Property Values

So, let's see what happens when we update a property – starting with the simplest one.

Changing the innerText Property

In the next screen shot, you can see that we've changed the `innerText` property:

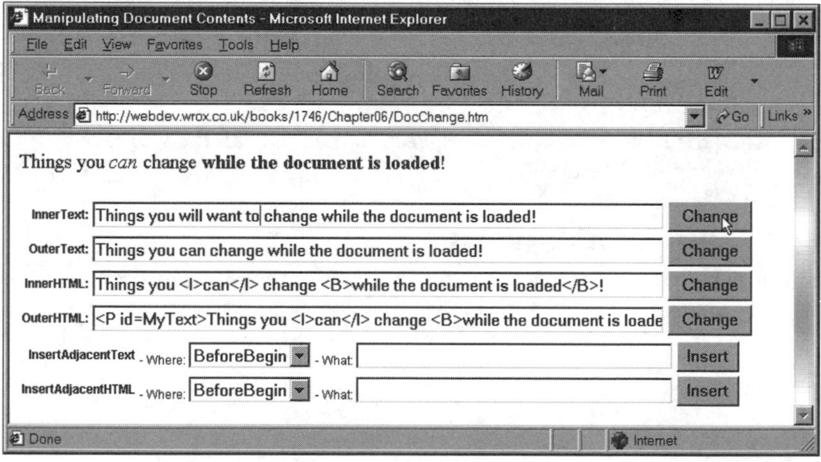

Clicking the Change button updates the property of the `<P>` element named `MyText` and then updates all four property text boxes to reflect the new values:

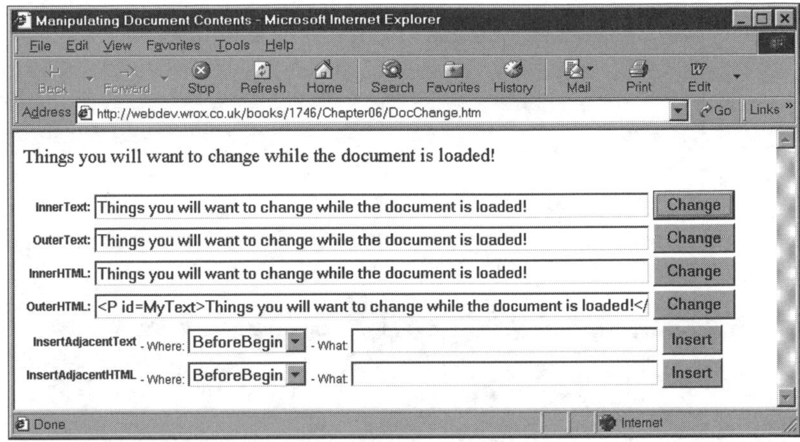

The first thing to notice is that, as we'd expect, all four properties have changed. However, the text itself has lost its formatting, and in the outerHTML property you can actually see that the <I> and <B> tags have disappeared. This is, of course, because we've assigned only text to the contents of the element – replacing the original text and HTML. Also, because the text is now unformatted the innerHTML property contains the correct text but has lost all of the HTML tags.

The UpdateProperties() Function

The `UpdateProperties()` function updates the properties – it's simple enough, and follows the same pattern as the `DisplayProperties()` function we looked at earlier. There is a major difference, which uses the fact that each Change button provides a reference to itself as a parameter to our function, using the `this` keyword:

```
<TD><INPUT ID=cmdIText TYPE=BUTTON VALUE="Change"
          ONCLICK="UpdateProperties(this)"></TD>
```

In the function, we use this parameter to find the `ID` of the button, and we can then use this `ID` to decide which text property to update. Once we've done that, we call the `DisplayProperties()` function to update all four text boxes again:

```
function UpdateProperties(objButton)
{
  strButtonID = objButton.id;
  objNewSample = document.all["MyText"];
  if (objNewSample == null)
  {
    document.all["txtIText"].value = null;
    document.all["txtOText"].value = null;
    document.all["txtIHTML"].value = null;
    document.all["txtOHTML"].value = null
  }
  else
  {
    if (strButtonID == "cmdIText")
       objNewSample.innerText = document.all["txtIText"].value;
    if (strButtonID == "cmdOText")
       objNewSample.outerText = document.all["txtOText"].value;
```

```
    if (strButtonID == "cmdIHTML")
      objNewSample.innerHTML = document.all["txtIHTML"].value;
    if (strButtonID == "cmdOHTML")
      objNewSample.outerHTML = document.all["txtOHTML"].value;
  }
  DisplayProperties()
}
```

Changing the outerText Property

So now let's try changing the `outerText` property. Here, we've Refreshed the page, then edited the outerText text box, and we are ready to click the Change button:

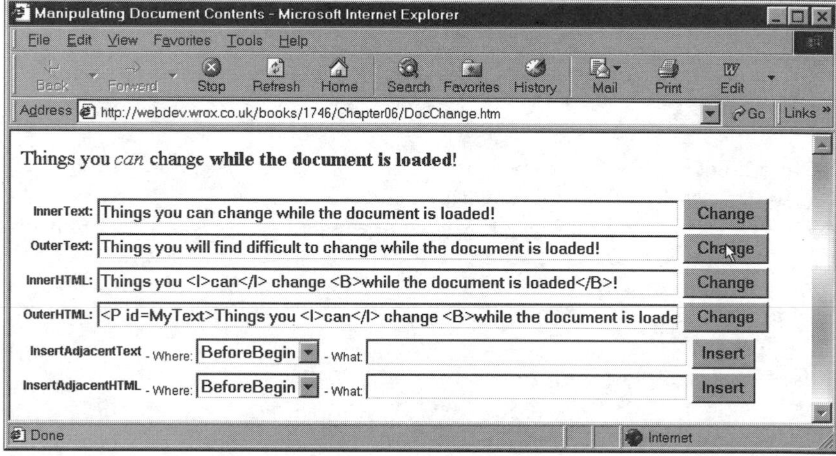

The result may come as a bit of a shock – all the properties are now `null`:

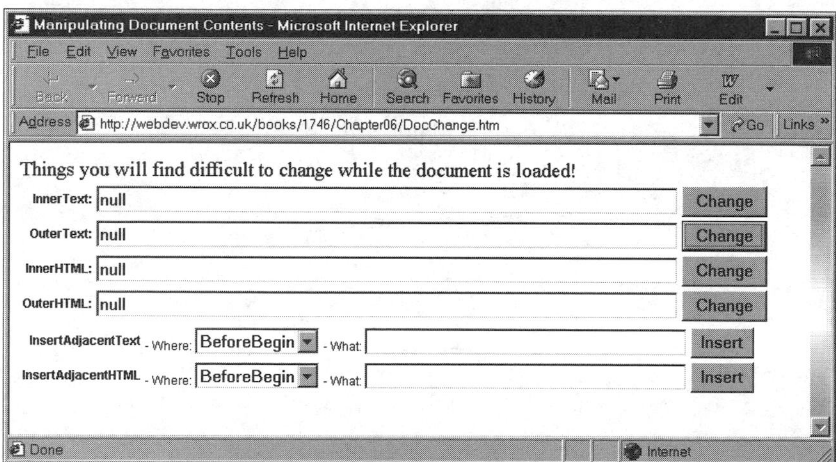

What's happened is that we've replaced the entire element with just text, removing the start `<P>` and end `</P>` tags:

```
objNewSample = document.all["MyText"];
...
  if (strButtonID == "cmdOText")
    objNewSample.outerText = document.all["txtOText"].value;
```

By removing the <P> tag, we've also removed the object's `ID` – and consequently the element no longer exists within the document. (It's still in the original HTML source, but it has been removed from the browser's `document` object.) Only the new text we assigned to the property remains. When we test for the existence of the element in our `DisplayProperties()` function, we find that it has been removed (it's null).

Thus, the `outerText` property is useful when we want to remove elements from the page altogether.

Changing the innerHTML Property

OK, it's time to get to the really clever stuff. This time, we'll add some new HTML to the page, within the existing tag. When we change the `innerHTML` property, the new value is interpreted by the browser as HTML. Therefore, we can do almost anything we like as long as it doesn't contravene the structure rules of HTML (for example, we can't place a <P> tag within another <P>..</P> element). You'll first need to reload the original HTML source again for this part of the example – just do this by hitting the Refresh button.

In the screen shot, you can see that we've edited the innerHTML text box to insert an <IMG> tag within the property:

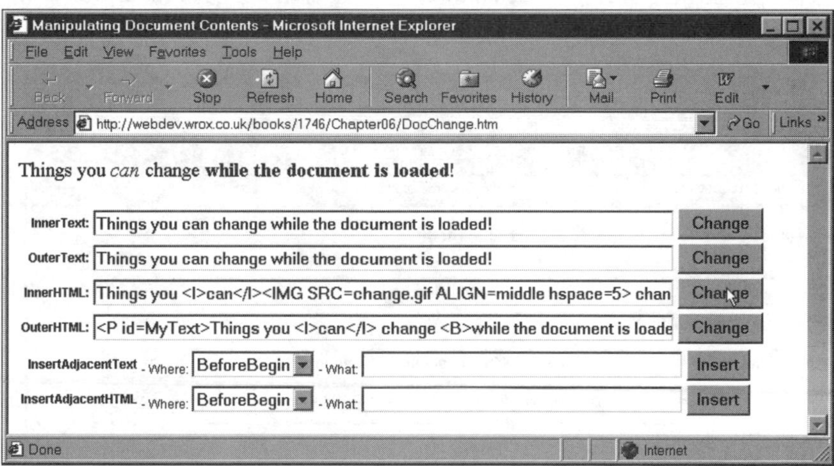

Clicking Change updates the property, and displays the new <P> element with our graphic included. It also, of course, displays the values of all four content properties as they now stand:

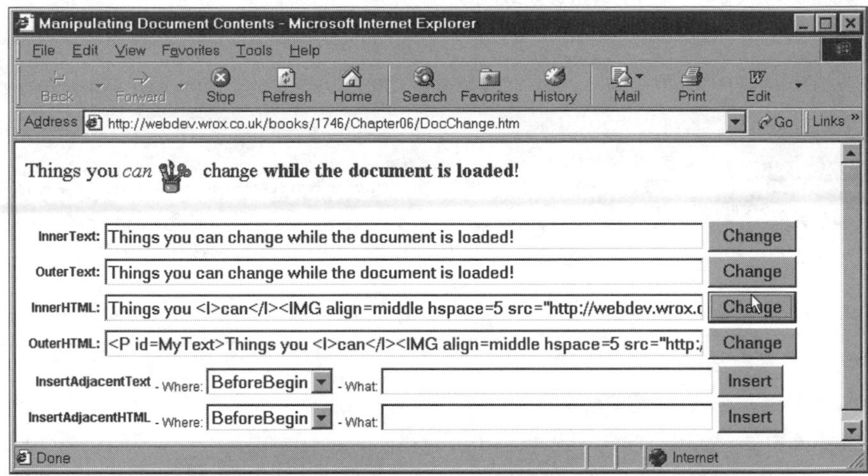

Notice how the innerHTML and outerHTML properties now include the new <IMG> tag, but not in the same format as that we entered – the ordering of the attributes is different and they are now all lower-case. Internet Explorer 5 is interpreting the HTML and placing it in its own internal representation of the page in its own format.

Changing the outerHTML Property

The final property we can change is outerHTML. Refresh the page one more time; then simply change the <P> and </P> tags into <H3> and </H3> tags in the OuterHTML text box (in this screen shot, </H3> is just off the textbox):

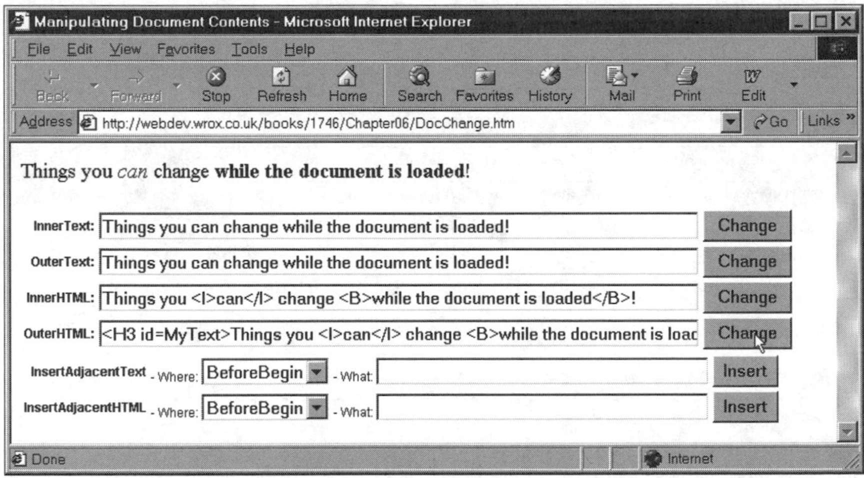

Clicking the Change button produces the result that you will be expecting:

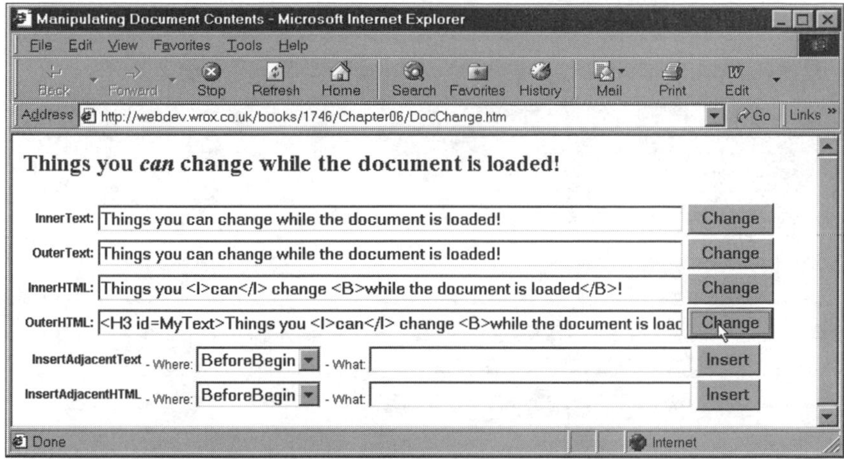

Of course, we can't change the `ID` of the element in our example, because the `DisplayProperties()` function would then fail: the `MyText` element it was looking for would not exist. However, there is no reason why we can't change the `ID` in other pages we create, allowing us complete freedom to redesign the page dynamically while it is loaded.

The insertAdjacentText and insertAdjacentHTML Methods

The sample page also allows us to experiment with the `insertAdjacentText` and `insertAdjacentHTML` methods. For each one, we can select where we want to insert the new values from a drop-down list.

Using the insertAdjacentText Method

In the screen shot below, we're adding some text after the beginning of our `MyText` element with the `insertAdjacentText` method:

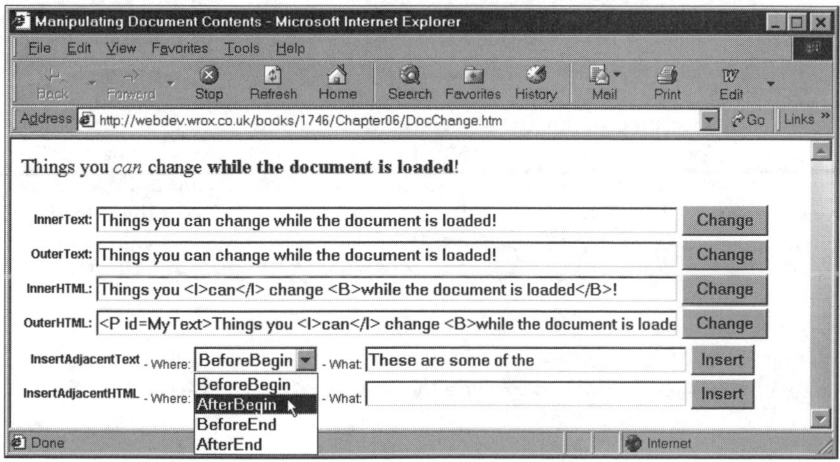

Here's the result. You can see that the four content properties are also updated, as you'd expect:

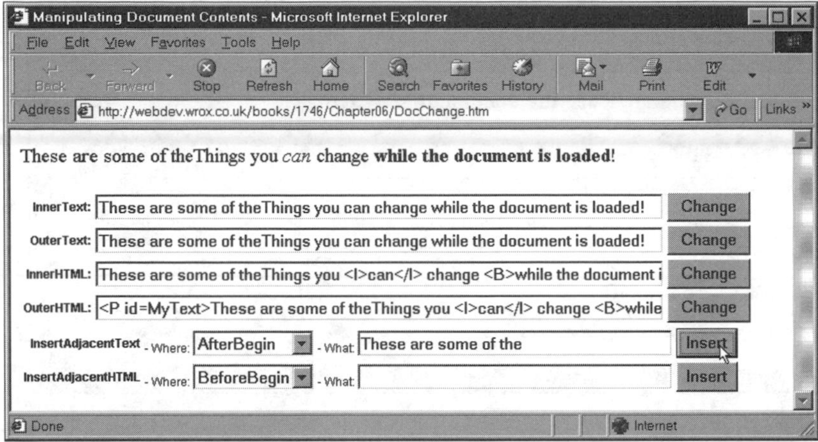

The InsAdjText() Function

The execution of the `insertAdjacentText` method is done by a function in the `<SCRIPT>` section of our page, which runs when the appropriate Insert button is clicked:

```
<INPUT TYPE=BUTTON VALUE="Insert" ONCLICK="InsAdjText()">
```

The function itself is simple enough:

```
function InsAdjText()
{
  objNewSample = document.all["MyText"];
  if (objNewSample == null)
    return;
  intPosn = document.all["lstTPosn"].selectedIndex;
  strPosn = document.all["lstTPosn"].options[intPosn].text;
  strText = document.all["txtInsText"].value;
  objNewSample.insertAdjacentText(strPosn, strText)
  DisplayProperties()
}
```

Here, we create a reference to the `MyText` element first using the `all` collection of the `document` object as before. Then we retrieve the `selectedIndex` property of the drop-down Where: list to find out the index of the currently selected option. Using this index with the list element's `options` collection gives us the value of the selection as a text string – in our case it's `"AfterBegin"`. Then we can retrieve the value of the What: text box and call the `insertAdjacentText` method of the `MyText` heading object.

The function for the `insertAdjacentHTML` method is almost identical, but uses the other set of controls on the page to provide the arguments to the method.

Using the insertAdjacentHTML Method

The `insertAdjacentHTML` method is very useful when we want to add HTML *as well as* text, or when we want to create a new element in the page. In the next screen shot, we've used it to add a new `<H2>` heading line above our existing `<P>` element:

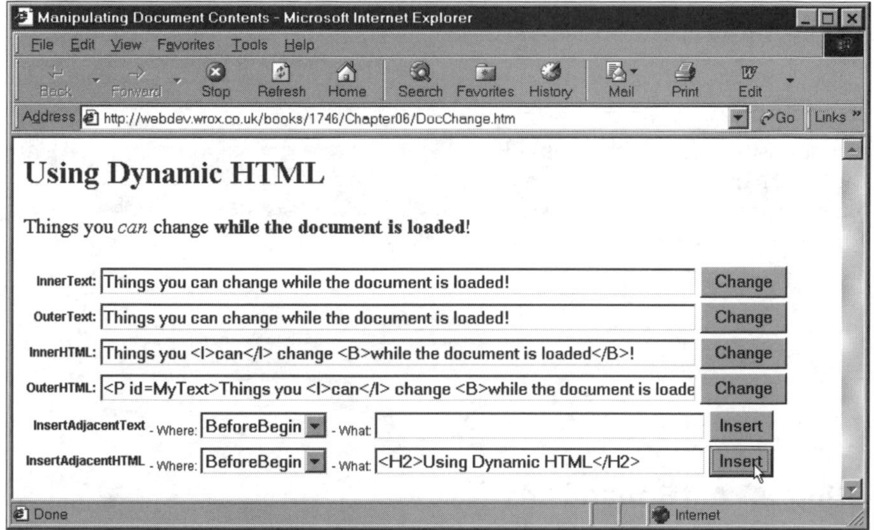

The `insertAdjacentHTML` method is useful if we need to add new elements to our pages. It generally does this more reliably than the `outerHTML` property, since it will not remove the existing element as setting the `outerHTML` property will do. The big advantage of the `insertAdjacent...` methods is that we don't have to read the existing property and add the new text or HTML to it first. However, if we want to just change part of the content of the element, it's often easier to read the `innerHTML` or `outerHTML` properties and manipulate them in code, then write them back to the element.

> *Here's one thing to watch out for when you add or remove elements in a page – note that all the element collections are updated at the same time. So, if you remove the third image from a page, the* `images` *collection will shrink by one, and what was previously* `document.images[3]` *will become* `document.images[2]`*! If you have stored the collection index in a variable, you'll get the wrong element when you access it later in your code.*

Working with TextRanges

As we mentioned at the top of the chapter, there are two ways to manipulate the contents of the page dynamically. The first uses the `inner...`, `outer...` and `insertAdjacent...` methods discussed above; the second is the `TextRange` object. We very briefly mentioned text ranges back in Chapter 4. They provide another method of adding and removing elements from a page, and changing the contents of a document. We'll be using them throughout the remainder of this chapter.

What is the TextRange Object?

The `TextRange` object is really just a block of text in a document referred to by its start and end points. It's very important to remember that the `TextRange` object doesn't actually hold a copy of the text and elements it encloses – it points to the beginning and the end of a block of text that is part of the document. By using its properties and methods, we can manipulate the text and elements that are encompassed by these references.

As a simple graphical example, consider the diagram opposite. It shows conceptually how the `TextRange` object keeps track of the contents of the document, and can therefore retrieve or change them as required:

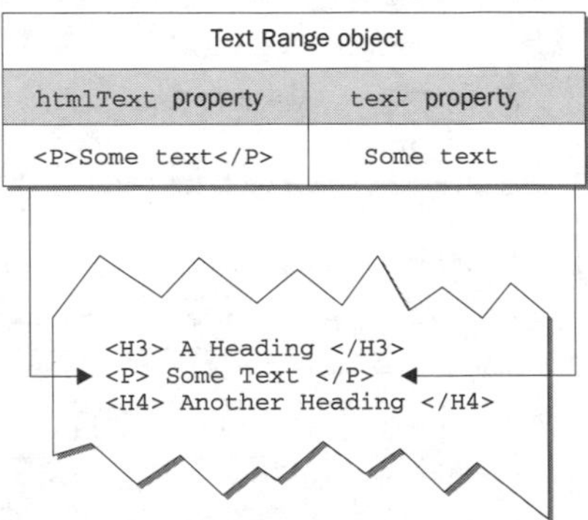

Creating a TextRange

We can create a `TextRange` object in three different ways, as outlined below.

Using the createTextRange Method

First, we can use the `createTextRange` method on the document's `BODY` element to create a range covering the entire body of the document, or on an individual `TEXTAREA`, `BUTTON` or `INPUT` (with its `TYPE` set to `button`, `hidden`, `password`, `reset`, `submit` or `text`) element in the page. These are the only elements that support the `createTextRange` method:

```
objMyBodyRange = document.body.createTextRange();
objMyTextAreaRange = document.all["MyTextArea"].createTextRange();
objMyButtonRange = document.all["MyButton"].createTextRange();
objMyTextInputRange = document.all["MyInput"].createTextRange();
```

Every visible element has an `isTextEdit` property, which is `true` only for the elements that support the `createTextRange` method.

Using the duplicate Method

Alternatively, we can create a copy of an existing `TextRange` using the `duplicate` method:

```
objCopyOfRange = objMyRange.duplicate;
```

Using the createRange Method on a selection

Finally, we can create a `TextRange` object from a `selection` object. This allows us to modify the text in a selection using the methods of the `TextRange` object:

```
objTRSelection = document.selection.createRange;
```

Moving a TextRange

We can change the contents of a `TextRange` by moving the start and end positions. This means that we are effectively reselecting the text and elements that the `TextRange` refers to, but *not* changing the actual text itself. We can do this with the following techniques:

- Using the `expand`, `collapse`, `move`, `moveStart`, `moveEnd` or `setEndPoint` methods to change either the start position, end position, or both together
- Using the `moveToBookmark`, `moveToElementText` or `moveToPoint` methods to change the `TextRange` to cover a different part of the document
- Using the `findText` method to move the `TextRange` to cover some text that we've searched for in the page

We'll look at some of these methods in the following subsections.

The expand Method

The `expand` method accepts a string parameter indicating the range that we want to expand the existing `TextRange` by. The parameter can be `"character"`, `"word"`, `"sentence"` and `"textedit"`. For example, if you want to ensure that a `TextRange` encompassed an entire sentence, you could call the `expand` method with a parameter of `sentence`. This would move the start of the text range to the beginning of the first word in the sentence and move the end of the range to after the terminating punctuation:

```
blnSuccess = objMyRange.expand("sentence");
```

The last of these possible parameter values, `"textedit"`, resets the range to its original position, when it was first created.

The move... Methods

The three `move...` methods (`move`, `moveStart` and `moveEnd`) accept an optional string parameter indicating the unit we want to move the start or end position by, and the number of these units that we want to move. The parameter can be `"character"`, `"word"`, `"sentence"` and `"textedit"`. Each of the `move...` methods returns a number that indicates how many units were actually moved by the method. Notice that we can specify a negative number in the second parameter – this allows us to move things backwards in the document (if we omit the optional second argument the value 1 is assumed). When the unit is `"textedit"`, the second argument is never required.

```
lngNumberMoved = objMyRange.move("word");
lngNumberMoved = objMyRange.move("sentence", 3);
lngNumberMoved = objMyRange.moveStart("character", -10);
lngNumberMoved = objMyRange.moveEnd("textedit");
```

The setEndPoint Method

If we want to move the start or end of a range to a position occupied by the start or end of a second `TextRange` object, we can use the `setEndPoint` method instead. The `setEndPoint` method is used as shown below: its first argument indicates which end of the first range to move, and which end of the second range to use:

```
objMyRange.setEndPoint("StartToStart", objOtherRange);
objMyRange.setEndPoint("EndToEnd", objOtherRange);
objMyRange.setEndPoint("StartToEnd", objOtherRange);
objMyRange.setEndPoint("EndToStart", objOtherRange);
```

Thus, for example, the last of these commands moves the end position of `objMyRange` to coincide with the start position of `objOtherRange`.

The collapse Method

We can shrink a `TextRange` to a single point (by moving the end to coincide with the start, or *vice versa*) – to do this we use the `collapse` method. After calling this method, the `start` and `end` properties will refer to the same point. We specify `true` or `false` for the *start* parameter, to decide which end to collapse it to:

```
objMyRange.collapse(true);  // collapse to start of the current range
objMyRange.collapse(false); // collapse to end of the current range
```

Using Bookmarks

We can create a **bookmark** in a document, so that this refers to the text that is currently referenced by a `TextRange` object. Then, later on in our code, we can move this or another existing `TextRange` object to reference the same parts of the document:

```
strMyBookmark = objMyRange.getBookmark();
blnSuccess = objMyRange.moveToBookmark(strMyBookmark);
```

Moving to an Element or a Point

Alternatively, we can move an existing `TextRange` object to reference a particular element within our page. This element must already be within an existing `TextRange`, which we effectively shrink to cover just the element. The easiest way to do this is to create a `TextRange` covering the entire `BODY` of the page first:

```
objMyBodyRange = document.body.createTextRange();
objMyBodyRange.moveToElementText(MyElement);
```

If we want to pick out the word or part of a document that is at a particular point in the page, such as under the mouse pointer, we can use a two-step approach. First, use the `moveToPoint` method to shrink a `TextRange` object to a single character (the start and end positions are the same) at the *x* and *y* positions we provide as arguments. Second, use the expand method to expose the relevant element.

Note that the `moveToPoint` method only works if the point lies within the existing range of the `TextRange` object – so again, the easiest way to use this method is to create a `TextRange` covering the entire `BODY` of the page first:

```
objMyBodyRange = document.body.createTextRange();
objMyBodyRange.moveToPoint(event.x, event.y);
objMyBodyRange.expand("sentence");
```

This code uses the mouse pointer position, as stored in the `x` and `y` properties of the `event` object, and then expands the `TextRange` to cover the word under the mouse pointer.

Finding Text in a Range

The `findText` method takes a single string argument – the text to be searched for – and positions the range to cover that text:

```
blnSuccess = objMyRange.findText("Find This Text");
```

If it doesn't find a match, it returns `false` and doesn't move the range. Since the `TextRange` object can include HTML as well as displayed text, you can use this to search for HTML elements.

Determining TextRectangle objects for the Range

The `TextRange` object supports the same methods for determining its `TextRectangle` objects as do HTML elements. We looked at this in Chapter 5. The `getClientRects` method will return a collection of `TextRectangle` objects that bound each line in the `TextRange`.

Getting Information About a TextRange

Once we've created our `TextRange` object, or moved it to a new position, we can get information about the current text and elements it refers to, in the following ways:

- By querying the `text` or `htmlText` properties to get the contents of the range as a string
- By using the `parentElement` method to retrieve the element that completely contains all of the text range
- By using the `compareEndPoints`, `isEqual` and `inRange` methods to see if the current range is equal to, or contains, another range
- By determining the dimensions of a rectangle encompassing a `TextRange` on the page by using the bounding properties
- By using the `offsetLeft` and `offsetTop` properties to determine if the `TextRange` is visible (or if it has scrolled off the screen)

We'll look at a couple of these possibilities in the following subsections.

Comparing Ranges

The `compareEndPoints` method accepts a string parameter, rather like the `setEndPoint` method, that defines which ends of the two `TextRange` objects are to be compared:

```
objMyRange.compareEndPoints("StartToStart", objOtherRange);
objMyRange.compareEndPoints("EndToEnd", objOtherRange);
objMyRange.compareEndPoints("StartToEnd", objOtherRange);
objMyRange.compareEndPoints("EndToStart", objOtherRange);
```

The `compareEndPoints` method returns a value: -1 if the existing `TextRange` endpoint is before the other one in the document, 0 if it is the same, and 1 if it is after the other one.

If two `TextRange` object cover exactly the same part of a document, the `isEqual` and `inRange` methods both return `true`. However, if the first range is smaller than (and completely within) the second range, only the `inRange` method will return `true`:

```
objMyRange.isEqual(objOtherRange);
objMyRange.inRange(objOtherRange);
```

Bounding Rectangles for Text Ranges

A new feature of text ranges in Internet Explorer 5 is the support for a bounding rectangle. As you saw in Chapter 5, a bounding rectangle will give you the coordinates that surround an object. You can also get that information about a `TextRange` object. There are four properties that define the bounding rectangle:

Property	Description
`boundingTop`	The top coordinate of the bounding rectangle, with respect to the parent container (in pixels)
`boundingLeft`	The left coordinate of the bounding rectangle, with respect to the parent container (in pixels)
`boundingHeight`	The height of the bounding rectangle (in pixels)
`boundingWidth`	The width of the bounding rectangle (in pixels)

These properties are read-only, so you can't change the position of a `TextRange` on the page by modifying these properties.

Manipulating the Contents of a TextRange

We can also use three other of the `TextRange` object's methods:

- If the range is outside the visible area of the window, we can bring it into view in the browser by using the `scrollIntoView` method.
- We can highlight the contents of the range on the screen (as though the user had dragged over it with the mouse) with the `select` method.
- We can replace the contents of the range with our own text and HTML using the `pasteHTML` method, or by assigning a new string to the `text` property.

Using Range Commands

One feature of text ranges that we won't be covering in detail is the ability to carry out a command on the text. This is designed for situations where the browser is being used as an embedded object, or control, within another application, and allows the application to edit the text in the page without worrying about the HTML format.

For example, the application could make the text within a `TextRange` object bold by executing the `execCommand` method of the `TextRange` object. There are also matching methods that determine if a command is supported and enabled, what state it is in, and the text representation and value of the command.

```
if (objMyRange.queryCommandEnabled)
  objMyRange.execCommand("Italic")
```

TextRange Object Summary

Here's a list of the properties and methods of the `TextRange` object that we use most often. You'll find a full alphabetical listing of them all in Appendix A of this book.

Property	Description
`boundingHeight`	Retrieves the height of the rectangle that bounds the object.
`boundingLeft`	Retrieves the left of the rectangle that bounds the object.
`boundingTop`	Retrieves the top of the rectangle that bounds the object.
`boundingWidth`	Retrieves the width of the rectangle that bounds the object.
`htmlText`	Returns the contents of a text range as text and HTML source.
`offsetLeft`	Returns the calculated left position of the object relative to its parent, as affected by the scrolled window position.
`offsetTop`	Returns the calculated top position of the object relative to its parent, as affected by the scrolled window position.
`text`	Returns the plain text contained within the text range.

Method	Description
`collapse`	Shrinks a text range to either the start or end of the current range.
`compareEndPoints`	Compares two text ranges and returns a value indicating the result.
`duplicate`	Returns a duplicate of a text range object.
`expand`	Expands a text range by a character, word, sentence or textedit so that partial units are completely contained.
`findText`	Sets the start and end points of a text range to cover the text, if found within the current document.
`getBookmark`	Returns a unique bookmark value to identify that position in the document.
`getBoundingClientRect`	Retrieve a rectangle that bounds all of the `TextRectangle` objects in the range.
`getClientRects`	Returns a collection of `TextRectangle` objects that encompass the range.
`inRange`	Denotes if the specified text range is within or equal to the current text range.
`isEqual`	Denotes if the specified text range is equal to the current text range.
`move`	Changes the start and end points of a text range to cover different text.
`moveEnd`	Causes the text range to grow or shrink from the end of the range.
`moveStart`	Causes the text range to grow or shrink from the beginning of the range.
`moveToBookmark`	Moves a text range to encompass the range referenced a bookmark value previously defined with `getBookmark`
`moveToElementText`	Moves a text range to encompass the text in the element specified.
`moveToPoint`	Moves and collapses a text range to the point specified in x and y relative to the document.
`parentElement`	Returns the parent element that completely encloses the current text range.

Method	Description
`pasteHTML`	Pastes HTML and/or plain text into the current text range.
`scrollIntoView`	Scrolls the text range into view in the browser, optionally at the top of the window.
`select`	Makes the active highlighted selection in the page equal to the current text range.
`setEndPoint`	Sets the start or end point of the text range based on the start or end point of another range.

A TextRange Example Page

To give you a better idea of how we use the `TextRange` object, try this example that is available from our web site at http://webdev.wrox.co.uk/books/1746. It displays some text about an exciting new authoring language, while demonstrating some of the things the `TextRange` object can easily achieve:

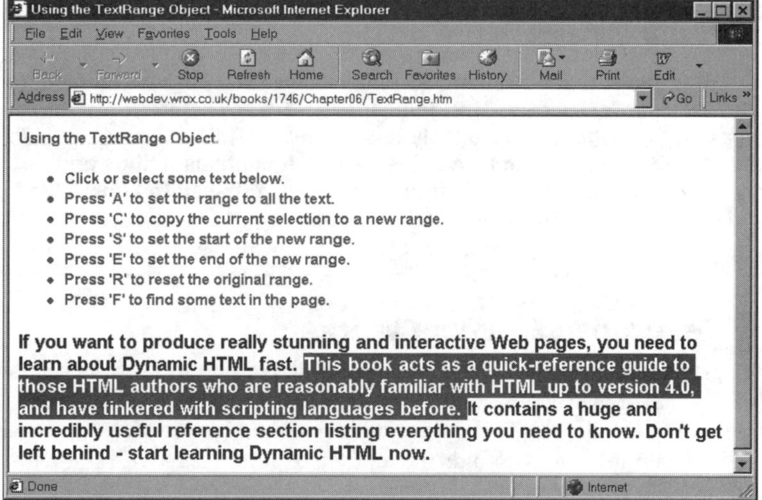

What the TextRange Example Does

In the screenshot, we've selected a text block (or text range) by clicking on the paragraph (before This) and pressing the *S* key, then clicking again (after before.) and finally pressing the *E* key. The code in the page turns this text white with a red background. We can get the same effect by dragging over the text to select part of it in the usual way, then pressing *C*. We can also change the selection by changing the start and end points afterwards. Pressing the *R* key removes all highlighting from the text, while pressing *A* selects all the text in the paragraph.

Finally, we can search for text in the whole page by pressing the *F* key. This brings up an input box, where we enter the text to find. Clicking OK selects the found text (this time in green) and displays it in the window's status bar:

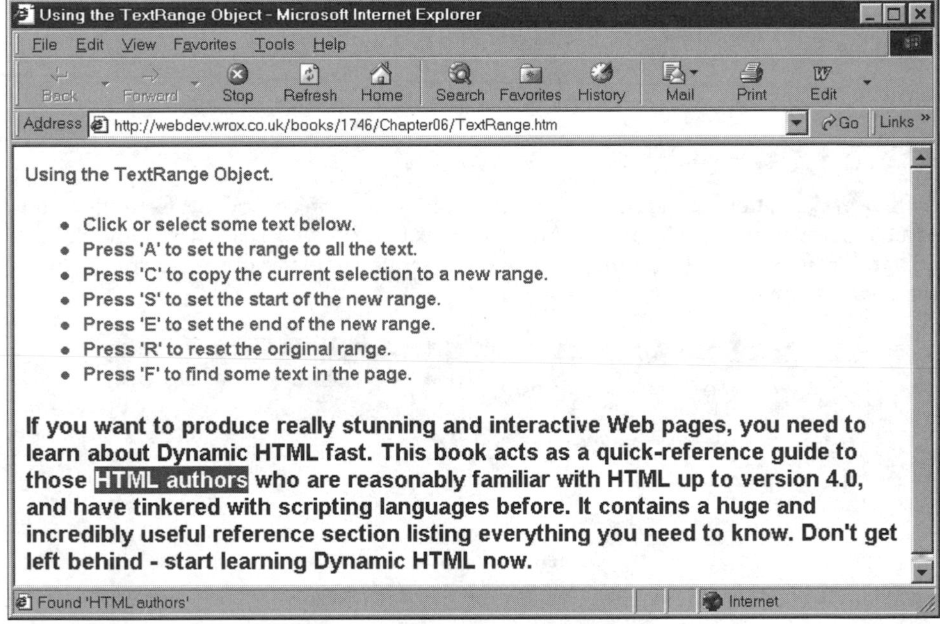

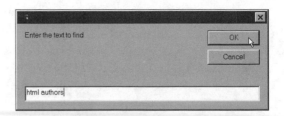

How the TextRange Example Works

The visible part of the page itself is simple, consisting of an `<H3>` heading section, a `<UL>` unordered list of instructions and a paragraph of text. We've used a `<STYLE>` tag to define the style of the text in the heading tag. We define the style separately for the single `<P>` paragraph tag that holds the text we're going to be working with:

```
<P ID=MyText STYLE="font-family:Arial, sans-serif; font-weight:bold">
If you want to produce really stunning and interactive Web pages, you need to
learn about Dynamic HTML fast. etc...
</P>

<SCRIPT LANGUAGE=VBSCRIPT>

Dim objMyRange
Dim objSavedRange
Dim strOriginalText

Set objSavedRange = document.body.createTextRange()
objSavedRange.moveToElementText(MyText)
strOriginalText = objSavedRange.HTMLtext
...
```

Inside the `<SCRIPT>` section, we've defined three variables that will be **global** – these will retain their values while the page is displayed. The last three lines shown above are also outside any subroutine or function, and so will be executed as the page is loaded. The first two create a new `TextRange` object from the body element and then shrink it to cover just the `MyText` paragraph element. This `TextRange` object is assigned to the global variable `objSavedRange`. The final line here retrieves the HTML and text from that range – the original text in the page once it has loaded – using the `HTMLtext` property. This is stored in the global variable `strOriginalText`.

Responding to a Key Press

Our page works by responding to a key-press from the user, so we need to create a routine to handle the `onkeypress` event for either the `<P>` element or the `document` object. We've chosen to react to the `document`'s event, so that we can show you how the `parentElement` method works. Here's the main event handler routine, with the code for each key-stroke removed for clarity:

```
...
Sub document_onkeypress()
  Set objSelRange = document.selection.createRange
  strTagName = objSelRange.parentElement.tagName
  if window.event.keyCode = 82 or window.event.keyCode = 114 then _
    ' "R" - reset text to original style
    Set objMyRange = document.body.createTextRange()
    objMyRange.moveToElementText(MyText)
    objMyRange.pasteHTML strOriginalText & "</P>"
    objMyRange.collapse True     'go to start of text
    Exit Sub
  end if

  If strTagName = "P" Or strTagName = "FONT" Then
    If IsEmpty(objMyRange) Then
      Set objMyRange = objSelRange.duplicate
    End If

    Select Case window.event.keyCode
      Case 65, 97          ' "A" - set range to all text
        ... code for key-stroke A here ...
      Case 67, 99          ' "C" - copy all selection to range
      ...   code for key-stroke C here ...
      Case 83, 115          ' "S" - set start of range
      ...   code for key-stroke S here ...
      Case 69, 101          ' "E" - set end of range
      .  .. code for key-stroke E here ...
      Case 70 , 102          ' "F" - find text in objMyRange
        ... code for key-stroke F here ...
    End Select
    document.selection.empty
  End if
End Sub
```

Each time we detect a downward key-stroke, we start by saving the user's current selection from the page into a `TextRange` object named `objSelRange`, by calling the `createRange` method of the `selection` object. We saw this done back in Chapter 4, where we examined the `selection` object in some depth. It gives us a reference to where the text cursor is on the screen, even if the user hasn't dragged to highlight any text – but it only works if they have clicked on the paragraph first.

Tracking Down the parentElement

Next, we need to check if the selection we've retrieved is within our `MyText` paragraph element. The `parentElement` method returns the closest (or innermost) element for the current selection, and we use the `tagName` property to get the text name of the tag. It will be `P` when we start off, but might at some point – as you'll see in a while – be `FONT`. If it matches one of these two, then we will continue our processing:

```
  strTagName = objSelRange.parentElement.tagName
...
  If strTagName = "P" Or strTagName = "FONT" Then
```

Notice that the `tagName` property always returns the tag as upper case, even if it's lower-case in the HTML source of the page.

Checking for an Empty Object Variable

If our code is still running at this point, we know we have something to do – so we can check if we've got an existing `TextRange` set up from the last time the user pressed a key. Because we're saving the `TextRange` between key-presses in a global variable, we have to see if this is the first key-press since the page was loaded. If it is, we need to initialize our `TextRange` this time only, and we do this by checking if the global variable is storing an object reference or is 'empty'. The VBScript `IsEmpty` function returns `true` if the variable we specify as its argument does not refer to an object. In this case, we assign a copy of the current contents of the `objSelRange` (the current selection) to it:

```
    If IsEmpty(objMyRange) Then
      Set objMyRange = objSelRange.duplicate
    End If
```

The final section of the code is just the `Select Case` construct that determines which code will be executed, depending on the ASCII value of the key-stroke. This is retrieved from the `event` object's `keyCode` property, as you saw in Chapter 5.

Setting the Start or End Position

If the user pressed *S* (start of range) or *E* (end of range), we need to change the start or end position of the current `TextRange` object, `objMyRange`. This is done using the `setEndPoint` method of the `TextRange` object, which means that we need an existing range that has the correct start or end point already. The answer, as before, is the `selection` object. At the start of the event routine we set it to the current selection on the page, so we know where the text cursor is within our paragraph:

```
  Set objSelRange = document.selection.createRange
```

To change the start of the current range in `objMyRange`, we simply execute the `setEndPoint` method with the value `"StartToStart"` or `"EndToEnd"`, depending on which end we want to set:

```
Case 83, 115         ' "S" - set start of range
  objMyRange.setEndPoint "StartToStart", objSelRange
  strNewText = "<FONT STYLE=""color:white; background:red"">" & _
                            objMyRange.text & "</FONT>"
  objMyRange.pasteHTML strNewText
Case 69, 101         ' "E" - set end of range
  objMyRange.setEndPoint "EndToEnd", objSelRange
  strNewText = "<FONT STYLE=""color:white; background:red"">" & _
                            objMyRange.text & "</FONT>"
  objMyRange.pasteHTML strNewText
```

Displaying the Selection

Once we've got our `TextRange` object pointing to the correct text, we can create the string that will produce the white-on-red text to indicate the current range. We simply enclose the current text, retrieved from the `objMyRange` object's `text` property, in a `<FONT>` tag – specifying the style we want for it. Then we replace the current text with the new string using the `pasteHTML` method.

> **In fact this doesn't always work, because it leaves existing `<FONT>` and `</FONT>` tags in the HTML – before and after the new range. This means that after a few operations, the page stops responding correctly, as you may have discovered. Also, if you set the end of a range to the end of a word, then the space gets dropped because it is ignored by the HTML parser. However, it serves to demonstrate the techniques without clouding the issue with extra complexity.**

Selecting All the Text

If the user presses the *A* key, we need to change our current range to include the whole paragraph. We've done this by simply re-creating the `TextRange` object to point to the complete paragraph `MyText`, then pasting into it the `<FONT>` tags and the existing text and HTML from the `text` property. This removes any leftover `<FONT>` and `</FONT>` tags that might have been embedded into the page previously. Because the user is selecting all the range, and some of it might be off-screen if they have resized the browser window, we finish up by using the `scrollIntoView` method to bring it into view:

```
Case 65, 97          ' "A" - set range to all text
  Set objMyRange = document.body.createTextRange()
  objMyRange.moveToElementText(MyText)
  strNewText = "<FONT STYLE=""color:white; background:red"">" & _
                            objMyRange.text & "</FONT>"
  objMyRange.pasteHTML strNewText
  objMyRange.scrollIntoView
```

Copying the Current Selection

Pressing *C* makes the current range equal to the users on-screen selection. All we have to do is to `duplicate` the copy of the user's screen selection from `objSelRange`, and add the `<FONT>` tags and paste it into the page:

```
Case 67, 99          ' "C" - copy all selection to range
  Set objMyRange = objSelRange.duplicate
  strNewText = "<FONT STYLE=""color:white; background:red"">" & _
                            objMyRange.text & "</FONT>"
  objMyRange.pasteHTML strNewText
```

Resetting and Removing the Highlighted Range

Pressing *R* removes all the highlighting from the page, and sets the current range to a single point in the paragraph. This is done early in the event handler so that it works even if nothing has been selected. We do it by creating a new range in objMyRange from the MyText paragraph element, then paste into it the text we originally saved in strOriginalText when the page was loaded. Then we shrink our range to the start of the paragraph using the collapse method:

```
if window.event.keyCode = 82 or window.event.keyCode = 114 then
  ' "R" - reset text to original style
  Set objMyRange = document.body.createTextRange()
  objMyRange.moveToElementText(MyText)
  objMyRange.pasteHTML strOriginalText & "</P>"
  objMyRange.collapse True    'go to start of text
  Exit Sub
end if
```

Finding Text in the Document

The final user option is to search for text in the whole document by pressing the *F* key. In this case, we first set the current range to the entire text block named MyText, then display an input box to collect the string to search for. Providing the user doesn't leave it empty ("") we can look for it in the document.

To search for the given string, we create a new TextRange object that covers our <P> paragraph element, as before. This time we've named it objFoundRange. Then we can display the InputBox, and check if we got any input. If the user clicks Cancel, or doesn't enter any text, the result will be an empty string:

```
  Case 70 , 102        ' "F" - find text in objMyRange
    Set objFoundRange = document.body.createTextRange()
    objFoundRange.moveToElementText(MyText)
    strFind = InputBox("Enter the text to find", "")
    If strFind <> "" Then
      If objFoundRange.findText(strFind) Then
        strNewText = "<FONT STYLE=""color:white; background:green"">" & _
                               objFoundRange.text & "</FONT>"
        window.status = "Found '" & objFoundRange.text & "'"
        objFoundRange.pasteHTML strNewText
        objFoundRange.scrollIntoView
      End If
    End If
```

Providing we've got a string to search for, we just have to call the findText method of the TextRange object. It returns true if the text was found, and we can go on to surround it in the <FONT> tag we want this time, and paste it into the page. The final task is to update the status bar, and scroll the found text into view in the browser.

Creating Dynamic Tables

Working with HTML tables and their contents isn't a whole lot different from working with the plain text in the page. This shouldn't be surprising, because tables are just a heap of HTML <TABLE>, <TH>, <TR> and <TD> tags anyway. We can use the techniques we've seen in this chapter to manipulate them as easily as we manipulate text.

The rows and cells Collections

What makes tables interesting, however, is that Dynamic HTML finally brings the concept of rows and columns to a table created with HTML tags. We can use the `rows` and `cells` collections to access individual rows and cells in a table whenever we like:

`rows`	Collection of all the rows in the table, including those in the <THEAD>, <TBODY> and <TFOOT> sections.
`cells`	Collection of all the <TH> and <TD> cells in the row of a table.

Using the Collections

These collections work in the same way as the collections we've met throughout the book. We can access individual rows in the `rows` collection using the `ID` of the <TR> element for that row, or using an index number (starting at zero for the first row). We can loop through the rows using the `For Next` construct. Each row in the `rows` collection is an element representing that <TR> tag, and has its own `cells` collection representing the cells in that row.

The `cells` collection is accessed in the same way, using the `ID` of the <TD> or <TH> tag, or using an index number (that representing the cell's position in the row – the left-most cell is indexed zero). Each object in the `cells` collection is an element representing the <TD> or <TH> tag.

A Dynamic Table Sample Page

We've provided a sample page named `Table.htm` that demonstrates how we can use the `rows` and `cells` collections, and follows up on the techniques we've seen earlier in this chapter. You can run it directly from our web site at http://webdev.wrox.co.uk/books/1746.

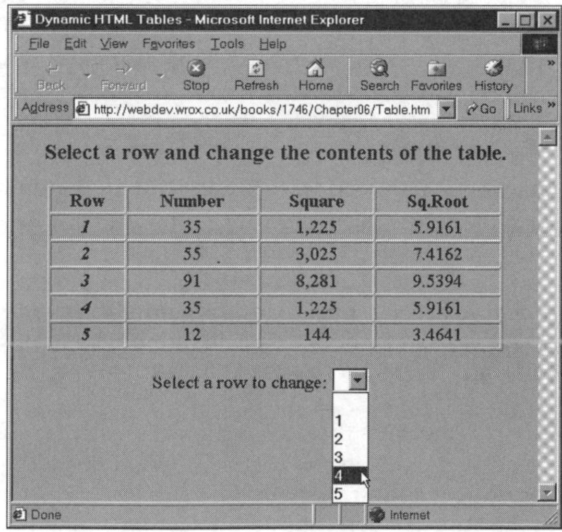

The Initial Page

As you can see, the page consists of a simple table containing five numbered rows. Each row contains a whole number between 0 and 100, plus the value of its square and square root. The numbers change each time you refresh the page, and so we've got a dynamic page that is obviously not created by ordinary HTML. In fact, it uses techniques that have been impossible with scripting code in earlier versions of HTML.

Writing a Dynamic Page

To create the table, we used script code plus VBScript's random number generator. Here's the HTML for the first part of the page, starting with the normal HTML `<TABLE>` tag and the `<TH>` tags for the heading row:

```
...
<TABLE ID=MyTable WIDTH=90% ALIGN=CENTER BORDER=1>
<TR><TH>Row</TH><TH>Number</TH><TH>Square</TH><TH>Sq.Root</TH></TR>

<SCRIPT LANGUAGE=VBSCRIPT>
'Create the initial table using random numbers
Randomize
For intRow = 1 To 5
  intNumber = CInt(Rnd * 100) + 1
  strTableRow = "<TR ALIGN=CENTER><TD ID=MyRow" & CStr(intRow) & "><I><B>" _
              & FormatNumber(intRow, 0) & "</B></I></TD>" _
              & "<TD ID=MyNumber" & CStr(intRow) & ">" _
              & FormatNumber(intNumber, 0) & "</TD>" _
              & "<TD ID=MySquareNumber" & CStr(intRow) & ">" _
              & FormatNumber(intNumber * intNumber, 0) & "</TD>" _
              & "<TD ID=MySqrtNumber" & CStr(intRow) & ">" _
              & FormatNumber(Sqr(intNumber), 4) & "</TD></TR>"
  document.write strTableRow
Next
</SCRIPT>

</TABLE>
...
```

After the heading row you'll see there is a script section containing a `For..Next` loop, which is executed as the page is being rendered. With each iteration, the code in the loop creates a string `strTableRow`, which contains the complete HTML code for one row in the table. Then it just has to display it in the page using the `write` method of the `document` object.

Creating the Initial Table Rows

Before starting the loop, we use `Randomize` to seed the random number generator, and prevent the same results appearing every time. Then the code in our `For...Next` loop is repeated five times to get the five numbered rows.

First it calls the `Rnd` function, which returns a random number greater than or equal to zero and less than one. We convert this into a whole number by multiplying by 100, taking the integer result, and adding one.

Now we can create the table row. First there's a center-aligned `<TR>` tag, and then a `<TD>` tag with the `ID` set to `MyRow`*x* – where *x* is the row number. Then we insert the row number itself, formatting it as a string with the `FormatNumber` function. We're using a simple form of this function here, supplying just the numeric value to convert and a parameter indicating the number of decimal places we require.

The latest version of VBScript (5.0), as supported by Dynamic HTML and Active Server Pages, provides several number formatting functions. `FormatNumber` *is a very useful function, and allows us to specify the number of decimal places to include, whether to include leading zeros, how negative numbers should be represented, and how to group the digits. There are also new functions to format dates, percentages and currency values.*

We continue adding the `<TD>` tags for each cell to the string, including an `ID` for each one. As we go along, we use the random number calculated for that row, and the calculated square and square root values. In the final cell, we format the value to four decimal places.

Adding the Row Selector

Once the table is complete, we add a document division containing the HTML drop-down list element. This contains the row numbers, plus an empty option so that no number is displayed when the page is first loaded. As we are going to respond to the list's `onchange` event, we need the user to make a choice in the list to start our code running:

```
...
<DIV ID=MyDiv STYLE="position:absolute; top:260; left:150;
                     width:300; height:100">
Select a row to change:
<SELECT ID=lstSelect STYLE="width=40">
  <OPTION VALUE=0></OPTION>
  <OPTION VALUE=1>1</OPTION>
  <OPTION VALUE=2>2</OPTION>
  <OPTION VALUE=3>3</OPTION>
  <OPTION VALUE=4>4</OPTION>
  <OPTION VALUE=5>5</OPTION>
</SELECT>
</DIV>
...
```

Updating the Table Contents

That's the original page complete, and now we need to consider how we update a row. Making a choice in the row selector drop-down displays an input box. This shows the row number and the current value, and allows a new value to be entered. The current value is also highlighted in the original table:

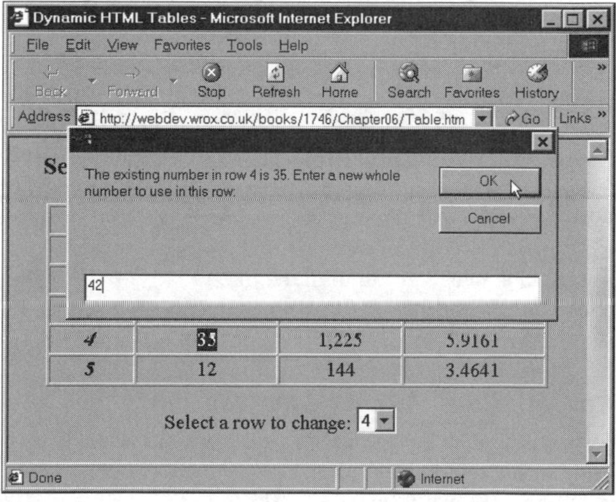

Retrieving the Current Value

Here's the code that runs when a selection is made in the drop-down list. First we collect the user's row selection from this list, which is a string, and convert it into a number. If they have selected the empty entry at the top of the list, we just exit from the routine. Otherwise, the value is stored in the variable `intRow`. Then, we can start the process of retrieving the current value from the table:

```
...
<SCRIPT LANGUAGE=VBSCRIPT>
Sub lstSelect_onchange()
  intRow = CInt(lstSelect.value)
  If intRow = 0 Then Exit Sub
  Set colTheRow = document.all("MyTable").Rows(intRow)
  Set objTheCell = colTheRow.Cells(1)
  Set rngExisting = document.body.createTextRange()
  rngExisting.moveToElementText(objTheCell)
  rngExisting.select
...
```

The `all` collection of the `document` object holds all the elements in the page. One of these is the table we created, and named `MyTable` in the `ID` attribute of the `<TABLE>` tag. This table element is the parent of all the rows in the table, and it has a `rows` collection. We use this to get an object reference to the selected row into a variable `colTheRow`. Once we've got the row, we can reference the members of the `cells` collection for that row. We want the cell indexed `1` (which is in the second column), and we've assigned it to the object variable `objTheCell`.

The next part of the code should look familiar. Once we've got a reference to an element, we can create a `TextRange` for it like we did in our earlier examples. Once this is done, we highlight it on screen using the `select` method of our new `rngExisting` object.

Why Don't We Use the 'Content' Properties?

You may be wondering why we've used `TextRanges` again here to get at the contents of a table cell. There are two reasons for this. First, we want to be able to select the cell contents, so that they are highlighted on screen. This can only be done using the `select` method of a `TextRange` object.

Second, we intend to change the text that makes up the contents of the cell. For most visible elements, we would do this by assigning a new string to the `innerHTML` property. In the prior versions of DHTML, the `<TD>` tag, and most other parts of a table, didn't support this property – they only supported the `innerText` property. But with the release of IE5 and its version of DHTML, this restriction has been removed.

In our case, we're going to make the updated row of the table display in bold. We could use either the `innerHTML` property, or use a `TextRange`. For this example, we will be using a `TextRange`.

Collecting and Validating the New Value

Now it's time to get the new value from our user. We display an `InputBox`, and check that they didn't leave it blank, or press the Cancel key. If they did, the `If..Then` statement skips the rest of the routine.

Next we check if the text they entered can be converted to a valid number – and if it can, that it's between 1 and 99. If either of these tests fail, a suitable message box is displayed. If all is still OK, we can get on and update the table:

```
  strPrompt = "The existing number in row " & intRow _
            & " is " & rngExisting.text & ". Enter a new whole" _
            & " number to use in this row:"
  strNewNumber = InputBox(strPrompt, "")
  If strNewNumber <> "" Then
    If IsNumeric(strNewNumber) Then
      intNewNumber = CInt(strNewNumber)
      If (intNewNumber > 0) And (intNewNumber < 100) Then
        'code to update the table cell in the page
      Else
        MsgBox "Number must be between 1 and 99.", vbOKOnly + vbExclamation
      End If
    Else
      MsgBox "'" & strNewNumber & "' is not a number!", vbOKOnly + _
             vbExclamation
    End If
  End If
End Sub
</SCRIPT>
```

Creating the New Value in the Table

The chunk of code missing from the routine above is what does all the work of creating the new values for the table row, and putting them into the table. Here's how it works. We just need to format our new value into a string, and paste it onto the `TextRange` object `rngExisting` together with the new `<B>` and `</B>` tags that will make it bold:

```
      If (intNewNumber > 0) And (intNewNumber < 100) Then
        strNewNumber = FormatNumber(intNewNumber, 0)
        rngExisting.pasteHTML "<B>" & strNewNumber & "</B>"
        For intCell = 2 To 3
          Set objTheCell = colTheRow.cells(intCell)
          Set rngExisting = document.body.createTextRange()
          rngExisting.moveToElementText(objTheCell)
          If intCell = 2 Then
            strNewNumber = FormatNumber(intNewNumber * intNewNumber, 0)
          Else
            strNewNumber = FormatNumber(Sqr(intNewNumber), 4)
          End If
          rngExisting.pasteHTML "<B>" & strNewNumber & "</B>"
        Next
      Else
```

Now we can update the other two columns. As you'll see from the code, the technique is much the same as when we retrieved the value from the second column earlier on. We've used a `For..Next` loop, because the code for each of the two cells we're interested in is very similar. This also allows us to use the loop index variable, `intCell`, in the line that references the `cells` collection. We've already got a reference to the `cells` collection in `colTheRow`, so we can just `Set` the `objTheCell` variable to refer to it.

With the reference to the cell, we can then re-create a `TextRange` object called `rngExisting`, and move it to reference that cell. Then we only have to paste in the new value. We've used the value of the loop variable again here to decide how to calculate the new value – it's the square in column 3 and the square root in column 4. The next screen shot shows the result:

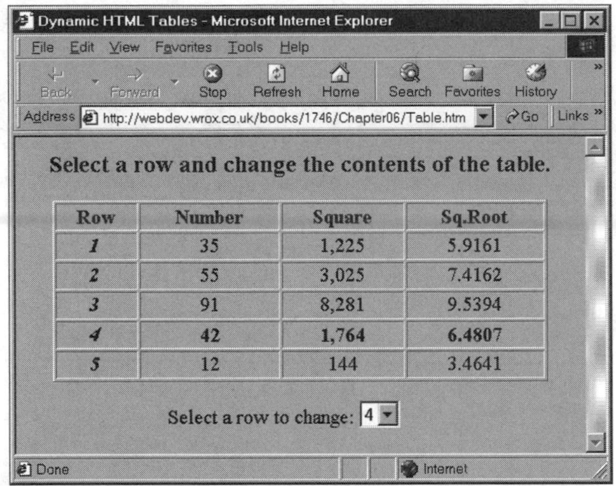

Mathematical Error Prevention

When we come to play with mathematical functions like this, there's an increased chance of errors arising in our code. Users can type any text into an `InputBox`, so it's always a good plan to check it's valid before trying to do arithmetic with it. This is where the `IsNumeric` function, and a timely message box, come in.

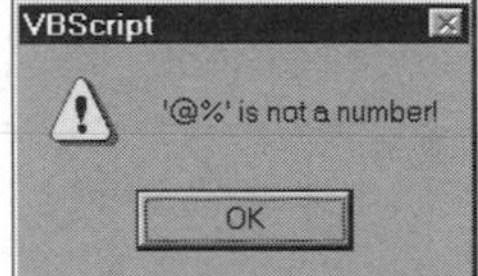

In our example page, we've also limited the user's entry to positive numbers less than 99 on purpose. Anything larger than 181 would have caused an error message to appear, because we are using integer numbers and the `CInt` function – which only accepts positive values up to 32767. (The square of 182 is 33124.) And if you're a mathematician, you might like to ponder on the result of calculating the square root of a negative number.

Summary

In this chapter, we've looked at the different ways that we can actually modify the contents of the page while it is displayed, rather than just playing with the properties or styles of the elements. We've seen how we can remove elements, add new ones, or modify the contents of existing ones. All in all, we now have the techniques available to completely rewrite a loaded HTML page within the browser if we wish.

We've seen how we can:

- Read and assign values to the 'content' properties of the elements, such as `innerText`, `outerText`, `innerHTML` and `outerHTML`, to change the contents, or the entire elements
- Use the `insertAdjacentText` and `insertAdjacentHTML` properties of elements to add text and HTML before or after the element, or at the beginning or end of the existing content
- Reference the elements and their contents in a page with a `TextRange` object, and retrieve the contents using this object's text and HTML text properties
- Change the displayed contents of the page by pasting new text and HTML into a `TextRange` object using the `pasteHTML` method
- Use a `TextRange` object to search for text in a page, through its `findText` method
- Use `TextRange` objects to retrieve and manipulate the contents of all kinds of elements, including cells in tables
- Reference the contents of tables using the `<TABLE>` element's `rows` and `cells` collections

In the next chapter, we'll be looking at a mixture of other techniques that add even more power to our pages. We'll see how Dynamic HTML provides new opportunities to work with windows, dialogs, forms and data.

7

Dialogs, Forms and Data Binding

With the introduction of third-generation browsers (IE3, Netscape Navigator 3 and the like) came technology that allows us to extend the interactivity of the browser through the use of external objects. These objects were developed as Java applets and ActiveX controls. While these technologies have had some success in providing additional functionality such as multimedia, they have not met with overwhelming success as user interfaces.

With the advent of Dynamic HTML in Internet Explorer 4 and beyond, the use of these extensions of the browser is no longer necessary when deploying a user interface. In this chapter, we'll look at why this is a good thing and how we use these features in our pages – in particular, how we can now build interactive forms far more easily. We'll also show you the difference between a modal dialog and a new browser window, and we'll look at the features of Dynamic HTML that we can use to display both.

There will always be tasks to perform that *can't* be achieved using Dynamic HTML alone, so we'll also look at some of the ways that objects can be used. Some of these tasks are those that involve databases and multimedia. We won't be looking at the multitude of Java applets and ActiveX controls that are available, but we will cover the generic way that these and other objects can be added to make your pages more usable and exciting. We'll also briefly outline the techniques for data binding, where the controls in an HTML form can be dynamically linked to a data source on the server.

So, we'll be covering:

- How we create separate windows and dialogs to display individual pages
- Ways of getting the most from Dynamic HTML when creating forms
- The tags and attributes that make building interactive forms easier
- How we use embedded Java applets and ActiveX controls in our pages
- An introduction to the data-binding abilities of Dynamic HTML

To start, we'll look at how we can create new browser windows and dialog windows.

Creating New Windows and Dialogs

One way to make your web site appear different from the rest is to create a new, additional browser window in which to display some of the pages. For example, you might open a new window to display the details of a product when a viewer selects that product in a page in the main browser window. This means that they can see the original page and the new page simultaneously.

This is already possible using traditional HTML methods and with scripting code in older browsers. However, not only does Dynamic HTML support and expand on these methods, it adds some additional ones as well. You can now display a different page either as a **modal dialog window**, or in a special help dialog. We'll look at examples in this chapter.

New Browser Windows

To open a new browser window we have two choices. The first method is to use a normal HTML `<A>` tag, specifying the appropriate value for the `TARGET` attribute. If we specify the `TARGET` attribute to be the name of an existing frame or window then the page will open there, but if we specify a *new* name for `TARGET`, a new browser window (with this name) will be created. For example, this code creates a new window named `MyNewWindow`, and loads the *Wrox* home page into it:

```
<A HREF="http://www.wrox.com" TARGET="MyNewWindow">
  Wrox Press Limited
</A>
```

Alternatively we can do the same kind of thing using script code, by executing the `window` object's `open` method. We supply the address of the page to be loaded into the new window, the name for the new window, and a string containing the settings (or **features**) that we want the new window to have. The `open` method returns a reference to the new window, which we can use later in our code (if we wish) by assigning it to a variable. For example, using JScript:

```
<SCRIPT LANGUAGE=JSCRIPT>
strFeatures = "top=100,left=100,width=450,height=265,"
              + "toolbar=no,menubar=no,location=no,directories=no";
objNewWindow = window.open("myPage.htm", "MyWin", strFeatures);
</SCRIPT>
```

This code would look similar in VBScript, but we'd need to use the `Set` statement to assign the results of the `window.open` method to a variable.

```
<SCRIPT LANGUAGE=VBSCRIPT>
strFeatures = "top=100,left=100,width=450,height=265," & _
               "toolbar=no,menubar=no,location=no,directories=no"
Set objNewWindow = window.open("myPage.htm", "MyWin", strFeatures)
</SCRIPT>
```

As you can see from the code, the `window.open` method gives us a lot more control over what the new window looks like, and where it appears on the screen. In our example, we've positioned the new window 100 pixels from the top and left of the screen, set the size to 450 by 265 pixels, and turned off display of the toolbar, menus, address text box (`location`) and the directory buttons.

The second argument (`MyWin` in our example) acts like the `TARGET` attribute in an `<A>` tag, in that it allows us to target an existing window instead of creating a new one. We can also add the optional `replace` argument to the method call. Setting it to `true` causes the document being loaded to replace any current entry in the window's history list. If we're sending a new page to an existing window, we don't need to specify the 'features' for the existing window:

```
objNewWindow = window.open("myPage.htm", "MyWin", "", true);
```

The Open Method Features – Summary

Here's a full list of all the available 'feature' arguments for use with the `window` object's `open` method. The 'features' are used to set the attributes of the window itself, such as its size, location, and visual characteristics, like scroll bars and a title bar:

Attribute	Values	Description
`channelmode`	`yes` | `no` | `1` | `0`	Show the channel controls (default is `no`)
`directories`	`yes` | `no` | `1` | `0`	Include directory buttons (default is `yes`)
`fullscreen`	`yes` | `no` | `1` | `0`	Maximize the new window (default is `no`)
`height`	*number*	Height of window, in pixels
`left`	*number*	Position of left of the window on the screen, in pixels
`location`	`yes` | `no` | `1` | `0`	The URL Address text box (default is `yes`)
`menubar`	`yes` | `no` | `1` | `0`	The default browser menus (default is `yes`)
`resizeable`	`yes` | `no` | `1` | `0`	Window can be resized by user (default is `yes`)
`scrollbars`	`yes` | `no` | `1` | `0`	Horizontal and vertical scrollbars (default is `yes`)
`status`	`yes` | `no` | `1` | `0`	The default status bar (default is `yes` for untrusted dialog windows and `no` for trusted dialog windows)
`titlebar`	`yes` | `no` | `1` | `0`	Display a title bar – only used for HTML Applications (default is `yes`)

Table Continued on Following Page

Attribute	Values	Description
`toolbar`	`yes` | `no` | `1` | `0`	Include the browser toolbars (default is `yes`)
`top`	*number*	Position of top of the window on the screen, in pixels
`width`	*number*	Width of window, in pixels

Modal Dialog Windows

In Dynamic HTML, we can also open a new window using the `showModalDialog` method of the `window` object. This uses a 'features' string like the `open` method, but the attributes are different and the format of the string is more specific. The other differences in usage are that the `showModalDialog` method doesn't require a window name or the optional *`replace`* argument; instead, it *does* accept an *`arguments`* argument (if you see what we mean!). We'll see some examples in a moment.

What are Modal Dialog Windows?

The big difference between using the `open` and `showModalDialog` methods to open a window is the way in which the new window behaves with respect to the existing one. Using `open` creates an independent window, as a new instance of the browser: and as you'd expect, if the user closes the original window then the new window remains.

However, when we create a window using `showModalDialog`, the behavior is totally different. As the name of the method suggests, the new window becomes **modal** with respect to the original window. This means that the user cannot activate the original window until they close the new modal window. It's similar to the way that application dialogs and message boxes operate. It provides a window that is more like a form in Visual Basic.

Here's an example (using JScript again). Note that the `showModalDialog` returns a simple value, which we've assigned to an ordinary variable called `result`, rather than referencing the new window as we would have done using the `open` method. You'll see how we use this value later on:

```
strFeatures = "dialogWidth=500px;dialogHeight=320px;"
                                        + "center=yes;help=no;status=no";
result = window.showModalDialog("mydlg.htm", "MyDialog", strFeatures);
```

Like the `open` method, the first argument of `showModalDialog` is the URL of the page we want to open (note that we could specify a full HTTP URL here). The second is the *`arguments`* argument that we mentioned above – this is a value that will be passed to the new dialog window once it's opened. The third argument is the 'features' string – notice that the format requires semi-colons rather than commas between entries. You can also use colons instead of 'equals' signs, in the same format as a style sheet entry:

```
... "dialogWidth:500px;dialogHeight:320px; ..."
```

We can use this dialog window in any number of ways. We can place controls on it to prompt for information; we can allow the user to make selections; we can even create a Wizard, like the ones we see in many modern applications. We've used it as a book selector in our example, which you'll see at the end of this section.

The ShowModalDialog Features Summary

The options available in the 'features' string for the `showModalDialog` method are subtly different to those for the `open` method. The following table lists them all:

Attribute	Values	Description
`center`	`yes` | `no` | `1` | `0`	Center window on browser (default is `yes`)
`dialogHeight`	*number + units*	Height of the dialog window
`dialogLeft`	*number + units*	Left position of window on desktop
`dialogTop`	*number + units*	Top position of window on desktop
`dialogWidth`	*number + units*	Width of the dialog window
`help`	`yes` | `no` | `1` | `0`	Include Help button in title bar (default is `yes`)
`status`	`yes` | `no` | `1` | `0`	Include a status bar at the bottom of the window (default is `yes`)
`resizeable`	`yes` | `no` | `1` | `0`	User is able to resize the dialog window (default is `no`)

Notice also that the dialog window size and position attributes require a CSS unit to be specified. If you don't specify a unit, you get the default value (which is the full size of the screen).

Modeless Dialog Windows

When a modal dialog box is displayed, all script execution and interaction with other windows of the browser is suspended until the modal dialog is closed. In many instances this is the desired effect. For example, if critical information is required, and the system can't proceed without it, then a modal dialog box is appropriate. But what if you want to keep a dialog window open and *still* allow the user to interact with the browser?

You can achieve this by using a **modeless** dialog box. It appears on top of the browser window just like a modal dialog, but the user can switch focus back to the browser and interact with the page there while the modeless dialog box is open. This can be very useful for displaying step-by-step help, or for displaying search and replace dialogs.

We use the showModelessDialog method to create a modeless dialog box – it has exactly the same parameters as the showModalDialog method, and the available display characteristics are also exactly the same. Here's an example:

```
strFeatures = "dialogWidth=500px;dialogHeight=320px;"
                                      + "center=yes;help=no;status=no";
result = window.showModelessDialog("mydlg.htm", "MyDialog", strFeatures);
```

Since modeless dialog boxes are used throughout the Windows operating system, a number of display conventions are generally used when displaying a modeless dialog box:

- No scrollbars should be shown. In the BODY tag of the document being displayed, set the SCROLL attribute to no
- Turn off the status bar, by setting the status feature to no
- Do not allow the window to be resized. Set the resizable feature to no

A Windows and Dialogs Example

So that you can see how we use new windows and modal dialogs, we've provided a sample page NewWin.htm on our web site at http://webdev.wrox.co.uk/books/1746. It displays a normal HTML page containing two links. Each link opens the same new page - one as a new browser window and the other as a dialog:

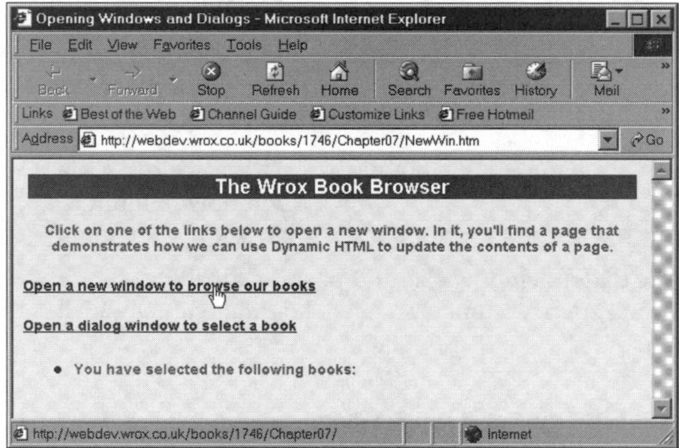

The Initial Book Browser Page

This page uses two <A> tags to create the links. Each one has the HREF set to an empty string, because we're going to look after the opening of the new window ourselves in code – rather than letting the browser open a default new window:

```
<P> <A HREF="" ONCLICK="return OpenWindow()">
  Open a new window to browse our books</A></P>
<P> <A HREF="" ONCLICK="return OpenDialog()">
  Open a dialog window to select a book</A></P>
```

(Of course, we could have easily used buttons rather than links.) Within each <A> tag is the connection to an event handler that will be executed when the link is clicked.

In fact, there's an interesting little problem that arises when using `<A>` tags like this. When the user clicks on a link, and after the `ONCLICK` code has executed, the original browser window will attempt to load the page referenced in the `HREF`. Since our `HREF` is empty, this will cause an error. To prevent this, we need to ensure that the `ONCLICK` code returns a value of `false` to the browser. Then (as you can see in the code above) the `<A>` tag captures that return value and ensures that the browser won't follow the link.

All we need to do now is ensure that our functions return `false` – we'll see this in the code for the `OpenWindow` and `OpenDialog` functions.

Opening the New Browser Window

The first link in the page opens a new browser window in the traditional way, using the following code. You can see that the routine contains a line that displays the message **Opened a new browser window** in the status bar of the main window. You'll see why as we go along:

```
function OpenWindow()
{
  window.status = "";
  strFeatures = "top=100,left=100,width=450,height=305,toolbar=no,"
             + "menubar=no,location=no,directories=no";
  objNewWindow = window.open("dialog.htm", "MyNewWindow", strFeatures);
  window.status = "Opened a new browser window.";
  window.event.cancelBubble = true;
  window.event.returnValue = false;
}
```

Notice that we have set the `cancelBubble` property of the `event` object to `true` to prevent the event being passed back up through the `document` object hierarchy. More importantly, we set the event object's `returnValue` property to `false`. This will return the `false` value we want to the `<A>` tag in the page, and will prevent the browser trying to load another page.

> *Alternatively, we could have used the line `return false` in the function. Either technique will work in this situation, though we prefer to use the `event` object's `returnValue` property.*

Clicking the **Open a new window to browse our books** link displays a small new window, with the features (or lack of them) that we specified in our code:

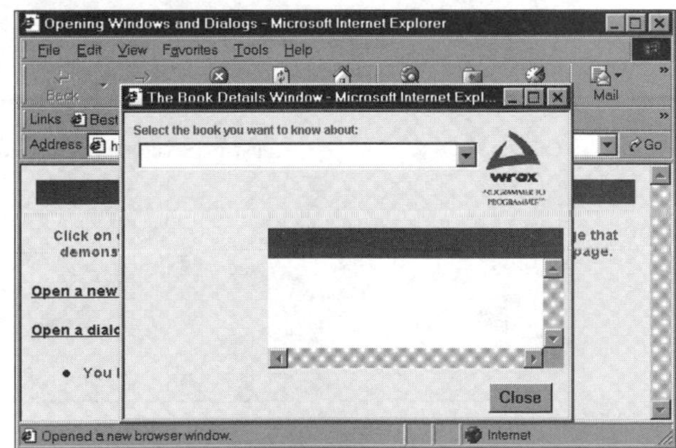

OK, so the new window doesn't look much at the moment, but it is another Dynamic HTML page – we'll look at its code in a moment. Notice that the status bar of the main window shows the message Opened a new browser window. You can switch between the two windows, and even load a different page into the main window without changing the new window. They act independently.

Opening the Modal Dialog Window

Before we go any further, click the Close button to close the new window, then click the Open a dialog window to select a book link. The same new page is displayed (with an extra button), but this time it's a modal dialog window, and you can't go back to the original window without closing the modal window – clicking on the original *doesn't* bring it to the front.

This is the code that opens the new dialog window in response to the click on the second link:

```
function OpenDialog()
{
  window.status = "";
  strFeatures = "dialogWidth=500px;dialogHeight=360px;scrollbars=no;"
              + "center=yes;border=thin;help=no;status=no"
  strTitle = window.showModalDialog("dialog.htm", "MyDialog", strFeatures);
  window.status = "Opened a modal dialog window.";
// code here to handle the returned value
  ...
}
```

Code Execution and Modal Windows

If you're used to programming in other languages then you'll be expecting the second difference between new windows and modal windows – but if you've only used VBScript or JavaScript before then it may come as a surprise. When we open the dialog window, the code in the main page stops at the `showModalDialog` method. If you look at status bar in the main page while the modal dialog window is open, you'll see that the message does *not* display the words Opened a modal dialog window:

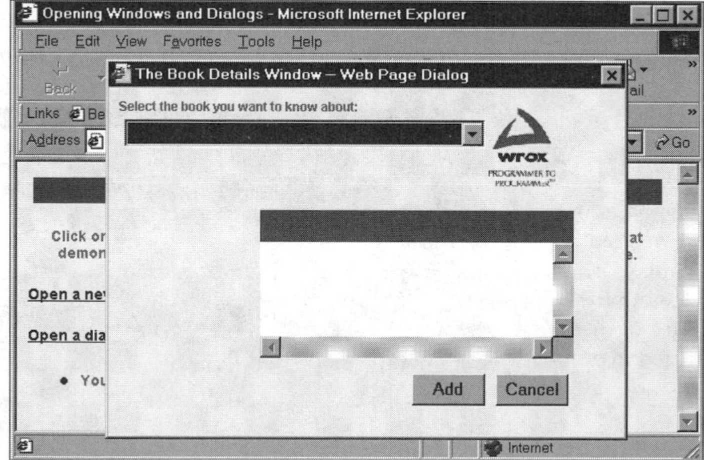

The reason is that the code line `window.status = "Opened a modal dialog window."` is not executed until *after* the modal dialog is closed. When the modal dialog is closed, the status message will appear. This also means that the *original* window's code will be able to use values entered (or selected) by the user in the modal dialog. You can see from the comment in the code above that this is what our example does.

It is a bit trickier with a modeless dialog box. Since the script code that follows the `showModelessDialog` method is executed immediately, we don't have a set point in the script where we know the values will be returned. You would need to have a special function in the page to open a window that the modeless dialog box can call just before it is closed. This method can be used to pass back any values captured by the modeless dialog.

The Dynamic New Window Page

As you've seen, we're loading the same page into both the new browser window and the modal dialog – it's a Dynamic HTML document called `dialog.htm`. We've designed it using absolute positioning, as demonstrated back in Chapter 2, and incorporated some effects that were difficult (or even impossible) to achieve in traditional HTML – even using ActiveX controls. Here's the first part of the HTML for `dialog.htm`:

```
...
<BODY BGCOLOR="LemonChiffon">
<DIV ID=divMain STYLE="position:absolute; top:10;
                       left:10; width:450; height:300">
  <P>Select the book you want to know about:</P>
  <SELECT ID=lstBooks ONCHANGE="BookListChange()"
     STYLE="position:absolute; font-weight:light; width:345; top:20; left:5">
   <OPTION VALUE=0></OPTION>
   <OPTION VALUE=1266>Professional Active Server Pages 2.0</OPTION>
   <OPTION VALUE=138X>Instant DHTML Scriptlets</OPTION>
   <OPTION VALUE=1460>Professional MTS/MSMQ with VB and ASP</OPTION>
   <OPTION VALUE=1568>Instant HTML Programmer's Reference</OPTION>
   <OPTION VALUE=1894>JavaScript Objects</OPTION>
  </SELECT>
  <IMG SRC="wroxp2p.gif"
       STYLE="position:absolute; top:5; left:345" WIDTH="80" HEIGHT="80">
  <IMG SRC="" ID=imgCover
       STYLE="position:absolute; top:60; left:5; visibility:hidden">
  <DIV ID=divTitle
       STYLE="position:absolute; margin:5; top:100;
              left:130; width:300; height:30;
              background-color:red; overflow:hidden">
    <P ID=pTitle CLASS="main"
       TITLE="Visit our Web site for more information"></P>
  </DIV>
  <DIV ID=divText
       STYLE="position:absolute; margin:5; top:130;
              left:130; width:300; height:110;
              background-color:white; overflow:scroll">
    <P ID=pText CLASS="text"
       TITLE="Visit our Web site for more information"></P>
  </DIV>
...
  // code here for the buttons at the bottom of the page
  ...
</DIV>
</BODY>
```

The page consists of a main document division, placed 10 pixels in from the top and left of the window and filling the rest of it. Inside this are two more divisions. The first, with a red background, will display the title of the book selected in the list, and the second will display the descriptive text for that book. In both cases, there is an empty paragraph section within the division that sets the style `class` for that text. These style classes are defined at the top of the page, and not shown here:

```
<P ID=pTitle CLASS="main"
       TITLE="Visit our Web site for more information"></P>
...
<P ID=pText CLASS="text"
       TITLE="Visit our Web site for more information"></P>
```

It's into these `<P>` elements that we'll be placing the title and description of each book as the user selects it from the drop-down list at the top of the page.

The Add, Cancel and Close Buttons

At the bottom of the page that's displayed in our new window or dialog are buttons that allow you to close the window (or dialog) and return to the original window. You may have noticed that different buttons appear, depending on whether you've opened a new window or a dialog:

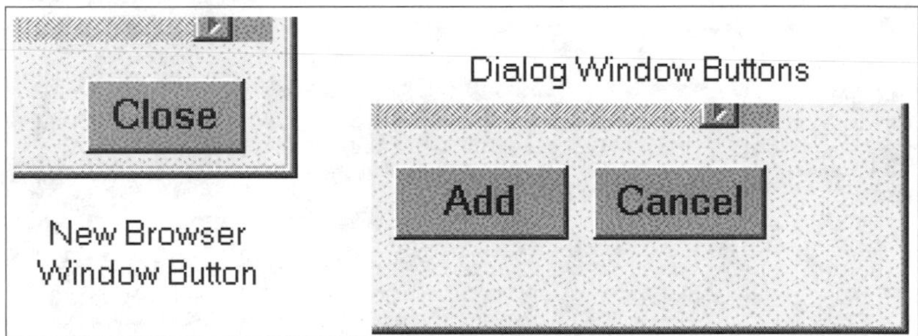

This raises two questions. How do we know which buttons to display in the new windows, and how do we actually display different ones anyway?

The answer lies in a piece of script within the new document, that is executed as the page is being rendered. To tell which buttons we want, we use the *`arguments`* argument that is available in the `showModalDialog` method. You may recall from our earlier discussion that we set this to the string value `"MyDialog"` in the function that opened the dialog window:

```
strTitle = window.showModalDialog("dialog.htm", "MyDialog", strFeatures);
```

This value is passed across to the new window, and we can access it within the new page. While we've only used a simple string, there is no reason why you can't use a different type of value, such as an array or a series of values in delimited format. Remember that this is very different from the way the `open` method works, where the second argument is used to provide a name for the window so that we can target pages to it using an `<A>` tag or script. In a modal dialog, the second parameter is passed to the window as a value for use in our script.

Using the window.dialogArguments Property

So, we can tell if we are displaying our new page in a dialog or a separate browser window by examining this value. It becomes available in the new page as the `dialogArguments` property of the new `window` object. Here's how we've used it to create the *appropriate* buttons in the page (note that if we are opening the page in a new browser window, the `window.dialogArguments` property will be `null`):

```
  ...
<SCRIPT LANGUAGE="JAVASCRIPT">
   // add the buttons we want to the bottom of the page
   if (window.dialogArguments == "MyDialog")
   {
     strButtons = '<INPUT TITLE="Add book to order '
                + 'and return to main window" '
                + 'ID=cmdOK TYPE=BUTTON VALUE="Add" '
                + 'ONCLICK="AddClicked()" '
                + 'STYLE="position:absolute; top:260; '
                + 'left:280; width:70">'
                + '<INPUT TITLE="Return to main window '
                + 'without adding book to order" '
                + 'ID=cmdClose TYPE=BUTTON VALUE="Cancel" '
                + 'ONCLICK="CloseClicked()" '
                + 'STYLE="position:absolute; top:260; '
                + 'left:360; width:70">';
   }
   else
   {
     strButtons = '<INPUT TITLE="Return to main window" '
                + 'ID=cmdClose TYPE=BUTTON VALUE="Close" '
                + 'ONCLICK="CloseClicked()" '
                + 'STYLE="position:absolute; top:260; left:360">';
   }
   document.write(strButtons);
</SCRIPT>
</DIV>
</BODY>
```

The Title Selector List

Now that we've got our new page displayed, we'll look at some of its features. Near the top of the page is a `<SELECT>` tag that creates a normal HTML drop-down list box, and fills it with book titles. For each one, it sets the `VALUE` to the book's code number, and it includes a blank entry at the top of the list:

```
<SELECT ID=lstBooks ONCHANGE="BookListChange()"
   STYLE="position:absolute; font-weight:light; width:345; top:20; left:5">
 <OPTION VALUE=0></OPTION>
 <OPTION VALUE=1266>Professional Active Server Pages 2.0</OPTION>
 <OPTION VALUE=138X>Instant DHTML Scriptlets</OPTION>
 <OPTION VALUE=1460>Professional MTS/MSMQ with VB and ASP</OPTION>
 <OPTION VALUE=1568>Instant HTML Programmer's Reference</OPTION>
 <OPTION VALUE=1894>JavaScript Objects</OPTION>
</SELECT>
```

One extra trick here is to use the `STYLE` attribute to set the `width` of the element – something we couldn't do in HTML, and which often resulted in the end of the selected entry being cut off by the 'drop' button. The drop-down list looks like this.

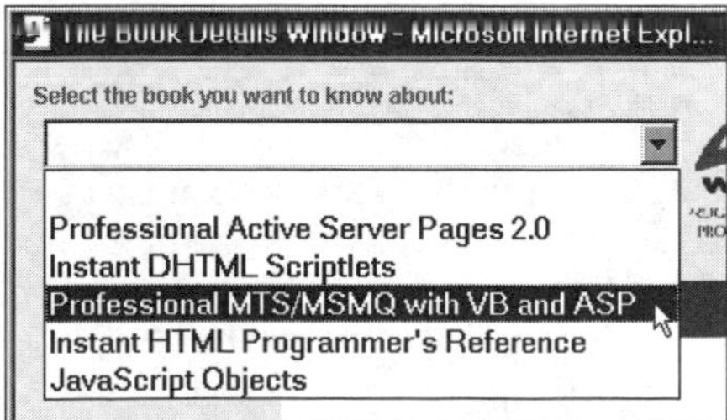

An Invisible Image Control

The page also contains an `<IMG>` tag with an `ID` of `imgCover`, and a `SRC` that is an empty string. This is where we'll display a picture of the book's cover, but we want it to be blank when the page is first opened. If we don't supply an `SRC` for the element, we'll get a 'missing picture' frame displayed in the page. To get round this, we can use the `visibility` style property. In the HTML source, we set it to `hidden` so that the image element is not visible when the page is first displayed:

```
<IMG SRC="" ID=imgCover
       STYLE="position:absolute; top:60; left:5; visibility:hidden">
```

Displaying the Selected Book Details

All we have to do now is to respond to the user selecting a book title in the drop-down list, and display the details and cover picture on the page. Here's the first part of the script section in the page. In it, we define two variables `strTitle` and `strText`, which will hold the title and description of the selected book. Declaring them first like this, outside any of the subroutines or functions in the page, means that they are **in scope** (i.e. available and will retain their values) the whole time the page is displayed:

```
<SCRIPT LANGUAGE="JAVASCRIPT">

var strTitle = "";   // the book title
var strText = "";    // the text description
...
function BookListChange()
{
  objCoverImage = document.all["imgCover"];// get the book cover image
  strBookID = document.all["lstBooks"].value;    // get the selected book
  if (strBookID == "0")
    // hide the imgCover element
    objCoverImage.style.visibility = "hidden"
  else
  {
    // put picture in imgCover and make it visible
    objCoverImage.src = strBookID + ".gif";
    objCoverImage.style.visibility = "visible";
  }
  //set the new text and title
  SetBookText(strBookID);
  // put title and text into <P> tags
  document.all["pTitle"].innerText = strTitle
  document.all["pText"].innerText = strText
}
...
```

The rest of the code shown above is in an event handler that responds to the `onchange` event of the drop-down list box `lstBooks`. It will run when the user selects a book from the list. In it, we first create a reference to our invisible `imgCover` image element in `objCoverImage`, so that we can access it easily afterwards. Then we retrieve the user's selection from the list into a variable `strBookID`. This will be the currently selected `VALUE` – in other words, the book's code number. We've been clever enough to name the cover image files using this book code, so we can retrieve the correct one easily.

Next, we check that the selection isn't 0 (the blank entry at the top of the list). If it isn't we can then create the filename of the image, assign it to the `imgCover` element's `src` property to load it into the `<IMG>` element, and finally make it visible by setting the element's visibility property to `visible`. If the user did select the blank entry, however, we just have to set the visibility property back to `hidden`.

Getting the Book Title and Description

The next line in our event handler calls another function, which we've named `SetBookText`. It takes as a parameter the book code number `strBookID`, as selected in the drop-down list. This function simply sets the value of the `strTitle` and `strText` variables to the appropriate ones (we've omitted the text and some of the `if` statements here to save repetition):

```
...
function SetBookText(strBookID)
{
  strTitle = "";
  strText = "";
  if (strBookID == "1266")
  {
    strTitle = "Professional Active Server Pages 2.0";
    strText = "Active Server Pages is simply the ... etc.";
  }
  if (strBookID == "138X")
  {
    strTitle = "Instant DHTML Scriptlets";
    strText = "Scriptlets give you the ability to ... etc. ";
  }
  ... 'if' statements for the other books here ...
}
```

Inserting Text into the Page

Up until now, much of this has been stuff you could easily do in earlier versions of browsers that supported VBScript or JavaScript. The next part, however, is one of the things that make Dynamic HTML special. We need to insert the book title and description, currently held in two string variables, into the page. We've previously set aside two empty `<P>` elements in the HTML source ready to receive them. But how do we get the text into them?

As you saw in Chapter 6, it's easy. We just assign the text we want to the `innerText` property of the appropriate element:

```
// put title and text into <P> tags
  document.all["pTitle"].innerText = strTitle
  document.all["pText"].innerText = strText
```

And here's the result, with the page opened as a new browser window. Notice the effect of setting the `overflow` property to `scroll` for the `<DIV>` that contains the book description:

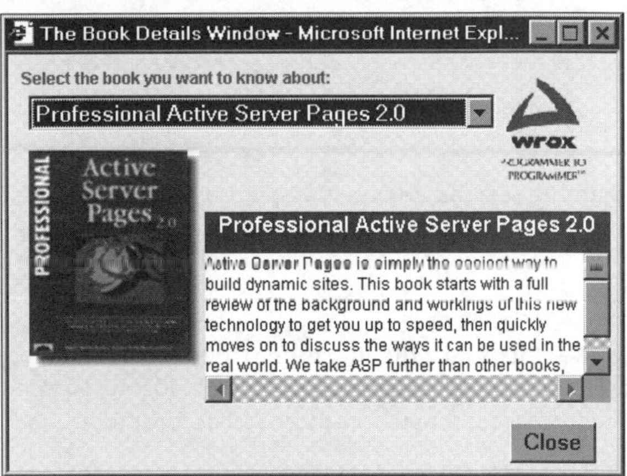

Displaying Tooltips for Elements

You'll see from the next screenshot that we have also arranged for the various elements to display 'tooltips' when the mouse pointer pauses over them – including the `<P>` element that holds our book description. This is easily done for any element by simply specifying the text of the tooltip in the tag's `TITLE` property. We have set it in the HTML source, but it could just as easily be set and changed in code, like any other property:

```
<P ID=pText CLASS="text" TITLE="Visit our Web site for more information"></P>
```

It also works for the buttons at the bottom of the window, which we created using script when the page was loaded. Instead of having an element with a `TITLE` attribute, we dynamically created the `INPUT` element, including a `TITLE` element, and then added it to the page with a `document.write` method;

```
    strButtons = '<INPUT TITLE="Add book to order '
               + 'and return to main window" '
               + 'ID=cmdOK TYPE=BUTTON VALUE="Add" '
               + .....">';
    .....
  document.write(strButtons);
```

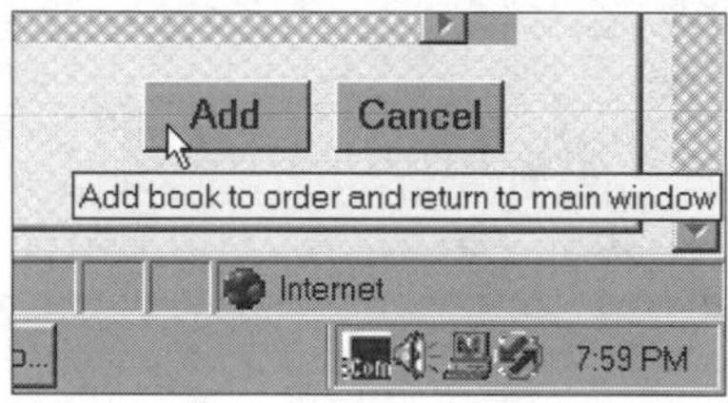

Closing the New Window

The final two sections of code in this page are used to close the new window or dialog when the appropriate button is clicked. This could be either the Close button in the new browser window page, or the Add or Cancel buttons in the dialog window page. In fact, the Close and Cancel buttons both use the same function, named `CloseClicked()`:

```
function CloseClicked()
{
  window.returnValue = "";
  window.close()
}
```

It simply sets the `returnValue` property of the `window` object (not the `event` object this time) to an empty string, and calls the `close` method of the `window` object. This works the same way for both new browser windows and modal dialogs.

The Add button that appears in the dialog window uses slightly different code. Here, we want to return the title of the currently selected book, so that we can use it in our original page. The string `strTitle` holds the last book title selected, and so we just need to assign it to the `returnValue` property:

```
function AddClicked()
{
  window.returnValue = strTitle;
  window.close()
}
```

> **Take care to use the correct object when returning values from a dialog window. Both the `window` object itself and the global `event` object have a `returnValue` property. The `event.returnValue` property is a `true/false` value that the event returns to the browser, and is used to cancel the default action for that event. The `window.returnValue` property is a value that is passed back to the object as the return value of the `showModalDialog` method.**

Using the Returned Value

Our new dialog page returns a value to the original window that opened it, by assigning that value to the `window.returnValue` property. As we saw earlier, the code in the original page stops executing at the call to the `showModalDialog` method, and only resumes when the dialog is closed. At this point, the `returnValue` becomes available as the value that is returned by the `showModalDialog` method.

So, we can use this value in our code. In the Book List example page we've been working with, we add it to the original page – inside an unordered list. Each time the dialog is closed, the current book title is added:

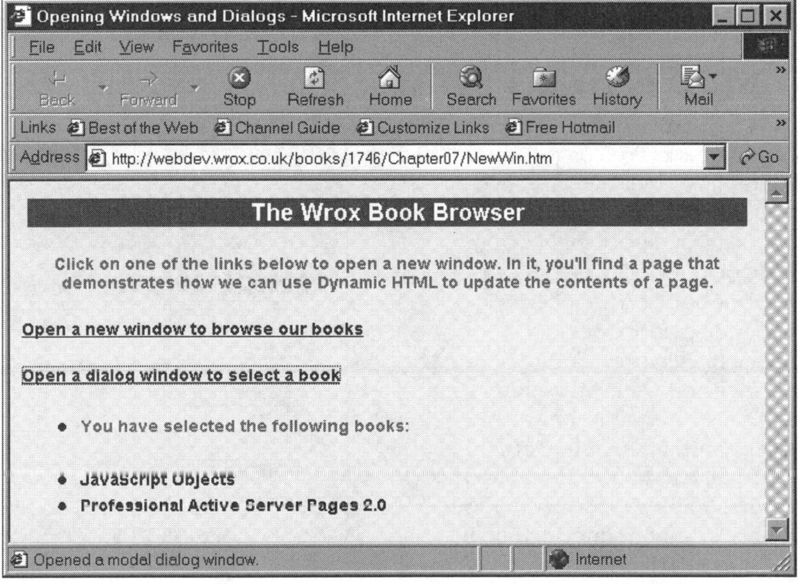

Inserting the Titles into the Page

Back in the original `NewWin.htm` page, where we opened the dialog window in the first place, the code that adds the title to the list is simple enough. Here, we've highlighted it within the complete function. It simply uses the `insertAdjacentHTML` method we discussed in Chapter 6, and adds a new `<LI>` element (containing the book title) into the `<UL>` element (with `ID=ListTag`) that we provided in the page:

```
function OpenDialog()
{
  window.status = "";
  strFeatures = "dialogWidth=500px;dialogHeight=360px;scrollbars=no;"
              + "center=yes;border=thin;help=no;status=no"
  strTitle = window.showModalDialog("dialog.htm", "MyDialog", strFeatures);
  window.status = "Opened a modal dialog window.";
  if (strTitle != null && strTitle != "")
  {
    objList = document.all["ListTag"];
    objList.insertAdjacentHTML("AfterEnd", "<LI>" + strTitle + "</LI>");
  }
  window.event.cancelBubble = true;
  window.event.returnValue = false;
}
```

Now we have the techniques we need to build pages that offer separate dialogs that get information from a user. These could be used to offer a 'shopping cart' facility, or a pop-up options dialog, or almost any kind of task where we need to collect information from a user before accomplishing a task. Because the original page remains loaded and waiting in the background, we can treat the dialog window as a separate page. When it comes time to close the dialog, we don't have to do anything special to the page that launched the dialog – its state remains the same as before we opened the dialog. These techniques are also useful when we come to use forms in our pages, as you'll see in the next section.

Dynamic HTML Forms

The use of forms in web pages is still growing rapidly, and there are several reasons behind this. First and foremost is the explosion of electronic commerce on the web, which means that people are submitting their orders, shipping addresses and credit card details to web sites like Amazon.com and Dell. Also, more companies are offering technical and product support, often in the form of a feedback page in which they collect information. Many sites even offer the opportunity to submit information, if its only your favorite joke. The days of the Web being purely a one-way content provider are long gone. Now you are expected to 'get involved' and provide information of your own.

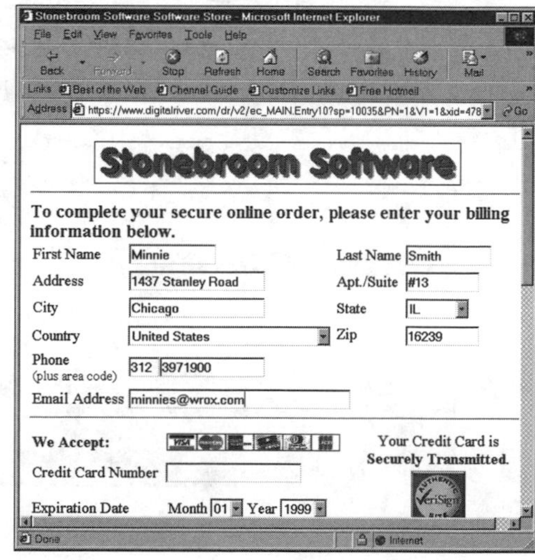

However, there is a stronger underlying trend that makes web-based forms a requirement in a web site, rather than just an add-on. As corporate developers have seen the explosion in the Internet, they have begun to deploy these same technologies for obtaining intra-company information – and we've seen the birth of the intranet. More and more web-based Intranet applications are being designed with a Web browser as the front end or **interface**. This means that a few text boxes and option buttons are no longer enough. We need to provide the kind of rich, attractive and responsive interface that users have become accustomed to in traditional Windows applications.

These rich user interfaces have already started to appear, especially in the world of the intranet – where bandwidth is generally not a problem and everyone is using the same browser. On the Internet as a whole, however, there are some problems with previous versions of HTML. While using the latest features of HTML and adding applets and controls to pages is a great way to produce a richer experience, there is a considerable down-side – as we'll see in the following sections.

Balancing the Needs of Compatibility

Web page authors have always faced the problem of which version of HTML they should write to. Early versions of HTML didn't offer anything like the control of layout and text formatting that is possible in more recent versions – for example, there were no tables or frames. Thus, a page created using the latest version of HTML might well look a mess (or even be unviewable) on older browsers. There is also the issue of the two leading browsers – Internet Explorer and Netscape Navigator – supporting two different versions of Dynamic HTML.

The Internet itself is mainly a Unix-based system underneath, as well as being cross-platform as far as the client is concerned. The browser could be running on almost anything – a green-on-black text-only terminal, or a Macintosh, or a Cray – with Windows nowhere in sight. It's likely that, in many of the more esoteric environments, your carefully crafted Dynamic HTML pages will look like they were designed by a gorilla.

Hopefully, the winds have begun blowing towards a standard Dynamic HTML – HTML 4.0. IE5 supports HTML 4.0 better than any browser out there. Netscape has promised that Netscape 5 will have support for DHTML as well. But now, we have three versions of both Netscape and Internet Explorer in use. For a time, the situation may not improve – you still have to worry about what your page will look like on earlier Windows-based browsers, such as versions 3 and 4 of both Internet Explorer and Netscape Navigator. The redeeming factor is that it's likely we'll see an accepted and more universal standard evolve as HTML 4.0, based on Dynamic HTML.

The Embedded Object Dilemma

And if you think HTML versions can cause a problem, then just consider objects. We already encounter two different types on a regular basis – Java applets and ActiveX controls. Java applets are **cross-platform**, so will run on any machine that implements the correct environment. This is simply an interpreter that understands the byte-codes that make up the applet. Hence, in theory, the same Java applet works on any machine with an appropriate interpreter.

ActiveX controls are not cross-platform, but instead are **cross-language** objects. They can be written in any one of several different programming languages, but are specific to a particular operating system. You have to provide a different control for each platform where you want your page to be available. Worse than that, they'll only work on browsers that have a suitable environment, which means at least Internet Explorer 3, since no other browsers have any kind of robust support for ActiveX controls.

In both cases, the browser has to download the object and install it on the user's system, unless it is already available there. This increases the download times of the page, often annoys users, and may not work at all depending on the settings in their browser or the proxy server on their network. While this is technologically a wonderful system, it doesn't score well in usability terms generally, unless you stick to using the common objects that are likely to be installed on the user's system by default. Instead, it would be nice if we could do without them altogether.

Creating Dynamic Forms

So, let's see how HTML 4.0 can help to limit our requirements for non-HTML controls. It still implements the set of intrinsic HTML controls supported by earlier versions: `<INPUT>`, `<SELECT>`, `<OPTION>` and `<TEXTAREA>`. On top of this, it also supports HTML's new `<BUTTON>`, `<FIELDSET>`, `<LEGEND>` and `<LABEL>` tags, plus some new features that extend the capabilities of existing controls. And of course, these are useful not only in forms on a normal Web page, but in the new dialog windows we saw earlier in this chapter.

Absolute Positioning in Forms

If you've ever created forms in IE3, you were able to take advantage of an ActiveX control called the **Layout Control**. This was designed to provide an absolute positioning feature in HTML for third-generation browsers. Embedding a Layout Control in a page effectively creates a document division, in which other controls can be accurately positioned and overlapped. However, to work, it requires a separate file containing the definition of the division, and then a whole series of other ActiveX controls.

In Dynamic HTML, we can do without any of this. As you've seen in earlier chapters, we can create a document division using the `<DIV>` tag, and then position almost any other elements inside the division using the `top`, `left` and `z-index` style properties. And more than that, we can get a lot more control over the size of the elements by using the element's `width` and `height` properties – as you saw earlier in this chapter.

New Tags and Properties

We can create generic command (push) buttons using the new `<BUTTON>` tag, as well as with the existing `<INPUT>` tag, and group controls like option buttons together with the `<FIELDSET>` and `<LEGEND>` tags. You'll see examples of all these shortly.

And to add to the list of ingredients for more usable forms, all the HTML controls have gained some new attributes (and therefore properties). We can set the `tabIndex` of a control, which means we no longer depend on the order of the controls in the page to determine the way the focus (or text cursor) moves between them. We can also create a 'hot-key' to activate a control, using its `accessKey` property; and we can make a control read-only by setting its `readOnly` property. We can include a text `title` for the elements, as you saw earlier in this chapter, to provide a pop-up tool-tip, and use the `disabled` property to enable and disable controls as required.

More Events Supported

The final new ingredient for building application interface-type pages is the extended number of events that the HTML controls respond to. Back in HTML 3.2, the list was limited to `onclick`, `onblur`, `onfocus`, `onchange` and `onselect` (depending on the type of control), but with HTML 4.0, we have more than 20 additional events to react to in our code. These include keyboard events like `onkeypress` and `onhelp`, focus events like `onbeforeeditfocus`, `onfocus` and `onblur`, update events `onbeforeupdate` and `onafterupdate`, and a range of mouse events – including `onmousemove`, `ondblclick`, `onlosecapture` and `onmousedown`.

If you have programmed in a traditional language like Visual Basic, Delphi, or C++, you'll be used to using most these in your interface code. Now, you can do much the same in a web page using VBScript, JavaScript and other scripting languages. In the example coming up later in the chapter, you'll see many of these new events used – and all of it without an applet or ActiveX control in sight. But first, we'll look at the additional tags and attributes in HTML 4.0 that make it possible.

The <BUTTON> Tag

When we create buttons using the `<INPUT>` tag, we have little real control over the appearance of the button itself. The `<BUTTON>` element allows us to create buttons which more closely resemble those seen in normal Windows or other GUI-based operating system applications. We can include other elements, such as images, as well as text on the button itself.

To make it possible, the `<BUTTON>` tag has a closing tag, `</BUTTON>`, and anything between the opening and closing tags is rendered on the button face. For example, we can create a button that contains a picture instead of text like this:

```
<BUTTON>
  <IMG SRC="mypic.gif">
</BUTTON>
```

The button tag also provides absolute positioning through a `STYLE` attribute, so we can size and place it accurately on the page:

```
<BUTTON STYLE="position:absolute; top:200; width:80; left:325;">
  <IMG SRC="mypic.gif">
</BUTTON>
```

The button is sized automatically so that all of its contents are displayed, unless you specify the button's width and/or height style attributes explicitly.

We can also include more than one element on the button. In the next code fragment we're adding a text caption. Normally (as in a HTML page) the contents are laid out next to each other. To get the text onto the next line we include a <BR> tag. Each 'line' of elements is centered on the button face by default:

```
<BUTTON STYLE="position:absolute; top:200; width:80; left:325">
  <IMG SRC="mypic.gif" STYLE="height:30; width:25;"><BR>Stop
</BUTTON>
```

Notice that we've also included the `width` and `height` style attributes – both of the button and of the image within. The image's `width` and `height` style attributes allow us to force the picture to a new size, and therefore prevent the original image being cropped if it is larger than the button size we want. On top of that, they prevent the button being resized as the image loads, by informing the browser what the actual size will be – as when placing an image in the page in the usual way.

Finally, we'll generally also include an `ID` attribute, so that we can refer to the button in our code. And by including an `ID` for the <IMG> tag as well, we can access the image element at run-time, and change the picture it displays. This is what we've done in the example you'll see later on:

```
<BUTTON ID=cmdStop STYLE="position:absolute; top:200; width:80; left:325">
  <IMG ID=imgbtnStop SRC="mypic.gif" STYLE="height:30; width:25;"><BR>Stop
</BUTTON>
```

The <FIELDSET> and <LEGEND> Tags

When we create groups of controls, especially things like a set of related option buttons or checkboxes, we would often like to enclose them in a 'box' of some type, in the same way as most standard Windows applications do. This can be done using document divisions (with the `border` properties set to provide a border around the controls), but the <FIELDSET> and <LEGEND> tags provide a much neater solution.

The new <FIELDSET> tag works in a similar way to a <DIV> tag, in that it can create a container to hold the controls. The <FIELDSET> will generally include a <LEGEND> element for the group, which defines the text to be placed at the top of the 'box':

```
<FIELDSET ID=fldFruit>
  <LEGEND>Select a fruit</LEGEND>
  <INPUT TYPE=RADIO NAME=Fruit VALUE=Orange> Oranges <BR>
  <INPUT TYPE=RADIO NAME=Fruit VALUE=Banana> Bananas <BR>
  <INPUT TYPE=RADIO NAME=Fruit VALUE=Mango> Mango, my favorite <BR>
</FIELDSET>
```

Here's what it looks like in the browser:

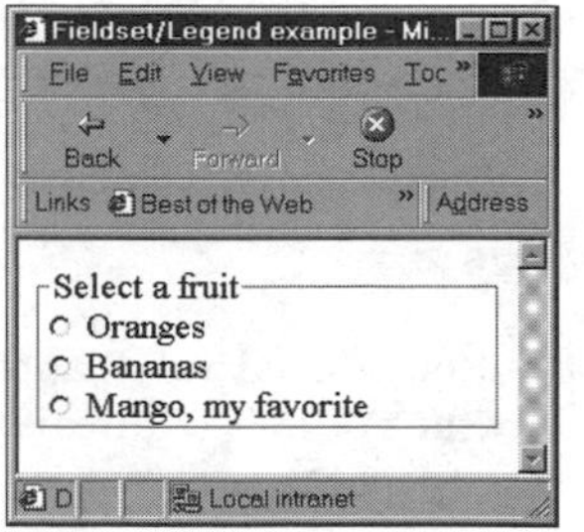

The <LABEL> Tag

The usual way to add a text caption to other control elements is to place text before or after it in the HTML source, or position it using a table. When we come to place controls using absolute positioning, this is a lot more difficult. We have to create a separate `<DIV>` for each caption, and position it as required.

To get round this, HTML 4.0 includes the `<LABEL>` tag. This will place any text (or other elements contained in the `<LABEL>` tag) next to a control automatically. The label effectively acts as a container for the control element:

```
<LABEL>
  Enter your name:
  <INPUT TYPE=TEXT ID=txtYourName>
</LABEL>
```

The ACCESSKEY and TABINDEX Attributes

One of the things that users appreciate in an application is the ability to press a 'hot-key', or short-cut key to place the focus on a particular control. This saves tabbing to it, or reaching for the mouse each time. While we can create this effect by reacting to the `onkeydown` event of the document – as suggested in earlier chapters – a better way is now available. This involves the `ACCESSKEY` attribute.

Here's the Stop button we looked at earlier, with the access key set to *T*: pressing *Alt T* sets the focus on the button.

```
<BUTTON ACCESSKEY="T" ID=cmdStop TABINDEX=13
        STYLE="position:absolute; top:200; width:80; left:325">
  <IMG ID=imgbtnStop SRC="stop.gif" WIDTH=25 HEIGHT=30><BR>Stop
</BUTTON>
```

You can also see that the `TABINDEX` attribute has been added, setting this control to be the thirteenth in the tab order of the form. This useful technique allows us to control the tab order when the page is created, and change it dynamically while the page is open if required.

A Dynamic Form Example

This example page is a simplified mock-up of an interface for a web-based client/server application that controls the cutting plant in a factory. It demonstrates just how much more we can achieve using the integral controls that are part of Dynamic HTML. It's called the Cutting List Controller (`CutList.htm`), and you can run or download it from our web site at http://webdev.wrox.co.uk/books/1746.

This is how it looks when you first open it:

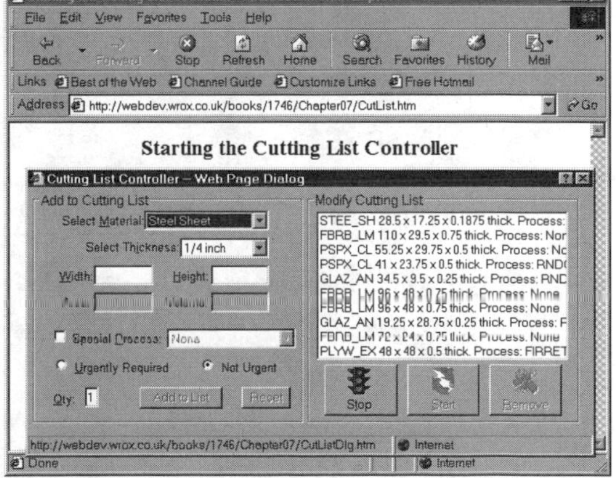

The original page, `CutList.htm`, uses the `showModalDialog` method we looked at in the previous section to open the form in a dialog window. This allows us to control which parts of the browser window will be visible, so we can make it look more like an application's form by omitting the toolbars, location bar, etc. This time, we've also included the 'Help' button in the title bar, by including the attribute `help=yes` in the 'features' string (note that this is actually the default for the `help` attribute):

```
<BODY ONLOAD="OpenCutListPage()">
  <H3 ALIGN="CENTER"> Starting the Cutting List Controller</H3>
</BODY>

<SCRIPT LANGUAGE=JAVASCRIPT>
function OpenCutListPage()
{
  showModalDialog("CutListDlg.htm", "MyDialog",
                  "dialogWidth=630px;dialogHeight=320px;"
                  + "center=yes;border=thin;help=yes");
  event.cancelBubble = true
}
</SCRIPT>
```

New Properties and Control Settings

As you can see from the screenshot, the form in the dialog window looks more like a 'real' compiled application than a web page. Many of the techniques it demonstrates are just not possible in earlier versions of HTML without resorting to external embedded controls, such as those from the Microsoft Forms ActiveX controls range.

The Left-hand 'Input Area' Controls

When creating the controls themselves we've used absolute positioning. We also placed those in the left-hand side of the dialog inside a `<FORM>` element, so that we can use a `RESET` button to clear the values. Here's part of the HTML that creates the controls (we've removed some of the code here to avoid unnecessary repetition):

```
<! The Input controls section >
<FIELDSET ID=Input STYLE="position:absolute; width:300;
                          height:255; top:5; left:5; font-size:9pt">
  <LEGEND> Add to Cutting List </LEGEND>
  <FORM ID=frmInput>
    <SELECT ID=cboMaterial ACCESSKEY="M" TABINDEX=1
            TITLE="Select the type material you require"
            STYLE="position:absolute; width=140; top=20; left=120;
                   font-size:9pt">
      <OPTION VALUE="PSPX_CL">Clear Perspex</OPTION>
...
      <OPTION VALUE="PLYW_EX">Exterior Plywood</OPTION>
    </SELECT>
    <SELECT ID=cboThickness ACCESSKEY="I" TABINDEX=2
            TITLE="Select the thickness of the material you require"
            STYLE="position:absolute; width=100; top=50; left=160;
                   font-size:9pt">
      <OPTION VALUE=0.1875>3/16 inch</OPTION>
...
      <OPTION VALUE=0.75>3/4 inch</OPTION>
    </SELECT>
    <INPUT TYPE=TEXT ID=txtWidth ACCESSKEY="W" TABINDEX=3
           TITLE="Enter the width of the material"
           STYLE="position:absolute; width=65; top=80; left=65;
                  font-size:9pt">
    <INPUT TYPE=TEXT ID=txtHeight ACCESSKEY="H" TABINDEX=4
           TITLE="Enter the height of the material"
           STYLE="position:absolute; width=65; top=80; left=195;
                  font-size:9pt">
...
```

We also make some of the controls read-only, and change the background color to indicate this to the user:

```
    ...
    <INPUT TYPE=TEXT ID=txtArea READONLY
           STYLE="position:absolute; width=65; top=110; left=65;
                  background-color:silver; font-size:9pt">
...
```

The buttons at the bottom of the left-hand control area are created using the traditional `<INPUT>` tag, with a type of `BUTTON`. This emphasizes the differences between this and the new `<BUTTON>` tag that we're using in the right-hand area. To make the buttons disabled when the page loads, we just have to include the `DISABLED` attribute:

```
    ...
    <INPUT TYPE=BUTTON ID=cmdAdd VALUE="Add to List" ACCESSKEY="A"
                                   TABINDEX=10 DISABLED
           TITLE="Add the current cutting entry to the cutting list"
           STYLE="position:absolute; top=215; left=115; font-size:9pt">
    <INPUT TYPE=RESET ID=cmdReset ACCESSKEY="E" TABINDEX=11
           TITLE="Clear the current cutting entry details" DISABLED
           STYLE="position:absolute; top=215; left=230; font-size:9pt">
  </FORM>
</FIELDSET>
```

In all these, notice how we assign a hot-key to them using the `ACCESSKEY` attribute, provide a pop-up tool-tip by setting the `TITLE` attribute, and set the tab order by providing a `TABINDEX` attribute. Notice also that we've only provided the form elements themselves here, and the accompanying labels (e.g. Select Material) are absent: we'll be adding these labels using the `<LABEL>` tag later in the code.

The Right-hand 'Cutting List' Control Area

The right-hand control area contains a list and three buttons. To make the `<SELECT>` tag show as an open list, instead of a drop-down combo box, we just need to set the `SIZE` attribute. We've also provided some entries in the list when the page is first loaded, so that you can see it working:

```
<! The Cutting List controls>
<FIELDSET ID=Output STYLE="position:absolute; width:300; height:255;
                            top:5; left:310; font-size:9pt">
  <LEGEND> Modify Cutting List </LEGEND>
  <SELECT ID=lstCutting SIZE=12 TABINDEX=12
          TITLE="Select an item in the list and click 'Remove' to delete it"
          STYLE="position:absolute; width=280; height=170; top=20;
                 left=7; font-size:7pt">
    <OPTION>STEE_SH 28.5 x 17.25 x 0.1875 thick. Process: VITREN</OPTION>
...
    <OPTION>PLYW_EX 48 x 48 x 0.5 thick. Process: FIRRET</OPTION>
  </SELECT>
...
```

You can also see the code to create our three picture buttons here. The last two are disabled when the form first loads. We've defined the access key for each one, the tab index, and the text for the pop-up tool-tip that appears when the mouse pointer pauses over the control:

```
...
<BUTTON ID=cmdStop ACCESSKEY="T" TABINDEX=13
        TITLE="Stop the cutting process"
        STYLE="position:absolute; top=190; width:80; left=17;
               font-size:9pt">
  <IMG ID=imgbtnStop SRC="stop.gif" WIDTH=25 HEIGHT=30>
    <BR>S<U>t</U>op
</BUTTON>
<BUTTON ID=cmdStart DISABLED ACCESSKEY="S" TABINDEX=14
        TITLE="Restart the cutting process"
        STYLE="position:absolute; top=190; width:80; left=108;
               font-size:9pt">
  <IMG ID=imgbtnStart SRC="lightoff.gif" WIDTH=25 HEIGHT=30>
    <BR><U>S</U>tart
</BUTTON>
<BUTTON ID=cmdRemove DISABLED ACCESSKEY="R" TABINDEX=15
        TITLE="Remove an item from cutting list"
        STYLE="position:absolute; top=190; width:80; left=199;
               font-size:9pt">
  <IMG ID=imgbtnRemove SRC="remgray.gif" WIDTH=28 HEIGHT=30>
    <BR><U>R</U>emove
</BUTTON>
</FIELDSET>
```

Pre-Loading and Caching Images

As well as the pictures that are visible on the buttons as the page loads, we'll be using others when the button state changes – i.e. when the disabled ones become enabled and vice versa. To prevent a delay while the new picture is loaded the first time, we force the browser to cache them by loading them into hidden `<IMG>` controls on the page:

```
<! Pre-load the other button pictures in hidden image controls >
<IMG SRC="remove.gif" STYLE="visibility:hidden">
<IMG SRC="lightoff.gif" STYLE="visibility:hidden">
```

We'll see these images being used later on.

The Control Labels

Finally, we place all the labels for the controls in the two control areas. Again, we assign a hot-key for the control attached to the label by using the `ACCESSKEY` attribute:

```
<! The Labels for the Input controls>
<LABEL STYLE="position:absolute; width=140; top=28; left=13; font-size:8pt"
       ID=lblMaterial FOR="cboMaterial" ACCESSKEY="M">
       Select <U>M</U>aterial:</LABEL>
<LABEL STYLE="position:absolute; width:150; height:20; top:57; left:40;
              font-size:8pt"
       ID=lblThickness ACCESSKEY="I" FOR="cboThickness">
       Select Th<U>i</U>ckness:</LABEL>
<LABEL STYLE="position:absolute; width:60; height:20; top:89; left:23;
              font-size:8pt"
       ID=lblWidth ACCESSKEY="W" FOR="txtWidth">
       <U>W</U>idth:</LABEL>
...
```

The Script That Makes It Work

As you may have guessed, the page contains quite a lot of script code. We'll look at the important routines to show you how it works, but we won't print it all here. Many of the techniques are duplicated across controls, and the whole thing is fully commented. You can view the source of the page, or download it with the rest of the samples to run and examine on your own system. We've implemented this example in VBScript, so that you get the chance see both languages in action throughout the book and the example pages.

Referring to the Form

Because all the controls in the right-hand area are in a `<FORM>`, we've created a global variable to reference the form. We set this when the page first loads – in the `window_onload()` event. At the same time, we place the text cursor in the top Select Material list and start the cutting timer running. Like the Dancing Buttons page we looked at in Chapter 5, this page uses a timer created with the `setInterval` method:

```
<SCRIPT LANGUAGE=VBSCRIPT>
Dim gInputForm   'global reference to the Input form
Dim gCutTimer    'global interval timer reference

Sub window_onLoad()
  Set gInputForm = Document.Forms("frmInput")  'set the form reference.
  gInputForm.cboMaterial.focus                 'set the text cursor focus
  gCutTimer = window.setInterval("CutTimer_Interval()", 5000)
End Sub
```

From this point on, we can refer to any control on the form by using the `gInputForm` variable.

Calculating the Area and Volume

When you enter values for a new entry, the Area and Volume controls are filled in as soon as the cursor leaves the appropriate control. The four controls that contribute to this are Width, Height, Thickness and Quantity, and the calculation is only done when they all have legitimate values. At the same time, the Add to List and Reset buttons become available:

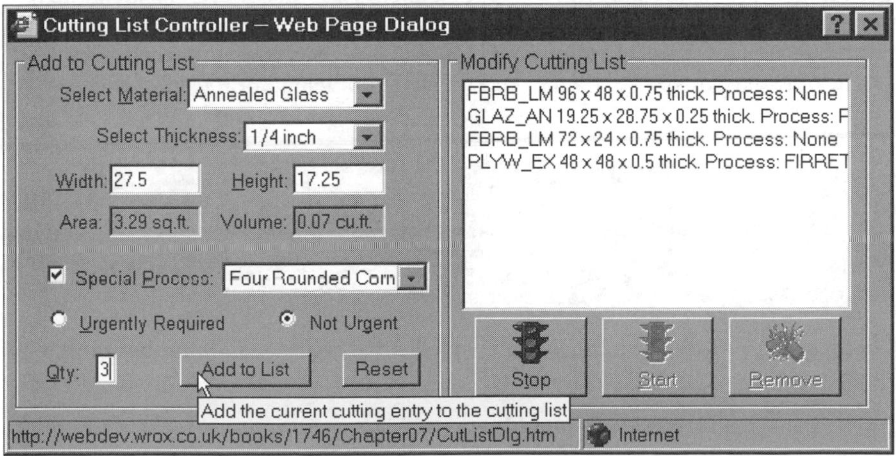

To do this, we have to react to the onchange event for the four controls that supply the values for the calculation. In each one (txtWidth, txtHeight, txtQty and cboThickness) we call a separate subroutine named UpdateAreaVol, which performs the calculation and updates the page once you tab or move to the next control:

```
Sub txtWidth_onchange()        'occurs when Width changed in text box
  UpdateAreaVol                'call the UpdateAreaVol subroutine
End Sub                        'similar code for txtHeight_onchange(),
                               'cboThickness_onchange() and txtQty_onChange()
...
```

Here's the UpdateAreaVol subroutine in full. To simplify the code we've omitted any checking for out-of-range result values, and we check only that the values are numeric:

```
Sub UpdateAreaVol()      'runs when the height, width or thickness change
  If IsNumeric(gInputForm.txtWidth.Value) _
  And IsNumeric(gInputForm.txtHeight.Value) _
  And IsNumeric(gInputForm.txtQty.Value) Then
    'set the values of the Area and Volume text boxes
    sngResult = gInputForm.txtWidth.Value * gInputForm.txtHeight.Value / 144
    gInputForm.txtArea.Value = FormatNumber(sngResult, 2) & " sq.ft."
    sngresult = sngResult * gInputForm.cboThickness.Value  / 12
    gInputForm.txtVolume.Value = FormatNumber(sngResult, 2) & " cu.ft."
    'enable the Add and Reset buttons
    gInputForm.cmdAdd.Disabled = False
    gInputForm.cmdReset.Disabled = False
  Else
    'disable the Add and Reset buttons
    gInputForm.cmdAdd.Disabled = True
    gInputForm.cmdReset.Disabled = True
    'clear the Area and Volume text boxes
    gInputForm.txtArea.Value = ""
    gInputForm.txtVolume.Value = ""
  End If
End Sub
```

If the values are numeric, we set the appropriate text boxes. Otherwise, we force the Area and Volume controls to blank out and we disable the Add and Reset buttons.

Using the VALUE property of a <SELECT> Element

You can see that the UpdateAreaVol code first checks that the Width, Height and Qty controls contain valid numbers. Notice that we don't check the Thickness list for a valid number. When we created it in the HTML, we used decimal numbers for the VALUE attribute of each <OPTION> tag, and the text equivalent for the entry the user sees:

```
    <SELECT ID=cboThickness ... >
      <OPTION VALUE=0.1875>3/16 inch</OPTION>
      <OPTION VALUE=0.25 SELECTED>1/4 inch</OPTION>
      <OPTION VALUE=0.3125>5/16 inch</OPTION>
      <OPTION VALUE=0.5>1/2 inch</OPTION>
      <OPTION VALUE=0.75>3/4 inch</OPTION>
    </SELECT>
```

Now, because it's a drop-down list, we know we'll always get a valid number for the value property.

Enabling and Disabling Buttons and Controls

The final part of the `UpdateAreaVol` routine enables or disables the buttons at the bottom of the left-hand control area, depending on the outcome of the update process. If the calculation is possible, the results are placed in the Area and Volume controls, and the two buttons have their `disabled` property set to `false`. If we don't have enough information, we set the `disabled` property to `true`, and clear the contents of the Area and Volume controls.

A similar technique is used to set the `disabled` state of the Special Process drop-down list. Here, we react to the user clicking on the checkbox `chkSpecial`, and examine its `checked` property to decide if we need to enable or disable the drop-down list `cboProcess`:

```
Sub chkSpecial_onclick()          'Special Process' checkbox clicked
  If gInputForm.chkSpecial.Checked Then
    gInputForm.cboProcess.Disabled = False    'enable the combo list
  Else
    gInputForm.cboProcess.Disabled = True     'disable the combo
    gInputForm.cboProcess.SelectedIndex = 0   'and set it to 'None'
  End If
  UpdateAreaVol
End Sub
```

If we are disabling it, we can also change the setting to None simply by assigning a new value to the control's `selectedIndex` property. The entry we want is the first in the list, so it has an `index` of zero. Of course, we can set it to any appropriate value using this technique.

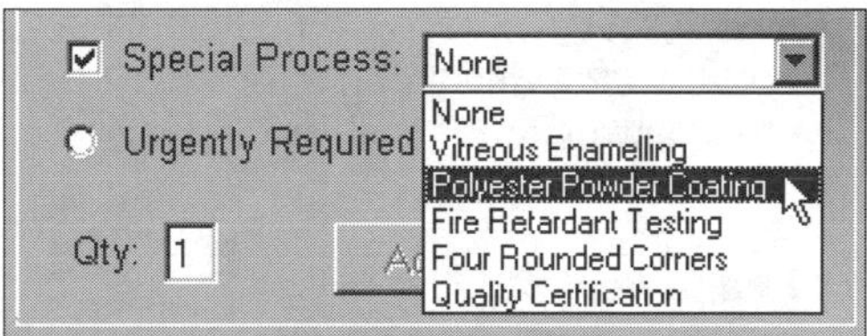

Adding the Entry to the Cutting List

The next task we need to consider is how we add an item to the list. If you've been watching the right-hand list, you'll see that it keeps shrinking. Items are removed automatically every five seconds or so, to simulate the processing in the factory. This is something new in HTML 4.0 – we couldn't change the contents of a `<SELECT>` list while a page was loaded in HTML 3.2, without using an embedded control.

To understand how it works, we need to look at how the list stores its entries. When we create the control in HTML, we use a series of `<OPTION>` tags to define the contents. Like all other elements in Dynamic HTML, we can change the contents of the HTML source dynamically while the page is displayed. The clever bit is that this includes adding `<OPTION>` tags to (and removing then from) a `<SELECT>` list.

The Options Collection

The <SELECT> tag stores its entries in a collection called `options`, which represents the <OPTIONS> tags within the HTML source. All we need to do is add new members to the collection, or remove existing ones. We can also tell how many members there are at any time by querying the collection's `length` property. We'll come to removing members in a while; in the meantime, let's consider how we go about adding them. Here's the code that runs when the Add to List button is clicked:

```
Sub cmdAdd_onclick()                          'Add' button pressed
  gInputForm.cmdAdd.Disabled = True           'disable the button
  'create the new string for the cutting list
  strEntry = gInputForm.cboMaterial.Value & " " _
          & gInputForm.txtWidth.Value & "in x " _
          & gInputForm.txtHeight.Value & "in x " _
          & gInputForm.cboThickness.Value & "in thick. " _
          & "Process: " & gInputForm.cboProcess.Value
  intQty = gInputForm.txtQty.Value    'get the quantity
  For intLoop = 1 To intQty
    'create a new element of type OPTION for the cutting list
    Set objEntry = document.createElement("OPTION")
    objEntry.text = strEntry      'set the text string to show in the list
    If gInputForm.optUrgent.checked Then
      lstCutting.add objEntry, 0      'add it to the top of the list
    Else
      lstCutting.add objEntry         'add it to the end of the list
    End If
  Next
End Sub
```

The first thing it does is disable the Add to List button so that the user can't accidentally add the same item twice. Then it builds up the text for the new entry in a string `strEntry`. Now we have to consider how we add it to the options collection. Each member of the collection is an `OPTION` element object, not just a string. It has an `index` and a `value` (as set by the `VALUE` attribute), as well as the `text` property that we see in the list.

Creating New Elements in a Collection

We can create an instance of an HTML element object using the `document` object's `createObject` method – here we're creating a new `OPTION` element object:

```
    Set objEntry = document.createElement("OPTION")
```

Then we can assign the values we want for its properties. In our case, we don't need the `value` property, but we do need the `text` property to be shown in the list. This, of course, is `strEntry`:

```
    objEntry.text = strEntry      'set the text string to show in the list
```

Now we can add the new element to the `options` collection using the `add` method. In our example, we'll add it at the top of the cutting list form element if it's urgent, by using the optional second `index` parameter:

```
      lstCutting.add objEntry, 0      'add it to the top of the list
```

Otherwise, we add it to the end by omitting this parameter:

```
      lstCutting.add objEntry         'add it to the end of the list
```

Removing Cutting List Entries

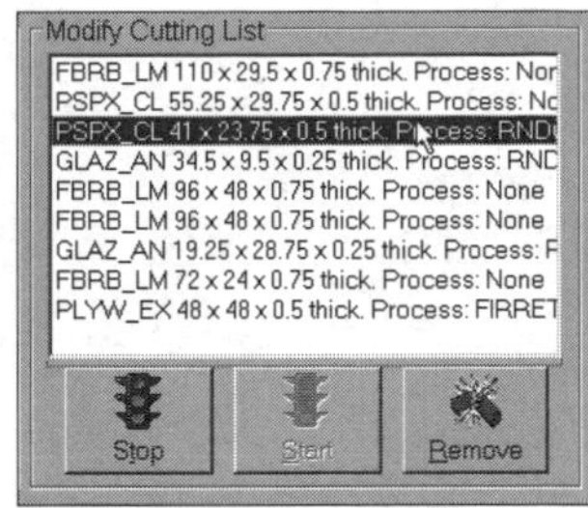

The entries in the cutting list are removed every five seconds or so automatically, but the user can also select and remove them using the Remove button in the right-hand area of the page. This button is disabled until they click on the list to select an entry.

So, we need to respond to a click on the list, and enable the Remove button. This is easy enough – we use the `onclick` event of the list, and set the button's `disabled` property as appropriate. But how do we know which one they selected? We use the `selectedIndex` property of the list (this is `-1` if nothing is selected) or the `index` of the selected item (starting from zero for the first one).

Of course, the task is more than just setting the `disabled` property, like we did with the buttons in the left-hand control area. Here, we also have to change the picture they display. We've provided the pictures for each button as both a color image and a grayed-out version. When we disable the button, we just have to change the `src` property of the `<IMG>` tag as appropriate as well, to load the picture which we cached earlier:

```
Sub lstCutting_onclick()                          'click in the cutting list
  If lstCutting.SelectedIndex >= 0 Then           'existing entry selected
    cmdremove.Disabled = False                    'enable the 'Remove' button
    document.all("imgbtnRemove").src = "remove.gif"
  Else
    cmdremove.Disabled = True                     'disable the 'Remove' button
    document.all("imgbtnRemove").src = "remgray.gif"
  End If
End Sub
```

Removing Elements from a Collection

Once we've enabled the button, we can respond to it being clicked by removing the item and disabling the button again. Removing an item from a collection is done with the `remove` method. It takes a single parameter, namely the `index` of the item to be removed – and again we get this from the list's `selectedIndex` property:

```
Sub cmdRemove_onclick()                              'Remove' button pressed
  lstCutting.remove lstCutting.SelectedIndex         'remove the selected entry
  lstCutting_onclick                                 'and update the buttons
End Sub
```

Then we can update the enabled states of the buttons by simply calling the `lstCutting_onclick` routine.

Stopping and Starting the Cutting Process

The other two buttons in the right-hand section of the page allow the user to stop and restart the cutting process as required. To stop it, all we have to do is clear the interval timer that we started running when we loaded the page. Of course, we have to change the enabled state of the Stop and Start buttons as appropriate as well:

```
Sub cmdStop_onclick()          'Stop' button pressed
  window.clearInterval gCutTimer 'stop the timer running
  cmdStop.Disabled = True       'disable the 'Stop' button
  cmdStart.Disabled = False     'enable the 'Start' button
  document.all("imgbtnStop").src = "lightoff.gif"
  document.all("imgbtnStart").src = "go.gif"
End Sub
```

To re-start the process, we just reverse the actions we took to stop it. However, we also need to make sure that there are some items in the list first, and we'll remove the first one straight away to indicate that cutting has restarted:

```
Sub cmdStart_onclick()          'Start' button pressed
  If lstCutting.length > 0 Then
    lstCutting.remove 0         'remove top item and start timer
    gCutTimer = window.setInterval("CutTimer_Interval()", 5000)
    cmdStop.Disabled = False    'enable the 'Stop' button
    cmdStart.Disabled = True    'disable the 'Start' button
    document.all("imgbtnStop").src = "stop.gif"
    document.all("imgbtnStart").src = "lightoff.gif"
  End If
End Sub
```

The Interval Timer Code

While the cutting process is running, the `setInterval` method calls our `CutTimer_Interval` routine every five seconds. Here, we simply remove the top item from the cutting list, and if it's now empty we call the `cmdStop` button routine. This looks after changing the enabled state of the buttons for us:

```
Sub CutTimer_Interval()   'timer interval over
  lstCutting.remove 0     'remove top entry from cutting list
  lstCutting_onclick      'update the buttons
  'if list is empty then stop the timer
  If lstCutting.length = 0 Then cmdStop_onclick
End Sub
```

You'll notice in several of these routines that we've created our own 'pseudo-events' by running other event handler routines directly. This technique often saves us from having to write so much code, and makes maintenance much easier. What you have to watch out for, however, is not to create a loop where an event handler calls another one, which itself calls the first one. This is a good way to lock up the browser and prevent your pages working at all!

Providing Context Sensitive Help

The final technique we want to look at in the Cutting List Controller page is the new support for context-sensitive help in a web page. If we are going to build interactive applications that use a browser as the front end, we need to be able to mirror as much of the functionality of a normal Windows application as possible.

One thing that makes any application easier to use, especially for newcomers, is the provision of easy-to-access help – plus tips on the way that the application works. We've already seen how to implement the pop up tool-tips that are used in almost all new applications, by setting the `TITLE` attribute for the element within the HTML.

Another way that we can provide help is by using the What's This? button at the top of a dialog window. Clicking this in a normal application, then clicking somewhere in the dialog, provides a pop-up window containing more information about the dialog and its contents. Placing the text cursor in a control and pressing the *F1* key usually has the same effect.

Reacting to the onhelp Event

We can respond to the What's This? button and the *F1* key in our web pages by using the new `onhelp` event that is supported for nearly all visible elements. Our page displays some specific help in a message box when you click the What's This? button and click on a control or its label, or press the *F1* key when a control has the input focus:

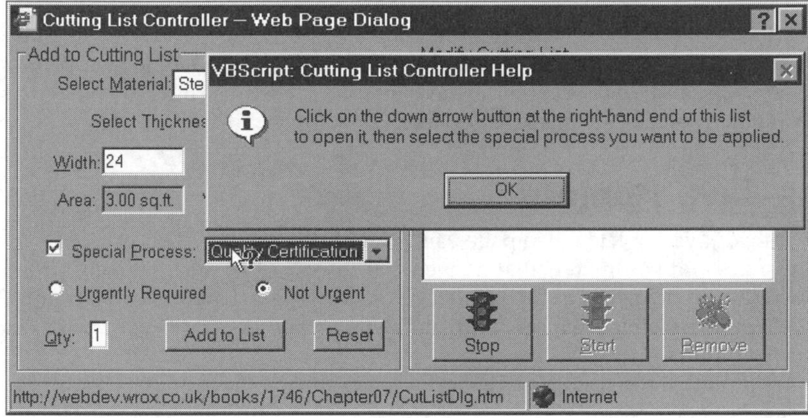

How it Works

When the `onhelp` event occurs, we can look for the source element using the `event` object's `srcElement` property. However, in our example, we're being a bit cleverer than that. We want a click on a control's label to display the help message as well, so we've made sure that each control and label have `ID` properties that vary only in the first three characters.

For example, the Quantity text box has the `ID` property `txtQty`, while its label has the `ID` property `lblQty`. By chopping off the first three characters, we can use a `Select Case` statement that gives the same result for each control and its label:

```
Sub document_onhelp()      'Window's help event occurred
  'this may be with the ? button at the top of the window, or by pressing F1
  'first set the default help message
  strHelpMesg = "No more information is available for this item."
  'find source element ID and remove first three letters This means (for
  'example) that lblMaterial and cboMaterial will show the same message.
  strSourceID = Mid(window.event.srcElement.id, 4)
  Select Case strSourceID
    Case "Material"
      strHelpMesg = "Click on the down arrow button at the ... etc."
    Case "Thickness"
      strHelpMesg = "Click on the down arrow button at the ... etc."
    ... other messages ...
```

```
    Case "Remove"
      strHelpMesg = "Use this button to remove an item from ... etc."
  End Select
  'display the help message
  MsgBox strHelpMesg, vbInformation, "Cutting List Controller Help"
  window.event.cancelBubble = true
End Sub
```

Using Objects and Controls

Of course, there are times when we want to achieve effects that aren't possible using just the HTML controls. In these cases, we still end up needing to use an ActiveX control or a Java applet to carry a particular task that even Dynamic HTML can't manage on its own. Although there are lots of improvements in the way that forms work – and extra properties, methods and events exposed that we can use in our code – they may not be able to give us exactly what we need.

It's at this point that we have to make a decision as to how we implement an 'outside' object in our page. We've already made a brief comparison between Java applets and ActiveX controls, and this is the point where you decide which route to take. To help you, we'll look briefly at the possibilities here.

Using Java Applets

We can embed Java applets into a page using the <APPLET> tag. This accepts a special set of attributes and parameters that define what the object is, where it comes from, and how it should be used. On top of that are the more usual attributes that control the size of the applet's visible representation on the page, and the positioning with respect to the surrounding elements.

The <APPLET> Tag

To use the <APPLET> tag, we add the attributes that define the location of the applet's code and its appearance within the page inside the opening tag. Then, between this and the closing </APPLET> tag, we can provide parameters which define the custom properties for that applet:

```
<APPLET WIDTH=100 HEIGHT=50 ALIGN=CENTER ID=MyApplet ALT="Wrox Applet"
        CODEBASE="http://www.wrox.com/java/" CODE="WroxApp.class">
  <PARAM NAME="STARTCOLOR" VALUE="green">
  <PARAM NAME="RATINGLEVEL" VALUE=24>
  <PARAM NAME="FAILUREMSG" VALUE="Whoops">
</APPLET>
```

In this example, we're using a fictitious object whose code file WroxApp.class is stored in the server directory http://www.wrox.com/java. It provides three properties that we need to set when we start the object running in the page: STARTCOLOR, RATINGLEVEL and FAILUREMSG. We use <PARAM> tags to set the values of these within the <APPLET> tag.

Once the page is downloaded, the browser fetches the applet code from our server, creates an instance of the object that the code defines, sets the properties using the <PARAM> tag values, and starts its execution.

The <APPLET> Attributes

Here's a list of commonly-used attributes supported by the `<APPLET>` tag in Dynamic HTML (for a complete list, see Appendix C):

Attribute	Description
`ACCESSKEY`	Sets a key to be used as the 'short-cut key'.
`ALIGN`	The alignment of the object horizontally and vertically on the page.
`CLASS`	The style class to associate with the element to control its appearance.
`CODEBASE`	The URL where the class file can be downloaded from if required.
`DATAFLD`	Defines the field in the data source for data-bound controls.
`DATASRC`	Defines the data source for data-bound controls.
`DISABLED`	When set to true prevents the object code from executing.
`HSPACE`	Sets the horizontal distance between the object and surrounding elements.
`ID`	Provides an ID string to refer to the object by.
`NAME`	Provides a name to refer to the object by.
`SRC`	Defines the URL of file that provides the applet's data.
`STYLE`	The CSS style properties for the object's container.
`TITLE`	The text for the tool-tip displayed when the mouse pointer is over the object.
`VSPACE`	Sets the vertical distance between the object and surrounding elements.

While some applets may be simply decorative animations, the more recent are aimed at achieving something more useful. The common ones are things like stock tickers and graphic manipulation objects, but the range of available applets is huge. To see more, visit http://www.gamelan.com or http://www.jars.com.

Object and Container Properties, Methods and Events

To be of real use in a dynamic page, an object needs to provide properties, methods and events. However, when an object is embedded into the page, you have to remember that there are two distinct sets of properties, methods and events available:

- The HTML page provides a **container** which holds the object, and this container has properties, methods and events that are the same in all cases – irrespective of the object it contains

- The **object** that runs inside this container may also expose its own properties, methods and events. These are separate from those of the container, and can be different for each object

The **properties** of the <APPLET> tag (the container), as listed above, are set by the attributes of the tag, and can be manipulated in code like any other properties. However, it's worth noting in passing that the two mainline browsers, Internet Explorer and Netscape's Navigator/Communicator, implement the connection between the object and the script in the page in different ways.

Working with Applets in Internet Explorer

In Microsoft's Internet Explorer browser, Java applets are 'wrapped' in an ActiveX/COM interface when they are instantiated in the page. This makes them appear to the browser like any other integral object, which has a set of properties, methods and events that mirror those in the control and those of the container.

For example, the applet adopts the standard Dynamic HTML set of **methods** such as `scrollIntoView`, `getAttribute`, and so on, through its container element (the <APPLET> tag). The object may also provide its own properties, methods and events for use in our code. For example we might want to change the object's `RATINGLEVEL` property while our page is displayed, or react to the object's `ratinglevelchange` event:

```
MyApplet.ratinglevel = 36  'change the rating level
```

```
Sub MyApplet_ratinglevelchange()
  'runs when the user changes the rating level in the applet
  ...
  'code to respond to the event goes here
  ...
End Sub
```

Using ActiveX Controls

To insert an ActiveX control into our page, we use an <OBJECT> tag. Internet Explorer supported ActiveX controls from version 3 onwards. Because the ActiveX standard is a development of the existing Microsoft OLE technology, there are hundreds of ActiveX controls available for use in our pages – and many are provided as standard with Internet Explorer. A gallery showing some of those that are available is at http://www.activex.com.

The <OBJECT> Tag

The basic principles of using ActiveX controls and the <OBJECT> tag are similar to the <APPLET> tag we looked at earlier. We use the normal HTML attributes to set the size and relative position of the visible portion of the object in the page, and a series of <PARAM> tags to set its properties. Notice that we use the `ID` attribute (rather than the `NAME` attribute) to set the object's 'identity', so that we can refer to it in our code:

```
<OBJECT ID="timMove" WIDTH=39 HEIGHT=39
  CLASSID="CLSID:59CCB4A0-727D-11CF-AC36-00AA00A47DD2"
  CODEBASE="http://activex.microsoft.com/controls/iexplorer/timer.ocx">
  <PARAM NAME="Interval" VALUE="4000">
  <PARAM NAME="Enabled" VALUE="False">
</OBJECT>
```

The CODEBASE attribute defines the URL or location of the object's code, in case it is not already available on the client and has to be downloaded – just like a Java class file. As objects are downloaded, they are registered on the client in Windows registry so that the system can find and use them the next time, without having to download them again.

To ensure that each one has a unique registered identity, it contains a CLASSID string – created inside the object when it is built and guaranteed to be unique. Using just a name would provide too many opportunities for clashes when two designers used the same name for their different controls.

The <OBJECT> Attributes

Here is a full list of the attributes for the <OBJECT> tag. The valid values for each one, where applicable, are given in Appendix C. We'll be coming back to the data-binding attributes (DATA, DATAFLD and DATASRC) later in this chapter.

Attribute	Description
ACCESSKEY	Defines the 'hot-key' that can be used to activate the control.
ALIGN	The alignment of the object horizontally and vertically on the page.
CLASS	The style class to associate with the element to control its appearance.
CLASSID	The unique registry value to identify the control.
CODE	The class name of a Java applet, if this is the object source.
CODEBASE	The URL or location where the object code file can be downloaded from.
CODETYPE	Defines the type of the object, and the way the operating system handles it.
DATA	Defines the URL of the data source for data-bound controls.
DATAFLD	Defines the field in the data source for data-bound controls.
DATASRC	Defines the data source for data-bound controls.
DIR	Sets the reading order for the object – left-to-right or right-to-left.
HEIGHT	Sets the height of the object on the page.
HSPACE	Sets the horizontal distance between the object and surrounding elements.
ID	Provides an ID string to refer to the object by.
LANG	Defines the language to use, such as en for English or fr for French.

Table Continued on Following Page

Attribute	Description
LANGUAGE	Defines the language name for the object container events, either "VBSCRIPT", "JAVASCRIPT", or "XML".
NAME	Provides a name to refer to the object by.
STYLE	The CSS style properties for the object's container.
TABINDEX	The tab index for the object's container.
TITLE	The text for the tooltip displayed when the mouse pointer is over the object.
TYPE	Defines the Mime type for the object, as defined in the registry.
VSPACE	Sets the vertical distance between the object and surrounding elements.
WIDTH	Sets the width of the object on the page.

Object and Container Properties, Methods and Events

The <OBJECT> tag provides a set of properties, methods and events for the container, and the object can provide its own set of properties, methods and events as well. The container properties are the attributes you've seen above, and the methods are the standard Dynamic HTML methods such as `scrollIntoView`, `getAttribute`, and so on.

The <OBJECT> tag also provides a wide range of events for the container. There are 30 in all, and for visible controls we can react to them in code in the same way as we would for an ordinary HTML element. However, they will not all be available for non-visible controls:

onbeforeeditfocus	onblur	oncellchange
ondataavailable	ondatasetchanged	ondatasetcomplete
ondrag	ondragend	ondragenter
ondragover	ondragstart	ondrop
onfocus	onkeydown	onkeypress
onlosecapture	onpropertychange	onreadystatechange
onrowenter	onrowexit	onrowsdelete
onscroll	onselectstart	onclick
ondblclick	ondragleave	onerror
onkeyup	onresize	onrowsinserted

And, of course, the object itself will usually provide us with its own events. The <OBJECT> tag example we used earlier inserts a Microsoft **Timer** ActiveX control into the page. It has just one event of its own, and two properties, that we can use in our code:

```
Sub timMove_Timer()
  'occurs regularly every 'Interval' number of milliseconds
End Sub
```

```
timMove.Interval = 5000   'set the Interval to 5 seconds
timMove.Enabled = True    'and set the timer running
```

If an object exposes properties, methods or events that have the same name as the container (i.e. the <OBJECT> element) we have a problem. By default, accessing the object through the ID of the <OBJECT> tag will provide a reference to the container's property, method or event if one exists with that name. To get round this, we use the object syntax:

```
MyObject.width = 100;        // sets the object container's width property
MyObject.object.width = 75; // sets the object's width property
```

There are two ActiveX controls that you will no doubt meet in Internet Explorer 4 and beyond as you start to develop your own site. These provide us with a way of connecting our pages to a database, and are the subject of the next section.

Data Binding in Dynamic HTML

A great deal of browser use, especially on a corporate Intranet or web-based client/server application interface, is to do with viewing and manipulating the contents of databases. These may be databases in the traditional sense (systems like Oracle, SQL Server or Access) or other specialist implementations. To achieve this task, the traditional route has been through some type of server-side programming – perhaps CGI, scripting languages like Perl, or more specialist methods like Active Server Pages.

The Downside of Server-Side Processing

Server-side processing is an excellent solution in most situations, for many reasons – for example, because the server executes the code at its end, and sends the client the final HTML-only page. We won't extol all the virtues here – that's another book.

However, there is a downside. When the user wants to interact with the database – perhaps updating information or just scrolling through the records – it involves repeated server-side processing and the regular transfer of data and instructions between the server and the browser.

This isn't usually a problem on a local network or Intranet, unless the demands on the server are so high as to absorb all its processing capacity. Out on the Web, however, the repeated connections and data transfer demand a more elegant approach.

Caching Data Client-side

One obvious solution is to **cache** the data at the client (browser) – so instead of only sending extracts each time, we allow the browser to extract what it wants and display it. This adds another advantage in that the user can update several rows of a data set (i.e. several records), then send back the complete package of changes in one go.

Providing a Data Source

To achieve data binding in a Dynamic HTML page, there has to be a way of connecting the controls on the page with a data source. In our example, we're using a very simple source – a small text file containing nutritional information. In fact, the screen shot opposite shows our 'database':

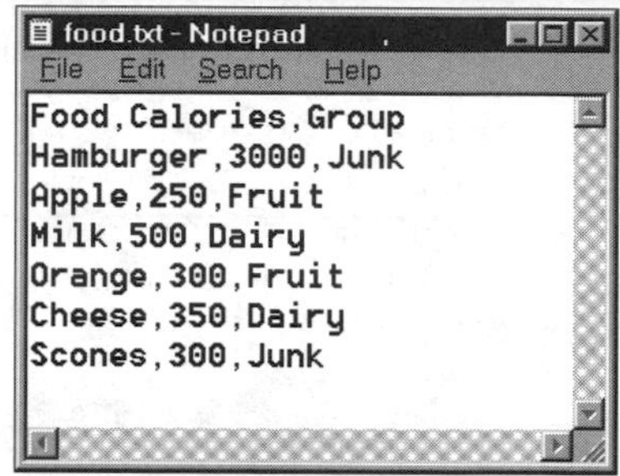

The first step is to connect this database to our page, so that the controls in the page can access the data. This requires a connector component that can read the data and access our page. IE5 provides five of these controls:

- Microsoft **Remote Data Service** (RDS) control
- JDBC Applet control
- XML Data Source control
- MSHTML Data Source object
- **Tabular Data Control** (TDC) control

The RDS control is designed to access ODBC-equipped data sources, and offers the ability to update the data from within the browser. The JDBC Applet control provides similar functionality to the RDS control, but it is implemented as a Java applet. This means that it can be used in browsers such as Netscape, that do not support ActiveX Controls.

The XML Data Source control provides access to client-side or server-side data that is stored in XML format. XML is becoming a leading data description format, and we will look at it in Chapter 8. The MSHTML Data Source object will expose the contents of an HTML page as a read-only recordset. This allows you to work with the contents as the page in the same way that you would a database.

For this example, we only have Tabular Data, so we'll use the TDC control. For more detailed information on the other data source controls, take a look at ADO 2.0 Programmer's Reference *(Wrox, ISBN 1-861001-83-5)*.

Inserting the Tabular Data Control

We insert the data connector control (in our case the Tabular Data control) using a normal <OBJECT> tag – we've given it an ID of food. We've specified our database food.txt (in the same directory as the page) for the DataURL property, and we've set the FieldDelim property to a comma – this is the field delimiter within our file's 'records'. The final <PARAM> tag sets the UseHeader property to True, because our database has the field names in the first record (or row):

```
<OBJECT ID="food" WIDTH=100 HEIGHT=51
  CLASSID="CLSID:333C7BC4-460F-11D0-BC04-0080C7055A83">
  <PARAM NAME="FieldDelim" VALUE=",">
  <PARAM NAME="DataURL" VALUE="food.txt">
  <PARAM NAME="UseHeader" VALUE=True>
</OBJECT>
```

Once the page is loaded, the browser will fetch the data from the DataURL and create a connection to it.

Data Binding Attributes

To connect the fields in the database with controls on our page, we use the tag attributes DATASRC, DATAFLD and DATAFORMATAS. These are available for a range of tags, as shown in Appendix C. To understand why they apply to some tags and not others, we need to delve a little deeper.

The concept behind data binding is that, once a connection is made to a data source, the browser has two options. It can either show individual values from this source in separate controls (called **single-valued data binding**), or it can display lists of whole or partial records in a set of table controls (called **tabular data binding**). We'll look at single-value data binding first.

Single-Value Data Binding

To bind individual controls to a data source, we have to provide two items of information: a reference to the connector object for that data source, and the name of a field within the data source for this control. For example, we can bind an <INPUT> tag to the Calories field in our food data source like this:

```
<INPUT TYPE="TEXT" DATASRC="#food" DATAFLD="Calories">
```

The value of DATASRC is related to the fact that food is the ID of the TDC control we inserted into our page (it's not related to the name of the database file). It is preceded by a hash sign (#) to indicate this.

When the page is loaded, the control will display the value of that field for the first record in our database. We'll see how to display other records in a while.

This method works for different kinds of controls, depending on the type of data the data source contains:

- We can display text or numeric data in TEXT-type INPUT controls, SELECT lists, TEXTAREA and MARQUEE controls, plus ordinary document SPAN and DIV controls.
- We can use it as a PARAM to an object tag, if the control is an ActiveX control or Java applet.
- If the text is the name of an image file, we can use it in an IMG tag.
- True/False values can be displayed in CHECKBOX- and RADIO-type INPUT controls, as well as in the PARAM tag of an object.

This example page – available at http://webdev.wrox.co.uk/books/1746 – shows how we can display the contents of a record from our food database. It also contains buttons to move around the recordset created by the TDC control:

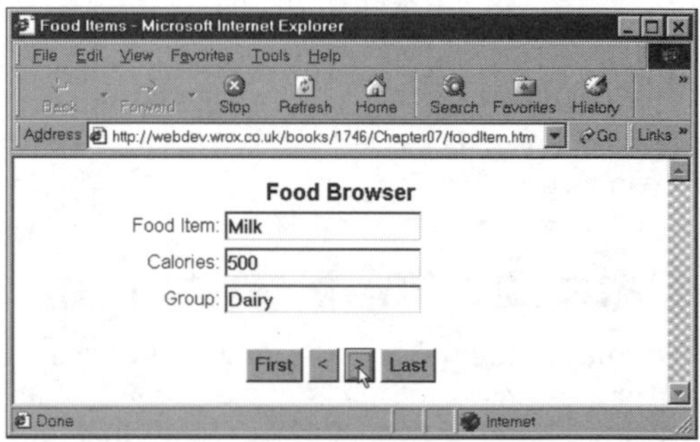

Here's an extract of the HTML source for the page. It uses two tables. The first holds the heading and the three text <INPUT> tags. The second holds the four navigation buttons:

```
<TABLE WIDTH=100%>
<TR>
  <TH COLSPAN=2> Food Browser </TH>
</TR>
<TR>
  <TD ALIGN=RIGHT> Food Item: </TD>
  <TD> <INPUT TYPE="TEXT" DATASRC="#food" DATAFLD="Food"> </TD>
</TR>
<TR>
  <TD ALIGN=RIGHT> Calories: </TD>
  <TD> <INPUT TYPE="TEXT" DATASRC="#food" DATAFLD="Calories"> </TD>
</TR>
<TR>
  <TD ALIGN=RIGHT> Group: </TD>
  <TD> <INPUT TYPE="TEXT" DATASRC="#food" DATAFLD="Group"> </TD>
</TR>
</TABLE><P>
<TABLE WIDTH=100%>
<TR>
  <TD ALIGN=CENTER>
    <INPUT NAME="cmdFirst" TYPE="BUTTON" VALUE="First">
    <INPUT NAME="cmdPrevious" TYPE="BUTTON" VALUE=" < ">
    <INPUT NAME="cmdNext" TYPE="BUTTON" VALUE=" > ">
    <INPUT NAME="cmdLast" TYPE="BUTTON" VALUE="Last">
  </TD>
</TR>
</TABLE>
```

Navigating the Recordset

To move through the records, we use objects and methods exposed by the TDC control. These are similar to those provided by most Microsoft (and other) database technologies. The control provides a `recordset` object that represents our data, and this has methods that allow us to manipulate it:

```
Sub cmdPrevious_onclick()
If Not food.recordset.bof Then food.recordset.movePrevious
End Sub

Sub cmdNext_onclick()
If Not food.recordset.eof Then food.recordset.moveNext
End Sub

Sub cmdFirst_onclick()
 food.recordset.moveFirst
End Sub

Sub cmdLast_onclick()
 food.recordset.moveLast
End Sub
```

These methods will automatically refresh the input controls as well. Notice here that we check the `bof` (beginning of file) and `eof` (end of file) properties before we move to the previous or next record. When we are at the first record in the recordset, we can still `movePrevious` without an error, and the controls display an 'empty' record. At this point the `bof` property becomes `True`, and any further attempt to `movePrevious` produces as error. The same kind of process works at the end of the file, with `eof`.

Tabular Data Binding

When we want to display the contents of several records, in a tabular view, we need to repeat certain parts of our page once for each record. There's more than one way to do this; the most usual is to create a document division and use a table with the special tags that define the heading and body sections of the table.

Here's an example. We use a `<DIV>` tag to denote an area of the page as a division, and we build a table inside it. This time, we use the `DATASRC` attribute in the `<TABLE>` tag, to indicate that the whole table is bound to the data connector control we named `food`:

```
<DIV ALIGN=CENTER>
<TABLE ID=Data WIDTH=75% DATASRC=#food>
  <THEAD>
    <TH> Group </TH> <TH> Food </TH> <TH> Calories </TH>
  </THEAD>
  <TBODY>
    <TR>
      <TD ALIGN=CENTER> <SPAN DATAFLD="Group"> </SPAN> </TD>
      <TD ALIGN=CENTER> <SPAN DATAFLD="Food"> </SPAN> </TD>
      <TD ALIGN=CENTER> <SPAN DATAFLD="Calories"> </SPAN> </TD>
    </TR>
  </TBODY>
</TABLE>
</DIV>
```

Inside the table, we want to display the field names (the headings of the columns) then repeat the data from the records – one per table row. To indicate to the browser which section of the table is which, we use <THEAD> and <TBODY> tags. The <THEAD> section will only appear once, but the <TBODY> section will be repeated for each record in our recordset.

However, we can't provide the field value to the <TD> tag, as we did earlier with the <INPUT> tag – it doesn't accept 'values' as such. Instead, we just place a <SPAN> (or <DIV>) tag in the appropriate position and set *its* DATAFLD attribute to the field name. We'll see this in action in a moment.

Sorting and Filtering

Sometimes, we don't want to display all the records in the data source, or we may want to display them in a different order from the order they exist in the data source. In our earlier single-value data binding example, it would be easier to find a particular food if the records appeared in alphabetical order. If we are listing records in tabular format, it would be handy if we could just list records that matched certain criteria – calorie values below 250, for example.

We can do both of these things, and more, by setting other properties of our data connector control. Here, we're filtering on the field (or column) named `Group`, and selecting only values where it is equal to `"Dairy"`. We're also sorting the resulting recordset by the value in the field named `Food`:

```
<OBJECT ID="food" WIDTH=100 HEIGHT=51
  CLASSID="CLSID:333C7BC4-460F-11D0-BC04-0080C7055A83">
  <PARAM NAME="FieldDelim" VALUE=",">
  <PARAM NAME="DataURL" VALUE="food.txt">
  <PARAM NAME="UseHeader" VALUE=True>
  <PARAM NAME="FilterColumn" VALUE="Group">
  <PARAM NAME="FilterCriterion" VALUE="=">
  <PARAM NAME="FilterValue" VALUE="Dairy">
  <PARAM NAME="SortColumn" VALUE="Food">
</OBJECT>
```

When combined with the earlier code to create a tabular format, this is what we get:

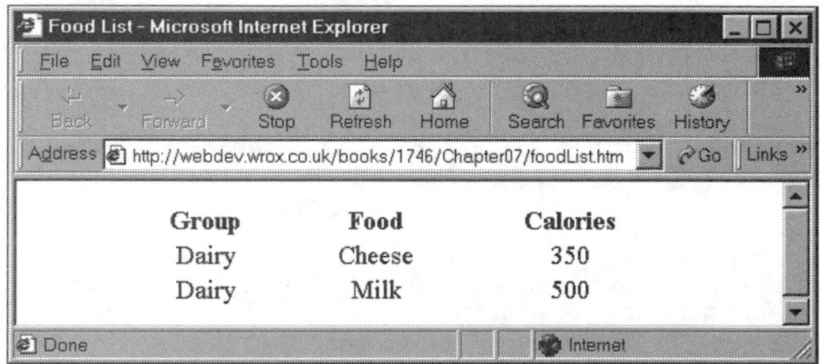

Of course, this is only a taster of what data binding can achieve. For example, it's possible to arrange for the data source to be updated – the cached 'local' data is returned to the server. To find out more about data binding, and client/server programming with data binding, look for the aforementioned *ADO 2.0 Programmer's Reference* from Wrox Press.

Summary

In this chapter, we began by looking at how we can create new browser windows, and started to think about working with HTML controls such as the <SELECT> drop-down list control. We also started looking at how Dynamic HTML makes it possible to build more interactive web-based pages – including forms – without having to resort to using embedded ActiveX controls or Java applets.

The new properties, methods and events provided for the intrinsic HTML form controls gives us a lot more freedom in building really dynamic forms, and we used these to build a sample client/server front end using Dynamic HTML in the browser.

However, as we discovered, there are times when the standard HTML controls just can't cut it. At this point, you have to know how to take advantage of the hundreds of pre-built objects that are now available. We looked briefly at the issues of compatibility between browsers that affect their use, and how the two tags <APPLET> and <OBJECT> can be used to insert them into our pages.

Finally, we ended the chapter by using a special ActiveX control that provides data-binding capabilities to Dynamic HTML. We briefly introduced the way that this new technology can be used to make working with databases in the browser much more responsive and user-friendly. In all, the main points of this chapter are that we can:

- Create new windows and dialogs to display individual pages, using the `open`, `showModalDialog` and `showModelessDialog` methods of the current `window` object
- Build interactive forms using just HTML controls and standard tags, within a dialog window if required
- Use the new HTML tags, and the new properties and events of the existing HTML controls, to make our forms more usable and dynamic
- Provide context-sensitive help in web pages, using the new `onhelp` event
- Insert ActiveX controls and Java applets into our pages, to cope with the inevitable situations where Dynamic HTML alone cannot provide what we need
- Bind a server or client-based data source to our web pages using data binding, allowing access to different formats of data, including ODBC databases, XML formatted files, and even HTML files, as well as providing different ways to display the information in the browser

We have now looked at the core technologies that make of HTML 4.0 and its implementation in Internet Explorer 5. These technologies allow us to develop web pages that are far beyond what was possible just a few short years ago. Next, we will take a look at two of the newest technologies that are moving to the forefront of the Internet world. The first, eXtensible Markup Language (XML), is quickly becoming the data lingua franca of the web and we will look at the support that IE5 has for this new technology. Also, we will look at the concept of Behaviors, which allow the interactivity of VBScript or JavaScript to be packaged in a reusable component, and then easily applied to elements in different web pages.

8

Introducing XML and Behaviors

One of the hottest buzzwords right now in the world of the Internet is **XML** – eXtensible Markup Language. XML is a powerful data description language that is optimized for delivery over the web. It allows for the data that is being passed from server to browser (or even from server to server) to be self-describing. XML provides a structured mechanism for labeling each piece of data that is being passed between the two systems.

Internet Explorer 5 offers significant native support for XML. It allows for the direct viewing of XML files, support for formatting XML data using style sheets, and also the ability to directly embed XML inside of HTML files themselves.

XML is also used to support another new technology of IE5 – **behaviors**. In the past, when developers wrote cool client-side scripting code for a web page, they had very few options to reuse that code in other pages. Techniques such as ActiveX controls, Java applets, or scriptlets all had their drawbacks. Behaviors have been introduced in IE5 to separate the interaction code from the display code, so that the interaction code can be used on different elements, even among different pages.

In order to describe what behaviors can do, Microsoft has chosen to use XML as the language to describe the capabilities of behaviors. So, to get started, we first need to look at what XML is and how it is supported in IE5.

Introduction to XML

As we discussed in Chapter 1, HTML is a markup language – in fact, HTML stands for HyperText Markup Language. A markup language is a set of special codes that are placed into a document in order to provide additional information about something in the document. It can describe what the information is, what it is related to, or how to display it. As a markup language, HTML is optimized to describe how a document is displayed.

HTML is based on the Standardized Generalized Markup Language – SGML. In fact, HTML is a very simplified version of SGML, since the full set of SGML is an incredibly huge specification.

XML is another simplified version of SGML. XML came about primarily due to the explosion of the Web and the use of HTML in creating documents. As HTML became more widely used, people began to use it for things besides hypertext markup. This quickly uncovered some drawbacks in HTML that made it difficult for it to grow and expand.

An example of this was the 'Tag Wars' of the mid-1990s. Because there was no mechanism for expanding the set of tags in HTML other than the standards committees, Microsoft and Netscape both took it upon themselves to add new features through the use of new tags. Internet Explorer's `<MARQUEE>` tag was good example of this. The `<MARQUEE>` tag was a Microsoft technology, so it was never supported in Netscape, and there was no way for a document to tell Netscape that it was using the `<MARQUEE>` tag, or how to support it.

Let's consider the main limitations of HTML:

- A fixed tag set – you could not create your own tag and hope that others were able to interpret what you meant by it.
- Presentation based – HTML was only concerned with how a document looked when shown in a browser. There was no way to determine the meaning of any of the content between a specific set of tags.
- Browsers as application platforms – HTML is ill-suited to moving data from a server to a browser and back again.

All of these drawbacks were beginning to cause problems for people who wanted to use browsers and the web for more than just looking at documents. XML is the result of their work.

XML Terminology

As with any new language, there are some new terms that we have to learn. These terms relate to parts of the XML document, and to ways that we interact with XML documents.

Element

An **element** in XML is the same as an element in HTML. It is defined to be a set of tags plus the text contained between them. In HTML, we have tags such as `<BODY>`, `<P>`, `<DIV>`, and `<OBJECT>`. An element in HTML would look like:

```
<DIV>This is some text in an element</DIV>
```

In XML, we can create tags that have any name we like – for example `<PERSON>`, `<AUTHOR>`, `<CATALOG>`, `<LINE-ITEM>` or `<BIGSTUFF>`. So an element in XML would look like:

```
<AUTHOR>J. Brian Francis</AUTHOR>
```

Attribute

Each tag can have a set of associated data known as an **attribute**. In HTML, the attributes of the `<BODY>` tag include `CLASS`, `ID`, `STYLE`, `BGCOLOR` and `LINK`. Each of these attributes, if used, has a value associated with it. Tags in XML can possess attributes in much the same way.

Document Type Definition

Since the 'extensible' part of the XML language means that people can create their own tags, we will need a method that allows them to also describe what the tags mean. The XML specification used **Document Type Definitions** (DTDs) as a way of defining new tags. The DTD describes what constitutes a markup tag and what that markup means. Each tag, and each attribute of each tag, must be fully defined in the DTD for a document. Without proper definition, the system trying to interpret the file will not know how properly to deal with the undefined element.

Style Sheets

XML is used to describe data. The information contained in the DTD will tell the program what the data is, but it will not describe how the data should be displayed. This is the job of the **style sheet**. With XML, there are two types of style sheet that can be used. We can use the Cascading Style Sheet (CSS) specification to tell a browser how to display XML data. Alternatively, a newer language called Extensible Stylesheet Language (XSL) can also be used to describe how XML data should be displayed. XSL is generally considered to be the future of style sheets, but for the moment there is broader support for CSS than there is for XSL.

Parsers

In order for XML information to be displayed, the system that is trying to display it must first interpret the information. This is the job of the **XML parser**. The XML file contains a reference to a DTD; the parser reads the XML file and uses the information contained in the DTD to create a document tree that represents the information. The browser can then take the document tree and use it for displaying the information, or for other purposes.

> *The **document tree** is an object hierarchy representing all of the elements and their relationships.*

The parser can also be used to check the validity of the XML document. This means that the parser checks to ensure that the XML data conforms to the XML standards. You've probably noticed that, in the past, the validation of HTML documents has not been very rigid – most browsers are quite forgiving when it comes to malformed HTML code. The creators of XML have tried to change that, and are therefore recommending much closer compliance with the XML standard.

Viewing XML

Since XML is just data, there needs to be a way to view that data. The 4.0 versions of Netscape and Internet Explorer contained very rudimentary XML parsers, which could be used (along with a good bit of code) to display XML in the browser. There were also plug-ins available for both browsers, which enhanced the parser (although these didn't provide consistent support).

With IE5, Microsoft has added the ability to use XML data in a number of different ways within the browser. We will take a look at some of these in this chapter.

Uses for XML

XML is very versatile, and the key to its flexibility is that the XML file is marked up in a way that *describes* its contents. HTML, on the other hand, is specifically designed for the *display* of content. XML achieves this versatility in two ways:

- First, the creators of an XML document can create their own tags that specifically relate to the content of their document.
- Second, XML is used only to describe the data; there is nothing in an XML file that tells the application how the data should be displayed.

This allows different applications to use the same XML data in different ways. One application might display the data within a browser. Another application might use the same data to populate a local database that could then be searched by the user. XML makes this very efficient, because – unlike HTML – there is no display code going along with the data.

These days, many people are using Microsoft Office as their productivity tool – but not so long ago there was a much wider variety of word processing applications on the market. Each of these applications had its own data format, and you had to have a special program in order for one application to read the data format of another. In some instances, such cross-platform activity simply wasn't possible.

XML is the first step in changing this. Since XML contains both data and the description of the data, it can be used as a universal data exchange language. So, your word processor of tomorrow shouldn't need to be able to read all of the different formats of the other word processors; instead, it could simply read an XML file. All other word processors could save their data using XML as the format; then, no matter what application was available to the intended reader, they would be able to interpret the information.

XML in IE5

As we said before, IE5 dives feet-first into the world of XML. There are a number of places inside of IE5 that utilize XML. IE5 allows users to view XML using XSL or CSS, in exactly the same way that they view HTML documents. IE5 also includes a high-performance validating XML engine. This engine can actually be used by other applications (that is, not just IE5) to work with XML data – this gives the entire Windows platform access to XML information.

XML information can also be embedded directly into an HTML file – so in essence, the XML becomes an island of data within the file. And as mentioned in Chapter 7, XML data can be bound to elements on an HTML page in the same way that database data can.

Data Islands and XML Files

As XML has become more widely used as a data description language, people have recognized the need to include XML inside of HTML files. Two implementations of this include the Resource Definition Format (RDF) and MathML. RDF is a framework for metadata and can be used for many things – including cataloging, content rating, intellectual property and collaboration. It is included as XML-formatted data within an HTML file.

Recognizing that more and more people were going to be adding XML-formatted data to HTML, the W3C decided to set a standard way for inserting XML into an HTML file – the `<XML>` tag. With the standardization of the inclusion method, any browser that recognizes the information will know how to access the XML data islands, while those that don't recognize the data islands will be unaffected.

Here is an example of an XML data island within an HTML file:

```
<HTML>
<XML ID=XMLData>
  <book genre="computers">
    <title>IE5 DHTML Programmer's Reference</title>
    <author>
      <first-name>Brian</first-name>
      <last-name>Francis</last-name>
    </author>
    <price>24.99</price>
  </book>
</XML>
<BODY>
<H1>This page has some XML in it</H1>
</BODY>
</HTML>
```

In addition to including the XML data directly in the HTML file, you can also reference XML data in an external file. To do this, the `XML` tag has a `SRC` property, which you can set to point to the XML data. This works in the same way as the `SCRIPT` tag's `SRC` property:

```
<XML SRC="http://localhost/xmlFile.xml"></XML>
```

The `XML` element now becomes part of the Document Object Model of IE5. This means that you can retrieve a reference to it in the `document.all()` collection. For more information on how to manipulate the XML object model in IE5, take a look at *XML IE5 Programmer's Reference* by Alex Homer (Wrox Press, ISBN 1-861001-57-6).

XML Data Binding

In Chapter 7, we took a look at data binding. This IE technology allows us to bind an element (or set of elements) in an HTML page to a data source. In Chapter 7 we saw how the Tabular Data Control, with its data source objects (DSOs), allows us to bind to a delimited text file. Well, in IE5 we can use the same technique to bind to XML data. The XML data can be contained either in an XML data island, or in a separate XML file.

There are actually two DSOs that allow us to bind to XML data. The first one is written in Java, and was actually made available for use in IE4. It provides read-only access to a client-based or server-based file that holds data in an XML format. The code to create an instance of this object uses the normal <APPLET> tag:

```
<APPLET CODE="com.ms.xml.dso.XMLDSO.class" ID="dsoFoods"
                                           WIDTH=0 HEIGHT=0 MAYSCRIPT=true>
  <PARAM NAME="URL" VALUE="foods.xml">
</APPLET>
```

With the release of IE5, Microsoft has also included a high-performance DSO for XML that is written in C++. As well as having better performance than the Java DSO, it also provides the ability to bind to an XML data island. To insert this DSO into an HTML page, you use this element:

```
<XML ID=xmlFoods src="foods.xml"></XML>
<TABLE DATASRC="#xmlFoods" BORDER=1>
```

The C++ DSO gives you the ability to create XML-driven Web applications in a completely declarative fashion. It is still possible to write scripts against the XML document object. In fact, with the C++ DSO, you can use both the ADO and XML object models.

Using XML Data Binding

In Chapter 7 we also looked at an example that showed simple data binding to a text file using the Tabular Data Control DSO. We will now take that example and convert it to read the same data stored in XML format. The first step is to convert the text data file into an XML file.

This is the original text file, `food.txt`:

```
Food,Calories,Group
Hamburger,3000,Junk
Apple,250,Fruit
Milk,500,Dairy
Orange,300,Fruit
Cheese,350,Dairy
Scones,300,Junk
```

Now we will convert this file to XML. We'll call this file `food.xml`. Notice that, in the interests of making sure that our tags are relevantly named, we have changed the name of the `Food` column heading to `Name`:

```
<FoodList>
  <Food>
    <Name>Hamburger</Name>
    <Calories>3000</Calories>
```

```
    <Group>Junk</Group>
  </Food>
  <Food>
    <Name>Apple</Name>
    <Calories>250</Calories>
    <Group>Fruit</Group>
  </Food>
  <Food>
    <Name>Milk</Name>
..  <Calories>500</Calories>
    <Group>Dairy</Group>
  </Food>
...
</FoodList>
```

The final step is to modify the two example programs to access this new data file instead of the old text-based data file. As you probably noticed above, it is very simple to use an XML data source. In the original `foodItem.htm` and `foodList.htm` in Chapter 7, we had a TDC object that looked like this:

```
<OBJECT ID="food" WIDTH=100 HEIGHT=51
  CLASSID="CLSID:333C7BC4-460F-11D0-BC04-0080C7055A83">
  <PARAM NAME="FieldDelim" VALUE=",">
  <PARAM NAME="DataURL" VALUE="food.txt">
  <PARAM NAME="UseHeader" VALUE=True>
</OBJECT>
```

Part of the complexity of the TDC stems from the fact that the data is relatively unstructured. In the beginning of this chapter, we saw that one of the great advantages of XML is that it includes both the data itself, and a description of the data. Since the data is self-describing, the XML DSO does not need to be given information such as the field delimiter value.

Adapting foodlist.htm

First, let's look at the changes we made to the `foodList.htm` file. We will be calling our new file `xFoodList.htm`:

```
<HTML>
<HEAD>
<TITLE>Food List</TITLE>
</HEAD>
<XML ID=food SRC=food.xml></XML>

<BODY>
<DIV ALIGN=CENTER>
<TABLE ID=Data WIDTH=75% DATASRC=#food>
  <THEAD>
    <TH> Group </TH> <TH> Food </TH> <TH> Calories </TH>
  </THEAD>
  <TBODY>
    <TR>
      <TD ALIGN=CENTER> <SPAN DATAFLD="Group"> </SPAN> </TD>
      <TD ALIGN=CENTER> <SPAN DATAFLD="Name"> </SPAN> </TD>
      <TD ALIGN=CENTER> <SPAN DATAFLD="Calories"> </SPAN> </TD>
    </TR>
  </TBODY>
</TABLE>
</DIV>
</BODY>
</HTML>
```

The first change is the inclusion of the <XML>..</XML> HTML tags, which tell us where to look for the data. By setting the `ID` property of the `XML` element, we will be able to reference this data later in the file. We also use the `SRC` property of the `XML` element to reference XML data stored in a separate file. The `TABLE` element is unchanged from the file that used the TDC. This is because we have set the name of the XML data to be the same as the TDC DSO in the previous example.

We did have to make one small change to one of the columns. In the TDC example, the column that contained the name of the food was called `food`. In our XML file, we have defined the `Food` element to be the three pieces of information that described a particular food. In order to keep the naming consistent, we now refer to the name of the food as `Name`. This means that the `DATAFLD` property of the `SPAN` that contains the name will need to be changed as well.

Finally, since the TDC DSO is no longer needed, we can delete it from the HTML file. If we view this file in our browser, it looks like this. As you can see, the page itself looks exactly the same as the page that was generated from the TDC Data Source Object.

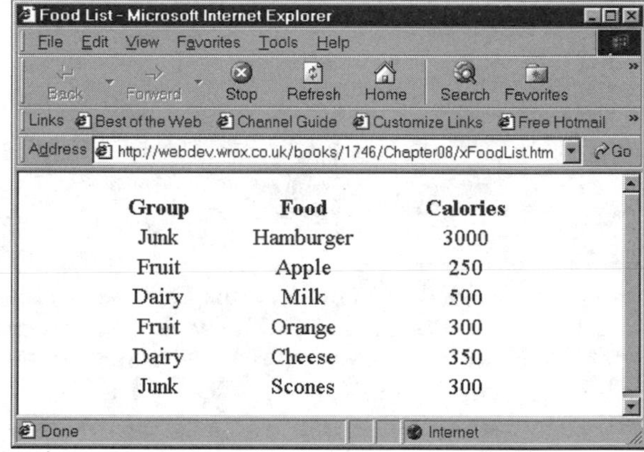

Before we move on, it's worth noting that that we could implement our XML data island by writing the data into the `.htm` file, instead of importing the `food.xml` file. To do this, we'd make the following change to the code above:

```
<HTML>
<HEAD>
<TITLE>Food List</TITLE>
</HEAD>
<XML ID=food>
  <FoodList>
    <Food>
       <Name>Hamburger</Name>
       <Calories>3000</Calories>
       <Group>Junk</Group>
    </Food>
    <Food>
      <Name>Apple</Name>
      <Calories>250</Calories>
      <Group>Fruit</Group>
    </Food>
    ... other food details ...
  </FoodList>
</XML>
<BODY>
    ... rest of file as before...
```

Adapting fooditem.htm

Next, let's take a look at how we modified the `foodItem.htm` page from Chapter 7 to use XML as its data source:

```
<HTML>
<HEAD>
<TITLE>Food Items</TITLE>
</HEAD>
<STYLE>
  TD {font-family:"Arial, sans-serif"; font-size:10pt }
  TH {font-family:"Arial, sans-serif"; font-size:12pt; font-weight:bold }
</STYLE>
<XML SRC="food.xml" ID=food></XML>
<BODY>

<TABLE WIDTH=100%>
<TR>
  <TH COLSPAN=2> Food Browser </TH>
</TR>
<TR>
  <TD ALIGN=RIGHT> Food Item: </TD>
  <TD> <INPUT TYPE="TEXT" DATASRC="#food" DATAFLD="Name"> </TD>
</TR>
<TR>
  <TD ALIGN=RIGHT> Calories: </TD>
  <TD> <INPUT TYPE="TEXT" DATASRC="#food" DATAFLD="Calories"> </TD>
</TR>
<TR>
  <TD ALIGN=RIGHT> Group: </TD>
  <TD> <INPUT TYPE="TEXT" DATASRC="#food" DATAFLD="Group"> </TD>
</TR>
</TABLE><P>
<TABLE WIDTH=100%>
<TR>
  <TD ALIGN=CENTER>
    <INPUT NAME="cmdFirst" TYPE="BUTTON" VALUE="First">
    <INPUT NAME="cmdPrevious" TYPE="BUTTON" VALUE=" < ">
    <INPUT NAME="cmdNext" TYPE="BUTTON" VALUE=" > ">
    <INPUT NAME="cmdLast" TYPE="BUTTON" VALUE="Last">
  </TD>
</TR>
</TABLE>

<SCRIPT LANGUAGE=VBSCRIPT>
   ...scripts as before ...
</SCRIPT>
  'no need for the TDC DSO object...
</BODY>
</HTML>
```

There are three changes that were made to this to convert it from accessing data from a text file to accessing data from an XML file. First, we were able to remove the reference to the TDC Data Source Object. Next, we need to add our XML data island, which we do again using the XML element and the SRC property of the XML element to reference XML data stored in a separate file.

Finally, we need to make the same type of change that was made in the previous example. Since the name of the food is now referred to as `Name` instead of `Food`, we need to change the `DATAFLD` property of the `INPUT` field that is displaying that data. When we look at this page in the browser, it will look exactly the same as the page generated by the TDC DSO.

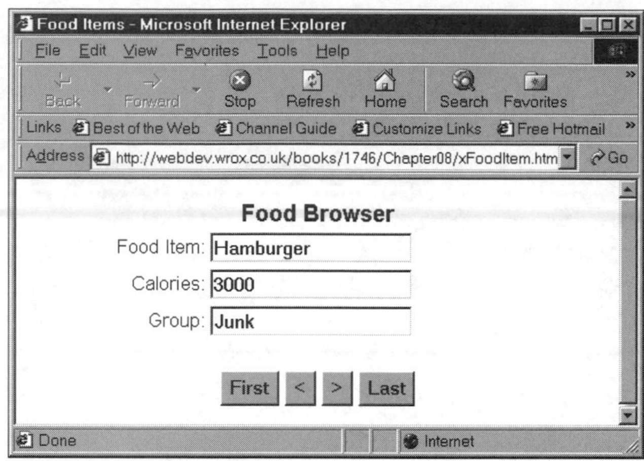

You can see that using XML as a data source for data bound controls is just as simple – maybe even simpler – than using the Tabular Data Control. The same ADO script code that allowed you to move through the data with the TDC control works exactly the same for the XML control. This flexibility and ease of use make the use of XML as the data format for data bound controls a natural choice.

Next, we will switch gears and take a look at another new technology in IE5 – behaviors.

Introduction to Behaviors

As HTML pages have become dynamic through the introduction of more and more scripting functionality, the role of **code reuse** has become increasingly important. For example, consider a web page creator who is ill-at-ease with programming matters, and who is faced with an ever-increasing demand to write scripting code. For such an author, adding scripting functionality means trying to figure out how to borrow and adapt script from books or from other web pages, or enlisting the help of an experienced programmer.

As another example, consider the many trained developers attracted to writing HTML scripting code by the advent of development tools like Active Server Pages, but let down by the lack of provision of language support that developers are used to.

In DHTML prior to IE5, client-side scripting was just that: script code that was sent to the client and run there. Unfortunately, code reuse was difficult: the scripting code could only execute if the code was explicitly written for the elements on that page. It's true that you could use the `<SCRIPT>` tag with a `SRC` property to reference script code in another page, but that code was still tied to the elements on the page where the script was included.

In IE4, Microsoft also introduced a technology called **scriptlets**. Scriptlets allowed developers to encapsulate HTML and scripting code into a reusable and distributable COM object. However, scriptlets still demanded a close coupling between the interactivity (the script) and the presentation (the HTML).

Something better was called for. So IE5 has provided us with a new technology – behaviors – which is both easier to use and inherently more flexible.

DHTML with Behaviors

With the introduction of **behaviors** in IE5, developers now have a way of encapsulating the scripting logic that makes DHTML pages dynamic. However, this encapsulation is much more than just saving the script into its own little file.

A behavior is defined by its interface – in much the same way that a COM object is defined by its interface. Thus, this interface allows a set of properties, methods, and events to be exposed by the behavior. A behavior can also listen for events that happen in the document that is hosting it, and react to those events by performing actions. The key difference between a behavior and a scriptlet is that a behavior has no display whatsoever.

In fact, the term 'behavior' is rather descriptive of what a behavior can do for you. It allows a web page developer to attach (one or more) elements of his page to a behavior – and those elements will 'behave' in the way defined by the behavior. For example, suppose you have a piece of code that causes a part of your DHTML page to react when a mouse moves over it. This is a specific behavior of that element. By putting that interactivity code into a behavior, we can use that code on *any* page.

Moreover, this allows a developer to create the required interactivity and package it up into a behavior. Then, the web page designer can simply apply that behavior to an element in exactly the same way that they assign a `style` property such as `color` or `font`. The code that used to be replicated in many pages across a site can now exist in one place. Each of the pages that want to utilize its functionality will simply reference the stored functionality within the behavior.

Building and using Behaviors

Now that we have an understanding of what behaviors can be used for, we can set out to create behaviors of our own. At its core, a behavior is simply a component that we can use to extend and enhance Internet Explorer. Since it is a component, it has many of the same characteristics as other COM components. One of the most important of these characteristics is that it can be created in a multitude of languages.

You may well be familiar with ActiveX controls that can be used with Internet Explorer. These are components that extend the functionality of IE in some way. At first, these ActiveX controls were only written using C++, but with the advent of Visual Basic 5.0 and Visual J++, in became possible to write the same type of component using these higher-level languages. In Internet Explorer 5, the capability to write these components has been extend to any of the ActiveX scripting engines supported by IE5. For most of us, this means VBScript or JScript.

When we create components using one of these scripting languages, we are creating what is known as an **HTML component (HTC)**. These files are saved with a `.htc` extension and contain the script for the component as well as some XML entries that are used to define the component.

With the first beta release of IE5, behaviors were implemented using HTML scriptlets. As I've said, scriptlets were first introduced in IE4, and allowed for the encapsulation of HTML and scripts into a component that could be reused in other HTML files.

HTML components are the new technology, introduced by Microsoft with the official release of IE5, and designed to encapsulate just script.

A Working Example of Behaviors

In the remainder of this chapter, we will build up a working example that introduces the concepts necessary to build and use behaviors. This example behavior will provide text rollover effects for any element to which it is attached. To get started building our behavior, we first need to create the HTML component file that will contain the script for the behavior. We'll begin to do that just as soon as we've taken a look at the XML elements.

XML Elements

In order to define what the HTML component interface looks like, we will be using a set of XML tags. These tags will allow us to define the HTC and set up what events it will monitor, along with the properties, methods, and events that the behavior will support.

XML Element	Parent	Description
`COMPONENT`	none	This XML tag identifies this document as an HTML component.
`ATTACH`	`COMPONENT`	Used to bind a function in the HTC to an event fired in the hosting document
`EVENT`	`COMPONENT`	Defines an event that the behavior can fire, which can be handled by the hosting document.
`METHOD`	`COMPONENT`	Defines a method that the hosting document can call on the behavior.
`PROPERTY`	`COMPONENT`	Defines a property that the hosting document can get or set on the behavior

The `COMPONENT` element is used to uniquely identify the HTC file. It has three properties. The `URN` (uniform resource name) property contains a string that uniquely identifies it. This is important, because there could be multiple behaviors associated with a single element. We can access the the `URN` of the behavior currently acting on the element, using the `window.event.srcURN` property.

The other two properties are optional properties. The NAME property defines the name by which the property is referred to in the containing document. This helps us to distinguish between multiple behaviors attached to one element, but is less rigorously defined than the value of URN. The ID property is similar to the ID property found in most HTML elements – it provides a reference that allows us to manipulate the behavior through script.

Creating an HTC – Part 1

An HTC file is just like an HTML file; the only external difference is that it has an .htc extension, instead of an .htm or .html extension. This makes it very easy for us to use our existing HTML editing tool to create the HTC.

Here is the beginning of an HTC file that will create a behavior:

```
<PUBLIC:COMPONENT URN="WroxIE5BehaviorExample">
</PUBLIC:COMPONENT>
...
```

Notice the XML syntax that requires every opening tag to have a corresponding closing tag. So here, the opening <PUBLIC:COMPONENT> is matched with the closing </PUBLIC:COMPONENT>.

Events

One of the key functions of behaviors is that they are able to work with events. Much of the dynamic nature of HTML is based on events being fired by some occurrence. To function in this environment, a behavior needs to be able to perform the appropriate action whenever an event is fired in the hosting document. It also needs to be capable of firing events of its own, which can then be handled by script within the hosting document.

Handling Events

As we know, one of the most common ways of designing a Dynamic HTML page is to have certain operations perform whenever a certain event fires in the browser. Just about any action will fire an event – from a movement of the mouse to the completion of a document download. Most of these events just pass right on by. With scripting and the Document Object Model, we can write event handlers to capture whatever events we're interested in, and have them process the appropriate operations when those events occur. Our behaviors can also be designed to take advantage of events in order to perform some processing.

However, there is a difference in the way that a behavior deals with an event. Ordinarily, an event handler is written for a particular event occurring for a particular element – thus it is the *one and only* function that is called when that event is fired on that element. But what if our behavior's events were to be handled in this manner? In that case, any event handler that was part of the hosting document would either not be called, or it would supercede the behavior's event handler.

For a behavior to work properly, it needs to join with any other existing event handlers so that they *both* can deal with a particular event. This is known as **attaching an event**. When you attach an event handler to an event, you are telling Internet Explorer to add this method to the beginning of the list of methods that it will call when an event occurs. In this way, all event handlers will be fired.

There are two ways that a behavior can be attached to an event. First, through the use of an XML tag, the event handler can be defined declaratively. Alternatively, the event can be attached explicitly using script. We'll look at both possibilities here.

The ATTACH Element

This ATTACH element is an XML element; it's part of the header of the HTC. It allows us to select an event that is generated from the hosting document, and to assign a function in the behavior to handle that event. We do this by using the following syntax within the HTC file:

```
<PUBLIC:ATTACH
  EVENT = sEvent
     FOR = "document" | "window" | "element"
  ONEVENT = sEventHandler
  ID = sID
/>
```

The attributes of the ATTACH element are as follows:

Attribute	Use
EVENT	*Required* The name of the DHTML event that the behavior is bound to
FOR	*Optional* The source of the event – refers to the document or window object, or the element to which the behavior is attached. The default is element
ONEVENT	*Required* The inline script or function to be called to handle the event
ID	*Optional* A unique reference that allows us to manipulate the behavior through script

So, each ATTACH element is listening for the event that is specified in its EVENT parameter. This event can be any of the standard DHTML events. There are also two HTC-specific events that can be handled:

Event	Use
oncontentchange	Fired when the element affected by this behavior is first loaded, or when its contents change
ondocumentready	Fired when the hosting document has been first loaded

The `FOR` parameter defines the element in the hosting document that is generating the event. The default value is "`element`" – this refers to the element that this behavior is affecting. The behavior can also attach to events generated by the hosting document's document object, as well as its window object.

Creating an HTC – Part 2

Let's look at how to extend the behavior that we started earlier, to handle some events fired by the hosting document:

```
<PUBLIC:COMPONENT URN="WroxIE5BehaviorExample">
  <PUBLIC:ATTACH EVENT="onmouseover" HANDLER="doMouseOver" />
  <PUBLIC:ATTACH EVENT="onmouseout" HANDLER="doMouseOut" />
</PUBLIC:COMPONENT>
...
```

This will add two event handlers to our behavior. The `doMouseOver()` event handler will be fired whenever the `onmouseover` event occurs in the element to which our behavior is attached. Similarly, when the `onmouseout` event occurs in the element, the `doMouseOut()` event handler will be fired. Remember that any event handler that is written in the hosting document will also be called, but *after* the behavior event is called.

The attachEvent and detachEvent methods

The alternative to using the declarative method to attach the behavior to the event of a particular object, is to use a method called `attachEvent` from script code. This is functionally identical to the declarative method, and uses the following syntax:

```
bSuccess = object.attachEvent(sEventHandler, fpNotify)
```

This method will return a `TRUE` if it is successful in attaching to the event, or a `FALSE` if it is not. The name of the event being attached to is passed in as a string in the *`sEventHandler`* parameter. The difference between this and the declarative version is that the name of the function that will handle the event needs to be passed as a function pointer, rather than a string containing the name of the function. Thankfully, function pointers are passed simply by giving the name of the function without any quotes around it.

The `attachEvent` method is actually a method of the object that will be firing the event to which you want to react. By calling this method on the `document` or `window` object, the event fired by that object will be attached.

> *Note that in a DHTML page, the default element is the `window` – so any method or property that does not specifically reference an element will be part of the `window` element. By contrast, in a behavior, the default object is the element to which the behavior is attached.*

If you want to detach a behavior from an event of an element using script, you can use the `detachEvent` method:

```
object.detachEvent(sEventHandler, fpNotify)
```

The `detachEvent` method has the same parameters as the `attachEvent` method.

Creating an HTC – Part 3 (Handling the Event)

One we have attached to a set of events to be handled, the next step is to write the script code that will be called when each of the events is fired. This scripting is exactly the same as scripting within a DHTML page, except that the default element is the element to which the behavior is attached.

Let's build up our example HTC some more, by adding the functionality to our event handlers:

```
<PUBLIC:COMPONENT URN="WroxIE5BehaviorExample">
  <PUBLIC:ATTACH EVENT="onmouseover" HANDLER="doMouseOver" />
  <PUBLIC:ATTACH EVENT="onmouseout" HANDLER="doMouseOut" />
  <SCRIPT LANGUAGE=JSCRIPT>
    var oldTextColor, oldTextFont;
    var bDocReady;

    function doMouseOver()
    {
      oldTextColor = style.color;
      oldTextFont = style.fontFamily;
      style.color = "Green";
      style.fontFamily = "Tahoma";
    }

    function doMouseOut()
    {
      style.color = oldTextColor;
      style.fontFamily = oldTextFont;
    }
  </SCRIPT>
</PUBLIC:COMPONENT>
```

This script looks very similar to some of the DHTML script that we've already seen in this book. It will simply save the current color and font of the element and replace them with the color green and the Tahoma font. Notice that we do not need to reference the element explicitly, since it is the default object in a behavior.

Firing Events – the EVENT Element

In addition to being able to handle events fired by the hosting document, a behavior can also generate its own events that can be in turn handled by the hosting document. This will allow a behavior to notify its hosting document of an event occurring in the behavior. To define an event we will use a declarative XML statement, similar to the one used to attach to an event. This time we use the `EVENT` element. The syntax is as follows:

```
<PUBLIC:EVENT
  NAME = sEventName
  ID = sEventID
/>
```

The `EVENT` element's attributes are as follows:

Attribute	Use
NAME	*Required* Defines the name of the event that will be exposed by the behavior
ID	*Optional* Provides a unique reference allowing you to manipulate the behavior through script

In order to fire an event in a behavior, you will need to create an event object, set its result property, and then fire the event. The first step is to create an event object:

```
oEvent = createEventObject();
oEvent.result = EventResult;
rcID.fire (oEvent);
```

The createEventObject method is used to create a new event object that will be used to fire the event. This object has a result property, which is set with the value that the event will return to the hosting document. Finally, we call the fire method of the event that was declared earlier, with the event object being passed as its parameter.

Creating an HTC – Part 4 (Adding an Event)

Let's look at our example behavior and add an event to it:

```
<PUBLIC:COMPONENT URN="WroxIE5BehaviorExample">
  <PUBLIC:ATTACH EVENT="onmouseover" HANDLER="doMouseOver" />
  <PUBLIC:ATTACH EVENT="onmouseout" HANDLER="doMouseOut" />
  <PUBLIC:EVENT NAME="onBackToNormal" ID=idBTN />
  <SCRIPT LANGUAGE=JSCRIPT>
    var oldTextColor, oldTextFont;
    var bDocReady;

    function doMouseOver()
    {
      ...function code in here as before...
    }

    function doMouseOut()
    {
      style.color = oldTextColor;
      style.fontFamily = oldTextFont;
      var oEvent;
      oEvent = createEventObject();
      oEvent.result = "Mouse Out Fired";
      idBTN.fire (oEvent);
    }
  </SCRIPT>
</PUBLIC:COMPONENT>
```

Properties – the PROPERTY Element

A behavior can expose its internal values using properties, in just the same way that an object can. In addition to exposing the property value itself, we can set and retrieve property values using accessor functions.

A property will need to be defined declaratively, using XML syntax:

```
<PUBLIC:PROPERTY
  NAME = sName
  ID = sPropertyID
  INTERNALNAME = sInternalName
  GET = sGetFunction
  PUT = sPutFunction
  PERSIST = bPersist
  VALUE = vValue
/>
```

The attributes to the `PROPERTY` element are described as follows:

Attribute	Use
`NAME`	External identification of the property. This is what the hosting document refers to the property by. If the `INTERNALNAME` property is not specified, then the `NAME` attribute is also used internally (within the behavior).
`ID`	*Optional* Identifies the property object within the behavior
`INTERNALNAME`	*Optional* Used to refer to the property value itself within the behavior
`GET`	*Optional* Function that will be called whenever the property is read by the hosting document
`PUT`	*Optional* Function that will be called whenever the property is set by the hosting document
`PERSIST`	*Optional* Boolean value that determines if the value of this property will be automatically persisted as long as the page is persisted.
`VALUE`	*Optional* Specifies the default value of the property, if any.

Whenever a property's value is changed, the hosting document should be notified of this change. This is done automatically if you have not defined a `PUT` accessor function. If you are defining your own `PUT` accessor function, then you will need to send this notification manually. To do this, you will call the `fireChange()` method of the property object. Here's the syntax for the method call:

```
sPropertyID.fireChange();
```

The *`sPropertyID`* object refers to the property object `ID` defined in the `<PUBLIC:PROPERTY>` element. In either case, when a property value changes, the `onpropertychange` event is fired in the hosting document.

Creating an HTC – Part 5 (Adding a Property)

Let's build on our existing example behavior by adding a property to the HTC:

```
<PUBLIC:COMPONENT URN="WroxIE5BehaviorExample">
  <PUBLIC:ATTACH EVENT="onmouseover" HANDLER="doMouseOver" />
  <PUBLIC:ATTACH EVENT="onmouseout" HANDLER="doMouseOut" />
  <PUBLIC:EVENT NAME="onBackToNormal" ID=idBTN />
  <PUBLIC:PROPERTY NAME="color" />
  <SCRIPT LANGUAGE=JSCRIPT>
    var oldTextColor, oldTextFont;
    var bDocReady;

    function doMouseOver()
    {
      oldTextColor = style.color;
      oldTextFont = style.fontFamily;
      style.color = color;
      style.fontFamily = "Tahoma";
    }

    function doMouseOut()
    {
      ...function code in here as before...
    }
  </SCRIPT>
</PUBLIC:COMPONENT>
```

Methods – the METHOD Element

There's one more way that we can interact with a behavior – through the use of a method. A behavior method will allow the hosting document to explicitly execute some code within the behavior. To declare a method within a behavior, you will again use the XML declarative method. Here's the syntax:

```
<PUBLIC:METHOD
  NAME = sName
  INTERNALNAME = sInternalName
  ID = sID
/>
```

The `METHOD` element has the following attributes:

Attribute	Use
`NAME`	*Required* External identification of the method. This is what the hosting document refers to the method with. If you want the behavior to override an existing method, then just give it the same name as the existing method. If the `INTERNALNAME` property is not specified, then the `NAME` attribute is also used internally (within the behavior).
`INTERNALNAME`	*Optional* Used to refer to the method name itself within the behavior
`ID`	*Optional* Identifies the property object within the behavior

Once you've declared a method using the `METHOD` element above, you will need to add the method itself to the behavior. This method has no special characteristics, and looks like any other method within the behavior.

Creating an HTC – Part 6 (Adding a Method)

To add a method to our example behavior, we could make the following amendments to our HTC:

```
<PUBLIC:COMPONENT URN="WroxIE5BehaviorExample">
  <PUBLIC:ATTACH EVENT="onmouseover" HANDLER="doMouseOver" />
  <PUBLIC:ATTACH EVENT="onmouseout" HANDLER="doMouseOut" />
  <PUBLIC:EVENT NAME="onBackToNormal" ID=idBTN />
  <PUBLIC:PROPERTY NAME="color" />
  <PUBLIC:METHOD NAME="blinkIt" />
  <PUBLIC:METHOD NAME="blinkOff" />
  <SCRIPT LANGUAGE=JSCRIPT>
    var oldTextColor, oldTextFont;
    var bBlinked, bMouseOver=false;
    var bDocReady;

    function doMouseOver()
    {
      bMouseOver = true;
      if (!bBlinked)
      {
         oldTextColor = style.color;
         oldTextFont = style.fontFamily;
      }
      style.color = color;
      style.fontFamily = "Tahoma";
    }

    function doMouseOut()
    {
      bMouseOver = false;
      style.color = oldTextColor;
      style.fontFamily = oldTextFont;
      var oEvent;
      oEvent = createEventObject();
      oEvent.result = "Mouse Out Fired";
      idBTN.fire (oEvent);
    }

    function blinkIt()
    {
      if (!bMouseOver)
      {
        doMouseOver();
        bBlinked = true;
        window.setTimeout(uniqueID + ".blinkOff();", 300);
      }
    }

    function blinkOff()
    {
      bBlinked = false;
      doMouseOut();
    }
  </SCRIPT>
</PUBLIC:COMPONENT>
```

Using Behaviors

Once a behavior has been created, the fun really begins. Before behaviors, if you were to create some cool DHTML scripting code, the only way that you could move it from page to page was to lift the code completely and copy it to the new file. And even that wasn't foolproof – you'd still have to modify any of the references that the script made to elements on the page.

With behaviors, all of this scripting logic is in the HTML component. All that is left for the page developer to do is reference the behavior and assign it to one or more elements on their page.

You can see some of the following in action by running the example on http://webdev.wrox.co.uk/books/1746:

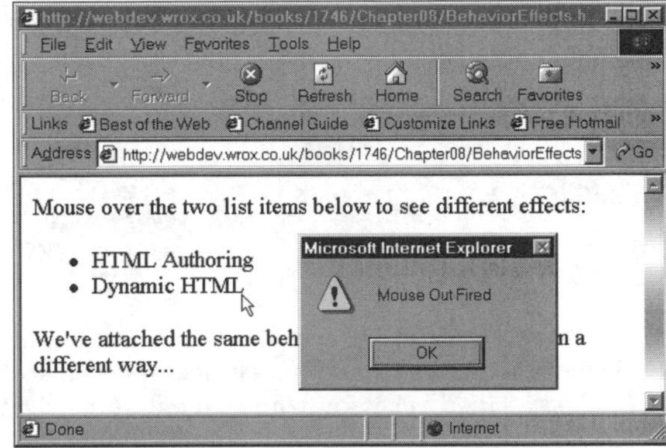

Referencing the Behavior from the Page

When referencing a behavior from a page, you will use an enhancement to the CSS syntax:

```
behavior:url(filename.htc)
```

Here, `filename.htc` indicates the location of the HTML component file. This can be a simple file name, which is the case if HTC file is in the same directory as the HTML file. It's more common (and often more tidy) to store all HTC files in a common directory on your site – in this case, the *`filename`* parameter would include a relative path from the HTML file to the HTC file. It is also possible to reference an HTML component that lives on a separate site – in which case the *`filename`* parameter would specify a full URL to the file.

There are five ways that a behavior can be referenced from a page:

- **Inline Style.** A behavior can be attached to a particular element in a page by putting it in an inline style reference:

```
<P STYLE="behavior:url(AttachEvent.htc)">We've attached the ... etc. </P>
```

- **Embedded Style.** You can attach the behavior to a standard HTML element in the `<STYLE>` block. This will cause all instances of that element in the page to take on the characteristics of the behavior:

```
<STYLE>
  LI {behavior:url(AttachEvent.htc)}
</STYLE>
```

- **Style Class.** You can define a style class in the `<STYLE>` block that contains the behavior. This class can then be applied to any element on the page. That element would then take on the characteristics of the behavior:

```
<STYLE>
  .rollover {behavior:url(AttachEvent.htc)}
</STYLE>
```

- **The `style` Object.** To apply behaviors dynamically, you can use the element's style object to access its behavior property. For example:

```
<SCRIPT>
  function window.onload()
  {
    myElem1.style.behavior = "url(AttachEvent.htc)";
    myElem2.style.behavior = "url(AttachEvent.htc)";
  }
</SCRIPT>
```

- **Adding and removing behaviors in script.** You can also add and remove behaviors to an element within your script. The `addBehavior` method will add the specified behavior to an element. If the element already has a behavior applied, then this method will simply add this new behavior – the other applied behaviors will be unaffected (and to remove a behavior, you can use the `removeBehavior` method):

```
<SCRIPT>
  function window.onload()
  {
    myElem1.addBehavior("AttachEvent.htc");
    myElem2.addBehavior("AttachEvent.htc");
  }
</SCRIPT>
```

Multiple Behaviors

To define multiple behaviors for an element or a style, you can simply add multiple `url` parameters to the behavior declaration. For example:

```
<STYLE>
  LI {behavior:url(AttachEvent.htc) url(AnotherBehavior.htc)}
</STYLE>
```

Once you have attached a behavior to an element, it will take on all of the characteristics defined by that element. In addition to responding to events generated by the hosting document, a behavior can also expose its own properties, methods and events.

Accessing Properties

To access a property of a behavior, you have two choices. First, you can set the property inline with the declaration of the application. To do this, add another parameter to the element tag that has the name of the property exposed by the behavior. In our example, we want to set our highlight color property to the value `#800080` (purple):

```
<LI color="#800080" ID=HTMLA>HTML Authoring</LI>
```

The value for the property will be passed to the behavior. If a `PUT` function is declared in the behavior, then it will be called. This method of accessing a property will only allow you set the value of the property.

As well as using scripting to set the value of the property, you can use it to read the value of a property. Internet Explorer will expose the behavior property as an `expando` property of the element object. As with the element declaration method, setting or accessing a property using script will cause the accessor function, if one exists, to be called:

```
<SCRIPT>
   HTMLA.color = "Yellow"
   alert("The color property of the behavior is " + HTMLA.color);
</SCRIPT>
```

Calling Methods

Calling a custom method of a behavior is similar to accessing a property value using script. The method name is exposed as a method of the element's object. To call the method, simply call it the same way you would call an intrinsic method of the element. In this example, we want the behavior's `blinkIt` method to be called whenever the user clicks their mouse anywhere in the document:

```
<SCRIPT>
  function document.onclick()
  {
    HTMLA.blinkIt();
  }
</SCRIPT>
```

Handling Events

The events that are fired by behaviors are handled in the same way that events that are fired by the elements themselves. This means that the event handlers can be specified in the same way. You can specify the event handler in the element tag itself:

```
<LI onbacktonormal="doBackToNormal()">Dynamic HTML</LI>
```

You can also set an event handler using script.

Behavior Object Model Extensions

In order to support behaviors, there have been a number of extensions to the Dynamic HTML object model. These extensions have been added to support the implementation of behaviors in HTML components, and also utilize the components in the DHTML file. These extensions have been proposed to the W3C as extensions to the CSS standard, but for now they are specific to Internet Explorer 5 and above.

Extension	Use
CSS `behavior` property	Used in a style definition to set the location of the HTML component defining the behavior
`attachEvent` method, `detachEvent` method	Tells an HTML component to listen for (resp. stop listening for) a particular event happening in the containing document, by defining the method that will be called
`uniqueID` property	Allows the element utilizing the behavior to be uniquely identified. Used when setting a method to be called, normally a `setTimeout`, and needing to refer to the actual element itself.
`event.srcURN`	Specifies the `URN` of the behavior that fired this event.
`addBehavior` method, `removeBehavior` method	Allow a script in the hosting document to dynamically add (resp. remove) a behavior from an element. These are methods of the element itself.

There are some nice behavior resources on the web – for example, take a look at the resources at http://www.developer.com/downloads/behaviors/.

Summary

In this chapter, we have looked at two new technologies that are an important part of Internet Explorer 5.0. These technologies are used to enhance the interactivity and information being presented in a web page. By integrating XML into IE5, web page developers now have access to a very robust data representation model. With behaviors, IE5 now allows web page designers to design the page they want and add interactivity in exactly the same way that they add a color or set a font. Behaviors also allow developers to script a particular interaction and then make that interaction available to anyone who wants to use it.

Specifically, this chapter has focused on:

- What XML is, and why is it so important to IE5 and to the web community
- How XML data islands and the XML Data Source Object give robust access to client-side data
- The problems with reusing the script code that makes web pages dynamic and how using behaviors can solve that program

- How to develop an HTML component, which hosts the functionality of a behavior
- How to use the behavior in a web page
- Extensions to the HTML object model for supporting behaviors

As far as the topics of XML and behaviors are concerned, we really have only just skimmed the surface here. We haven't begun to mention about XML schemas, the XML Document Object Model, the IE5 default and custom behaviors, and so on. If you want to know more about these subjects, you could try *XML IE5 Programmer's Reference* (Wrox Press, ISBN 1-861001-75-6).

Now that we have reached the end of our tour through the functionality of Internet Explorer 5, you can see that Microsoft has once again set the standard in terms of browser performance and functionality. With the integration of new technologies (such as XML and behaviors) in particular, IE5 is becoming much more that just a web browser.

This chapter is the last in the 'teaching' part of this book. The reference section that follows is intended both to support the chapters of this book, and as an independent and complete quick-reference to using Dynamic HTML in IE5.

HTML

The Reference Section

This section of the book is designed to help you to find the information you need while working with Dynamic HTML. To achieve this, we've split it up into separate but related appendices.

For example, when working with a `<DIV>` tag, you can look in Appendix C to find a full list of the attributes that it supports.

If you need to match a property to an attribute that you can use within the HTML tag, or to a CSS property, you'll find that information in Appendix B. Alternatively, if you need a description of any property, method or event, you'll find it listed in Appendix B too.

If you then need to know how to reference the layer, using the browser's object model, you can see the overall structure and look up individual objects within the hierarchy in Appendix A.

Appendix A - The Browser Object Model

This appendix covers the **object model** that is available in the browser through Dynamic HTML. It contains a view of the overall structure, and a list of all the **objects** and **collections** that are provided. It goes on to show lists of the properties, methods and events supported by each object.

Appendix B – DHTML Properties, Methods and Events

The list of **properties** includes the equivalent HTML **attributes** and **CSS styles**, plus the type of data or individual values you can use with each one. The list of methods also gives the syntax for using each method

Appendix C - Dynamic HTML Tags

An alphabetical list of all the **HTML Tags** that can be used in Dynamic HTML files. The entry for each tag provides the following information:

- A short description of the tag
- Usage for all its available attributes.
- Some sample code, where appropriate, to show you how it is used

Appendix D – Common HTML Tags by Category

This appendix will help you to find which tag you need. It lists all the HTML tags by name, divided into **categories** like **tables**, **graphics**, **forms**, etc.

Appendix E – CSS Properties

This listing contains all the attributes and values that can be used in **Cascading Style Sheets**, `STYLE` sections of a page, and in-line HTML `<STYLE>` tags.

Appendix F - HTML Color Names and Values

Many Dynamic HTML properties and methods expect you to provide a **color value**. This can be one of the accepted color names, or a numeric value that indicates the red green and blue (RGB) components of the color (also known as the hexadecimal value). This appendix lists all the color names, and shows the equivalent RGB values.

Appendix G - Special Characters in HTML

Many of the **common symbols** we use in web pages cannot be transmitted as ASCII code because HTTP only supports 7-bit characters. Instead we use special codes in the page to indicate which of the **special characters** we want the browser to display. This appendix lists all the available characters and their equivalent codes.

Appendix H - VBScript Tutorial

Dynamic HTML is available in any **scripting language** that is supported by the browser. This appendix contains a tutorial to help those not so familiar with the language.

Appendix I - VBScript Language Reference

This appendix contains a reference to the **VBScript language**, listing all the keywords, functions, statements, built-in constants, etc.

Appendix J - JScript Language Reference

JScript is Microsoft's implementation of the JavaScript language, and is fully supported by IE5. This appendix contains a reference to the **JScript language**, including the built-in objects, functions, keywords and constants.

Appendix K - Support and Errata

Explains in detail how to contact us for support on this book, and how to log any errata that you may find in it.

The Browser Object Model

The IE5 Dynamic HTML object model contains 23 **objects** and 29 **collections**. Most of these are organized into a strict hierarchy that allows HTML authors to access all the parts of the browser, and the pages that are loaded, from a scripting language like JavaScript or VBScript.

The Object Model In Outline

The diagram (overleaf) shows the object hierarchy in graphical form. It is followed by a list of the objects and collection, with a brief description. Then, each object is documented in detail, showing the properties, methods, and events it supports.

Note that we haven't included all of the objects and collections in the diagram. Some are not part of the overall object model, but are used to access other items – such as dialogs and HTML elements.

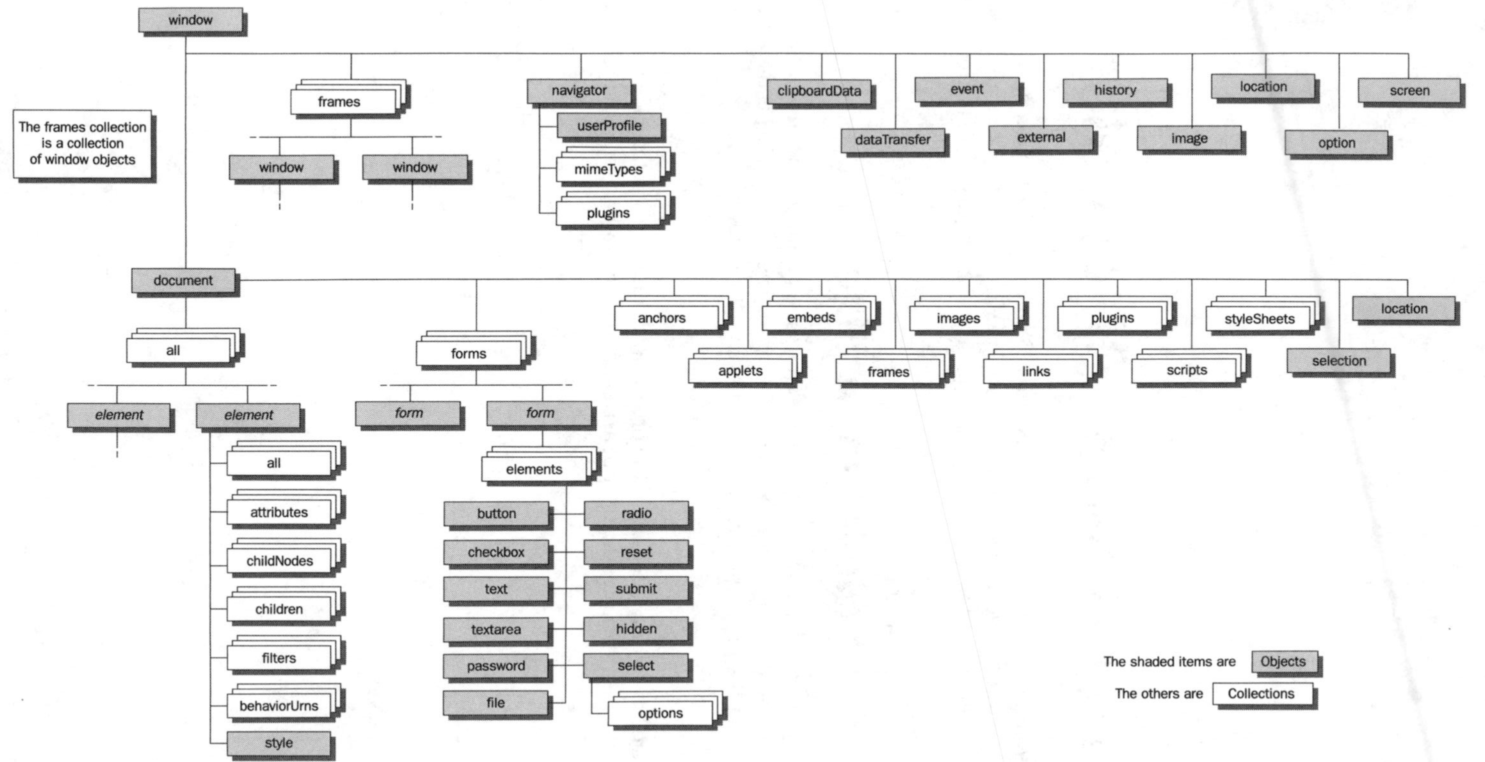
window
frames
window
window
navigator
userProfile
mimeTypes
plugins
clipboardData
dataTransfer
event
external
history
image
location
option
screen
The frames collection is a collection of window objects
document
all
element
element
all
attributes
childNodes
children
filters
behaviorUrns
style
forms
form
form
elements
button
checkbox
text
textarea
password
file
radio
reset
submit
hidden
select
options
anchors
applets
embeds
frames
images
links
plugins
scripts
styleSheets
selection
location
The shaded items are Objects
The others are Collections

Object Name	Description
`Attribute`	An object-representation of an attribute or property.
`clipboardData`	Used with editing operations to provide access to data contained on the clipboard.
`currentStyle`	Represents the cascaded format and style of its parent object.
`custom`	A user-defined element.
`dataTransfer`	Used with drag-and-drop operations to provide access to data contained on the clipboard.
`document`	An object that exposes the contents of the HTML document through a number of collections and properties.
`event`	A global object that exposes properties that represent the parameters of all events as they occur.
`external`	Allows access to the object model of any application hosting Internet Explorer components.
`history`	Exposes information about the URLs that the client has previously visited.
`location`	Exposes information about the currently displayed document's URL.
`mimeType`	An object that provides information about a MIME type.
`navigator`	Exposes properties that provide information about the browser, or user agent.
`rule`	A style (i.e. a selector and one or more declarations) within a cascading style sheet (CSS).
`runtimeStyle`	Represents the cascaded format and style of its parent object, overriding global stylesheets, inline styles and HTML attributes. Overwrites the values of the `currentStyle` object but not the `style` object.
`screen`	Exposes information about the client's monitor screen and system rendering abilities.
`selection`	Represents the currently active selection on the screen in the document.
`style`	Represents an individual style element within a style sheet.

Table Continued on Following Page

Object Name	Description
styleSheet	Exposes all the styles within a single style sheet in the styleSheets collection.
textNode	A string of text, represented as a node on the document hierarchy.
textRange	Represents sections of the text stream making up the HTML document.
textRectangle	A set of the four coordinates that represent the rectangle containing a line of text of TextRange object.
userProfile	Allows a script to request read access to and perform read actions on a user's profile.
window	Exposes properties, methods and events connected to the browser window or a frame.

Collection Name	Description
all	Collection of all the tags and elements in the body of the document.
anchors	Collection of all the anchors in the document.
applets	Collection of all the objects in the document, including intrinsic controls, images, applets, embeds, and other objects.
areas	Collection of all the areas that make up the image map.
attributes	Collection of all the attributes of the object.
behaviorUrns	Collection of all the behaviors attached to the element (as a set of URN strings).
bookmarks	Collection of all the ADO bookmarks tied to the rows affected by the current event.
boundElements	Collection of all the elements on the page that are bound to a dataset.
cells	Collection of all the <TH> and <TD> cells in the row of a table.
childNodes	Collection of all the object's children.
children	Collection of all the object's direct descendents.
controlRange	Collection of the BODY's elements.
elements	Collection of all controls and elements in the form.

Collection Name	Description
embeds	Collection of all the embed tags in the document.
filters	Collection of all the filter objects for an element.
forms	Collection of all the forms in the page.
frames	Collection of all the frames defined within a <FRAMESET> tag.
images	Collection of all the images in the page.
imports	Collection of all the imported style sheets defined for a stylesheet object.
links	Collection of all the links and <AREA> blocks in the page.
mimeTypes	Collection of all the document and file types supported by the browser.
options	Collection of all the items in a <SELECT> element.
plugins	An alias for collection of all the embeds in the page.
rows	Collection of all the rows in the table, including <THEAD>, <TBODY>, and <TFOOT>.
rules	Collection of all the rule objects defined in a styleSheet.
scripts	Collection of all the <SCRIPT> sections in the page.
stylesheets	Collection of all the individual style property objects defined for a document.
tBodies	Collection of all TBODY objects in the table.
TextRectangle	Collection of all the TextRectangle objects in the object.

The Objects in Detail

This section lists all the properties, methods and events available for each object in the browser hierarchy. Brief descriptions of these properties, methods and events can be found in Appendix B, and the collections are briefly described above.

It's worth noting that there's a set of attributes that are common to almost all of the DHTML elements. These attributes provide properties, methods, and events for manipulating the specific object. This commonality makes it simpler to use the exact same scripting style and techniques to deal with nearly every element in the document object model. Thus, you'll see a certain amount of repetition in these lists.

The Attribute Object

An object-representation of an attribute or property.

Properties nodeName nodeType nodeValue specified

Methods None

Events None

Collections None

The clipboardData Object

Used with editing operations to provide access to data contained on the clipboard.

Properties None

Methods None

Events None

Collections None

The currentStyle Object

Represents the cascaded format and style of its parent object.

Properties backgroundAttachment backgroundColor backgroundImage backgroundPositionX backgroundPositionY backgroundRepeat borderBottomColor borderBottomStyle borderBottomWidth borderColor borderLeftColor borderLeftStyle borderLeftWidth borderRightColor borderRightStyle borderRightWidth borderStyle borderTopColor borderTopStyle borderTopWidth borderWidth bottom clear clipBottom clipLeft clipRight clipTop color cursor direction display fontFamily fontSize fontStyle fontVariant fontWeight height layoutGrid layoutGridChar layoutGridCharSpacing layoutGridLine layoutGridMode layoutGridType left letterSpacing lineHeight listStyleImage listStylePosition listStyleType margin marginBottom marginLeft marginRight marginTop overflow overflowX overflowY padding paddingBottom paddingLeft paddingRight paddingTop pageBreakAfter pageBreakBefore position right styleFloat tableLayout textAlign textDecoration textIndent textTransform top unicodeBidi verticalAlign visibility width zIndex

Methods None

Events None

Collections None

The custom Object

A user-defined element.

Properties accessKey canHaveChildren className clientHeight clientLeft clientTop clientWidth currentStyle dir document id innerHTML innerText isTextEdit lang language offsetHeight offsetLeft offsetParent offsetTop offsetWidth outerHTML outerText parentElement parentTextEdit readyState recordNumber runtimeStyle scopeName scrollHeight scrollLeft scrollTop scrollWidth sourceIndex style tabIndex tagName tagUrn title

Methods addBehavior applyElement attachEvent blur clearAttributes click componentFromPoint contains createControlRange detachEvent doScroll focus getAdjacentText getAttribute getBoundingClientRect getClientRects getElementsByTagName getExpression insertAdjacentHTML insertAdjacentText mergeAttributes releaseCapture removeAttribute removeBehavior removeExpression replaceAdjacentText scrollIntoView setAttribute setCapture setExpression

Events onafterupdate onbeforecopy onbeforecut onbeforeeditfocus onbeforepaste onbeforeupdate onblur onclick oncontextmenu oncopy oncut ondblclick ondrag ondragend ondragenter ondragleave ondragover ondragstart ondrop onerrorupdate onfilterchange onfocus onhelp onkeydown onkeypress onkeyup onlosecapture onmousedown onmousemove onmouseout onmouseover onmouseup onpaste onpropertychange onreadystatechange onresize onscroll onselectstart

Collections all behaviorUrns children filters

The dataTransfer Object

Used with drag-and-drop operations to provide access to data contained on the clipboard.

Properties dropEffect effectAllowed

Methods clearData getData setData

Events None

Collections None

The document Object

An object that exposes the contents of the HTML document through a number of collections and properties.

Properties `activeElement aLinkColor bgColor cookie defaultCharset designMode documentElement domain expando fgColor fileCreatedDate fileModifiedDate fileSize lastModified linkColor location parentWindow protocol readyState referrer selection uniqueID URL vlinkColor`

Methods `attachEvent clear clearAttributes close createElement createStyleSheet createTextNode detachEvent elementFromPoint execCommand getElementById getElementsByName getElementsByTagName mergeAttributes open queryCommandEnabled queryCommandIndeterm queryCommandState queryCommandSupported queryCommandValue recalc releaseCapture write writeln`

Events `onbeforecut onbeforeeditfocus onbeforepaste onclick oncontextmenu oncut ondblclick ondrag ondragend ondragenter ondragleave ondragover ondragstart ondrop onhelp onkeydown onkeypress onkeyup onmousedown onmousemove onmouseout onmouseover onmouseup onpaste onpropertychange onreadystatechange onstop`

Collections `all anchors applets childNodes children embeds forms frames images links scripts styleSheets`

The event Object

A global object that exposes properties that represent the parameters of all events as they occur.

Properties `altKey button cancelBubble clientX clientY ctrlKey dataFld dataTransfer fromElement keyCode offsetX offsetY propertyName qualifier reason recordset repeat returnValue screenX screenY shiftKey srcElement srcFilter srcUrn toElement type x y`

Methods None

Events None

Collections `bookmarks boundElements`

The external Object

Allows access to the object model of any application hosting Internet Explorer components.

Properties `menuArguments`

Methods `AddChannel AddDesktopComponent AddFavorite AutoCompleteSaveForm AutoScan ImportExportFavorites IsSubscribed NavigateAndFind ShowBrowserUI`

Events None

Collections None

The history Object

Exposes information about the URLs that the client has previously visited.

Properties `length`

Methods `back` `forward` `go`

Events None **Collections** None

The location Object

Exposes information about the currently displayed document's URL.

Properties `hash` `host` `hostname` `href` `pathname` `port` `protocol` `search`

Methods `assign` `reload` `replace`

Events None **Collections** None

The mimeType

An object that provides information about a MIME type.

Properties `description` `enabledPlugin` `name`

Methods None

Events None **Collections** `suffixes`

The navigator Object

Exposes properties that provide information about the browser, or user agent.

Properties `appCodeName` `appMinorVersion` `appName` `appVersion` `browserLanguage` `cookieEnabled` `cpuClass` `onLine` `platform` `systemLanguage` `userAgent` `userLanguage` `userProfile`

Methods `javaEnabled` `taintEnabled`

Events None

Collections `plugins`

The rule Object

A style (i.e. a selector and one or more declarations) within a cascading style sheet (CSS).

Properties `readOnly` `runtimeStyle` `selectorText` `style`

Methods None

Events None **Collections** None

The runtimeStyle Object

Represents the cascaded format and style of its parent object, overriding global stylesheets, inline styles and HTML attributes. Overwrites the values of the `currentStyle` object but not the `style` object.

Properties `background` `backgroundAttachment` `backgroundColor` `backgroundImage` `backgroundPosition` `backgroundPositionX` `backgroundPositionY` `backgroundRepeat` `border` `borderBottom` `borderBottomColor` `borderBottomStyle` `borderBottomWidth` `borderColor` `borderLeft` `borderLeftColor` `borderLeftStyle` `borderLeftWidth` `borderRight` `borderRightColor` `borderRightStyle` `borderRightWidth` `borderStyle` `borderTop` `borderTopColor` `borderTopStyle` `borderTopWidth` `borderWidth` `bottom` `clear` `clip` `color` `cssText` `cursor` `direction` `display` `filter` `font` `fontFamily` `fontSize` `fontStyle` `fontVariant` `fontWeight` `height` `layoutGrid` `layoutGridChar` `layoutGridCharSpacing` `layoutGridLine` `layoutGridMode` `layoutGridType` `left` `letterSpacing` `lineHeight` `listStyle` `listStyleImage` `listStylePosition` `listStyleType` `margin` `marginBottom` `marginLeft` `marginRight` `marginTop` `overflow` `overflowX` `overflowY` `padding` `paddingBottom` `paddingLeft` `paddingRight` `paddingTop` `pageBreakAfter` `pageBreakBefore` `pixelBottom` `pixelHeight` `pixelLeft` `pixelRight` `pixelTop` `pixelWidth` `posBottom` `posHeight` `position` `posLeft` `posRight` `posTop` `posWidth` `right` `styleFloat` `tableLayout` `textAlign` `textDecoration` `textDecorationBlink` `textDecorationLineThrough` `textDecorationNone` `textDecorationOverline` `textDecorationUnderline` `textIndent` `textTransform` `top` `unicodeBidi` `verticalAlign` `visibility` `width` `zIndex`

Methods None

Events None

Collections None

The screen Object

Exposes information about the client's monitor screen and system rendering abilities.

Properties `availHeight` `availWidth` `bufferDepth` `colorDepth` `fontSmoothingEnabled` `height` `updateInterval` `width`

Methods None

Events None

Collections None

The selection Object

Represents the currently active selection on the screen in the document.

Properties `type`

Methods `clear` `createRange` `empty`

Events None

Collections None

The style Object

Represents an individual style element within a style sheet.

Properties `background` `backgroundAttachment` `backgroundColor` `backgroundImage` `backgroundPosition` `backgroundPositionX` `backgroundPositionY` `backgroundRepeat` `border` `borderBottom` `borderBottomColor` `borderBottomStyle` `borderBottomWidth` `borderColor` `borderLeft` `borderLeftColor` `borderLeftStyle` `borderLeftWidth` `borderRight` `borderRightColor` `borderRightStyle` `borderRightWidth` `borderStyle` `borderTop` `borderTopColor` `borderTopStyle` `borderTopWidth` `borderWidth` `bottom` `clear` `clip` `color` `cssText` `cursor` `direction` `display` `filter` `font` `fontFamily` `fontSize` `fontStyle` `fontVariant` `fontWeight` `height` `layoutGrid` `layoutGridChar` `layoutGridCharSpacing` `layoutGridLine` `layoutGridMode` `layoutGridType` `left` `letterSpacing` `lineHeight` `listStyle` `listStyleImage` `listStylePosition` `listStyleType` `margin` `marginBottom` `marginLeft` `marginRight` `marginTop` `overflow` `overflowX` `overflowY` `padding` `paddingBottom` `paddingLeft` `paddingRight` `paddingTop` `pageBreakAfter` `pageBreakBefore` `pixelBottom` `pixelHeight` `pixelLeft` `pixelRight` `pixelTop` `pixelWidth` `posBottom` `posHeight` `position` `posLeft` `posRight` `posTop` `posWidth` `right` `styleFloat` `tableLayout` `textAlign` `textDecoration` `textDecorationBlink` `textDecorationLineThrough` `textDecorationNone` `textDecorationOverline` `textDecorationUnderline` `textIndent` `textTransform` `top` `unicodeBidi` `verticalAlign` `visibility` `width` `zIndex`

Methods `getExpression` `removeExpression` `setExpression`

Events None

Collections None

The styleSheet Object

Exposes all the styles within a single style sheet in the `styleSheets` collection.

Properties `disabled` `id` `owningElement` `parentStyleSheet` `readOnly` `type`

Methods `addImport` `addRule` `removeRule`

Events None

Collections `imports` `rules`

The textNode Object

A string of text, represented as a node on the document hierarchy.

Properties `data` `length` `nextSibling` `nodeName` `nodeType` `nodeValue` `previousSibling`

Methods `splitText`

Events None

Collections None

The textRange Object

Represents sections of the text stream making up the HTML document.

Properties `boundingHeight` `boundingLeft` `boundingTop` `boundingWidth` `htmlText` `offsetLeft` `offsetTop` `text`

Methods `collapse` `compareEndPoints` `duplicate` `execCommand` `expand` `findText` `getBookmark` `getBoundingClientRect` `getClientRects` `inRange` `isEqual` `move` `moveEnd` `moveStart` `moveToBookmark` `moveToElementText` `moveToPoint` `parentElement` `pasteHTML` `queryCommandEnabled` `queryCommandIndeterm` `queryCommandState` `queryCommandSupported` `queryCommandValue` `scrollIntoView` `select` `setEndPoint`

Events None

Collections None

The textRectangle Object

A set of the four coordinates that represent the rectangle containing a line of text of `TextRange` object.

Properties `bottom` `left` `right` `top`

Methods None

Events None

Collections None

The userProfile Object

Allows a script to request read access to and perform read actions on a user's profile.

Properties None

Methods `addReadRequest clearRequest doReadRequest getAttribute`

Events None

Collections None

The window Object

Exposes properties, methods and events connected to the browser window or a frame.

Properties `clientInformation clipboardData closed defaultStatus dialogArguments dialogHeight dialogLeft dialogTop dialogWidth document event external history length location name navigator offscreenBuffering opener parent returnValue screen screenLeft screenTop self status top`

Methods `alert attachEvent blur clearInterval clearTimeout close confirm detachEvent execScript focus moveBy moveTo navigate open print prompt resizeBy resizeTo scroll scrollBy scrollTo setInterval setTimeout showHelp showModalDialog showModelessDialog`

Events `onafterprint onbeforeprint onbeforeunload onblur onerror onfocus onhelp onload onresize onunload`

Collections `Frames`

HTML and Form Controls Cross Reference

Dynamic HTML provides the same integral control types as HTML 3.2. However, there are many more different properties, methods and events available now for all the controls.

The following tables show those that are most relevant to controls. For a full list and description of the properties, methods and events for each element check out Appendices **A** and **B**.

Control Properties	checked	dataFld	dataFormatAs	dataSrc	defaultChecked	defaultValue	maxLength	readOnly	recordNumber	selectedIndex	size	status	type	value
HTML button	✗	✓	✓	✓	✗	✓	✗	✗	✓	✗	✓	✗	✓	✓
HTML checkbox	✓	✓	✗	✓	✓	✓	✗	✗	✓	✗	✓	✓	✓	✓
HTML file	✗	✓	✗	✓	✗	✓	✗	✗	✓	✗	✓	✗	✓	✓
HTML hidden	✗	✓	✗	✓	✗	✓	✗	✗	✓	✗	✗	✗	✓	✓
HTML image	✗	✓	✗	✓	✗	✓	✗	✗	✓	✗	✓	✗	✓	✓
HTML password	✗	✓	✗	✓	✗	✓	✓	✓	✓	✗	✓	✗	✓	✓
HTML radio	✓	✓	✗	✓	✓	✓	✗	✗	✓	✗	✓	✓	✓	✓
HTML reset	✗	✓	✗	✓	✗	✓	✗	✗	✓	✗	✓	✗	✓	✓
HTML submit	✗	✓	✗	✓	✗	✓	✗	✗	✓	✗	✓	✗	✓	✓
HTML text	✗	✓	✗	✓	✗	✓	✓	✓	✓	✗	✓	✗	✓	✓
APPLET tag	✗	✓	✗	✓	✗	✗	✗	✗	✓	✗	✗	✗	✗	✗
BUTTON tag	✗	✓	✓	✓	✗	✗	✗	✗	✓	✗	✗	✗	✓	✓
FIELD SET tag	✗	✗	✗	✗	✗	✗	✗	✗	✓	✗	✗	✗	✗	✗
LABEL tag	✗	✓	✓	✓	✗	✗	✗	✗	✓	✗	✗	✗	✗	✗
LEGEND tag	✗	✗	✗	✗	✗	✗	✗	✗	✗	✗	✗	✗	✗	✗
SELECT tag	✗	✓	✗	✓	✗	✗	✗	✗	✓	✓	✓	✗	✓	✗
TEXTAREA tag	✗	✓	✗	✓	✗	✓	✗	✓	✗	✗	✗	✗	✓	✓
XML tag	✗	✗	✗	✗	✗	✗	✗	✗	✗	✗	✗	✗	✗	✗

Control Methods	add	blur	click	createTextRange	focus	item	remove	select
HTML button	✗	✓	✓	✓	✓	✗	✗	✓
HTML checkbox	✗	✓	✓	✗	✓	✗	✗	✓
HTML file	✗	✓	✓	✗	✓	✗	✗	✓
HTML hidden	✗	✗	✗	✓	✗	✗	✗	✗
HTML image	✗	✓	✓	✗	✓	✗	✗	✓
HTML password	✗	✓	✓	✓	✓	✗	✗	✓
HTML radio	✗	✓	✓	✗	✓	✗	✗	✓
HTML reset	✗	✓	✓	✓	✓	✗	✗	✓
HTML submit	✗	✓	✓	✓	✓	✗	✗	✓
HTML text	✗	✓	✓	✓	✓	✗	✗	✓
APPLET tag	✗	✓	✓	✗	✓	✗	✗	✗
BUTTON tag	✗	✓	✓	✓	✓	✗	✗	✗
FIELDSET tag	✗	✓	✓	✗	✓	✗	✗	✗
LABEL tag	✗	✓	✓	✗	✓	✗	✗	✗
LEGEND tag	✗	✓	✓	✗	✓	✗	✗	✗
SELECT tag	✗	✓	✓	✗	✓	✗	✗	✗
TEXTAREA tag	✗	✓	✓	✓	✓	✗	✗	✓
XML tag	✗	✗	✗	✗	✗	✗	✗	✗

Control Events

	onafterupdate	onbeforeupdate	onblur	onchange	onclick	ondblclick	onfocus	onrowenter	onrowexit	onselect
HTML button	✗	✗	✓	✗	✓	✓	✓	✗	✗	✗
HTML checkbox	✓	✓	✓	✗	✓	✓	✓	✗	✗	✗
HTML file	✗	✗	✓	✗	✓	✓	✓	✗	✗	✗
HTML hidden	✗	✗	✗	✗	✗	✗	✓	✗	✗	✗
HTML image	✗	✗	✓	✗	✓	✓	✓	✗	✗	✗
HTML password	✗	✗	✓	✗	✓	✓	✓	✗	✗	✗
HTML radio	✗	✗	✓	✗	✓	✓	✓	✗	✗	✗
HTML reset	✗	✗	✓	✗	✓	✓	✓	✗	✗	✗
HTML submit	✗	✗	✓	✗	✓	✓	✓	✗	✗	✗
HTML text	✗	✗	✓	✓	✓	✓	✓	✗	✗	✓
APPLET tag	✗	✗	✓	✗	✓	✓	✓	✓	✓	✗
BUTTON tag	✗	✗	✓	✗	✓	✓	✓	✗	✗	✗
FIELDSET tag	✗	✗	✓	✗	✓	✓	✓	✗	✗	✗
LABEL tag	✗	✗	✓	✗	✓	✓	✓	✗	✗	✗
LEGEND tag	✗	✗	✓	✗	✓	✓	✓	✗	✗	✗
SELECT tag	✗	✗	✓	✓	✓	✓	✓	✗	✗	✗
TEXTAREA tag	✓	✓	✓	✓	✓	✓	✓	✗	✗	✓
XML tag	✗	✗	✗	✗	✗	✗	✗	✓	✓	✗

B

DHTML Properties, Methods and Events

This appendix consists of three tables; the listing of Properties, Attributes and CSS Equivalents below, a listing of Dynamic HTML Methods and a listing of Dynamic HTML Events. Where there is more than one possible use/description for an item there will sometimes be more than one entry for it in the table. To find out more about any of the items listed here, check out the Microsoft Dynamic HTML Authoring reference section at http://msdn.microsoft.com/workshop/author/default.asp.

The notation for the CSS Values is as follows:

- One vertical bar | means *exclusive or*; that is, only one of the items is allowed.
- Two vertical bars || means *inclusive or*; that is, any number of the items are allowed.
- <>mean the actual value of the items needs to be substituted, for example `#FFCC00` for `<color>`.
- `[]` indicate grouping.
- `{}` denote each style sheet within the `STYLE` tag, which have to be enclosed between braces.
- `{A,B}` within the CSS Values indicate that the preceding group must be repeated between `A` and `B` times, for example within `padding`, `{1,4` indicates that the individual values may be specified up to four times top, right, bottom and left respectively.
- An asterisk means that the preceding group is repeated zero or more times
- A question mark indicates that the preceding group is optional.

List of Properties, Attributes and CSS Equivalents

This table lists properties, with their associated attributes and CSS equivalents where appropriate. Not all properties have attributes, and occasionally you will find an entry for a CSS equivalent which has neither a property nor an attribute associated with it.

Property Name	Attribute Name	CSS Values	Description
		`!important`	Used in a CSS rule definition, to specify that it should be preferred to any alternative rules
		`@charset <characterset>`	Specifies the character set for an external style sheet
		`@font-face{font-family: <font-family>; url:(<url>);}`	Specifies a font to embed in your HTML document. Allows you to use fonts not found locally.
		`@import url(<url>)`	Specifies a style sheet to import.
		`@media <mediatype> <rules>`	Specifies the media type(s) for a set of style sheet rules
accessKey	ACCESSKEY		Specifies an accelerator or 'hot key' for the element.
action	ACTION		The URL for the ACTION of the form. If not specified document's base URL is used.
activeElement			Identifies the element that has the focus.
align	ALIGN		Specifies how the element is aligned with respect to the rest of the page.
aLink	ALINK		The color for active links in the element - i.e. while the mouse button is held down.

<table>
<tr><td>aLinkColor</td><td></td><td></td><td>The color for active links in the document - i.e. while the mouse button is held down.</td></tr>
<tr><td>alt</td><td>ALT</td><td></td><td>Text to be used as an alternative to the object in non-graphical environments.</td></tr>
<tr><td>altHTML</td><td></td><td></td><td>Specifies alternative HTML code to be used if the object fails to load.</td></tr>
<tr><td>altKey</td><td></td><td></td><td>Returns the state of the ALT key when an event occurs.</td></tr>
<tr><td>appCodeName</td><td></td><td></td><td>The code name of the browser.</td></tr>
<tr><td>appMinorVersion</td><td></td><td></td><td>Returns the application's minor version value.</td></tr>
<tr><td>appName</td><td></td><td></td><td>The product name of the browser.</td></tr>
<tr><td>appVersion</td><td></td><td></td><td>The version of the browser.</td></tr>
<tr><td>autocomplete</td><td>AUTOCOMPLETE</td><td></td><td>Specifies whether the object has autocomplete enabled.</td></tr>
<tr><td>availHeight</td><td></td><td></td><td>Height, in pixels, of the screen's working area.</td></tr>
<tr><td>availWidth</td><td></td><td></td><td>Width, in pixels, of the screen's working area.</td></tr>
<tr><td>background (BODY, TABLE, TH, TD)</td><td>BACKGROUND</td><td></td><td>Specifies a background picture that is tiled behind text and graphics.</td></tr>
<tr><td>background (others)</td><td></td><td>{ background: transparent | <color> || <url> || <repeat> || <scroll> || <position>}</td><td>Specifies the other background properties (q.v.) all at once.</td></tr>
<tr><td>backgroundAttachment</td><td></td><td>{ background-attachment: scroll | fixed}</td><td>Defines if a background image should be fixed on the page or scroll with the content.</td></tr>
<tr><td>backgroundColor</td><td></td><td>{ background-color: <color> | transparent}</td><td>Specifies the background color of the page or element.</td></tr>
<tr><td>backgroundImage</td><td></td><td>{ background-image: <url> | none}</td><td>Specifies a URL for the background image for the page or element.</td></tr>
</table>

<table>
<tr><th>PropertyName</th><th>AttributeName</th><th>CSSValues</th><th>Description</th></tr>
<tr><td>backgroundPosition</td><td></td><td>{ background-position: [<position> | <length>] {1,2} | [top | center | bottom] || [left | center | right]}</td><td>The initial position of a background image on the page.</td></tr>
<tr><td>backgroundPositionX</td><td></td><td></td><td>The x-coordinate of the background image in relation to the containing window.</td></tr>
<tr><td>backgroundPositionY</td><td></td><td></td><td>The y-coordinate of the background image in relation to the containing window.</td></tr>
<tr><td>backgroundRepeat</td><td></td><td>{ background-repeat: repeat | repeat-x | repeat-y | no-repeat}</td><td>Defines if and how a background image is repeated on the page.</td></tr>
<tr><td>balance</td><td>BALANCE</td><td></td><td>Returns the left-to-right balance value for a background sound.</td></tr>
<tr><td>behavior (MARQUEE)</td><td>BEHAVIOR</td><td></td><td>Specifies how the text scrolls in a marquee element.</td></tr>
<tr><td>behavior (others)</td><td>BEHAVIOR</td><td>{ behavior : url(sLocation) | url (#objID) | url(#default#behaviorName) }</td><td>Specifies the location of the DHTML behavior.</td></tr>
<tr><td>bgColor</td><td>BGCOLOR</td><td>{ background-color: <color> | transparent}</td><td>Specifies the background color to be used for an element.</td></tr>
<tr><td>bgProperties</td><td>BGPROPERTIES</td><td>{ background-attachment: scroll | fixed}</td><td>Sets or retrieves properties for the background picture.</td></tr>
<tr><td>body</td><td>BODY</td><td></td><td>Read-only reference to the document's implicit body object, as defined by the <BODY> tag.</td></tr>
<tr><td>border (FRAMESET, IMG, TABLE)</td><td>BORDER</td><td></td><td>Specifies the border to be drawn around the element or between frame.</td></tr>
</table>

<table>
<tr><td>border
(others)</td><td></td><td>{ border: <border-width> || <border-style> || <color>}</td><td>Specifies the border-width, -style and –color properties (q.v.) to be drawn around the element.</td></tr>
<tr><td>borderBottom</td><td></td><td>{ border-bottom: <border-bottom-width> || <border-style> || <color>}</td><td>Used to specify several attributes of the bottom border of an element.</td></tr>
<tr><td>borderBottomColor</td><td></td><td>{ border-bottom-color: <color>}</td><td>The color of the bottom border for an element.</td></tr>
<tr><td>borderBottomStyle</td><td></td><td>{ border-bottom-style: none | dotted | dashed | solid | double | groove | ridge | inset | outset}</td><td>The style of the bottom border for an element.</td></tr>
<tr><td>borderBottomWidth</td><td></td><td>{ border-bottom-width: thin| medium| thick | <length>}</td><td>The width of the bottom border for an element.</td></tr>
<tr><td>borderCollapse</td><td></td><td>{ border-collapse : separate | collapse }</td><td>Specifies whether the row and cell borders of a table are joined into a single border or detached.</td></tr>
<tr><td>borderColor
(FRAME, FRAMESET, TABLE, TD, TH, TR)</td><td>BORDERCOLOR</td><td></td><td>The color of all or some of the borders for an element.</td></tr>
<tr><td>borderColor
(others)</td><td></td><td>{ border-color: <color> {1,4}}</td><td>The color of all or some of the borders for an element.</td></tr>
<tr><td>borderColorDark</td><td>BORDERCOLORDARK</td><td></td><td>The color used to draw the bottom and right borders for a 3-D element border.</td></tr>
<tr><td>borderColorLight</td><td>BORDERCOLORLIGHT</td><td></td><td>The color used to draw the top and left borders for a 3-D element border.</td></tr>
<tr><td>borderLeft</td><td></td><td>{ border-left: <border-left-width> || <border-style> || <color>}</td><td>Used to specify several attributes of the left border of an element.</td></tr>
</table>

<table>
<tr><th>opertyName</th><th>AttributeName</th><th>CSSValues</th><th>Description</th></tr>
<tr><td>borderLeftColor</td><td></td><td>{ border-left-color: <color>}</td><td>The color of the left border for an element.</td></tr>
<tr><td>borderLeftStyle</td><td></td><td>{ border-left-style: none | dotted | dashed | solid | double | groove | ridge | inset | outset}</td><td>The style of the left border for an element.</td></tr>
<tr><td>borderLeftWidth</td><td></td><td>{ border-left-width: thin | medium| thick | <length>}</td><td>The width of the left border for an element.</td></tr>
<tr><td>borderRight</td><td></td><td>{ border-right: <border-right-width> || <border-style> || <color>}</td><td>Used to specify several attributes of the right border of an element.</td></tr>
<tr><td>borderRightColor</td><td></td><td>{ border-right-color: <color>}</td><td>The color of the right border for an element.</td></tr>
<tr><td>borderRightStyle</td><td></td><td>{ border-right-style: none | dotted | dashed | solid | double | groove | ridge | inset | outset}</td><td>The style of the right border for an element.</td></tr>
<tr><td>borderRightWidth</td><td></td><td>{ border-right-width: thin | medium| thick | <length>}</td><td>The width of the right border for an element.</td></tr>
<tr><td>borderStyle</td><td></td><td>{ border-style: none | dotted | dashed | solid | double | groove | ridge | inset | outset}</td><td>Used to specify the style of one or more borders of an element.</td></tr>
<tr><td>borderTop</td><td></td><td>{ border-top: <border-top-width> || <border-style> || <color>}</td><td>Used to specify several attributes of the top border of an element.</td></tr>
</table>

borderTopColor		{ border-top-color: <color>}	The color of the top border for an element.
borderTopStyle		{ border-top-style: none | dotted | dashed | solid | double | groove | ridge | inset | outset}	The style of the top border for an element.
borderTopWidth		{ border-top-width: thin | medium| thick | <length>}	The width of the top border for an element.
borderWidth		{ border-width: [thin | medium | thick | <length>] {1,4}}	Used to specify the width of one or more borders of an element.
bottom (TextRectangle)			Returns the bottom coordinate of the object.
bottom (others)		{ bottom: auto | <length> | <percentage> }	Specifies the bottom coordinate of the object (relative to the next object in the hierarchy).
bottomMargin	BOTTOMMARGIN		Sets or returns the bottom margin for the entire page. Overrides default margin.
boundingHeight			Height of the rectangle that bounds the TextRange object.
boundingLeft			Left coordinate of the rectangle that bounds the TextRange object.
boundingTop			Top coordinate of the rectangle that bounds the TextRange object.
boundingWidth			Width of the rectangle that bounds the TextRange object.
browserLanguage			Current browser language.
bufferDepth			Specifies if and how an off-screen bitmap buffer should be used.

PropertyName	AttributeName	CSSValues	Description
button			The mouse button, if any, that was pressed to fire the event.
cancelBubble			Set to prevent the current event from bubbling up the hierarchy.
canHaveChildren			Specifies whether object can have children.
caption			Returns the CAPTION object of the TABLE.
cellIndex			Position of the object in the cells collection of a given row.
cellPadding	CELLPADDING		Specifies the amount of space between the border of the cell and its contents.
cellSpacing	CELLSPACING		Specifies the amount of space between cells in a table.
charset			Sets or returns the character set of the document.
checked	CHECKED		For check boxes and radio buttons, indicates that they are selected.
classid	CLASSID		Used to specify the class identifier for the object.
className	CLASS		Specifies the class of the tag, used to associate a sub-classed style sheet with the tag.
clear	CLEAR		Specifies which sides of the current object (BR) should be kept clear of any floating objects.
clear (others)		{ clear: none | left | right | both}	Specifies which sides of the current object should be kept clear of any floating objects.
client			A reference that returns the navigator object for the browser, used to retrieve information on the browser name and version.

clientHeight			Returns the height of the element, excluding borders, margins, padding, scrollbars, etc.
clientInformation			Returns the navigator object.
clientLeft			Distance, in pixels, between the `offsetLeft` and the true left side of the client area.
clientTop			Distance, in pixels, between the `offsetTop` and the true top of the client area.
clientWidth			Returns the width of the element, excluding borders, margins, padding, scrollbars, etc.
clientX			Returns the x-coordinate of the element, excluding borders, margins, padding, scrollbars, etc.
clientY			Returns the y-coordinate of the element, excluding borders, margins, padding, scrollbars, etc.
clip		{ clip: <shape> | auto}	Specifies how an element's contents should be displayed if larger that the available client area.
clipBottom			Bottom coordinate of the object clipping region.
clipLeft			Left coordinate of the object clipping region.
clipRight			Right coordinate of the object clipping region.
clipTop			Top coordinate of the object clipping region.
closed			Indicates if a window is closed.
code	CODE		The name of the file containing the compiled Java class.
codeBase	CODEBASE		The URL where the code implementation of the object can be found if required.
codeType	CODETYPE		The media type of the code for an externally implemented object.

PropertyName	AttributeName	CSSValues	Description
color (BASEFONT, FONT, HR)	COLOR		The text or foreground color of an element.
color (others)		{ color: <color>}	The text or foreground color of an element.
colorDepth			Returns the number of bits per pixel of the user's display device or screen buffer.
cols	COLS		The number of columns in the table or a frameset, or the number of characters in an input element.
colSpan	COLSPAN		Specifies the number of columns in the table that this cell should span.
compact	COMPACT		Specifies that the list should be compacted to remove extra space between its elements.
complete			Indicates whether the contents of the image have finished loading.
content	CONTENT		Information in a <META> tag to be associated with the given name or HTTP response header.
cookie			The string value of a cookie stored by the browser.
cookieEnabled			Indicates if client-side cookies are enabled in the browser.
coords	COORDS		The coordinates that define the hot spot's shape in a client-side image map.
cpuClass			CPU class as a string.
cssText			The text value of the element's entire STYLE attribute.

ctrlKey			Returns the state of the *CTRL* key when an event occurs.
cursor		{ cursor: auto | crosshair | default | hand | move | e-resize | ne-resize | nw-resize | n-resize | se-resize | sw-resize | s-resize | w-resize | text | wait | help}	Specifies the type of cursor to display when the mouse pointer is over the element.
data (OBJECT)	DATA		Specifies a URL that references the source of the object's data.
data (TextNode)			Specifies the text of a TextNode object.
dataFld	DATAFLD		Specifies the column or field name in the object's data source bound to this element.
dataFormatAs	DATAFORMATAS		Specifies the format of the data, can be 'text', 'html', or 'none'.
dataPageSize	DATAPAGESIZE		Defines the maximum number of records to be displayed at one time, as pages.
dataSrc	DATASRC		Specifies the source of the object's data for data binding.
defaultCharset			Default character set of the document.
defaultChecked			Denotes if this control element is checked (on) by default.
defaultSelected			Denotes if this list option is selected by default.
defaultStatus			The default message displayed in the status bar at the bottom of the window.
defaultValue			The text that is displayed as the initial contents of a control.

<table>
<tr><th>PropertyName</th><th>AttributeName</th><th>CSSValues</th><th>Description</th></tr>
<tr><td>defer</td><td>DEFER</td><td></td><td>Specifies whether the script contains an inline executable function.</td></tr>
<tr><td>designMode</td><td></td><td></td><td>Toggles between browsing and editing the document.</td></tr>
<tr><td>dialogArguments</td><td></td><td></td><td>Returns the arguments that were passed into a dialog window, as an array.</td></tr>
<tr><td>dialogHeight</td><td></td><td></td><td>Sets or returns the height of a dialog window.</td></tr>
<tr><td>dialogLeft</td><td></td><td></td><td>Sets or returns the x coordinate of a dialog window.</td></tr>
<tr><td>dialogTop</td><td></td><td></td><td>Sets or returns the y coordinate of a dialog window.</td></tr>
<tr><td>dialogWidth</td><td></td><td></td><td>Sets or returns the width of a dialog window.</td></tr>
<tr><td>dir</td><td>DIR</td><td></td><td>Reading order of the object (left-to-right or right-to-left).</td></tr>
<tr><td>direction (MARQUEE)</td><td>DIRECTION</td><td></td><td>Specifies which direction the text should scroll in a <MARQUEE>.</td></tr>
<tr><td>direction (others)</td><td></td><td>{ direction: ltr | rtl | inherit}</td><td>Specifies the reading order of the object.</td></tr>
<tr><td>disabled</td><td>DISABLED</td><td></td><td>Sets or returns whether an element is disabled.</td></tr>
<tr><td>display</td><td></td><td>{ display: block | none | inline | list-item | table-header-group | table-footer-group }</td><td>Specifies if the element will be visible (displayed) in the page.</td></tr>
<tr><td>document</td><td></td><td></td><td>Read-only reference to the window's document object.</td></tr>
</table>

<table>
<tr><td>documentElement</td><td></td><td></td><td>Returns a reference to the root node of the document.</td></tr>
<tr><td>domain</td><td></td><td></td><td>Sets or returns the domain of the document for use in cookies and security.</td></tr>
<tr><td>dropEffect</td><td></td><td></td><td>Type of drag-and-drop operation.</td></tr>
<tr><td>duration</td><td></td><td></td><td>Sets the default length of time a filter transition will take to complete.</td></tr>
<tr><td>dynsrc</td><td>DYNSRC</td><td></td><td>Specifies the address of a dynamic source (video clip or VRML) be displayed in the element.</td></tr>
<tr><td>effectAllowed</td><td></td><td></td><td>Permitted data transfer operations for the object.</td></tr>
<tr><td>encoding</td><td>ENCTYPE</td><td></td><td>The type of encoding to apply to the contents of a form when submitted.</td></tr>
<tr><td>event</td><td><event_name></td><td></td><td>Name of the event handler to be called when the specified event occurs.</td></tr>
<tr><td>event</td><td>EVENT</td><td></td><td>Read-only reference to the global event object.</td></tr>
<tr><td>expando</td><td></td><td></td><td>Specifies whether an object can be expanded by the creation of arbitrary variables.</td></tr>
<tr><td>face</td><td>FACE</td><td>{ font-family: [[<family-name> | <generic-family>] ,]* [<family-name> | <generic-family>] }</td><td>Sets the typeface of the current font.</td></tr>
<tr><td>fgColor</td><td>TEXT</td><td></td><td>Sets the color of the document foreground text.</td></tr>
<tr><td>fileCreatedDate</td><td></td><td></td><td>Date the file was created.</td></tr>
<tr><td>fileModifiedDate</td><td></td><td></td><td>Date the file was last modified.</td></tr>
<tr><td>fileSize</td><td></td><td></td><td>File size.</td></tr>
<tr><td>fileUpdatedDate</td><td></td><td></td><td>Date the file was last updated.</td></tr>
</table>

<table>
<tr><th>PropertyName</th><th>AttributeName</th><th>CSSValues</th><th>Description</th></tr>
<tr><td>filter</td><td></td><td>{ filter: blendtrans | revealtrans | alpha | blur | chroma | dropshadow | fliph | flipv | glow | gray | invert | light | mask | shadow | wave | xray }</td><td>Sets or returns an array of all the filters specified in the element's style property.</td></tr>
<tr><td>firstChild</td><td></td><td></td><td>Returns a reference to the first child in the childNodes collection of the object.</td></tr>
<tr><td>font</td><td></td><td>{ font: caption | icon | menu | messagebox | smallcaption | statusbar | [<font-style> || <font-variant> || <font-weight>] <font-size> [<line-height>] <font-family> }</td><td>Defines various attributes of the font for an element, or imports a font.</td></tr>
<tr><td>fontFamily</td><td></td><td>{ font-family: <family-name> | <generic-family> [, <family-name> | <generic-family>] }</td><td>Specifies the name of the typeface, or 'font family'.</td></tr>
<tr><td>fontSize</td><td></td><td>{ font-size: [xx-large | x-large | large | medium | small | x-small | xx-small] | [larger | smaller] | <percentage> | <length>}</td><td>Specifies the font size.</td></tr>
<tr><td>fontSmoothingEnabled</td><td></td><td></td><td>Specifies whether the user has enabled font smoothing in the Display control panel.</td></tr>
<tr><td>fontStyle</td><td></td><td>{ font-style: normal | italic | oblique}</td><td>Specifies the style of the font, i.e. normal or italic.</td></tr>
</table>

<table>
<tr><td>fontVariant</td><td></td><td>{ font-variant: normal | small-caps}</td><td>Specifies the use of small capitals for the text.</td></tr>
<tr><td>fontWeight</td><td></td><td>{ font-weight: normal | bold | bolder | lighter | 100 | 200 | 300 | 400 | 500 | 600 | 700 | 800 | 900}</td><td>Specifies the weight (boldness) of the text.</td></tr>
<tr><td>form</td><td></td><td></td><td>Returns a reference to the form that contains the element.</td></tr>
<tr><td>frame</td><td>FRAME</td><td></td><td>Controls the appearance of the border frame around a table.</td></tr>
<tr><td>frameBorder</td><td>FRAMEBORDER</td><td></td><td>Controls the appearance of the border frame around a frame.</td></tr>
<tr><td>frameSpacing</td><td>FRAMESPACING</td><td></td><td>Specifies the spacing between frames in a frameset.</td></tr>
<tr><td>fromElement</td><td></td><td></td><td>Returns the element being moved from for an onmouseover or onmouseout event.</td></tr>
<tr><td>hash</td><td></td><td></td><td>The string following the # symbol in the URL.</td></tr>
<tr><td>height (screen)</td><td></td><td></td><td>Returns the height of the user's display screen in pixels.</td></tr>
<tr><td>height (others)</td><td>HEIGHT</td><td>{ height: <length> | <percentage> | auto}</td><td>Specifies the height at which the element is to be drawn, and sets the posHeight property.</td></tr>
<tr><td>hidden</td><td>HIDDEN</td><td></td><td>Forces the embedded object to be invisible in an <EMBED> tag.</td></tr>
<tr><td>history</td><td></td><td></td><td>Read-only reference to the window's history object.</td></tr>
<tr><td>host</td><td></td><td></td><td>The hostname:port part of the location or URL.</td></tr>
<tr><td>hostname</td><td></td><td></td><td>The hostname part of the location or URL.</td></tr>
</table>

PropertyName	AttributeName	CSSValues	Description
href (style, location)			The URL of the stylesheet as a string.
href (A, AREA, LINK)	HREF		The destination or anchor as a string.
href (BASE)	HREF		A URL which that forms the base for other relative paths.
hspace	HSPACE		Specifies the horizontal spacing or margin between an element and its neighbors.
htmlFor	FOR		Specifies the element that the event script or label is linked to.
htmlText			Returns the contents of a TextRange as text and HTML source.
httpEquiv	HTTP-EQUIV		Used to bind the content of the element to an HTTP response header.
id	ID		Identifier or name for an element in a page or style sheet, or as the target for hypertext links.
imeMode		{ ime-mode: auto | active | inactive | disabled }	State of an Input Method Editor (IME) that allows a user to enter Chinese, Japanese, and Korean characters.
indeterminate			Sets the value of a checkbox to a gray background, representing an indeterminate state.
index			Returns the ordinal position of the option in a list box.
innerHTML			Sets or returns the text and HTML between an element's opening and closing tags in the HTML source.

<table>
<tr><td>innerText</td><td></td><td></td><td>Sets or returns only the text between an element's opening and closing tags in the HTML source.</td></tr>
<tr><td>isMap</td><td>ISMAP</td><td></td><td>Identifies the picture as being a server-side image map.</td></tr>
<tr><td>isTextEdit</td><td></td><td></td><td>Indicates if the element can be used as the source to create a TextRange object.</td></tr>
<tr><td>keyCode</td><td></td><td></td><td>ASCII code of the key being pressed. Changing it sends a different character to the object.</td></tr>
<tr><td>lang</td><td>LANG</td><td></td><td>The ISO description of the language for the element, as in "text/javascript"</td></tr>
<tr><td>language</td><td>LANGUAGE</td><td></td><td>The browser-specific description of the scripting language in use, such as "javascript".</td></tr>
<tr><td>lastChild</td><td></td><td></td><td>Returns a reference to the last child in the childNodes collection of an object.</td></tr>
<tr><td>lastModified</td><td></td><td></td><td>The date that the source file for the page was last modified, as a string, where available.</td></tr>
<tr><td>layoutGrid</td><td></td><td>{ layout-grid: <Mode> || <Type> || <Line> || <Char> || <Space> }</td><td>Sets or retrieves the composite document grid properties (layoutGridMode, layoutGridType, layoutGridLine, layoutGridChar, and layoutGridCharSpacing) used to specify the layout of text characters.</td></tr>
<tr><td>layoutGridChar</td><td></td><td>{ layout-grid-char: none | auto | <length> | <percentage> }</td><td>Size of the character grid to use for rendering the text contents of an element.</td></tr>
<tr><td>layoutGridCharSpacing</td><td></td><td>{ layout-grid-char-spacing: auto | <length> | <percentage> }</td><td>Character spacing to use for rendering the text contents of an element with the layout-grid-type attribute set to loose.</td></tr>
</table>

<table>
<tr><th>PropertyName</th><th>AttributeName</th><th>CSSValues</th><th>Description</th></tr>
<tr><td>layoutGridLine</td><td></td><td>{ layout-grid-line: none | auto | <length> | <percentage> }</td><td>Line grid value for rendering the text contents of an element.</td></tr>
<tr><td>layoutGridMode</td><td></td><td>{ layout-grid-mode: none | line | char | both }</td><td>Specifies whether the text layout grid uses two dimensions.</td></tr>
<tr><td>layoutGridType</td><td></td><td>{ layout-grid-type: loose | strict | fixed }</td><td>Type of grid to use for rendering the text contents of an element.</td></tr>
<tr><td>left (TextRectangle)</td><td></td><td></td><td>Specifies the position of the left of the element.</td></tr>
<tr><td>left (others)</td><td></td><td>{ left: <length> | <percentage> | auto}</td><td>Specifies the position of the left of the element, and sets the posLeft property.</td></tr>
<tr><td>leftMargin</td><td>LEFTMARGIN</td><td>{ margin-left: [<length> | <percentage> | auto] }</td><td>Specifies the left margin for the entire body of the page, over-riding the default margin.</td></tr>
<tr><td>length (TextNode)</td><td></td><td></td><td>Returns the length of the data.</td></tr>
<tr><td>length (others)</td><td></td><td></td><td>Returns the number of elements in a collection.</td></tr>
<tr><td>letterSpacing</td><td></td><td>{ letter-spacing: normal | <length>}</td><td>Indicates the additional space to be placed between characters in the text.</td></tr>
<tr><td>lineBreak</td><td></td><td>{ line-break : normal | strict }</td><td>Line-breaking behavior for Japanese text.</td></tr>
<tr><td>lineHeight</td><td></td><td>{ line-height: normal | <number> | <length> | <percentage>}</td><td>The distance between the baselines of two adjacent lines of text.</td></tr>
<tr><td>link</td><td>LINK</td><td></td><td>Color of the document links for the object.</td></tr>
<tr><td>linkColor</td><td></td><td></td><td>The color for links in the page.</td></tr>
</table>

<table>
<tr><td>listStyle</td><td></td><td>{ list-style: <type> || <position> || <url>}</td><td>Allows several style properties of a list element to be set in one operation.</td></tr>
<tr><td>listStyleImage</td><td></td><td>{ list-style-image: <url> | none}</td><td>Defines the image used as a background for a list element.</td></tr>
<tr><td>listStylePosition</td><td></td><td>{ list-style-position: inside | outside}</td><td>Defines the position of the bullets used in a list element.</td></tr>
<tr><td>listStyleType</td><td></td><td>{ list-style-type: disk | circle | square | decimal | lower-roman | upper-roman | lower-alpha | upper-alpha | none}</td><td>Defines the design of the bullets used in a list element.</td></tr>
<tr><td>location</td><td></td><td></td><td>The full URL of the document.</td></tr>
<tr><td>loop</td><td>LOOP</td><td></td><td>Number of times sound or video clips should play when activated, or text in a MARQUEE should loop.</td></tr>
<tr><td>lowsrc</td><td>LOWSRC</td><td></td><td>Specifies the URL of a lower resolution image to display.</td></tr>
<tr><td>map</td><td></td><td></td><td>Identifies the element as representing an image map.</td></tr>
<tr><td>margin</td><td></td><td>{ margin: [<length> | <percentage> | auto] {1,4}}</td><td>Allows all four margins to be specified with a single attribute.</td></tr>
<tr><td>marginBottom</td><td></td><td>{ margin-bottom: [<length> | <percentage> | auto]}</td><td>Specifies the bottom margin for the page or text block.</td></tr>
<tr><td>marginHeight</td><td>MARGINHEIGHT</td><td></td><td>Specifies the top and bottom margins for displaying text in a frame.</td></tr>
<tr><td>marginLeft</td><td></td><td>{ margin-left: [<length> | <percentage> | auto]}</td><td>Specifies the left margin for the page or text block.</td></tr>
</table>

PropertyName	AttributeName	CSSValues	Description
marginRight		{ margin-right: [<length> | <percentage> | auto] }	Specifies the right margin for the page or text block.
marginTop		{ margin-top: [<length> | <percentage> | auto] }	Specifies the top margin for the page or text block.
marginWidth	MARGINWIDTH		Specifies the left and right margins for displaying text in a frame.
maxLength	MAXLENGTH		Indicates the maximum number of characters that can be entered into a text control.
media	MEDIA		Media type.
menuArguments			Window object where the context menu item was executed.
method	METHOD		Indicates how the form data should be sent to the server; either GET or POST
Methods	METHODS		Provides information about the functions that the user may perform on an object.
mimeTypes			An array of MimeTypes supported by the browser. Returns an empty collection in IE4.
multiple	MULTIPLE		Indicates that multiple items in the select list can be selected.
name	NAME		Specifies the name of the window, frame, element, control, bookmark, or applet.
nameProp			File name specified in the href or src property of the object.
navigator			Read-only reference to the window's navigator object.

nextSibling		Returns a reference to the next child of the parent for the specified object.
nodeName		Name of a particular type of node.
nodeType		Type of requested node.
nodeValue		Value of a node.
noHref	NOHREF	Indicates that clicks in this region of an image map should cause no action.
noResize	NORESIZE	Indicates that a frame is not resizable by the user.
noShade	NOSHADE	Draws the horizontal rule without 3-D shading.
noWrap	NOWRAP	Indicates that the browser should not perform automatic word wrapping of the text.
object	OBJECT	Reference to the object contained in an <OBJECT> tag, for use with duplicated property names.
offScreenBuffering		Specifies whether to use off-screen buffering for the document.
offsetHeight		Returns the total height of the content of an element in pixels, including that not currently visible without scrolling.
offsetLeft		Returns the x coordinate of the left of the content of an element in pixels, relative to the containing element.
offsetParent		Returns a reference to the element that contains this element, and that defines the top and left positions.

<table>
<tr><th>PropertyName</th><th>AttributeName</th><th>CSSValues</th><th>Description</th></tr>
<tr><td>offsetTop</td><td></td><td></td><td>Returns the y coordinate of the top of the content of an element in pixels, relative to the containing element.</td></tr>
<tr><td>offsetWidth</td><td></td><td></td><td>Returns the total width of the content of an element in pixels, including that not currently visible without scrolling.</td></tr>
<tr><td>offsetX</td><td></td><td></td><td>Returns the x coordinate of the mouse pointer when an event occurs, relative to the containing element.</td></tr>
<tr><td>offsetY</td><td></td><td></td><td>Returns the y coordinate position of the mouse pointer when an event occurs, relative to the containing element.</td></tr>
<tr><td>onLine</td><td></td><td></td><td>Specifies whether the system is in global offline mode</td></tr>
<tr><td>opener</td><td></td><td></td><td>Returns a reference to the window that created the current window.</td></tr>
<tr><td>outerHTML</td><td></td><td></td><td>Sets or returns the text and HTML for an element, including the opening and closing tags in the HTML source.</td></tr>
<tr><td>outerText</td><td></td><td></td><td>Sets or returns only the text for an element, including the opening and closing tags in the HTML source.</td></tr>
<tr><td>overflow</td><td></td><td>{ overflow: visible | scroll | hidden | auto}</td><td>Defines how text that overflows the element is handled.</td></tr>
<tr><td>overflowX</td><td></td><td>{ overflow-x: visible | scroll | hidden | auto }</td><td>Specifies how to manage the content of the object when the content exceeds the width of the object.</td></tr>
</table>

<table>
<tr><td>overflowY</td><td></td><td>{ overflow-y: visible | scroll | hidden | auto }</td><td>Specifies how to manage the content of the object when the content exceeds the height of the object.</td></tr>
<tr><td>owningElement</td><td></td><td></td><td>Returns the style sheet that imported or referenced the current style sheet, usually through a <LINK> tag.</td></tr>
<tr><td>padding</td><td></td><td>{ padding: [<length> | <percentage>] {1,4}}</td><td>Sets the amount of space between the border and content for up to four sides of an element in one operation.</td></tr>
<tr><td>paddingBottom</td><td></td><td>{ padding-bottom: [<length> | <percentage>] }</td><td>Sets the amount of space between the bottom border and content of an element.</td></tr>
<tr><td>paddingLeft</td><td></td><td>{ padding-left: [<length> | <percentage>] }</td><td>Sets the amount of space between the left border and content of an element.</td></tr>
<tr><td>paddingRight</td><td></td><td>{ padding-right: [<length> | <percentage>] }</td><td>Sets the amount of space between the right border and content of an element.</td></tr>
<tr><td>paddingTop</td><td></td><td>{ padding-top: [<length> | <percentage>] }</td><td>Sets the amount of space between the top border and content of an element.</td></tr>
<tr><td>pageBreakAfter</td><td></td><td>{ page-break-after: auto | always }</td><td>Specifies if a page break should occur after the element.</td></tr>
<tr><td>pageBreakBefore</td><td></td><td>{ page-break-before: auto | always }</td><td>Specifies if a page break should occur before the element.</td></tr>
<tr><td>palette</td><td>PALETTE</td><td></td><td>Defines a palette to be used with an embedded document.</td></tr>
<tr><td>parent</td><td></td><td></td><td>Returns the parent window or frame in the window/frame hierarchy.</td></tr>
<tr><td>parentElement</td><td></td><td></td><td>Returns the parent element. The top-most element returns null for its parent.</td></tr>
<tr><td>parentNode</td><td></td><td></td><td>Parent object in the document hierarchy.</td></tr>
</table>

<table>
<tr><th>PropertyName</th><th>AttributeName</th><th>CSSValues</th><th>Description</th></tr>
<tr><td>parentStyleSheet</td><td></td><td></td><td>Returns the style sheet that imported the current style sheet, or null for a non-imported stylesheet.</td></tr>
<tr><td>parentTextEdit</td><td></td><td></td><td>Returns the closest parent of the element that can be used as the source to create a TextRange object.</td></tr>
<tr><td>parentWindow</td><td></td><td></td><td>Returns the parent window that contains the document.</td></tr>
<tr><td>pathname</td><td></td><td></td><td>The file or object path name following the third slash in a URL.</td></tr>
<tr><td>pixelBottom</td><td></td><td></td><td>Sets or returns the bottom style property of the element in pixels, as a pure number, rather than a string.</td></tr>
<tr><td>pixelHeight</td><td></td><td>{ height: <length> | auto}</td><td>Sets or returns the height style property of the element in pixels, as a pure number rather than a string.</td></tr>
<tr><td>pixelLeft</td><td></td><td>{left: <length | <percentage> | auto}</td><td>Sets or returns the left style property of the element in pixels, as a pure number, rather than a string.</td></tr>
<tr><td>pixelRight</td><td></td><td></td><td>Sets or returns the right style property of the element in pixels, as a pure number, rather than a string.</td></tr>
<tr><td>pixelTop</td><td></td><td>{top: <length | <percentage> | auto}</td><td>Sets or returns the top style property of the element in pixels, as a pure number, rather than a string.</td></tr>
<tr><td>pixelWidth</td><td></td><td>{width: <length | <percentage> | auto}</td><td>Sets or returns the width style property of the element in pixels, as a pure number, rather than a string.</td></tr>
</table>

<table>
<tr><td>platform</td><td></td><td></td><td>Name of user's operating system.</td></tr>
<tr><td>plugins</td><td></td><td></td><td>An array of plugins available in the browser. Returns an empty collection in IE4.</td></tr>
<tr><td>pluginspage</td><td>PLUGINSPAGE</td><td></td><td>Defines the plug-in to be used with an embedded document.</td></tr>
<tr><td>port</td><td></td><td></td><td>The port number in a URL.</td></tr>
<tr><td>posBottom</td><td></td><td></td><td>Returns the value of the bottom style property in its last specified units, as a pure number rather than a string.</td></tr>
<tr><td>posHeight</td><td></td><td>{ height: <length> | auto}</td><td>Returns the value of the height style property in its last specified units, as a pure number rather than a string.</td></tr>
<tr><td>position</td><td></td><td>{ position: absolute | relative | static}</td><td>Returns the value of the position style property, defining whether the element can be positioned.</td></tr>
<tr><td>posLeft</td><td></td><td>{left: <length | <percentage> | auto}</td><td>Returns the value of the left style property in its last specified units, as a pure number rather than a string.</td></tr>
<tr><td>posRight</td><td></td><td></td><td>Returns the value of the right style property in its last specified units, as a pure number rather than a string.</td></tr>
<tr><td>posTop</td><td></td><td>{top: <length | <percentage> | auto}</td><td>Returns the value of the top style property in its last specified units, as a pure number rather than a string.</td></tr>
<tr><td>posWidth</td><td></td><td>{width: <length | <percentage> | auto}</td><td>Returns the value of the width style property in its last specified units, as a pure number rather than a string.</td></tr>
<tr><td>protocol</td><td></td><td></td><td>The initial substring up to and including the first colon, indicating the URL's access method.</td></tr>
</table>

PropertyName	AttributeName	CSSValues	Description
qualifier			Name of the data member provided by a data source object.
readOnly	READONLY		Indicates that an element's contents are read only, or that a rule in a style sheet cannot be changed.
readyState			Specifies the current state of an object being downloaded.
reason			Indicates whether data transfer to an element was successful, or why it failed.
recordNumber			Returns the ordinal number of the current record for a data-bound table element.
recordset			Returns the recordset for the object, if the object is a data provider.
	REF		Indicates that the value is a URL.
referrer			The URL of the page that referenced (loaded) the current page.
rel	REL		Relationship described by a hypertext link from an anchor to the target. Opposite of rev.
repeat			Specifies whether an event is being repeated.
returnValue			Allows a return value to be specified for the event or a dialog window.
rev	REV		Relationship described by a hypertext link from the target to its anchor. Opposite of rel.
right (TextRectangle)			Specifies the position of the right of the element.

<table>
<tr><td>right
(others)</td><td></td><td>{ right: <length> | <percentage> | auto}</td><td>Specifies the position of the right of the element, and sets the posRight property.</td></tr>
<tr><td>rightMargin</td><td>RIGHTMARGIN</td><td></td><td>Specifies the right margin for the entire body of the page, over-riding the default margin.</td></tr>
<tr><td>rowIndex</td><td></td><td></td><td>Position of the object in the rows collection for the TABLE.</td></tr>
<tr><td>rows</td><td>ROWS</td><td></td><td>Number of rows in a TEXTAREA control, or the height of the frames in a frameset.</td></tr>
<tr><td>rowSpan</td><td>ROWSPAN</td><td></td><td>Specifies the number of rows in the table that this cell should span.</td></tr>
<tr><td>rubyAlign</td><td></td><td>{ ruby-align: auto | left | center | right | distribute-letter | distribute-space | line-edge }</td><td>Alignment of the ruby text specified by the RT object.</td></tr>
<tr><td>rubyOverhang</td><td></td><td>{ ruby-overhang: auto | whitespace | none }</td><td>Overhang of the ruby text specified by the RT object.</td></tr>
<tr><td>rubyPosition</td><td></td><td>{ ruby-position: above | inline }</td><td>Position of the ruby text specified by the RT object.</td></tr>
<tr><td>rules</td><td>RULES</td><td></td><td>Specifies which dividing lines (inner borders) are displayed in a table.</td></tr>
<tr><td>screen</td><td></td><td></td><td>Read-only reference to the global screen object.</td></tr>
<tr><td>screenLeft</td><td></td><td></td><td>Left edge of the client's position in screen coordinates.</td></tr>
<tr><td>screenTop</td><td></td><td></td><td>Top edge of the client's position in screen coordinates.</td></tr>
<tr><td>screenX</td><td></td><td></td><td>Returns the x coordinate of the mouse pointer when an event occurs, in relation to the screen.</td></tr>
</table>

PropertyName	AttributeName	CSSValues	Description
screenY			Returns the y coordinate of the mouse pointer when an event occurs, in relation to the screen.
scroll	SCROLL		Turns on or off the scrollbars in a frame.
scrollAmount	SCROLLAMOUNT		Number of pixels that the text scrolls between each subsequent drawing of the MARQUEE.
scrollDelay	SCROLLDELAY		Specifies the time between redraws of the MARQUEE in milliseconds.
scrollHeight			Total height in pixels of the content of an element that can be viewed without moving any scroll bars.
scrolling	SCROLLING		Specifies whether a frame can be scrolled.
scrollLeft			The scrolled distance in pixels between the left edge of the content of an element and the left edge of its container.
scrollTop			The scrolled distance in pixels between the top edge of the content of an element and the top edge of its container.
scrollWidth			Total width in pixels of the content of an element that can be viewed without moving any scroll bars.
search			The contents of the query string or form data following the ? in the complete URL.
sectionRowIndex			Position of the object in the TBODY, THEAD, TFOOT, or rows collection.
selected	SELECTED		Indicates that this item is the default and will be selected in a select list.

selectedIndex		An integer specifying the index of the currently selected option in a select list.
selection		Read-only reference to the document's `selection` object.
selectorText		Returns a string that identifies what elements the corresponding rule applies to.
self		Provides a reference to the current window.
shape	SHAPE	Specifies the type of shape used in a client-side image map.
shiftKey		Returns the state of the *SHIFT* key when an event occurs.
size (HR)		Specifies the height of an `HR` object.
size (others)	SIZE	Specifies the size of the control, horizontal rule, or font.
sourceIndex		Returns the ordinal position of the element in the source order, and in the `all` collection.
span	SPAN	Specifies how many columns are in a `COLGROUP`.
specified		Specifies whether an object has been specified.
src	SRC	Specifies an external file that contains the source data for the element.
srcElement		Returns the element deepest in the object hierarchy that a specified event occurred over.
srcFilter		Returns the filter that caused the element to produce an `onfilterchange` event.
srcUrn		Universal resource name (URN) of the behavior that fired the event.

PropertyName	AttributeName	CSSValues	Description
start	START		Sets or returns the start number of a list.
start			Specifies when a video clip should begin playing.
status			Text displayed in the window's status bar, or an alias for the value of an option button.
status			Returns the current status of the filter transition.
style	STYLE		Specifies an in-line style sheet (or set of style properties) for the element.
styleFloat		{ float: left | right | none}	Specifies if the element will float above the other elements in the page, or cause them to flow round it.
systemLanguage			Default language that the system is running.
tabIndex	TABINDEX		Sets the Tab index for the element within the tabbing order of the page.
tableLayout		{ table-layout : auto | fixed }	Specifies whether the table layout is fixed.
tagName			Returns the HTML tag as a lower-case string, without the < and > delimiters.
tagUrn			Longer Uniform Resource Name (URN) specified in the namespace declaration.
target	TARGET		Specifies the window or frame where the new page will be loaded.
text (BODY)	TEXT		Sets or retrieves the color of the foreground text in the page.
text (other)			The plain text contained within a block element, a TextRange or an <OPTION> tag.

<table>
<tr><td>textAlign</td><td>{ text-align: left | right | center | justify}</td><td>Indicates how text should be aligned within the element.</td></tr>
<tr><td>textAutospace</td><td>{ text-autospace : none | ideograph-alpha | ideograph-numeric | ideograph-parenthesis | ideograph-space }</td><td>Autospacing and narrow space width adjustment of text.</td></tr>
<tr><td>textDecoration</td><td>{ text-decoration: none | [underline || overline || line-through]}</td><td>Specifies several font decorations (underline, overline, strikethrough) added to the text of an element.</td></tr>
<tr><td>textDecorationBlink</td><td></td><td>Specifies if the font should blink or flash. Has no effect in IE4.</td></tr>
<tr><td>textDecorationLineThrough</td><td></td><td>Specifies if the text is displayed as strikethrough, i.e. with a horizontal line through it.</td></tr>
<tr><td>textDecorationNone</td><td></td><td>Specifies if the text is displayed with no additional decoration.</td></tr>
<tr><td>textDecorationOverline</td><td></td><td>Denotes if the text is displayed as overline, i.e. with a horizontal line above it.</td></tr>
<tr><td>textDecorationUnderline</td><td></td><td>Denotes if the text is displayed as underline, i.e. with a horizontal line below it.</td></tr>
<tr><td>textIndent</td><td>{ text-indent: <length> | <percentage>}</td><td>Specifies the indent for the first line of text in an element, and may be negative.</td></tr>
<tr><td>textJustify</td><td>{ text-justify : inter-word | newspaper | distribute | distribute-all-lines | inter-ideograph | auto }</td><td>Determines the type of alignment used to justify text in the object.</td></tr>
<tr><td>textTransform</td><td>{ text-transform: capitalize | uppercase | lowercase | none}</td><td>Specifies how the text for the element should be capitalized.</td></tr>
</table>

<table>
<tr><th>PropertyName</th><th>AttributeName</th><th>CSSValues</th><th>Description</th></tr>
<tr><td>tFoot</td><td></td><td></td><td>TFOOT object of the table.</td></tr>
<tr><td>tHead</td><td></td><td></td><td>THEAD object of the table.</td></tr>
<tr><td>title (LINK)</td><td>TITLE</td><td></td><td>Specifies the title of a stylesheet.</td></tr>
<tr><td>title (others)</td><td>TITLE</td><td></td><td>Provides advisory information about the element, such as when loading or as a tooltip.</td></tr>
<tr><td>toElement</td><td></td><td></td><td>Returns the element being moved to for an onmouseover or onmouseout event.</td></tr>
<tr><td>top (TextRectangle)</td><td></td><td></td><td>Returns the top coordinate of the rectangle.</td></tr>
<tr><td>top (window)</td><td></td><td></td><td>Returns the topmost parent window object.</td></tr>
<tr><td>top (others)</td><td></td><td>{ top: <length> | <percentage> | auto}</td><td>Position of the top of the element, sets the posTop property.</td></tr>
<tr><td>topMargin</td><td>TOPMARGIN</td><td>{ margin-top: [<length> | <percentage> | auto] }</td><td>Specifies the margin for the top of the page, over-riding the default top margin.</td></tr>
<tr><td>trueSpeed</td><td>TRUESPEED</td><td></td><td>Specifies how a MARQUEE element calculates the scrolling speed, compared to IE3.</td></tr>
<tr><td>type (event)</td><td></td><td></td><td>Returns the name of the event as a string, without the 'on' prefix, such as 'click' instead of 'onclick'.</td></tr>
<tr><td>type (selection, stylesheet)</td><td></td><td></td><td>Returns the selection type or the CSS language of the stylesheet.</td></tr>
<tr><td>type (others)</td><td>TYPE</td><td></td><td>Specifies the type of list style, link, selection, control, button, Mime-type, rel, or the CSS language.</td></tr>
</table>

unicodeBidi		{ unicode-bidi : normal | embed | bidi-override }	Level of embedding with respect to the bidirectional algorithm.
uniqueID			Returns an auto-generated unique identifier for the object.
units	UNITS		Units for the height and width of the EMBED object.
updateInterval			Sets or returns the interval between screen updates on the client.
url	URL		Uniform Resource Locator (address) for the current document or in a <META> tag.
urn	URN		Uniform Resource Name for a target document.
useMap	USEMAP		Identifies the picture as a client-side image map, and indicates the map to be used with it.
userAgent			The user-agent (browser name) header sent in the HTTP protocol from the client to the server.
userLanguage			Current user language.
vAlign	VALIGN		Specifies how the contents should aligned at the top or bottom of an element.
value (TEXTAREA)			The default value of text/numeric controls, or the value when control is 'on' for boolean controls.
value (others)	VALUE		The default value of text/numeric controls, or the value when control is 'on' for boolean controls.
vcard_name	VCARD_NAME		vCard value of the object to use for the AutoComplete box.

<table>
<tr><th>PropertyName</th><th>AttributeName</th><th>CSSValues</th><th>Description</th></tr>
<tr><td>verticalAlign</td><td></td><td>{ vertical-align: baseline | sub | super | top | text-top | middle | bottom | text-bottom | <percentage>}</td><td>Sets or returns the vertical alignment style property for an element.</td></tr>
<tr><td>visibility</td><td></td><td>{ visibility: visible | hidden | inherit}</td><td>Indicates if the element or contents are visible on the page.</td></tr>
<tr><td>vLink</td><td>VLINK</td><td></td><td>Color of links in the object that have already been visited.</td></tr>
<tr><td>vlinkColor</td><td></td><td></td><td>The color for visited links in the page.</td></tr>
<tr><td>volume</td><td>VOLUME</td><td></td><td>Returns the volume setting for a background sound.</td></tr>
<tr><td>vspace</td><td>VSPACE</td><td></td><td>Specifies the vertical spacing or margin between an element and its neighbors.</td></tr>
<tr><td>whitespace</td><td>WHITESPACE</td><td></td><td>Property not implemented.</td></tr>
<tr><td>width (screen)</td><td></td><td></td><td>Returns the width of the user's display screen in pixels.</td></tr>
<tr><td>width (others)</td><td>WIDTH</td><td>{ width: <length> | <percentage> | auto}</td><td>Specifies the width at which the element is to be drawn, and sets the posWidth property.</td></tr>
<tr><td>window</td><td></td><td></td><td>Read-only reference to the current window object, same as _self.</td></tr>
<tr><td>wordBreak</td><td></td><td>{ word-break : normal | break-all | keep-all }</td><td>Line-breaking behavior within words, particularly where multiple languages appear in the object.</td></tr>
<tr><td>wordSpacing</td><td></td><td>{ word-spacing: normal | length }</td><td>Amount of additional space between words in the object.</td></tr>
</table>

wrap	WRAP		Specifies how wrapping is handled in a Textarea control element.
x			Returns the x coordinate of the mouse pointer relative to a positioned parent, or otherwise to the window.
XMLDocument			Returns a reference to the XML Document Object Model (DOM) exposed by the object.
y			Returns the y coordinate of the mouse pointer relative to a positioned parent, or otherwise to the window.
zIndex		{ z-index: auto | <number>}	Sets or returns the z-index for the element, indicating whether it appears above or below other elements.

Listing of Dynamic HTML Methods

Method Name	Syntax	Description
add	*object*.add(*element* [, *index*])	Adds an area or option element to the appropriate collection.
addAmbient	*object*.style.filters.Light(*n*). addAmbient(*R,G,B,strength*)	Adds an ambient light to the Lights Filter Effect object.
addBehavior	*id* = *object*.addBehavior(*url*)	Adds a behavior to the element.
AddChannel	*window.external*.AddChannel(*URLToCDF*)	Allows the user to add the specified channel (or change the existing channel URL) via a dialog box.
addCone	*object*.style.filters.Light(*n*). addCone(*x1,y1,z1,x2,y2,R,G,B, strenth,spread*)	Adds a cone light to the Lights Filter Effect object to cast a directional light on the page.
AddDesktopComponent	*window.external*.AddDesktopComponent (*URL*, *Type* [, *Left*, *Top*, *Width*, *Height*])	Adds a website or image to the active desktop.
AddFavorite	*external*.AddFavorite(*URL* [, *Title*])	Displays dialog box that allows the user to add the specified URL to the Favorites list.
addImport	*Integer* = *stylesheet*.addImport *(url* [, *index*] *)*	Adds a style sheet from *url* to the current document, optionally at *index* In the styleSheets collection.
addPoint	object.style.filters.Light(n). addPoint(*x,y,z,R,G,B,strength*)	Adds a point light source to the Lights Filter Effect object.
AddReadRequest	*Success* = *userProfile*.addReadRequest (*AttributeName* [, *Reserved*])	Adds an entry to the queue for read requests.
addRule	*object*.addRule *(selector, style* [, *index*])	Adds a new property rule to a style sheet.

`alert`	*object*.alert([*message*])	Displays an Alert dialog box with a message and an OK button.
`appendChild`	*Element* = *object*.appendChild(*Node*)	Appends an element as a child to the *object*.
`apply`	*object*.style.filters.transition (*index*).apply	Applies a transition to the designated *object*.
`applyElement`	*object*.applyElement(*NewElement* [, *where*])	Makes the *NewElement* a child or parent of the *object*.
`assign`	*object*.assign(*url*)	Loads another page. Equivalent to changing the `window.location.href` property.
`attachEvent`	*Success* = *object*.attachEvent(*Event*, *Notify*)	Binds the specified function, *Notify*, to an event – so that the function is called whenever the event fires on the *object*.
`AutoCompleteSaveForm`	*window.external*.AutoCompleteSaveForm (*form*)	Saves the *form* in the AutoComplete data store.
`AutoScan`	*window.external*.AutoScan(*UserQuery* [, *URL*, *Target*])	Attempts to connect to a Web server by passing the user's query through completion templates.
`back`	*object*.back([*distance*])	Looks back a specified number of steps in the browser's history list, and loads the URL found there.
`blur`	*object*.blur( )	Causes a control to lose focus and fire its `onblur` event.
`changeColor`	*object*.style.filters.Light(*n*).changeColor(*lightnumber,r,g,b, fAbsolute*)	Changes the light color for any light on the page.
`changeStrength`	*object*.style.filters.Light(*n*).changeStrength(*lightnumber, strength,fAbsolute*)	Changes the intensity of the light.
`clear`	*object*.style.filters.Light(*n*).clear	Deletes all lights associated with the specified Light Filter.
`clear`	*object*.clear( )	Clears the contents of a `selection` or `document` object.

MethodName	Syntax	Description
`clearAttributes`	*object*.`clearAttributes()`	Removes all the attributes and values from the *object*.
`clearData`	*object*.`clearData(`[*DataFormat*]`)`	Removes one or more data formats (`Text`, `URL`, `File`, `HTML`, `Image`) from the `dataTransfer` or `clipboardData` object.
`clearInterval`	*object*.`clearInterval(`*intervalID*`)`	Cancels an interval timer that was set with the `setInterval` method.
`clearRequest`	*userProfile*.`clearRequest()`	Clears all requests in the read-requests queue to prepare for future requests for profile information.
`clearTimeout`	*object*.`clearTimeout(`*timeoutID*`)`	Cancels a timeout that was set with the `setTimeout` method.
`click`	*object*.`click( )`	Simulates a click on an element, and fires its `onclick` event.
`cloneNode`	*Clone* = *object*.`cloneNode(`*CloneChildren*`)`	Copies a reference from the document hierarchy to the object. *CloneChildren* specifies whether or not to copy children also.
`close`	*object*.`close( )`	Closes a document forcing written data to be displayed, or closes the browser window.
`collapse`	*object*.`collapse(`[*start*]`)`	Shrinks a `TextRange` to either the start or end of the current range.
`compareEndPoints`	*object*.`compareEndPoints` `(`*comparetype, range*`)`	Compares two text ranges and returns a value indicating the result.
`componentFromPoint`	*ScrollComponent* = *object*. `componentFromPoint(`*CoordX, CoordY*`)`	Returns the component located at the given coordinates.
`confirm`	*object*.`confirm(`[*message*]`)`	Displays a Confirm dialog box with a message and OK and Cancel buttons.
`contains`	*Boolean* = *object*.`contains(`*element*`)`	Denotes if another element is contained within the current element.

createCaption	*Caption* = *TABLE*.createCaption()	Creates an empty caption element in the given table.
createControlRange	*ControlRange* = *document.body*.createControlRange()	Creates a controlRange collection of nontext elements.
createElement	*element* = *object*.createElement(*tag*)	Creates an instance of an image or option element object.
createRange	*object*.createRange( )	Returns a copy of the current selection in the document.
createStyleSheet	*Stylesheet* = *document*.createStyleSheet([*URL*] [, *Index*])	Creates a style sheet for the *document*.
createTextNode	*TextNode* = *document*.createTextNode([*Text*])	Creates a text string from the given *Text*.
createTextRange	*TextRange* = *object*.createTextRange( )	Returns a new TextRange from the document or a text-based control.
createTFoot	*TFoot* = *TABLE*.createTFoot()	Creates an empty TFOOT in the TABLE.
createTHead	*THead* = *TABLE*.createTHead()	Creates an empty THEAD in the TABLE.
deleteCaption	*TABLE*.deleteCaption()	Deletes the CAPTION element from the TABLE.
deleteCell	*TR*.deleteCell([*Index*])	Deletes the specified TD (table cell) element from the table row, and removes the cell from the cells collection.
deleteRow	*object*.deleteRow([*RowIndex*])	Deletes the specified TR (table row) element from the TABLE, and removes the row from the rows collection.
deleteTFOOT	*TABLE*.deleteTHead()	Deletes the THEAD element and its contents from the TABLE.
deleteTHEAD	*TABLE*.deleteTFoot()	Deletes the TFOOT element and its contents from the TABLE.
detachEvent	*object*.detachEvent(*Event*, *Notify*)	Opposite of attachEvent: unbinds the specified function, *Notify*, from the event, so that the function stops receiving notifications when the event fires on the object.

MethodName	Syntax	Description
doReadRequest	*Success* = *userProfile*.doReadRequest (*vUsageCode* [, *vFriendlyName*][, *vDomain*] [, *vPath*][, *vExpiration*][, *vReserved*])	Performs all requests located in the read-requests queue.
doScroll	*object*.doScroll([*ScrollAction*])	Simulates a click on a scroll-bar.
duplicate	*TextRange* = *object*.duplicate( )	Returns a copy of a TextRange object.
elementFromPoint	*element* = *object*.elementFromPoint (*x*, *y*)	Returns the element at the specified x and y coordinates with respect to the window.
empty	*object*.empty( )	Deselects the current selection. Sets selection type to none and the item property to null.
execCommand	*Boolean* = *object*.execCommand(*command* [, *bool* [, *value*]])	Executes a command over the document selection or range.
execScript	*object*.execScript(*expression* [, *language*])	Executes a script in the language defined.. The default language is JScript.
expand	*Boolean* = *object*.expand(*unit*)	Expands the range by a character, word, sentence or story so that partial units are completely contained.
findText	*Boolean* = *object*.findText(*text*)	Sets the range start and end points to cover the text if found within the current document.
firstPage	*TABLE*.firstPage()	Moves to the first page in the data set, and scrolls it into view.
focus	*object*.focus( )	Causes a control to receive the focus and fire its onfocus event.
forward	*object*.forward( )	Loads the next URL in the browser's history list.
getAdjacentText	*object*.getAdjacentText(*Where*)	Returns the first adjacent text character.
getAttribute	*Variant* = *object*.getAttribute (*attrName* [, *caseSensitive*])	Returns the value of an attribute defined in an HTML tag.

<table>
<tr><td>getBookmark</td><td>String = object.getBookmark( )</td><td>Sets String to a unique bookmark value to identify that position in the document.</td></tr>
<tr><td>getBoundingClientRect</td><td>[Rect =] object.getBoundingClientRect()</td><td>Retrieves an object containing four integer properties, that specify the bounds of a collection of TextRectangle objects.</td></tr>
<tr><td>getClientRects</td><td>[collRect =] object.getClientRects()</td><td>Returns a collection of rectangles that describes the layout of the contents of an object or range. Each rectangle describes a single line.</td></tr>
<tr><td>getData</td><td>RetrieveData = object.getData(DataFormat)</td><td>Retrieves the data in the specified format (Text or URL) from the dataTransfer or clipboardData objects.</td></tr>
<tr><td>getElementById</td><td>Element = document.getElementById (IDValue)</td><td>Returns a reference to the first object with the specified ID.</td></tr>
<tr><td>getElementsByName</td><td>Objects = document.getElementsByName (NameValue)</td><td>Returns a collection containing objects with the specified NAME.</td></tr>
<tr><td>getElementsByTagName</td><td>Objects = document.getElementsByTagName (TagName)</td><td>Returns a collection containing objects with the specified element name.</td></tr>
<tr><td>getExpression</td><td>Expression = object.getExpression (PropertyName)</td><td>Returns the expression for the given property.</td></tr>
<tr><td>go</td><td>object.go(delta | location)</td><td>Loads the specified URL from the browser's history list.</td></tr>
<tr><td>hasChildNodes</td><td>ChildNodes = object.hasChildNodes()</td><td>Returns whether the object has children.</td></tr>
<tr><td>ImportExportFavorites</td><td>window.external.ImportExportFavorites (ImportExport [, ImportExportPath])</td><td>Imports or exports information about the Favorites.</td></tr>
<tr><td>inRange</td><td>Boolean = object.inRange (compareRange)</td><td>Denotes if the specified range is within or equal to the current range.</td></tr>
<tr><td>insertAdjacentElement</td><td>Element = object.insertAdjacentElement (Where, Element)</td><td>Inserts an element at the location specified.</td></tr>
</table>

MethodName	Syntax	Description
`insertAdjacentHtml`	*object*.`insertAdjacentHtml` (*where*, *html*)	Inserts text and HTML into the *object* at the location specified, parsing the HTML.
`insertAdjacentText`	*object*.`insertAdjacentText` (*where*, *text*)	Inserts text into the *object* at the location specified. Any HTML tags in the *text* are displayed as text (i.e. not parsed as HTML).
`insertBefore`	*Element* = *object*.`insertBefore`(*NewNode* [, *ChildNode*])	Inserts an *element* into the document hierarchy.
`insertCell`	*TD* = *TR*.`insertCell`([*Index*])	Creates a new cell at the specified position in the table row (`TR`), and adds the cell to the `cells` collection.
`insertRow`	*oTR* = *object*.`insertRow`([*iIndex*])	Creates a new row (`TR`) at the specified line in the table, and adds the row to the `rows` collection.
`isEqual`	*Boolean* = *object*.`isEqual` (*compareRange*)	Denotes if the specified range is equal to the current range.
`IsSubscribed`	*Subscribed* = *window.external*.`IsSubscribed` (*URLToCDF*)	Returns whether the client is subscribed to the given channel.
`item`	*element* = *object*.`item`(*index* [, *subindex*])	Returns an object from a collection using its index. If the element returned is a collection, a subindex can be used.
`javaEnabled`	*Boolean* = *object*.`javaEnabled( )`	Returns True or False, depending on whether a Java VM is installed and enabled.
`lastPage`	*TABLE*.`lastPage()`	Moves to the last page in the data set, and scrolls it into view.
`mergeAttributes`	*object*.`mergeAttributes`(*Source*)	Copies all read/write attributes to the specified element.
`move`	*Long* = *object*.`move`(*unit* [, *count*])	Changes the start and end points of a `TextRange` to cover different text.

`moveBy`	*window*.`moveBy`(*iX*, *iY*)	Moves the screen position of the window by the specified x- and y-offsets relative to its current position.
`moveEnd`	*Long* = *object*.`moveEnd`(*unit* [, *count*])	Causes the range to grow or shrink from the end of the range.
`moveLight`	*object*.`style.filters.Light`(*n*).`moveLight`(*x,y,z,fAbsolute*)	Moves the light effect on the page.
`moveStart`	*Long* = *object*.`moveStart`(*unit* [, *count*])	Causes the range to grow or shrink from the beginning of the range.
`moveTo`	*window*.`moveTo`(*X*, *Y*)	Moves the (*X*, *Y*) pixel position of the window to the upper-left corner of the screen.
`moveToBookmark`	*Boolean* = *object*.`moveToBookmark`()	Moves range to encompass the range with a bookmark value previously defined in String.
`moveToElementText`	*object*.`moveToElement`(*Element*)	Moves range to encompass the text in the element specified.
`moveToPoint`	*object*.`moveToPoint`(*x*, *y*)	Moves and collapses range to the point specified in x and y relative to the document.
`namedRecordset`	*Recordset* = *object*.`namedRecordset`(*Qualifier* [, *SubChapter*])	Retrieves the `recordset` object, *Qualifier*, from a data source object.
`navigate`	*object*.`navigate`(*url*)	Loads another page (VBScript only). Equivalent to changing the `window.location.href` property.
`NavigateAndFind`	*window.external*.`NavigateAndFind`(*Location*, *Query*, *TargetFrame*)	Opens a web page and highlights a specific text string.
`nextPage`	*object*.`nextPage`( )	Displays the next page of records in a repeated databound table element.
`open`	*object*.`open`( )	Opens the document as a a stream to collect output of `write` or `writeln` methods.

MethodName	Syntax	Description
`open`	*window* = *object*.`open`(*url* [, *name* [, *features* [, *replace*]]])	Opens a new browser window and loads the document defined in the *url* parameter.
`parentElement`	*element* = *object*.`parentElement()`	Returns the parent element that completely encloses the current range.
`pasteHTML`	*object*.`pasteHTML(htmlText)`	Pastes HTML and/or plain text into the current range.
`play`	*object*.`style.filters.transition.play`(*duration*)	Plays the transition.
`previousPage`	*object*.`previousPage( )`	Displays the previous page of records in a repeated databound table element.
`print`	*window*.`print()`	Prints the document associated with the specified `window` object.
`prompt`	*object*.`prompt`([*message* [, *inputDefault*]])	Displays a Prompt dialog box with a message and an input field.
`queryCommandEnabled`	*Boolean* = *object*.`queryCommandEnabled`(*command*)	Denotes whether the specified command is available for a document or `TextRange`.
`queryCommandIndeterm`	*Boolean* = *object*.`queryCommandIndeterm`(*command*)	Denotes whether the specified command is in the indeterminate state.
`queryCommandState`	*Boolean* = *object*.`queryCommandState`(*command*)	Returns the current state of the command for a document or `TextRange` object.
`queryCommandSupported`	*Boolean* = *object*.`queryCommandSupported`(*command*)	Denotes whether the specified command is supported for a document or `TextRange` object.
`queryCommandText`	*String* = *object*.`queryCommandText`(*command*)	Returns the string associated with a command for a document or `TextRange` object.
`queryCommandValue`	*String* = *object*.`queryCommandValue`(*command*)	Returns the value of the command specified for a document or `TextRange` object.
`recalc`	*document*.`recalc`([*ForceAll*])	Recalculates the dynamic properties in the `document` object.

refresh	*object*.refresh( )	Refreshes the contents of the table.
releaseCapture	*object*.releaseCapture()	Removes mouse capture from the object in the current document.
reload	*object*.reload( )	Reloads the current page.
remove	*object*.remove(*index*)	Removes an element from an areas or options collection.
removeAttribute	*Boolean* = *object*.removeAttribute (*attrName* [, *caseSensitive*])	Causes the specified attribute to be removed from the HTML element and the current page.
removeBehavior	*Success* = *object*.removeBehavior(*ID*)	Detaches a behavior from the specified element.
removeChild	*Remove* = *object*.removeChild(*Node*)	Removes a child node from the specified element.
removeExpression	*Success* = *object*.removeExpression (*PropertyName*)	Removes an expression from the given property.
removeNode	*Removed* = *object*.removeNode(*RemoveChildren*)	Removes the *object* (and its children, optionally) from the document hierarchy.
removeRule	*styleSheet*.removeRule[*Index*]	Deletes an existing style rule for the styleSheet object and makes the appropriate adjustment to the rules collection.
replace	*object*.replace(*url*)	Loads a document, replacing the current document's session history entry with its URL.
replaceAdjacentText	*object*.replaceAdjacentText (*Where*, *ReplaceText*)	Replaces the adjacent text character.
replaceChild	*Replace* = *object*.replaceChild (*NewNode*, *OldNode*)	Replaces an existing child element with a new one.
replaceNode	*oReplace* = *object*.replaceNode(*oNewNode*)	Replaces the object with another element.
reset	*object*.reset( )	Simulates a mouse click on a RESET button in a form.
resizeBy	*window*.resizeBy(*X*, *Y*)	Changes the current size of the window by the specified horizontal and vertical pixel values.

MethodName	Syntax	Description
`resizeTo`	*window*.`resizeTo`(*Width*, *Height*)	Sets the size of the window to the specified width and height (in pixels).
`scroll`	*object*.`scroll`(*x*, *y*)	Scrolls the window to the specified x and y offset relative to the entire document.
`scrollBy`	*window*.`scrollBy`(*X*, *Y*)	Causes the window to scroll by the specified horizontal and vertical pixel values (relative to the current scrolled position).
`scrollIntoView`	*object*.`scrollIntoView`([*start*])	Scrolls the element or `TextRange` into view in the browser, optionally at the top of the window.
`scrollTo`	*window*.`scrollTo`(*X*, *Y*)	Scrolls the window to the specified pixel position.
`select`	*object*.`select`( )	Makes the active selection equal to the current object, or highlights the input area of a form element.
`setAttribute`	*object*.`setAttribute`(*attrName*, *value* [, *caseSensitive*])	Adds and/or sets the value of an attribute in a HTML tag.
`setCapture`	*object*.`setCapture`([*ContainerCapture*])	Sets the mouse capture to the *object* belonging to the current document.
`setData`	*Success* = *object*.`setData`(*DataFormat*, *Data*)	Assigns data in a specified format (`Text` or `URL`) to the `dataTransfer` or `clipboardData` object.
`setEndPoint`	*object*.`setEndPoint`(*type*, *range*)	Sets the end point of the range based on the end point of another range.
`setExpression`	*object*.`setExpression`(*PropertyName*, *Expression2*, *sLanguage*)	Sets an expression for a given *object*.
`setInterval`	*intervalID* = *object*.`setInterval`(*expression*, *msec* [, *language*])	Denotes a code routine to execute repeatedly every specified number of milliseconds.
`setTimeout`	*timeoutID* = *object*.`setTimeout`(*expression*, *msec* [, *language*])	Denotes a code routine to execute a specified number of milliseconds after loading the page.

`showBrowserUI`	*vReturn* = *window.external*.`ShowBrowserUI (`*UI*`, null)`	Opens the specified browser dialog box (`LanguageDialog` or `OrganizeFavorites`).
`showHelp`	*object*`.showHelp(`*url* `[,` *arguments*`])`	Opens a window to display a Help file.
`showModalDialog`	*Variant* = *object*`.showModalDialog (`*url* `[,` *arguments* `[,` *features*`]])`	Displays an HTML dialog window, and returns the `returnValue` property of its document when closed.
`showModelessDialog`	*ReturnValue* = *window*`.showModelessDialog (`*URL* `[,` *Arguments*`][,` *Features*`])`	Creates a modeless dialog box.
`splitText`	*SplitNode* = *TextNode*`.splitText(`*Index*`)`	Divides a text node at the specified index.
`start`	*object*`.start( )`	Begins scrolling the text in a `MARQUEE`.
`stop`	*object*`.stop( )`	Stops scrolling the text in a `MARQUEE`.
`stop`	*object*`.style.filters.transition. (`*index*`)stop`	Stops the transition playback.
`submit`	*object*`.submit( )`	Submits a form, and fires the `onsubmit` event.
`swapMode`	*Swapped* = *object*`.swapNode(`*Node*`)`	Swaps the locations of two objects in the document hierarchy.
`tags`	*element* = *object*`.tags(`*tag*`)`	Returns a collection of all the elements for the specified tagname.
`taintEnabled`	*Boolean* = *object*`.taintEnabled( )`	Returns False, included for compatibility with Netscape Navigator
`urns`	*collObjects* = *object*`.urns(`*Urn*`)`	Retrieves a collection of all objects to which a specified behavior is attached.
`write`	*object*`.write(`*string*`)`	Writes text and HTML to a document in the specified window.
`writeln`	*object*`.writeln(`*string*`)`	Writes text and HTML to a document in the specified window, followed by a carriage return.
`zOrder`	*object*`.zOrder([`*position*`])`	Sets the z-index or layering in fixed layout regions.

Listing of Dynamic HTML Events

EventName	Description
onabort	Occurs if the user aborts the downloading of the image.
onafterprint	Occurs on the object, immediately after its associated document prints.
onafterupdate	Occurs when transfer of data from the element to the data provider is complete.
onbeforecopy	Occurs on the source object, before the selection is copied to the system clipboard.
onbeforecut	Occurs on the source object, before the selection is deleted from the document.
onbeforeeditfocus	Occurs just before a control enters a UI-activated state.
onbeforepaste	Occurs on the target object, before the selection is pasted from the clipboard to the document.
onbeforeprint	Occurs on the object, just before its associated document prints.
onbeforeunload	Occurs just before the page is unloaded, allowing the unload to be cancelled.
onbeforeupdate	Occurs before transfer of changed data to the data provider when an element loses focus or the page is unloaded.
onblur	Occurs when the control loses the input focus.
onbounce	Occurs in a <MARQUEE>when BEHAVIOR is ALTERNATE, and the contents reach the edge.
oncellchange	Occurs whenever data changes in a data provider.
onchange	Occurs when the contents of the element have changed.
onclick	Occurs when the user clicks the mouse button on an element, or when the value of a control is changed.
oncontextmenu	Occurs when the right mouse button is clicked (within the client area).
oncopy	Fires on the source element when the object or selection is duplicated and added to the system clipboard.
oncut	Occurs on the source element, when the object or selection is cut from the document and added to the clipboard.

ondataavailable	Occurs periodically while data is arriving from an asynchronous data source.
ondatasetchanged	Occurs when the dataset changes, such as when a different data filter is applied.
ondatasetcomplete	Occurs once all the data is available from the data source object.
ondblclick	Occurs when the user double-clicks on an element.
ondrag	Occurs continuously on the source object during a drag.
ondragend	Occurs on the source object, when the mouse is released at the end of a drag.
ondragenter	Occurs on the target element, when the object being dragged enters a valid drop target.
ondragleave	Occurs on the target object, when the mouse moves out of a valid drop target during a drag.
ondragover	Occurs continuously on the target element while dragging the object over a valid drop target.
ondragstart	Occurs when the user first starts to drag an element or selection.
ondrop	Occurs on the target object when the mouse button is released during a drag-and-drop.
onerror	Occurs when an error loading a document or image arises.
onerrorupdate	Occurs when an on `beforeupdate` event cancels update of the data, replacing the `onafterupdate` event.
onfilterchange	Occurs when a filter changes state, or when a filter transition is complete.
onfilterevent	Occurs when a specified transition is complete.
onfinish	Occurs when looping is complete in a `<MARQUEE>` element.
onfocus	Occurs when a control receives the input focus.
onhelp	Occurs when the user presses the F1 or Help key.
onkeydown	Occurs when the user presses a key.
onkeypress	Occurs when the user presses a key and a character is available.
onkeyup	Occurs when the user releases a key.
onload	Occurs when the element has completed loading.
onlosecapture	Occurs when the object loses the mouse capture.
onmousedown	Occurs when the user presses a mouse button.

EventName	Description
onmousemove	Occurs when the user moves the mouse.
onmouseout	Occurs when the mouse pointer leaves the element.
onmouseover	Occurs when the mouse pointer first enters the element.
onmouseup	Occurs when the user releases a mouse button.
onpaste	Occurs on the target object, when the data is transferred from the clipboard to the document.
onpropertychange	Occurs when a property changes on the object.
onreadystatechange	Occurs when the readyState for an object has changed.
onreset	Occurs when the RESET button on a form is clicked or a form is reset.
onresize	Occurs when the element or object is resized by the user.
onrowenter	Occurs when data in the current row has changed and new values are available.
onrowexit	Occurs before the data source changes data in the current row.
onrowsdelete	Occurs when rows are about to be deleted from the recordset.
onrowsinserted	Occurs just after new rows are inserted to the current recordset.
onscroll	Occurs when the user scrolls a page or element.
onselect	Occurs when the current selection in an element is changed.
onselectstart	Occurs when the user first starts to select contents of an element.
onstart	Occurs in a <MARQUEE> when looping begins, or a bounce occurs when BEHAVIOR is ALTERNATE.
onstop	Occurs when the **Stop** button is clicked or the document is unloaded.
onsubmit	Occurs when the SUBMIT button on a form is clicked or a form is submitted.
onunload	Occurs immediately before the page is unloaded.

Dynamic HTML Tags

!--

Denotes a comments that is ignored by the HTML parser.

Can be a single tag containing a comment, or span several lines. Often used to hide features that may not be supported in older browsers.

```
<!-- this is a comment that will be ignored-->

<SCRIPT LANGUAGE=VBSCRIPT>
<!-- hide the script from older browsers
Sub DoSomething()
   ...
End Sub
-->
</SCRIPT>
```

!DOCTYPE

Declares the type and content format of the document.

A rigorous HTML-checking program will reject any documents that do not contain this tag. However, most browsers are not so fussy, and most documents on the Web do not include this tag, even though it is required by the HTML 4.0 standard.

It must be the first item in the document. For documents written strictly to HTML 4.0 standard use:

```
<!DOCTYPE HTML PUBLIC "-//W3C//DTD HTML 4.0 Strict//EN">
```

A

Defines a hypertext link. The HREF or the NAME attribute must be specified.

ACCESSKEY = *sAccessKey*
CLASS = *sClass*
DATAFLD = *sField*
DATASRC = *sID*
DIR = "ltr" | "rtl"
<event_name> = *name of script*
HREF = *sURL*
ID = *sID*
LANG = *sLanguage*
LANGUAGE = "JScript" | "javascript" | "vbs" | "vbscript" | "XML" | *sLanguage*
METHODS = *sMethod*
NAME = *sName*
REL = *sRelation*
REV = "Alternate" || "Stylesheet" || "Start" || "Next" || "Prev" || "Contents" || "Index" || "Glossary" || "Copyright" || "Chapter" || "Section" || "Subsection" || "Appendix" || "Help" || "Bookmark"
STYLE = *sStyle*
TABINDEX = *iIndex*
TARGET = *sTarget* | "_blank" | "_parent" | "_search" | "_self" | "_top"
TITLE = *sTitle*
URN = *sURN*

```
<AHREF = "http://www.wrox.com"onclick="MsgBox 'Switching to the Wrox web site'">
Click here to go to Wrox!</A>
```

ACRONYM

Indicates an acronym abbreviation.

ACCESSKEY = *sAccessKey*
CLASS = *sClass*
DIR = "ltr" | "rtl"
ID = *sID*
LANG = *sLanguage*
LANGUAGE = "JScript" | "javascript" | "vbs" | "vbscript" | "XML" | *sLanguage*
STYLE = *sStyle*
TABINDEX = *iIndex*
TITLE = *sTitle*

```
<ACRONYM>ISBN</ACRONYM>
```

ADDRESS

Specifies information such as address, signature and authorship.

ACCESSKEY = *sAccessKey*
CLASS = *sClass*
DIR = "ltr" | "rtl"
<event_name> = *name of script*
ID = *sID*
LANG = *sLanguage*
LANGUAGE = "JScript" | "javascript" | "vbs" | "vbscript" | "XML" | *sLanguage*
STYLE = *sStyle*
TABINDEX = *iIndex*
TITLE = *sTitle*

Normally displays text in italics:

```
Produced by:
<ADDRESS>
  Wrox Press Limited, US
  1512 North Fremont
  Suite 103
  Chicago
  IL 60622
</ADDRESS>
```

APPLET

Places a Java applet or other executable content in the page.

ACCESSKEY = *sAccessKey*
ALIGN = "absbottom" | "absmiddle" | "baseline" | "bottom" | "left" | "middle" | "right" | "texttop" | "top"
ALT = *sTxt*
CLASS = *sClass*
CODE = *sURL*
CODEBASE = *sURL*[#version=a,b,c,d]
DATAFLD = *sField*
DATASRC = *sID*
HSPACE = *iMargin*
ID = *sID*
LANG = *sLanguage*
LANGUAGE = "JScript" | "javascript" | "vbs" | "vbscript" | "XML" | *sLanguage*
NAME = *sName*
SRC = *sURL*
STYLE = *sStyle*
TABINDEX = *iIndex*
TITLE = *sTitle*
VSPACE = *iMargin*
WIDTH = *sWidth*[%]

AREA

Specifies the shape of a 'hot spot' in a client-side image map.

ACCESSKEY = *sAccessKey*
ALT = *sTxt*
CLASS = *sClass*
COORDS = *sCoords*
DIR = "ltr" | "rtl"
<event_name> = *name of script*
HREF = *sURL*
ID = *sID*
LANG = *sLanguage*
LANGUAGE = "JScript" | "javascript" | "vbs" | "vbscript" | "XML" | *sLanguage*
NOHREF
SHAPE = "circ" | "circle" | "poly" | "polygon" | "rect" | "rectangle"
STYLE = *sStyle*
TABINDEX = *iIndex*
TARGET = *sTarget* | "_blank" | "_parent" | "_search" | "_self" | "_top"
TITLE = *sTitle*

See also MAP.

```
<MAP NAME = "toolbar">
<AREA SHAPE="RECT" COORDS = "12,216,68,267" HREF = "wrox.html">
</MAP>
```

B

Renders text in boldface where available.

ACCESSKEY = *sAccessKey*
CLASS = *sClass*
DIR = "ltr" | "rtl"
<event_name> = *name of script*
ID = *sID*
LANG = *sLanguage*
LANGUAGE = "JScript" | "javascript" | "vbs" | "vbscript" | "XML" | *sLanguage*
STYLE = *sStyle*
TABINDEX = *iIndex*
TITLE = *sTitle*

The following example will produce the word **BOLD** in bold font:

```
<B>BOLD</B>
```

BASE

Specifies the document's base URL.

CLASS = *sClass*
HREF = *sURL*
ID = *sID*
LANG = *sLanguage*
TARGET = *sTarget* | "_blank" | "_parent" | "_search" | "_self" | "_top"
TITLE = *sTitle*

This is the address used to reference other resources, such as documents, graphics, etc., which do not specify a full URL. For example:

```
<IMG SRC = "MyGraphic.gif">
```

If you have set up a <BASE> tag defining the base directory, MyGraphic.gif will be loaded from the directory defined by the <BASE> tag.

BASEFONT

Sets a base font value to be used as the default font when rendering text.

CLASS = *sClass*
COLOR = *sColor*
FACE = *sTypeface*
ID = *sID*
SIZE = *iSize*
TITLE = *sTitle*

Once the BASEFONT for a document has been set, you can use relative sizes for the font in different places, or specify individual sizes as required:

```
<BASEFONT SIZE = 4 FACE = "Arial,Tahoma,sans-serif">
...
<FONT SIZE = -1> A bit smaller font than the base </FONT>
...
<FONT SIZE = -3> A larger font than the base will be used here </FONT>
...
<FONT SIZE = 2> This is small and not related to BASEFONT </FONT>
```

See also FONT.

BDO

Allows authors to disable the bidirectional algorithm for selected fragments of text.

ACCESSKEY = *sAccessKey*
CLASS = *sClass*
DIR = "ltr" | "rtl"
ID = *sID*
LANG = *sLanguage*
LANGUAGE = "JScript" | "javascript" | "vbs" | "vbscript" | "XML" | *sLanguage*
TABINDEX = *iIndex*
TITLE = *sTitle*

BGSOUND

Specifies a background sound to be played while the page is loaded.

BALANCE = *iBalance*
CLASS = *sClass*
ID = *sID*
LANG = *sLanguage*
LOOP = *iLoop*
SRC = *sURL*
TITLE = *sTitle*
VOLUME = *iVolume*

The SRC attribute identifies the file through a URL, and the LOOP attribute defines how often it will be played. Setting LOOP to -1 or the special value INFINITE causes the sound to be repeated all the time the page is displayed:

```
<BGSOUND SRC = "http://www.wrox.com/sounds/crash.wav LOOP = INFINITE>
<BGSOUND SRC = "http://www.wrox.com/sounds/crash.wav LOOP = -1>
```

Otherwise, LOOP can be set to a value starting at 1 to play the file that many times:

```
<BGSOUND SRC = "http://www.wrox.com/sounds/crash.wav LOOP = 3>
```

BIG

Renders text in a relatively larger font than the current font.

ACCESSKEY = *sAccessKey*
CLASS = *sClass*
DIR = "ltr" | "rtl"
<event_name> = *name of script*
ID = *sID*
LANG = *sLanguage*
LANGUAGE = "JScript" | "javascript" | "vbs" | "vbscript" | "XML" | *sLanguage*
STYLE = *sStyle*
TABINDEX = *iIndex*
TITLE = *sTitle*

Normally displays text in italics:

```
<BIG> This text will be one size larger than the rest. </BIG>
```

BLOCKQUOTE

Denotes a quotation in text.

ACCESSKEY = *sAccessKey*
CLASS = *sClass*
DIR = "ltr" | "rtl"
<event_name> = *name of script*
ID = *sID*
LANG = *sLanguage*
LANGUAGE = "JScript" | "javascript" | "vbs" | "vbscript" | "XML" | *sLanguage*
STYLE = *sStyle*
TABINDEX = *iIndex*
TITLE = *sTitle*

Normally displays text indented:

```
<HTML>
  <HEAD></HEAD>
  <BODY>
    This is normal text.
    <BR>
    <BLOCKQUOTE>This is a blockquote which will produce indented text.
    </BLOCKQUOTE>
  </BODY>
</HTML>
```

BODY

Defines the beginning and end of the body section of the page.

ACCESSKEY = *sAccessKey*
ALINK = *sColor*
BACKGROUND = *sURL*
BGCOLOR = *sColor*
BGPROPERTIES = "fixed"
BOTTOMMARGIN = *sPixels*
CLASS = *sClass*
DATAFLD = *sField*
DATAFORMATAS = "text" | "html"
DATASRC = *sID*
DIR = "ltr" | "rtl"
<event_name> = *name of script*
ID = *sID*
LANG = *sLanguage*
LANGUAGE = "JScript" | "javascript" | "vbs" | "vbscript" | "XML" | *sLanguage*
LEFTMARGIN = *sMargin*
LINK = *sColor*
NOWRAP
RIGHTMARGIN = *sMargin*
SCROLL = "yes" | "no"
STYLE = *sStyle*
TABINDEX = *iIndex*
TEXT = *sColor*
TITLE = *sTitle*
TOPMARGIN = *iMargin*
VLINK = *sColor*

To set the colors of the links in the page, we include the LINK and VLINK attributes in the BODY tag. To set the color of the page itself, and the color of the text, we use the BGCOLOR and TEXT attributes:

```
<BODY BGCOLOR = "red" TEXT = "white" LINK = "blue" ALINK = "maroon">
```

Alternatively, we can specify the colors using their RGB values:

```
<BODY BGCOLOR = "#ff0000" TEXT = "#ffffff" LINK = "#ff" ALINK = "#ff00ff">
```

To display a picture on the page as a background, we use the BACKGROUND attribute:

```
<BODY BACKGROUND = "bgpattern.gif">
```

We can also align the text in the page, and set the margins:

```
<BODY ALIGN=LEFT LEFTMARGIN = 100>
```

Finally, we can also prevent the image used as the page background from scrolling with the page by setting the BGPROPERTIES attribute, and remove the default scroll bars with the SCROLL attribute:

```
<BODY BACKGROUND = "bgpattern.gif" BGPROPERTIES=FIXED SCROLL=NO>
```

BR

Inserts a line break.

CLASS = *sClass*
CLEAR = "all" | "left" | "right" | "none"
ID = *sID*
LANGUAGE = "JScript" | "javascript" | "vbs" | "vbscript" | "XML" | *sLanguage*
STYLE = *sStyle*
TITLE = *sTitle*

If we want the line break to move following text or elements down past another element, such as an image, which is left or right aligned, we use the CLEAR attribute. Without it, the following text or elements would continue to wrap around the other element.

To move the following elements below a left-aligned image, for example, we can use:

```
<BR CLEAR=LEFT>
```

To move the following elements below both left and right-aligned images we use:

```
<BR CLEAR=ALL>
```

BUTTON

Renders an HTML button with the text or other elements between the opening and closing tags being rendered as the button face.

ACCESSKEY = *sAccessKey*
CLASS = *sClass*
DATAFLD = *sField*
DATAFORMATAS = "text" | "html"
DATASRC = *sID*
DISABLED
<event_name> = *name of script*
ID = *sID*
LANG = *sLanguage*
LANGUAGE = "JScript" | "javascript" | "vbs" | "vbscript" | "XML" | *sLanguage*
NAME = *sName*
STYLE = *sStyle*
TABINDEX = *iIndex*
TITLE = *sTitle*
TYPE = "button" | "reset" | "submit"
VALUE = *sValue*

```
<BUTTON>Button Caption</BUTTON>
```

```
<BUTTONID = MyBTN>
  <IMG SRC = "ButtonPic.gif" WIDTH = 100 HEIGHT=100> <BR>
  My Button
</BUTTON>
```

We can even specify what the button should do when it is clicked:

```
<BUTTON onclick="alert'You just clicked the button'">Button Caption</BUTTON>
```

CAPTION

Specifies a caption for a table.

ACCESSKEY = *aAccessKey*
ALIGN = "bottom" | "center" | "left" | "right" | "top"
CLASS = *sClass*
DIR = "ltr" | "rtl"
<event_name> = *name of script*
ID = *sID*
LANG = *sLanguage*
LANGUAGE = "JScript" | "javascript" | "vbs" | "vbscript" | "XML" | *sLanguage*
STYLE = *sStyle*
TABINDEX = *iIndex*
TITLE = *sTitle*
VALIGN = "top" | "bottom"

See also TABLE.

```
<TABLE>
  <CAPTION ALIGN=LEFT> This is the table caption </CAPTION>
  <TR><TD>table content</TD></TR>
</TABLE>
```

CENTER

Causes subsequent text and other elements to be centered on the page.

ACCESSKEY = *sAccessKey*
CLASS = *sClass*
DIR = "ltr" | "rtl"
<event_name> = *name of script*
ID = *sID*
LANG = *sLanguage*
LANGUAGE = "JScript" | "javascript" | "vbs" | "vbscript" | "XML" | *sLanguage*
STYLE = *sStyle*
TABINDEX = *iIndex*
TITLE = *sTitle*

```
<CENTER>
  This text will be centered on the page.
  <H1>So will this heading </H1>
  <IMG SRC = "MyImage.gif"> <P>
  And so will the image above.
</CENTER>
```

The CENTER tag is still available for backward compatibility purposes, but the W3C recommendation is that you use ALIGN instead.

CITE

Renders text in italics, as a citation. Often used for copyright statements.

ACCESSKEY = *sAccessKey*
CLASS = *sClass*
DIR = "ltr" | "rtl">
<event_name> = *name of script*
ID = *sID*
LANG = *sLanguage*
LANGUAGE = "JScript" | "javascript" | "vbs" | "vbscript" | "XML" | *sLanguage*
STYLE = *sStyle*
TABINDEX = *iIndex*
TITLE = *sTitle*

```
<CITE>&copy;1999 Wrox Press Limited, UK</CITE>
```

CODE

Renders text as a code sample in a fixed width font.

CLASS = *sClass*
DIR = "ltr" | "rtl"
<event_name> = *name of script*
ID = *sID*
LANG = *sLanguage*
LANGUAGE = "JScript" | "javascript" | "vbs" | "vbscript" | "XML" | *sLanguage*
STYLE = *sStyle*
TITLE = *sTitle*

```
<CODE> <!--The following is rendered as a code listing on the screen -->
  Sub MyRoutine(datToday)
    If datToday = "Saturday" Then
      strDestination = "The beach."
    Else
      strDestination = "The office again."
    End If
  End Sub
</CODE>
```

COL

Used to specify column based defaults for a table.

ALIGN = "center" | "justify" | "left" | "right"
BGCOLOR = *sColor*
CLASS = *sClass*
DIR = "ltr" | "rtl"
ID = *sID*
LANG = *sLanguage*
SPAN = *iSpan*
STYLE = *sStyle*
TITLE = *sTitle*
VALIGN = "middle" | "center" | "baseline" | "bottom" | "top"
WIDTH = *sWidth*

```
<TABLE>
  <COLGROUP>
  <COL ALIGN=LEFT WIDTH=100 SPAN=2>
  <COLGROUP ALIGN=LEFT WIDTH=100 SPAN=4>
  ...
  <TR><TD> table content </TD></TR>
  ...
</TABLE>
```

COLGROUP

Used as a container for a group of columns.

ALIGN = "center" | "justify" | "left" | "right"
BGCOLOR = *sColor*
CLASS = *sClass*
DIR = "ltr" | "rtl"
ID = *sID*
LANG = *sLanguage*
SPAN = *iSpan*
STYLE = *sStyle*
TITLE = *sTitle*
VALIGN = "middle" | "center" | "baseline" | "bottom" | "top"
WIDTH = *sWidth*[%]

COMMENT

Denotes a comment that will not be displayed.

CLASS = *sClass*
ID = *sID*
LANG = *sLanguage*
TITLE = *sTitle*

```
<COMMENT>
  Anything here will be ignored by the browser while rendering the page.
  The COMMENT tag is good for commenting out several lines at a time.
</COMMENT>
```

custom

Represents a user-defined element.

ACCESSKEY = *sAccessKey*
CLASS = *sClass*
DIR = "ltr" | "rtl"
ID = *sID*
LANG = *sLanguage*
LANGUAGE = "JScript" | "javascript" | "vbs" | "vbscript" | "XML" | *sLanguage*
STYLE = *sStyle*
TABINDEX = *iIndex*
TITLE = *sTitle*

DD

The DD tag is used inside a definition list to provide the definition of the text in the DT tag. It may contain block elements, but also plain text and markup. The end tag is optional, as it's always clear from the context where the tag's contents end.

ACCESSKEY = *sAccessKey*
CLASS = *sClass*
DIR = "ltr" | "rtl"
<event_name> = *name of script*
ID = *sID*
LANG = *sLanguage*
LANGUAGE = "JScript" | "javascript" | "vbs" | "vbscript" | "XML" | *sLanguage*
NOWRAP
STYLE = *sStyle*
TABINDEX = *iIndex*
TITLE = *sTitle*

See also DL and DT.

```
<DL>
  <DT>Wrox</DT>
  <DD>The publisher of IE5 Dynamic HTML Programmer's Reference</DD>
</DL>
```

DEL

Indicates text that has been deleted from the document.

ACCESSKEY = *sAccessKey*
CLASS = *sClass*
DIR = "ltr" | "rtl"
ID = *sID*
LANG = *sLanguage*
LANGUAGE = "JScript" | "javascript" | "vbs" | "vbscript" | "XML" | *sLanguage*
STYLE = *sStyle*
TABINDEX = *iIndex*
TITLE = *sTitle*

DFN

DFN is used to mark out terms which are being used for the first time. These are often rendered in italics so that the user can see that this is where the term was used for the first time.

ACCESSKEY = *sAccessKey*
CLASS = *sClass*
DIR = "ltr" | "rtl"
<event_name> = *name of script*
ID = *sID*
LANG = *sLanguage*
LANGUAGE = "JScript" | "javascript" | "vbs" | "vbscript" | "XML" | *sLanguage*
STYLE = *sStyle*
TABINDEX = *iIndex*
TITLE = *sTitle*

```
DHTML -
<DFN>Dynamic HTML</DFN>
```

DIR

Renders text as a directory listing.

ACCESSKEY = *sAccessKey*
CLASS = *aClass*
DIR = "ltr" | "rtl"
<event_name> = *name of script*
ID = *sID*
LANG = *sLanguage*
LANGUAGE = "JScript" | "javascript" | "vbs" | "vbscript" | "XML" | *sLanguage*
STYLE = *sStyle*
TABINDEX = *iIndex*
TITLE = *sTitle*

```
<DIR>
  properties.doc   421,564
  methods.doc       23,518
  events.doc         6,386
</DIR>
```

DIV

Defines a logical division within a document.

ACCESSKEY = *sAccessKey*
ALIGN = "center" | "justify" | "left" | "right"
CLASS = *sClass*
DATAFLD = *sField*
DATAFORMATAS = "text" | "html"
DATASRC = *sID*
DIR = "ltr" | "rtl"
<event_name> = *name of script*
ID = *sID*
LANG = *sLanguage*
LANGUAGE = "JScript" | "javascript" | "vbs" | "vbscript" | "XML" | *sLanguage*
NOWRAP
STYLE = *sStyle*
TABINDEX = *iIndex*
TITLE = *sTitle*

```
<DIV ID=MyDiv STYLE="position:absolute;top:20;left:50;width:500;height:100>
This text is inside an absolutely positioned document division.
</DIV>
```

DL

DL is used to provide a list of items with associated definitions. Every item should be put in a DT, with its definition in the DD immediately following it. This list is typically rendered without bullets of any kind. While it is legal to have a DL with only DD or DT tags, it doesn't make much sense - what good is a definition without a term? - and you should not expect it to get rendered as a normal list.

ACCESSKEY = *sAccessKey*
CLASS = *sClass*
COMPACT
DIR = "ltr" | "rtl"
<event_name> = *name of script*
ID = *sID*
LANG = *sLanguage*
LANGUAGE = "JScript" | "javascript" | "vbs" | "vbscript" | "XML" | *sLanguage*
STYLE = *sStyle*
TABINDEX = *iIndex*
TITLE = *sTitle*

```
<DL>
  <DT>Wrox</DT>
  <DD>The publisher of IE5 Dynamic HTML Programmer's Reference</DD>
</DL>
```

See also DT, DD.

DT

The DT tag is used inside HYPERLINK "../list/dl.html" DL. It marks up a term whose definition is provided by the next DD. The DT tag may only contain text-level markup.

ACCESSKEY = *sAccessKey*
CLASS = *sClass*
DIR = "ltr" | "rtl"
<event_name> = *name of script*
ID = *sID*
LANG = *sLanguage*
LANGUAGE = "JScript" | "javascript" | "vbs" | "vbscript" | "XML" | *sLanguage*
NOWRAP
STYLE = *sStyle*
TABINDEX = *iIndex*
TITLE = *sTitle*

```
<DL>
  <DT>Wrox</DT>
  <DD>The publisher of IE5 Dynamic HTML Programmer's Reference</DD>
</DL>
```

See also DD, DL.

EM

Renders text as emphasized, usually in italics.

ACCESSKEY = *sAccessKey*
CLASS = *sClass*
DIR = "ltr" | "rtl"
<event_name> = *name of script*
ID = *sID*
LANG = *sLanguage*
LANGUAGE = "JScript" | "javascript" | "vbs" | "vbscript" | "XML" | *sLanguage*
STYLE = *sStyle*
TABINDEX = *iIndex*
TITLE = *sTitle*

```
The word <EM>emphasis</EM> will be emphasized by being rendered in italics
```

EMBED

Embeds documents of any type in the page, to be viewed in another suitable application.

ACCESSKEY = *sAccessKey*
ALIGN = "absbottom" | "absmiddle" | "baseline" | "bottom" | "left" | "middle" | "right" | "texttop" | "top"
ALT = *sTxt*
CLASS = *sClass*
CODE = *sURL*
CODEBASE = *sURL*[#version=a,b,c,d]
DIR = "ltr" | "rtl"
HEIGHT = *sHeight*["%"]
HSPACE = *iMargin*
ID = *sID*
NAME = *sName*
LANG = *sLanguage*
LANGUAGE = "JScript" | "javascript" | "vbs" | "vbscript" | "XML" | *sLanguage*
PLUGINSPAGE = *sURL*
SRC = *sURL*
STYLE = *sStyle*
TABINDEX = *iIndex*
TITLE = *sTitle*
UNITS = *sUnits*
VSPACE = *iMargin*
WIDTH = *sWidth*[%]

```
<EMBED SRC="MyMovie.mov" WIDTH=300 HEIGHT=200>
<EMBED SRC="Letter.doc" WIDTH=600 HEIGHT=400 ALIGN=CENTER>
```

FIELDSET

Draws a box around the contained elements to indicate related items.

ACCESSKEY = *sAccessKey*
ALIGN = "absbottom" | "absmiddle" | "baseline" | "bottom" | "left" | "middle" | "right" | "texttop" | "top"
CLASS = *sClass*
DIR = "ltr" | "rtl"
<event_name> = *name of script*
ID = *sID*
LANG = *sLanguage*
LANGUAGE = "JScript" | "javascript" | "vbs" | "vbscript" | "XML" | *sLanguage*
STYLE = *sStyle*
TABINDEX = *iIndex*
TITLE = *sTitle*

FONT

Specifies the font face, size and color for rendering the text.

ACCESSKEY = *sAccessKey*
CLASS = *sClass*
COLOR = *sColor*
DIR = "ltr" | "rtl"
<event_name> = *name of script*
FACE = *sTypeface*
ID = *sID*
LANG = *sLanguage*
LANGUAGE = "JScript" | "javascript" | "vbs" | "vbscript" | "XML" | *sLanguage*
SIZE = *iSize*
STYLE = *sStyle*
TABINDEX = *iIndex*
TITLE = *sTitle*

We can change the size in relation to the current BASEFONT setting. For example, this code will render the word font as slightly bigger than the other text:

```
<FONT SIZE = "+1">font</FONT>
```

We can also specify the font face (fontname) and color. The following code will render the word font in slightly larger, white Arial font:

```
<FONT FACE = "ARIAL" SIZE = "+1" COLOR = "#FFFFFF">font</FONT>
```

FORM

Denotes a form on the page that can contain other controls and elements.

ACTION = *sURL*
AUTOCOMPLETE = "off"
CLASS = *sClass*
DIR = "ltr" | "rtl"
ENCTYPE = *sType*
<event_name> = *name of script*
ID = *sID*
LANG = *sLanguage*
LANGUAGE = "JScript" | "javascript" | "vbs" | "vbscript" | "XML" | *sLanguage*
METHOD = "get" | "post"
NAME = *sName*
STYLE = *sStyle*
TABINDEX = *iIndex*
TARGET = *sTarget* | "_blank" | "_parent" | "_search" | "_self" | "_top"
TITLE = *sTitle*

```
<FORM NAME="MyForm"  ACTION="http://mysite.com/scripts/handler.pl">
  This is a form which can be submitted to the server.
  Enter Your Opinion: <INPUT TYPE="TEXT" NAME = "txtOpinion">
  <INPUT TYPE="SUBMIT" VALUE="Send Opinion">
  <INPUT TYPE="RESET" VALUE="Clear Form">
</FORM>
```

FRAME

Specifies an individual frame within a frameset.

APPLICATION = "yes" | "no"
BORDERCOLOR = *sColor*
CLASS = *sClass*
DATAFLD = *sField*
DATASRC = *sID*
<event_name> = *name of script*
FRAMEBORDER = "1" | "0" | "no" | "yes"
HEIGHT = *sHeight*[%]
ID = *sID*
LANG = *sLanguage*
LANGUAGE = "JScript" | "javascript" | "vbs" | "vbscript" | "XML" | *sLanguage*
MARGINHEIGHT = *iHeight*
MARGINWIDTH = *iWidth*
NAME = *sName*
NORESIZE
SCROLLING = "auto" | "no" | "yes"
SRC = *sURL*
TITLE = *sTitle*
WIDTH = *sWidth*[%]

See also FRAMESET.

```
<FRAMESET FRAMESPACING=0 COLS=140,*" BORDER=1>
  <FRAME SRC="menu.htm" NAME="menuframe" MARGINWIDTH=0 SCROLLING=NO NORESIZE>
  <FRAME SRC="menu.htm" NAME="menuframe" MARGINWIDTH=10 MARGINHEIGHT=10>
</FRAMESET>
```

FRAMESET

Specifies a frameset containing multiple frames and other nested framesets.

BORDER = *iSpace*
BORDERCOLOR = *sColor*
CLASS = *sClass*
COLS = *iWidth* [% | *] [, *iWidth* [% | *] ...]
FRAMEBORDER = "1" | "0" | "no" | "yes"
FRAMESPACING = *sPixels*
ID = *sID*
LANG = *sLanguage*
LANGUAGE = "JScript" | "javascript" | "vbs" | "vbscript" | "XML" | *sLanguage*
ROWS = *iHeight* [, *iHeight*...]
TABINDEX = *iIndex*
TITLE = *sTitle*

```
<FRAMESET FRAMESPACING=0 COLS=140,*" BORDER=1>
  <FRAME SRC="menu.htm" NAME="menuframe" MARGINWIDTH=0 SCROLLING=NO NORESIZE>
  <FRAME SRC="menu.htm" NAME="menuframe" MARGINWIDTH=10 MARGINHEIGHT=10>
</FRAMESET>
```

HEAD

Contains tags holding unviewed information about the document.

CLASS = *sClass*
ID = *sID*
LANG = *sLanguage*
TITLE = *sTitle*

Usually only contains TITLE, META, BASE, BASEFONT, BGSOUND, ISINDEX, LINK, NEXTID, SCRIPT and STYLE tags.

```
<HEAD>
  <TITLE> My Web Page </TITLE>
  <META NAME="Updated" CONTENT="15-Aug-97">
  <BASE HREF="http://mysite.com/pages/thispage.htm">
</HEAD>
```

H*n*

Renders text as a heading style (H1 to H6).

ACCESSKEY = *sAccessKey*
ALIGN = "center" | "justify" | "left" | "right"
CLASS = *sClass*
DIR = "ltr" | "rtl"
<event_name> = *name of script*
ID = *sID*
LANG = *sLanguage*
LANGUAGE = "JScript" | "javascript" | "vbs" | "vbscript" | "XML" | *sLanguage*
STYLE = *sStyle*
TABINDEX = *iIndex*
TITLE = *sTitle*

```
<H1> This is the largest size of heading </H1>
<H6> This is the smallest size of heading </H6>
<H4> And this is somewhere in between </H4>
```

HR

Places a horizontal rule in the page.

ACCESSKEY = *sAccessKey*
ALIGN = "center" | "justify" | "left" | "right"
CLASS = *sClass*
COLOR = *sColor*
<event_name> = *name of script*
ID = *sID*
LANG = *sLanguage*
LANGUAGE = "JScript" | "javascript" | "vbs" | "vbscript" | "XML" | *sLanguage*
NOSHADE
SIZE = *iSize*
SRC = *sURL*
STYLE = *sStyle*
TABINDEX = *iIndex*
TITLE = *sTitle*
WIDTH = *sWidth*[%]

For a red horizontal rule half the page width, five pixels deep, and with no 3-D effect, we can use:

```
<HR SIZE=5 WIDTH=50% COLOR="#ff0000" NOSHADE>
```

HTML

Identifies the document as containing HTML elements.

CLASS = *sClass*
ID = *sID*
LANG = *language*
TITLE =*sTitle*
XMLNS:*sNamespace* [= *sUrn*]

A standard HTML document *must be* enclosed by the HTML tags. Inside these, the HEAD and BODY tags are used to divide the document up into sections.

The HEAD section contains information about the document, specifies how it should be displayed, and issues other instructions to the browser.

The BODY section contains the elements of the document designed to be displayed by the browser.

```
<!DOCTYPE ...>
<HTML>
  <HEAD>
    <META ... >
    <TITLE> Page title goes here </TITLE>
  </HEAD>
  <BODY>
    ...
      This is the main visible part of the page
    ...
  </BODY>
</HTML>
```

The XMLNS section contains a namespace for a custom tag, and is based on the W3C XML Namespace Specification. Multiple namespace decarations are allowed:

```
<HTML XMLNS:Namepace1 XMLNS:Namespace2="www.wrox.com">
```

I

Renders text in an italic font where available.

ACCESSKEY = *sAccessKey*
CLASS = *sClass*
DIR = "ltr" | "rtl"
<event_name> = *name of script*
ID = *sID*
LANG = *sLanguage*
LANGUAGE = "JScript" | "javascript" | "vbs" | "vbscript" | "XML" | *sLanguage*
STYLE = *sStyle*
TABINDEX = *iIndex*
TITLE = *sTitle*

```
<I> This text will be displayed in italic font style. </I>
```

IFRAME

Used to create in-line floating frames within the page.

ALIGN = "absbottom" | "absmiddle" | "baseline" | "bottom" | "left" | "middle" | "right" | "texttop" | "top"
APPLICATION = "yes" | "no"
BORDER = *iSpace*
BORDERCOLOR = *sColor*
CLASS = *sClass*
DATAFLD = *sField*
DATASRC = *sID*
<event_name> = *name of script*
FRAMEBORDER = "1" | "0" | "no" | "yes"
FRAMESPACING = *sPixels*
HEIGHT = *sHeight*[%]
HSPACE = *iMargin*
ID = *sID*
LANG = *sLanguage*
LANGUAGE = "JScript" | "javascript" | "vbs" | "vbscript" | "XML" | *sLanguage*
MARGINHEIGHT = *iHieght*
MARGINWIDTH = *iWidth*
NAME = *sName*
NORESIZE
SCROLLING = "auto" | "no" | "yes"
SRC = *sURL*
STYLE = *sStyle*
TABINDEX = *iIndex*
TITLE = *sTitle*
VSPACE = *iMargin*
WIDTH = *sWidth*[%]

IMG

Embeds an image or a video clip in the document. Most browsers only support `GIF` and `JPEG` file types for inline images. Video clips are more usually handled by the `EMBED` tag.

ACCESSKEY = sAccessKey
ALIGN = "absbottom" | "absmiddle" | "baseline" | "bottom" | "left" | "middle" | "right" | "texttop" | "top"
ALT = *sTxt*
BORDER = *iBorder*
CLASS = *sClass*
DATAFLD = *sField*
DATASRC = *sID*
DIR = "ltr" | "rtl"
DYNSRC = *sURL*
<event_name> = *name of script*
HEIGHT = *sHeight*["%"]
HSPACE = *iMargin*
ID = *sID*
ISMAP
LANG = *sLanguage*
LANGUAGE = "JScript" | "javascript" | "vbs" | "vbscript" | "XML" | *sLanguage*
LOOP = *iLoop*
LOWSRC = *sURL*
NAME = *sName*
SRC = *sURL*
STYLE = *sStyle*
TABINDEX = *iIndex*
TITLE = *sTitle*
USEMAP = *sURL*
VSPACE = *iMargin*
WIDTH = *sWidth*[%]

This example inserts an image named `MyDog.gif` into the page:

```
<IMG SRC = "MyDog.gif">
```

We can speed up the loading of the image by setting the size for it in the page:

```
<IMG SRC = "MyDog.gif" WIDTH = 200 HEIGHT=100>
```

We can also supply text that is displayed if the image is not loaded:

```
<IMG SRC = "MyDog.gif" WIDTH = 200 HEIGHT=100 ALT = "Picture of my dog">
```

The `IMG` tage can also display `.avi` files in Internet Explorer. This example will play the AVI file `MyDog.avi` if possible, or include the picture `MyDog.gif` if not. If the video can be shown it will start when the page opens and repeat indefinitely:

```
<IMG DYNASRC = "MyDog.avi" SRC = "MyDog.gif" START=FILEOPEN LOOP = INFINITE>
```

INPUT

Specifies a form input control.

ACCESSKEY = *sAccessKey*
ALIGN = "absbottom" | "absmiddle" | "baseline" | "bottom" | "left" | "middle" | "right" | "texttop" | "top"
AUTOCOMPLETE = "off"
CHECKED
CLASS = *sClass*
DATAFLD = sField
DATAFORMATAS = "text" | "html"
DATASRC = *sID*
DIR = "ltr" | "rtl"
DISABLED
<event_name> = *name of script*
ID = *sID*
LANG = *sLanguage*
LANGUAGE = "JScript" | "javascript" | "vbs" | "vbscript" | "XML" | *sLanguage*
MAXLENGTH = *iLength*
NAME = *sName*
READONLY
SIZE = *iSize*
SRC = *sURL*
STYLE = *sStyle*
TABINDEX = *iIndex*
TITLE = *sTitle*
TYPE = *sType*
VALUE = *sValue*
VCARD_NAME = *sVCard*

The INPUT tag is used to create a range of HTML controls, depending on the setting of the TYPE attribute.

The VALUE attribute provides the default value for a text-type control, or the caption for a button-type control:

```
<INPUT TYPE="TEXT" NAME = "txtFavorite" VALUE="Enter your Favorite" SIZE =
       30>
<INPUT TYPE="BUTTON" NAME = "btnOK" VALUE="OK" ONCLICK="MyClickCode()">
<INPUT TYPE="CHECKBOX" NAME = "chkYes" CHECKED>
<INPUT TYPE="SUBMIT" NAME = "btnSubmit" VALUE="Send Details">
<INPUT TYPE="RESET" NAME = "btnReset" VALUE="Clear Form">
<INPUT TYPE="HIDDEN" NAME = "hidMyValue" VALUE="Hidden from view">
<INPUT TYPE="PASSWORD" NAME = "txtPassword">
```

When creating sets of RADIO type controls, or option buttons, use the same NAME attribute if you want only one of the controls to be set at any time:

```
<INPUT TYPE="RADIO" NAME = "optColor" VALUE="RED" CHECKED>
<INPUT TYPE="RADIO" NAME = "optColor" VALUE="YELLOW">
<INPUT TYPE="RADIO" NAME = "optColor" VALUE="GREEN">
```

When controls are placed on a form, their values are sent to the server when a SUBMIT-type button is clicked:

```
<FORM NAME = "MyForm"  ACTION="http://mysite.com/scripts/handler.pl">
  This is a form which can be submitted to the server.
  Enter Your Opinion: <INPUT TYPE="TEXT" NAME = "txtOpinion">
  <INPUT TYPE="SUBMIT" VALUE="Send Opinion">
</FORM>
```

INS

Indicates text that has been inserted into the document.

ACCESSKEY = *sAccessKey*
CLASS = *sClass*
DIR = "ltr" | "rtl"
ID = *sID*
LANG = *sLanguage*
LANGUAGE = "JScript" | "javascript" | "vbs" | "vbscript" | "XML" | *sLanguage*
STYLE = *sStyle*
TABINDEX = *iIndex*
TITLE = *sTitle*

ISINDEX

Causes the browser to display a dialog window that prompts the user for a single line of input.

ACCESSKEY = *sAccessKey*
CLASS = *sClass*
ID = *sID*
LANG = *sLanguage*
LANGUAGE = "JScript" | "javascript" | "vbs" | "vbscript" | "XML" | *sLanguage*
STYLE = *sStyle*
TABINDEX = *iIndex*

KBD

KBD is used to indicate text which should be entered by the user. It is often drawn in a monospaced font, although this is not required. It differs from CODE in that CODE indicates code fragments and KBD indicates input.

ACCESSKEY = *sAccessKey*
CLASS = *sClass*
DIR = "ltr" | "rtl"
<event_name> = *name of script*
ID = *sID*
LANG = *sLanguage*
LANGUAGE = "JScript" | "javascript" | "vbs" | "vbscript" | "XML" | *sLanguage*
STYLE = *sStyle*
TABINDEX = *iIndex*
TITLE = *sTitle*

```
This tag is useful to indicate that <KBD> something </KBD> is to be typed.
```

LABEL

Defines the text of a label for a control-like element.

ACCESSKEY = *sAccessKey*
CLASS = *sClass*
DATAFLD = *sField*
DATAFORMATAS = "text" | "html"
DATASRC = *sID*
DIR = "ltr" | "rtl"
<event_name> = *name of script*
FOR = *sID*
ID = *sID*
LANG = *sLanguage*
LANGUAGE = "JScript" | "javascript" | "vbs" | "vbscript" | "XML" | *sLanguage*
STYLE = *sStyle*
TABINDEX = *iIndex*
TITLE = *sTitle*

```
<LABEL ACCESSKEY = F FOR="txtFavorite" ID = "MyLabel">
  Favorite Color:
  <INPUT TYPE=""TEXT" NAME = txtFavorite>
</LABEL>
```

LEGEND

Defines the text to place in the box created by the `FIELDSET` tag.

`ACCESSKEY` = *sAccessKey*
`ALIGN = "bottom" | "center" | "left" | "right" | "top"`
`CLASS` = *sClass*
`DIR = "ltr" | "rtl"`
`<event_name>` = *name of script*
`ID` = *sID*
`LANG` = *sLanguage*
`LANGUAGE = "JScript" | "javascript" | "vbs" | "vbscript" | "XML" |` *sLanguage*
`STYLE` = *sStyle*
`TABINDEX` = *iIndex*
`TITLE` = *sTitle*
`VALIGN = BOTTOM | TOP`

LI

Denotes one item within an ordered or unordered list.

`ACCESSKEY` = *sAccessKey*
`CLASS` = *sClass*
`DIR = "ltr" | "rtl"`
`<event_name>` = *name of script*
`ID` = *sID*
`LANG` = *sLanguage*
`LANGUAGE = "JScript" | "javascript" | "vbs" | "vbscript" | "XML" |` *sLanguage*
`STYLE` = *sStyle*
`TABINDEX` = *iIndex*
`TITLE` = *sTitle*
`TYPE = "1" | "a" | "A" | "i" | "I"`
`VALUE` = *sValue*

Used to create indented lists of items, either in an ordered or unordered list. Tags can be nested to provide sub-lists:

See also `UL`, `OL`.

```
<OL>
  <LI> This is item one in an ordered list
  <LI> This is item two in an ordered list
</OL>
```

LINK

LINK is used to indicate relationships between documents. REL indicates a normal relationship to the document specified in the URL. The TITLE attribute can be used to suggest a title for the referenced URL or relation.

DISABLED
HREF = *sURL*
ID = *sID*
MEDIA = "screen" | "print" | "all"
NAME = *sName*
REL = *sRelation*
REV = "Alternate" || "Stylesheet" || "Start" || "Next" || "Prev" || "Contents" || "Index" || "Glossary" || "Copyright" || "Chapter" || "Section" || "Subsection" || "Appendix" || "Help" || "Bookmark"
TITLE = *sTitle*
TYPE = *sType*

The following LINK tags allow advanced browsers to automatically generate a navigational buttonbar for the site. For each possible value, the URL can be either absolute or relative.

REL = "copyright"	Indicates the location of a page with copyright information for information and such on this site.
REL = "glossary"	Indicates the location of a glossary of terms for this site.
REL = "help"	Indicates the location of a help file for this site. This can be useful if the site is complex, or if the current document may require explanation to be used correctly (for example, a large fill-in form)
REL = "home"	Indicates the location of the homepage, or starting page in this site.
REL = "index"	Indicates the location of the index for this site. This doesn't have to be the same as the table of contents. The index could be alphabetical, for example.
REL = "next"	Indicates the location of the next document in a series, relative to the current document.
REL = "previous"	Indicates the location of the previous document in a series, relative to the current document.
REL = "toc"	Indicates the location of the table of contents, or overview of this site.
REL = "up"	Indicates the location of the document which is logically directly above the current document.

```
<LINK REL = "stylesheet" HREF = "http://mysite.com/styles/mystyle.css">

<LINK REL = "subdocument" HREF = "http://mysite.com/docs/subdoc.htm">
```

LISTING

Renders text in fixed-width type. This tag is no longer recommended – use the PRE or SAMP tag instead.

ACCESSKEY = sAccessKey
CLASS = *sClass*
DIR = "ltr" | "rtl"
<event_name> = *name of script*
ID = *sID*
LANG = *sLanguage*
LANGUAGE = "JScript" | "javascript" | "vbs" | "vbscript" | "XML" | *sLanguage*
STYLE = *sStyle*
TABINDEX = *iIndex*
TITLE = *sTitle*

```
<LISTING> <!-- following is rendered at a code listing on the screen -->
  Sub MyRoutine(datToday)
    If datToday = "Saturday" Then
      strDestination = "The beach."
    Else
      strDestination = "The office again."
    End If
  End Sub
</LISTING>
```

MAP

Specifies a collection of hot spots for a client-side image map.

CLASS = *sClass*
DIR = "ltr" | "rtl"
<event_name> = *name of script*
ID = *sID*
LANG = *sLanguage*
LANGUAGE = "JScript" | "javascript" | "vbs" | "vbscript" | "XML" | *sLanguage*
NAME = *sName*
STYLE = *sStyle*
TITLE = *sTitle*

```
<MAP NAME = "toolbar">
  <AREA SHAPE="RECT" COORDS = "12,216,68,267" HREF = "wrox.html">
  <AREA SHAPE="CIRCLE" COORDS = "100,200,50" HREF = "index.html">
</MAP>
```

MARQUEE

Creates a scrolling text marquee in the page.

ACCESSKEY = *sAccessKey*
BEHAVIOR = "scroll" | "alternate" | "slide"
BGCOLOR = *sColor*
CLASS = *sClass*
DATAFLD = *sField*
DATAFORMATAS = "text" | "html"
DATASRC = *sID*
DIR = "ltr" | "rtl"
DIRECTION = "left" | "right" | "down" | "up"
<event_name> = *name of script*
HEIGHT = *sHeight* ["%"]
HSPACE = *iMargin*
ID = *sID*
LANG = *sLanguage*
LANGUAGE = "JScript" | "javascript" | "vbs" | "vbscript" | "XML" | *sLanguage*
LOOP = *iLoop*
SCROLLAMOUNT = *iAmount*
SCROLLDELAY = *iDelay*
STYLE = *sStyle*
TABINDEX = *iIndex*
TITLE = *sTitle*
TRUESPEED
VSPACE = *iMargin*
WIDTH = *sWidth*[%]

MENU

Renders the following block of text as individual items.

ACCESSKEY = *sAccessKey*
CLASS = *sClass*
DIR = "ltr" | "rtl"
<event_name> = *name of script*
ID = *sID*
LANG = *sLanguage*
STYLE = *sStyle*
TABINDEX = *iIndex*
TITLE = *sTitle*

```
<MENU>
  <LI> This is an item in a menu
  <LI> This is another item in a menu
  <LI> And so is this one
</MENU>
```

META

Provides various types of unviewed information or instructions to the browser.

CONTENT = *sDescription* [; *iRefresh*] [; URL = *sURL*]
[; *sMimeType*] [; CHARSET = *sCharset*]
HTTP-EQUIV = *sInformation*
NAME = *sName*
TITLE = *sTitle*
URL = *url*

To store information in a document so that it can be read automatically by search engines or automated web crawlers:

```
<META NAME = "Updated" CONTENT "15-AUG-97">
<META NAME = "Author" CONTENT="Wrox Press Limited">
<META NAME = "Keywords" CONTENT="HTML Dynamic Web Internet">
<META NAME = "Description" CONTENT="A page about Dynamic HTML">
```

A popular use for the META tag is to set HTTP values and redirect the browser to another page.

```
<META HTTP-EQUIV="REFRESH" CONTENT="10;URL=http://www.wrox.com">
<META HTTP-EQUIV="EXPIRES" CONTENT="Fri, 15 Aug 1997 12:00:00 GMT">
```

NEXTID

Defines a parameter in the <HEAD> of the page for use by text editing software.

TITLE = *sTitle*

NOBR

Renders text without any text wrapping in the page.

CLASS = *sClass*
DIR = "ltr" | "rtl"
ID = *sID*
LANG = *sLanguage*
LANGUAGE = "JScript" | "javascript" | "vbs" | "vbscript" | "XML" | *sLanguage*
STYLE = *sStyle*
TITLE = *sTitle*

NOFRAMES

Defines the HTML to be displayed by browsers that do not support frames.

ID = *sID*
STYLE = *sStyle*
TITLE = *sTitle*

NOSCRIPT

Defines the HTML to be displayed in browsers that do not support scripting.

ID = *sID*
STYLE = *sStyle*
TITLE = *sTitle*

OBJECT

Inserts an object or other non-intrinsic HTML control into the page.

ACCESSKEY = *sAccessKey*
ALIGN = "absbottom" | "absmiddle" | "baseline" | "bottom" | "left" | "middle" | "right" | "texttop" | "top"
CLASS = *sClass*
CLASSID = *sID*
CODE = *sURL*
CODEBASE = *sURL*[#version=a,b,c,d]
CODETYPE = *sType*
DATA = *sURL*
DATAFLD = *sField*
DATASRC = *sID*
DIR = "ltr" | "rtl"
<event_name> = *name of script*
HEIGHT = *sHeight*["%"]
HSPACE = *iMargin*
ID = *sID*
LANG = *sLanguage*
LANGUAGE = "JScript" | "javascript" | "vbs" | "vbscript" | "XML" | *sLanguage*
NAME = *sName*
STYLE = *sStyle*
TABINDEX = *iIndex*
TITLE = *sTitle*
TYPE = *sType*
VSPACE = *iMargin*
WIDTH = *sWidth*[%]

```
<OBJECT ID = "MyObject" CLASSID = "clsid:AA45-6575-5C1E-7788-BB632C9E3453"
  WIDTH = 200 HEIGHT=100 TYPE="application/x-oleobject"
  CODEBASE="http://mysite.com/activex/controls/controll.ocx">
  <PARAM NAME = "StartValue" VALUE="12">
  <PARAM NAME = "EndValue" VALUE="42">
  <PARAM NAME = "ErrorMsg" VALUE="Panic">
</OBJECT>
```

OL

Renders lines of text with <LI> tags as an ordered list.

ACCESSKEY = *sAccessKey*
CLASS = *sClass*
DIR = "ltr" | "rtl"
<event_name> = *name of script*
ID = *sID*
LANG = *sLanguage*
LANGUAGE = "JScript" | "javascript" | "vbs" | "vbscript" | "XML" | *sLanguage*
START = *iStart*
STYLE = *sStyle*
TABINDEX = *iIndex*
TITLE = *sTitle*
TYPE = "1" | "a" | "A" | "i" | "I"

See also LI, UL.

```
<OL>
  <LI> This is item one in an ordered list
  <LI> This is item two in an ordered list
</OL>
```

OPTION

Denotes one choice in a SELECT element.

CLASS = *sClass*
DIR = "ltr" | "rtl"
<event_name> = *name of script*
ID = *sID*
LANG = *sLanguage*
LANGUAGE = "JScript" | "javascript" | "vbs" | "vbscript" | "XML" | *sLanguage*
SELECTED
TITLE = *sTitle*
VALUE = *sValue*

```
<SELECT SIZE = 1 ID = "MyDropList">
  <OPTION VALUE="0.25"> 1/4 inch thick
  <OPTION VALUE="0.5"> 1/2 inch thick
  <OPTION VALUE="0.75" SELECTED> 3/4 inch thick
  <OPTION VALUE="1"> 1 inch thick
</SELECT>
```

```
<SELECT SIZE = 12 ID = MySelectList" MULTIPLE>
  <OPTION VALUE="0723"> Active Server Pages
  <OPTION VALUE="0448"> VBScript Programming
  <OPTION VALUE="0464"> ActiveX Web Databases
  <OPTION VALUE="0707"> Professional DHTML
</SELECT>
```

P

Denotes a paragraph.

`ACCESSKEY =` *sAccessKey*
`ALIGN = "center" | "justify" | "left" | "right"`
`CLASS =` *sClass*
`DIR = "ltr" | "rtl"`
`<event_name> =` *name of script*
`ID =` *sID*
`LANG =` *sLanguage*
`LANGUAGE = "JScript" | "javascript" | "vbs" | "vbscript" | "XML" |` *sLanguage*
`STYLE =` *sStyle*
`TABINDEX =` *iIndex*
`TITLE =` *sTitle*

The `P` tag can be used on its own:

```
This sentence is separated from the next.<P> This is another paragraph.
```

or to enclose the text in a paragraph:

```
<P> This is one paragraph. </P> <P> This is another paragraph. </P>
```

PARAM

Used in an OBJECT tag to set the object's properties.

DATAFLD = *sField*
DATAFORMATAS = "text" | "html"
DATASRC = *sID*
NAME = *sName*
VALUE = *sValue*

See also OBJECT, APPLET.

```
<OBJECT ID = "MyObject" CLASSID = "clsid:AA45-6575-5C1E-7788-BB632C9E3453"
  WIDTH = 200 HEIGHT=100 TYPE="application/x-oleobject"
  CODEBASE="http://mysite.com/activex/controls/controll.ocx">
  <PARAM NAME = "StartValue" VALUE="12">
  <PARAM NAME = "EndValue" VALUE="42">
  <PARAM NAME = "ErrorMsg" VALUE="Panic">
</OBJECT>
```

PLAINTEXT

Renders text in fixed-width type without processing tags.

ACCESSKEY = *sAccessKey*
CLASS = *sClass*
DIR = "ltr" | "rtl"
<event_name> = *name of script*
ID = *sID*
LANG = *sLanguage*
LANGUAGE = "JScript" | "javascript" | "vbs" | "vbscript" | "XML" | *sLanguage*
STYLE = *sStyle*
TABINDEX = *iIndex*
TITLE = *sTitle*

```
<PLAINTEXT>
  All the text and HTML tags here will be rendered on the page without
  being processed by the browser. This means it will look like this on
  screen, and a <B> tag will show as a tag, and not change the text to
  bold. All the text will be in a fixed width font as well.
</PLAINTEXT>
```

PRE

Renders text in fixed-width type.

ACCESSKEY = *sAccessKey*
CLASS = *sClass*
DIR = "ltr" | "rtl"
<event_name> = *name of script*
ID = *sID*
LANG = *sLanguage*
LANGUAGE = "JScript" | "javascript" | "vbs" | "vbscript" | "XML" | *sLanguage*
STYLE = *sStyle*
TABINDEX = *iIndex*
TITLE = *sTitle*

```
<PRE>
  Text here will be rendered in a fixed width font and the line breaks
  will be maintained, so this part will be on the second line.
</PRE>
```

Q

Sets apart a quotation in text.

ACCESSKEY = *sAccessKey*
CLASS = *sClass*
DIR = "ltr" | "rtl"
ID = *sID*
LANG = *sLanguage*
LANGUAGE = "JScript" | "javascript" | "vbs" | "vbscript" | "XML" | *sLanguage*
STYLE = *sStyle*
TABINDEX = *iIndex*
TITLE = *sTitle*

RT

Designates the ruby text for the RUBY element.

ACCESSKEY = *sAccessKey*
CLASS = *sClass*
DIR = "ltr" | "rtl"
ID = *sID*
LANG = *sLanguage*
LANGUAGE = "JScript" | "javascript" | "vbs" | "vbscript" | "XML" | *sLanguage*
NAME = *sName*
STYLE = *sStyle*
TABINDEX = *iIndex*
TITLE = *sTitle*

RUBY

Designates an annotation or pronunciation guide to be placed above or inline with a string of text.

ACCESSKEY = *sAccessKey*
CLASS = *sClass*
DIR = "ltr" | "rtl"
LANG = *sLanguage*
LANGUAGE = "JScript" | "javascript" | "vbs" | "vbscript" | "XML" | *sLanguage*
NAME = *sName*
STYLE = *sStyle*
TABINDEX = *iIndex*
TITLE = *sTitle*

S

Renders text in strikethrough type.

ACCESSKEY = *sAccessKey*
CLASS = *sClass*
DIR = "ltr" | "rtl"
<event_name> = *name of script*
ID = *sID*
LANG = *sLanguage*
LANGUAGE = "JScript" | "javascript" | "vbs" | "vbscript" | "XML" | *sLanguage*
STYLE = *sStyle*
TABINDEX = *iIndex*
TITLE = *sTitle*

```
We can show a word in <S> strikethrough </S> format like this.
```

SAMP

Renders text as a code sample listing.

ACCESSKEY = *sAccessKey*
CLASS = *sClass*
DIR = "ltr" | "rtl"
<event_name> = *name of script*
ID = *sID*
LANG = *sLanguage*
LANGUAGE = "JScript" | "javascript" | "vbs" | "vbscript" | "XML" | *sLanguage*
STYLE = *sStyle*
TABINDEX = *iIndex*
TITLE = *sTitle*

```
<SAMP>
  …
  x = sqr(y + b * 2^e
  result = (x + y) / cos(t)
  …
</SAMP>
```

SCRIPT

Specifies a script for the page that will be interpreted by a script engine.

CLASS = *sClass*
DEFER
EVENT = *sEvent*
<event_name> = *name of script*
FOR = *oObject*
ID = *sID*
LANG = *sLanguage*
LANGUAGE = "JScript" | "javascript" | "vbs" | "vbscript" | "XML" | *sLanguage*
SRC = *sURL*
TITLE = *sTitle*
TYPE = "text/ecmascript" | "text/Jscript" | "text/javascript" | "text/vbs" | "text/vbscript" | "text/xml"

SELECT

Defines a list box or dropdown list.

ACCESSKEY = *sAccessKey*
ALIGN = "absbottom" | "absmiddle" | "baseline" | "bottom" | "left" | "middle" | "right" | "texttop" | "top"
CLASS = *sClass*
DATAFLD = *sField*
DATASRC = *sID*
DIR = "ltr" | "rtl"
DISABLED
<event_name> = *name of script*
ID = *sID*
LANG = *sLanuage*
LANGUAGE = "JScript" | "javascript" | "vbs" | "vbscript" | "XML" | *sLanguage*
MULTIPLE
NAME = *sName*
SIZE = *iSize*
STYLE = *sStyle*
TABINDEX = *iIndex*
TITLE = *sTitle*
TYPE = *sType*

```
<SELECT SIZE = 12 ID = MySelectList" MULTIPLE>
  <OPTION VALUE="0723"> Active Server Pages
  <OPTION VALUE="0448"> VBScript Programming
  <OPTION VALUE="0464"> ActiveX Web Databases
  <OPTION VALUE="0707"> Professional DHTML
</SELECT>
```

SMALL

Specifies that text should be displayed with a relatively smaller font than the current font.

ACCESSKEY = *sAccessKey*
CLASS = *sClass*
DIR = "ltr" | "rtl"
<event_name> = *name of script*
ID = *sID*
LANG = *sLanguage*
LANGUAGE = "JScript" | "javascript" | "vbs" | "vbscript" | "XML" | *sLanguage*
STYLE = *sStyle*
TABINDEX = *iIndex*
TITLE = *sTitle*

```
We can show <SMALL>some of the text</SMALL> in a smaller font.
```

SPAN

Used with a style sheet to define non-standard attributes for text on the page.

ACCESSKEY = *sAccessKey*
CLASS = *sClass*
DATAFLD = *sField*
DATAFORMATAS = "text" | "html"
DATASRC = *sID*
DIR = "ltr" | "rtl"
<event_name> = *name of script*
ID = *sID*
LANG = *sLanguage*
LANGUAGE = "JScript" | "javascript" | "vbs" | "vbscript" | "XML" | *sLanguage*
STYLE = *sStyle*
TABINDEX = *iIndex*
TITLE = *sTitle*

```
<STYLE>
  SPAN {color:white; background-color:red}
</STYLE>

<P STYLE = "color:green">
  In a green paragraph, we can change <SPAN>some of the text to
  white on red</SPAN> without changing anything else.
</P>
```

STRIKE

Renders text in strikethrough type.

ACCESSKEY = *sAccessKey*
CLASS = *sClass*
DIR = "ltr" | "rtl"
<event_name> = *name of script*
ID = *sID*
LANG = *sLanguage*
LANGUAGE = "JScript" | "javascript" | "vbs" | "vbscript" | "XML" | *sLanguage*
STYLE = *sStyle*
TABINDEX = *iIndex*
TITLE = *sTitle*

```
We can show a word in <STRIKE>strikethrough</STRIKE> format like this.
```

STRONG

Renders text in boldface.

ACCESSKEY = *sAccessKey*
CLASS = *sClass*
DIR = "ltr" | "rtl"
<event_name> = *name of script*
ID = *sID*
LANG = *sLanguage*
LANGUAGE = "JScript" | "javascript" | "vbs" | "vbscript" | "XML" | *sLanguage*
STYLE = *sStyle*
TABINDEX = *iIndex*
TITLE = *sTitle*

STYLE

Specifies the style sheet for the page.

behavior : url(*sLocation*) | url(#*objID*) | url(#*default#behaviorName*)
DISABLED
MEDIA = "screen" | "print" | "all"
TITLE = *sTitle*
TYPE = *sType*

SUB

Renders text as a subscript using a smaller font than the current font.

ACCESSKEY = *sAccessKey*
CLASS = *sClass*
DIR = "ltr" | "rtl"
<event_name> = *name of script*
ID = *sID*
LANG = *sLanguage*
LANGUAGE = "JScript" | "javascript" | "vbs" | "vbscript" | "XML" | *sLanguage*
STYLE = *sStyle*
TABINDEX = *iIndex*
TITLE = *sTitle*

```
To calculate the result multiply x<SUB>1</SUB> by x<SUB>2</SUB>.
```

SUP

Renders text as a superscript using a smaller font than the current font.

ACCESSKEY = *sAccessKey*
CLASS = *sClass*
DIR = "ltr" | "rtl"
<event_name> = *name of script*
ID = *sID*
LANG = *sLanguage*
LANGUAGE = "JScript" | "javascript" | "vbs" | "vbscript" | "XML" | *sLanguage*
STYLE = *sStyle*
TABINDEX = *iIndex*
TITLE = *sTitle*

```
To calculate the result use x<SUP>3</SUP> - y<SUP>2</SUP>.
```

TABLE

Denotes a section of TR, TD and TH tags organized into rows and columns.

ACCESSKEY = *sAccessKey*
ALIGN = "left" | "center" | "right"
BACKGROUND = *sURL*
BGCOLOR = *sColor*
BORDER = *iBorder*
BORDERCOLOR = *sColor*
BORDERCOLORDARK = *sColor*
BORDERCOLORLIGHT = *sColor*
CELLPADDING = *iPadding* [%]
CELLSPACING = *iSpacing* [%]
CLASS = *sClass*
COLS = *iCount*
DATAPAGESIZE = *iSize*
DATASRC = *sID*
DIR = "ltr" | "rtl"
<event_name> = *name of script*
FRAME = "void" | "above" | "below" | "border" | "box" | "hsides" | "lhs" | "rhs" | "vsides"
HEIGHT = *sHeight* ["%"]
ID = *sID*
LANG = *sLanguage*
LANGUAGE = "JScript" | "javascript" | "vbs" | "vbscript" | "XML" | *sLanguage*
RULES = "all" | "cols" | "groups" | "none" | "rows"
STYLE = *sStyle*
TABINDEX = *iIndex*
TITLE = *sTitle*
WIDTH = *sWidth* [%]

```
<TABLE BACKGROUND = "wrox.gif" BORDER=1 WIDTH = 100%>
  <THEAD>
    <TR>
      <TH COLSPAN=2> This is a heading cell</TH>
    </TR>
  </THEAD>
  <TBODY ALIGN-CENTER>
    <TR BGCOLOR = aliceblue>
      <TD This is a body detail cell</TD>
      <TD> And so is this one</TD>
    </TR>
  </TBODY>
  <TFOOT>
    <TR>
      <TD NOWRAP> This is a footer detail cell</TD>
      <TD> And so is this one</TD>
    </TR>
  </TFOOT>
<TABLE>
```

TBODY

Denotes a section of `TR` `TD` and `TH` tags forming the body of the table.

`ACCESSKEY =` *sAccessKey*
`ALIGN = "center" | "justify" | "left" | "right"`
`BGCOLOR =` *sColor*
`CLASS =` *sClass*
`DIR = "ltr" | "rtl"`
`<event_name> =` *name of script*
`ID =` *sID*
`LANG =` *sLanguage*
`LANGUAGE = "JScript" | "javascript" | "vbs" | "vbscript" | "XML" |` *sLanguage*
`STYLE =` *sStyle*
`TABINDEX =` *iIndex*
`TITLE =` *sTitle*
`VALIGN = "middle" | "center" | "baseline" | "bottom" | "top"`

TD

Specifies a cell in a table.

ACCESSKEY = *sAccessKey*
ALIGN = "center" | "justify" | "left" | "right"
BACKGROUND = *sURL*
BGCOLOR = *sColor*
BORDERCOLOR = *sColor*
BORDERCOLORDARK = *sColor*
BORDERCOLORLIGHT = *sColor*
CLASS = *sClass*
COLSPAN = *iCount*
DIR = "ltr" | "rtl"
<event_name> = *name of script*
HEIGHT = *sHeight* ["%"]
ID = *sID*
LANG = *sLanguage*
LANGUAGE = "JScript" | "javascript" | "vbs" | "vbscript" | "XML" | *sLanguage*
NOWRAP
ROWSPAN = *iRows*
STYLE = *sStyle*
TABINDEX = *iIndex*
TITLE = *sTitle*
VALIGN = "middle" | "center" | "baseline" | "bottom" | "top"
WIDTH = *sWidth*[%]

TEXTAREA

Specifies a multi-line text input control.

ACCESSKEY = *sAccessKey*
ALIGN = "absbottom" | "absmiddle" | "baseline" | "bottom" | "left" | "middle" | "right" | "texttop" | "top"
CLASS = *sClass*
COLS = *iCount*
DATAFLD = *sField*
DATASRC = *sID*
DIR = "ltr" | "rtl"
DISABLED
<event_name> = *name of script*
ID = *sID*
LANG = *sLanguage*
LANGUAGE = "JScript" | "javascript" | "vbs" | "vbscript" | "XML" | *sLanguage*
NAME = *sName*
READONLY
ROWS = *iRows*
STYLE = *sStyle*
TABINDEX = *iIndex*
TITLE = *sTitle*
TYPE = *sType*
WRAP = "soft" | "hard" | "off"

TFOOT

Denotes a set of rows to be used as the footer of a table.

ACCESSKEY = *sAccessKey*
ALIGN = "center" | "justify" | "left" | "right"
BGCOLOR = *sColor*
CLASS = *sClass*
DIR = "ltr" | "rtl"
<event_name> = *name of script*
ID = *sID*
LANG = *sLanguage*
LANGUAGE = "JScript" | "javascript" | "vbs" | "vbscript" | "XML" | *sLanguage*
STYLE = *sStyle*
TABINDEX = *iIndex*
TITLE = *sTitle*
VALIGN = "middle" | "center" | "baseline" | "bottom" | "top"

```
<TABLE BACKGROUND = "wrox.gif" BORDER=1 WIDTH = 100%>
  <THEAD>
    <TR>
      <TH COLSPAN=2> This is a heading cell</TH>
    </TR>
  </THEAD>
  <TBODY ALIGN-CENTER>
    <TR BGCOLOR = aliceblue>
      <TD This is a body detail cell</TD>
      <TD> And so is this one</TD>
    </TR>
  </TBODY>
  <TFOOT>
    <TR>
      <TD NOWRAP> This is a footer detail cell</TD>
      <TD> And so is this one</TD>
    </TR>
  </TFOOT>
<TABLE>
```

TH

Denotes a header row in a table. Contents are centered within each cell and are bold.

ACCESSKEY = *sAccessKey*
ALIGN = "center" | "justify" | "left" | "right"
BACKGROUND = *sURL*
BGCOLOR = *sColor*
BORDERCOLOR = *sColor*
BORDERCOLORDARK = *sColor*
BORDERCOLORLIGHT = *sColor*
CLASS = *sClass*
COLSPAN = *iCount*
DIR = "ltr" | "rtl"
<event_name> = *name of script*
HEIGHT = *sHeight* ["%"]
ID = *sID*
LANG = *sLanguage*
LANGUAGE = "JScript" | "javascript" | "vbs" | "vbscript" | "XML" | *sLanguage*
NOWRAP
ROWSPAN = *iRows*
STYLE = *sStyle*
TABINDEX = *iIndex*
TITLE = *sTitle*
VALIGN = "middle" | "center" | "baseline" | "bottom" | "top".
WIDTH = *sWidth* [%]

THEAD

Denotes a set of rows to be used as the header of a table.

ACCESSKEY = *sAccessKey*
ALIGN = "center" | "justify" | "left" | "right"
BGCOLOR = *sColor*
CLASS = *sClass*
DIR = "ltr" | "rtl"
<event_name> = *name of script*
ID = *sID*
LANG = *sLanguage*
LANGUAGE = "JScript" | "javascript" | "vbs" | "vbscript" | "XML" | *sLanguage*
STYLE = *sStyle*
TABINDEX = *iIndex*
TITLE = *sTitle*
VALIGN = "middle" | "center" | "baseline" | "bottom" | "top"

```
<TABLE BACKGROUND = "wrox.gif" BORDER=1 WIDTH = 100%>
  <THEAD>
    <TR>
      <TH COLSPAN=2> This is a heading cell</TH>
    </TR>
    </THEAD>
  <TBODY ALIGN-CENTER>
    <TR BGCOLOR = aliceblue>
      <TD This is a body detail cell</TD>
      <TD> And so is this one</TD>
    </TR>
  </TBODY>
  <TFOOT>
    <TR>
      <TD NOWRAP> This is a footer detail cell</TD>
      <TD> And so is this one</TD>
    </TR>
  </TFOOT>
<TABLE>
```

TITLE

Denotes the title of the document, and used in the browser's window title bar.

ID = *sID*
LANG = *sLanguage*
TITLE = *sTitle*

```
<HTML>
  <HEAD>
    <TITLE> My new web page </TITLE>
  </HEAD>
  <BODY>
    Page contents
  </BODY>
</HTML>
```

TR

Specifies a row in a table.

ACCESSKEY = *sAccessKey*
ALIGN = "center" | "justify" | "left" | "right"
BGCOLOR = *sColor*
BORDERCOLOR = *sColor*
BORDERCOLORDARK = *sColor*
BORDERCOLORLIGHT = *sColor*
CLASS = *sClass*
DIR = "ltr" | "rtl"
<event_name> = *name of script*
HEIGHT = *sHeight* ["%"]
ID = *sID*
LANG = *sLanguage*
LANGUAGE = "JScript" | "javascript" | "vbs" | "vbscript" | "XML" | *sLanguage*
STYLE = *sStyle*
TABINDEX = *iIndex*
TITLE = *sTitle*
VALIGN = "middle" | "center" | "baseline" | "bottom" | "top"
WIDTH = *sWidth* [%]

TT

Renders text in fixed-width type.

ACCESSKEY = *sAccessKey*
CLASS = *sClass*
DIR = "ltr" | "rtl"
<event_name> = *name of script*
ID = *sID*
LANG = *sLanguage*
LANGUAGE = "JScript" | "javascript" | "vbs" | "vbscript" | "XML" | *sLanguage*
STYLE = *sStyle*
TABINDEX = *iIndex*
TITLE = *sTitle*

```
<TT>
This text will be shown in a fixed width font.
It comes from when documents were usually sent
from place to place on a teletype machine.
</TT>
```

U

Renders text underlined.

ACCESSKEY = *sAccessKey*
CLASS = *sClass*
DIR = "ltr" | "rtl"
<event_name> = *name of script*
ID = *sID*
LANG = *sLanguage*
LANGUAGE = "JScript" | "javascript" | "vbs" | "vbscript" | "XML" | *sLanguage*
STYLE = *sStyle*
TABINDEX = *iIndex*
TITLE = *sTitle*

```
We can use this tag to <U> underline </U> some words.
```

UL

Renders lines of text with LI tags as a bulleted list.

ACCESSKEY = *sAccessKey*
CLASS = *sClass*
DIR = "ltr" | "rtl"
<event_name> = *name of script*
ID = *sID*
LANG = *sLanguage*
LANGUAGE = "JScript" | "javascript" | "vbs" | "vbscript" | "XML" | *sLanguage*
STYLE = *sStyle*
TABINDEX = *iIndex*
TITLE = *sTitle*
TYPE = "1" | "a" | "A" | "i" | "I"

```
<UL>
  <LI> This is an item in an un-ordered list
  <LI> This is another item in an un-ordered list
</UL>
```

Se also LI, OL.

VAR

Renders text as a small fixed-width font.

ACCESSKEY = *sAccessKey*
CLASS = *sClass*
DIR = "ltr" | "rtl"
<event_name> = *name of script*
ID = *sID*
LANG = *sLanguage*
LANGUAGE = "JScript" | "javascript" | "vbs" | "vbscript" | "XML" | *sLanguage*
STYLE = *sStyle*
TABINDEX = *iIndex*
TITLE = *sTitle*

```
Used to show the names of variables like <VAR>strTheValue</VAR> in the text
```

WBR

Inserts a soft line break in a block of NOBR text.

CLASS = *sClass*
ID = *sID*
LANGUAGE = "JScript" | "javascript" | "vbs" | "vbscript" | "XML" | *sLanguage*
STYLE = *sStyle*
TITLE = *sTitle*

```
<NOBR>
  This text will not break onto two lines in the browser window.
  This text will only break here <WBR>, and only if it won't fit on one line.
</NOBR>
```

There are no Methods or Events for this tag.

XML

Defines an XML data island on an HTML page.

ID = *sID*
SRC = *sURL*

XMP

Renders text in fixed-width type used for example text.

ACCESSKEY = *sAccessKey*
CLASS = *sClass*
DIR = "ltr" | "rtl"
<event_name> = *name of script*
ID = *sID*
LANG = *sLanguage*
LANGUAGE = "JScript" | "javascript" | "vbs" | "vbscript" | "XML" | *sLanguage*
STYLE = *sStyle*
TABINDEX = *iIndex*
TITLE = *sTitle*

```
<XMP>
  …
  x = sqr(y + b) * 2^e
  result = (x + y) / cos(t)
  …
</XMP>
```

General Element Attributes

There's a set of attributes that are common to almost all of the DHTL elements. These attributes provide properties, methods, and events for manipulating the specific object. This commonality makes it simpler to use the exact same scripting style and techniques to deal with nearly every element in the document object model.

This section lists those common attributes:

Properties

```
className  clientHeight  clientLeft  clientTop  clientWidth
firstChild  id  lastChild  nextSibling  nodeName  nodeType
nodeValue  offsetHeight  offsetLeft  offsetTop  offsetWidth
offsetParent  parentElement  parentNode  previousSibling
readyState  runtimeStyle  scopeName  scrollHeight  scrollLeft
scrollTop  scrollWidth  sourceIndex  style  tagName  uniqueID
```

General Methods

```
appendChild  attachEvent  blur  applyElement  clearAttributes
click  cloneNode  contains  detachEvent  doScroll  getAttribute
getElementsByTagName  hasChildNodes  insertAdjacentElement
insertBefore  mergeAttributes  removeAttribute  removeChild
removeNode  replaceChild  replaceNode  scrollIntoView
setAttribute  swapNode
```

Events

```
onbeforecopy  onbeforecut  onbeforeeditfocus  onbeforepaste
onbeforeupdate  onafterupdate  onblur  onclick  oncopy  oncut
ondblclick  ondrag  ondragend  ondragenter  ondragleave
ondragover  ondragstart  ondrop  onfilterchange  onfocus  onhelp
onkeydown  onkeypress  onkeyup  onlosecapture  onmousedown
onmousemove  onmouseout  onmouseover  onmouseup  onpaste
onpropertychange  onreadystatechange  onresize  onselectstart
```

Collections

```
attributes  childNodes  children  filters
```

Common HTML Tags by Category

Here, we have listed some of the most commonly-used tags by the following categories:

Document Structure	Titles and Headings	Paragraphs and Lines
Text Styles	Lists	Tables
Links	Graphics, Objects, Multimedia and Scripts	
Forms	Frames	

When you know what you want to do, but you're not sure which tag will achieve the desired effect, use the reference tables below to put you on the right track.

Document Structure

Tag	Meaning
`<!>`	Allows authors to add comments to code.
`<!DOCTYPE>`	Defines the document type. This is required by all HTML documents.
`<BASE>`	Specifies the document's base URL – its original location. It's not normally necessary to include this tag. It may only be used in `HEAD` section.
`<BODY>`	Contains the main part of the HTML document.
`<COMMENT>`	Allows authors to add comments to code. No longer recommended, use `<!>`.
`<DIV>`	Defines a block division of the `BODY` section of the document.

Table Continued on Following Page

Tag	Meaning
<HEAD>	Contains information about the document itself.
<HTML>	Signals the beginning and end of an HTML document.
<LINK>	Defines the current document's relationship with other resources. Used in HEAD section only.
<META>	Describes the content of a document.
<NEXTID>	Defines a parameter in the HEAD section of the document.
<SPAN>	Defines an area for reference by a style sheet.
<STYLE>	Specifies the style sheet for the page.
<XML>	Defines an XML data island on the HTML page.

Titles and Headings

Tag	Meaning
<H1>	Heading level 1.
<H2>	Heading level 2.
<H3>	Heading level 3.
<H4>	Heading level 4.
<H5>	Heading level 5.
<H6>	Heading level 6.
<TITLE>	Identifies the contents of the document.

Paragraphs and Lines

Tag	Meaning
 	Inserts a line break.
<CENTER>	Centers subsequent text/images.
<HR>	Draws a horizontal rule.
<NOBR>	Prevents a line of text breaking.
<P>	Defines a paragraph.
<WBR>	Inserts a soft line break in a block of NOBR text.

Text Styles

Tag	Meaning
<ACRONYM>	Indicates an acronym.
<ADDRESS>	Indicates an address, typically displayed in italics.
<B>	Emboldens text.
<BASEFONT>	Sets font size to be used as default.
<BIG>	Changes the physical rendering of the font to one size larger.
<BLOCKQUOTE>	Formats a quote – typically by indentation.
<BDO>	Allows the Unicode bidirectional algorithm (which reverses the order of embedded character sequences) to be disabled.
<CITE>	Renders text in italics.
<CODE>	Renders text in a font resembling computer code.
<DEL>	Denotes text that has been deleted from the document.
<DFN>	Indicates the first instance of a term or important word.
<EM>	Emphasized text – usually italic.
<FONT>	Changes font properties.
<I>	Defines italic text.
<INS>	Denotes text that has been inserted into the document.
<KBD>	Indicates typed text. Useful for instruction manuals etc.
<LISTING>	Renders text in a fixed-width font. No longer recommended - use `<PRE>`.
<PLAINTEXT>	Renders text in a fixed-width font without processing any other tags it may contain. May not be consistently supported across browsers - use `<PRE>`.
<PRE>	Pre-formatted text. Renders text exactly how it is typed, i.e. carriage returns, styles etc., *will* be recognized.
<Q>	Sets a quotation.
<RT>	Specifies the ruby text (i.e. the annotation text) that annotates the content of the RUBY tag.

Table Continued on Following Page

Tag	Meaning
<RUBY>	Defines an pronunciation guide through which a block of text can be annotated using the RT tag.
<S> <STRIKE>	Strike through. Renders the text as 'deleted' (crossed out).
<SAMP>	Specifies sample code and renders it in small font.
<SMALL>	Changes the physical rendering of a font to one size smaller.
<STRONG>	Strong emphasis – usually bold.
<STYLE>	Specifies the style sheet for the page.
<SUB>	Subscript.
<SUP>	Superscript.
<TT>	Renders text in fixed width, typewriter style font.
<U>	Underlines text. Not widely supported at present, and not recommended, as it can cause confusion with hyperlinks, which also normally appear underlined.
<VAR>	Indicates a variable.
<XMP>	Renders text in fixed width type, used for example text. No longer recommended, use <PRE> or <SAMP>.

Lists

Tag	Meaning
<DD>	Definition description. Used in definition lists with DT to define the term.
<DIR>	Denotes a directory list by indenting the text.
<DL>	Defines a definition list.
<DT>	Defines a definition term within a definition list.
<LI>	Defines a list item in any type of list other than a definition list.
<MENU>	Defines a menu list.
<OL>	Defines an ordered (numbered) list.
<UL>	Defines an unordered (bulleted) list.

Tables

Tag	Meaning
<CAPTION>	Puts a title above a table.
<COL>	Defines column width and properties for a table.
<COLGROUP>	Defines properties for a group of columns in a table.
<TABLE>	Defines a series of columns and rows to form a table.
<TBODY>	Defines the table body.
<TD>	Specifies a cell in a table.
<TFOOT>	Defines table footer.
<TH>	Specifies a header column. Text will be centered and bold.
<THEAD>	Used to designate rows as the table's header.
<TR>	Defines the start of a table row.

Links

Tag	Meaning
<A>	Used to insert an anchor, which can be either a local reference point or a hyperlink to another URL.
<A HREF="url">	Hyperlink to another document.
<A NAME="name">	Link to a local reference point.

Graphics, Objects, Multimedia and Scripts

Tag	Meaning
<APPLET>	Inserts an applet.
<AREA>	Specifies the shape of a "hot spot" in a client-side image map.
<BGSOUND>	Plays a background sound.
<EMBED>	Defines an embedded object in an HTML document.
<IMG>	Embeds an image or a video clip in a document.
<MAP>	Specifies a collection of hot spots for a client-side image map.
<MARQUEE>	Sets a scrolling marquee.

Table Continued on Following Page

Tag	Meaning
<NOSCRIPT>	Specifies HTML to be displayed in browsers which don't support scripting.
<OBJECT>	Inserts an object.
<PARAM>	Sets the property value for a given object.
<SCRIPT>	Inserts a script.

Forms

Tag	Meaning
<BUTTON>	Creates an HTML-style button.
<FIELDSET>	Draws a box around a group of controls.
<FORM>	Defines part of the document as a user fill-out form.
<INPUT>	Defines a user input box. There are input controls: `button`, `checkbox`, `file`, `hidden`, `image`, `password`, `radio`, `reset`, `submit`, `text`.
<ISINDEX>	Causes the browser to display a dialog containing a single-line prompt. (Deprecated in HTML 4.0 – use `INPUT` instead.)
<LABEL>	Defines a label for a control.
<LEGEND>	Defines the text label to use in box created by a `FIELDSET` tag.
<OPTION>	Used within the `SELECT` tag to present the user with a number of options.
<SELECT>	Denotes a list box or drop-down list.
<TEXTAREA>	Defines a text area inside a `FORM` element.

Frames

Tag	Meaning
<FRAME>	Defines a single frame in a frameset.
<FRAMESET>	Defines the main container for a frame.
<IFRAME>	Defines a 'floating' frame within a document.
<NOFRAMES>	Allows for backward compatibility with non-frame compliant browsers.

CSS Properties

This appendix lists the properties of CSS Level 2 (which includes all the properties of CSS1). However, not all these properties are implemented by IE5, although the level of support is likely to be increased with successive releases. As ever, to see if a property works, just try it!

I shall cover the properties under the same headings you'll find in the specification:

- Box Model
- Visual Formatting Model
- Visual Formatting Model Details
- Visual Effects
- Generated Content, Automatic Numbering and Lists
- Paged Media
- Colors and Backgrounds
- Font Properties
- Text Properties
- Tables
- User Interface
- Aural Style Sheets

The tables on the following pages list all the properties that can be applied to HTML and XML elements through a CSS style sheet. For more information about each of the properties, you should refer to the specification that may be found at http://www.w3.org/TR/1998/REC-CSS2/. You could also take a look at the Wrox Press title *Professional Style Sheets for HTML and XML* (1-861001-65-7).

Box Model

These properties are covered in Section 8 of the CSS2 specification.

Property Name	Possible Values	Initial Value	Applies to	Inherited
`margin-top`	**<length> | <percentage> | auto** <**percentage**> refers to the parent element's width. Negative values are permitted.	0	All	No
`margin-right`	*as above*	0	All	No
`margin-bottom`	*as above*	0	All	No
`margin-left`	*as above*	0	All	No
`margin`	**[<length> | <percentage> | auto]{1,4}** If 4 values are given they apply to top, right, bottom, left, in that order. 1 value applies to all 4. If 2 or 3 values are given, the missing value is taken from the opposite side. <**percentage**> refers to the parent element's width. Negative values are permitted.	Undefined	All	No
`padding-top`	**<length> | <percentage>** <**percentage**> refers to the parent element's width. Negative values are *not* permitted.	0	All	No
`padding-right`	*as above*	0	All	No
`padding-bottom`	*as above*	0	All	No
`padding-left`	*as above*	0	All	No

<table>
<tr><td>padding</td><td>[<length> | <percentage>]{1,4}
If 4 values are given they apply to top, right, bottom, left, in that order.
1 value applies to all 4.
If 2 or 3 values are given, the missing value is taken from the opposite side.
<percentage> refers to the parent element's width.
Negative values are not permitted.</td><td>0</td><td>All</td><td>No</td></tr>
<tr><td>border-top-width</td><td>thin | medium | thick | <length></td><td>medium</td><td>All</td><td>No</td></tr>
<tr><td>border-right-width</td><td>thin | medium | thick | <length></td><td>medium</td><td>All</td><td>No</td></tr>
<tr><td>border-bottom-width</td><td>thin | medium | thick | <length></td><td>medium</td><td>All</td><td>No</td></tr>
<tr><td>border-left-width</td><td>thin | medium | thick | <length></td><td>medium</td><td>All</td><td>No</td></tr>
<tr><td>border-width</td><td>[thin | medium | thick | <length>]{1,4}
If 4 values are given they apply to top, right, bottom, left, in that order.
1 value applies to all 4.
If 2 or 3 values are given, the missing value is taken from the opposite side.</td><td>Undefined</td><td>All</td><td>No</td></tr>
<tr><td>border-top-color</td><td><color></td><td>The element's color property</td><td>All</td><td>No</td></tr>
<tr><td>border-right-color</td><td><color></td><td>The element's color property</td><td>All</td><td>No</td></tr>
<tr><td>border-bottom-color</td><td><color></td><td>The element's color property</td><td>All</td><td>No</td></tr>
<tr><td>border-left-color</td><td><color></td><td>The element's color property</td><td>All</td><td>No</td></tr>
</table>

<table>
<tr><th>Property Name</th><th>Possible Values</th><th>Initial Value</th><th>Applies to</th><th>Inherited</th></tr>
<tr><td>border-color</td><td><color>{1,4} | transparent
If 4 values are given they apply to top, right, bottom, left, in that order.
1 value applies to all 4.
If 2 or 3 values are given, the missing value is taken from the opposite side.</td><td>The element's color property</td><td>All</td><td>No</td></tr>
<tr><td>border-top-style</td><td>none | hidden | dotted | dashed | solid | double | groove | ridge | inset | outset</td><td>none</td><td>All</td><td>No</td></tr>
<tr><td>border-right-style</td><td>none | hidden | dotted | dashed | solid | double | groove | ridge | inset | outset</td><td>none</td><td>All</td><td>No</td></tr>
<tr><td>border-bottom-style</td><td>none | hidden | dotted | dashed | solid | double | groove | ridge | inset | outset</td><td>none</td><td>All</td><td>No</td></tr>
<tr><td>border-left-style</td><td>none | hidden | dotted | dashed | solid | double | groove | ridge | inset | outset</td><td>none</td><td>All</td><td>No</td></tr>
<tr><td>border-style</td><td>[none | hidden | dotted | dashed | solid | double | groove | ridge | inset | outset]{1,4}</td><td>none</td><td>All</td><td>No</td></tr>
<tr><td>border-top</td><td><border-top-width> || <border-top-style> || <color></td><td>Undefined</td><td>All</td><td>No</td></tr>
<tr><td>border-right</td><td><border-right-width> || <border-right-style> || <color></td><td>Undefined</td><td>All</td><td>No</td></tr>
<tr><td>border-bottom</td><td><border-bottom-width> || <border-bottom-style> || <color></td><td>Undefined</td><td>All</td><td>No</td></tr>
<tr><td>border-left</td><td><border-left-width> || <border-left-style> || <color></td><td>Undefined</td><td>All</td><td>No</td></tr>
<tr><td>border</td><td><border-width> || <border-style> || <color></td><td>Undefined</td><td>All</td><td>No</td></tr>
</table>

Visual Formatting Model

This is a new category of property in CSS2, and is covered in Section 9 of the specification.

Property Name	Possible Values	Initial Value	Applies to	Inherited
`display`	`block | inline | list-item | none | run-in | compact | marker | table | inline-table | table-row-group | table-column-group | table-header-group | table-footer-group | table-row | table-cell | table-caption | table-column`	`inline`	All	No
`position`	`static | relative | absolute | fixed`	`static`	All (but not generated content)	No
`top` (box offsets)	`<length> | <percentage> | auto` `<length>`: the box offset is a fixed distance from the reference edge. `<percentage>`: the box offset is a percentage of the containing block's width (for `left` or right) or height (for `top` and `bottom`). `auto`: the value depends on which of the other box offset properties are `auto` as well.	`auto`	Positioned elements	No
`left` (box offsets)	*as above*	`auto`	Positioned elements	No
`bottom` (box offsets)	*as above*	`auto`	Positioned elements	No

Property Name	Possible Values	Initial Value	Applies to	Inherited
right (box offsets)	*as above*	**auto**	Positioned elements	No
float	**left | right | none** Note: **float** removes inline elements from the line.	**none**	All but positioned elements and generated content	No
clear	**block | inline | list-item | none**	**none**	Block elements	No
z-index	**auto | <integer>**	**auto**	Positioned elements	No
direction	**ltr | rtl** **ltr**: left-to-right **rtl**: right-to-left	**ltr**	All	Yes
unicode-bidi	**normal | embed | bidi-override**	**normal**	All	No

Visual Formatting Model Details

This is another new Section in CSS2, and is covered in Section 10 of the CSS2 specification.

Property Name	Possible Values	Initial Value	Applies to	Inherited
width	**<length> | <percentage> | auto** <**percentage**> refers to parent element's width.	**auto**	All but non-replaced inline elements, table columns and column groups	No
min-width	**<length> | <percentage>**	Depends on user agent	All but non-replaced inline elements and table elements	No

<table>
<tr><td>max-width</td><td><length> | <percentage> | none</td><td>none</td><td>All but non-replaced inline elements and table elements</td><td>No</td></tr>
<tr><td>height</td><td><length> | <percentage> | auto</td><td>auto</td><td>All but non-replaced inline elements, table rows and row groups</td><td>No</td></tr>
<tr><td>min-height</td><td><length> | <percentage></td><td>0</td><td>All but non-replaced inline elements and table elements</td><td>No</td></tr>
<tr><td>max-height</td><td><length> | <percentage> | none</td><td>none</td><td>All but non-replaced inline elements and table elements</td><td>No</td></tr>
<tr><td>line-height</td><td>normal | <number> | <length> | <percentage>
<number>:-
line-height = font-size x num.
<percentage> is relative to font-size.</td><td>normal</td><td>All</td><td>Yes</td></tr>
<tr><td>vertical-align</td><td>baseline | sub | super | top | text-top | middle | bottom | text-bottom | <percentage> | <length>
<percentage> is relative to element's line-height property</td><td>baseline</td><td>Inline and table-cell elements</td><td>No</td></tr>
</table>

Visual Effects

This is a new category of property in CSS2. It is covered in Section 11 of the specification.

Property Name	Possible Values	Initial Value	Applies to	Inherited
`overflow`	`visible | hidden | scroll | auto`	`visible`	Block-level and replaced elements	No
`clip`	`<shape> | auto`	`auto`	Block-level and replaced elements	No
`visibility`	`visible | hidden | collapse | inherit`	`inherit`	All	No

Generated Content, Automatic Numbering and Lists

Again, this is a new category of property in CSS2, covered in Section 12 of the specification. In CSS2 it is possible to generate content in several ways:

- Using the `content` property in conjunction with the `:before` and `:after` pseudo-elements.
- In conjunction with the `cue-before` and `cue-after` aural properties
- Elements with a value of `list-item` for the `display` property

The style and location of generated content is specified with the `:before` and `:after` pseudo-elements. These are used in conjunction with the `content` property, which specifies what is inserted. Unsurprisingly, `:before` and `:after` pseudo-elements specify content before and after an element's document tree content. See the specification (Section 12) for further details.

<table>
<tr><th>Property Name</th><th>Possible Values</th><th>Initial Value</th><th>Applies to</th><th>Inherited</th></tr>
<tr><td>content</td><td>[<string> | <uri> | <counter> | attr(X) | open-quote | close-quote | no-open-quote | no-close-quote]+</td><td>empty string</td><td>:before and :after pseudo-elements</td><td>No</td></tr>
<tr><td>quotes</td><td>[<string> <string>]+ | none</td><td>Depends on user agent</td><td>All</td><td>Yes</td></tr>
<tr><td>counter-reset</td><td>[<identifier> <integer>?]+ | none</td><td>none</td><td>All</td><td>No</td></tr>
<tr><td>counter-increment</td><td>[<identifier> <integer>?]+ | none</td><td>none</td><td>All</td><td>No</td></tr>
<tr><td>marker-offset</td><td><length> | auto</td><td>auto</td><td>Elements with the display property set to marker</td><td>No</td></tr>
<tr><td>list-style-type</td><td>disc | circle | square | decimal | decimal-leading-zero | lower-roman | upper-roman | lower-greek | lower-alpha | upper-alpha | none | lower-latin | upper-latin | hebrew | armenian | georgian | cjk-ideographic | hiragana | katakana | hiragana-iroha | katakana-iroha</td><td>disc</td><td>Elements with the display property set to list-item</td><td>Yes</td></tr>
<tr><td>list-style-image</td><td><uri> | none</td><td>none</td><td>List-items</td><td>Yes</td></tr>
<tr><td>list-style-position</td><td>inside | outside</td><td>outside</td><td>List-items</td><td>Yes</td></tr>
<tr><td>list-style</td><td><list-style-type> || <list-style-position> || <list-style-image></td><td>Undefined</td><td>List-items</td><td>Yes</td></tr>
</table>

Paged Media

All the following paged media properties are new to CSS2 and are covered in Section 13 of the specification.

Property Name	Possible Values	Initial Value	Applies to	Inherited
`size`	`<length>{1, 2}	auto	portrait	landscape`	`auto`	Page context	N/A
`marks` (crop marks)	`[crop		cross]	none`	`none`	Page context	N/A
`page-break-before`	`auto	always	avoid	left	right`	`auto`	Block-level elements	No
`page-break-after`	`auto	always	avoid	left	right`	`auto`	Block-level elements	No
`page-break-inside`	`avoid	auto`	`auto`	Block-level elements	Yes
`page` (for using named pages)	`<identifier>	auto`	`auto`	Block level elements	Yes
`orphans`	`<integer>`	2	Block-level elements	Yes
`widows`	`<integer>`	2	Block-level elements	Yes

Colors and Backgrounds

These properties (which are unchanged from CSS1) are in Section 12 of the CSS2 specification.

<table>
<tr><th>Property Name</th><th>Possible Values</th><th>Initial Value</th><th>Applies to</th><th>Inherited</th></tr>
<tr><td>color</td><td>keyword | numerical RGB specification</td><td>Depends on user agent</td><td>All</td><td>Yes</td></tr>
<tr><td>background-color</td><td><color> | transparent</td><td>transparent</td><td>All</td><td>No</td></tr>
<tr><td>background-image</td><td><uri> | none</td><td>none</td><td>All</td><td>No</td></tr>
<tr><td>background-repeat</td><td>repeat | repeat-x | repeat-y | no-repeat</td><td>repeat</td><td>All</td><td>No</td></tr>
<tr><td>background-attachment</td><td>scroll | fixed</td><td>scroll</td><td>All</td><td>No</td></tr>
<tr><td>background-position</td><td>[[<length> | <percentage>]{1,2} | [top | center | bottom] || [left | center | right]]</td><td>0%, 0%</td><td>Block and replaced elements</td><td>No</td></tr>
<tr><td>background</td><td>[<background-color> || <background-image> || <background-repeat> || <background-attachment> || <background-position>]</td><td>Undefined</td><td>All</td><td>No</td></tr>
</table>

Font Properties

These properties are unchanged in CSS2 from CSS1, and are covered in Section 15 of the specification.

<table>
<tr><th>Property Name</th><th>Possible Values</th><th>Initial Value</th><th>Applies to</th><th>Inherited</th></tr>
<tr><td>font-family</td><td>[[<family-name> | <generic-family>],]* [<family-name> | <generic-family>]
Use any font family name.
<generic-family> values are:
serif
sans-serif
cursive
fantasy
monospace</td><td>Depends on user agent</td><td>All</td><td>Yes</td></tr>
<tr><td>font-style</td><td>normal | italic | oblique</td><td>normal</td><td>All</td><td>Yes</td></tr>
<tr><td>font-variant</td><td>normal | smallcaps</td><td>normal</td><td>All</td><td>Yes</td></tr>
<tr><td>font-weight</td><td>normal | bold | bolder | lighter | 100 | 200 | 300 | 400 | 500 | 600 | 700 | 800 | 900</td><td>normal</td><td>All</td><td>Yes</td></tr>
<tr><td>font-stretch</td><td>normal | wider | narrower | ultra-condensed | extra-condensed | condensed | semi-condensed | semi-expanded | expanded | extra-expanded | ultra-expanded</td><td>normal</td><td>All</td><td>Yes</td></tr>
</table>

<table>
<tr><td>'font-size'</td><td><absolute-size> | <relative-size> | <length> | <percentage>

<absolute-size>:
xx-small | x-small | small | medium | large | x-large | xx-large

<relative-size>:
larger | smaller

<percentage>:
In relation to parent element</td><td>medium</td><td>All</td><td>Yes</td></tr>
<tr><td>font-size-adjust</td><td><number> | none</td><td>none</td><td>All</td><td>Yes</td></tr>
<tr><td>font</td><td>[[<font-style> || <font-variant> || <font-weight>]? <font-size> [/<line-height>]? <font-family>] | caption | icon | menu | message-box | small-caption | status-bar</td><td>Undefined</td><td>All</td><td>Yes</td></tr>
</table>

Text Properties

The text properties are covered in Section 16 of the CSS2 specification.

<table>
<tr><th>Property Name</th><th>Possible Values</th><th>Initial Value</th><th>Applies to</th><th>Inherited</th></tr>
<tr><td>text-indent</td><td><length> | <percentage></td><td>0</td><td>Block elements</td><td>Yes</td></tr>
<tr><td>text-align</td><td>left | right | center | justify | <string></td><td>Depends on user agent and writing direction</td><td>Block elements</td><td>Yes</td></tr>
<tr><td>text-decoration</td><td>none | [underline || overline || line-through || blink]</td><td>none</td><td>All</td><td>No</td></tr>
<tr><td>text-shadow</td><td>none | [<color> || <length> <length> <length>? ,]* [<color> || <length> <length> <length>?]</td><td>none</td><td>All</td><td>No</td></tr>
<tr><td>letter-spacing</td><td>normal | <length></td><td>normal</td><td>All</td><td>Yes</td></tr>
<tr><td>word-spacing</td><td>normal | <length></td><td>normal</td><td>All</td><td>Yes</td></tr>
<tr><td>text-transform</td><td>none | capitalize | uppercase | lowercase</td><td>none</td><td>All</td><td>Yes</td></tr>
<tr><td>white-space</td><td>normal | pre | nowrap</td><td>normal</td><td>Block elements</td><td>Yes</td></tr>
</table>

Tables

All the `table` properties are new to CSS2 and can be found in Section 17 of the specification.

<table>
<tr><th>Property Name</th><th>Possible Values</th><th>Initial Value</th><th>Applies to</th><th>Inherited</th></tr>
<tr><td>caption-side</td><td>top | bottom | left | right</td><td>top</td><td>Table-caption elements</td><td>Yes</td></tr>
<tr><td>border-collapse</td><td>collapse | separate</td><td>collapse</td><td>Table and in-line-table elements</td><td>Yes</td></tr>
<tr><td>border-spacing</td><td><length> <length></td><td>0</td><td>Table and in-line-table elements</td><td>yes</td></tr>
<tr><td>table-layout</td><td>fixed | auto</td><td>auto</td><td>Table and in-line-table elements</td><td>No</td></tr>
<tr><td>empty-cells</td><td>show | hide</td><td>show</td><td>Table-cell elements</td><td>Yes</td></tr>
<tr><td>speak-header</td><td>once | always</td><td>once</td><td>Elements that have header information</td><td>Yes</td></tr>
</table>

User Interface

The user interface properties are new to CSS2 and can be found in Section 18 of the specification.

<table>
<tr><th>Property Name</th><th>Possible Values</th><th>Initial Value</th><th>Applies to</th><th>Inherited</th></tr>
<tr><td>cursor</td><td>[[<uri>,]* [auto | crosshair | default | pointer | move | e-resize | ne-resize | nw-resize | n-resize | se-resize | sw-resize | s-resize | w-resize| text | wait | help]]</td><td>auto</td><td>All</td><td>Yes</td></tr>
<tr><td>outline</td><td><outline-color> || <outline-style> || <outline-width></td><td>See individual properties</td><td>All</td><td>No</td></tr>
<tr><td>outline-width</td><td>border-width</td><td>medium</td><td>All</td><td>No</td></tr>
<tr><td>outline-style</td><td>border-style</td><td>none</td><td>All</td><td>No</td></tr>
<tr><td>outline-color</td><td>border-color | invert</td><td>invert</td><td>All</td><td>No</td></tr>
</table>

Aural Style Sheets

These are a new addition in CSS2 and can be seen in further detail in Section 19 of the specification.

<table>
<tr><th>Property Name</th><th>Possible Values</th><th>Initial Value</th><th>Applies to</th><th>Inherited</th></tr>
<tr><td>volume</td><td><number> | <percentage> | silent | x-soft | soft | medium | loud | x-loud</td><td>medium</td><td>All</td><td>Yes</td></tr>
<tr><td>speak</td><td>normal | none | spell-out</td><td>normal</td><td>All</td><td>Yes</td></tr>
<tr><td>pause-before</td><td><time> | <percentage></td><td>Depends on user agent</td><td>All</td><td>No</td></tr>
<tr><td>pause-after</td><td><time> | <percentage></td><td>Depends on user agent</td><td>All</td><td>No</td></tr>
<tr><td>pause</td><td>[[<time> | <percentage>] {1, 2}]</td><td>Depends on user agent</td><td>All</td><td>No</td></tr>
<tr><td>cue-before</td><td><uri> | none</td><td>none</td><td>All</td><td>No</td></tr>
<tr><td>cue-after</td><td><uri> | none</td><td>none</td><td>All</td><td>No</td></tr>
<tr><td>cue</td><td>[<cue-before> || <cue-after>]</td><td>Undefined</td><td>All</td><td>No</td></tr>
<tr><td>play-during</td><td><uri> mix? repeat? | auto | none</td><td>auto</td><td>All</td><td>No</td></tr>
<tr><td>azimuth</td><td><angle> | [[left-side | far-left | left | center-left | center | center-right | right | far-right | right-side] || behind] | leftwards | rightwards</td><td>center</td><td>All</td><td>Yes</td></tr>
</table>

<table>
<tr><th>Property Name</th><th>Possible Values</th><th>Initial Value</th><th>Applies to</th><th>Inherited</th></tr>
<tr><td>elevation</td><td><angle> | below | level | above | higher | lower</td><td>level</td><td>All</td><td>Yes</td></tr>
<tr><td>speech-rate</td><td><number> | x-slow | slow | medium | fast | x-fast | faster | slower</td><td>medium</td><td>All</td><td>Yes</td></tr>
<tr><td>voice-family</td><td>[[<specific-voice> | <generic-voice>],]* [<specific-voice> | <generic-voice>]</td><td>Depends on user agent</td><td>All</td><td>Yes</td></tr>
<tr><td>pitch</td><td><frequency> | x-low | low | medium | high | x-high</td><td>medium</td><td>All</td><td>Yes</td></tr>
<tr><td>pitch-range</td><td><number></td><td>50</td><td>All</td><td>Yes</td></tr>
<tr><td>stress</td><td><number></td><td>50</td><td>All</td><td>Yes</td></tr>
<tr><td>richness</td><td><number></td><td>50</td><td>All</td><td>Yes</td></tr>
<tr><td>speak-punctuation</td><td>code | none</td><td>none</td><td>All</td><td>Yes</td></tr>
<tr><td>speak-numeral</td><td>digits | continuous</td><td>continuous</td><td>All</td><td>Yes</td></tr>
</table>

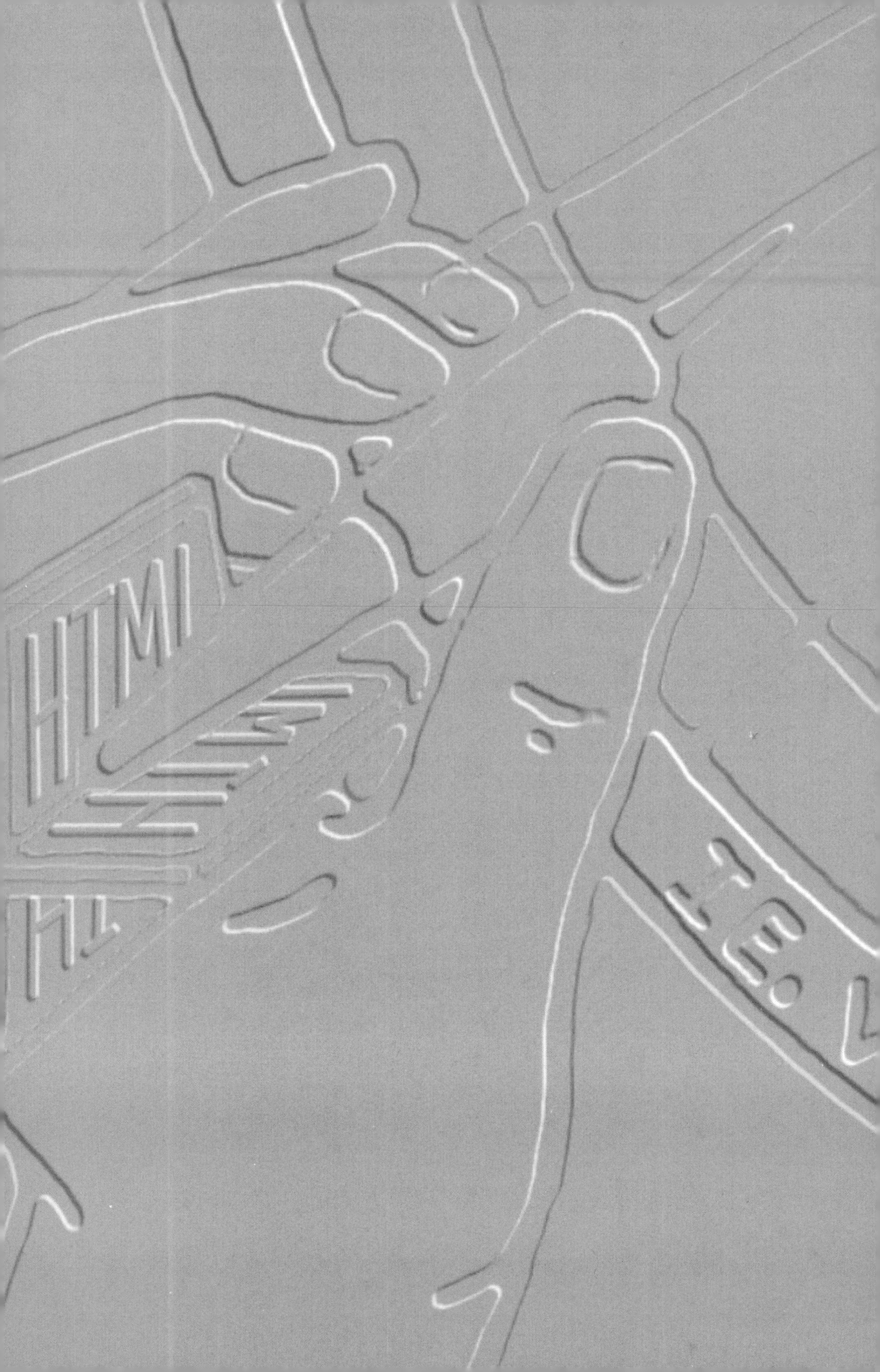

HTML Color Names and Values

Colors Sorted by Name

Color Name	Value	IE5 Color Constant
aliceblue	F0F8FF	htmlAliceBlue
antiquewhite	FAEBD7	htmlAntiqueWhite
aqua	00FFFF	htmlAqua
aquamarine	7FFFD4	htmlAquamarine
azure	F0FFFF	htmlAzure
beige	F5F5DC	htmlBeige
bisque	FFE4C4	htmlBisque
black	000000	htmlBlack
blanchedalmond	FFEBCD	htmlBlanchedAlmond
blue	0000FF	htmlBlue
blueviolet	8A2BE2	htmlBlueViolet
brown	A52A2A	htmlBrown
burlywood	DEB887	htmlBurlywood
cadetblue	5F9EA0	htmlCadetBlue

Table Continued on Following Page

Color Name	Value	IE5 Color Constant
chartreuse	7FFF00	htmlChartreuse
chocolate	D2691E	htmlChocolate
coral	FF7F50	htmlCoral
cornflowerblue	6495ED	htmlCornflowerBlue
cornsilk	FFF8DC	htmlCornsilk
crimson	DC143C	htmlCrimson
cyan	00FFFF	htmlCyan
darkblue	00008B	htmlDarkBlue
darkcyan	008B8B	htmlDarkCyan
darkgoldenrod	B8860B	htmlDarkGoldenRod
darkgray	A9A9A9	htmlDarkGray
darkgreen	006400	htmlDarkGreen
darkkhaki	BDB76B	htmlDarkKhaki
darkmagenta	8B008B	htmlDarkMagenta
darkolivegreen	556B2F	htmlDarkOliveGreen
darkorange	FF8C00	htmlDarkOrange
darkorchid	9932CC	htmlDarkOrchid
darkred	8B0000	htmlDarkRed
darksalmon	E9967A	htmlDarkSalmon
darkseagreen	8FBC8F	htmlDarkSeaGreen
darkslateblue	483D8B	htmlDarkSlateBlue
darkslategray	2F4F4F	htmlDarkSlateGray
darkturquoise	00CED1	htmlDarkTurquoise
darkviolet	9400D3	htmlDarkViolet
deeppink	FF1493	htmlDeepPink
deepskyblue	00BFFF	htmlDeepSkyBlue
dimgray	696969	htmlDimGray
dodgerblue	1E90FF	htmlDodgerBlue
firebrick	B22222	htmlFirebrick

Color Name	Value	IE5 Color Constant
floralwhite	FFFAF0	htmlFloralWhite
forestgreen	228B22	htmlForestGreen
fuchsia	FF00FF	htmlFuchsia
gainsboro	DCDCDC	htmlGainsboro
ghostwhite	F8F8FF	htmlGhostWhite
gold	FFD700	htmlGold
goldenrod	DAA520	htmlGoldenRod
gray	808080	htmlGray
green	008000	htmlGreen
greenyellow	ADFF2F	htmlGreenYellow
honeydew	F0FFF0	htmlHoneydew
hotpink	FF69B4	htmlHotPink
indianred	CD5C5C	htmlIndianRed
indigo	4B0082	htmlIndigo
ivory	FFFFF0	htmlIvory
khaki	F0E68C	htmlKhaki
lavender	E6E6FA	htmlLavender
lavenderblush	FFF0F5	htmlLavenderBlush
lawngreen	7CFC00	htmlLawnGreen
lemonchiffon	FFFACD	htmlLemonChiffon
lightblue	ADD8E6	htmlLightBlue
lightcoral	F08080	htmlLightCoral
lightcyan	E0FFFF	htmlLightCyan
Lightgoldenrod yellow	FAFAD2	HtmlLightGoldenrod Yellow
lightgreen	90EE90	htmlLightGreen
lightgrey	D3D3D3	htmlLightGrey
lightpink	FFB6C1	htmlLightPink
lightsalmon	FFA07A	htmlLightSalmon

Table Continued on Following Page

Color Name	Value	IE5 Color Constant
lightseagreen	20B2AA	htmlLightSeaGreen
lightskyblue	87CEFA	htmlLightSkyBlue
lightslategray	778899	htmlLightSlateGray
lightsteelblue	B0C4DE	htmlLightSteelBlue
lightyellow	FFFFE0	htmlLightYellow
lime	00FF00	htmlLime
limegreen	32CD32	htmlLimeGreen
linen	FAF0E6	htmlLinen
magenta	FF00FF	htmlMagenta
maroon	800000	htmlMaroon
mediumaquamarine	66CDAA	HtmlMedium Aquamarine
mediumblue	0000CD	htmlMediumBlue
mediumorchid	BA55D3	htmlMediumOrchid
mediumpurple	9370DB	htmlMediumPurple
mediumseagreen	3CB371	htmlMediumSeaGreen
mediumslateblue	7B68EE	htmlMediumSlateBlue
mediumspringgreen	00FA9A	HtmlMediumSpring Green
mediumturquoise	48D1CC	htmlMediumTurquoise
mediumvioletred	C71585	htmlMediumVioletRed
midnightblue	191970	htmlMidnightBlue
mintcream	F5FFFA	htmlMintCream
mistyrose	FFE4E1	htmlMistyRose
moccasin	FFE4B5	htmlMoccasin
navajowhite	FFDEAD	htmlNavajoWhite
navy	000080	htmlNavy
oldlace	FDF5E6	htmlOldLace
olive	808000	htmlOlive
olivedrab	6B8E23	htmlOliveDrab
orange	FFA500	htmlOrange

Color Name	Value	IE5 Color Constant
orangered	FF4500	htmlOrangeRed
orchid	DA70D6	htmlOrchid
palegoldenrod	EEE8AA	htmlPaleGoldenRod
palegreen	98FB98	htmlPaleGreen
paleturquoise	AFEEEE	htmlPaleTurquoise
palevioletred	DB7093	htmlPaleVioletRed
papayawhip	FFEFD5	htmlPapayaWhip
peachpuff	FFDAB9	htmlPeachPuff
peru	CD853F	htmlPeru
pink	FFC0CB	htmlPink
plum	DDA0DD	htmlPlum
powderblue	B0E0E6	htmlPowderBlue
purple	800080	htmlPurple
red	FF0000	htmlRed
rosybrown	BC8F8F	htmlRosyBrown
royalblue	4169E1	htmlRoyalBlue
saddlebrown	8B4513	htmlSaddleBrown
salmon	FA8072	htmlSalmon
sandybrown	F4A460	htmlSandyBrown
seagreen	2E8B57	htmlSeaGreen
seashell	FFF5EE	htmlSeashell
sienna	A0522D	htmlSienna
silver	C0C0C0	htmlSilver
skyblue	87CEEB	htmlSkyBlue
slateblue	6A5ACD	htmlSlateBlue
slategray	708090	htmlSlateGray
snow	FFFAFA	htmlSnow
springgreen	00FF7F	htmlSpringGreen
steelblue	4682B4	htmlSteelBlue

Table Continued on Following Page

Color Name	Value	IE5 Color Constant
tan	D2B48C	htmlTan
teal	008080	htmlTeal
thistle	D8BFD8	htmlThistle
tomato	FF6347	htmlTomato
turquoise	40E0D0	htmlTurquoise
violet	EE82EE	htmlViolet
wheat	F5DEB3	htmlWheat
white	FFFFFF	htmlWhite
whitesmoke	F5F5F5	htmlWhiteSmoke
yellow	FFFF00	htmlYellow
yellowgreen	9ACD32	htmlYellowGreen

Colors Sorted by Group

Color Name	Value	IE5 Color Constant
Blues		
azure	F0FFFF	htmlAzure
aliceblue	F0F8FF	htmlAliceBlue
lavender	E6E6FA	htmlLavender
lightcyan	E0FFFF	htmlLightCyan
powderblue	B0E0E6	htmlPowderBlue
lightsteelblue	B0C4DE	htmlLightSteelBlue
paleturquoise	AFEEEE	htmlPaleTurquoise
lightblue	ADD8E6	htmlLightBlue
blueviolet	8A2BE2	htmlBlueViolet
lightskyblue	87CEFA	htmlLightSkyBlue
skyblue	87CEEB	htmlSkyBlue

Color Name	Value	IE5 Color Constant
mediumslateblue	7B68EE	htmlMediumSlateBlue
slateblue	6A5ACD	htmlSlateBlue
cornflowerblue	6495ED	htmlCornflowerBlue
cadetblue	5F9EA0	htmlCadetBlue
indigo	4B0082	htmlIndigo
mediumturquoise	48D1CC	htmlMediumTurquoise
darkslateblue	483D8B	htmlDarkSlateBlue
steelblue	4682B4	htmlSteelBlue
royalblue	4169E1	htmlRoyalBlue
turquoise	40E0D0	htmlTurquoise
dodgerblue	1E90FF	htmlDodgerBlue
midnightblue	191970	htmlMidnightBlue
aqua	00FFFF	htmlAqua
cyan	00FFFF	htmlCyan
darkturquoise	00CED1	htmlDarkTurquoise
deepskyblue	00BFFF	htmlDeepSkyBlue
darkcyan	008B8B	htmlDarkCyan
blue	0000FF	htmlBlue
mediumblue	0000CD	htmlMediumBlue
darkblue	00008B	htmlDarkBlue
navy	000080	htmlNavy
Greens		
mintcream	F5FFFA	htmlMintCream
honeydew	F0FFF0	htmlHoneydew
greenyellow	ADFF2F	htmlGreenYellow
yellowgreen	9ACD32	htmlYellowGreen
palegreen	98FB98	htmlPaleGreen
lightgreen	90EE90	htmlLightGreen

Table Continued on Following Page

Color Name	Value	IE5 Color Constant
darkseagreen	8FBC8F	htmlDarkSeaGreen
olive	808000	htmlOlive
aquamarine	7FFFD4	htmlAquamarine
chartreuse	7FFF00	htmlChartreuse
lawngreen	7CFC00	htmlLawnGreen
olivedrab	6B8E23	htmlOliveDrab
mediumaquamarine	66CDAA	HtmlMedium Aquamarine
darkolivegreen	556B2F	htmlDarkOliveGreen
mediumseagreen	3CB371	htmlMediumSeaGreen
limegreen	32CD32	htmlLimeGreen
seagreen	2E8B57	htmlSeaGreen
forestgreen	228B22	htmlForestGreen
lightseagreen	20B2AA	htmlLightSeaGreen
springgreen	00FF7F	htmlSpringGreen
lime	00FF00	htmlLime
Mediumspring green	00FA9A	HtmlMediumSpring Green
teal	008080	htmlTeal
green	008000	htmlGreen
darkgreen	006400	htmlDarkGreen
Pinks and Reds		
lavenderblush	FFF0F5	htmlLavenderBlush
mistyrose	FFE4E1	htmlMistyRose
pink	FFC0CB	htmlPink
lightpink	FFB6C1	htmlLightPink
orange	FFA500	htmlOrange
lightsalmon	FFA07A	htmlLightSalmon
darkorange	FF8C00	htmlDarkOrange
coral	FF7F50	htmlCoral

Color Name	Value	IE5 Color Constant
hotpink	FF69B4	htmlHotPink
tomato	FF6347	htmlTomato
orangered	FF4500	htmlOrangeRed
deeppink	FF1493	htmlDeepPink
fuchsia	FF00FF	htmlFuchsia
magenta	FF00FF	htmlMagenta
red	FF0000	htmlRed
salmon	FA8072	htmlSalmon
lightcoral	F08080	htmlLightCoral
violet	EE82EE	htmlViolet
darksalmon	E9967A	htmlDarkSalmon
plum	DDA0DD	htmlPlum
crimson	DC143C	htmlCrimson
palevioletred	DB7093	htmlPaleVioletRed
orchid	DA70D6	htmlOrchid
thistle	D8BFD8	htmlThistle
indianred	CD5C5C	htmlIndianRed
mediumvioletred	C71585	htmlMediumVioletRed
mediumorchid	BA55D3	htmlMediumOrchid
firebrick	B22222	htmlFirebrick
darkorchid	9932CC	htmlDarkOrchid
darkviolet	9400D3	htmlDarkViolet
mediumpurple	9370DB	htmlMediumPurple
darkmagenta	8B008B	htmlDarkMagenta
darkred	8B0000	htmlDarkRed
purple	800080	htmlPurple
maroon	800000	htmlMaroon

Table Continued on Following Page

Color Name	Value	IE5 Color Constant
Yellows		
lightgoldenrod yellow	FAFAD2	HtmlLightGoldenRod Yellow
ivory	FFFFF0	htmlIvory
lightyellow	FFFFE0	htmlLightYellow
yellow	FFFF00	htmlYellow
floralwhite	FFFAF0	htmlFloralWhite
lemonchiffon	FFFACD	htmlLemonChiffon
cornsilk	FFF8DC	htmlCornsilk
gold	FFD700	htmlGold
khaki	F0E68C	htmlKhaki
darkkhaki	BDB76B	htmlDarkKhaki
Beiges and Browns		
snow	FFFAFA	htmlSnow
seashell	FFF5EE	htmlSeashell
papayawhite	FFEFD5	htmlPapayaWhite
blanchedalmond	FFEBCD	htmlBlanchedAlmond
bisque	FFE4C4	htmlBisque
moccasin	FFE4B5	htmlMoccasin
navajowhite	FFDEAD	htmlNavajoWhite
peachpuff	FFDAB9	htmlPeachPuff
oldlace	FDF5E6	htmlOldLace
linen	FAF0E6	htmlLinen
antiquewhite	FAEBD7	htmlAntiqueWhite
beige	F5F5DC	htmlBeige
wheat	F5DEB3	htmlWheat
sandybrown	F4A460	htmlSandyBrown
palegoldenrod	EEE8AA	htmlPaleGoldenRod

Color Name	Value	IE5 Color Constant
burlywood	DEB887	htmlBurlywood
goldenrod	DAA520	htmlGoldenRod
tan	D2B48C	htmlTan
chocolate	D2691E	htmlChocolate
peru	CD853F	htmlPeru
rosybrown	BC8F8F	htmlRosyBrown
darkgoldenrod	B8860B	htmlDarkGoldenRod
brown	A52A2A	htmlBrown
sienna	A0522D	htmlSienna
saddlebrown	8B4513	htmlSaddleBrown
Whites and Grays		
white	FFFFFF	htmlWhite
ghostwhite	F8F8FF	htmlGhostWhite
whitesmoke	F5F5F5	htmlWhiteSmoke
gainsboro	DCDCDC	htmlGainsboro
lightgrey	D3D3D3	htmlLightGrey
silver	C0C0C0	htmlSilver
darkgray	A9A9A9	htmlDarkGray
gray	808080	htmlGray
lightslategray	778899	htmlLightSlateGray
slategray	708090	htmlSlateGray
dimgray	696969	htmlDimGray
darkslategray	2F4F4F	htmlDarkSlateGray
black	000000	htmlBlack

Colors Sorted by Depth

Color Name	Value	IE5 Color Constant
white	FFFFFF	htmlWhite
ivory	FFFFF0	htmlIvory
lightyellow	FFFFE0	htmlLightYellow
yellow	FFFF00	htmlYellow
snow	FFFAFA	htmlSnow
floralwhite	FFFAF0	htmlFloralWhite
lemonchiffon	FFFACD	htmlLemonChiffon
cornsilk	FFF8DC	htmlCornsilk
seashell	FFF5EE	htmlSeashell
lavenderblush	FFF0F5	htmlLavenderBlush
papayawhip	FFEFD5	htmlPapayaWhip
blanchedalmond	FFEBCD	htmlBlanchedAlmond
mistyrose	FFE4E1	htmlMistyRose
bisque	FFE4C4	htmlBisque
moccasin	FFE4B5	htmlMoccasin
navajowhite	FFDEAD	htmlNavajoWhite
peachpuff	FFDAB9	htmlPeachPuff
gold	FFD700	htmlGold
pink	FFC0CB	htmlPink
lightpink	FFB6C1	htmlLightPink
orange	FFA500	htmlOrange
lightsalmon	FFA07A	htmlLightSalmon
darkorange	FF8C00	htmlDarkOrange
coral	FF7F50	htmlCoral
hotpink	FF69B4	htmlHotPink
tomato	FF6347	htmlTomato
orangered	FF4500	htmlOrangeRed

Color Name	Value	IE5 Color Constant
deeppink	FF1493	htmlDeepPink
fuchsia	FF00FF	htmlFuchsia
magenta	FF00FF	htmlMagenta
red	FF0000	htmlRed
oldlace	FDF5E6	htmlOldLace
Lightgoldenrod yellow	FAFAD2	HtmlLightGoldenrod Yellow
linen	FAF0E6	htmlLinen
antiquewhite	FAEBD7	htmlAntiqueWhite
salmon	FA8072	htmlSalmon
ghostwhite	F8F8FF	htmlGhostWhite
mintcream	F5FFFA	htmlMintCream
whitesmoke	F5F5F5	htmlWhiteSmoke
beige	F5F5DC	htmlBeige
wheat	F5DEB3	htmlWheat
sandybrown	F4A460	htmlSandyBrown
azure	F0FFFF	htmlAzure
honeydew	F0FFF0	htmlHoneydew
aliceblue	F0F8FF	htmlAliceBlue
khaki	F0E68C	htmlKhaki
lightcoral	F08080	htmlLightCoral
palegoldenrod	EEE8AA	htmlPaleGoldenRod
violet	EE82EE	htmlViolet
darksalmon	E9967A	htmlDarkSalmon
lavender	E6E6FA	htmlLavender
lightcyan	E0FFFF	htmlLightCyan
burlywood	DEB887	htmlBurlywood
plum	DDA0DD	htmlPlum
gainsboro	DCDCDC	htmlGainsboro

Table Continued on Following Page

Color Name	Value	IE5 Color Constant
crimson	DC143C	htmlCrimson
palevioletred	DB7093	htmlPaleVioletRed
goldenrod	DAA520	htmlGoldenRod
orchid	DA70D6	htmlOrchid
thistle	D8BFD8	htmlThistle
lightgrey	D3D3D3	htmlLightGrey
tan	D2B48C	htmlTan
chocolate	D2691E	htmlChocolate
peru	CD853F	htmlPeru
indianred	CD5C5C	htmlIndianRed
mediumvioletred	C71585	htmlMediumVioletRed
silver	C0C0C0	htmlSilver
darkkhaki	BDB76B	htmlDarkKhaki
rosybrown	BC8F8F	htmlRosyBrown
mediumorchid	BA55D3	htmlMediumOrchid
darkgoldenrod	B8860B	htmlDarkGoldenRod
firebrick	B22222	htmlFirebrick
powderblue	B0E0E6	htmlPowderBlue
lightsteelblue	B0C4DE	htmlLightSteelBlue
paleturquoise	AFEEEE	htmlPaleTurquoise
greenyellow	ADFF2F	htmlGreenYellow
lightblue	ADD8E6	htmlLightBlue
darkgray	A9A9A9	htmlDarkGray
brown	A52A2A	htmlBrown
sienna	A0522D	htmlSienna
yellowgreen	9ACD32	htmlYellowGreen
darkorchid	9932CC	htmlDarkOrchid
palegreen	98FB98	htmlPaleGreen
darkviolet	9400D3	htmlDarkViolet
mediumpurple	9370DB	htmlMediumPurple

Color Name	Value	IE5 Color Constant
lightgreen	90EE90	htmlLightGreen
darkseagreen	8FBC8F	htmlDarkSeaGreen
saddlebrown	8B4513	htmlSaddleBrown
darkmagenta	8B008B	htmlDarkMagenta
darkred	8B0000	htmlDarkRed
blueviolet	8A2BE2	htmlBlueViolet
lightskyblue	87CEFA	htmlLightSkyBlue
skyblue	87CEEB	htmlSkyBlue
gray	808080	htmlGray
olive	808000	htmlOlive
purple	800080	htmlPurple
maroon	800000	htmlMaroon
aquamarine	7FFFD4	htmlAquamarine
chartreuse	7FFF00	htmlChartreuse
lawngreen	7CFC00	htmlLawnGreen
mediumslateblue	7B68EE	htmlMediumSlateBlue
lightslategray	778899	htmlLightSlateGray
slategray	708090	htmlSlateGray
olivedrab	6B8E23	htmlOliveDrab
slateblue	6A5ACD	htmlSlateBlue
dimgray	696969	htmlDimGray
mediumaquamarine	66CDAA	HtmlMedium Aquamarine
cornflowerblue	6495ED	htmlCornflowerBlue
cadetblue	5F9EA0	htmlCadetBlue
darkolivegreen	556B2F	htmlDarkOliveGreen
indigo	4B0082	htmlIndigo
mediumturquoise	48D1CC	htmlMediumTurquoise
darkslateblue	483D8B	htmlDarkSlateBlue
steelblue	4682B4	htmlSteelBlue

Table Continued on Following Page

Color Name	Value	IE5 Color Constant
royalblue	4169E1	htmlRoyalBlue
turquoise	40E0D0	htmlTurquoise
mediumseagreen	3CB371	htmlMediumSeaGreen
limegreen	32CD32	htmlLimeGreen
darkslategray	2F4F4F	htmlDarkSlateGray
seagreen	2E8B57	htmlSeaGreen
forestgreen	228B22	htmlForestGreen
lightseagreen	20B2AA	htmlLightSeaGreen
dodgerblue	1E90FF	htmlDodgerBlue
midnightblue	191970	htmlMidnightBlue
aqua	00FFFF	htmlAqua
cyan	00FFFF	htmlCyan
springgreen	00FF7F	htmlSpringGreen
lime	00FF00	htmlLime
Mediumspring green	00FA9A	HtmlMediumSpring Green
darkturquoise	00CED1	htmlDarkTurquoise
deepskyblue	00BFFF	htmlDeepSkyBlue
darkcyan	008B8B	htmlDarkCyan
teal	008080	htmlTeal
green	008000	htmlGreen
darkgreen	006400	htmlDarkGreen
blue	0000FF	htmlBlue
mediumblue	0000CD	htmlMediumBlue
darkblue	00008B	htmlDarkBlue
navy	000080	htmlNavy
black	000000	htmlBlack

Special Characters in HTML

The following table gives you the codes you need to display special characters in your HTML documents. You can insert a character by using its decimal code or the mnemonic name – for example, the registered trademark character can be written in HTML as `®` or `®`.

Character	Decimal Code	HTML	Description
"	`"`	`"`	Quotation mark
&	`&`	`&`	Ampersand
<	`<`	`<`	Less than
>	`>`	`>`	Greater than
	` `	` `	Non-breaking space
¡	`¡`	`¡`	Inverted exclamation
¢	`¢`	`¢`	Cent sign
£	`£`	`£`	Pound sterling
¤	`¤`	`¤`	General currency sign
¥	`¥`	`¥`	Yen sign
¦	`¦`	`¦`	Broken vertical bar
§	`§`	`§`	Section sign
¨	`¨`	`¨`	Diæresis/umlaut

Table Continued on Following Page

Character	Decimal Code	HTML	Description
©	©	©	Copyright
ª	ª	ª	Feminine ordinal
«	«	«	Left angle quote,
¬	¬	¬	Not sign
-			Soft hyphen
®	®	®	Registered trademark
¯	¯	¯	Macron accent
°	°	°	Degree sign
±	±	±	Plus or minus
²	²	²	Superscript two
³	³	³	Superscript three
´	´	´	Acute accent
µ	µ	µ	Micro sign
¶	¶	¶	Paragraph sign
·	·	·	Middle dot
¸	¸	¸	Cedilla
¹	¹	¹	Superscript one
º	º	º	Masculine ordinal
»	»	»	Right angle quote
¼	¼	¼	Fraction one quarter
½	½	½	Fraction one half
¾	¾	¾	Fraction three-quarters
¿	¿	¿	Inverted question mark
À	À	À	Capital A, grave accent
Á	Á	Á	Capital A, acute accent
Â	Â	Â	Capital A, circumflex
Ã	Ã	Ã	Capital A, tilde
Ä	Ä	Ä	Capital A, diæresis/umlaut

Character	Decimal Code	HTML	Description
Å	Å	Å	Capital A, ring
Æ	Æ	Æ	Capital AE, ligature
Ç	Ç	Ç	Capital C, cedilla
È	È	È	Capital E, grave accent
É	É	É	Capital E, acute accent
Ê	Ê	Ê	Capital E, circumflex
Ë	Ë	Ë	Capital E, diæresis/umlaut
Ì	Ì	Ì	Capital I, grave accent
Í	Í	Í	Capital I, acute accent
Î	Î	Î	Capital I, circumflex
Ï	Ï	Ï	Capital I, diæresis/umlaut
Ð	Ð	Ð	Capital Eth, Icelandic
Ñ	Ñ	Ñ	Capital N, tilde
Ò	Ò	Ò	Capital O, grave accent
Ó	Ó	Ó	Capital O, acute accent
Ô	Ô	Ô	Capital O, circumflex
Õ	Õ	Õ	Capital O, tilde
Ö	Ö	Ö	Capital O, diæresis/umlaut
×	×	×	Multiplication sign
Ø	Ø	Ø	Capital O, slash
Ù	Ù	Ù	Capital U, grave accent
Ú	Ú	Ú	Capital U, acute accent
Û	Û	Û	Capital U, circumflex
Ü	Ü	Ü	Capital U, diæresis/umlaut
Ý	Ý	Ý	Capital Y, acute accent
Þ	Þ	Þ	Capital Thorn, Icelandic

Table Continued on Following Page

Character	Decimal Code	HTML	Description
ß	`ß`	`ß`	German sz
à	`à`	`à`	Small a, grave accent
á	`á`	`á`	Small a, acute accent
â	`â`	`â`	Small a, circumflex
ã	`ã`	`ã`	Small a, tilde
ä	`ä`	`ä`	Small a, diæresis/umlaut
å	`å`	`å`	Small a, ring
æ	`æ`	`æ`	Small ae ligature
ç	`ç`	`ç`	Small c, cedilla
è	`è`	`è`	Small e, grave accent
é	`é`	`é`	Small e, acute accent
ê	`ê`	`ê`	Small e, circumflex
ë	`ë`	`ë`	Small e, diæresis/umlaut
ì	`ì`	`ì`	Small i, grave accent
í	`í`	`í`	Small i, acute accent
î	`î`	`î`	Small i, circumflex
ï	`ï`	`ï`	Small i, diæresis/umlaut
ð	`ð`	`ð`	Small eth, Icelandic
ñ	`ñ`	`ñ`	Small n, tilde
ò	`ò`	`ò`	Small o, grave accent
ó	`ó`	`ó`	Small o, acute accent
ô	`ô`	`ô`	Small o, circumflex
õ	`õ`	`õ`	Small o, tilde
ö	`ö`	`ö`	Small o, diæresis/umlaut
÷	`÷`	`÷`	Division sign
ø	`ø`	`ø`	Small o, slash
ù	`ù`	`ù`	Small u, grave accent
ú	`ú`	`ú`	Small u, acute accent

Character	Decimal Code	HTML	Description
û	`û`	`û`	Small u, circumflex
ü	`ü`	`ü`	Small u, diæresis/umlaut
ý	`ý`	`ý`	Small y, acute accent
þ	`þ`	`þ`	Small thorn, Icelandic
ÿ	`ÿ`	`ÿ`	Small y, diæresis/umlaut

Remember, if you want to show HTML code in a browser, you have to use the special character codes for the angled brackets in order to avoid the browser interpreting them as start and end of tags.

HTML

A Tutorial in VBScript

In this appendix, we'll walk through the fundamentals, and along the way you will learn how to add VBScript to your existing web pages, the structure of the VBScript language, and how to use **event-driven** programming within your HTML documents. There's a more detailed language VBScript reference section in Appendix I.

What is VBScript?

VBScript, Microsoft's Visual Basic Scripting Edition, is a scaled down version of Visual Basic. While it doesn't offer the full functionality of Visual Basic, it does provide a powerful, easy to learn tool that can be used to add interaction to your web pages. If you are already experienced in either Visual Basic or Visual Basic for Applications, you will find working with VBScript easy and should be immediately productive. Don't be concerned if you haven't worked in another version of Visual Basic. VBScript is easy to learn, even for the novice developer.

How to Use this Tutorial

This tutorial is a stand-alone introduction to VBScript. It is laid out in a series of five lessons. Each lesson introduces you to a new segment of the VBScript language. Along the way you will learn how to add calculations, formatting and validations to your web pages. At the end of each lesson is an exercise where you, the reader, get to try out your newly acquired knowledge by building web pages utilizing VBScript. The topics of the lessons are:

- **An Introduction to VBScript.** You will learn how to add VBScript into a web page, and different methods for linking scripts with HTML
- **Working with Variables.** What would any language be without variables? Here you learn how to define and use variables in your script routines
- **Using Objects with VBScript.** Java applets and ActiveX controls extend the HTML environment. In this lesson you will learn how to tie these objects together using VBScript

- **Controlling Your VBScript Routines.** Conditional statements (If...Then...Else, Select...Case) and looping (For...Next and Do...Loop) are the topic of this section
- **Using VBScript with Forms.** With VBScript you can validate forms before they are submitted. You see how in this final lesson

Step-by-Step Exercises

As mentioned above, each of the five lessons has a worked exercise, which demonstrates how to use the topics that were presented. Along the way you will find descriptions of each component of the example, so that by the end you will have a sound understanding of the lesson's topic.

A copy of the completed exercises can be found on the Wrox Press web site at http://webdev.wrox.co.uk/books/1746. Each lesson will have two or more completed examples that are referenced in the step-by-step instructions.

Lesson 1: Adding VBScript to Web Pages

Scripting languages like JScript and VBScript are designed as an extension to HTML. The web browser receives scripts along with the rest of the web document, and it is the browser's responsibility to parse and process the scripts. HTML was extended to include a tag that is used to incorporate scripts into HTML – the <SCRIPT> tag.

The <SCRIPT> Tag

You add scripts into your web pages within a pair of <SCRIPT> tags. The <SCRIPT> tag signifies the start of the script section, while </SCRIPT> marks the end. An example of this is shown below:

```
<HTML>
<HEAD>
<TITLE>Working With VBScript</TITLE>
<SCRIPT LANGUAGE="VBScript">
  MsgBox "Welcome to my Web page!"
</SCRIPT>
</HEAD>
</HTML>
```

The beginning <SCRIPT> tag includes a LANGUAGE argument that indicates the scripting language that will be used. The LANGUAGE argument is required because there is more than one scripting language. Without the LANGUAGE argument, a web browser would not know if the text between the tags was JavaScript, VBScript or another scripting language.

While technically you can place scripts throughout an HTML document using pairs of <SCRIPT> tags, scripts are typically found at either the top or bottom of a web document. This provides for easy reference and maintenance. Placing script at the top guarantees that the script is fully loaded before it needs to be called.

Handling Non-Supporting Browsers

Not all browsers support scripting languages. Some only support JavaScript. Only Microsoft's Internet Explorer supports VBScript. You might be wondering what happens to your scripts when non-supporting browsers encounter them. Usually, browsers will do what they do most frequently with text: they will display your scripts as part of the web page. Obviously, this isn't the result you had hoped for. One simple way to address this problem is to encase your scripts in comment tags (<!-- and -->). Below is our example script as it appears with the addition of the comment tags:

```
<HTML>
<HEAD>
<TITLE>Working With VBScript</TITLE>
<SCRIPT LANGUAGE="VBScript">
<!--
  MsgBox "Welcome to my Web page!"
-->
</SCRIPT>
</HEAD>
</HTML>
```

Now, when a browser that does not support VBScript processes this page, it will view your script as a comment and simply ignore it.

Exercise 1: Adding VBScript to a Web page

The easiest way to learn any language is to work with it. So let's get right into Exercise 1 and expose you to the process of using VBScript in your web pages. Just follow along with the step-by-step instructions to create your first script-enabled web page.

In this exercise, you will create an HTML document and add a simple script to respond to a click event generated by a command button. You will need to be familiar with creating and testing an HTML document. A completed copy of this part of the exercise can be found in the file `exer1_v1.htm`.

Part 1: Creating the HTML Document

1 Open up a text editor application and insert the following HTML code:

```
<HTML>
<HEAD>
<TITLE>Working With VBScript: Exercise 1</TITLE>
</HEAD>
<BODY>
  <H1>Your First VBScript Exercise</H1>
  <P> By utilizing VBScript you can give your web pages actions.
  Click on the button below to see what we mean. </P>
  <FORM NAME="frmExercise1">
    <INPUT TYPE="Button" NAME="cmdClickMe" VALUE="Click Me">
  </FORM>
</BODY>
</HTML>
```

2 Save the file and test it by loading it into Internet Explorer. The resulting page should be similar to the screenshot.
Try out the Click Me button. Does anything happen?

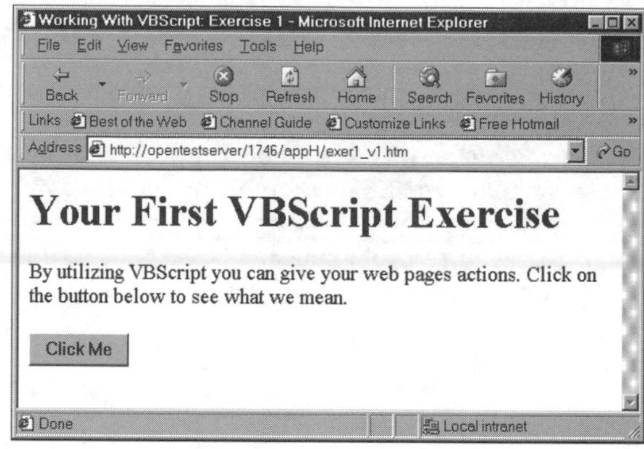

In the next part we will add a script to provide functionality for the Click Me command button. A completed copy of this part of the exercise can be found in the file `exer1_v2.htm`.

Part 2: Adding VBScript

3 Re-open the HTML document that you created in Part 1, if necessary. Modify the document adding the lines shown with shading below:

```
<HTML>
<HEAD>
<TITLE>Working With VBScript: Exercise 1</TITLE>
</HEAD>
<BODY>
  <H1>Your First VBScript Exercise</H1>
  <P> By utilizing VBScript you can give your Web pages actions.
  Click on the button below to see what we mean. </P>
  <FORM NAME="frmExercise1">
    <INPUT TYPE="Button" NAME="cmdClickMe" VALUE="Click Me">
    <SCRIPT FOR="cmdClickMe" EVENT="onClick" LANGUAGE="VBScript">
      MsgBox "A simple example of VBScript in action."
    </SCRIPT>
  </FORM>
</BODY>
</HTML>
```

4 Save the file and test it by loading it into Internet Explorer. Then try out the Click Me button. The result is shown here.

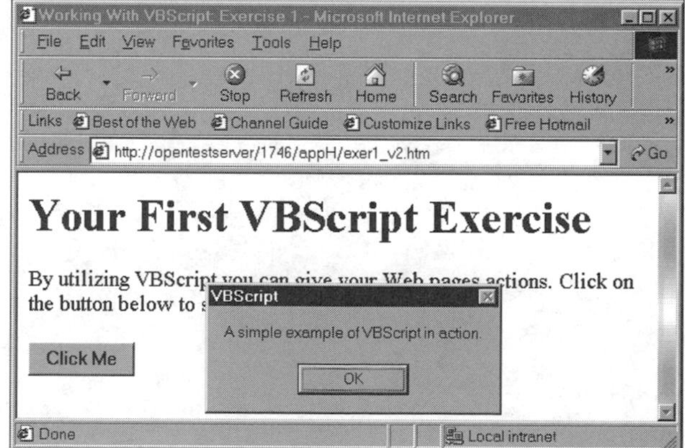

How It Works

Let's take a look at the three lines of code that you added. We want you to have a firm understanding of what the VBScript code is doing and how it is implemented within the HTML document. The first line defines a script:

```
<SCRIPT FOR="cmdClickMe" EVENT="onClick" LANGUAGE="VBScript">
```

The `FOR` argument specifies that this script is for the button named `cmdClickMe`, the name we have given our command button with the HTML `<INPUT>` tag. The `EVENT` argument says that this script should be run when the button is clicked. The `LANGUAGE` argument states that this is a VBScript module.

The second line is the only line of VBScript in this HTML document. The `MsgBox` function simply displays a message dialog. You will see more of the `MsgBox` function later in this tutorial. The third line marks the end of our script.

Part 3: Preferred Method of Including VBScript

In the code above, we simply inserted the VBScript module right after the HTML tag that defined the command button. While this method is functional, it is not the preferred approach. The HTML alone can be confusing to read with all of its tags and text; adding VBScript into the middle of all this just makes it even more complicated. A more organized alternative is to place all of your script together within the HTML document. The following steps introduce you to this approach.

A completed copy of this part of the exercise can be found in the file `exer1_v3.htm`.

5 Re-open the HTML document that you created in Part 2, if necessary, and remove the lines that you added there:

```
<SCRIPT FOR="cmdClickMe" EVENT="onClick" LANGUAGE="VBScript">
  MsgBox "A simple example of VBScript in action."
</SCRIPT>
```

6 Modify the document by adding the scripting lines as shown in the light shading below:

```
<HTML>
<HEAD>
<TITLE>Working With VBScript: Exercise 1</TITLE>
<SCRIPT LANGUAGE="VBScript">
<!-- Instruct non-IE browsers to skip over VBScript modules.
  Sub cmdClickMe_OnClick
    MsgBox "A simple example of VBScript in action."
  End Sub
-->
</SCRIPT>
</HEAD>
<BODY>
  <H1>Your First VBScript Exercise</H1>
  <P> By utilizing VBScript you can give your Web pages actions.
  Click on the button below to see what we mean. </P>
  <FORM NAME="frmExercise1">
    <INPUT TYPE="Button" NAME="cmdClickMe" VALUE="Click Me">
  </FORM>
</BODY>
</HTML>
```

7 Save the file and test it by loading it into Internet Explorer. When you try out the Click Me button, the result is the same as the previous code.

How It Works

This second method starts with the same `<SCRIPT>` tag as the previous example. At the center of this script are three lines that provide the functionality for our page. The first line defines a sub-procedure called `cmdClickMe_OnClick`, which will be executed any time that the control `cmdClickMe` is clicked:

```
Sub cmdClickMe_OnClick
```

This type of procedure is referred to as an **event** procedure. The event is the user clicking the button, and the procedure that we associate with this event is executed every time the button is clicked.

On the second line we find the `MsgBox` function again, while the third line marks an end to our subroutine.

Don't get too hung up on understanding all of the details of this right now – you will see plenty more examples along the way.

Summary

That's it – you just created your first VBScript-enabled web page. Along the way you have learned:

- How to add VBScript into your web pages
- Ways to tie HTML and VBScript together to provide functionality to your pages
- Why you should encase your VBScript modules within HTML comments

Next up, we will look at what VBScript has to offer in the way of variables.

Lesson 2: Working with Variables

A **variable** is a named location in computer memory that you can use for storage of data during the execution of your scripts. You can use variables to:

- Store input from the user gathered via your web page
- Save data returned from functions
- Hold results from calculations

An Introduction to Variables

Let's look at a simple VBScript example to clarify the use of variables:

```
Sub cmdVariables_OnClick
  Dim Name
  Name = InputBox("Enter your name: ")
  MsgBox "The name you entered was " & Name
End Sub
```

The first line of this example defines a sub procedure named `cmdVariables`, which is associated with the `onclick` event of a command button.

On the second line we declare a variable named `Name`. We are going to use this variable to store the name of the user when it is entered. The third line uses the `InputBox` function to first prompt for, and then return, the user's name. You'll see more of the `InputBox` function later in this tutorial. The name it returns is stored in the `Name` variable.

The fourth line uses the `MsgBox` function to display the user's name. The sub procedure completes on the fifth line.

Exactly how and where variables are stored is not important. What is important is what you use them for and how you use them. That's what we will be looking at next.

Declaring Variables

There are two methods for declaring variables in VBScript – **explicitly** and **implicitly**. You usually declare variables explicitly with the `Dim` statement:

```
Dim Name
```

This statement declares the variable `Name`. You can also declare multiple variables on one line as shown below:

```
Dim Name, Address, City, State
```

Variables can be declared implicitly by simply using the variable name within your script. This practice is not recommended. It leads to code that is prone to errors and more difficult to debug.

You can force VBScript to require all variables to be explicitly declared by including the statement `Option Explicit` at the start of every script. Any variable that is not explicitly declared will then generate an error.

Variable Naming Rules

When naming variables the following rules apply:

- They must begin with an alphabetic character.
- They cannot contain embedded periods.
- They must be unique within the same scope. (There's more on scopes later in this lesson.)
- They must be no longer than 255 characters.

Variants and Subtypes

VBScript has a single data type called a **variant**, which has the ability to store different types of data. The types of data that a variant can store are referred to as **subtypes**. The table below describes the subtypes supported by VBScript.

Subtype	Description of Uses for Each Subtype
`Byte`	Integer numbers between 0 to 255
`Boolean`	`True` and `False`
`Currency`	Monetary values
`Date`	Date and time
`Double`	Extremely large numbers with decimal points
`Empty`	Indicates that a Variant has been declared, but not assigned a value
`Error`	An error number
`Integer`	Large integers between –32,768 and 32,767
`Long`	Extremely large integers (between –2,147,483,648 and 2,147,483,647)
`Object`	Objects
`Null`	No valid data
`Single`	Large numbers with decimal points
`String`	Character strings

Assigning Values

You assign a value to a variable by using the following format:

`Variable_name = value`

The following examples demonstrate assigning values to variables:

```
Name = "Larry Roof"
HoursWorked = 50
Overtime = True
```

Scope of Variables

The scope of a variable dictates where it can be used in your script. A variable's scope is determined by where it is declared. If it is declared within a procedure, it is referred to as a **procedure-level** variable and can only be used within that procedure. If it is declared outside of any procedure, it is a **script-level** variable and can be used throughout the script.

The example below demonstrates both script-level and procedure-level variables:

```
<SCRIPT>
  Dim counter
  Sub cmdButton_onClick
    Dim temp
  End Sub
</SCRIPT>
```

The variable `counter` is a script-level variable and can be utilized throughout the script. The variable `temp` exists only within the `cmdButton_onClick` sub-procedure.

Constants

Constants can be declared in VBScript using the following syntax:

`Const` *`constname`* `=` *`expression`*

For example, we can assign values or strings as follows:

```
Const MyNumber = 99.9
Const MyString = "constant"
```

You could also assign constant values to variables that you have defined, as shown in the example below. Here, `TAX_RATE` is our constant:

```
<SCRIPT>
  Dim TAX_RATE
  TAX_RATE = .06
  Function CalculateTaxes
    CalculateTaxes = CostOfGoods * TAX_RATE
  End Function
</SCRIPT>
```

Arrays

The VBScript language provides support for arrays. You declare an array using the `Dim` statement, just as you did with variables:

```
Dim States(50)
```

The statement above creates an array with 51 elements. Why 51? Because VBScript arrays are **zero-based**, meaning that the first array element is indexed 0 and the last is the number specified when declaring the array.

You assign values to the elements of an array just as you would a variable, but with an additional reference (the **index**) to the element in which it will be stored:

```
States(5) = "California"
States(6) = "New York"
```

Arrays can have multiple dimensions – VBScript supports up to 60 dimensions. Declaring a two-dimensional array for storing 51 states and their capitals could be done as follows:

```
Dim StateInfo(50,1)
```

To store values into this array you would then reference both dimensions.

```
StateInfo(18,0) = "Michigan"
StateInfo(18,1) = "Lansing"
```

VBScript also provides support for arrays whose size may need to change as the script is executing. These arrays are referred to as **dynamic arrays**. A dynamic array is declared without specifying the number of elements it will contain:

```
Dim Customers()
```

The `ReDim` statement is then used to change the size of the array from within the script:

```
ReDim Customers(100)
```

There is no limit to the number of times an array can be re-dimensioned during the execution of a script. To preserve the contents of an array when you are re-dimensioning, use the `Preserve` keyword:

```
ReDim Preserve Customers(100)
```

Exercise 2: Working with Variables

We will now create a page that performs a simple calculation involving sub-totals, sales tax and final totals. Follow the step-by-step instructions that will introduce you to using variables with VBScript.

In this exercise you will create an HTML document which contains a script that will retrieve data from a web page, perform calculations and output a result.

Part 1: Creating the HTML Document

A completed copy of this part of the exercise can be found in the file `exer2_v1.htm`.

1 Open up a text editor and insert the following HTML code:

```
<HTML>
<HEAD>
<TITLE>Working With VBScript: Exercise 2</TITLE>
</HEAD>
<BODY>
<H1>Your Second VBScript Exercise</H1>
<P> Variables can be used to store and manipulate values. To
see a demonstration of this enter a quantity and unit price
in the fields below and click the "Calculate Cost" button.</P>
<FORM NAME="frmExercise2">
  <TABLE>
    <TR>
      <TD><B>Quantity:</B></TD>
      <TD><INPUT TYPE="Text" NAME="txtQuantity" SIZE=5></TD>
    </TR>
    <TR>
      <TD><B>Unit price:</B></TD>
      <TD><INPUT TYPE="Text" NAME="txtUnitPrice" SIZE=5></TD>
    </TR>
  </TABLE>
```

```
  <BR>
  <INPUT TYPE="Button" NAME="cmdCalculate" VALUE="Calculate Cost">
</FORM>
</BODY>
</HTML>
```

2 Save the file, and load it into Internet Explorer. The result is shown is this screenshot.

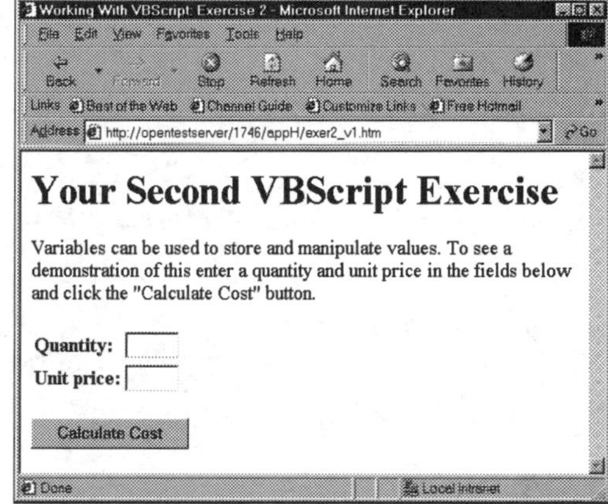

Part 2: Adding VBScript

In the following section, we will be adding a script to provide functionality for when the Calculate Cost command button is clicked. A completed copy of this part of the exercise can be found in the file `exer2_v2.htm`.

3 Re-open the HTML document that you created in Part 1, if necessary. Modify the document adding the scripting lines as shown by the shading:

```
<HTML>
<HEAD>
<TITLE>Working With VBScript: Exercise 2</TITLE>
<SCRIPT LANGUAGE="VBScript">
<!-- Add this to instruct non-IE browsers to skip over VBScript modules.
Option Explicit

Sub cmdCalculate_OnClick
  Dim AmountofTax
  Dim CRLF
  Dim Message
  Dim Subtotal
  Dim TABSPACE
  Dim TAX_RATE
  Dim TotalCost

' Define our constant values.
  TAX_RATE = 0.06
  CRLF = Chr(13) & Chr(10)
  TABSPACE = Chr(9)

' Perform order calculations.
  Subtotal = document.frmExercise2.txtQuantity.value _
           * document.frmExercise2.txtUnitPrice.value
  AmountofTax = Subtotal * TAX_RATE
  TotalCost = Subtotal + AmountofTax
```

```
' Display the results.
  Message = "The total for your order is:"
  Message = Message & CRLF & CRLF
  Message = Message & "Subtotal:" & TABSPACE & "$" & Subtotal & CRLF
  Message = Message & "Tax:" & TABSPACE & "$" & AmountofTax & CRLF
  Message = Message & "Total:" & TABSPACE & "$" & TotalCost
  MsgBox Message,,"Your Total"
End Sub
-->
</SCRIPT>
</HEAD>
<BODY>
...
```

The apostrophes (') are there to comment out code – there's more on this in a moment. The underscore (_) at the end of the line `Subtotal = document.frmExercise2.txtQuantity.value_` *is a coding convention which is used to instruct VBScript to join this line and the next one together for processing. This has the same effect typing the code of these two lines on a single line, discarding the _.*

4 Save the file and test it by loading it into Internet Explorer. Enter 100 into the Quantity field and 10 into the Unit Price field. Try out the Calculate Cost button. The result is shown in the screenshot.

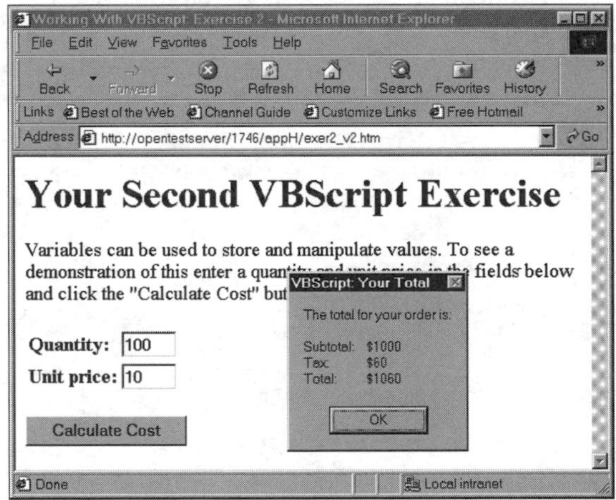

How It Works

What should be obvious right from the start is that this script is far more involved than the one used with Exercise 1. Don't be intimidated by its size – as with the previous lesson, we will work through this script line-by-line.

After the starting `<SCRIPT>` tag and HTML comment we find:

```
Option Explicit
```

Remember what this statement does: it forces you to declare all of your variables.

Next we create a sub procedure for the click event of the cmdCalculate button:

```
Sub cmdCalculate_OnClick
```

Following that we declare seven variables, three of which we are going to use as constants. The constants can be identified by the fact that they are all in uppercase. Case doesn't matter in VBScript (although it does in JavaScript) – we are using it to make the script easier to read. Are the variables procedure-level or script-level variables? They are procedure-level since they are declared within a procedure.

In VBScript, anything to the right of an apostrophe is a comment. These comments are ignored when the script is processed. A comment can appear on a line by itself or at the end of a line of script. Comments at the end of a line are referred to as inline comments:

```
' Define our constant values.
```

The constants are assigned values in the following lines:

```
CRLF = Chr(13) & Chr(10)
TABSPACE = Chr(9)
```

Chr() is a VBScript function that returns the character associated with a specified ANSI code. ANSI codes 13, 10 and 9 are carriage return, line feed and tab, respectively.

The next line demonstrates how values are taken from a form on a web page, and used within a script. The two fields on our form were named txtQuantity and txtUnitPrice in their HTML <INPUT> tags. The form is named frmExercise2. Here we are referencing our web document, then the form, then the input field and finally the value of that field. The value associated with each field contains what the user entered into that field on the web page. The * says to multiply the value of the first field, txtQuantity, by the second field, txtUnitPrice.

> **The commonly-used VBScript operands are + for addition, - for subtraction, * for multiplication and / for division.**

The result of this calculation is then stored in the variable Subtotal. Next we perform some additional calculations. Finally, we display the result of our calculations using the MsgBox function. The ampersand character, &, is used to concatenate two strings.

As we said in Lesson 1, don't get too worried about understanding all of the details of this example right now. You will pick up the language as you continue to work with VBScript.

Summary

That completes Exercise 2. You just created a web page that interacts with the user to gather data, perform calculations and present results – the fundamental components of most applications. Along the way you have learned:

- The types of variables that VBScript supports
- How to declare and use variables within a script
- A technique to work around the absence of constants in VBScript
- What a comment line is in a script

In the next lesson we'll look at objects. You will learn what they are and how they are used with VBScript.

Lesson 3: Objects and VBScript

Objects, both in the form of Java applets and ActiveX controls, enhance the functionality that is provided with HTML. By using VBScript you can extend the capabilities of these controls, integrating and manipulating them from within your scripts. In this lesson we will look at how you can utilize the power of objects with VBScript.

Scripting with objects involves two steps:

- Adding the object to your web page using HTML
- Writing script procedures to respond to events that the object provides

Adding Objects to Your Web Pages

Since this is a VBScript tutorial (rather than an HTML tutorial), we will offer only a limited discussion of how to add an object to a web page. Objects (whether they're Java applets or ActiveX controls) are added to a page with the `<OBJECT>` tag. The properties, or characteristics, of the object are configured using the `<PARAM>` tag. Typically you will see an object implemented using a single `<OBJECT>` tag along with several `<PARAM>` tags. The following HTML code demonstrates how an ActiveX control might appear when added to a page:

```
<OBJECT ID="lblTotalPay" WIDTH=45 HEIGHT=24
          CLASSID="CLSID:978C9E23-D4B0-11CE-BF2D-00AA003F40D0">
  <PARAM NAME="ForeColor" VALUE="0">
  <PARAM NAME="BackColor" VALUE="16777215">
  <PARAM NAME="Caption" VALUE="">
  <PARAM NAME="Size" VALUE="1582;635">
  <PARAM NAME="SpecialEffect" VALUE="2">
  <PARAM NAME="FontHeight" VALUE="200">
  <PARAM NAME="FontCharSet" VALUE="0">
  <PARAM NAME="FontPitchAndFamily" VALUE="2">
  <PARAM NAME="FontWeight" VALUE="0">
</OBJECT>
```

Linking VBScript with Objects

Once you have added a control to your web page, it can be configured, manipulated and responded to through its properties, methods and events. **Properties** are the characteristics of an object. They include items like a caption, the foreground color and the font size. **Methods** cause an object to perform a task. **Events** are actions that are recognized by an object. For instance, a command button recognizes an `onclick` event.

For the most part, you will be focusing on properties and events. The following is an example of setting properties for a label control:

```
<SCRIPT LANGUAGE="VBScript">
Sub cmdCalculatePay_onClick
   Dim HoursWorked
   Dim PayRate
   Dim TotalPay

   HoursWorked = InputBox("Enter hours worked: ")
   PayRate = InputBox("Enter pay rate: ")
   TotalPay = HoursWorked * PayRate

   document.lblTotalPay.caption = TotalPay
End Sub
</SCRIPT>
```

The `caption` property of the label control `lblTotalPay` is set equal to the results of our calculation with the script line:

```
   document.lblTotalPay.caption = TotalPay
```

Object properties are referenced within your scripts using the same format shown in Exercise 2.

Exercise 3: Working with Objects

In Exercise 3 we modify the web page created in Exercise 2. These modifications will be made so that we can display the results of our calculations not with the `MsgBox` function, but rather to ActiveX objects that are part of the page. Just follow the step-by-step instructions below to begin learning how to use VBScript with ActiveX.

In this exercise, you will create an HTML document that contains a script that will retrieve data from a web page, perform calculations and output a result back to the web page.

Part 1: Testing the HTML Document

1 Load the file `exer3_v1.htm` into a text editor. This is the HTML component of this exercise already typed in for you. Look over the HTML document. It contains three ActiveX label controls named `lblSubtotal`, `lblTaxes` and `lblTotalCost`. Save the file under a different name. We are going to be modifying this source and wouldn't want to work with the original.

2 Test the file by loading it into Internet Explorer. The result is shown below. I'd have you try out the Calculate Cost button, but you have probably already figured out from the previous two exercises that it doesn't do anything.

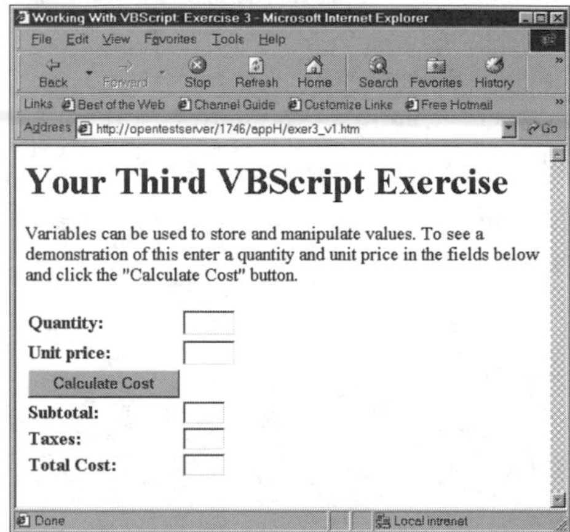

Part 2: Adding VBScript

As we did in Exercise 2, we will now add a script to provide functionality for the Calculate Cost command button's click event. A completed copy of this part of the exercise can be found in the file `exer3_v2.htm`.

3 We're going to modify the document, by adding the scripting lines as shown by the shading below:

```
<HTML>
<HEAD>
<TITLE>Working With VBScript: Exercise 3</TITLE>
<SCRIPT LANGUAGE="VBScript">
<!-- Add this to instruct non-IE browsers to skip over VBScript modules.
Option Explicit

Sub cmdCalculate_OnClick
  Dim AmountofTax
  Dim Subtotal
  Dim TAX_RATE
  Dim TotalCost

' Define our constant values.
  TAX_RATE = 0.06

' Perform order calculations.
  Subtotal = document.frmExercise3.txtQuantity.value _
           * document.frmExercise3.txtUnitPrice.value
  AmountofTax = Subtotal * TAX_RATE
  TotalCost = Subtotal + AmountofTax

' Display the results.
  document.frmExercise3.lblSubtotal.caption = Subtotal
  document.frmExercise3.lblTaxes.caption = AmountofTax
  document.frmExercise3.lblTotalCost.caption = TotalCost
End Sub
-->
</SCRIPT>
</HEAD>
...
```

4 Save the file and test it by loading it into Internet Explorer. Enter 100 into the Quantity field and 10 into the Unit Price field. Try out the Calculate Cost button. The result is shown in the screenshot.

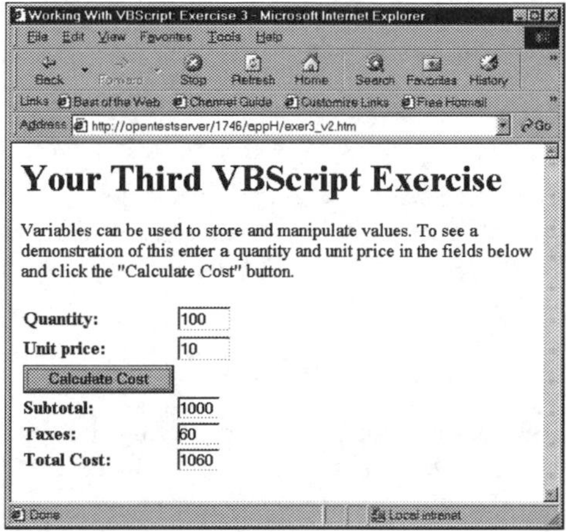

How It Works

Exercise 3 is just a modification of Exercise 2. As such, we will focus on what's different, rather than going over the script line by line again.

There were minimal changes involving variable declarations and the defining of constant values. We simply didn't need them in this version, so they were removed:

```
   Dim AmountofTax
   Dim Subtotal
   Dim TAX_RATE
   Dim TotalCost

'  Define our constant values.
   TAX_RATE = 0.06
```

We won't discuss the method used to calculate the subtotal, taxes and total amount, as it is identical in both exercises.

The way results are displayed is different in Example 3. The script has been modified to remove the `MsgBox` function, and in its place we set the `caption` property of three label controls:

```
'  Display the results.
   document.frmExercise3.lblSubtotal.caption = Subtotal
   document.frmExercise3.lblTaxes.caption = AmountofTax
   document.frmExercise3.lblTotalCost.caption = TotalCost
```

The format used when referencing these properties is:

`document`	Our web document
`frmExercise3`	The form on which the ActiveX controls were placed
`lblTaxes`	The name of the control
`caption`	The property to set

Hopefully, by this point you are starting to get comfortable reading and working with VBScript. The best way to strengthen your knowledge of VBScript is to take some of the examples that we have been working with in the first three lessons and modify them to suit your own needs.

Summary

Well, that's it for Exercise 3. I know, objects are a pretty hefty topic for a small lesson. What we wanted to do was to give you an exposure to objects and how they can be utilized in VBScript. Along the way, you have learned:

- What objects are and how they could be used with VBScript
- About properties, methods and events

Next is a lesson in how you can control your script files using conditional and looping statements.

Lesson 4: Controlling Your VBScript Routines

VBScript allows you to control how your scripts process data through the use of **conditional** and **looping** statements. By using conditional statements you can develop scripts that evaluate data and use criteria to determine what tasks to perform. Looping statements allow you to repetitively execute lines of a script. Each offers benefits to the script developer in the process of creating more complex and functional web pages.

Conditional Statements

VBScript provides two forms of conditional statements: `If..Then..Else` and `Select..Case`.

If..Then..Else

The `If..Then..Else` statement is used to evaluate a condition to see if it is true or false and then, depending upon this result, to execute a statement or set of statements. Rather than discussing an `If` statement in theory, we will examine some examples to see how they work.

The simplest version of an `If` statement is one that contains only a condition and a single statement:

```
If AmountPurchased > 10000 Then DiscountAmount = AmountPurchased * .10
```

In this example statement the condition is:

```
If AmountPurchased > 10000
```

which simply checks to see if the contents of the variable `AmountPurchased` is greater than 10,000. If it is, the condition is true. In this simple version of the `If` statement, when the condition is true the following statement is executed:

```
DiscountAmount = AmountPurchased * .10
```

Now let's look at a more complicated version of the `If` statement. In this version we will perform a series of statements when the condition is true:

```
If AmountPurchased > 10000 Then
  DiscountAmount = AmountPurchased * .10
  Subtotal = AmountPurchased - DiscountAmount
End If
```

In this form of the `If` statement, one or more statements can be executed when the condition is true, by placing them between the `If` statement on the top and the `End If` statement on the bottom.

The next form of the `If` statement uses the `If..Then..Else` format. This version of the `If` statement differs from the two previous versions in that it will perform one set of statements if the condition is true and another set when the condition is false:

```
If AmountPurchased > 10000 Then
  DiscountAmount = AmountPurchased * .10
  Subtotal = AmountPurchased - DiscountAmount
Else
  HandlingFee = AmountPurchased *.03
  Subtotal = AmountPurchased + HandlingFee
End If
```

In this example, when the customer's order is over $10,000 (that is, the condition is true) they receive a 10% discount. When the order is under $10,000, they are charged a 3% handling fee.

The final version of the `If` statement that we will look at is the `If..Then..ElseIf`. In this form the `If` statement checks each of the conditions until it finds either one that is true or an `Else` statement:

```
If AmountPurchased > 10000 Then
  DiscountAmount = AmountPurchased * .10
  Subtotal = AmountPurchased - DiscountAmount
ElseIf AmountPurchased > 5000 Then
  DiscountAmount = AmountPurchased * .05
  Subtotal = AmountPurchased - DiscountAmount
Else
  HandlingFee = AmountPurchased *.03
  Subtotal = AmountPurchased + HandlingFee
End If
```

In this example the customer receives a 10% discount for orders over $10,000, a 5% discount for orders over $5000 or a handling fee of 3% for orders under $5000. Note that only *one* of these three possibilities is actually executed.

As you see, VBScript offers you plenty of options when it comes to `If` statements.

Select Case

The `Select Case` statement provides an alternative to the `If..Then..Else` statement, providing additional control and readability when evaluating complex conditions. It is well suited for situations where there are a number of possible conditions for the value being checked. Like the `If` statement, the `Select Case` structure checks a condition and, based upon that condition being true, executes a series of statements.

The syntax of the `Select Case` statement is:

```
Select Case condition
  Case value
    statements
  Case value
    statements
  ...
  Case Else
    statements
End Select
```

For example, the following `Select` statement assigns a shipping fee based upon the state where the order is being sent:

```
Select Case Document.frmOrder.txtState.Value
  Case "California"
    ShippingFee= .04
  Case "Florida"
    ShippingFee = .03
  Case Else
    ShippingFee = .02
End Select
```

The `Select Case` statement checks each of the `Case` statements until it finds one that will result in the condition being true. If none are found to be true, it executes the statements within the `Case Else`.

Even though it is not required, always include a `Case Else` when working with `Select Case` statements to process conditions that you may not have considered possible. For these conditions you can display something as simple as a message dialog, informing you that a branch was executed that you hadn't planned for.

Looping Statements

VBScript provides four forms of looping statements, which can be divided into two groups. The `For..Next` and `For Each..Next` statements are best used when you want to perform a loop a specific number of times. The `Do..Loop` and `While..Wend` statements are best used to perform a loop an undetermined number of times.

For..Next

The `For..Next` structure is used when you want to perform a loop a specific number of times. It uses a counter variable, which is incremented or decremented with each repetition of the loop. The following example demonstrates a simple `For` loop, with a counter that is incremented with each iteration:

```
For counter = 1 To 12
  result = 5 * counter
  MsgBox counter & " times 5 is " & result
Next
```

The variable `counter` is the numeric value being incremented or decremented. The number 1 defines the start of the loop, 12 the end of the loop. When this loop executes it will display twelve dialog box messages, each containing the product of multiplying five times the counter as it runs from 1 to 12.

In this example, the variable `counter` is incremented by 1 with each loop. Optionally, we could control how we wanted the counter to be modified through the addition of the `Step` argument:

```
For counter = 1 To 12 Step 2
  result = 5 * counter
  MsgBox counter & " times 5 is " & result
Next
```

This slight modification to the loop results in only the products of the odd numbers between 1 and 12 being displayed. If you want to create a countdown loop (where the number is decremented with each loop), simply use a negative value with the `Step` argument as shown in the following example:

```
For counter = 12 To 1 Step -1
  result = 5 * counter
  MsgBox counter & " times 5 is " & result
Next
```

Note that, in a decrementing loop, the starting number is greater than the ending number.

For Each..Next

The `For Each..Next` is similar to the `For..Next` loop, but instead of repeating a loop for a certain number of times, it repeats the loop for each member of a specified collection. The discussion of collections and their use is outside of the scope of this tutorial. The `For Each..Next` structure is detailed elsewhere in the book.

Do..Loop

The `Do..Loop` structure repeats a block of statements until a specified condition is met. Normally, when using a `Do..Loop`, the condition being checked is the result of some operation being performed within the structure of the loop. Two versions of this structure are provided – the `Do..While` and the `Do..Until`.

Do..While

A `Do` loop that contains the `While` keyword will be performed as long as the condition being tested is true. You have the option of checking the condition at the start of the loop, as in the form:

```
Do While condition
  statements
Loop
```

or at the end of the loop, as shown in the following example:

```
Do
  statements
Loop While condition
```

The difference between these two formats is that the first example may never perform the statements included within its structure, while the second example will always perform its statements at least once.

Do..Until

A `Do` loop that contains the `Until` keyword will continue to loop as long as the condition being tested is false. As with the `Do..While` structure, you have the option of checking the condition at the start of the loop, as in the form:

```
Do Until condition
  statements
Loop
```

or at the end of the loop, as shown in the following example:

```
Do
  statements
Loop Until condition
```

One use for a `Do Until..Loop` is shown in the example below:

```
password = InputBox("Enter your password:")
Do Until password = "letmein"
  Msgbox "Invalid password - please try again."
  password = InputBox("Enter you password:")
Loop
```

In this example we ask the user to enter a password before performing the conditional part of the `Do..Loop` the first time. The result is that, if they enter the correct password the first time, the statements within the loop's structure will never be performed. If the user were to enter an invalid password then the statements within the `Do..Loop` structure would be performed, a message would be displayed and the user would be prompted to re-enter their password.

While..Wend

The `While..Wend` structure loops as long as the condition being checked is true. If the condition is true, the `While..Wend` statement operates similar to the `Do..Loop` structure, but without its flexibility. The structure for the `While..Wend` statement is:

```
While condition
  statements
Wend
```

Exercise 4: Working with Conditional and Looping Statements

In this exercise we continue to extend the functionality of our web page. New features provided by this exercise are:

- A combo box from which the user can select products
- Automatic pricing of products as they are selected
- Discounting purchase prices based upon the size of the order

As with the first three exercises simply follow the step-by-step instructions below to begin to learn how to use conditional and looping statements with your scripts.

We will create an HTML document containing a script that will retrieve data from a web page, perform calculations and output a result back to the web page. In addition, it will look up prices for products and provide discounts based upon the order size.

Part 1: Testing the HTML Document

1 Open up a text editor application and load the file `exer4_v1.htm`. This is the HTML component of this exercise already typed in for you.

2 Look over the HTML document. Note the addition of an ActiveX combo box control, `cmbProducts`, and additional label controls. Scroll to the bottom of the document where you will find a script that fills the combo box with the available products as shown in the following code fragment:

```
<SCRIPT LANGUAGE="VBScript">
<!--
  Document.frmExercise4.cmbProducts.Additem "NEC MultiSync E1100"
  Document.frmExercise4.cmbProducts.Additem "NEC MultiSync P1150"
  Document.frmExercise4.cmbProducts.Additem "NEC MultiSync E750"
-->
</SCRIPT>
```

3 Test the file by loading it into Internet Explorer. The resulting page is shown here. You can forget about testing the Calculate Cost button: we've been down that road before.

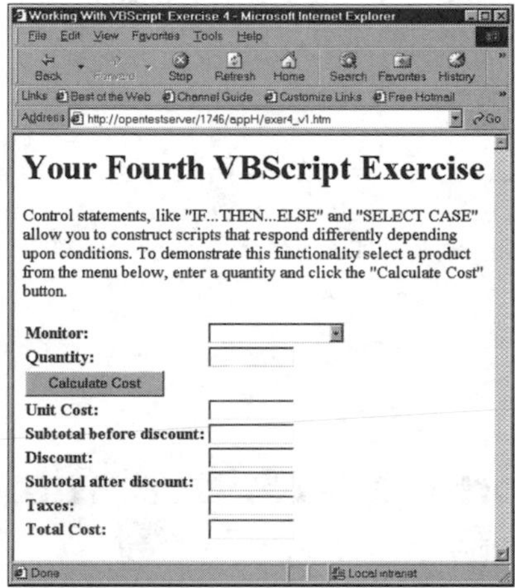

Part 2: Adding VBScript

We will now add a script to provide functionality for the Calculate Cost command button, as well as when a product is selected from the combo box control. A completed copy of this part of the exercise can be found in the file `exer4_v2.htm`.

4 Modify the document by adding the shaded lines of script:

```
<HTML>
<HEAD>
<TITLE>Working With VBScript: Exercise 4</TITLE>
<SCRIPT LANGUAGE="VBScript">
<!-- Add this to instruct non-IE browsers to skip over VBScript modules.
Option Explicit

Sub cmdCalculate_OnClick
  Dim AmountofDiscount
  Dim AmountofTax
  Dim DISCOUNT_LIMIT
  Dim DISCOUNT_RATE
  Dim SubtotalBefore
  Dim SubtotalAfter
  Dim TAX_RATE
  Dim TotalCost
```

```
' Define our constant values.
  DISCOUNT_LIMIT = 1000
  DISCOUNT_RATE = .10
  TAX_RATE = 0.06

' Calculate the subtotal for the order.
  SubtotalBefore = document.frmExercise4.txtQuantity.value _
                 * document.frmExercise4.lblUnitCost.caption

' Check to see if the order is large enough to offer discounts.
  If (SubtotalBefore > DISCOUNT_LIMIT) Then
    AmountofDiscount = SubtotalBefore * DISCOUNT_RATE
  Else
    AmountofDiscount = 0
  End If
  SubtotalAfter = SubtotalBefore - AmountofDiscount

' Calculate taxes and total cost.
  AmountofTax = SubtotalAfter * TAX_RATE
  TotalCost = SubtotalAfter + AmountofTax

' Display the results.
  document.frmExercise4.lblSubtotalBefore.caption = SubtotalBefore
  document.frmExercise4.lblDiscount.caption = AmountofDiscount
  document.frmExercise4.lblSubtotalAfter.caption = SubtotalAfter
  document.frmExercise4.lblTaxes.caption = AmountofTax
  document.frmExercise4.lblTotalCost.caption = TotalCost
End Sub

Sub cmbProducts_Change()
  Select Case document.frmExercise4.cmbProducts.value
    Case "NEC MultiSync E1100"
      document.frmExercise4.lblUnitCost.caption = 1590
    Case "NEC MultiSync P1150"
      document.frmExercise4.lblUnitCost.caption = 880
    Case "NEC MultiSync E750"
      document.frmExercise4.lblUnitCost.caption = 1940
    Case Else
      document.frmExercise4.lblUnitCost.caption = 0
  End Select
End Sub
-->
</SCRIPT>
</HEAD>
...
```

5 Save the file, and test it in Internet Explorer. Select a product (say NEC MultiSync E1100) from the combo box. Notice how the Unit Cost field is automatically updated as shown in the screenshot.

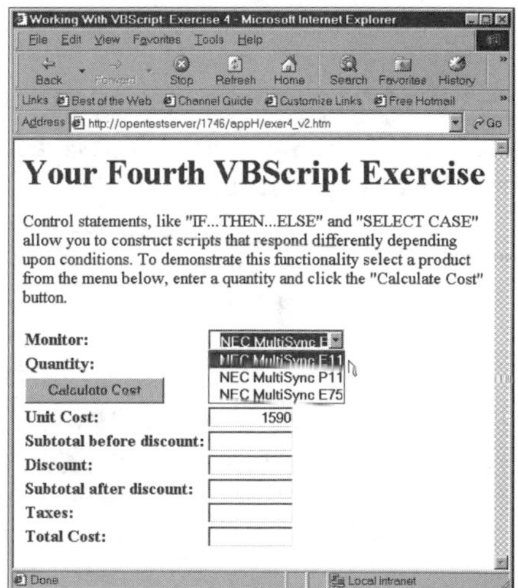

6 Enter 10 into the Quantity field, and try out the Calculate Cost button. The result is shown here.

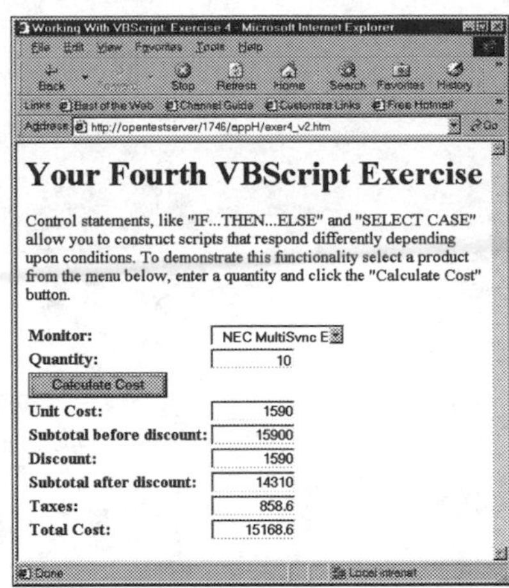

Exercise 4 has two new features: the automatic price lookup and the discount feature. We will look at how each is implemented separately.

Product Lookup: How It Works

The lookup feature is implemented via the `cmbProducts_Change` event procedure. As you might have remembered, the ActiveX combo box control that we added to your HTML document was given the name `cmbProducts`. This control supports a `change` event, which is triggered every time the user selects an item from the list. We simply make use of the `Select Case` statement to check the value of the control:

```
Sub cmbProducts_Change()
  Select Case document.frmExercise4.cmbProducts.value
    Case "NEC MultiSync E1100"
      document.frmExercise4.lblUnitCost.caption = 1590
    Case "NEC MultiSync P1150"
      document.frmExercise4.lblUnitCost.caption = 880
    Case "NEC MultiSync E750"
      document.frmExercise4.lblUnitCost.caption = 1940
    Case Else
      document.frmExercise4.lblUnitCost.caption = 0
  End Select
End Sub
```

Now, in our example, these values are hard coded. In a real life application we would normally pull these from a data source.

Even though the combo box control can only contain one of the three monitors, we still employ a `Case Else` *branch. This is simply a good programming habit to develop.*

Discounting Orders: How It Works

The script used to implement discounts begins by defining some constants, setting the discount limit at $1000 and a discount rate of 10%. Our discounting process begins by calculating the subtotal of the order before discounts and taxes are applied.

Discounting is then applied through the use of an `If..Then..Else` statement. We compare our subtotal amount against the constant `DISCOUNT_LIMIT`. If our amount is greater than the limit, the discount amount is calculated and stored in the variable `AmountofDiscount`. If it is less than, or equal to, the limit, the discount amount is set to 0:

```
' Check to see if the order is large enough to offer discounts.
  If (SubtotalBefore > DISCOUNT_LIMIT) Then
    AmountofDiscount = SubtotalBefore * DISCOUNT_RATE
  Else
    AmountofDiscount = 0
  End If
  SubtotalAfter = SubtotalBefore - AmountofDiscount
```

The value of the variable `AmountofDiscount` is subsequently subtracted from the subtotal. Next we calculate the taxes and total cost of the order. We complete the script by displaying the order information on the web page.

Extending this application

In this example I set the discount limit at $1,000. What would we have to change in our script to set the limit at a more reasonable amount of say, $100,000?

Summary

Can you believe how far our original application has progressed? Now we have a page that receives user input, performs price lookups, calculates discount amounts and displays the complete order information on the web page, all without having to go back to the web server.

In this section you were introduced to:

- Conditional statements, which allow you to selectively execute blocks of statements
- Looping statements, which provide you with a way to repetitively execute blocks of statements

Now that we can input, manipulate and display data, it is time to learn how to validate the data, before sending it on to a web server.

Lesson 5: Using VBScript with Forms

As the popularity of web page forms increase, so does the need to be able to validate data before the client browser submits it to the web server. As a scripting language, VBScript is well suited for this task. Once the form has been validated, the same script can be used to forward the data on to the server. In this lesson we will look at both the process of validating and submitting forms.

Validating Your Forms

The process of validating forms involves checking the form to see if:

- All of the required data is provided
- The data provided is valid

Meticulous data validation scripts can be tedious to code but are well worth their return in verifying the quality of the data.

The validation example that we will be examining does not contain anything new in the way of VBScript. We are simply using the elements that we have learned in the previous lessons in a new way. Before reading any further you may find it beneficial to ponder how you would validate an HTML form using the VBScript techniques that you have learned.

Okay, are you through pondering? Let's look at an example to give you an idea of what is possible when it comes to validating forms.

Checking Form Input

This example is pretty simple. It has a single field in which the user can enter their age, and a single command button that is used to submit their age to the server. A copy of this example can be found in `exam_5a.htm`.

```
<HTML>
<HEAD>
<TITLE>Working With VBScript: Example 5a</TITLE>

<SCRIPT LANGUAGE="VBScript">
<!-- Add this to instruct non-IE browsers to skip over VBScript modules.
Option Explicit

Sub cmdSubmit_OnClick

' Check to see if the user entered anything.
  If (Len(Document.frmExample5a.txtAge.Value) = 0) Then
    MsgBox "You must enter your age before submitting."
    Exit Sub
  End If

' Check to see if the user entered a number.
  If (Not(IsNumeric(Document.frmExample5a.txtAge.Value))) Then
    MsgBox "You must enter a number for your age."
    Exit Sub
  End If

' Check to see if the age entered is valid.
  If (Document.frmExample5a.txtAge.Value < 0) OR _
     (Document.frmExample5a.txtAge.Value > 100) Then
    MsgBox "The age you entered is invalid."
    Exit Sub
  End If

' Data looks okay so submit it.
  MsgBox "Thanks for providing your age."
  Document.frmExample5a.Submit

End Sub

-->
</SCRIPT>

</HEAD>

<BODY>
<H1>A VBScript Example on Variables</H1>
<P>
This example demonstrates validation techniques in VBScript.
```

```
</P>
<FORM NAME="frmExample5a">
  <TABLE>
    <TR>
      <TD>Enter your age:</TD>
      <TD><INPUT TYPE="Text" NAME="txtAge" SIZE="2"></TD>
    </TR>
    <TR>
      <TD><INPUT TYPE="Button" NAME="cmdSubmit" VALUE="Submit"></TD>
      <TD></TD>
    </TR>
  </TABLE>
</FORM>

</BODY>
</HTML>
```

How It Works

The heart of this validation script is found in the click event procedure for the `cmdSubmit` command button. We start by checking if the user entered anything at all into the field using VBScript's `Len` function. This function returns the length of a string. If the length is 0, the data is invalid. We inform the user and exit the submit procedure via the `Exit Sub` statement:

```
' Check to see if the user entered anything.
  If (Len(Document.frmExample5a.txtAge.Value) = 0) Then
    MsgBox "You must enter your age before submitting."
    Exit Sub
  End If
```

Next we check to see if what the user entered is a numeric value. The VBScript function `IsNumeric` returns a true value when it is a number. If not, we tell the user and exit:

```
' Check to see if the user entered a number.
  If (Not(IsNumeric(Document.frmExample5a.txtAge.Value))) Then
    MsgBox "You must enter a number for your age."
    Exit Sub
  End If
```

Our final check involves verifying that the age they entered seems reasonable for our environment. I have determined that no age less than 0 or greater than 100 is acceptable. Using an `If..Then` statement, we can check the value of the input field against this criteria:

```
' Check to see if the age entered is valid.
  If (Document.frmExample5a.txtAge.Value < 0) OR _
     (Document.frmExample5a.txtAge.Value > 100) Then
    MsgBox "The age you entered is invalid."
    Exit Sub
  End If
```

That's it. While this example is by no means the most detailed validation script you will encounter, it provides you with a basis of what is possible with VBScript.

Submitting Your Forms

Compared to validation, the process of submitting a form is simple. In our example we've used a normal HTML button with the Submit caption that is tied to an event procedure that both validates and, at the same time, submits the form. In Chapter 5, we've demonstrated how to use function `MyButton_onSubmit`, as an alternative.

The code that we would have to add to our previous example to submit the form is shown below:

```
' Data looks okay so submit it.
  MsgBox "Thanks for providing your age."
  Document.frmExample5a.Submit
```

The `MsgBox` statement lets the user know that their data has been processed. The form is then submitted by invoking the Submit method of the form object. As we saw in Lesson 3 on objects, methods cause an object to perform a task. Here we are using the `submit` method of our form to cause the form to submit its data, just as if we had used a `submit` control.

Exercise 5: How to Validate and Submit a Form

With this exercise we will add scripts to validate and submit the form that we have been constructing in the previous four lessons.

In this exercise you will create an HTML document containing a script that will retrieve data from a web page, perform calculations, and output results back to the web page. Additionally it will lookup prices for products and provide discounts based upon the order size. Finally, it will validate data and submit the web page form to a server.

Part 1: Testing the HTML Document

1 Open up the file `exer5_v1.htm` in a text editor. This is the HTML component of this exercise. Look over the HTML document. Note the addition of a command button `cmdSubmit`, which will be used to submit our form to a web server, after validation. Load the file up into Internet Explorer and it should look like the illustration below:

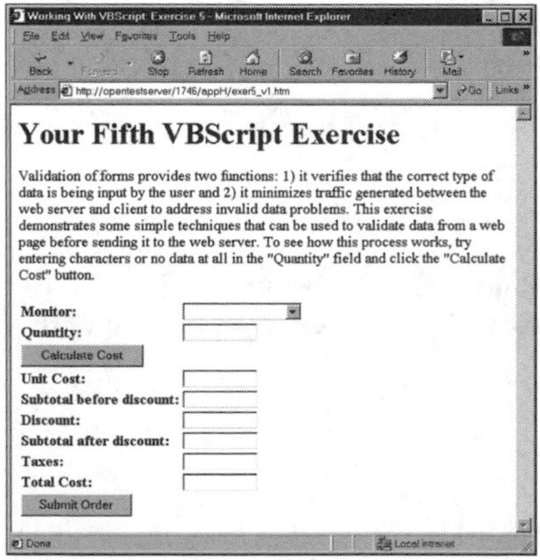

Part 2: Adding VBScript

Next, we will add the script that will handle the validation and submit our form. A completed copy of this part of the exercise can be found in the file exer5_v2.htm.

2 Modify the document by adding the shaded lines of script:

```
Sub cmdCalculate_OnClick
  Dim AmountofDiscount
  Dim AmountofTax
  Dim DISCOUNT_LIMIT
  Dim DISCOUNT_RATE
  Dim SubtotalBefore
  Dim SubtotalAfter
  Dim TAX_RATE
  Dim TotalCost

' Perform validation checks before process anything. While this is not
' everything that we could check, it provides an example of how you can
' validate data.
  If (Len(document.frmExercise5.txtQuantity.value) = 0) Then
    MsgBox "You must enter a quantity."
    Exit Sub
  End If

  If (Not IsNumeric(document.frmExercise5.txtQuantity.value)) Then
    MsgBox "Quantity must be a numeric value."
    Exit Sub
  End If

  If (Len(document.frmExercise5.cmbProducts.value) = 0) Then
    MsgBox "You must select a product."
    Exit Sub
  End If

' Define our constant values.
  DISCOUNT_LIMIT = 1000
  DISCOUNT_RATE = .10
  TAX_RATE = 0.06

' Calculate the subtotal for the order.
  SubtotalBefore = document.frmExercise5.txtQuantity.Value _
                 * document.frmExercise5.lblUnitCost.Caption

' Check to see if the order is large enough to offer discounts.
  If (SubtotalBefore > DISCOUNT_LIMIT) Then
    AmountofDiscount = SubtotalBefore * DISCOUNT_RATE
  Else
    AmountofDiscount = 0
  End If
  SubtotalAfter = SubtotalBefore - AmountofDiscount

' Calculate taxes and total cost.
  AmountofTax = SubtotalAfter * TAX_RATE
  TotalCost = SubtotalAfter + AmountofTax

' Display the results.
  Document.frmExercise5.lblSubtotalBefore.Caption = SubtotalBefore
  Document.frmExercise5.lblDiscount.Caption = AmountofDiscount
  Document.frmExercise5.lblSubtotalAfter.Caption = SubtotalAfter
  Document.frmExercise5.lblTaxes.Caption = AmountofTax
  Document.frmExercise5.lblTotalCost.Caption = TotalCost
End Sub

' Submit this order for processing.
Sub cmdSubmit_onClick
  MsgBox "Your order has been submitted."
  document.frmExercise5.submit
End Sub
```

```
Sub cmbProducts_Change()
  Select Case Document.frmExercise5.cmbProducts.Value
    Case "NEC MultiSync E1100"
      Document.frmExercise5.lblUnitCost.Caption = 1590
    Case "NEC MultiSync P1150"
      Document.frmExercise5.lblUnitCost.Caption = 880
    Case "NEC MultiSync E750"
      Document.frmExercise5.lblUnitCost.Caption = 1940
    Case Else
      Document.frmExercise5.lblUnitCost.Caption = 0
  End Select
End Sub
```

3 Save the file and test it by loading it into Internet Explorer. Without entering anything into the Quantity field click the Calculate Costs button. This dialog will be displayed.

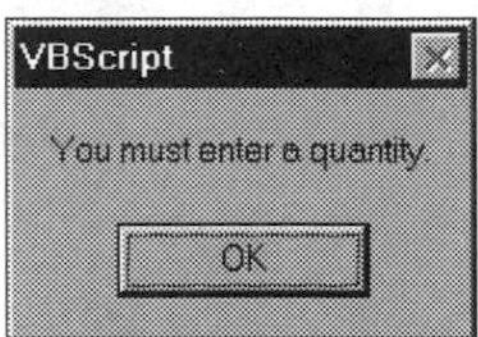

4 Enter the letter A into the Quantity field and click the Calculate Costs button. Now you'll see this dialog.

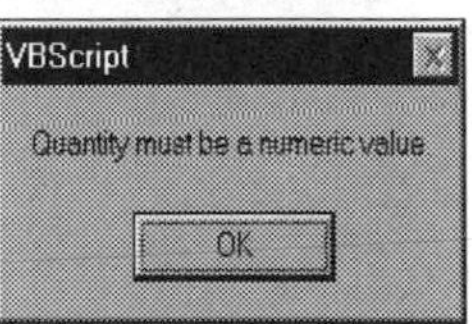

5 Enter a value of 10 into the Quantity field and once again click the Calculate Costs button. This time you will see this dialog.

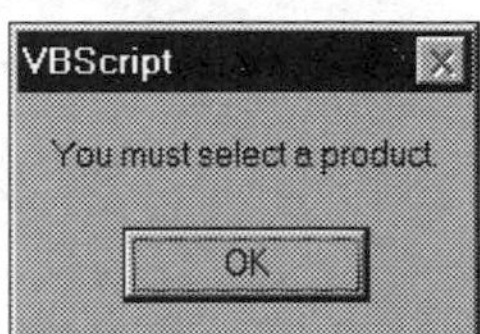

6 Finally, select the NEC MultiSync E1100 monitor from the combo box. Clicking the Calculate Costs button followed by the Submit Order button will leave you with the following:

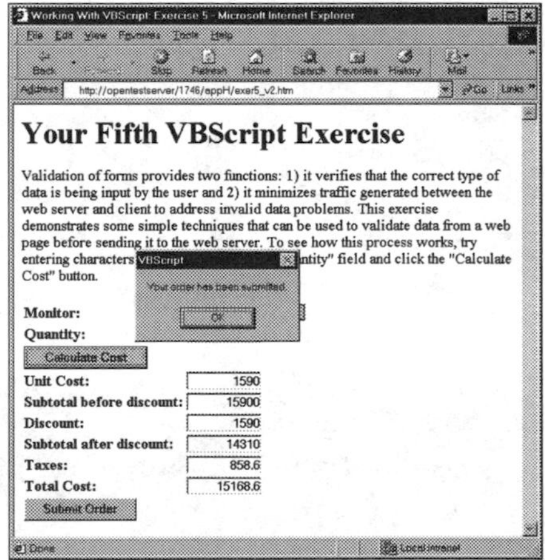

The script that was added to Exercise 5 has two components, one which validates the form and one that submits the form. We will look at each component separately.

Form Validation: How It Works

The validation of our form is handled by the event procedure associated with the button named `cmdCalculate`. You should note that this is only an example of what is possible in the way of validation and is by no means a comprehensive validation script.

We start by checking the length of the Quantity field to determine if the user has entered anything. VBScript's `Len` function is well suited for this purpose. If we find that the length is zero, the user is informed and we exit the event procedure.

Next we check to make sure that the Quantity field contains a numeric value. For this we use VBScript's `IsNumeric` function. An order would never be valid without selecting a product first, so we check the value of the Monitor combo box, again using the `Len` function.

If we pass all of these validations the cost of the order is calculated and displayed.

Submitting the Form How It Works

The submitting of the form is handled within the event procedure for the button named `cmdSubmit`. When the user clicks this button first a message box is displayed to confirm with the user that the order has been processed and then the form is submitted.

> **Normally we would include the script for both validating a form and submitting it in the same event procedure. I chose to separate them in this example so that it would be easier to understand.**

Summary

That wraps up our application and our tutorial on VBScript. In this short space we've covered some of the basic ways you can use VBScript in a web page. We started with a simple example that displayed a message box and built it into a program that accepted, processed, displayed, validated and submitted data. What's left for you? Coupled with the reference and the examples in the book, you can try modifying and tweaking some of the examples. Take some of the techniques that were presented and integrate them into your own web pages. Script writing, like any development skill, requires practice and perseverance.

HTML

VBScript Reference

Array Handling

`Dim` – declares a variable. An array variable can be static, with a defined number of elements, or dynamic, and can have up to 60 dimensions.
`ReDim` – used to change the size of an array variable which has been declared as dynamic.
`Preserve` – keyword used to preserve the contents of an array being resized (otherwise data is lost when `ReDim` is used). If you need to use this then you can only re-dimension the rightmost index of the array.
`Erase` – reinitializes the elements of a fixed-size array or empties the contents of a dynamic array:

```
Dim arEmployees ()
ReDim arEmployees (9,1)

arEmployees (9,1) = "Phil"

ReDim arEmployees (9,2)            'loses the contents of element (9,1)
arEmployees (9,2) = "Paul"

ReDim Preserve arEmployees (9,3)   'preserves the contents of (9,2)
arEmployees (9,3) = "Smith"

Erase arEmployees                  'now we are back to where we started -
                                   'empty array
```

`LBound` – returns the smallest subscript for the dimension of an array. Note that arrays always start from the subscript zero so this function will always return the value zero.
`UBound` – used to determine the size of an array:

```
Dim strCustomers (10, 5)
intSizeFirst = UBound (strCustomers, 1)       'returns SizeFirst = 10
intSizeSecond = UBound (strCustomers, 2)      'returns SizeSecond = 5
```

The actual number of elements is always one greater than the value returned by `UBound` because the array starts from zero.

Assignments

Let – used to assign values to variables (optional).
Set – used to assign an object reference to a variable.

```
Let intNumberOfDays = 365

Set txtMyTextBox = txtcontrol
txtMyTextBox.Value = "Hello World"
```

Constants

Empty – an empty variable is one that has been created, but has not yet been assigned a value.
Nothing – used to remove an object reference:

```
Set txtMyTextBox = txtATextBox        'assigns object reference
Set txtMyTextBox = Nothing            'removes object reference
```

Null – indicates that a variable is not valid. Note that this isn't the same as Empty.
True – indicates that an expression is true. Has numerical value –1.
False – indicates that an expression is false. Has numerical value 0.

Error constant

Constant	Value
vbObjectError	&h80040000

System Color constants

Constant	Value	Description
vbBlack	&h000000	Black
vbRed	&hFF0000	Red
vbGreen	&h00FF00	Green
vbYellow	&hFFFF00	Yellow
vbBlue	&h0000FF	Blue
vbMagenta	&hFF00FF	Magenta
vbCyan	&h00FFFF	Cyan
vbWhite	&hFFFFFF	White

Comparison constants

Constant	Value	Description
vbBinaryCompare	0	Perform a binary comparison.
vbTextCompare	1	Perform a textual comparison.

Date and Time constants

Constant	Value	Description
vbSunday	1	Sunday
vbMonday	2	Monday
vbTuesday	3	Tuesday
vbWednesday	4	Wednesday
vbThursday	5	Thursday
vbFriday	6	Friday
vbSaturday	7	Saturday
vbFirstJan1	1	Use the week in which January 1 occurs (default).
vbFirstFourDays	2	Use the first week that has at least four days in the new year.
vbFirstFullWeek	3	Use the first full week of the year.
vbUseSystem	0	Use the format in the regional settings for the computer.
vbUseSystemDayOfWeek	0	Use the day in the system settings for the first weekday.

Date Format constants

Constant	Value	Description
vbGeneralDate	0	Display a date and/or time in the format set in the system settings. For real numbers display a date and time. For integer numbers display only a date. For numbers less than 1, display time only.

Table Continued on Following Page

Constant	Value	Description
vbLongDate	1	Display a date using the long date format specified in the computer's regional settings.
vbShortDate	2	Display a date using the short date format specified in the computer's regional settings.
vbLongTime	3	Display a time using the long time format specified in the computer's regional settings.
vbShortTime	4	Display a time using the short time format specified in the computer's regional settings.

Message Box Constants

Constant	Value	Description
vbOKOnly	0	Display OK button only.
vbOKCancel	1	Display OK and Cancel buttons.
vbAbortRetryIgnore	2	Display Abort, Retry, and Ignore buttons.
vbYesNoCancel	3	Display Yes, No, and Cancel buttons.
vbYesNo	4	Display Yes and No buttons.
vbRetryCancel	5	Display Retry and Cancel buttons.
vbCritical	16	Display Critical Message icon.
vbQuestion	32	Display Warning Query icon.
vbExclamation	48	Display Warning Message icon.
vbInformation	64	Display Information Message icon.
vbDefaultButton1	0	First button is the default.
vbDefaultButton2	256	Second button is the default.
vbDefaultButton3	512	Third button is the default.
vbDefaultButton4	768	Fourth button is the default.
vbApplicationModal	0	Application modal.
vbSystemModal	4096	System modal.

String constants

Constant	Value	Description
vbCr	Chr(13)	Carriage return only
vbCrLf	Chr(13) & Chr(10)	Carriage return and linefeed (Newline)
vbFormFeed	Chr(12)	Form feed only
vbLf	Chr(10)	Line feed only
vbNewLine	-	Newline character as appropriate to a specific platform
vbNullChar	Chr(0)	Character having the value 0
vbNullString	-	String having the value zero (not just an empty string)
vbTab	Chr(9)	Horizontal tab
vbVerticalTab	Chr(11)	Vertical tab

Tristate constants

Constant	Value	Description
TristateUseDefault	-2	Use default setting
TristateTrue	-1	True
TristateFalse	0	False

VarType constants

Constant	Value	Description
vbEmpty	0	Uninitialized (default)
vbNull	1	Contains no valid data
vbInteger	2	Integer subtype
vbLong	3	Long subtype
vbSingle	4	Single subtype
vbDouble	5	Double subtype
vbCurrency	6	Currency subtype
vbDate	7	Date subtype

Table Continued on Following Page

Constant	Value	Description
vbString	8	String subtype
vbObject	9	Object
vbError	10	Error subtype
vbBoolean	11	Boolean subtype
vbVariant	12	Variant (used only for arrays of variants)
vbDataObject	13	Data access object
vbDecimal	14	Decimal subtype
vbByte	17	Byte subtype
vbArray	8192	Array

Control Flow

For...Next – executes a block of code a specified number of times:

```
Dim intSalary (10)
For intCounter = 0 to 10
   intSalary (intCounter) = 20000
Next
```

For Each...Next – repeats a block of code for each element in an array or collection:

```
For Each Item In Request.QueryString("MyControl")
  Response.Write Item & "<BR>"
Next
```

Do...Loop – executes a block of code while a condition is true or until a condition becomes true. Note that the condition can be checked either at the beginning or the end of the loop: the difference is that the code will be executed at least once if the condition is checked at the end.

```
Do While strDayOfWeek <> "Saturday" And strDayOfWeek <> "Sunday"
   MsgBox ("Get Up! Time for work")
   ...
Loop
```

```
Do
   MsgBox ("Get Up! Time for work")
   ...
Loop Until strDayOfWeek = "Saturday" Or strDayOfWeek = "Sunday"
```

We can also exit from a Do...Loop using Exit Do:

```
Do
   MsgBox ("Get Up! Time for work")
   ...
   If strDayOfWeek = "Sunday" Then
      Exit Do
   End If
Loop Until strDayOfWeek = "Saturday"
```

`If...Then...Else` – used to run various blocks of code depending on conditions:

```
If intAge < 20 Then
   MsgBox ("You're just a slip of a thing!")
ElseIf intAge < 40 Then
   MsgBox ("You're in your prime!")
Else
   MsgBox ("You're older and wiser")
End If
```

`Select Case` – used to replace `If...Then...Else` statements where there are many conditions:

```
Select Case intAge
Case 21,22,23,24,25,26
   MsgBox ("You're in your prime")
Case 40
   MsgBox ("You're fulfilling your dreams")
Case Else
   MsgBox ("Time for a new challenge")
End Select
```

`While...Wend` – executes a block of code while a condition is true:

```
While strDayOfWeek <> "Saturday" AND strDayOfWeek <> "Sunday"
   MsgBox ("Get Up! Time for work")
   ...
Wend
```

`With` – executes a series of statements for a single object:

```
With myDiv.style
   .posLeft = 200
   .posTop = 300
   .color = Red
End With
```

Functions

VBScript contains several inbuilt functions that can be used to manipulate and examine variables. These have been subdivided into these general categories:

- Conversion functions
- Date/time functions
- Math functions
- Object management functions
- Script engine identification functions
- String functions
- Variable testing functions

For a full description of each function and the parameters it requires, see the Microsoft web site at http://msdn.microsoft.com/scripting/.

Conversion Functions

These functions are used to convert values in variables between different types:

Function	Description
`Abs`	Returns the absolute value of a number.
`Asc`	Returns the numeric ANSI (or ASCII) code number of the first character in a string.
`AscB`	As above, but provided for use with byte data contained in a string. Returns result from the first byte only.
`AscW`	As above, but provided for Unicode characters. Returns the `Wide` character code, avoiding the conversion from Unicode to ANSI.
`Chr`	Returns a string made up of the ANSI character matching the number supplied.
`ChrB`	As above, but provided for use with byte data contained in a string. Always returns a single byte.
`ChrW`	As above, but provided for Unicode characters. Its argument is a `Wide` character code, thereby avoiding the conversion from ANSI to Unicode.
`CBool`	Returns the argument value converted to a `Variant` of subtype `Boolean`.
`CByte`	Returns the argument value converted to a `Variant` of subtype `Byte`.
`CCur`	Returns the argument value converted to a `Variant` of subtype `Currency`
`CDate`	Returns the argument value converted to a `Variant` of subtype `Date`.
`CDbl`	Returns the argument value converted to a `Variant` of subtype `Double`.
`CInt`	Returns the argument value converted to a `Variant` of subtype `Integer`.
`CLng`	Returns the argument value converted to a `Variant` of subtype `Long`
`CSng`	Returns the argument value converted to a `Variant` of subtype `Single`
`CStr`	Returns the argument value converted to a `Variant` of subtype `String`.

Function	Description
`Fix`	Returns the integer (whole) part of a number. If the number is negative, `Fix` returns the first negative integer greater than or equal to the number
`Hex`	Returns a string representing the hexadecimal value of a number.
`Int`	Returns the integer (whole) portion of a number. If the number is negative, `Int` returns the first negative integer less than or equal to the number.
`Oct`	Returns a string representing the octal value of a number.
`Round`	Returns a number rounded to a specified number of decimal places.
`Sgn`	Returns an integer indicating the sign of a number.

Date/Time Functions

These functions return date or time values from the computer's system clock, or manipulate existing values:

Function	Description
`Date`	Returns the current system date.
`DateAdd`	Returns a date to which a specified time interval has been added.
`DateDiff`	Returns the number of days, weeks, or years between two dates.
`DatePart`	Returns just the day, month or year of a given date.
`DateSerial`	Returns a `Variant` of subtype `Date` for a specified year, month and day.
`DateValue`	Returns a `Variant` of subtype `Date`.
`Day`	Returns a number between `1` and `31` representing the day of the month.
`Hour`	Returns a number between `0` and `23` representing the hour of the day.
`Minute`	Returns a number between `0` and `59` representing the minute of the hour.
`Month`	Returns a number between `1` and `12` representing the month of the year.

Table Continued on Following Page

Function	Description
MonthName	Returns the name of the specified month as a string.
Now	Returns the current date and time.
Second	Returns a number between 0 and 59 representing the second of the minute.
Time	Returns a Variant of subtype Date indicating the current system time.
TimeSerial	Returns a Variant of subtype Date for a specific hour, minute, and second.
TimeValue	Returns a Variant of subtype Date containing the time.
Weekday	Returns a number representing the day of the week.
WeekdayName	Returns the name of the specified day of the week as a string.
Year	Returns a number representing the year.

Math Functions

These functions perform mathematical operations on variables containing numerical values:

Function	Description
Atn	Returns the arctangent of a number.
Cos	Returns the cosine of an angle.
Exp	Returns e (the base of natural logarithms) raised to a power.
Log	Returns the natural logarithm of a number.
Randomize	Initializes the random-number generator.
Rnd	Returns a random number.
Sin	Returns the sine of an angle.
Sqr	Returns the square root of a number.
Tan	Returns the tangent of an angle.

Miscellaneous Functions

Function	Description
`Eval`	Evaluates an expression and returns a boolean result (e.g. treats `x=y` as an *expression* which is either true or false).
`Execute`	Executes one or more statements (e.g. treats `x=y` as a *statement* which assigns the value of y to x).
`RGB`	Returns a number representing an RGB color value

Object Management Functions

These functions are used to manipulate objects, where applicable:

Function	Description
`CreateObject`	Creates and returns a reference to an ActiveX or OLE Automation object.
`GetObject`	Returns a reference to an ActiveX or OLE Automation object.
`LoadPicture`	Returns a picture object.

Script Engine Identification

These functions return the version of the scripting engine:

Function	Description
`ScriptEngine`	A string containing the major, minor, and build version numbers of the scripting engine.
`ScriptEngineMajor _Version`	The major version of the scripting engine, as a number.
`ScriptEngineMinor _Version`	The minor version of the scripting engine, as a number.
`ScriptEngineBuild _Version`	The build version of the scripting engine, as a number.

String Functions

These functions are used to manipulate string values in variables:

Function	Description
`Filter`	Returns an array from a string array, based on specified filter criteria.
`FormatCurrency`	Returns a string formatted as currency value.
`FormatDateTime`	Returns a string formatted as a date or time.
`FormatNumber`	Returns a string formatted as a number.
`FormatPercent`	Returns a string formatted as a percentage.
`InStr`	Returns the position of the first occurrence of one string within another.
`InStrB`	As above, but provided for use with byte data contained in a string. Returns the byte position instead of the character position.
`InstrRev`	As `InStr`, but starts from the end of the string.
`Join`	Returns a string created by joining the strings contained in an array.
`LCase`	Returns a string that has been converted to lowercase.
`Left`	Returns a specified number of characters from the left end of a string.
`LeftB`	As above, but provided for use with byte data contained in a string. Uses that number of bytes instead of that number of characters.
`Len`	Returns the length of a string or the number of bytes needed for a variable.
`LenB`	As above, but is provided for use with byte data contained in a string. Returns the number of bytes in the string instead of characters.
`LTrim`	Returns a copy of a string without leading spaces.
`Mid`	Returns a specified number of characters from a string.
`MidB`	As above, but provided for use with byte data contained in a string. Uses that numbers of bytes instead of that number of characters.

Function	Description
`Replace`	Returns a string in which a specified substring has been replaced with another substring a specified number of times.
`Right`	Returns a specified number of characters from the right end of a string.
`RightB`	As above, but provided for use with byte data contained in a string. Uses that number of bytes instead of that number of characters.
`RTrim`	Returns a copy of a string without trailing spaces.
`Space`	Returns a string consisting of the specified number of spaces.
`Split`	Returns a one-dimensional array of a specified number of substrings.
`StrComp`	Returns a value indicating the result of a string comparison.
`String`	Returns a string of the length specified made up of a repeating character.
`StrReverse`	Returns a string in which the character order of a string is reversed.
`Trim`	Returns a copy of a string without leading or trailing spaces.
`UCase`	Returns a string that has been converted to uppercase.

Variable Testing Functions

These functions are used to determine the type of information stored in a variable:

Function	Description
`IsArray`	Returns a `Boolean` value indicating whether a variable is an array.
`IsDate`	Returns a `Boolean` value indicating whether an expression can be converted to a date.
`IsEmpty`	Returns a `Boolean` value indicating whether a variable has been initialized.

Table Continued on Following Page

Function	Description
IsNull	Returns a Boolean value indicating whether an expression contains no valid data
IsNumeric	Returns a Boolean value indicating whether an expression can be evaluated as a number.
IsObject	Returns a Boolean value indicating whether an expression references a valid ActiveX or OLE Automation object.
TypeName	Returns a string that provides Variant subtype information about a variable.
VarType	Returns a number indicating the subtype of a variable.

Variable Declarations

`Class` – Declares the name of a class, as well as the variables, properties, and methods that comprise the class.
`Const` – Declares a constant to be used in place of literal values.
`Dim` – declares a variable.

Error Handling

`On Error Resume Next` –indicates that if an error occurs, control should continue at the next statement.
`Err` – this is the error object that provides information about run-time errors.

Error handling is very limited in VBScript and the `Err` object must be tested explicitly to determine if an error has occurred.

Input/Output

This consists of `Msgbox` for output and `InputBox` for input:

MsgBox

This displays a message, and can return a value indicating which button was clicked.

```
MsgBox "Hello There",20,"Hello Message","c:\windows\MyHelp.hlp",123
```

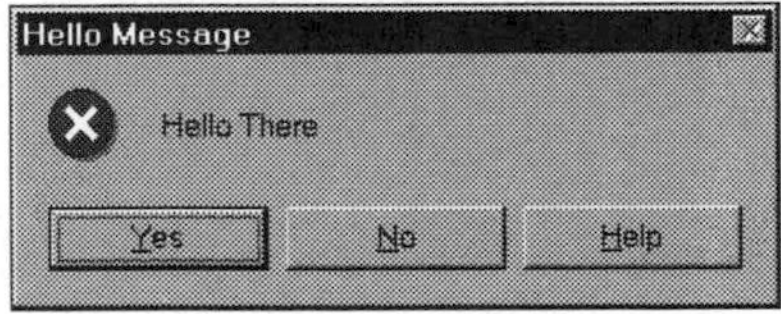

The parameters are:
`"Hello There"` – this contains the text of the message (the only obligatory parameter).
`20` – this determines which icon and buttons appear on the message box.
`"Hello Message"` – this contains the text that will appear as the title of the message box.
`"c:\windows\MyHelp.hlp"` – this adds a Help button to the message box and determines the help file that is opened if the button is clicked.
`123` – this is a reference to the particular help topic that will be displayed if the Help button is clicked.

The value of the icon and buttons parameter is determined using the following tables:

Constant	Value	Buttons
vbOKOnly	0	OK
vbOKCancel	1	OK Cancel
vbAbortRetry _Ignore	2	Abort Retry Ignore
vbYesNoCancel	3	Yes No Cancel
vbYesNo	4	Yes No
vbRetryCancel	5	Retry Cancel

Constant	Value	Buttons
vbDefaultButton1	0	The first button from the left is the default.
vbDefaultButton2	256	The second button from the left is the default.
vbDefaultButton3	512	The third button from the left is the default.
vbDefaultButton4	768	The fourth button from the left is the default.

Constant	Value	Description	Icon
vbCritical	16	Critical Message	
vbQuestion	32	Questioning Message	
vbExclamation	48	Warning Message	
vbInformation	64	Informational Message	
vbApplication Modal	0	Just the application stops until user clicks a button.	
vbSystemModal	4096	On Win16 systems the whole system stops until user clicks a button. On Win32 systems the message box remains on top of any other programs.	

To specify which buttons and icon are displayed you simply add the relevant values. So, in our example we add together `4 + 0+ 16` to display the **Yes** and **No** buttons, with **Yes** as the default, and the `Critical` icon. If we used `4 + 256 + 16` we could display the same buttons and icon, but have **No** as the default.

You can determine which button the user clicked by assigning the return code of the `MsgBox` function to a variable:

```
intButtonClicked = MsgBox ("Hello There",35,"Hello Message")
```

Notice that brackets enclose the `MsgBox` parameters when used in this format. The following table determines the value assigned to the variable `intButtonClicked`:

Constant	Value	Button Clicked	Constant	Value	Button Clicked
vbOK	1	OK	vbIgnore	5	Ignore
vbCancel	2	Cancel	vbYes	6	Yes
vbAbort	3	Abort	vbNo	7	No
vbRetry	4	Retry			

InputBox

This accepts text entry from the user and returns it as a string.

```
strName = InputBox ("Please enter your name","Login","John Smith",500,500)
```

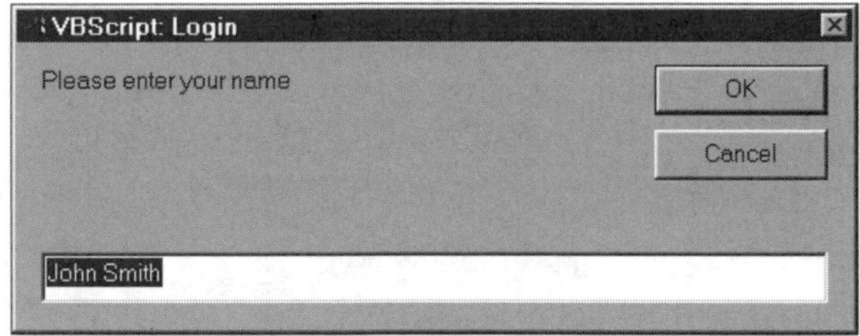

The parameters are:
`"Please enter your name"` – this is the prompt displayed in the input box.
`"Login"` – this is the text displayed as the title of the input box.
`"John Smith"` – this is the default value displayed in the input box.
`500` – specifies the x position of the input box in relation to the screen.
`500` – specifies the y position of the input box in relation to the screen.

As with the `MsgBox` function, you can also specify a help file and topic to add a Help button to the input box.

Procedures

`Call` – optional method of calling a subroutine.
`Function` – used to declare a function.
`Sub` – used to declare a subroutine.

Other Keywords

`Rem` – old style method of adding comments to code (it's now more usual to use an apostrophe (`'`).)
`Option Explicit` – forces you to declare a variable before it can be used (if used, it must appear before any other statements in a script).

Visual Basic Run-time Error Codes

The following error codes also apply to VBA code and many will not be appropriate to an application built completely around VBScript. However, if you have built your own components then these error codes may well be brought up when such components are used.

Code	Description
3	Return without GoSub
5	Invalid procedure call
6	Overflow

Table Continued on Following Page

Code	Description
7	Out of memory
9	Subscript out of range
10	This array is fixed or temporarily locked
11	Division by zero
13	Type mismatch
14	Out of string space
16	Expression too complex
17	Can't perform requested operation
18	User interrupt occurred
20	Resume without error
28	Out of stack space
35	Sub or Function not defined
47	Too many DLL application clients
48	Error in loading DLL
49	Bad DLL calling convention
51	Internal error
52	Bad file name or number
53	File not found
54	Bad file mode
55	File already open
57	Device I/O error
58	File already exists
59	Bad record length
61	Disk full
62	Input past end of file
63	Bad record number
67	Too many files
68	Device unavailable

Code	Description
70	Permission denied
71	Disk not ready
74	Can't rename with different drive
75	Path/File access error
76	Path not found
91	Object variable not set
92	`For` loop not initialized
93	Invalid pattern string
94	Invalid use of Null
322	Can't create necessary temporary file
325	Invalid format in resource file
380	Invalid property value
423	Property or method not found
424	Object required
429	OLE Automation server can't create object
430	Class doesn't support OLE Automation
432	File name or class name not found during OLE Automation operation
438	Object doesn't support this property or method
440	OLE Automation error
442	Connection to type library or object library for remote process has been lost. Press OK for dialog to remove reference.
443	OLE Automation object does not have a default value
445	Object doesn't support this action
446	Object doesn't support named arguments
447	Object doesn't support current locale setting
448	Named argument not found
449	Argument not optional

Table Continued on Following Page

Code	Description
450	Wrong number of arguments or invalid property assignment
451	Object not a collection
452	Invalid ordinal
453	Specified DLL function not found
454	Code resource not found
455	Code resource lock error
457	This key is already associated with an element of this collection
458	Variable uses an OLE Automation type not supported in Visual Basic
462	The remote server machine does not exist or is unavailable
481	Invalid picture
500	Variable is undefined
501	Cannot assign to variable
502	Object not safe for scripting
503	Object not safe for initializing
504	Object not safe for creating
505	Invalid or unqualified reference
506	Class not defined
1001	Out of memory
1002	Syntax error
1003	Expected ':'
1004	Expected ';'
1005	Expected '('
1006	Expected ')'
1007	Expected ']'
1008	Expected '{'
1009	Expected '}'
1010	Expected identifier
1011	Expected '='

Code	Description
1012	Expected 'If'
1013	Expected 'To'
1014	Expected 'End'
1015	Expected 'Function'
1016	Expected 'Sub'
1017	Expected 'Then'
1018	Expected 'Wend'
1019	Expected 'Loop'
1020	Expected 'Next'
1021	Expected 'Case'
1022	Expected 'Select'
1023	Expected expression
1024	Expected statement
1025	Expected end of statement
1026	Expected integer constant
1027	Expected 'While' or 'Until'
1028	Expected 'While', 'Until' or end of statement
1029	Too many locals or arguments
1030	Identifier too long
1031	Invalid number
1032	Invalid character
1033	Un-terminated string constant
1034	Un-terminated comment
1035	Nested comment
1036	'Me' cannot be used outside of a procedure
1037	Invalid use of 'Me' keyword
1038	'loop' without 'do'
1039	Invalid 'exit' statement

Table Continued on Following Page

Code	Description
1040	Invalid 'for' loop control variable
1041	Variable redefinition
1042	Must be first statement on the line
1043	Cannot assign to non-ByVal argument
1044	Cannot use parentheses when calling a Sub
1045	Expected literal constant
1046	Expected 'In'
1047	Expected 'Class'
1048	Must be defined inside a Class
1049	Expected Let or Set or Get in property declaration
1050	Expected 'Property'
1051	Number of arguments must be consistent across properties specification
1052	Cannot have multiple default property/method in a Class
1053	Class initialize or terminate do not have arguments
1054	Property set or let must have at least one argument
1055	Unexpected 'Next'
1056	'Default' can be specified only on 'Property' or 'Function' or 'Sub'
1057	'Default' specification must also specify 'Public'
1058	'Default' specification can only be on Property Get
5016	Regular Expression object expected
5017	Syntax error in regular expression
5018	Unexpected quantifier
5019	Expected ']' in regular expression
5020	Expected ')' in regular expression
5021	Invalid range in character set
32811	Element not found

For more information about VBScript, visit Microsoft's VBScript site, at http://msdn.microsoft.com/scripting.

HTML

JScript Reference

General Information

JScript is included in an HTML document with the <SCRIPT> tag. Here's an example:

```
<HTML>
<HEAD>

<SCRIPT LANGUAGE = "JScript">
<!-- wrap script in comments
      script code goes here
-->
</SCRIPT>

</HEAD>
<BODY>
      script goes here
</BODY>
</HTML>
```

The following points should be kept in mind:

- By placing JScript code in the <HEAD> section of the document you ensure that all the code has been loaded before an attempt is made to execute it.
- The script code should be wrapped in an HTML comment tag to stop older (non-JScript) browsers from displaying it.
- JScript is case sensitive.

Values

JScript recognizes the following data types:

- **strings** – e.g. "Hello World"
- **numbers** – both integers (86) and decimal values (86.235)
- **boolean** – `true` or `false` (case sensitive)

A null (*no value*) value is assigned with the keyword `null`.

JScript also makes use of 'special characters' in a similar way to the C++ programming language:

Character	Function
\n	newline
\t	tab
\f	form feed
\b	backspace
\r	carriage return

You may 'escape' other characters by preceding them with a backslash (\), to prevent the browser from trying to interpret them. This is most commonly used for quotes and backslashes, or to include a character by using its octal (base 8) value:

```
document.write("This shows a \"quote\" in a string.");
document.write("This is a backslash: \\");
document.write("This is a space character: \040.");
```

Variables

JScript is a **loosely typed** language. This means that variables do not have an explicitly defined variable type. Instead, every variable can hold values of various types. Conversions between types are done automatically when needed, as this example demonstrates:

```
x = 55;      // x is assigned to be the integer 55
y = "55";    // y is assigned to be the string "55"
y = '55';    // an alternative using single quotes

z = 1 + y;

/* because y is a string, z will be automatically
 converted to a string value, so the result is z = 155. */

document.write(x);
/* the number 55 will be written to the screen. Even
 though x is an integer and not a string, JScript will
 make the necessary conversion for you. */

n = 3.14159;  // assigning a real (fractional) number
n = 0546;     // numbers starting 0 assumed to be octal
n = 0xFFEC;   // numbers starting 0x assumed to be hex
n = 2.145E-5; // using exponential notation
```

The `parseInt()` and `parseFloat()` functions (discussed later in this appendix) can be used to convert strings for numeric addition.

Variable names must start with either a letter or an underscore. Beyond the first letter, variables may contain any combination of letters, underscores, and digits. JScript is case sensitive, so `this_variable` is not the same as `This_Variable`.

Variables do not need to be declared before they are used. However, you may use the var keyword to explicitly define a variable. This is especially useful when there is the possibility of conflicting variable names. When in doubt, use var.

```
var x = "55";
```

Assignment Operators

The following operators are used to make assignments in JScript:

Operator	Example	Result
=	x = y	x equals y
+=	x += y	x equals x plus y
-=	x -= y	x equals x minus y
*=	x *= y	x equals x multiplied by y
/=	x /= y	x equals x divided by y
%=	x %= y	x equals x modulus y

Each operator assigns the value on the right to the variable on the left.

```
x = 100;
y = 10;
x += y;  // x now is equal to 110
```

Equality Operators

Operator	Meaning
==	is equal to
!=	is not equal to
>	is greater than
>=	is greater than or equal to
<	is less than
<=	is less than or equal to

Other Operators

<table>
<tr><th>Operator</th><th>Meaning</th></tr>
<tr><td>+</td><td>Addition</td></tr>
<tr><td>-</td><td>Subtraction</td></tr>
<tr><td>*</td><td>Multiplication</td></tr>
<tr><td>/</td><td>Division</td></tr>
<tr><td>%</td><td>Modulus</td></tr>
<tr><td>++</td><td>Increment</td></tr>
<tr><td>--</td><td>Decrement</td></tr>
<tr><td>-</td><td>Unary Negation</td></tr>
<tr><td>&</td><td>Bitwise AND</td></tr>
<tr><td>|</td><td>Bitwise OR</td></tr>
<tr><td>^</td><td>Bitwise XOR</td></tr>
<tr><td><<</td><td>Bitwise left shift</td></tr>
<tr><td>>></td><td>Bitwise right shift</td></tr>
<tr><td>>>></td><td>Zero-fill right shift</td></tr>
<tr><td>&&</td><td>Logical AND</td></tr>
<tr><td>||</td><td>Logical OR</td></tr>
<tr><td>!</td><td>Not</td></tr>
</table>

String Operators

<table>
<tr><th>Operator</th><th>Meaning</th></tr>
<tr><td>+</td><td>Concatenates strings, so "abc" + "def" is "abcdef"</td></tr>
<tr><td>==</td><td rowspan="7">Compare strings in a case-sensitive way. A string is 'greater' than another based on the Latin ASCII code values of the characters, starting from the left of the string. So "DEF" is greater than "ABC" and "DEE", but less than "abc" (uppercase letters are before lowercase ones in the ASCII character set).</td></tr>
<tr><td>!=</td></tr>
<tr><td>></td></tr>
<tr><td>>=</td></tr>
<tr><td><</td></tr>
<tr><td><=</td></tr>
</table>

Comments

Operator	Meaning
`// a comment`	A single line comment
`/* this text is a multi-line comment */`	A multi-line comment

Input/Output

In JScript, there are three different methods of providing information to the user and getting a response back. (Note that these are methods of the window object, and not JScript function calls.)

Alert

This displays a message with an OK button:

```
alert("Hello World!");
```

Confirm

Displays a message with both an OK and a Cancel button. True is returned if the OK button is pressed, and false is returned if the Cancel button is pressed:

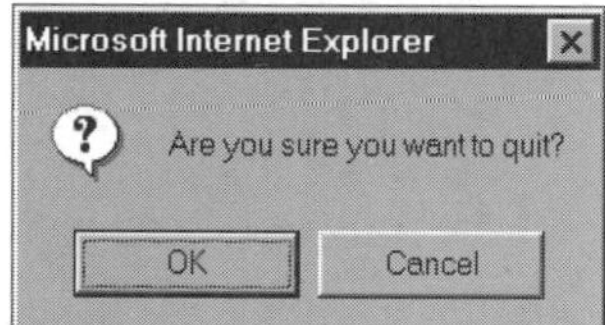


```
confirm("Are you sure you want to quit?");
```

Prompt

Displays a message and a text box for user input. The first string argument forms the text that is to be displayed above the text box. The second argument is a string, integer, or property of an existing object, which represents the default value to display inside the box. If the second argument is not specified, "<undefined>" is displayed inside the text box.

The string typed into the box is returned if the OK button is pressed. False is returned if the Cancel button is pressed:

```
prompt("What is your name?", "");
```

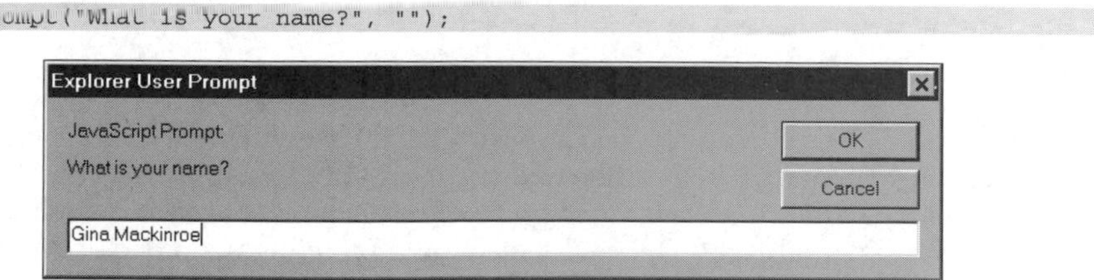

Control Flow

There are two ways of controlling the flow of a program in JScript. The first involves **conditional** statements, which follow either one branch of the program or another. The second way is to use a **repeated iteration** of a set of statements.

Conditional Statements

JScript has two conditional statements:

`if..then..else` – used to run various blocks of code, depending on conditions. These statements have the following general form in JScript:

```
if (condition)
{
  code to be executed if condition is true
}
else
{
  code to be executed if condition is false
};
```

In addition:

- The `else` portion is optional.
- `if` statements may be nested.
- Multiple statements must be enclosed by braces.

Here is an example:

```
person_type = prompt("What are you ?", "");
if (person_type == "cat")
  alert("Here, have some cat food.");
else
{
  if (person_type == "dog")
    alert("Here, have some dog food.");
  else
  {
    if (person_type == "human")
      alert("Here have some, er, human food!");
  }
};
```

Notice that the curly brackets are only actually required where there is more than one statement within the block. Like many other constructs, they can be omitted where single statements are used. (Although not necessary, it can sometimes be a good idea to include all of the semi-colons and brackets that could be used, as this makes the code easier to modify.)

All statements in JScript are supposed to have a semi-colon line terminator, because a statement can span more than one line without special continuation markers. However, JScript lets you leave it out in quite a few areas, as long as it can tell where a statement is supposed to end. The final semicolon is therefore not mandatory.

`switch` – used to run various blocks of code, depending on conditions. These statements have the following general form in JScript:

```
switch (expression) {
  case label1 :
    code to be executed if expression is equal to label1
    break;
  case label2 :
    code to be executed if expression is equal to label2
  ...
  default :
    code to be executed if expression is not equal to any of the
    case labels.
}
```

`break;` can be inserted following the code for a case, to prevent execution of the code running into the next case automatically

Loop Statements

`for` – executes a block of code a specified number of times:

```
for (initialization; condition; increment)
{
  statements to execute…
}
```

In the following example, `i` is initially set to zero, and is incremented by 1 at the end of each iteration. The loop terminates when the condition `i < 10` is false:

```
for (i = 0; i < 10; i++)
{
  document.write(i);
}
```

`while` – executes a block of code while a condition is true:

```
while (condition)
{
  statements to execute ...
}
```

`do...while` – executes a statement block once, and then repeats execution of the loop while a condition is true:

```
do
{
  statements to execute ...
}
while (condition);
```

`break` – will cause an exit from a loop regardless of the condition statement:

```
x = 0;
while (x != 10)
{
  n = prompt("Enter a number or 'q' to quit", "");
  if (n == "q")
  {
    alert("See ya");
    break;
  }
}
```

`break` can also be used in `switch`, `for` and `do...while` loops.

`continue` – will cause the loop to jump immediately back to the condition statement.

```
x = 0;
while (x != 1)
{
  if (!(confirm("Should I add 1 to n ?")))
  {
    continue;
    // the following x++ is never executed
    x++;
  }
  x++;
}
alert("Bye");
```

`with` – Establishes a default object for a set of statements. The code:

```
x = Math.cos(3 * Math.PI) + Math.sin(Math.LN10)
y = Math.tan(14 * Math.E)
```

can be rewritten as:

```
with (Math)
{
  x = cos(3 * PI) + sin (LN10)
  y = tan(14 * E)
}
```

When you use the `with` statement, the object passed as the parameter is the default object. Notice how this shortens each statement.

Error Handling Statements

JScript 5 now includes built-in error handling. This is done using the try…catch statement. It allows the developer to anticipate certain error messages, and provide a different code path to follow if that error occurs.

```
function ErrorHandler(x)
{
  try {
    try {
      if (x == 'OK')              // Evalute argument
        throw "Value OK";         // Throw an error
      else
        throw "Value not OK";     // Throw a different error
    }
    catch(e) {                    // Handle "x = OK" errors here
      if (e == "Value OK")        // Check for an error handled here
        return(e + " successfully handled.");
                                  // Return error message
      else                        // Can't handle error here
        throw e;                  // Rethrow the error for next
    }                             // error handler
  }
  catch(e) {                      // Handle other errors here
    return(e + " handled elsewhere.");
                                  // Return error message
  }
}
document.write(ErrorHandler('OK'));
document.write(ErrorHandler('BAD'));
```

The `throw` statement is used to generate error conditions that can then be handled by a `try...catch` block. The value that you throw can be any expression, including a string, Boolean or number.

Built-in Functions

JScript provides a number of built-in functions that can be accessed within code.

Function	Description
`escape(char)`	Returns a new string with all spaces, punctuation, accented characters and any non–ASCII characters encoded into the format %XX, where XX is their hexadecimal value.
`eval(expression)`	Returns the result of evaluating the JScript expression expression
`isFinite(value)`	Returns a Boolean value of `true` if value is any value other than `NaN` (not a number), negative infinity, or positive infinity.
`isNaN(value)`	Returns a Boolean value of `true` if value is not a legal number.
`parseFloat(string)`	Converts string to a floating-point number.
`parseInt(string, base)`	Converts string to an integer number with the base of base.
`typeOf(object)`	Returns the data type of object as a string, such as `"boolean"`, `"function"`, etc.
`unescape(char)`	Returns a string where all characters encoded with the %XX hexadecimal form are replaced by their ASCII character set equivalents.

Built-in Objects

JScript provides a set of built-in data-type objects, which have their own set of properties, and methods – and which can be accessed with JScript code.

ActiveXObject Object

The `ActiveXObject` object creates and returns a reference to an automation object. To create a new `ActiveXObject` object, use:

```
ExcelSheet = new ActiveXObject("Excel.Sheet");
   // create an automation object referring to an Excel Spreadsheet
```

Once you have created the object reference, you can interact with the object using it's methods and properties.

Array Object

The Array object specifies a method of creating arrays and working with them. To create a new array, use:

```
cats = new Array();     // create an empty array
cats = new Array(10);   // create an array of 10 items

// or create and fill an array with values in one go:
cats = new Array("Boo Boo", "Purrcila", "Sam", "Lucky");
```

Properties	Description
length	A read/write integer value specifying the number of elements in the array.

Methods	Description
array1.concat(array2)	Returns a new array consisting of the contents of two arrays.
join([string])	Returns a string containing each element of the array, optionally separated with string.
reverse()	Reverses the order of the array, without creating a new object.
slice(start, [end])	Returns a section of an array, starting at position start and going up to and including position end.
sort([function])	Sorts the array, optionally based upon the results of a function specified by function.
toString()	Returns the elements of an array converted to strings and concatenated, separated by commas.
valueOf()	Returns the elements of an array converted to strings and concatenated, separated by commas. Like toString.

Early versions of JScript had no explicit array structure. However, JScript's object mechanisms allow for easy creation of arrays:

```
function MakeArray(n)
{
  this.length = n;
  for (var i = 1; i <= n; i++)
    this[i] = 0;
  return this
}
```

With this function included in your script, you can create arrays with:

```
cats = new MakeArray(20);
```

You can then populate the array like this:

```
cats[0] = "Boo Boo";
cats[1] = "Purrcila";
cats[2] = "Sam";
cats[3] = "Lucky";
```

Boolean Object

The `Boolean` object is used to store simple yes/no, true/false values. To create a new Boolean object, use the syntax:

```
MyAnswer = new Boolean([value])
```

If *`value`* is `0`, `null`, omitted, or an empty string the new Boolean object will have the value `false`. All other values, *including the string* `"false"`, create an object with the value `true`.

Methods	Description
`toString()`	Returns the value of the Boolean as the string `true` or `false`.
`valueOf()`	Returns the primitive numeric value of the object for conversion in calculations.

Date Object

The `Date` object provides a method for working with dates and times inside of JScript. New instances of the `Date` object are invoked with:

```
newDateObject = new Date([dateInfo])
```

`dateInfo` is an optional specification for the date to set in the new object. If it is not specified, the current date and time are used. *`dateInfo`* can use any of the following formats:

`milliseconds` (since midnight GMT on January 1, 1970)
`year, month, day` (e.g. `1997, 0, 27` is January 27, 1997)
`year, month, day, hours, minutes, seconds`
(e.g. `1997, 8, 23, 08, 25, 30` is September 23 1997 at 08:25:30)

Times and dates are generally in **local time**, but the user can also specify Universal Coordinated Time (**UTC**, previously GMT).

Methods	Description
`getDate()` `getUTCDate()`	Returns the day of the month as an integer between 1 and 31, using local time or UTC.

Table Continued on Following Page

Methods	Description
`getDay()` `getUTCDay()`	Returns the day of the week as an integer between 0 (Sunday) and 6 (Saturday), using local time or UTC.
`getFullYear()` `getUTCFullYear()`	Returns the year as an Integer, using local time or UTC.
`getHours()` `getUTCHours()`	Returns the hours as an integer between 0 and 23, using local time or UTC.
`getMilliseconds()` `getUTCMilliseconds()`	Returns the milliseconds as an integer between 0 and 999, using local time or UTC.
`getMinutes()` `getUTCMinutes()`	Returns the minutes as an integer between 0 and 59, using local time or UTC.
`getMonth()` `getUTCMonth()`	Returns the month as an integer between 0 (January) and 11 (December), using local time or UTC.
`getSeconds()` `getUTCSeconds()`	Returns the seconds as an integer between 0 and 59, using local time or UTC.
`getTime()`	Returns the number of milliseconds between January 1, 1970 at 00:00:00 UTC and the current `Date` object as an integer.
`getTimeZoneOffset()`	Returns the number of minutes difference between local time and UTC as an integer.
`getVarDate()`	Returns the date in `VT_DATE` format, which is used to interact with ActiveX objects.
`getYear()`	Returns the year minus 1900 - i.e. only two digits) as an integer.
`parse(`*dateString*`)`	Returns the number of milliseconds in a date string, since Jan. 1, 1970 00:00:00 UTC.

Methods	Description
`setDate(`*dayValue*`)` `setUTCDate(`*dayValue*`)`	Sets the day of the month where *dayValue* is an integer between 1 and 31, using local time or UTC.
`setFullYear(`*yearValue*`)` `setUTCFullYear(`*yearValue*`)`	Sets the year where *yearValue* indicates the 4 digit year, using local time or UTC.
`setHours(`*hoursValue*`)` `setUTCHours(`*hoursValue*`)`	Sets the hours where *hoursValue* is an integer between 0 and 59, using local time or UTC.
`setMilliSeconds(`*msValue*`)` `setUTCMilliSeconds(`*msValue*`)`	Sets the milliseconds where *msValue* is an integer between 0 and 999, using local time or UTC.
`setMinutes(`*minutesValue*`)` `setUTCMinutes(`*minutesValue*`)`	Sets the minutes where *minutesValue* is an integer between 0 and 59, using local time or UTC.
`setMonth(`*monthValue*`)` `setUTCMonth(`*monthValue*`)`	Sets the month where *monthValue* is an integer between 0 and 11, using local time or UTC.
`setSeconds(`*secondsValue*`)` `setUTCSeconds(`*secondsValue*`)`	Sets the seconds where *secondsValue* is an integer between 0 and 59, using local time or UTC.
`setTime(`*timeValue*`)`	Sets the value of a `Date` object where *timeValue* is and integer representing the number of milliseconds in a date string, since Jan. 1, 1970 00:00:00 GMT.
`setYear(`*yearValue*`)`	Sets the year where *yearValue* is an integer (generally) greater than 1900.
`toGMTString()`	Converts a date to a string using GMT. Equivalent to `toUTCString`, and included only for backwards compatibility.
`toLocaleString()`	Converts a date to a string using local time.
`toUTCString()`	Converts a date to a string using UTC.
`UTC(`*year*`, `*month*`, `*day*`[,`*hrs*`][,`*min*`][,`*sec*`])`	Returns the number of milliseconds in a date object, since Jan. 1, 1970 00:00:00 UTC.

Enumerator Object

The `Enumerator` object is used to enumerate, or step through, the items in a collection. The `Enumerator` object provides a way to access any member of a collection, and behaves similarly to the `For...Each` statement in VBScript.

```
newEnumeratorObj = new Enumerator(collection)
```

Methods	Description
`atEnd()`	Returns a boolean value indicating if the enumerator is at the end of the collection
`item()`	Returns the current item in the collection
`moveFirst()`	Resets the current item to the first item in the collection
`moveNext()`	Changes the current item to the next item in the collection

Error Object

The `Error` object contains information about run-time errors generated in JScript code. The scripting engine automatically generates this object. You can also create it yourself if you want to generate your own custom error states.

```
newErrorObj = new Error(number)
```

Properties	Description
`description`	The descriptive string associated with a particular error
`number`	The number associated with a particular error

Function Object

The `Function` object provides a mechanism for compiling JScript code as a function. A new function is invoked with the syntax:

```
functionName = new Function(arg1, arg2, ..., functionCode)
```

where *`arg1`*, *`arg2`*, etc. are the argument names for the function object being created, and *`functionCode`* is a string containing the body of the function. This can be a series of JScript statements separated by semi-colons.

Properties	Description
`arguments[]`	A reference to the `arguments` array that holds the arguments that were provided when the function was called.
`caller`	Returns a reference to the function that invoked the current function.
`prototype`	Provides a way for adding properties to a `Function` object.

Methods	Description
toString()	Returns a string value representation of the function.
valueOf()	Returns the function.

Arguments Object

The `arguments` object is list (array) of arguments in a function.

Properties	Description
length	An integer specifying the number of arguments provided to the function when it was called.

Math Object

Provides a set of properties and methods for working with mathematical constants and functions. Simply reference the `Math` object, then the method or property required:

```
MyArea = Math.PI * MyRadius * MyRadius;
MyResult = Math.floor(MyNumber);
```

Properties	Description
E	Euler's Constant e (the base of natural logarithms).
LN10	The value of the natural logarithm of 10.
LN2	The value of the natural logarithm of 2.
LOG10E	The value of the base 10 logarithm of E.
LOG2E	The value of the base 2 logarithm of E.
PI	The value of the constant π (pi).
SQRT1_2	The value of the square root of a half.
SQRT 2	The value of the square root of two.

Methods	Description
abs(number)	Returns the absolute value of number.
acos(number)	Returns the arc cosine of number.
asin(number)	Returns the arc sine of number.
atan(number)	Returns the arc tangent of number.

Table Continued on Following Page

Methods	Description
`atan2(x, y)`	Returns the angle of the polar coordinate of a point `x, y` from the x-axis.
`ceil(number)`	Returns the next largest integer greater than number, i.e. rounds up.
`cos(number)`	Returns the cosine of number.
`exp(number)`	Returns the value of number as the exponent of e, as in e^{number}.
`floor(number)`	Returns the next smallest integer less than number, i.e. rounds down.
`log(number)`	Returns the natural logarithm of number.
`max(num1, num2)`	Returns the greater of the two values num1 and num2.
`min(num1, num2)`	Returns the smaller of the two values num1 and num2.
`pow(num1, num2)`	Returns the value of num1 to the power of num2.
`random()`	Returns a random number between 0 and 1.
`round(number)`	Returns the closest integer to number i.e. rounds up or down to the nearest whole number.
`sin(number)`	Returns the sin of number.
`sqrt(number)`	Returns the square root of number.
`tan(number)`	Returns the tangent of number.

Number Object

The `Number` object provides a set of properties that are useful when working with numbers:

```
newNumberObj = new Number(value)
```

Properties	Description
`MAX_VALUE`	The maximum numeric value represented in JScript (~1.79E+308).
`MIN_VALUE`	The minimum numeric value represented in JScript (~2.22E-308).
`NaN`	A value meaning 'Not A Number'.
`NEGATIVE_INFINITY`	A special value for negative infinity ("-Infinity").
`POSITIVE_INFINITY`	A special value for infinity ("Infinity").

Methods	Description
`toString([radix_base])`	Returns the value of the number as a string to a radix (base) of 10, unless specified otherwise in radix_base.
`valueOf()`	Returns the primitive numeric value of the object.

RegularExpression Object

The `RegularExpression` object contains a regular expression. A regular expression is used to search strings for character patterns.

```
function RegExpDemo()
{
  var s = "AaBbCcDdEeFfGgHhIiJjKkLlMmNnOoPp"
  var r = new RegExp("g", "i");
  var a = r.exec(s);
  document.write(a);
  r.compile("g");
  var a = r.exec(s);
  document.write(a);
}
```

Properties	Description
`lastIndex`	Character position at which to start the next match
`source`	Text of the regular expression

Methods	Description
`compile()`	Converts the regular expression into an internal format for faster execution
`exec()`	Executes the search for a match in a particular string
`test()`	Returns a boolean value indicating whether or not a pattern exists within a string

RegExp Object

The `RegExp` object stores information about regular expression pattern searches. It works in conjunction with the `RegularExpression` object. In the example below, even though the new method was called with the `RegExp` object as a parameter, a `RegularExpression` object was actually created:

```
function regExpDemo()
{
  var s;
  var re = new RegExp("d(b+)(d)","ig");
  var str = "cdbBdbsbdbdz";
  var arr = re.exec(str);
  s = "$1 contains: " + RegExp.$1 + "<BR>";
  s += "$2 contains: " + RegExp.$2 + "<BR>";
  s += "$3 contains: " + RegExp.$3;
  return(s);
}
```

Notice that when checking the properties for the RegExp object, we don't refer to an instance of that object. Rather the reference is made directly to the static RegExp object.

Properties	Description
$1...$9	The 9 most recently found portions during pattern matching
index	Character position where the first successful match begins
input	String against which the regular expression is searched
lastIndex	Character position where the last successful match begins

String Object

The String object provides a set of methods for text manipulation. To create a new string object, the syntax is:

```
MyString = new String([value])
```

where *value* is the optional text to place in the string when it is created. If this is a number, it is converted into a string first.

Properties	Description
length	An integer representing the number of characters in the string.

Methods	Description
anchor("nameAttribute")	Returns the original string surrounded by <A> and </A> anchor tags, with the NAME attribute set to "nameAttribute".
big()	Returns the original string enclosed in <BIG> and </BIG> tags.
blink()	Returns the original string enclosed in <BLINK> and </BLINK> tags.

Methods	Description
bold()	Returns the original string enclosed in <B> and </B> tags.
charAt(index)	Returns the single character at position index within the String object.
charCodeAt(index)	Returns the Unicode encoding of the character at position index.
concat(string2)	Returns a string containing string2 added to the end of the original string.
fixed()	Returns the original string enclosed in <TT> and </TT> tags.
fontcolor("color")	Returns the original string surrounded by <FONT> and </FONT> tags, with the COLOR attribute set to "color".
fontsize("size")	Returns the original string surrounded by <FONT> and </FONT> anchor tags, with the SIZE attribute set to "size".
fromCharCode(code1, _...coden)	Returns the string from a number of Unicode character values
indexOf(searchValue _[,fromIndex])	Returns first occurrence of the string searchValue starting at index fromIndex.
italics()	Returns the original string enclosed in <I> and </I> tags.
lastIndexOf(search _Value [,fromIndex])	Returns the index of the last occurrence of the string searchValue, searching backwards from index fromIndex.
link("hrefAttribute")	Returns the original string surrounded by <A> and </A> link tags, with the HREF attribute set to "hrefAttribute".
match(regExp)	Returns an array containing the results of a search using the regExp RegularExpression object.
replace(regExp, _replaceText)	Returns a string with text replaced using a regular expression
search(regExp)	Returns the position of the first substring match in a regular expression search
slice(start, [end])	Returns a section of a string starting at position start and ending at position end.

Table Continued on Following Page

Methods	Description
small()	Returns the original string enclosed in <SMALL> and </SMALL> tags.
split(separator)	Returns an array of strings created by separating the String object at every occurrence of separator.
strike()	Returns the original string enclosed in <STRIKE> and </STRIKE> tags.
sub()	Returns the original string enclosed in _{and} tags.
substr(start, [length])	Returns a substring starting at position start and having a length of length characters.
substring(indexA, indexB)	Returns the sub-string of the original String object from the character at indexA up to and including the one before the character at indexB.
sup()	Returns the original string enclosed in ^{and} tags.
toLowerCase()	Returns the original string with all the characters converted to lowercase.
toUpperCase()	Returns the original string with all the characters converted to uppercase.
toString()	Returns the value of the String object
valueOf()	Returns the string

VBArray Object

Provides access to an array created in VBScript. Since these arrays use a different memory structure than JScript arrays, it is necessary to use this object to access them. This object only provides read-only access.

```
<SCRIPT LANGUAGE="VBScript">
<!--
dim arVBArray
' populate this VBScript array…
-->
</SCRIPT>
<SCRIPT LANGUAGE="JScript">
<!--
function useVBArray()
{
  var arJSArray = new VBArray(arVBArray);
  var arArray = arJSArray.toArray();
// now arArray can be used like a JScript array
}
-->
</SCRIPT>
```

Methods	Description
dimensions()	Returns the number of dimensions in the VBArray
getItem(dim1, dim2,... dimn)	Returns the item at the specified location
lbound(dimension)	Returns the lowest index value used at the dimension specified by dimension.
toArray()	Returns a standard JScript array converted from the VBArray object.
ubound(dimension)	Returns the highest index value used at the dimension specified by dimension.

Reserved Words

The following are reserved words that can't be used for function, method, variable, or object names. Note that while some words in this list are not currently used as JScript keywords, they have been reserved for future use.

```
abstract    else         int          super
boolean     extends      interface    switch
break       false        long         synchronized
byte        final        native       this
case        finally      new          throw
catch       float        null         throws
char        for          package      transient
class       function     private      true
const       goto         protected    try
continue    if           public       typeof
default     implements   reset        var
delete      import       return       void
do          in           short        while
double      instanceof   static       with
```

Support and Errata

One of the most irritating things about any programming book is when you find that bit of code you've just spent an hour typing simply doesn't work. You check it a hundred times to see if you've set it up correctly and then you notice the spelling mistake in the variable name on the book page. Of course, you can blame the authors for not taking enough care and testing the code, the editors for not doing their job properly, or the proofreaders for not being eagle-eyed enough, but this doesn't get around the fact that mistakes do happen.

We try hard to ensure no mistakes sneak out into the real world, but we can't promise that this book is 100% error free. What we can do is offer the next best thing by providing you with immediate support and feedback from experts who have worked on the book and try to ensure that future editions eliminate these gremlins. The following section will take you step by step through the process of posting errata to our web site to get that help. The sections that follow, therefore, are:

- Wrox Developers Membership
- Finding a list of existing errata on the web site
- Adding your own errata to the existing list
- What happens to your errata once you've posted it (why doesn't it appear immediately)?

There is also a section covering how to e-mail a question for technical support. This comprises:

- What your e-mail should include
- What happens to your e-mail once it has been received by us

So that you only need view information relevant to yourself, we ask that you register as a Wrox Developer Member. This is a quick and easy process, that will save you time in the long-run. If you are already a member, just update your membership to include this book.

Wrox Developer's Membership

To get your FREE Wrox Developer's Membership click on Membership in the navigation bar of our home site – http://www.wrox.com. This is shown in the following screenshot:

Then, on the next screen (not shown), click on New User. This will display a form. Fill in the details on the form and submit the details using the Send Form button at the bottom. Before you can say 'The best read books come in Wrox Red' you will get the following screen:

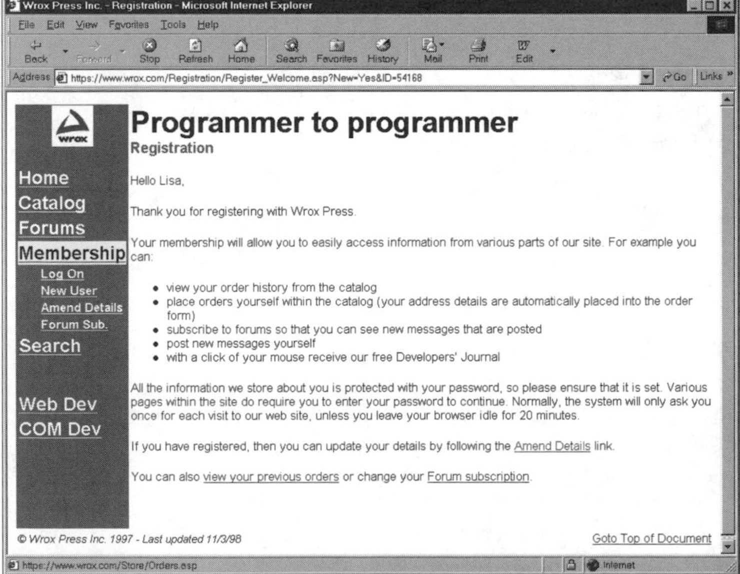

Finding an Errata on the Web Site

Before you send in a query, you might be able to save time by finding the answer to your problem on our web site – http://www.wrox.com.

Each book we publish has its own page and its own errata sheet. You can get to any book's page by clicking on Support from the left hand side navigation bar.

From this page you can locate any book's errata page on our site. Select your book from the pop-up menu and click on it.

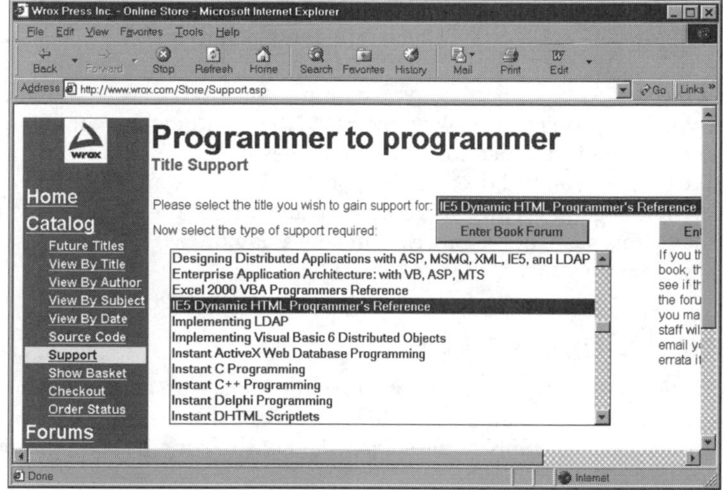

Then click on Enter Book Errata. This will take you to the errata page for the book. Select the criteria by which you want to view the errata, and click the Apply criteria... button. This will provide you with links to specific errata. For an initial search, you are advised to view the errata by page numbers. If you have looked for an error previously, then you may wish to limit your search using dates. We update these pages daily to ensure that you have the latest information on bugs and errors.

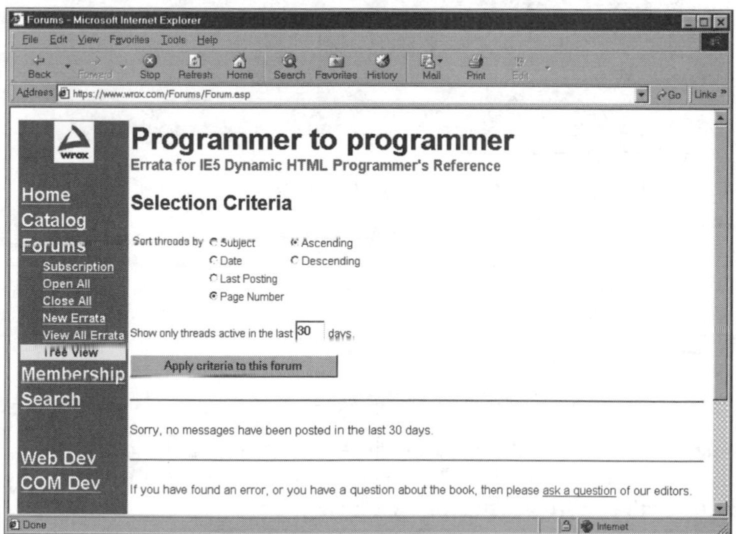

Adding an Errata to the Sheet Yourself

It's always possible that you may find your error is not listed, in which case you can enter details of the fault yourself. It might be anything from a spelling mistake to a faulty piece of code in the book. Sometimes you'll find useful hints that aren't really errors on the listing. By entering errata you may save another reader hours of frustration, and of course, you will be helping us provide even higher quality information. We're very grateful for this sort of advice and feedback. You can enter errata using the 'ask a question' of our editors link at the bottom of the errata page. Click on this link and you will get a form on which to post your message.

Fill in the subject box, and then type your message in the space provided on the form. Once you have done this, click on the Post Now button at the bottom of the page. The message will be forwarded to our editors. They'll then test your submission and check that the error exists, and that the suggestions you make are valid. Then your submission, together with a solution, is posted on the site for public consumption. Obviously this stage of the process can take a day or two, but we will endeavor to get a fix up sooner than that.

E-mail Support

If you wish to directly query a problem in the book with an expert who knows the book in detail then e-mail `support@wrox.com`, with the title of the book and the last four numbers of the ISBN in the subject field of the e-mail. A typical email should include the following things:

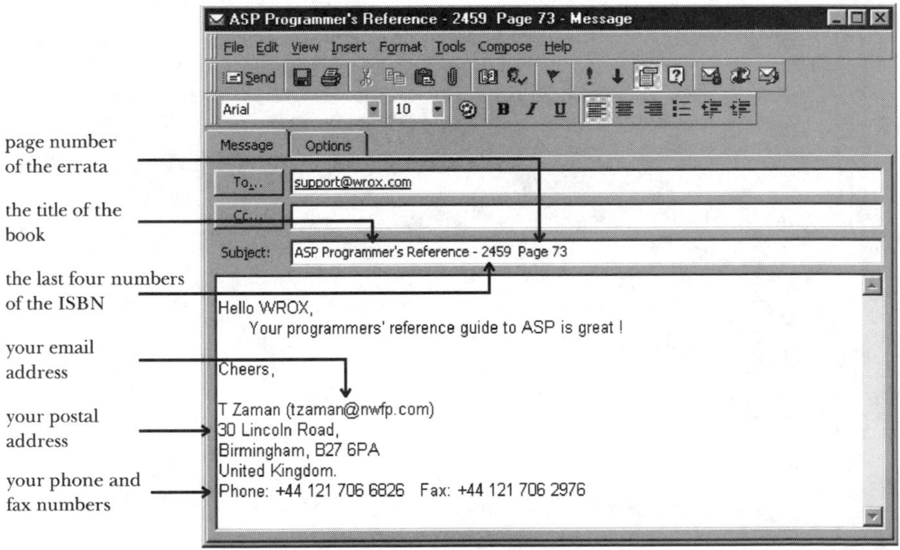

We won't send you junk mail. We need the details to save your time and ours. If we need to replace a disk or CD we'll be able to get it to you straight away. When you send an e-mail it will go through the following chain of support:

Customer Support

Your message is delivered to one of our customer support staff who are the first people to read it. They have files on most frequently asked questions and will answer anything general immediately. They answer general questions about the book and the web site.

Editorial

Deeper queries are forwarded to the technical editor responsible for that book. They have experience with the programming language or particular product and are able to answer detailed technical questions on the subject. Once an issue has been resolved, the editor can post the errata to the web site.

The Authors

Finally, in the unlikely event that the editor can't answer your problem, s/he will forward the request to the author. We try to protect the author from any distractions from writing. However, we are quite happy to forward specific requests to them. All Wrox authors help with the support on their books. They'll mail the customer and the editor with their response, and again all readers should benefit.

What We Can't Answer

Obviously with an ever growing range of books and an ever-changing technology base, there is an increasing volume of data requiring support. While we endeavor to answer all questions about the book, we can't answer bugs in your own programs that you've adapted from our code. So, while you might have loved the help desk systems in our Active Server Pages book, don't expect too much sympathy if you cripple your company with a live adaptation you customized from Chapter 12. But do tell us if you're especially pleased with the routine you developed with our help.

How to Tell Us Exactly What You Think

We understand that errors can destroy the enjoyment of a book and can cause many wasted and frustrated hours, so we seek to minimize the distress that they can cause.

You might just wish to tell us how much you liked or loathed the book in question. Or you might have ideas about how this whole process could be improved. In which case you should e-mail `feedback@wrox.com`. You'll always find a sympathetic ear, no matter what the problem is. Above all you should remember that we do care about what you have to say and we will do our utmost to act upon it.

Index

A

B

C

E

I

J

K

N

O

P

Q

R

S

T

U

V

W

X

Y

Z

HTML

WROX PRESS INC.

Wrox writes books for you. Any suggestions, or ideas about how you want information given in your ideal book will be studied by our team. Your comments are always valued at Wrox.

Free phone in USA 800-USE-WROX
Fax (312) 397 8990

UK Tel. (0121) 687 4100 Fax (0121) 687 4101

NB. If you post the bounce back card below in the UK, please send it to:
Wrox Press Ltd., Arden House, 1102 Warwick Road, Acocks Green, Birmingham. B27 6BH. UK.

E5 Dynamic HTML Programmer's Reference

Name ____________
Address ____________

City ________ State/Region ________
Country ________ Postcode/Zip ________
E-mail ____________
Occupation ____________

How did you hear about this book? ____________
- ☐ Book review (name) ____________
- ☐ Advertisement (name) ____________
- ☐ Recommendation ____________
- ☐ Catalog ____________
- ☐ Other ____________

Where did you buy this book? ____________
- ☐ Bookstore (name) ________ City ________
- ☐ Computer Store (name) ____________
- ☐ Mail Order ____________
- ☐ Other ____________

What influenced you in the purchase of this book?
- ☐ Cover Design
- ☐ Contents
- ☐ Other (please specify) ____________

How did you rate the overall contents of this book?
- ☐ Excellent
- ☐ Good
- ☐ Average
- ☐ Poor

What did you find most useful about this book? ____________

What did you find least useful about this book? ____________

Please add any additional comments. ____________

What other subjects will you buy a computer book on soon? ____________

What is the best computer book you have used this year? ____________

Note: This information will only be used to keep you updated about new Wrox Press titles and will not be used for any other purpose or passed to any other third party.

1746 *Check here if you DO NOT want to receive further support for this book.* ☐ 1746

NO POSTAGE
NECESSARY
IF MAILED
IN THE
UNITED STATES

BUSINESS REPLY MAIL

FIRST CLASS MAIL PERMIT#64 CHICAGO, IL

POSTAGE WILL BE PAID BY ADDRESSEE

WROX PRESS INC.
1512 NORTH FREMONT
SUITE 103
CHICAGO IL 60622-2567